Assessment Guide

Grade 6

Orlando • Boston • Dallas • Chicago • San Diego
www.harcourtschool.com

Printed in the United States of America

ISBN 0-15-320838-4

1 2 3 4 5 6 7 8 9 10 022 2004 2003 2002 2001

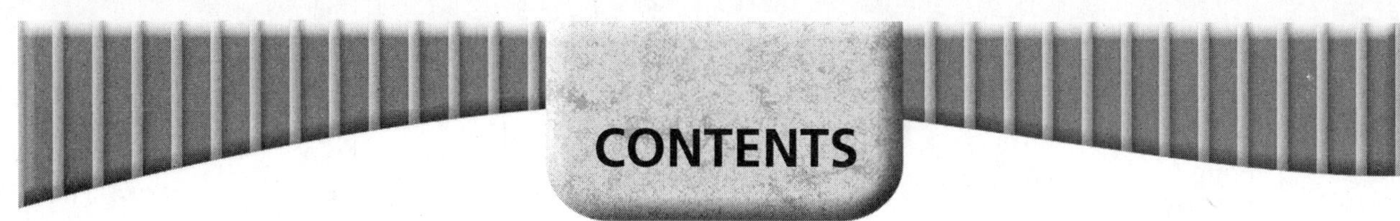

CONTENTS

TESTS

INTRODUCTION

"Assessment should be more than merely a test at the end of instruction to see how students perform under special conditions; rather, it should be an integral part of instruction that informs and guides teachers as they make instructional decisions. Assessment should not merely be done to *students; rather, it should also be done* for *students, to guide and enhance their learning." (Principles and Standards for School Mathematics, p. 22)*

Assessment in Harcourt Math

Harcourt Math provides a wide range of assessment tools to measure student achievement before, during, and after instruction. These tools include:

- Entry Level Assessment
- Progress Monitoring
- Summative Evaluation
- Test Preparation

Entry Level Assessment

Inventory Tests—These tests, provided on pages AG1–AG8 in this *Assessment Guide*, may be administered at the beginning of the school year to determine a baseline for student mastery of the grade-level objectives. The baseline may also be used to evaluate a student's future growth when compared to subsequent tests.

Assessing Prior Knowledge ("Check What You Know")—This feature appears at the beginning of every chapter in the *Harcourt Math* Pupil Edition. It may be used before chapter instruction begins to determine whether students possess crucial prerequisite skills. Tools for intervention are provided.

Pretests—The Chapter Tests, Form A (multiple choice) or Form B (free response), may be used as pretests to measure what students already may have mastered before instruction begins. These tests are provided in this *Assessment Guide*.

Progress Monitoring

Daily Assessment—These point-of-use strategies allow you to continually adjust instruction so that all students are constantly progressing toward mastery of the grade-level objectives. These strategies appear in every lesson of the *Harcourt Math* Teacher's Edition, and include the Quick Review, Mixed Review and Test Prep, and the Assess section of the lesson plan.

Intervention—While monitoring students' progress, you may determine that intervention is needed. The Intervention and Extension Resources page for each lesson in the Teacher's Edition suggests several options for meeting individual needs.

Student Self-Assessment—Students evaluate their own work through checklists, portfolios, and journals. Suggestions are provided in this *Assessment Guide*.

Summative Evaluation

Formal Assessment—Several options are provided to help the teacher determine whether students have achieved the goals defined by a given standard or set of standards. These options are provided at the end of each chapter and unit and at the end of the year. They include

Chapter Review/Test in the *Pupil Edition*
Chapter Tests in this *Assessment Guide*
Unit Tests in this *Assessment Guide*
Standardized Test Prep, in the *Pupil Edition*, for cumulative review

Performance Assessment—Two performance tasks for each unit are provided in the *Performance Assessment* book. Scoring rubrics and model papers are also provided in the *Performance Assessment* book. The tasks also appear in the *Pupil Edition* at the end of each unit.

Harcourt Electronic Test System—Math Practice and Assessment CD-ROM—This technology component provides the teacher with the opportunity to make and grade chapter tests electronically. The tests may be customized to meet individual needs or to create standards-based tests from a bank of test items. A management system for generating reports is also included.

Test Preparation

Test Prep—To help students prepare for tests, the Mixed Review and Test Prep, at the end of most lessons, provides items in standardized-test format. In addition, the Standardized Test Prep pages at the end of each chapter in the *Pupil Edition* provide practice in solving problems in a standardized test format. The Write What You Know questions provide students an opportunity to practice responding to written response questions of the type that may appear on a standardized test. These questions also appear in a consumable format in *Performance Assessment*. The Standardized Test Prep pages also include practical test-taking tips that give students ongoing strategies for analyzing problems and solving them.

ASSESSMENT OPTIONS AT A GLANCE

ASSESSING PRIOR KNOWLEDGE

Check What You Know, *PE*
Inventory Test, Form A, *AG*
Inventory Test, Form B, *AG*

DAILY ASSESSMENT

Quick Review, *PE*
Mixed Review and Test Prep, *PE*
Number of the Day, *PE*
Problem of the Day, *PE*
Lesson Quiz, *TE*

TEST PREPARATION

Standardized Test Prep, *PE*
Mixed Review and Test Prep, *PE*
Study Guide and Review, *PE*
Write What You Know, *PE*

PERFORMANCE ASSESSMENT

Performance Task A, *PA*
Performance Task B, *PA*
Write What You Know, *PA*

FORMAL ASSESSMENT

Chapter Review/Test, *PE*

Inventory Tests, *AG*
Pretest and Posttest Options
Chapter Test Form A, *AG*
Chapter Test Form B, *AG*
End-of-Year Tests, *AG*

Unit Test Form A, *AG*
Unit Test Form B, *AG*

Harcourt Electronic Test System—
Math Practice and
Assessment CD-ROM

STUDENT SELF-ASSESSMENT

How Did Our Group Do?, *AG*
How Well Did I Work in My Group?, *AG*
How Did I Do?, *AG*
A Guide to My Math Portfolio, *AG*
Math Journal, *TE*

Key: AG=*Assessment Guide*, TE=*Teacher's Edition*, PE=*Pupil Edition*, PA=*Performance Assessment*

PREPARING STUDENTS FOR SUCCESS

Assessing Prior Knowledge

Assessment of prior knowledge is essential to planning mathematics instruction and to ensure students' progress from what they already know to higher levels of learning. In *Harcourt Math*, each chapter begins with Check What You Know. This tool to assess prior knowledge can be used to determine whether students have the prerequisite skills to move on to the new skills and concepts of the subsequent chapter.

If students are found lacking in some skills or concepts, appropriate intervention strategies are suggested. The *Intervention Strategies and Activities* ancillary provides additional options for intervention. The *Teacher's Edition* of the textbook provides references for reteaching, practice, and challenge activities as well as suggestions for reaching students with a wide variety of learning abilities.

Test Preparation

With increasing emphasis today on standardized tests, many students feel intimidated and nervous as testing time approaches. Whether they are facing teacher-made tests, program tests, or state-wide standardized tests, students will feel more confident with the test format and content if they know what to expect in advance.

Harcourt Math provides multiple opportunities for test preparation. At the end of most lessons there is a Mixed Review and Test Prep, which provides items in a standardized-test format. Standardized Test Prep pages at the end of each chapter provide practice in problem solving presented in a standardized-test format. In the Student Handbook of the *Pupil Edition* there is a section on test-taking tips. Test-taking tips also appear in this *Assessment Guide* on pages AG xl and AG xli.

FORMAL ASSESSMENT

Formal assessment in *Harcourt Math* consists of a series of reviews and tests that assess how well students understand concepts, perform skills, and solve problems related to program content. Information from these measures (along with information from other kinds of assessment) is needed to evaluate student achievement and to determine grades. Moreover, analysis of results can help determine whether additional practice or reteaching is needed.

Formal assessment in *Harcourt Math* includes the following measures:

- Inventory Tests, in this *Assessment Guide*
- Chapter Review/Tests, in the *Pupil Edition*
- Chapter Tests, in this *Assessment Guide*
- Unit Tests, in this *Assessment Guide*
- End-of-Year Tests, in this *Assessment Guide*

The **Inventory Tests** assess how well students have mastered the objectives from the previous grade level. There are two forms of Inventory Tests—multiple choice (Form A) and free response (Form B). Test results provide information about the kinds of review students may need to be successful in mathematics at the new grade level. The teacher may use the Inventory Test at the beginning of the school year or when a new student arrives in your class.

The **Chapter Review/Test** appears at the end of each chapter in the *Pupil Edition*. It can be used to determine whether there is a need for more instruction or practice. Discussion of responses can help correct misconceptions before students take the chapter test.

The **Chapter Tests** are available in two formats—multiple choice (Form A) and free response (Form B). Both forms assess the same content. The two different forms permit use of the measure as a pretest and a posttest or as two forms of the posttest.

The **Unit Tests**, in both Form A and Form B, follow the chapter tests in each unit. Unit tests assess skills and concepts from the preceding unit.

The **End-of-Year Tests** assess how well students have mastered the objectives in the grade level. There are two forms of End-of-Year Tests—multiple choice and free response. Test results may provide a teacher help in recommending a summer review program.

The **Answer Key** in this *Assessment Guide* provides reduced replications of the tests with answers. Two record forms are available for formal assessment—an Individual Record Form (starting on page AG xxviii) and a Class Record Form (starting on page AG xxxvii).

Students may record their answers directly on the test sheets. However, for the multiple-choice tests, they may use the **Answer Sheet**, similar to the "bubble form" used for standardized tests. That sheet is located on page AG xlviii in this *Assessment Guide*.

DAILY ASSESSMENT

Daily Assessment is embedded in daily instruction. Students are assessed as they learn and learn as they are assessed. First you observe and evaluate your students' work on an informal basis, and then you seek confirmation of those observations through other program assessments.

Harcourt Math offers the following resources to support informal assessment on a daily basis:

- Quick Review in the *Pupil Edition* on the first page of each lesson
- Mixed Review and Test Prep in the *Pupil Edition* at the end of each skill lesson
- Number of the Day in the *Teacher's Edition* at the beginning of each lesson
- Problem of the Day in the *Teacher's Edition* at the beginning of each lesson
- Assess in the *Teacher's Edition* at the end of each lesson

Quick Review allows you to adjust instruction so that all students are progressing toward mastery of skills and concepts.

Mixed Review and Test Prep provides review and practice for skills and concepts previously taught. Some of the items are written in a multiple-choice format.

Number of the Day and **Problem of the Day** kick off the lesson with problems that are relevant both to lesson content and the students' world. Their purpose is to get students thinking about the lesson topic and to provide you with insights about their ability to solve problems related to it. Class discussion may yield clues about students' readiness to learn a concept or skill emphasized in the lesson.

Assess in the Teacher's Edition at the end of each lesson includes three brief assessments: Discuss and Write—to probe students' grasp of the main lesson concept, and Lesson Quiz—a quick check of students' mastery of lesson skills.

Depending on what you learn from students' responses to lesson assessments, you may wish to use **Problem Solving, Reteach, Practice**, or **Challenge** copying masters before starting the next lesson.

PERFORMANCE ASSESSMENT

Performance assessment can help reveal the thinking strategies students use to work through a problem. Students usually enjoy doing the performance tasks.

Harcourt Math offers the following assessment measures, scoring instruments, and teacher observation checklists for evaluating student performance.

- Unit Performance Assessments and Scoring Rubrics, in the *Performance Assessment* book
- Project Scoring Rubric in this *Assessment Guide*
- Portfolio Evaluation in this *Assessment Guide*
- Problem Solving Think Along Response Sheets and Scoring Guides in this *Assessment Guide*

The **Performance Assessment** book includes two tasks per unit. These tasks can help you assess students' ability to use what they have learned to solve everyday problems. This book also includes two written response questions per chapter. Students construct responses to these questions and often need to assimilate prior learning to fully answer the questions. For more information see the *Performance Assessment* book.

The **Project Scoring Rubric** can be used to evaluate an individual or group project. This rubric can be especially useful in evaluating the Problem Solving Project that appears in the *Teacher's Edition* at the beginning of every chapter. The project is an open-ended, problem-solving task that may involve activities such as gathering data, constructing a data table or graph, writing a report, building a model, or creating a simulation.

The **Problem Solving Think Along** is a performance assessment that is designed around the problem-solving method used in *Harcourt Math*. You may use either the Oral Response or Written Response form to evaluate the students. For more information see pages AG xxii–AG xxvi.

Portfolios can also be used to assess students' mathematics performance. For more information, see pages AG xviii–AG xx.

STUDENT SELF-ASSESSMENT

Research shows that self-assessment can have significant positive effects on students' learning. To achieve these effects, students must be challenged to reflect on their work and to monitor, analyze, and control their learning. Their ability to evaluate their behaviors and to monitor them grows with their experience in self-assessment.

Harcourt Math offers the following self-assessment tools:

- Math Journal, ideas for journal writing found in the *Teacher's Edition*
- Group Project Evaluation Sheet
- Individual Group Member Evaluation Sheet
- End-of-Chapter Individual Survey Sheet

The **Math Journal** is a collection of student writings that may communicate feelings, ideas, and explanations as well as responses to open-ended problems. It is an important evaluation tool in math even though it is not graded. Use the journal to gain insights about student growth that you cannot obtain from other assessments. Look for journal icons in your *Teacher's Edition* for suggested journal-writing activities.

The **Group Project Evaluation Sheet** ("How Did Our Group Do?") is designed to assess and build up group self-assessment skills. The Individual Group Member Evaluation ("How Well Did I Work in My Group?") helps the student evaluate his or her own behavior in and contributions to the group.

The **End-of-Chapter Survey** ("How Did I Do?") leads students to reflect on what they have learned and how they learned it. Use it to help students learn more about their own capabilities and develop confidence.

Discuss directions for completing each checklist or survey with the students. Tell them there are no "right" responses to the items. Talk over reasons for various responses.

Project Scoring Rubric

Check the indicators that describe a student's or group's performance on a project. Use the check marks to help determine the individual's or group's overall score.

Score 3 Indicators: The student/group

_______ makes outstanding use of resources.
_______ shows thorough understanding of content.
_______ demonstrates outstanding grasp of mathematics skills.
_______ displays strong decision-making/problem-solving skills.
_______ exhibits exceptional insight/creativity.
_______ communicates ideas clearly and effectively.

Score 2 Indicators: The student/group

_______ makes good use of resources.
_______ shows adequate understanding of content.
_______ demonstrates good grasp of mathematics skills.
_______ displays adequate decision-making/problem-solving skills.
_______ exhibits reasonable insight/creativity.
_______ communicates most ideas clearly and effectively.

Score 1 Indicators: The student/group

_______ makes limited use of resources.
_______ shows partial understanding of content.
_______ demonstrates limited grasp of mathematics skills.
_______ displays weak decision-making/problem-solving skills.
_______ exhibits limited insight/creativity.
_______ communicates some ideas clearly and effectively.

Score 0 Indicators: The student/group

_______ makes little or no use of resources.
_______ fails to show understanding of content.
_______ demonstrates little or no grasp of mathematics skills.
_______ does not display decision-making/problem-solving skills.
_______ does not exhibit insight/creativity.
_______ has difficulty communicating ideas clearly and effectively.

Overall score for the project. _______

Comments: ____

____

Project ______________________ Date ________

Group members ______________________

How Did Our Group Do?

Discuss the question. Then circle the score your group thinks it earned.

How well did our group	SCORE Great Job	 Good Job	 Could Do Better
1. share ideas?	3	2	1
2. plan what to do?	3	2	1
3. carry out plans?	3	2	1
4. share the work?	3	2	1
5. solve group problems without seeking help?	3	2	1
6. make use of resources?	3	2	1
7. record information and check for accuracy?	3	2	1
8. show understanding of math ideas?	3	2	1
9. demonstrate creativity and critical thinking?	3	2	1
10. solve the project problem?	3	2	1

Write your group's answer to each question.

11. What did our group do best? ______________________

____

____

12. How can we help our group do better? ______________________

____

____

Name ______________________ Date ______

Project ______________________

How Well Did I Work in My Group?

Circle **yes** if you agree. Circle **no** if you disagree.

1.	I shared my ideas with my group.	yes	no
2.	I listened to the ideas of others in my group.	yes	no
3.	I was able to ask questions of my group.	yes	no
4.	I encouraged others in my group to share their ideas.	yes	no
5.	I was able to discuss opposite ideas with my group.	yes	no
6.	I helped my group plan and make decisions.	yes	no
7.	I did my fair share of the group's work.	yes	no
8.	I understood the problem my group worked on.	yes	no
9.	I understood the solution to the problem my group worked on.	yes	no
10.	I can explain to others the problem my group worked on and its solution.	yes	no

Name ______________________ Date ______

Chapter ______________________

How Did I Do?

Write your response.

1. I thought the lessons in this chapter were

   ____

2. The lesson I enjoyed the most was

   ____

3. Something that I still need to work on is

   ____

4. One thing that I think I did a great job on was

   ____

5. I would like to learn more about

   ____

6. Something I understand now that I did not understand before these lessons is

   ____

7. I think I might use the math I learned in these lessons to

   ____

8. The amount of effort I put into these lessons was

   ____

   (very little some a lot)

PORTFOLIO ASSESSMENT

A portfolio is a collection of each student's work gathered over an extended period of time. A portfolio illustrates the growth, talents, achievements, and reflections of the learner and provides a means for the teacher to assess the student's performance and progress.

Building a Portfolio

There are many opportunities to collect students' work throughout the year as you use *Harcourt Math*. Suggested portfolio items are found throughout the *Teacher's Edition*. Give students the opportunity to select some work samples to be included in the portfolio.

- Provide a folder for each student with the student's name clearly marked.
- Explain to students that throughout the year they will save some of their work in the folder. Sometimes it will be their individual work; sometimes it will be group reports and projects or completed checklists.
- Have students complete "A Guide to My Math Portfolio" several times during the year.

Evaluating a Portfolio

The following points made with regular portfolio evaluation will encourage growth in self-evaluation:

- Discuss the contents of the portfolio as you examine it with each student.
- Encourage and reward students by emphasizing growth, original thinking, and completion of tasks.
- Reinforce and adjust instruction of the broad goals you want to accomplish as you evaluate the portfolios.
- Examine each portfolio on the basis of individual growth rather than in comparison with other portfolios.
- Use the Portfolio Evaluation sheet for your comments.
- Share the portfolios with families during conferences or send the portfolio, including the Family Response form, home with the students.

Name ________________________________

Date ________________________________

PORTFOLIO GUIDE

A Guide to My Math Portfolio

What is in My Portfolio	What I Learned
1.	
2.	
3.	
4.	
5.	

I organized my portfolio this way because ________________________________

____

____

Name ___________________________

Date ___________________________

Evaluating Performance	Evidence and Comments
1. What mathematical understandings are demonstrated?	
2. What skills are demonstrated?	
3. What approaches to problem solving and critical thinking are evident?	
4. What work habits and attitudes are demonstrated?	

Summary of Portfolio Assessment

For This Review			Since Last Review		
Excellent	Good	Fair	Improving	About the Same	Not as Good

Date ______________________

Dear Family,

This is your child's math portfolio. It contains work samples that your child and I have selected to show how his or her abilities in math have grown. Your child can explain what each sample shows.

Please look over the portfolio with your child and write a few comments in the blank space at the bottom of this sheet about what you have seen. Your child has been asked to bring the portfolio with your comments included back to school.

Thank you for helping your child evaluate his or her portfolio and for taking pride in the work he or she has done. Your interest and support is important to your child's success in school.

Sincerely,

____
(Teacher)

Response to Portfolio:

____
(Family member)

ASSESSING PROBLEM SOLVING

Assessing a student's ability to solve problems involves more than checking the student's answer. It involves looking at how students process information and how they work at solving problems. The problem-solving method used in *Harcourt Math*—Understand, Plan, Solve, and Check—guides the student's thinking process and provides a structure within which the student can work toward a solution. The following instruments can help you assess students' problem-solving abilities:

The **Oral Response Form** (page AG xxiii) can be used by a student or a group as a self-questioning instrument or as a guide for working through a problem. It can also be an interview instrument the teacher can use to assess students' problem-solving skills.

The analytic **Scoring Guide for Oral Responses** (page AG xxiv) has a criterion score for each section. It may be used to evaluate the oral presentation of an individual or group.

The **Written Response Form** (page AG xxv) provides a recording sheet for a student or group to record their responses as they work through each section of the problem-solving process.

The analytic **Scoring Guide for Written Responses** (page AG xxvi), which gives a criterion score for each section, will help you pinpoint the parts of the problem-solving process in which your students need more instruction.

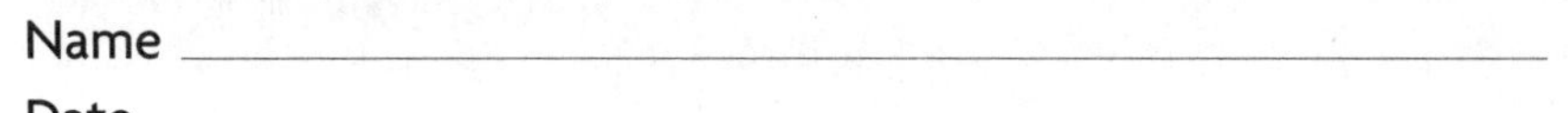
Name
Date

Problem-Solving Think Along: Oral Response Form

Solving problems is a thinking process. Asking yourself questions as you work through the steps in solving a problem can help guide your thinking. These questions will help you understand the problem, plan how to solve it, solve it, and then look back and check your solution. These questions will also help you think about other ways to solve the problem.

Understand

1. What is the problem about?
2. What is the question?
3. What information is given in the problem?

Plan

4. What problem-solving strategies might I try to help me solve the problem?
5. What is my estimated answer?

Solve

6. How can I solve the problem?
7. How can I state my answer in a complete sentence?

Check

8. How do I know whether my answer is reasonable?
9. How else might I have solved this problem?

Name ______________________________

Date ______________________________

Problem-Solving Think Along:
Scoring Guide • Oral Responses

Understand *Criterion Score 4/6* *Pupil Score* ______

______ **1.** *Restate the problem in his or her own words.*
2 points Complete problem restatement given.
1 point Incomplete problem restatement.
0 points No restatement given.

______ **2.** *Identify the question.*
2 points Complete problem restatement of the question given.
1 point Incomplete problem restatement of the question given.
0 points No restatement of the question given.

______ **3.** *State list of information needed to solve the problem.*
2 points Complete list given.
1 point Incomplete list given.
0 points No list given.

Plan *Criterion Score 3/4* *Pupil Score* ______

______ **1.** *State one or more strategies that might help solve the problem.*
2 points One or more useful strategies given.
1 point One or more strategies given but are poor choices.
0 points No strategies given.

______ **2.** *State reasonable estimated answer.*
2 points Reasonable estimate given.
1 point Unreasonable estimate given.
0 points No estimated answer given.

Solve *Criterion Score 3/4* *Pupil Score* ______

______ **1.** *Describe a solution method that correctly represents the information in the problem.*
2 points Correct solution method given.
1 point Incorrect solution method given.
0 points No solution method given.

______ **2.** *State correct answer in complete sentence.*
2 points Complete sentence given; answer to question is correct.
1 point Sentence given does not answer the question correctly.
0 points No sentence given.

Check *Criterion Score 3/4* *Pupil Score* ______

______ **1.** *State sentence explaining why the answer is reasonable.*
2 points Complete and correct explanation given.
1 point Sentence given with incomplete or incorrect reason.
0 points No solution method given.

______ **2.** *Describe another strategy that could have been used to solve the problem.*
2 points Another useful strategy described.
1 point Another strategy described, but strategy is a poor choice.
0 points No other strategy described.

TOTAL 13/18 *Pupil Score* ______

Name ______________________________
Date ______________________________

WRITTEN RESPONSE FORM

Problem Solving

Understand

1. Retell the problem in your own words. ______________________________

____

____

____

2. Restate the question as a fill-in-the-blank sentence. ______________________________

____

3. List the information needed to solve the problem. ______________________________

____

Plan

4. List one or more problem-solving strategies that you can use. ______________________________

____

5. Predict what your answer will be. ______________________________

____

Solve

6. Show how you solved the problem. ______________________________

____

7. Write your answer in a complete sentence. ______________________________

____

Check

8. Tell how you know your answer is reasonable. ______________________________

____

9. Describe another way you could have solved the problem. ______________________________

____

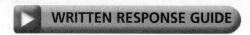

Problem-Solving Think Along:
Scoring Guide • Written Responses

Understand *Indicator 1:* Student restates the problem in his or her own words.	*Criterion Score 4/6* *Scoring:* 2 points Complete problem restatement written. 1 point Incomplete problem restatement written. 0 points No restatement written.
Indicator 2: Student restates the question as a fill-in-the-blank statement.	2 points Correct restatement of the question. 1 point Incorrect or incomplete restatement. 0 points No restatement written.
Indicator 3: Student writes a complete list of the information needed to solve the problem.	2 points Complete list made. 1 point Incomplete list made. 0 points No list made.
Plan *Indicator 1:* Student lists one or more problem-solving strategies that might be helpful in solving the. problem.	*Criterion Score 3/4* *Scoring:* 2 points One or more useful strategies listed. 1 point One or more strategies listed, but strategies are poor choices. 0 points No strategies listed.
Indicator 2: Student gives a reasonable estimated answer.	2 points Reasonable estimate given. 1 point Unreasonable estimate given. 0 points No estimated answer given.
Solve *Indicator 1:* Student shows a solution method that correctly represents the information in the problem.	*Criterion Score 3/4* *Scoring:* 2 points Correct solution method written. 1 point Incorrect solution method written. 0 points No solution method written.
Indicator 2: Student writes a complete sentence giving the correct answer.	2 points Sentence has correct answer and completely answers the question. 1 point Sentence has an incorrect numerical answer or does not answer the question. 0 points No sentence written.
Check *Indicator 1:* Student writes a sentence explaining why the answer is reasonable.	*Criterion Score 3/4* *Scoring:* 2 points Gives a complete and correct explanation. 1 point Gives an incomplete or incorrect reason. 0 points No sentence written.
Indicator 2: Student describes another strategy that could have been used to solve the problem.	2 points Another useful strategy described. 1 point Another strategy described, but it is a poor choice. 0 points No other strategy described.

TOTAL 13/18

MANAGEMENT FORMS

This *Assessment Guide* contains two types of forms to help you manage your record keeping and evaluate students in various types of assessment. On the following pages (AG xxviii–AG xxxvi) you will find Individual Record Forms that contain all of the Learning Goals for the grade level, divided by unit. After each Learning Goal are correlations to the items in Form A and Form B of the Chapter Tests. Criterion scores for each Learning Goal are given. The form provides a place to enter a single student's scores on formal tests and to indicate the objectives he or she has met. A list of review options is also included. The options include lessons in the *Pupil Edition* and *Teacher's Edition*, and activities in the Workbooks that you can assign to the student who is in need of additional practice.

The Class Record Form (pages AG xxxvii–AG xxxix) makes it possible to record the test scores of an entire class on a single form.

Individual Record Form

Grade 6 • Unit 1 **Number Sense and Operations**

Total	Chapter 1	Chapter 2	Chapter 3	Chapter 4	Unit 1 Test
Form A					
Form B					

Student Name ______________________

LEARNING GOALS		FORM A/B CHAPTER TEST				REVIEW OPTIONS				
Goal#	Learning Goal	Test Items	Criterion Score	Student's Score		PE/TE Lessons	Workbooks			
				Form A	Form B		P	R	C	PS
1A	To write whole number estimates	1–4	3/4			1.1	1.1	1.1	1.1	1.1
1B	To write whole number sums, differences, products, and quotients	5–12	6/8			1.2 1.3	1.2 1.3	1.2 1.3	1.2 1.3	1.2 1.3
1C	To evaluate expressions and to use mental math to solve equations involving addition, subtraction, multiplication, or division	17–25	6/9			1.5 1.6	1.5 1.6	1.5 1.6	1.5 1.6	1.5 1.6
1D	To solve problems by using an appropriate problem solving strategy such as *predict and test*	13–16	3/4			1.4	1.4	1.4	1.4	1.4
2A	To write whole number sums, differences, products, and quotients using number properties and mental math	1–6	4/6			2.1	2.1	2.1	2.1	2.1
2B	To evaluate expressions using exponents	7–10	3/4			2.2	2.2	2.2	2.2	2.2
2C	To evaluate expressions using order of operations	11–22	8/12			2.4	2.4	2.4	2.4	2.4
2D	To solve problems by using an appropriate problem solving skill such as *sequence and prioritize the information*	23–25	2/3			2.5	2.5	2.5	2.5	2.5
3A	To write, compare, and order decimals	1–11	8/11			3.1	3.1	3.1	3.1	3.1
3B	To write estimates of decimal sums, differences, products, and quotients	21–25	4/5			3.3	3.3	3.3	3.3	3.3
3C	To write decimals as percents and percents as decimals	12–16	4/5			3.4	3.4	3.4	3.4	3.4
3D	To solve problems by using an appropriate strategy such as *make a table*	17–20	3/4			3.2	3.2	3.2	3.2	3.2
4A	To write sums, differences, products, and quotients of decimals	1–12	8/12			4.1 4.2 4.4	4.1 4.2 4.4	4.1 4.2 4.4	4.1 4.2 4.4	4.1 4.2 4.4
4B	To evaluate expressions and use mental math to solve equations involving decimals	17–25	6/9			4.6	4.6	4.6	4.6	4.6
4C	To solve problems by using an appropriate problem solving skill such as *interpret the remainder*	13–16	3/4			4.5	4.5	4.5	4.5	4.5

Key: P-Practice, **R**-Reteach, **C**-Challenge, **PS**-Problem Solving

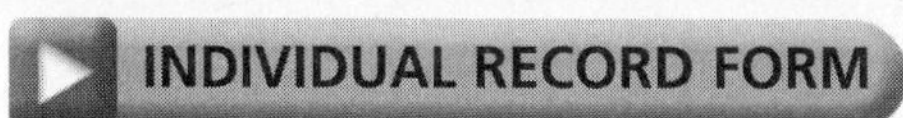

Individual Record Form

Grade 6 • Unit 2 **Statistics and Graphing**

Total	Chapter 5	Chapter 6	Unit 2 Test
Form A			
Form B			

Student Name ______________________________

LEARNING GOALS		FORM A/B CHAPTER TEST				REVIEW OPTIONS				
Goal#	**Learning Goal**	**Test Items**	**Criterion Score**	**Student's Score**		**PE/TE Lessons**	**Workbooks**			
				Form A	**Form B**		**P**	**R**	**C**	**PS**
5A	To identify types of samples and determine if they are representative of a given population or biased, and to draw conclusions about a set of data	1, 2, 9, 12	3/4			5.1 5.2 5.7	5.1 5.2 5.7	5.1 5.2 5.7	5.1 5.2 5.7	5.1 5.2 5.7
5B	To organize, read, interpret, and analyze data in frequency tables and line plots	10, 13	2/2			5.4	5.4	5.4	5.4	5.4
5C	To calculate and compare measures of central tendency with and without outliers	3–8, 11	5/7			5.5 5.6	5.5 5.6	5.5 5.6	5.5 5.6	5.5 5.6
5D	To solve problems by using an appropriate strategy such as *make a table*	14, 15	2/2			5.3	5.3	5.3	5.3	5.3
6A	To make and analyze different kinds of graphs and visual displays including circle graphs, bar graphs, stem-and-leaf plots, histograms, and box-and-whisker graphs	1–9, 11, 12, 16–23	13/19			6.1 6.3 6.5	6.1 6.3 6.5	6.1 6.3 6.5	6.1 6.3 6.5	6.1 6.3 6.5
6B	To estimate and solve for unknown values by using a graph, arithmetic, logical reasoning, and algebraic techniques	10, 24, 25	2/3			6.2	6.2	6.2	6.2	6.2
6C	To compare different types of graphs to determine if they are appropriate or misleading	13–15	2/3			6.6	6.6	6.6	6.6	6.6

Key: P-Practice, **R**-Reteach, **C**-Challenge, **PS**-Problem Solving

Individual Record Form

Grade 6 • Unit 3 **Fraction Concepts and Operations**

Total	Chapter 7	Chapter 8	Chapter 9	Chapter 10	Unit 3 Test
Form A					
Form B					

Student Name ____________________________

LEARNING GOALS		FORM A/B CHAPTER TEST				REVIEW OPTIONS				
Goal#	Learning Goal	Test Items	Criterion Score	Student's Score		PE/TE Lessons	Workbooks			
				Form A	Form B		P	R	C	PS
7A	To write and apply divisibility rules	1–4, 19	4/5			7.1	7.1	7.1	7.1	7.1
7B	To write and apply prime factorization in exponent form	6-9, 24	4/5			7.2	7.2	7.2	7.2	7.2
7C	To write and apply greatest common factors and least common multiples	5, 10, 11, 13, 14, 16–18, 21–23, 25	8/12			7.3	7.3	7.3	7.3	7.3
7D	To solve problems by using an appropriate problem solving strategy such as *make an organized list*	12, 15, 20	2/3			7.4	7.4	7.4	7.4	7.4
8A	To write fractions in equivalent and simplest form	1–6, 25	5/7			8.1	8.1	8.1	8.1	8.1
8B	To convert between, compare, and order fractions and mixed numbers	7–14, 21, 24	7/10			8.2 8.3	8.2 8.3	8.2 8.3	8.2 8.3	8.2 8.3
8C	To represent and use equivalent representations for fractions, decimals, and friendly percents	15–20, 22, 23	6/8			8.4 8.5	8.4 8.5	8.4 8.5	8.4 8.5	8.4 8.5
9A	To write estimates of sums and differences of fractions and mixed numbers	1–5	4/5			9.1	9.1	9.1	9.1	9.1
9B	To write fraction and mixed number sums and differences	6–12, 14–23	12/17			9.2 9.3 9.4 9.5 9.6	9.2 9.3 9.4 9.5 9.6	9.2 9.3 9.4 9.5 9.6	9.2 9.3 9.4 9.5 9.6	9.2 9.3 9.4 9.5 9.6
9C	To solve problems by using an appropriate problem solving strategy such as *draw a diagram*	13, 24, 25	2/3			9.7	9.7	9.7	9.7	9.7
10A	To estimate products and quotients of fractions and mixed numbers	1–4	3/4			10.1	10.1	10.1	10.1	10.1
10B	To write products and quotients of fractions and mixed numbers	5–17, 19, 20	10/14			10.2 10.3 10.4 10.5	10.2 10.3 10.4 10.5	10.2 10.3 10.4 10.5	10.2 10.3 10.4 10.5	10.2 10.3 10.4 10.5
10C	To evaluate expressions and to use mental math to solve equations involving addition, subtraction, multiplication, or division of fractions	18, 19, 21, 22, 25	4/5			10.7	10.7	10.7	10.7	10.7
10D	To solve problems by using an appropriate problem solving skill such as *choose the operation*	23, 24	2/2			10.6	10.6	10.6	10.6	10.6

Key: P-Practice, **R**-Reteach, **C**-Challenge, **PS**-Problem Solving

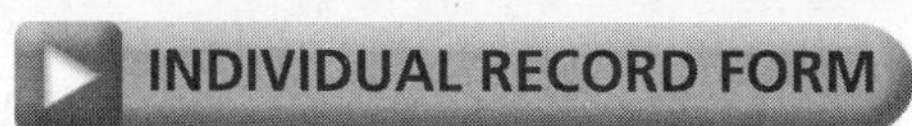

Individual Record Form

Grade 6 • Unit 4 Algebra: Integers

Total	Chapter 11	Chapter 12	Unit 4 Test
Form A			
Form B			

Student Name ______________________

LEARNING GOALS		FORM A/B CHAPTER TEST				REVIEW OPTIONS				
Goal#	Learning Goal	Test Items	Criterion Score	Student's Score		PE/TE Lessons	Workbooks			
				Form A	Form B		P	R	C	PS
11A	To identify and write integers, opposites, and absolute values	1–4	3/4			11.1	11.1	11.1	11.1	11.1
11B	To identify and represent relationships among sets of numbers by using a variety of methods, including number lines	5–10, 20	5/7			11.2	11.2	11.2	11.2	11.2
11C	To compare and order rational numbers	11, 14, 15, 18, 19	4/5			11.3	11.3	11.3	11.3	11.3
11D	To solve problems by using an appropriate strategy such as *use logical reasoning*	12, 13, 16, 17	3/4			11.4	11.4	11.4	11.4	11.4
12A	To write sums and differences of integers by using a variety of methods, including models and number lines	1–10, 17, 18, 23	9/13			12.1 12.2 12.3 12.4	12.2 12.4	12.2 12.4	12.2 12.4	12.2 12.4
12B	To write products and quotients of integers.	11–16, 24, 25	6/8			12.5	12.5	12.5	12.5	12.5
12C	To write sums, differences, products, and quotients of rational numbers and combinations of these operations.	19–22	3/4			12.6	12.6	12.6	12.6	12.6

Key: P-Practice, **R**-Reteach, **C**-Challenge, **PS**-Problem Solving

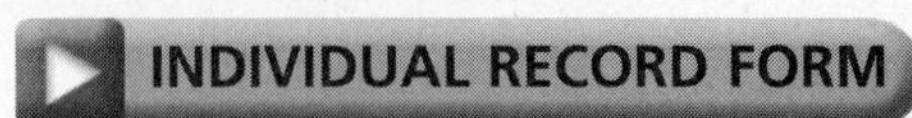

Individual Record Form

Grade 6 • Unit 5 **Algebra: Expressions and Equations**

Total	Chapter 13	Chapter 14	Chapter 15	Unit 5 Test
Form A				
Form B				

Student Name ______________________________

LEARNING GOALS		FORM A/B CHAPTER TEST				REVIEW OPTIONS				
Goal#	Learning Goal	Test Items	Criterion Score	Student's Score		PE/TE Lessons	Workbooks			
				Form A	Form B		P	R	C	PS
13A	To write and evaluate algebraic expressions	1–8, 10–11, 14, 16, 23–24	10/14			14.1 14.2 14.4	14.1 14.2 14.4	14.1 14.2 14.4	14.1 14.2 14.4	14.1 14.2 14.4
13B	To use models to find squares and square roots	9, 12, 13, 15, 17–22, 25	8/11			14.3	14.3	14.3	14.3	14.3
14A	To write verbal sentences as equations	1–6	4/6			15.1	15.1	15.1	15.1	15.1
14B	To use models to solve one-step equations	7–10	3/4			15.2	15.2	15.2	15.2	15.2
14C	To solve addition and subtraction equations	11–25	11/15			15.3 15.4	15.3 15.4	15.3 15.4	15.3 15.4	15.3 15.4
15A	To solve multiplication and division equations, and to use models to solve multiplication equations	1–10	7/10			16.1 16.2	16.1 16.2	16.1 16.2	16.1 16.2	16.1 16.2
15B	To solve real-world problems by using formulas	13–18, 21–23	6/9			16.3	16.3	16.3	16.3	16.3
15C	To use models to solve two-step equations	11, 12	2/2			16.4	16.4	16.4	16.4	16.4
15D	To solve problems by using an appropriate strategy such as *work backward*	19, 20, 24, 25	3/4			16.5	16.5	16.5	16.5	16.5

Key: P-Practice, **R**-Reteach, **C**-Challenge, **PS**-Problem Solving

Individual Record Form

Grade 6 • Unit 6 **Geometry and Spatial Reasoning**

Total	Chapter 16	Chapter 17	Chapter 18	Chapter 19	Unit 6 Test
Form A					
Form B					

Student Name ______________________________

LEARNING GOALS		FORM A/B CHAPTER TEST				REVIEW OPTIONS				
Goal#	Learning Goal	Test Items	Criterion Score	Student's Score		PE/TE Lessons	Workbooks			
				Form A	Form B		P	R	C	PS
16A	To identify, classify, and draw points, rays, lines, and planes	1–4, 10–12, 14, 20	6/9			17.1 17.4	17.1 17.4	17.1 17.4	17.1 17.4	17.1 17.4
16B	To identify, classify, measure, and draw angles	5–8, 16–18	5/7			17.2	17.2	17.2	17.2	17.2
16C	To recognize the relationships among angles	9, 13, 15, 19	3/4			17.3	17.3	17.3	17.3	17.3
17A	To identify, classify, and draw triangles, quadrilaterals, and other two-dimensional figures	1–15, 19, 21–23, 25	14/20			18.1 18.3 18.4	18.1 18.3 18.4	18.1 18.3 18.4	18.1 18.3 18.4	18.1 18.3 18.4
17B	To identify and measure parts of a circle	16–18, 20	3/4			18.5	18.5	18.5	18.5	18.5
17C	To solve problems by using appropriate strategies such as *find a pattern*	24	1/1			18.2	18.2	18.2	18.2	18.2
18A	To identify, classify, and draw solid figures	1–8,17	6/9			19.1	19.1	19.1	19.1	19.1
18B	To identify solid figures from different points of view	9, 10, 12–14	4/5			19.2	19.2	19.2	19.2	19.2
18C	To identify nets and patterns for solid figures	16, 18, 19	2/3			19.3	19.3	19.3	19.3	19.3
18D	To solve problems by using an appropriate strategy such as *solve a simpler problem*	11, 15, 20	2/3			19.4	19.4	19.4	19.4	19.4
19A	To identify and construct congruent line segments and congruent angles	1–6, 16	5/7			19.1	19.1	19.1	19.1	19.1
19B	To bisect line segments and angles	7–10, 17–20	6/8			19.2	19.2	19.2	19.2	19.2
19C	To identify and analyze congruent and similar figures	11–15	4/5			19.4	19.4	19.4	19.4	19.4

Key: P-Practice, **R**-Reteach, **C**-Challenge, **PS**-Problem Solving

Individual Record Form

Grade 6 • Unit 7 Ratio, Proportion, Percent and Probability

Student Name ______________________

Total	Chapter 20	Chapter 21	Chapter 22	Chapter 23	Unit 7 Test
Form A					
Form B					

LEARNING GOALS		FORM A/B CHAPTER TEST				REVIEW OPTIONS				
Goal#	Learning Goal	Test Items	Criterion Score	Student's Score		PE/TE Lessons	Workbooks			
				Form A	Form B		P	R	C	PS
20A	To write ratios, rates, unit rates, and proportions	1–5, 16	4/6			20.1 20.2	20.1 20.2	20.1 20.2	20.1 20.2	20.1 20.2
20B	To use ratios and proportions to solve problems involving similar figures, scale drawings, and maps	6, 8–11, 13–15, 17–20	8/12			20.4 20.5 20.6 20.7	20.4 20.5 20.6 20.7	20.4 20.5 20.6 20.7	20.4 20.5 20.6 20.7	20.4 20.5 20.6 20.7
20C	To solve problems by using an appropriate strategy such as *write an equation*	7, 12	2/2			20.3	20.3	20.3	20.3	20.3
21A	To write ratios as percents	1, 2	2/2			21.1	21.1	21.1	21.1	21.1
21B	To write equivalent forms of percents, decimals, and fractions	3–5	2/3			21.2	21.2	21.2	21.2	21.2
21C	To solve real-life and application percent problems such as those involving tips, discounts, sales tax, and simple interest and to estimate and find the percent of a number	6–16, 20	8/12			21.3 21.5 21.6	21.3 21.5 21.6	21.3 21.5 21.6	21.3 21.5 21.6	21.3 21.5 21.6
21D	To make circle graphs using percents	17–19	2/3			21.4	21.4	21.4	21.4	21.4
22A	To calculate the likelihood of an event, to find the theoretical probabilities of simple events, and to express probabilities as fractions, decimals, and percents	1–8	6/8			22.1	22.1	22.1	22.1	22.1
22B	To make predictions based on experimental probabilities	9–16	6/8			22.3 22.4	22.3 22.4	22.3 22.4	22.3 22.4	22.3 22.4
22C	To solve problems by using an appropriate skill, such as *too much or too little information*	17–20	3/4			22.2	22.2	22.2	22.2	22.2
23A	To identify and find the probabilities of compound, independent, and dependent events by using a variety of methods	1–7, 12–18	10/14			23.2 23.3	23.2 23.3	23.2 23.3	23.2 23.3	23.2 23.3
23B	To find probabilities, and to make predictions by using sample data	8–11	3/4			23.4	23.4	23.4	23.4	23.4
23C	To solve problems by using an appropriate strategy such as *make an organized list*	19, 20	2/2			23.1	23.1	23.1	23.1	23.1

Key: P-Practice, **R**-Reteach, **C**-Challenge, **PS**-Problem Solving

Individual Record Form

Grade 6 • Unit 8 **Measurement**

Total	Chapter 24	Chapter 25	Chapter 26	Chapter 27	Unit 8 Test
Form A					
Form B					

Student Name ______________________

LEARNING GOALS		FORM A/B CHAPTER TEST				REVIEW OPTIONS				
Goal#	Learning Goal	Test Items	Criterion Score	Student's Score		PE/TE Lessons	Workbooks			
				Form A	Form B		P	R	C	PS
24A	To convert between customary measures of length, weight, and capacity, and to convert between metric measures of length, mass, and capacity	1–8	6/8			24.1 24.2	24.1 24.2	24.1 24.2	24.1 24.2	24.1 24.2
24B	To estimate and write conversions between units in customary and metric systems	9–12	3/4			24.3	24.3	24.3	24.3	24.3
24C	To measure to a given degree of precision using appropriate units and tools	13–21	6/9			24.4	24.4	24.4	24.4	24.4
24D	To solve problems by using an appropriate skill such as *estimate or find exact answer*	22–25	3/4			24.5	24.5	24.5	24.5	24.5
25A	To estimate, measure, and calculate perimeters of plane figures	1–3, 6, 7, 10, 11, 15, 18, 19	7/10			25.1 25.2	25.1 25.2	25.1 25.2	25.1 25.2	25.1 25.2
25B	To find the circumference of a circle	4, 5, 8, 9, 13, 14, 16, 17	6/8			25.4 25.5	25.4 25.5	25.4 25.5	25.4 25.5	25.4 25.5
25C	To solve problems by using an appropriate strategy such as *draw a diagram*	12, 20	2/2			25.3	25.3	25.3	25.3	25.3
26A	To estimate and write the area of polygons	1, 3–6, 9, 11–14, 20	8/11			26.1 26.2	26.1 26.2	26.1 26.2	26.1 26.2	26.1 26.2
26B	To estimate and write the area of a circle	2, 8, 15, 16	3/4			26.3 26.4	26.3 26.4	26.3 26.4	26.3 26.4	26.3 26.4
26C	To write the surface area of prisms and pyramids	7, 10, 17–19	4/5			26.5	26.5	26.5	26.5	26.5
27A	To estimate and write the volume of triangular and rectangular prisms	1–3, 6, 7, 9, 14	5/7			27.1	27.1	27.1	27.1	27.1
27B	To estimate and write the volume of triangular and rectangular pyramids	4, 5, 8, 10	3/4			27.3	27.3	27.3	27.3	27.3
27C	To estimate and write the volume of cylinders	11–13, 15–18	5/7			27.4 27.5	27.4 27.5	27.4 27.5	27.4 27.5	27.4 27.5
27D	To solve problems by using an appropriate strategy such as *make a model*	19, 20	2/2			27.2	27.2	27.2	27.2	27.2

Key: P-Practice, **R**-Reteach, **C**-Challenge, **PS**-Problem Solving

Individual Record Form

Grade 6 • Unit 9 **Patterns and Relationships**

Total	Chapter 28	Chapter 29	Chapter 30	Unit 9 Test
Form A				
Form B				

Student Name ______________________

LEARNING GOALS		FORM A/B CHAPTER TEST				REVIEW OPTIONS				
Goal#	Learning Goal	Test Items	Criterion Score	Student's Score		PE/TE Lessons	Workbooks			
				Form A	Form B		P	R	C	PS
28A	To identify, extend, and make number patterns in function tables and sequences, and to write a rule to define a pattern	2–10, 13–16	9/13			28.2 28.3	28.2 28.3	28.2 28.3	28.2 28.3	28.2 28.3
28B	To identify and extend geometric patterns, and to write a rule to define a pattern	1, 17–20	4/5			28.4	28.4	28.4	28.4	28.4
28C	To solve problems by using an appropriate strategy such as *find a pattern*	11, 12	2/2			28.1	28.1	28.1	28.1	28.1
29A	To identify, analyze, and draw transformations of plane and solid figures	1–4, 9–12	6/8			29.1 29.4	29.1 29.4	29.1 29.4	29.1 29.4	29.1 29.4
29B	To identify, analyze, and make tessellations	5–8, 20	4/5			29.2	29.2	29.2	29.2	29.2
29C	To identify and analyze line and rotational symmetry in geometric figures	13–19	5/7			29.5	29.5	29.5	29.5	29.5
29D	To solve problems by using an appropriate strategy such as *make a model*					29.3	29.3	29.3	29.3	29.3
30A	To write, solve, and graph algebraic inequalities on a number line	2, 5–10	5/7			30.1	30.1	30.1	30.1	30.1
30B	To identify, locate, and graph points, relations, and transformations on a coordinate plane, and to write a rule for relations by using tables and graphs	1, 3, 4, 11–19	6/9			30.2 30.3 30.6	30.2 30.3 30.6	30.2 30.3 30.6	30.2 30.3 30.6	30.2 30.3 30.6
30C	To identify linear and nonlinear relationships		2/3			30.5	30.5	30.5	30.5	30.5
30D	To solve problems by using an appropriate skill such as *make generalizations*	20	1/1			30.4	30.4	30.4	30.4	30.4

Key: P-Practice, **R**-Reteach, **C**-Challenge, **PS**-Problem Solving

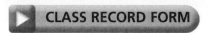

Formal Assessment

Class Record Form

CHAPTER TESTS

School											
Teacher											
NAMES	Date										

Formal Assessment

Class Record Form

UNIT TESTS

School											
Teacher											
NAMES	Date										

Formal Assessment

Class Record Form

INVENTORY/END-OF-YEAR TESTS

School											
Teacher											
NAMES	Date										

Test-Taking Tips

Being a good test taker is like being a good problem solver. When you answer test questions, you are solving problems. Remember to **UNDERSTAND, PLAN, SOLVE,** and **CHECK**.

Understand

Read the problem.

- Look for math terms and recall their meanings.
- Reread the problem and think about the question.
- Use the details in the problem and the question.
- Each word is important. Missing a word or reading it incorrectly could cause you to get the wrong answer.
- Pay attention to words that are in **bold** type, all CAPITAL letters, or *italics*.
- Some other words to look for are <u>round</u>, <u>about</u>, <u>only</u>, <u>best</u>, or <u>least to greatest</u>.

Plan

Think about how you can solve the problem.

- Can you solve the problem with the information given?
- Pictures, charts, tables, and graphs may have the information you need.
- Sometimes you may need to remember some information that is not given.
- Sometimes the answer choices have information to help you solve the problem.
- You may need to write a number sentence and solve it to answer the question.
- Some problems have two steps or more.
- In some problems you may need to look at relationships instead of computing an answer.
- If the path to the solution isn't clear, choose a problem-solving strategy.
- Use the strategy you chose to solve the problem.

Follow your plan, working logically and carefully.

- Estimate your answer. Look for unreasonable answer choices.
- Use reasoning to find the most likely choices.
- Make sure you solved all the steps needed to answer the problem.
- If your answer does not match one of the answer choices, check the numbers you used. Then check your computation.

Solve

Solve the problem.

- If your answer still does not match one of the choices, look for another form of the number such as decimals instead of fractions.
- If answer choices are given as pictures, look at each one by itself while you cover the other three.
- If you do not see your answer and the answer choices include NOT HERE, make sure your work is correct and then mark NOT HERE.
- Read answer choices that are statements and relate them to the problem one by one.
- Change your plan if it isn't working. You may need to try a different strategy.

Check

Take time to catch your mistakes.

- Be sure you answered the question asked.
- Check that your answer fits the information in the problem.
- Check for important words you may have missed.
- Be sure you used all the information you needed.
- Check your computation by using a different method.
- Draw a picture when you are unsure of your answer.

Don't forget!

Before the Test

- Listen to the teacher's directions and read the instructions.
- Write down the ending time if the test is timed.
- Know where and how to mark your answers.
- Know whether you should write on the test page or use scratch paper.
- Ask any questions you have before the test begins.

During the Test

- Work quickly but carefully. If you are unsure how to answer a question, leave it blank and return to it later.
- If you cannot finish on time, look over the questions that are left. Answer the easiest ones first. Then go back to the others.
- Fill in each answer space carefully and completely. Erase completely if you change an answer. Erase any stray marks.

Name ______________________ Date __________ HARCOURT MATH

Test Answer Sheet

Test Title ______________________

1.	Ⓐ Ⓑ Ⓒ Ⓓ	26.	Ⓕ Ⓖ Ⓗ Ⓙ
2.	Ⓕ Ⓖ Ⓗ Ⓙ	27.	Ⓐ Ⓑ Ⓒ Ⓓ
3.	Ⓐ Ⓑ Ⓒ Ⓓ	28.	Ⓕ Ⓖ Ⓗ Ⓙ
4.	Ⓕ Ⓖ Ⓗ Ⓙ	29.	Ⓐ Ⓑ Ⓒ Ⓓ
5.	Ⓐ Ⓑ Ⓒ Ⓓ	30.	Ⓕ Ⓖ Ⓗ Ⓙ
6.	Ⓕ Ⓖ Ⓗ Ⓙ	31.	Ⓐ Ⓑ Ⓒ Ⓓ
7.	Ⓐ Ⓑ Ⓒ Ⓓ	32.	Ⓕ Ⓖ Ⓗ Ⓙ
8.	Ⓕ Ⓖ Ⓗ Ⓙ	33.	Ⓐ Ⓑ Ⓒ Ⓓ
9.	Ⓐ Ⓑ Ⓒ Ⓓ	34.	Ⓕ Ⓖ Ⓗ Ⓙ
10.	Ⓕ Ⓖ Ⓗ Ⓙ	35.	Ⓐ Ⓑ Ⓒ Ⓓ
11.	Ⓐ Ⓑ Ⓒ Ⓓ	36.	Ⓕ Ⓖ Ⓗ Ⓙ
12.	Ⓕ Ⓖ Ⓗ Ⓙ	37.	Ⓐ Ⓑ Ⓒ Ⓓ
13.	Ⓐ Ⓑ Ⓒ Ⓓ	38.	Ⓕ Ⓖ Ⓗ Ⓙ
14.	Ⓕ Ⓖ Ⓗ Ⓙ	39.	Ⓐ Ⓑ Ⓒ Ⓓ
15.	Ⓐ Ⓑ Ⓒ Ⓓ	40.	Ⓕ Ⓖ Ⓗ Ⓙ
16.	Ⓕ Ⓖ Ⓗ Ⓙ	41.	Ⓐ Ⓑ Ⓒ Ⓓ
17.	Ⓐ Ⓑ Ⓒ Ⓓ	42.	Ⓕ Ⓖ Ⓗ Ⓙ
18.	Ⓕ Ⓖ Ⓗ Ⓙ	43.	Ⓐ Ⓑ Ⓒ Ⓓ
19.	Ⓐ Ⓑ Ⓒ Ⓓ	44.	Ⓕ Ⓖ Ⓗ Ⓙ
20.	Ⓕ Ⓖ Ⓗ Ⓙ	45.	Ⓐ Ⓑ Ⓒ Ⓓ
21.	Ⓐ Ⓑ Ⓒ Ⓓ	46.	Ⓕ Ⓖ Ⓗ Ⓙ
22.	Ⓕ Ⓖ Ⓗ Ⓙ	47.	Ⓐ Ⓑ Ⓒ Ⓓ
23.	Ⓐ Ⓑ Ⓒ Ⓓ	48.	Ⓕ Ⓖ Ⓗ Ⓙ
24.	Ⓕ Ⓖ Ⓗ Ⓙ	49.	Ⓐ Ⓑ Ⓒ Ⓓ
25.	Ⓐ Ⓑ Ⓒ Ⓓ	50.	Ⓕ Ⓖ Ⓗ Ⓙ

Name ______________________

Choose the best answer.

1. In which number does the 6 have the greatest value?

A 26,834
B 62,872
C 612,099
D 763,988

2. Which number should go in the ■ so that the numbers are in order from *least* to *greatest*?

199,153; ■; 203,471

F 199,089
G 199,149
H 200,865
J 204,003

3. Chris bought gasoline and paid $1.499 per gal. Which is the best estimate of how much she paid for 10 gal?

A $149
B $15.00
C $14.00
D $10.00

4. Choose the best estimate for 391 ÷ 8.

F 30
G 40
H 50
J 60

5. For which set of data do the mean and mode have the same value?

A 7, 7, 7, 9, 10
B 3, 8, 9, 10, 10
C 5, 8, 9, 9, 9
D 4, 8, 8, 9, 11

6. Mike earns $24.00 per week mowing lawns. Which expression represents the amount he earns in *n* weeks?

F $24 \times n$
G $n \div 24$
H $n + 24$
J $24 \div n$

7. The population of a city is 550,000 when rounded to the nearest ten thousand. Which city could it be?

A Boston: 555,447
B Austin: 552,434
C Seattle: 536,978
D Washington, DC: 523,124

8. The table shows the batting averages of 4 baseball players. Who has the highest average?

PLAYER	BATTING AVERAGE
Cruz	0.274
Gomez	0.302
Li	0.249
Jackson	0.310

F Cruz
G Li
H Gomez
J Jackson

9. Kevin wants to use a graph to compare the heights of five buildings. Which type of graph should he use?

A bar graph
B line plot
C circle graph
D line graph

10. The rainfall for two years was 42.71 in. and 54.38 in. Which is the best estimate of the total rainfall for these two years?

F 107 in.
G 97 in.
H 87 in.
J 80 in.

11. Which figure has all of its sides equal in length?

A rhombus
B rectangle
C trapezoid
D parallelogram

Go On

12. The sides of a number cube are numbered from 1 to 6. What is the probability of rolling a number greater than 4?

F $\frac{2}{6}$　　H $\frac{4}{6}$
G $\frac{3}{6}$　　J $\frac{5}{6}$

13. $0.5\overline{)0.35}$

A 70　　C 0.7
B 7　　D 0.07

14. Which number sentence is true?

F $\frac{1}{2} < \frac{3}{7}$　　H $\frac{5}{6} = \frac{10}{12}$
G $\frac{3}{4} = \frac{10}{12}$　　J $\frac{2}{5} > \frac{2}{3}$

15. $53\overline{)409}$

A 7 r38　　C 7 r59
B 7 r49　　D 8 r5

16. One winter morning, the temperature was $^{-}4$°F. By the afternoon, the temperature was $^{+}7$°F. What was the temperature change from morning to afternoon?

F $^{-}11$°F　　H $^{+}3$°F
G $^{-}3$°F　　J $^{+}11$°F

17. What are the coordinates of point *K*?

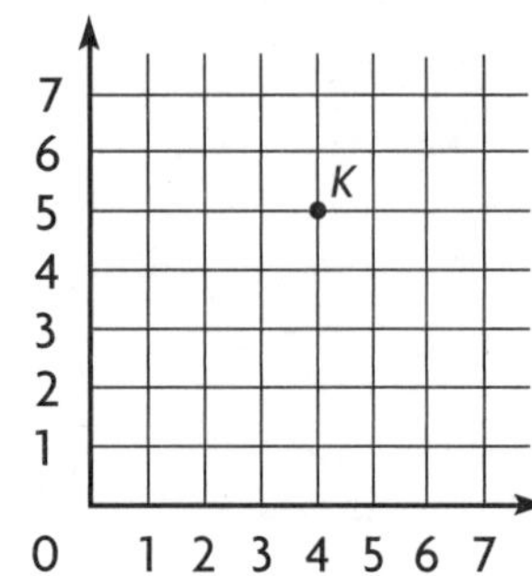

A (5,0)　　C (4,0)
B (5,4)　　D (4,5)

18. What is the rule for the table below?

x	3	6	9	12	15
y	6	12	18	24	30

F $y = x + 3$　　H $y = 2x$
G $x = y + 3$　　J $x = 2y$

19. During a song, Diana claps every third note and Matthew taps his foot every fourth note. Which is the first note when they will both participate?

A 6th note　　C 18th note
B 12th note　　D 24th note

20. Which sum is closest to 1?

F $\frac{7}{8} + \frac{5}{6}$　　H $\frac{2}{7} + \frac{1}{4}$
G $\frac{3}{5} + \frac{1}{2}$　　J $\frac{1}{8} + \frac{1}{8}$

21. Find $24 \times \frac{3}{8}$ in simplest form.

A $\frac{3}{4}$　　C 9
B $1\frac{1}{8}$　　D 64

22. Carol estimated a product to be 12,000. For which multiplication problem was she estimating the product?

F 63×19　　H 163×19
G 193×16　　J 603×19

23. $\begin{array}{r} 2.79 \\ \times\ 1.3 \\ \hline \end{array}$

A 0.3627
B 3.627
C 36.27
D 362.724

Go On

24. Twenty-four students in a class equally shared the $38.40 cost of 3 pizzas. How much did each student pay?

F $1.60
G $1.80
H $12.30
J $12.80

25. During the school year, Crystal's height increased by $2\frac{3}{8}$ in. Choose an equivalent way to name the change in Crystal's height.

A 0.238 in.
B 2.375 in.
C 2.38 in.
D 2.5 in.

26. The radius of a circle measures 8 cm. Which expression gives the length of the diameter?

F 8×2 cm
G $8 \times \pi$ cm
H $8 \div 2$ cm
J $8 \div \pi$ cm

27. On Monday, the high temperature was 8°F less than on Wednesday. If the high temperature on Wednesday was 23°F, which equation can be used to find the high temperature on Monday?

A $t - 8 = 23$
B $t = 23 - 8$
C $t - 23 = 8$
D $23 + t = 8$

28. Rachel ordered 3 medium pizzas for a party. Each was sliced into eighths. If $2\frac{3}{8}$ pizzas were eaten, how much was left?

F $\frac{3}{8}$ of a pizza
G $\frac{5}{8}$ of a pizza
H $1\frac{3}{8}$ pizzas
J $1\frac{5}{8}$ pizzas

29. Divide. Write the answer in simplest form.

$\frac{2}{3} \div \frac{4}{5}$

A $\frac{5}{12}$
B $\frac{8}{15}$
C $\frac{5}{6}$
D $1\frac{1}{5}$

30. Add. Write the answer in simplest form.

$\frac{2}{5} + \frac{1}{10}$

F $\frac{3}{15}$
G $\frac{1}{5}$
H $\frac{3}{10}$
J $\frac{1}{2}$

31. The length of George's desk is 85 cm, and the width is 40 cm. What is the perimeter of his desk?

A 125 cm
B 210 cm
C 250 cm
D 3,400 cm

32. A pencil is 5 in. long. What is the approximate length of the pencil in centimeters? (1 in. $\approx$ 2.54 cm)

F 12.7 cm
G 12.5 cm
H 1.27 cm
J 1.25 cm

33. Choose the ratio that compares the number of squares to the number of circles.

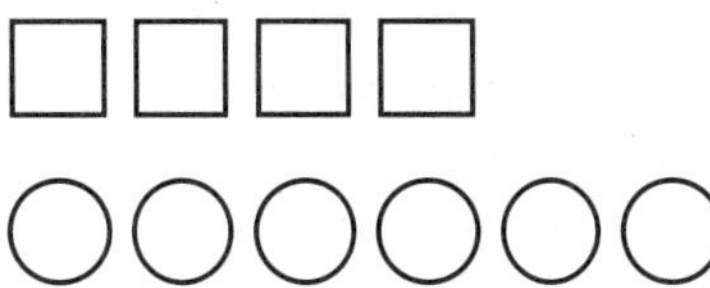

A 6 : 4
B 4 : 10
C 2 : 3
D 3 : 2

Go On

34. Which rectangles are congruent?

F

G

H

J

35. How many ways can you make 40 cents using only dimes and nickels?

A 5 ways C 3 ways
B 4 ways D 2 ways

36. How many of the small cubes make up the larger solid figure?

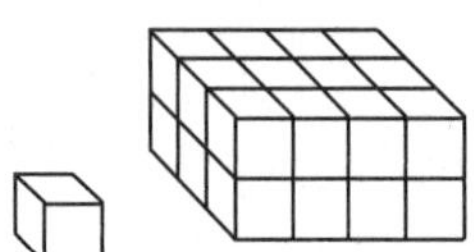

F 6 H 18
G 12 J 24

37. Which set shows three forms of the same number?

A $\frac{1}{4}$, 0.25, 2.5% C $\frac{3}{4}$, 0.75, 75%
B $\frac{3}{8}$, 0.38, 38% D $\frac{1}{2}$, 0.5, 5%

38. What is 30% of 90?

F 3 H 30
G 27 J 270

39. What is the probability that the pointer will land on the red section in this spinner?

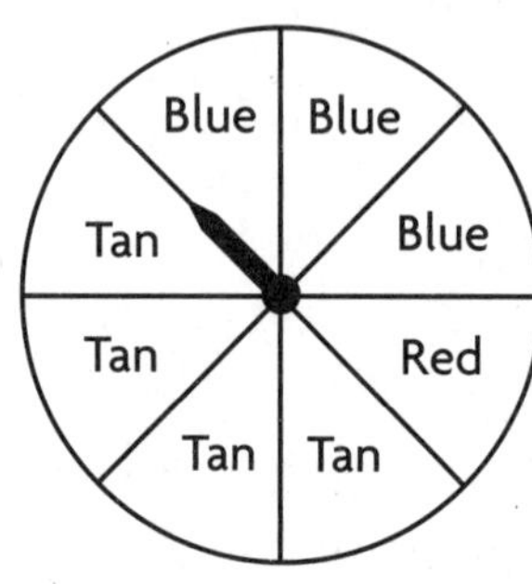

A $\frac{7}{8}$ C $\frac{1}{7}$
B $\frac{6}{7}$ D $\frac{1}{8}$

40. The table shows the number of blocks from school that students in one class live.

NUMBER OF BLOCKS	NUMBER OF STUDENTS
1	3
2	2
3	6
4	4
more than 4	7

How many students live at least 3 blocks from school?

F 5 students H 11 students
G 6 students J 17 students

Stop

Name ______________________________

Write the correct answer.

1. What is the value of the 8 in 678,253?

____

2. Order the numbers from *greatest* to *least*.

   199,417; 201,416; 200,415

____

3. Dennis paid $1.359 per gallon for gasoline. Estimate, to the nearest tenth of a dollar, how much he paid for 10 gal.

____

4. Estimate. 447 ÷ 9

____

5. Give the mean and mode for the set of data.

   8, 6, 9, 7, 7, 6, 5, 7, 8

   mean ________ mode ________

6. Delaney earns $18.00 per week delivering papers. Write an expression that represents the amount she earns in *d* weeks.

____

7. Round 345,012 to the nearest ten thousand.

____

8. The table shows the amount of rainfall for four days last week. On which day did the most rain fall?

DAY	RAIN (IN INCHES)
Monday	0.304
Tuesday	0.282
Wednesday	0.309
Thursday	0.299

____

9. Carly wants to use a graph to compare the lengths of six bridges. What type of graph should she use?

____

10. James bicycled 52.81 mi one week, and 47.28 mi the next week. Estimate, to the nearest whole number, the total distance he bicycled in those two weeks.

____

11. Which quadrilateral must have all sides equal in length, but does not have four equal angles?

____

Go On

Name ______________________________

12. The sides of a cube are numbered from 1 to 6. Express the probability of rolling a number greater than 2 as a fraction?

____

13. $0.6\overline{)0.42}$

____

14. Write an equivalent fraction for $\frac{3}{5}$.

____

15. $43\overline{)341}$

____

16. One afternoon, the temperature was $^{-}8$°F. By the evening, the temperature was $^{-}13$°F. What was the temperature change from afternoon to evening?

____

17. What are the coordinates of point *C*?

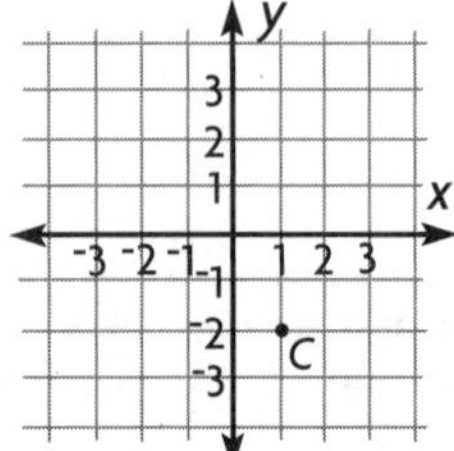

____

18. What is the rule for the table below?

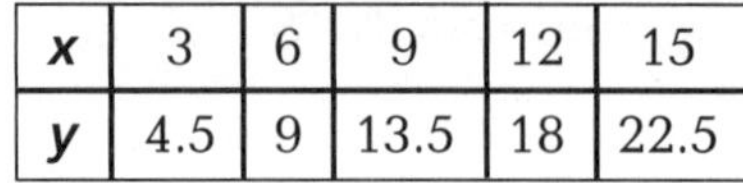

x	3	6	9	12	15
y	4.5	9	13.5	18	22.5

____

19. During a song, David claps every second note and Matthew taps his foot every sixth note. Which is the first note when they will both participate?

____

20. Add. Write the answer in simplest form.

$\frac{1}{4} + \frac{3}{8}$

____

21. Multiply. Write the answer in simplest form.

$30 \times \frac{2}{5}$

____

22. Estimate. 702×21

____

23.

$$\begin{array}{r} 3.28 \\ \times\ 1.7 \\ \hline \end{array}$$

____

Go On

Name ______________________________

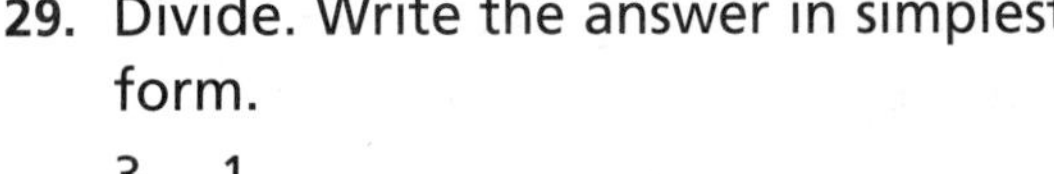

24. Twenty-eight students equally shared the $50.40 cost of supplies for a class party. How much did each student pay?

____

25. Name a decimal equivalent to $3\frac{5}{8}$.

____

26. The radius of a circle measures 7 in. Write an expression that gives the length of the diameter.

____

27. A share of stock in CMG Company sold for $7.00 more on Wednesday than it did on Monday. The price of the share on Wednesday was $65.00. Write an equation to find the price of the share on Monday.

____

28. Ms. Manning's class ordered 5 pizzas for a class picnic. The students ate $4\frac{1}{3}$ pizzas. How much was left?

____

29. Divide. Write the answer in simplest form.

$\frac{3}{4} \div \frac{1}{2}$

____

30. Add. Write the answer in simplest form.

$\frac{3}{8} + \frac{3}{4}$

____

31. The length of Bernie's beach towel is 205 cm, and the width is 80 cm. What is the perimeter of the towel?

____

32. A blackboard eraser is 6 in. long. What is the approximate length of the eraser in centimeters? (1 in. $\approx$ 2.54 cm)

____

33. Write a ratio that compares the number of triangles to the number of circles.

____

Go On

34. Circle two rectangles that are congruent.

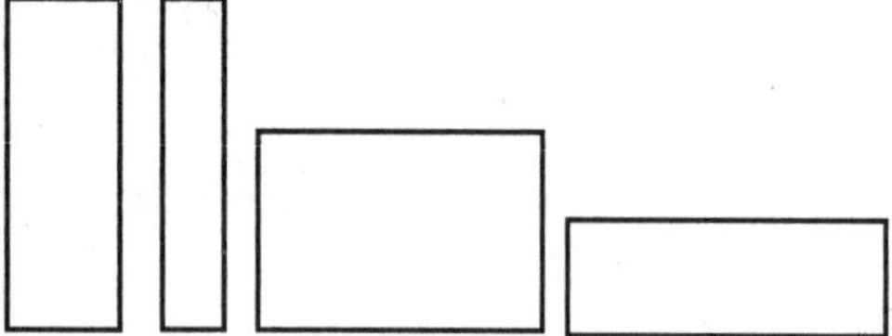

35. How many ways can you make 35¢, using only nickels and dimes?

______

36. How many small cubes make up the larger solid figure?

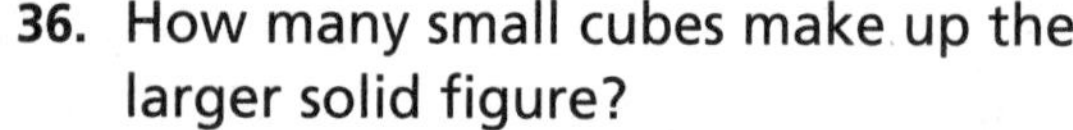

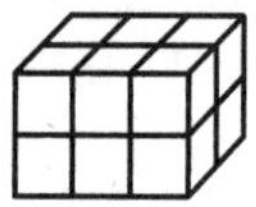

______

37. Name a decimal and fraction equivalent to 43%.

______

38. What is 40% of 80?

______

39. A spinner that is divided into 8 equal sections, has 2 blue, 3 orange, and 3 white sections. What is the probability that the pointer will land on a blue section?

______

40. The table shows the number of books that students in Mr. Brockelman's class read over the summer.

NUMBER OF BOOKS	NUMBER OF STUDENTS
1	2
2	5
3	6
4	7
more than 4	4

How many students read at least 3 books over the summer?

______

Stop

Name ______________________________

Choose the best answer.

For 1–4, estimate.

1. $617 - 285$

A 900
B 800
C 400
D 300

2. 2,391 ÷ 57

F 4
G 40
H 400
J 4,000

3. $3{,}134 + 2{,}876 + 2{,}945$

A 9,000
B 8,000
C 7,000
D 6,000

4. 863×48

F 32,000
G 36,000
H 45,000
J 50,000

For 5–8, find the sum or difference.

5. $132{,}534 + 389{,}145$

A 511,479
B 511,679
C 521,411
D 521,679

6. $876{,}611 + 454{,}686$

F 421,925
G 1,320,297
H 1,321,297
J 1,331,297

7. $998{,}355 - 366{,}541$

A 632,214
B 631,814
C 621,814
D 531,814

8. $782{,}561 - 485{,}192$

F 279,369
G 279,396
H 297,369
J 297,963

For 9–12, multiply or divide.

9. 4,267 × 22

A 17,068
B 83,874
C 92,674
D 93,874

10. 10,982 ÷ 19

F 578
G 587
H 600
J 10,963

11. 7,884 ÷ 12

A 656
B 657
C 658
D 3,942

12. 5,741 × 489

F 2,831,449
G 2,807,349
H 2,381,448
J 120,561

Go On

13. Mrs. Morris has 84 dance students. If she has five times as many teenage students as adult students, how many adult students does she have?

A 12
B 13
C 14
D 70

14. José has played 152 baseball games in the last 3 years. If he has won 7 times as many games as he has lost, how many games has he won?

F 133
G 132
H 22
J 19

15. Delia has 115 science fiction and mystery books. If she has 4 times as many mystery books as she has science fiction books, how many mystery books does she have?

A 4
B 23
C 92
D 115

16. Steve can play 153 songs on the piano or the guitar. If he can play twice as many songs on the piano as on the guitar, how many songs can he play on the piano?

F 104
G 102
H 98
J 51

For 17–20, evaluate each expression for the given value.

17. $d - 21$, for $d = 35$

A 14
B 16
C 54
D 66

18. $g \div 8 \times 2$, for $g = 40$

F 1
G 7
H 10
J 80

19. $126 \div z$, for $z = 9$

A 14
B 15
C 117
D 123

20. $238 + f$, for $f = 872$

F 634
G 646
H 1,110
J 1,111

For 21–25, solve each equation by using mental math.

21. $35 - t = 27$

A $t = 62$
B $t = 52$
C $t = 12$
D $t = 8$

22. $9 \times 8 = c - 42$

F $c = 30$
G $c = 98$
H $c = 106$
J $c = 114$

23. $35 \div r = 7$

A $r = 4$
B $r = 5$
C $r = 28$
D $r = 245$

24. $30 \times 12 = 3g$

F $g = 1{,}080$
G $g = 360$
H $g = 120$
J $g = 14$

25. $49 + k = 84$

A $k = 35$
B $k = 45$
C $k = 123$
D $k = 133$

Stop

Name ______________________

Write the correct answer.

For 1–4, use the given method to estimate.

1. Use rounding.

$$\begin{array}{r} 943 \\ -\ 678 \\ \hline \end{array}$$

____

2. Use compatible numbers.

1,586 ÷ 38

____

3. Use clustering.

$$\begin{array}{r} 8,959 \\ 9,124 \\ +\ 8,871 \\ \hline \end{array}$$

____

4. Overestimate.

$$\begin{array}{r} 487 \\ \times\ 36 \\ \hline \end{array}$$

____

For 5–8, find the exact sum or difference.

5.
$$\begin{array}{r} 723,458 \\ +\ 272,845 \\ \hline \end{array}$$

____

6.
$$\begin{array}{r} 855,589 \\ +\ 378,122 \\ \hline \end{array}$$

____

7.
$$\begin{array}{r} 842,705 \\ -\ 510,398 \\ \hline \end{array}$$

____

8.
$$\begin{array}{r} 667,346 \\ -\ 231,999 \\ \hline \end{array}$$

____

For 9–12, multiply or divide.

9.
$$\begin{array}{r} 6,422 \\ \times\ 88 \\ \hline \end{array}$$

____

10. $17\overline{)10,608}$

____

11. 6,570 ÷ 15

____

12. 6,454 × 645

____

Go On

Name ______________________________

13. Harry owns 216 CDs. If he has five times as many popular CDs as jazz CDs, how many popular CDs does he own?

____

14. Danielle is driving from New York to Los Angeles, which is about 3,200 miles. She has driven 1,950 miles in 3 days. How many miles has she averaged per day?

____

15. Pablo has 116 car and airplane models. If he has three times as many car models as airplane models, how many car models does he have?

____

16. A coach has 84 softballs and baseballs. If he has five times as many softballs as baseballs, how many baseballs does he have?

____

For 17–20, evaluate each expression.

17. $s - 62$, for $s = 548$

____

18. $p \div 60 \times 32$, for $p = 180$

____

19. $272 \div 16$

____

20. $522 + k$, for $k = 964$

____

For 21–25, solve each equation using mental math.

21. $62 - h = 56$

____

22. $4 \times 11 = j - 63$

____

23. $56 \div d = 8$

____

24. $0 \times 24 = 6s$

____

25. $61 + n = 92$

____

Stop

Name ______________________

Choose the best answer.

For 1–6, use mental math to find the value.

1. 19 + 254

A 263 C 273
B 265 D 275

2. $2 \times 7 \times 40$

F 280 H 560
G 360 J 650

3. 395 − 87

A 318 C 306
B 308 D 288

4. $225 \div 5$

F 45 H 35
G 41 J 31

5. $6{,}784 \times 1$

A 6,785 C 1
B 6,784 D 0

6. $20 \times 37 \times 5$

F 137 H 925
G 185 J 3,700

For 7–10, find the value.

7. 8^5

A 390,625 C 32,768
B 262,144 D 4,096

8. 5^6

F 15,625 H 3,125
G 5,600 J 25

9. 7^5

A 49 C 7,500
B 2,401 D 16,807

10. 6^4

F 216 H 7,776
G 1,296 J 46,656

For 11–15, evaluate the expression.

11. $3^3 + 4 \times 5$

A 29 C 155
B 47 D 180

12. $42 - (6 \div 3) \times (5 + 3)$

F 320 H 168
G 312 J 26

13. $33 \times (4 - 2) - 4^2$

A 50 C 82
B 58 D 560

14. $(44 \div 4) \times (2 + 3^2)$

F 39 H 110
G 55 J 121

15. $(72 \div 9) + 13^2 - 8$

A 22 C 169
B 42 D 433

Go On

16. Ling has written 8 pages each day for the last 30 days. If she has to write a total of 400 pages in 46 days, how many pages will she have to write per day during the remaining time in order to meet her goal?

F 10 pages **H** 25 pages
G 15 pages **J** 50 pages

17. Robin baby-sits 5 hours a week for $6 per hour. He mows lawns for $10 each twice a week. How much will he make in 12 weeks?

A $6,000 **C** $480
B $600 **D** $380

For 18–21, evaluate the expression for $a = 8$ and $b = 3$.

18. $9 + a^2 \div (12 - 4)$

F 64 **H** 11
G 17 **J** 3

19. $b \times 5 + 43$

A 58 **C** 144
B 88 **D** 645

20. $80 \div a \times (28 - 23)$

F 450 **H** 15
G 50 **J** 2

21. $48 \div b - 7$

A 23 **C** 10
B 11 **D** 9

22. Deborah's train ride takes 8 hours. She reads 30 pages per hour. How many pages will she read if she sleeps for 2 hours and reads the rest of the time?

F 300 pages **H** 180 pages
G 240 pages **J** 38 pages

For 23–25, use the following chart.

GUIDED TOUR TIMES	
1 Expressionists	10 A.M., 4 P.M.
2 American Painters	10 A.M., 3 P.M.
3 Dutch Painters	12 P.M., 3 P.M.
4 Sculpture	1 P.M, 4 P.M.
5 Impressionists	2 P.M., 4 P.M.

Each tour lasts 50 minutes.

23. Miranda wants to take the Sculpture tour at 1 P.M. If she arrives at the museum at 10 A.M. and leaves at 4 P.M., in which order could she take all of the tours?

A 1, 2, 3, 4, 5 **C** 2, 5, 4, 3, 1
B 1, 3, 4, 5, 2 **D** 5, 4, 3, 2, 1

24. Ivan wants to take the 12 P.M. Dutch Painters tour. If he takes the tour and then eats for 45 minutes, what other tour could he take before he leaves the museum at 3:00 P.M.?

F 1 **H** 4
G 3 **J** 5

25. Susan wants to take the 10 A.M. Expressionists tour. If she plans to leave the museum by 2 P.M., which other tours could she take?

A 3, 4 **C** 2, 3
B 1, 2 **D** 5, 4

Stop

Name ______________________

Write the correct answer.

For 1–6, use mental math to find the value of each expression.

1. $64 + 319$

____

2. $6 \times 4 \times 30$

____

3. $487 - 242$

____

4. $342 \div 6$

____

5. $9{,}208 \times 1$

____

6. $20 \times 64 \times 5$

____

For 7–15, evaluate the expression.

7. 7^5

____

8. 16^2

____

9. 4^8

____

10. 6^4

____

11. $42 + 8 \times 2$

____

12. $97 - 8^2 + (10 \times 5)$

____

13. $(13 \times 5 + 1) \div (4^2 - 5)$

____

14. $(72 \div 6) \times (3 + 1^2)$

____

15. $5^3 \div 25 \times (14 - 12)$

____

Go On

16. Bernardo has sold an average of 9 pairs of shoes per day for the last 20 days. He has to sell a total of 260 pairs of shoes in 30 days to get a bonus. How many pairs of shoes will he have to sell per day during the remaining time in order to get a bonus?

____

17. Martha weeds gardens 7 hours a week for \$8 per hour. She washes three cars a week for \$12 each. How much will she be able to make in the next 14 weeks?

____

For 18–21, evaluate the expression for $a = 6$ and $b = 4$.

18. $(6 + a^2) \div (10 - 3)$

____

19. $b \times 9 + 35$

____

20. $90 \div a \times (42 - 37)$

____

21. $64 \div b - 6$

____

22. Rick plants 15 bushes per hour. He is at work for 8 hours per day, but he gets 1 hour off for lunch and 2 half-hour breaks. How many bushes can Rick plant in a day?

____

For 23–25, use the following chart.

ACTIVITY SESSION TIMES	
Dancing	12 P.M., 3 P.M.
Gymnastics	10 A.M., 4 P.M.
Yoga	11 A.M., 4 P.M.
Volleyball	2 P.M.
Basketball	3 P.M., 4 P.M.

Each activity lasts 50 minutes.

23. Cyril wants to do yoga at 11 A.M. If he arrives at the sports center at 10 A.M. and leaves at 4 P.M., in what order could he do all the activities?

____

____

24. If Marina goes to the dancing class at noon and then takes a 1 hour 15 minute break for lunch, what other activity could she do before she leaves the sports center at 4 P.M.?

____

25. Amy plans to take gymnastics at 10 A.M. If she plans to leave the sports center by 12:30, what other activity could she do?

____

Stop

Name ______________________________

Choose the best answer.

1. Compare the numbers in each pair. For which pair is $>$ the correct symbol?

   A 43.27 ● 43.22
   B 43.77 ● 43.77
   C 3.22 ● 3.27
   D 43.22 ● 43.22

2. Compare the numbers in each pair. For which pair is $<$ the correct symbol?

   F 188.3 ● 188.03
   G 188.03 ● 188.3
   H 188.03 ● 188.03
   J 88.3 ● 88.3

3. Which is equal to 0.834?

   A 0.8340　　C 0.84
   B 0.843　　D 8.8340

4. Which is greater than 92.05?

   F 1.0005
   G 92.005
   H 92.05
   J 92.5

For 5–8, order the numbers from *least* to *greatest*.

5. 5.22, 5.81, 5.27, 5.041

   A 5.81, 5.27, 5.22, 5.041
   B 5.81, 5.041, 5.27, 5.22
   C 5.041, 5.27, 5.22, 5.81
   D 5.041, 5.22, 5.27, 5.81

6. 22.1, 22.7, 22.09, 22.078

   F 22.7, 22.1, 22.09, 22.078
   G 22.09, 22.7, 22.078, 22.1
   H 22.078, 22.09, 22.1, 22.7
   J 22.09, 22.078, 22.7, 22.1

7. 18.87, 18.45, 18.03, 18.30

   A 18.87, 18.45, 18.30, 18.03
   B 18.03, 18.87, 18.45, 18.30
   C 18.30, 18.45, 18.87, 18.03
   D 18.03, 18.30, 18.45, 18.87

8. 25.05, 25.80, 25.40, 25.99

   F 25.99, 25.80, 25.40, 25.05
   G 25.05, 25.40, 25.80, 25.99
   H 25.80, 25.40, 25.99, 25.05
   J 25.40, 25.80, 25.99, 25.05

For 9–11, find the value of the underlined digit.

9. $5.2\underline{3}94$

   A 3 ones
   B 3 tens
   C 3 hundredths
   D 3 thousandths

10. $37.66\underline{2}57$

   F 2 thousandths
   G 2 hundredths
   H 2 tenths
   J 2 ones

11. $0.\underline{3}0809$

   A 3 ones
   B 3 tenths
   C 3 hundredths
   D 3 thousandths

Go On

Name ______________________________

For 12–13, find the percent and the decimal for the shaded part.

12. 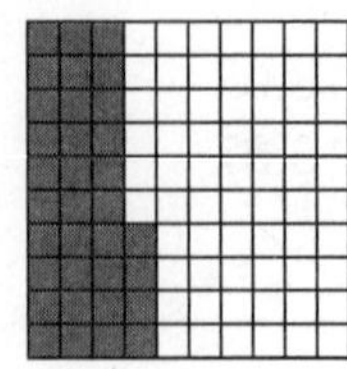

F 0.66%, 66
G 66%, 0.66
H 34%, 0.34
J 0.34%, 34

13. 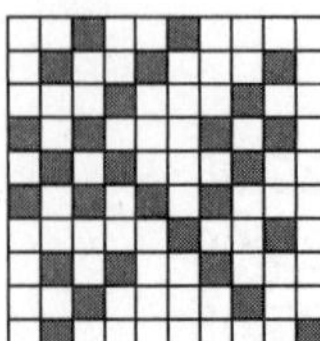

A 0.27%, 27
B 27%, 0.27
C 0.73%, 73
D 73%, 0.73

For 14–16, find the corresponding percent or decimal.

14. 0.07

F 700%
G 70%
H 7%
J 0.7%

15. 5%

A 5.0
B 0.5
C 0.05
D 0.005

16. 0.9

F 900%
G 90%
H 9%
J 0.9%

For 17–20, use the data in the chart below. The greater the number, the stronger the earthquake.

STRENGTH OF RECENT EARTHQUAKES (MAGNITUDE ON THE RICHTER SCALE)	
Los Angeles	3.4
Tokyo	3.1
San Francisco	4.1
Mexico City	4.2
New Delhi	3.6
Hong Kong	3.9

17. Which of these cities had the weakest earthquake?

A Hong Kong
B Tokyo
C San Francisco
D New Delhi

18. Which of these cities had the strongest earthquake?

F Mexico City
G San Francisco
H Hong Kong
J New Delhi

19. Which of these cities had the second weakest earthquake?

A Los Angeles
B Tokyo
C Mexico City
D Hong Kong

20. Which city had the second strongest earthquake?

F Tokyo
G New Delhi
H Mexico City
J San Francisco

For 21–25, estimate.

21. 4.8×7.2

A 28
B 35
C 40
D 3,500

22. $64.3 \div 8.1$

F 0.7
G 0.8
H 7
J 8

23. $38.9 + 162.3$

A 20
B 130
C 150
D 200

24. $5.13 + 4.97 + 4.88 + 5.04$

F 21
G 20
H 19
J 16

25. $80.7 - 2.5$

A 94
B 83
C 78
D 75

Stop

Name ______________________________

Write the correct answer.

For 1–4, compare the numbers in each pair. Write >, <, or =.

1. 83.09 ● 83.9

2. 3.0984 ● 3.0849

3. 8.80 ● 8.800

4. 48.75 ● 48.5

For 5–8, order the numbers from *least* to *greatest*.

5. 4.53, 4.091, 4.58, 4.12

6. 25.802, 25.8, 25.08, 25.818

7. 1.50, 1.05, 1.04, 1.45, 1.40

8. 7.54, 7.53, 7.08, 7.58

For 9–11, write the value of the underlined digit.

9. $8.09\underline{3}46$

10. $9.\underline{6}8723$

11. $8.2\underline{8}706$

Go On

For 12–13, write the percent and the decimal for the shaded part.

12. 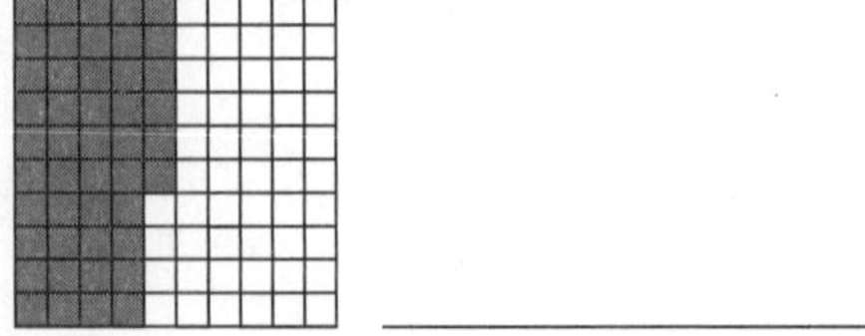 ____________

13. 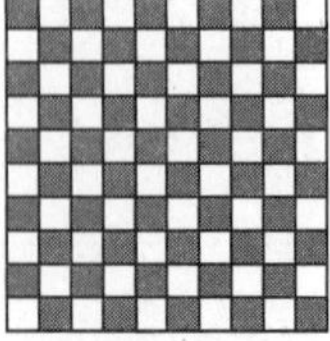 ____________

For 14–16, write the corresponding percent or decimal.

14. 0.03

____

15. 6%

____

16. 0.2

____

For 17–20, use the data in the chart below.

AVERAGE WIND SPEED (MILES PER HOUR)	
Boston, MA	12.5
Chicago, IL	10.4
Houston, TX	7.8
Mobile, AL	8.9
St. Louis, MO	9.7
San Diego, CA	7.0

17. Which city had the lowest average wind speed?

____

18. Which city had the highest average wind speed?

____

19. Which city had the second lowest average wind speed?

____

20. Which city had the second highest average wind speed?

____

For 21–25, estimate.

21. 6.3×8.2

____

22. $78.2 \div 8.5$

____

23. $62.5 + 127.7$

____

24. $3.25 + 4.08 + 7.62 + 9.13$

____

25. $43.8 - 6.1$

____

Stop

Name ______________________

Choose the best answer.

1. $\begin{array}{r} 75.9 \\ +\ 48.39 \\ \hline \end{array}$

A 27.51
B 123.29
C 124.29
D 1,243.2

2. $\begin{array}{r} 102.4 \\ -\ 89.72 \\ \hline \end{array}$

F 12.68
G 12.72
H 13.38
J 192.12

3. $18.2 - 5.68$

A 12.52
B 12.68
C 13.48
D 23.88

4. $4.7 + 0.25 + 6.09$

F 35.79
G 13.29
H 11.04
J 9.14

5. 5.9×4.2

A 3.54
B 24.78
C 247.8
D 2,478

6. 8.03×3.22

F 2.6726
G 24.8566
H 25.8566
J 258.566

7. 77.32×6.8

A 52.5776
B 70.52
C 84.12
D 525.776

8. 34.52×4.8

F 165.696
G 65.696
H 39.32
J 29.72

9. $9.03 \div 3$

A 30.1
B 6.03
C 3.1
D 3.01

10. $15.75 \div 4.5$

F 35
G 11.25
H 5.3
J 3.5

11. $45.9 \div 7.5$

A 61.2
B 38.4
C 6.12
D 6.02

12. $59.52 \div 0.96$

F 62
G 49.2
H 9.2
J 6.2

Go On

13. Gordy has 187 CDs. He wants to put them on shelves. Each shelf holds 42 CDs. How many shelves will he be able to completely fill with CDs?

A 2 C 4
B 3 D 5

14. Sasha is making craft projects to sell at the fair. Each project will take 3 days to finish. If she can spend 35 days working on the projects, how many projects can she complete?

F 32 H 11
G 12 J 5

15. Lee is buying cupcakes for his class picnic. If each cupcake costs $0.50 and he has $12.35, how many cupcakes can he buy?

A 25 C 12
B 24 D 5

16. Carole is making flower baskets. Each basket takes 35 minutes to make. She works from 9:00 AM to 5:00 PM. How many flower baskets can she finish?

F 14 H 12
G 13 J 3

For 17–20, evaluate each expression for the given value.

17. $e \times 7$ for $e = 5.6$

A 0.8 C 35.2
B 12.6 D 39.2

18. $g \div 4.3 \times 7$ for $g = 13.76$

F 30.1 H 13.76
G 22.4 J 10.2

19. $6.8 + c - 5.2$ for $c = 7.4$

A 25 C 9.4
B 19.4 D 9

20. $5.9 \times f + r$ for $f = 4.2$ and $r = 7.8$

F 32.58 H 16.98
G 32.08 J 3.258

For 21–25, solve each equation using mental math.

21. $5.7t = 17.1$

A 12.2 C 9
B 9.2 D 3

22. $2.8 \div c = 1.4$

F 38 H 2
G 18 J 1.876

23. $44.5 - d = 16.9$

A 2.76 C 27.6
B 16.9 D 61.4

24. $58.47 + y = 63.81$

F 122.28 H 5.34
G 55.34 J 0.534

25. $8.62 + k = 16.61$

A 7.99 C 16.61
B 8.62 D 25.13

Stop

Write the correct answer.

1. $\begin{array}{r} 34.4 \\ +\ 55.89 \\ \hline \end{array}$

____

2. $\begin{array}{r} 105.6 \\ -\ 58.91 \\ \hline \end{array}$

____

3. $16.4 - 8.59$

____

4. $6.05 + 0.78 + 2.1$

____

5. 3.7×2.9

____

6. 5.84×7.16

____

7. 53.29×4.6

____

8. 63.21×8.2

____

9. $16.08 \div 4$

____

10. $25.16 \div 3.7$

____

11. $50.73 \div 5.7$

____

12. $37.5 \div 6.25$

____

Go On

13. Betsy is making pizza for 35 people. Each pizza will serve 4 people. How many pizzas will she need to feed everyone?

____

14. Angelo has 22 muffins to serve for breakfast. Angelo will divide the muffins equally between 10 people. How many whole muffins can each person eat?

____

15. Joe invites 27 people to a party. He figures that each person will eat half of a submarine sandwich. How many whole sandwiches should he make?

____

16. Tonya is saving for a new computer. She can save $350 per month. The computer costs $1,650. How many months will it take her to save for the computer?

____

For 17–20, evaluate each expression for the given value.

17. $(4.7 + a) - 2.2$ for $a = 7.9$

____

18. $j \div 8.3 \times 3$ for $j = 26.56$

____

19. $4.5 \times q$ for $q = 2.8$

____

20. $33.2 \times k + m$ for $k = 6.7$ and $m = 7.3$

____

For 21–25, solve each equation using mental math.

21. $8.8j = 38.72$

____

22. $d \div 5 = 3.7$

____

23. $15.62 - h = 7.16$

____

24. $26.49 + s = 44.31$

____

25. $4.8 + p = 5.9 + 9.2$

____

Stop

Name ____________________

Choose the best answer.

1. An estimate that is greater than the exact answer is called a(n) __?__.

   A underestimate C error
   B overestimate D prediction

2. In the expression 4^7, the number 7 is called the __?__.

   F exponent H base
   G remainder J power

3. What is the value of the 5 in 3.1415926?

   A 5 millionths
   B 5 hundred-thousandths
   C 5 ten-thousandths
   D 5 thousandths

4. $2.7\overline{)72.9}$

   F 0.27
   G 2.7
   H 27
   J 270

5. Estimate.

$$\begin{array}{r} 2{,}497 \\ +\ 1{,}723 \\ \hline \end{array}$$

   A 5,000 C 3,500
   B 4,200 D 3,000

6. Find the value of $6 + 12 \div 3 - 2$.

   F 18 H 4
   G 8 J 2

7. Which list shows the numbers written in order from *least* to *greatest*?

   A 2.71, 2.7, 2.72, 2.718
   B 2.718, 2.7, 2.72, 2.71
   C 2.7, 2.71, 2.718, 2.72
   D 2.7, 2.71, 2.72, 2.718

8. 16.2×314.16

   F 5,089,392 H 50,893.92
   G 509,839.2 J 5,089.392

9. 125×25

   A 15,625 C 150
   B 3,125 D 5

10. Find the value of 6^6.

    F 279,936 H 7,776
    G 46,656 J 36

11. Estimate.

    $35.1 \div 6.85$

    A 9 C 7
    B 8 D 5

12. Evaluate $r \times (8.35 - t)$ for $r = 2.5$ and $t = 5.84$.

    F 15.035 H 8.775
    G 12.25 J 6.275

13. Estimate.

    $3{,}542 \div 72$

    A 50 C 60
    B 55 D 70

14. Evaluate $x^4 - y \bullet x$ for $x = 3$ and $y = 4$.

    F 756 H 69
    G 231 J 0

Go On

15. Which list shows the numbers in order from *least* to *greatest*?

0.240, 0.229, 0.251

A 0.251, 0.229, 0.240
B 0.251, 0.240, 0.229
C 0.229, 0.240, 0.251
D 0.240, 0.251, 0.229

16. Solve the equation by using mental math.

$p = 52.8 \div 5.28$

F $p = 10$
G $p = 100$
H $p = 110$
J $p = 1{,}000$

17. Juanita read a book in two weeks. She read for a total of 15 hr. She read twice as many hours the second week as the first week. How many hours did she read the second week?

A 10 hr
B 5 hr
C 3 hr
D 2 hr

18. Huang has $50 from delivering papers. He wants to buy 3 books at $7.95 each, a new pen for $5.49, and 2 maps for $3.75 each. How much money will he have left?

F $11.42
G $13.16
H $32.81
J $36.84

19. Which percent is equivalent to 0.28?

A 280%
B 28%
C 2.8%
D 0.28%

20. Kris finished a ski race in 53.27 sec. Tim finished in 51.84 sec. Who was faster and by how much?

F Kris; 2.43 sec
G Kris; 1.43 sec
H Tim; 1.43 sec
J Tim; 1.34 sec

21. Solve the equation using mental math.

$20x = 240$

A $x = 4{,}800$
B $x = 120$
C $x = 48$
D $x = 12$

22. Find the value of $25 \times (6 - 2)^2 + 4$.

F 10,004
G 804
H 404
J 204

23. Find a decimal and percent for the shaded area.

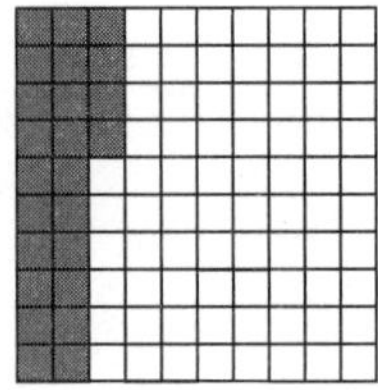

A 0.24, 24%
B 0.25, 25%
C 0.28, 28%
D 0.76, 76%

24. Jim can make one poster every 4.3 minutes. If he works non-stop from 8:00 A.M. to noon, how many posters can he finish?

F 240
G 60
H 56
J 55

25. Evaluate $a + b - 27$ for $a = 50$ and $b = 40$.

A 43
B 53
C 63
D 117

26. Find the value of $(3 + 4)^2$.

F 144
G 49
H 19
J 14

Go On

27. In a track event, Carl's time was 16.1 sec, Evan's was 16.13 sec, Ed's was 16.02 sec, and Phil's was 16.09 sec. Who came in third?

A Carl
B Evan
C Ed
D Phil

28. Notebooks cost $0.79 each, colored pencils are $0.29 each, and erasers are $0.24 each. Ms. Johnston wants to purchase 1 notebook, 2 colored pencils, and 1 eraser for each of the 33 students in her sixth-grade class. How much money will she need?

F $53.13
G $36.63
H $18.48
J $10.51

29. $\begin{array}{r} 321{,}456 \\ -\ 56{,}814 \\ \hline \end{array}$

A 378,270
B 335,442
C 264,642
D 264,462

30. Use mental math to find the value of $42 - (26 + 4)$.

F 74
G 66
H 64
J 12

31. Estimate.

597.993×48.817

A 30,000
B 29,192
C 25,000
D 20,000

32. Evaluate $k + 67.89$ for $k = 12.3$.

F 88.12
G 80.19
H 79.19
J 55.59

33. Kirk sold a total of 48 magazines in the last two days. He sold 12 more today than yesterday. How many magazines did he sell yesterday?

A 18
B 20
C 24
D 30

34. Jill, Sue, Fred, and Walt are going to a movie after they do their chores. The time it takes for each chore is shown below. To finish at the same time, in what order should they start?

Jill	Cleaning house	2 hr
Sue	Mowing lawn	3 hr
Fred	Washing dishes	1 hr
Walt	Washing clothes	4 hr

F Fred, Jill, Sue, Walt
G Sue, Walt, Jill, Fred
H Sue, Walt, Fred, Jill
J Walt, Sue, Jill, Fred

35. What is the value of 1 in 2.71828?

A 1 hundred
B 1 ten
C 1 tenth
D 1 hundredth

36. How many boxes of 12 calculators are needed for 369 students?

F 30
G 31
H 37
J 50

37. Use mental math to solve.

$360 = 12h$

A $h = 240$
B $h = 140$
C $h = 40$
D $h = 30$

38. Find the value of $(60 \div 5) + (8 - 5)^2$.

F 15
G 18
H 21
J 225

Go On

Name ______________________________

39. Liam learns that the first bus arrives at his bus stop at 7:27 A.M. Buses then come every 17 min. When will the sixth bus arrive?

A 9:09 A.M. **C** 8:50 A.M.
B 8:52 A.M. **D** 8:35 A.M.

40. $2.31 + 12.5 + 0.284$

F 64.0
G 17.65
H 15.094
J 15.0

41. Dorothy has 84 apples. She has three times as many red apples as she has green apples. How many red apples does she have?

A 84 **C** 42
B 63 **D** 21

42. Which of the following is the first step to evaluate $2 \times 3^4 - 18 \div 8$?

F 3^4 **H** 2×3
G $4 - 18$ **J** $18 \div 8$

43. Which is a decimal equivalent of 40%?

A 40.0 **C** 0.4
B 4.0 **D** 0.04

44. How many decimal places will be in the product 8.24×9.56?

F 2 **H** 5
G 4 **J** 6

45. Evaluate $21 \div a - b + 4$ for $a = 7$ and $b = 3$.

A 0 **C** 8
B 4 **D** 10

46. Find the value of $16 - 4^2$.

F 0 **H** 24
G 8 **J** 144

47. Zachary earned $9.75 raking leaves, $15.25 mowing lawns, $11.20 pruning shrubs, and $21.80 washing windows. Which is a reasonable estimate of his total earnings?

A $40 **C** $50
B $45 **D** $55

48. Jessica has to stack vegetable cans on shelves. She has 247 cans and each shelf holds 14 cans. How many complete shelves can she fill?

F 24 **H** 17
G 18 **J** 15

49. Find the value of $12 \times 12 \times 12$.

A 1,728 **C** 144
B 324 **D** 36

50. Pablo earns $3 for each car he washes and $7 for each car he waxes. If he washes 8 cars this month and waxes 5, how much will he earn?

F $10 **H** $39
G $31 **J** $59

Stop

Name ______________________________

Write the correct answer.

1. An estimate that is less than the exact answer is called a(n) __?__ .

____

2. In the expression 3^2, the number 3 is called the __?__ .

____

3. What is the value of the 5 in 8.675309?

____

4. $3.1\overline{)58.9}$

____

5. Estimate the sum.

$$\begin{array}{r} 3{,}807 \\ +\ 1{,}288 \\ \hline \end{array}$$

____

6. $9 - 16 \div 4 + 8$

____

7. Order the numbers from *greatest* to *least*.

   3.417, 3.471, 3.447, 3.474

____

8. 18.7×407.52

____

9. 250×15

____

10. Find the value of 4^5.

____

11. Estimate.

    $28.1 \div 7.35$

____

12. Evaluate $d \times (6.94 + g)$ for $d = 4.2$ and $g = 3.14$.

____

13. Estimate the quotient.

    $4{,}777 \div 81$

____

14. Evaluate $c^3 + m \times c$ for $c = 4$ and $m = 7$.

____

Go On

15. Order the numbers from *greatest* to *least*.

0.880, 0.804, 0.808

____

16. Solve the equation using mental math.

$c = 417 \div 4.17$

____

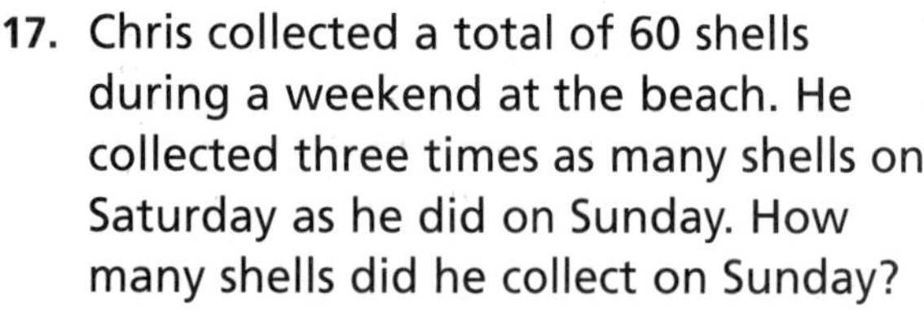

17. Chris collected a total of 60 shells during a weekend at the beach. He collected three times as many shells on Saturday as he did on Sunday. How many shells did he collect on Sunday?

____

18. Lynda began a craft project with a piece of copper wire 36 in. long. From this she cut 2 pieces that were each 3.5 in. long, 3 pieces that were each 4.75 in. long, and 1 piece that was 11.5 in. long. How much wire did she have left?

____

19. Write a percent that is equivalent to 0.54.

____

20. Maggie bought two CDs at the mall. One was priced $11.98, and the other was $13.45. What was the difference in their prices?

____

21. Solve the equation using mental math.

$30y = 360$

____

22. Evaluate the expression.

$48 \div (8 - 6)^2 + 11$

____

23. Write the decimal and percent for the shaded area.

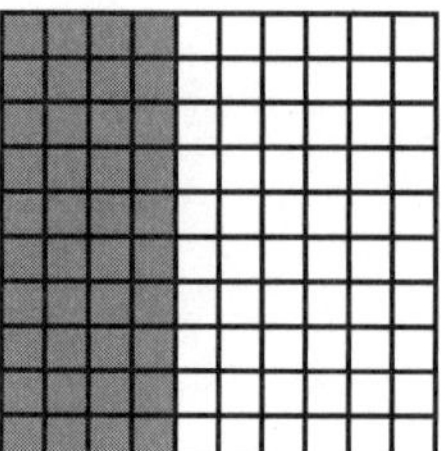

____

24. A pool is losing water through a leak at a constant rate of one gallon every 2.5 days. How much water does the pool lose in 4 weeks?

____

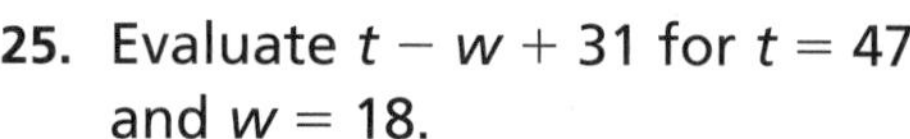

25. Evaluate $t - w + 31$ for $t = 47$ and $w = 18$.

____

26. $(4 + 2)^3$

____

Go On

27. At a gymnastics meet, Katherine scored 9.15 on the balance beam, 9.06 on the vault, and 9.10 on the uneven parallel bars. In which event did she receive the lowest score?

____

28. Michael's father made bags of party favors for the 12 friends that came to Michael's party. For each bag he bought 2 packs of baseball cards for \$1.59 each, 1 pack of bubblegum for \$0.49, and a kazoo for \$0.25. How much did he spend on party favors?

____

29.

$$\begin{array}{r} 456{,}391 \\ -\ \ 88{,}012 \\ \hline \end{array}$$

____

30. Use mental math to find the value of $28 + (41 - 9)$.

____

31. Estimate the product.

389.896×24.502

____

32. Evaluate $c + 56.78$ for $c = 23.4$.

____

33. It rained a total of 46 days in March and April. It rained 8 more days in April than in March. How many days did it rain in March?

____

34. David, Gary, Susan, and Walter are meeting at the mall. The time it takes for each to ride to the mall is shown below. To arrive at the same time, in what order should they leave their homes?

David	25 minutes
Gary	15 minutes
Susan	30 minutes
Walter	10 minutes

____

35. Write the value of the 2 in 8.32971.

____

36. How many complete rows of 15 parking spaces are needed to park 280 cars?

____

37. Use mental math to solve.

$440 = 11g$

____

38. $(56 \div 4) + (9 - 3)^2$

____

Go On

39. Diane saw on a schedule that the first tram leaving the parking lot departs at 8:42 A.M. Trams then depart every 12 min. When will the sixth tram depart?

____

40. $3.65 + 20.1 + 0.197$

____

41. Richard has 64 comic books in his collection. He has three times as many superhero comics as he has humor comics. How many superhero comic books does he have?

____

42. Which operation is the first step to evaluate $3 \times 2^4 + 25 \div 5$?

____

43. Write the decimal equivalent of 65%.

____

44. How many decimal places will be in the product 6.97×8.42?

____

45. Evaluate $42 \div d + g - 3$ for $d = 6$ and $g = 6$.

____

46. $36 - 6^2$

____

47. Vi spent $8.15 on Monday, $13.45 on Tuesday, $9.90 on Wednesday, and $18.65 on Thursday. What is a reasonable estimate of the amount of money he spent on these four days?

____

48. Wally has to pack his rock collection in cases. He has 165 rocks and each case holds 12 rocks. How many cases can he fill completely?

____

49. $11 \times 11 \times 11$

____

50. Bill earns $12 for each lawn he mows and $8 for each garden he weeds. If he mows 6 lawns this month and weeds 3 gardens, how much will he earn?

____

Stop

Name ______________________

Choose the best answer.

For 1–2, determine the type of sample used.

1. John randomly selected a student from his class and then every fifth student after that to determine the number of videos watched each week.

   A convenience
   B voluntary
   C random
   D systematic

2. Samantha randomly surveys 1 out of every 6 people in the movie theater to find the brand of popcorn most often eaten at home.

   F convenience
   G voluntary
   H random
   J systematic

For 3–7, use the table below, which shows the ages of teachers at Martin Luther King, Jr. School.

AGES OF TEACHERS				
24	53	32	48	28
35	41	29	33	51
40	29	31	25	28
38	47	52	29	27

3. What is the range of ages?

   A 3
   B 24
   C 29
   D 53

4. What is the mode?

   F 28
   G 29
   H 31
   J 53

5. What is the median?

   A 32
   B 32.5
   C 33
   D 53

6. What is the mean?

   F 24
   G 32.5
   H 36
   J 53

7. What is the sample size?

   A 20
   B 24
   C 63
   D 66

8. Which measure is best for describing the following data?

   2, 4, 3, 1, 4, 1, 87, 2, 3, 4, 3, 1, 2

   F median
   G mode
   H mean
   J range

9. Juanita wants to find out how much time sixth-grade students spend studying math. Which method of sampling is unbiased?

   A Survey her 2 best friends in the class.
   B Randomly survey the girls in her sixth-grade gym class.
   C Randomly survey 5 students from grades 3 through 6.
   D Randomly survey 40 sixth-grade students.

10. Find the mean of the data in the line plot.

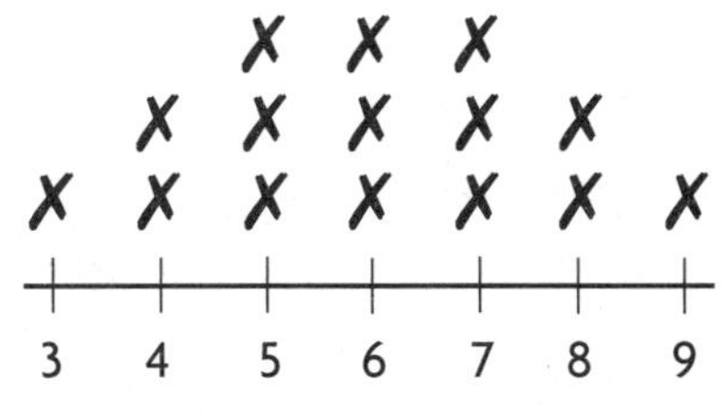

   F 3
   G 6
   H 15
   J 90

Go On

11. Meghan sells magazines. She sold 10 magazines the first week, 8 the second, and then had sales of 12, 14, 9, and 14 the following weeks. In the final week of sales, she sold 32 magazines. Which measure was most affected by the final week's sales?

A mean
B mode
C median
D mean and mode

12. Music can be purchased on CDs, cassettes, mini-discs, and CD-singles. From a survey of 500 randomly chosen teenagers, the following results were obtained.

Which is a possible conclusion?

F Cassettes were the most popular.
G Mini-discs were more popular than CD-singles.
H CD-singles were more popular than cassettes.
J CDs were the most popular.

13. The following frequency table lists the ratings given to a new science fiction movie.

SCIENCE FICTION MOVIE RATING		
Rating	Frequency	Cumulative Frequency
Excellent	25	25
Good	■	65
Fair	20	85
Poor	10	■
Disaster	5	100

What numbers are missing from the frequency column and the cumulative frequency column?

A 40, 85
B 40, 95
C 65, 10
D 65, 95

For 14–15, use the chart below. Jason recorded the kinds of cars parked in the school parking lot.

van	sports car	
sedan	SUV	sedan
sports car	sedan	mini-van
sedan	sedan	mini-van

14. How many rows would be needed to make a table that shows all the different kinds of cars?

F 2 rows
G 3 rows
H 4 rows
J 5 rows

15. How many of the cars were sports cars?

A 5 cars
B 4 cars
C 3 cars
D 2 cars

Stop

Name ______________________

Write the correct answer.

1. Fifty students are randomly selected from the 378 students at George Washington School for a survey. What are the 50 chosen students called?

____

2. A survey was conducted at a mall to determine how many families would consider buying a DVD player for their home. One shopper was selected and then every tenth shopper that entered the mall after her was surveyed. What type of sample was used?

____

3. Sales of special pizzas at a small pizza shop were recorded for the past two weeks. Find the mean, median, and mode for this data set.

NUMBER OF PIZZAS SOLD						
7	9	8	6	7	8	12
8	7	14	7	9	10	14

mean _____ median _____ mode _____

4. The annual wages in thousands of dollars for the owner and six workers at a small manufacturing company are:

   $25, $25, $20, $25, $25, $25, $100.

   What measure(s) of central tendency are most useful to describe this set of data?

____

5. The mean of two numbers is 15. When a third number is included, the mean increases to 20. What is the third number?

____

For 6–7, use this chart that lists the age of automobiles driven by counselors at the Community Center.

AGE OF AUTOMOBILE (IN YEARS)									
5	9	2	6	4	7	1	5	3	10
8	12	3	6	7	1	7	14	7	3

6. What is the range of ages for these automobiles?

____

7. What is the sample size?

____

8. What measure of central tendency best describes the data set below?

   5, 3, 7, 2, 6, 4, 75, 5, 3, 6, 2, 4, 2

____

9. José wants to know if students at his school spend as much time playing soccer as he does. He asks his three best friends how much time they spend playing soccer. Is this sampling method biased or unbiased? Explain.

____

____

Go On

Name ______________________________

10. Find the mean of the data in the following line plot.

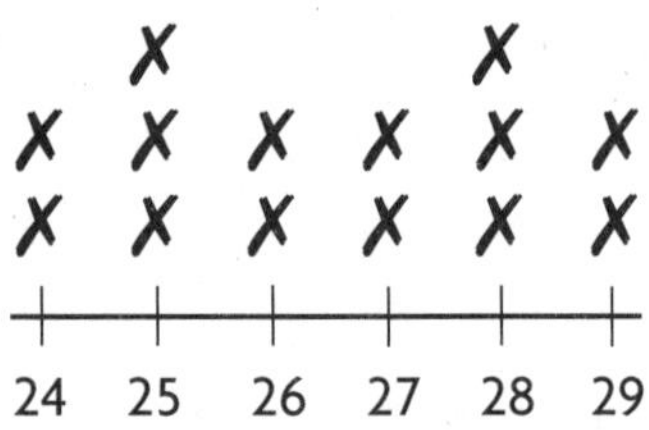

____

11. Cups and Cones sold 10 gal of ice cream the first day of summer, 8 gal the second day, and had sales of 12, 14, 9, and 14 gal the following days. On the seventh day, the store sold 32 gal of ice cream. What measure of central tendency was most affected by the seventh day's sales?

____

12. Popular movie rentals include VHS tapes, laser discs, and DVDs. The results of a survey of randomly chosen teens at the local video store are shown in the bar graph. What is a possible conclusion about the popularity of different ways to rent movies?

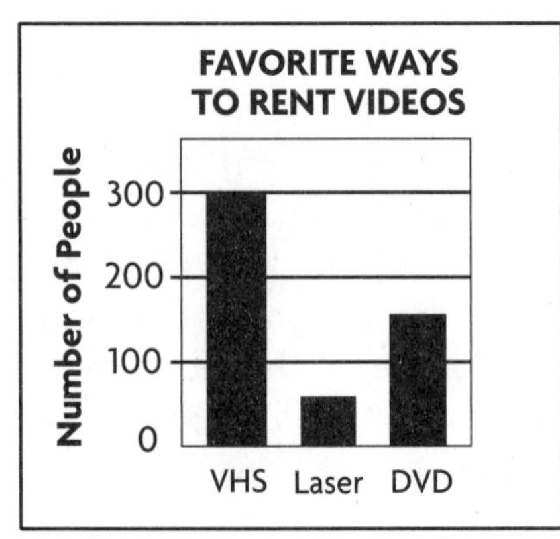

____

13. The following frequency table lists the ratings given to cafeteria food by sixth grade students. What numbers are missing from the frequency column and the cumulative frequency column?

CAFETERIA FOOD RATING		
Rating	**Frequency**	**Cumulative Frequency**
Excellent	5	5
Good	■	30
Fair	35	65
Poor	20	■
Disaster	15	100

____

For 14–15, use the chart below. It lists the music format most often listened to by the students in the music club.

CD	cassette	CD
mini-disc	CD	CD single
cassette	CD	mini-disc
CD single	cassette	CD

14. Make a table for this data.

15. How many students listened to cassettes?

____

Stop

Name ______________________________

Choose the best answer.

For 1–8, choose the best type of graph to show the given situation.

1. a stock price changing over time

   A histogram C bar graph
   B line graph D circle graph

2. the lengths of five different rivers

   F box-and-whisker H bar graph
   G line graph J circle graph

3. the number of visitors to a museum grouped by intervals

   A histogram C bar graph
   B box-and-whisker D circle graph

4. favorite music choices by percent

   F histogram H stem-and-leaf
   G line graph J circle graph

5. the season scores of a basketball team

   A histogram C stem-and-leaf
   B line graph D circle graph

6. how the extreme numbers are related to the median numbers

   F stem-and-leaf H bar graph
   G box-and-whisker J circle graph

7. to compare parts to the whole or to other parts

   A histogram C bar graph
   B box-and-whisker D circle graph

8. to show how data change over time

   F line graph H circle graph
   G histogram J bar graph

For 9–13, use the graph below.

9. Which month had the most tourists?

   A January C March
   B February D April

10. How many tourists would be a good prediction for July, if the trend continues?

   F 17,000 H 15,000
   G 16,000 J 14,000

11. How many tourists came in April?

   A 17 C 17,000
   B 18 D 18,000

12. Which other type of graph could be used to show the same data?

   F circle H bar
   G multiple-line J stem-and-leaf

13. Which of these changes could cause the graph to be misleading?

   A Use larger numbers.
   B Make the intervals unequal.
   C Double the intervals.
   D Start the scale at zero.

Go On

14. Choose the least biased question.

- F Do you think that vanilla is the favorite flavor, or is it chocolate?
- G Do you think chocolate is the favorite flavor, or is it vanilla?
- H Which do you think is the favorite flavor, chocolate or vanilla?
- J Isn't vanilla the favorite flavor, or is it chocolate?

15. Choose the least biased question.

- A Who is correct, Karen, Lars, or David?
- B Is Lars correct, or is it Karen or David?
- C Karen is correct, isn't she? Or is it Lars or David?
- D Do you think that David is correct, or is it Lars or Karen?

For 16–19, use the graph below.

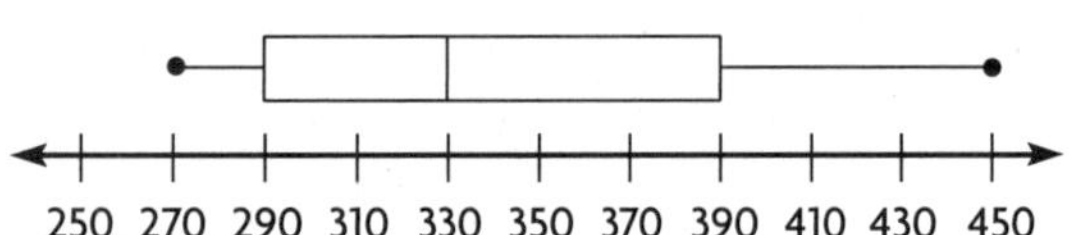

16. What is the lower quartile?

F 290 H 450
G 330 J 590

17. What is the median?

A 33 C 290
B 270 D 330

18. What is the lower extreme?

F 170 H 390
G 270 J 450

19. What is the upper quartile?

A 390 C 290
B 330 D 120

For 20–23, make a stem-and-leaf plot of the following scores.

87, 88, 94, 77, 98, 68, 72, 96, 80, 90, 79, 81, 69, 93, 92, 85, 99, 92, 83, 74

20. Which list shows the leaves for the stem 6?

F 9, 8, 0 H 2, 4, 7, 9
G 0, 1, 3, 5, 7, 8 J 8, 9

21. Which list shows the leaves for the stem 7?

A 8, 9 C 0, 1, 3, 5, 7, 8
B 2, 4, 7, 9 D 9, 7, 4, 2, 0

22. Which list shows the leaves for the stem 8?

F 2, 4, 7, 9 H 8, 9
G 0, 1, 3, 5, 7, 8 J 1, 3, 5, 7, 8

23. Which list shows the leaves for the stem 9?

A 0, 2, 2, 3, 4, 6, 8, 9 C 8, 9
B 0, 1, 3, 5, 7, 8 D 2, 4, 7, 9

For 24–25, use the table below.

DISTANCE ALLIE BICYCLED					
Week	1	2	3	4	5
Miles	65	80	95	115	135

24. If Allie continues her trend, estimate how far she will bike in week 6.

F 95 miles H 160 miles
G 130 miles J 240 miles

25. If the trend continues, in which week will Allie bike more than 200 miles?

A week 8 C week 10
B week 9 D week 11

Stop

Name ______________________________

Write the correct answer.

1. Which type of graph is best to show temperature changing over time?

____

2. Which type of graph is best to show the lengths of time cars were parked in a parking lot grouped by hourly intervals?

____

3. Which type of graph is best to show a family budget by percent?

____

4. Which type of graph is best to show every student's grade on a quiz?

____

5. Which type of graph is best to show how the amount of a person's savings changed over time?

____

6. Which type of graph is best to show the percentages of people surveyed who chose different candidates?

____

7. Which type of graph is best to show how the high and low test scores relate to the median?

____

8. Which type of graph is best to show how well different brands of orange juice sell?

____

For 9–13, use the graph below.

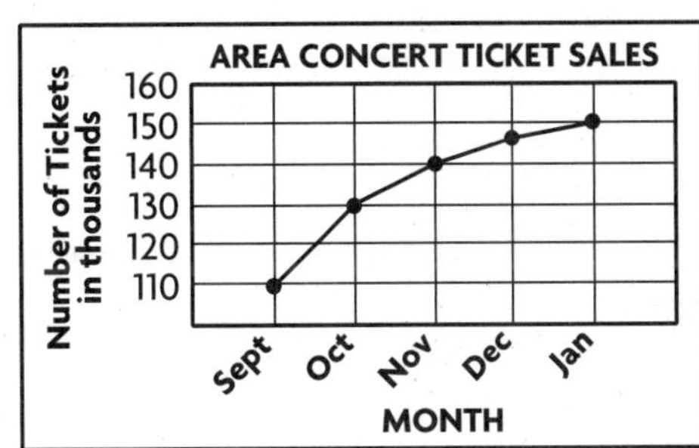

9. In which month were the most tickets sold?

____

10. How many tickets would be expected to be sold in February if the trend continued?

____

11. How many tickets were sold in October?

____

12. What other type of graph could be used to show the same data?

____

13. Explain why the graph would be less misleading if the scale started at 0?

____

____

Go On

For 14–15, rewrite the statement so that it is less biased.

14. Do you think that the Zebra is the best car ever made, or is it the Antelope or the Gazelle?

____

____

15. Is Saul the best athlete, or is it Mia or Andrew?

____

____

For 16–19, use the box-and-whisker graph below.

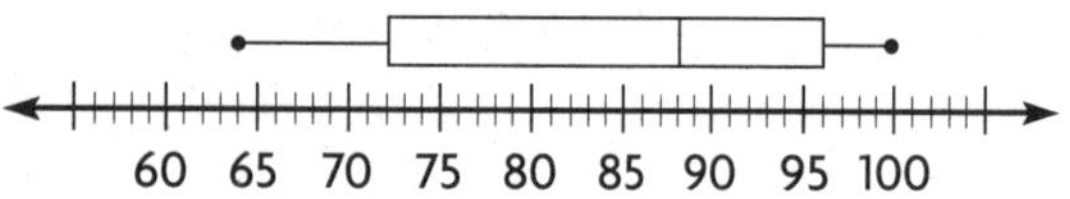

16. What is the upper extreme?

____

17. What is the lower quartile?

____

18. What is the median?

____

19. What is the upper quartile?

____

20. Make a stem-and-leaf plot for the following scores.

78, 56, 95, 48, 99, 87, 92, 79, 32, 94, 86, 85, 81, 76, 84, 55, 88, 88, 99, 68

For 21–23, use the stem-and-leaf plot you drew.

21. What are the leaves for the stem 9?

____

22. Which stem has the most leaves? List the leaves for that stem.

____

23. Which stem has only two leaves? List the leaves for that stem.

____

For 24–25, use the table below.

DISTANCE JOHN DROVE					
Week	1	2	3	4	5
Miles	280	300	330	370	420

24. Estimate how far John will drive in week 6 if he continues his trend.

____

25. In which week should John drive more than 600 miles if the trend continues?

____

Stop

Name ______________________________

Choose the best answer.

1. The entire group of individuals or objects for which data is collected is called the __?__.

   A sample C survey
   B population D cluster

2. The graph shows the price of a share of stock each day last week.

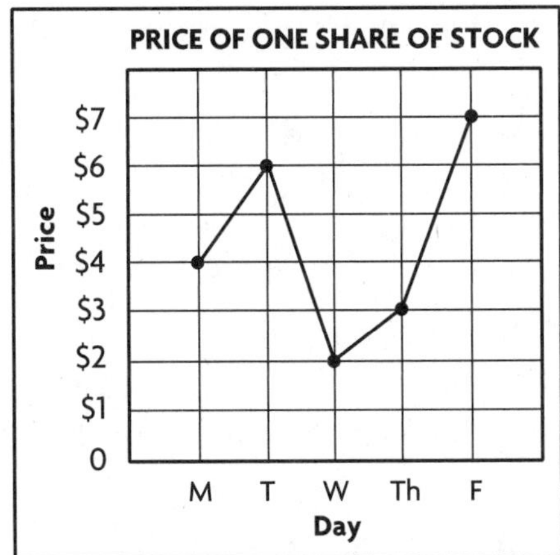

   What was the greatest price increase on any one day?

   F $4 G $2
   H $3 J $1

3. Which type of graph or plot would best show heights of students in a math class?

   A histogram C stem-and-leaf
   B line graph D circle graph

4. The best graph to show two or more sets of data on the same graph is a __?__ graph.

   F multiple-bar H line
   G bar J circle

5. Josh asked, "Do you agree that math teachers assign too much homework?" is __?__.

   A random C biased
   B unbiased D unclear

For 6–7, use the table showing how many nights a week some people eat out.

Number of Nights Eating Out	
1	𝍸 |||
2	𝍸 𝍸 |||
3	𝍸 |||
4					
5 or more	||

6. How many eat out 3 nights a week?

   F 14 H 5
   G 8 J 3

7. How many eat out at least 4 nights a week?

   A 9 C 4
   B 6 D 2

8. Which is the mean of this data?

   5, 5, 7, 15, 28

   F 5 H 10
   G 7 J 12

For 9–10, use the box-and-whisker graph below.

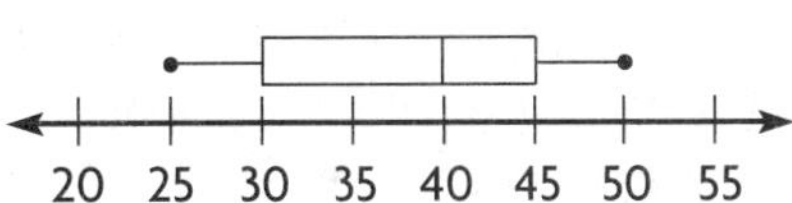

9. Which is the median?

   A 30 C 40
   B 37.5 D 45

10. Which is the upper extreme?

   F 30 H 45
   G 40 J 50

Go On

11. Which is the median number of fish caught?

NUMBER OF FISH CAUGHT
4, 2, 9, 3, 2, 2, 9, 4, 1

A 1
B 2
C 3
D 4

12. The median of the upper half of a set of data is called the __?__.

F upper quartile
G upper extreme
H lower quartile
J lower extreme

13. For the following set of data, what word describes the data value 15?

1, 1, 1, 2, 3, 3, 4, 5, 6, 6, 8, 15

A outlier
B data
C sample
D mode

14. Which type of graph shows all values in the set of data?

F histogram
G bar
H circle
J stem-and-leaf

15. Nine out of ten teenagers prefer action movies to dramas. Which conclusion is valid?

A Teenagers prefer action movies.
B Teenagers do not like dramas.
C A tenth of Linda's friends prefer action movies.
D Nine tenths of Linda's friends never watch dramas.

16. Which type of graph would be best to show a family's monthly budget?

F histogram
G circle graph
H line graph
J stem-and-leaf

For 17–18, use the circle graph below.

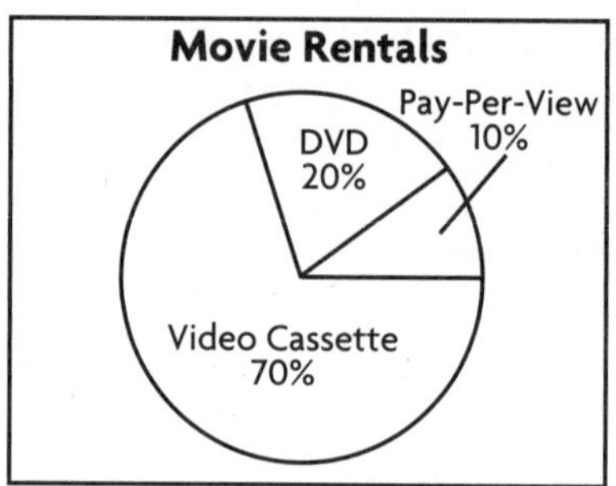

17. Which percent of people rented DVDs?

A 10%
B 20%
C 30%
D 70%

18. Which way to rent a movie was most preferred?

F DVD
G Pay-Per-View
H Video Cassette
J no preferred way

For 19–20, use the cumulative frequency table showing how people rated a new bike.

Rating	Frequency	Cumulative Frequency
Excellent	6	6
Good	?	14
Fair	5	?
Poor	3	22

19. How many people gave the bike a "Good" rating?

A 6
B 8
C 14
D 19

20. Which conclusion is valid for the data?

F Few gave an "Excellent" rating.
G 22 people gave a "Poor" rating.
H Most people liked the bike.
J No conclusion is possible.

Go On

21. Every fourth person entering a store is asked to name their favorite brand of jeans. What kind of sample is this?

A convenience C random
B systematic D cluster

For questions 22–24, use the bar graph showing this year's rainfall.

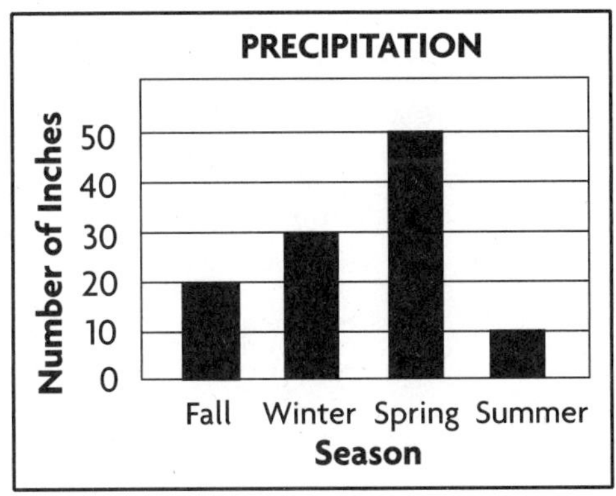

22. Which season had the most rainfall?

F spring H winter
G summer J fall

23. If next year is like this year, how much precipitation would be predicted for next summer?

A 50 in. C 20 in.
B 30 in. D 10 in.

24. Which change would make the graph misleading?

F Use larger numbers.
G Start the scale at zero.
H Double the intervals.
J Make the intervals unequal.

25. The mean age of 10 people is 20 years. When Mr. Wax's age is included, the mean age increases to 25. How old is Mr. Wax?

A 25 years C 50 years
B 30 years D 75 years

26. From her school of 285 students, Kim sampled 5 students and concluded that most students prefer beef. Why is her conclusion not valid?

F The sample is too random.
G The sample is too small.
H The sample is biased.
J The sample is not systematic.

For 27–29, make a stem-and-leaf plot of the following scores.

41, 34, 45, 22, 18, 28, 22, 34, 36,

22, 33, 25, 17, 26, 27, 46, 21, 32,

23, 14, 22, 25, 39, 39, 11, 16, 28

27. How many stems are in the stem-and-leaf plot?

A 5 C 3
B 4 D 2

28. Which are the leaves for the stem 3?

F 1, 4, 6, 7, 8
G 1, 2, 2, 2, 2, 3, 5, 5, 6, 7, 8, 8
H 2, 3, 4, 4, 6, 9, 9
J 1, 5, 6

29. Which is the median for the data?

A 22 C 27.6
B 26 D 28.5

30. Find the mode(s) for the data in the line plot.

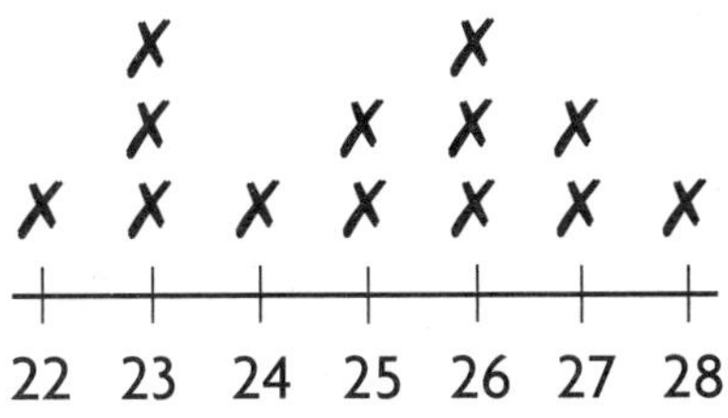

F 3 H 23 and 26
G 23 J 24.5

Go On

For 31–33, use the following stem-and-leaf plot of test score data.

Stem	Leaf
7	0 0 2 5 5 8 8 8 9
8	0 0 4 6 6 6 6 8
9	2 4 6 6 8

31. Which is the median?

A 78
B 79
C 80
D 82

32. Which is the range?

F 19
G 28
H 82
J 86

33. What other type of graph could be used to show the same data?

A line plot
B line graph
C circle graph
D bar graph

34. Which of the following should **not** be used to describe typical values in a set of data?

F outlier
G median
H mode
J mean

35. Which type of graph best shows how data is distributed?

A stem-and-leaf
B box-and-whisker
C circle bar
D line graph

36. In the first month of swimming class, Jordan swam 2 km. If she doubles her distance each month, how far will she swim in the fourth month?

F 4 km
G 8 km
H 16 km
J 32 km

37. Larry's savings deposits for the first 6 weeks of the new year were \$3, \$2, \$3, \$2, \$3, and \$2. If this trend continues, how much money will he have saved by the end of the 10th week?

A \$50
B \$47
C \$45
D \$25

38. Which is the upper quartile?

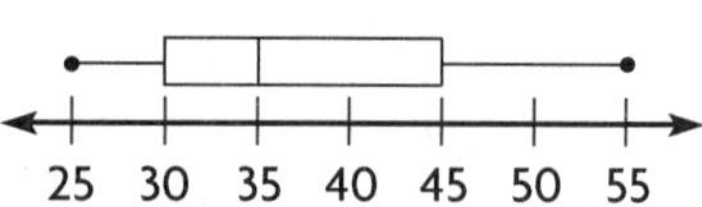

F 30
G 35
H 45
J 55

39. Which is the range of the data?

12, 19, 15, 22, 14

A 10
B 8
C 7
D 2

40. Which type of sample is most likely to give results that lead to invalid conclusions?

F convenience
G random
H systematic
J biased

Stop

Name ______________________________

Write the correct answer.

1. A __?__ is a method of gathering information about a group.

____

2. The graph shows the average temperature for each day last week. What was the greatest average temperature increase between any two days?

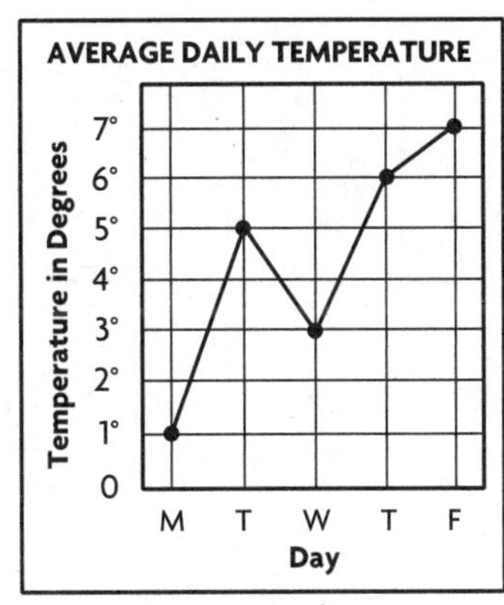

____

3. What type of graph would best show the number of visitors, grouped by age, to a theme park?

____

4. What type of graph would best show the numbers of points scored by players in a basketball game?

____

5. Rewrite the question so that it is less biased.

   Is Ms. Nathan the best teacher, or is it Mr. Gold or Mrs. Cone?

____

____

Use the data for 6–8. It shows the number of brothers and sisters each student in Mrs. Yokoi's class has.

0, 3, 2, 4, 0, 1, 1, 2, 5, 4, 6, 2, 3, 1, 0, 2, 5, 2, 1, 2, 0, 7, 4, 2, 1

6. Complete the tally table.

Number of Brothers and Sisters	
0	
1	
2	
3	
4	
5 or more	

7. How many students have at least 4 brothers and sisters?

____

8. What is the mean of the data?

____

For 9–10, use the box-and-whisker graph.

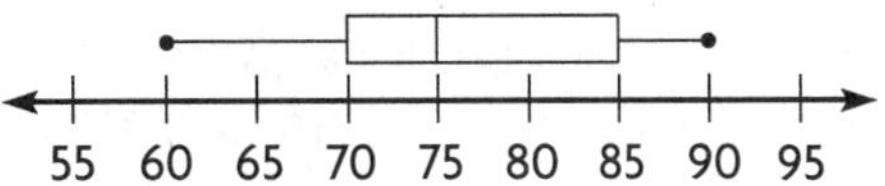

9. What is the median?

____

10. What is the lower extreme?

____

Go On

11. What is the median price for a pair of jeans?

PRICE OF JEANS								
$11	$12	$13	$13	$15	$16	$19	$22	$24

____

12. What is the median of the lower half of a set of data called?

____

13. For the following set of data, what word describes the value 13?

13, 20, 21, 23, 23, 25, 26, 28

____

14. Which type of graph would best show how the high and low scores of a soccer team relate to the median?

____

15. A random sample from one basketball team shows that the players prefer to wear two pairs of socks. Fati decides that all basketball players on the team prefer to wear two pairs of socks. Is the conclusion valid? Explain.

____

16. Which type of graph would best show how a baby gorilla's weight changed over time?

____

For 17–18, use the circle graph.

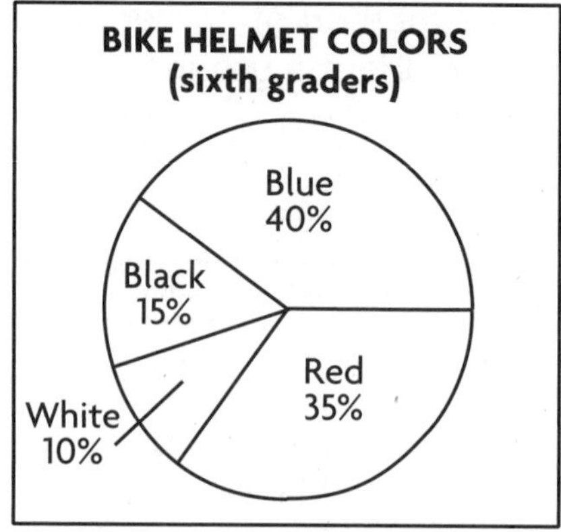

17. What percent of sixth graders have red bike helmets?

____

18. Which color of helmet is the most popular?

____

For 19–20, use the cumulative frequency table showing how people rated a new VCR.

19. Complete the table.

Rating	Frequency	Cumulative Frequency
Outstanding	3	3
Above Average	4	■
Average	■	12
Below Average	2	14

____

20. How many people rated the new VCR?

____

Go On

Name ____________________

21. A store surveyed the first 50 customers of the day. What type of sample was this?

____

For 22–24, use the bar graph showing this week's absences at Sojourner Truth Middle School.

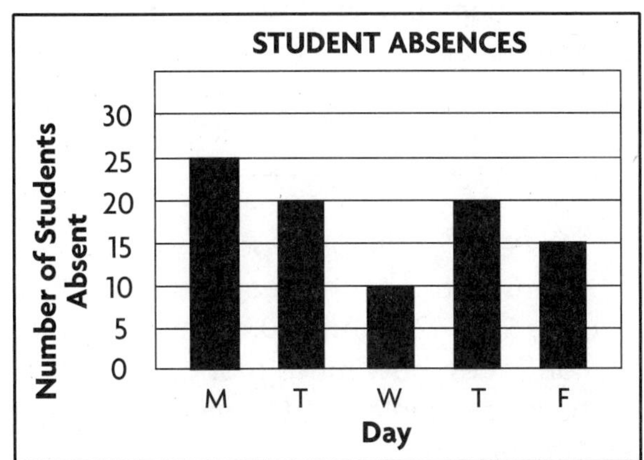

22. On which day were the fewest students absent?

____

23. If next week is similar to this week, how many absences would be predicted for Friday?

____

24. Why would it **not** be good to start the vertical scale at 5 instead of 0?

____

25. The mean age of 8 people is 16 years. When Mrs. Hernandez's age is included, the mean age increases to 20. How old is Mrs. Hernandez?

____

26. Andy randomly surveyed 30 children at the pet store to celebrate bird day. He concluded that children prefer birds as pets. Why is Andy's conclusion not valid?

____

____

27. Make a stem-and-leaf plot for the following scores.

23, 25, 29, 34, 33, 38, 42, 41, 40,

45, 49, 51, 53, 50, 50, 54, 60, 62,

70, 72, 76, 79, 76, 22, 23, 24, 45

For 28–29, use the stem-and-leaf plot you drew.

28. What is the median for the data?

____

29. What are the modes for the data?

____

Go On

Name ______________________________

30. What are the modes for the data in the line plot?

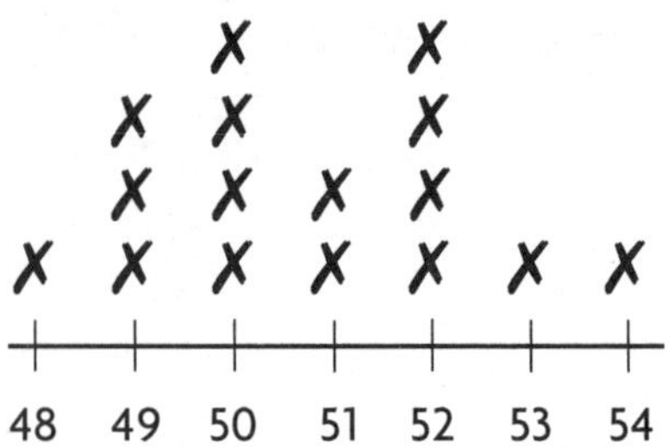

____

For 31–33, use the stem-and-leaf plot of test score data.

Stem	Leaves
1	0 0 1 3 3 3 4 5
2	0 2 6 6 8 9 9
3	1 2 4 5 7 7 8

31. What is the median score?

____

32. What is the range of the scores?

____

33. Could a histogram be used to show the same data? Explain.

____

34. Amy scored 65, 70, 75, 80, and 85 on her first 5 math quizzes. What does she have to score on the next quiz to increase her mean score by 2 points?

____

35. Which type of graph would best show the percent of votes all candidates in an election received?

____

36. In the first week of soccer training, Melissa did 20 crunches. If she doubles the number of crunches each week, how many crunches will she do in the fifth week?

____

37. Mr. Perez's savings deposits for the first 6 weeks of the year were $25, $20, $25, $20, $25, and $20. If this pattern continues, how much money will he have saved in all by the end of the 10th week?

____

38. What is the upper quartile of the data?

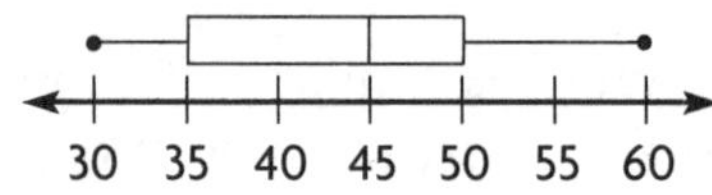

____

39. What is the range of the data?

64, 55, 72, 43, 36

____

40. A store surveyed every tenth customer during the day. What type of sample was this?

____

Stop

Name ____________________

Choose the best answer.

For 1–2, choose the list that contains all the numbers from 2 to 10 by which the given number is divisible.

1. 24

   A 2
   B 2, 3, 4
   C 2, 3, 4, 6, 8
   D 2, 3, 4, 6, 8, 9

2. 245

   F 2
   G 5, 7
   H 3, 5
   J 3, 5, 9

3. Which number is divisible by both 5 and 9?

   A 550
   B 801
   C 2,345
   D 4,005

4. Which pair of numbers is divisible by both 6 and 9?

   F 136 and 594
   G 234 and 458
   H 270 and 369
   J 414 and 630

5. What are the first five multiples of 21?

   A 1, 3, 7, 21, 63
   B 3, 7, 21, 63, 147
   C 21, 42, 63, 84, 105
   D 21, 42, 84, 168, 336

6. What is the prime factorization of 594 in exponent form?

   F $2^3 \times 3^2 \times 11$
   G $3^3 \times 4 \times 11$
   H $2 \times 3^3 \times 11$
   J $2^2 \times 3^2 \times 11$

7. What is the prime factorization of 936 in exponent form?

   A $2^3 \times 3^2$
   B $2^3 \times 3^2 \times 13$
   C $2^3 \times 3 \times 13$
   D $8 \times 9 \times 13$

8. What is the prime factorization of 52?

   F $2^2 \times 13$
   G 4×13
   H 2×26
   J $2 \times 3 \times 7$

9. Which number is prime?

   A 37
   B 54
   C 75
   D 91

10. Find the GCF of 52 and 195.

    F 780
    G 26
    H 15
    J 13

11. Find the LCM of 70 and 105.

    A 35
    B 42
    C 210
    D 7,350

12. Emily is making treats that need 1 chocolate bar and 1 marshmallow each. Chocolate bars come in packages of 12. Marshmallows come in packages of 30. What is the least number of packages of each she will have to buy in order to have equal numbers of chocolate bars and marshmallows?

    F 2 chocolate, 5 marshmallow
    G 5 chocolate, 2 marshmallow
    H 30 chocolate, 10 marshmallow
    J 60 chocolate, 60 marshmallow

13. Find a pair of numbers whose LCM is 360 and whose GCF is 3.

    A 15 and 18
    B 18 and 24
    C 24 and 45
    D 45 and 1,280

14. What is the 25th number in the pattern?

    137, 134, 131, 128, 125, ...

    F 26
    G 62
    H 65
    J 74

Go On

Name ______________________________

15. There are 12 cheerleaders and 45 band members. All of the cheerleaders and band members will work in groups at the car wash. Each group will have the same number of cheerleaders and the same number of band members. What is the greatest number of groups that can be formed?

A 3 **C** 6
B 5 **D** 12

16. Five weeks ago, Jules typed 8 words per min. During the next 4 weeks his speed increased to 12 words, 16 words, 20 words, and then 24 words per min. To get a job, Jules must type 60 words per min. If his improvement continues to follow this pattern, in how many more weeks will he reach 60 words per min?

F 12 weeks **H** 6 weeks
G 9 weeks **J** 3 weeks

17. If you fold a piece of paper in half once, there are 2 parts. Folding twice gives you 4 parts. Three folds gives you 8 parts, and so on. How many folds would be necessary to get 128 parts?

A 4 **C** 24
B 7 **D** 64

18. Find the LCM of 8, 12, and 18.

F 1,728 **H** 96
G 216 **J** 72

19. By which pair of numbers below is 16,728 divisible?

A 2 and 9 **C** 3 and 8
B 3 and 5 **D** 4 and 7

20. Joshua swims every 4 days and Katarina swims every 7 days. They both swam on July 4. How many more times will they swim on the same day by September 4?

F 1 **H** 5
G 2 **J** 10

21. Hot dogs are sold 12 in a package. Buns are sold 8 in a package. Ketchup packets come 100 in a box. What is the least number of each item you can buy and have the same number of hot dogs, buns, and ketchup packets?

A 4 **C** 1,200
B 600 **D** 9,600

22. Carbon-14 (C-14) has a half-life of about 6,000 yr. If you start with 6,400 g of C-14, there would be 3,200 g left after 6,000 yr, 1,600 g after 12,000 yr, and 800 g after 18,000 yr. How long would it be until only 100 g were left?

F 17,984 yr **H** 30,000 yr
G 24,000 yr **J** 36,000 yr

23. Find the GCF of 15, 18, and 54.

A 2 **C** 5
B 3 **D** 270

24. The prime factorization of 378 is $2 \times 3^n \times 7$. What is the value of n?

F 3 **H** 7
G 4 **J** 27

25. Which pair of numbers has 36 as the LCM?

A 3, 6 **C** 6, 9
B 3, 12 **D** 9, 12

Stop

Name ______________________________

Write the correct answer.

1. Write the numbers from 2 through 10 by which 36 is divisible.

____

2. Write the numbers from 2 through 10 by which 495 is divisible.

____

3. Which numbers between 100 and 200 are divisible by both 5 and 9?

____

4. Write *true* or *false*.

   Numbers that are even and divisible by 9 are also divisible by 6.

____

5. List the first five multiples of 17.

____

6. Write the prime factorization of 150 in exponent form.

____

7. Write the prime factorization of 531 in exponent form.

____

8. Find the prime factorization of 66.

____

9. A number *c* is a prime factor of both 35 and 98. What is the value of *c*?

____

10. Find the GCF of the numbers 12 and 20.

____

11. Find the LCM of the numbers 8 and 50.

____

12. Dr. Russell has 54 tape strips and 36 gauze pads. What is the greatest number of packages she can make if she puts the same numbers of tape strips and gauze pads in each package and uses all the strips and pads?

____

13. Find a pair of numbers whose LCM is 75 and whose GCF is 5.

____

14. What is the 26th number in the pattern?

    257, 253, 249, 245, 241, ...

____

Go On

15. Daniel has 12 quarters and 45 dimes to share among his friends at the arcade. He wants to give each friend the same number of quarters and the same number of dimes and not have any money left over. How many friends can he take to the arcade?

____

16. Mikael is in a training program assembling robot parts. He will finish the training when he can assemble 100 parts a day. He assembled 16 parts the first day, 22 the second day, 28 the third day, and 34 the fourth day. If he continues this pattern, when will he finish training?

____

17. A single cell amoeba reproduces by splitting into two cells. One cell reproduces to form 2 cells. Those cells split to form 4 cells. Then those cells split to form 8 cells, and so forth. How many times will a single cell have to split until there are more than 1,000 cells?

____

18. Find the LCM of the numbers 9, 18, and 27.

____

19. 20,202 is divisible by what numbers from 2 through 10?

____

20. Aaron works out at the gym every third day. Ashley works out only every five days. They meet at the gym for the first time on March 1. When will they meet at the gym for the third time?

____

21. Dimes are packaged 50 in a roll. Quarters come 40 in a roll. Susan B. Anthony dollars come in rolls of 25. How many rolls of each do you need to have an equal number of each coin?

____

____

22. It is possible for the amount of money in a savings account to double every 7 years. If you put $2,500 in a savings account of this type and never take any out, about how long would it take for your balance to be $80,000?

____

23. Find the GCF of the numbers 14, 42, and 63.

____

24. The prime factorization of 495 is $3^n \times 5 \times 11$. What is the value of n?

____

25. Find a pair of numbers that has 90 as the LCM and 15 as the GCF.

____

Stop

Name ___________________________________

Choose the best answer.

For 1–3, find the number that completes the equation.

1. $\frac{2}{3} = \frac{■}{15}$

A 5   C 12
B 10   D 18

2. $\frac{12}{24} = \frac{4}{■}$

F 72   H 6
G 8   J 2

3. $\frac{3}{■} = \frac{6}{8}$

A 16   C 4
B 5   D 2

4. Which fraction is in simplest form?

F $\frac{5}{12}$ H $\frac{9}{12}$
G $\frac{6}{12}$ J $\frac{10}{12}$

5. Which is $\frac{6}{30}$ in simplest form?

A $\frac{6}{5}$ C $\frac{1}{5}$
B $\frac{5}{6}$ D $\frac{1}{30}$

6. Which is $\frac{10}{16}$ in simplest form?

F $\frac{20}{32}$ H $\frac{4}{6}$
G $\frac{5}{8}$ J $\frac{5}{4}$

7. Which is $\frac{8}{3}$ as a mixed number?

A $\frac{2}{3}$ C $2\frac{1}{3}$
B 2   D $2\frac{2}{3}$

8. Which fraction is equal to 4?

F $\frac{20}{5}$ H $\frac{25}{5}$
G $\frac{22}{4}$ J $\frac{24}{4}$

9. Which is $2\frac{3}{4}$ as a fraction?

A $\frac{11}{4}$ C $\frac{9}{4}$
B $\frac{10}{4}$ D $\frac{8}{4}$

10. Which is $3\frac{5}{8}$ as a fraction?

F $\frac{5}{8}$ H $\frac{29}{8}$
G $\frac{16}{8}$ J $\frac{40}{8}$

For 11–14, find the number that makes the number sentence true.

11. $\frac{5}{6} = \frac{■}{12}$

A 2   C 10
B 6   D 11

12. $■ < \frac{11}{16}$

F $\frac{14}{16}$ H $\frac{6}{8}$
G $\frac{8}{10}$ J $\frac{5}{8}$

13. $■ > \frac{4}{7}$

A 0.3   C 0.5
B 0.4   D 0.6

14. $0.6 = ■$

F $\frac{60}{10}$ H $\frac{3}{5}$
G $\frac{10}{6}$ J $\frac{3}{50}$

Go On

15. Which is 0.3 as a fraction?

A $\frac{30}{10}$ C $\frac{3}{100}$
B $\frac{3}{10}$ D $\frac{3}{1,000}$

16. Which completes the equation?

$6\frac{7}{10} = \frac{670}{■}$

F 1,000 H 10
G 100 J 1

17. What is $\frac{3}{4}$ in decimal form? Tell whether the decimal terminates or repeats.

A 0.25; repeats
B 0.25; terminates
C 0.75; repeats
D 0.75; terminates

18. What is $\frac{8}{9}$ in decimal form?

F 0.9 H 0.8
G $0.\overline{8}$ J $0.\overline{3}$

19. What is $\frac{2}{5}$ written as a percent?

A 2% C 40%
B 20% D 45%

20. What is $\frac{19}{100}$ written as a percent?

F 190% H 1.9%
G 19% J 0.19%

21. In gym class, $\frac{1}{4}$ of the students voted to play soccer, $\frac{4}{12}$ voted to play baseball, $\frac{3}{8}$ voted to play volleyball, and $\frac{1}{24}$ voted to play basketball. Which activity got the greatest part of the votes?

A volleyball C basketball
B soccer D baseball

22. In a sixth-grade class, $\frac{7}{20}$ of the students got 100 on a test. What percent of the students got 100 on the test?

F 3.5% H 21%
G 5% J 35%

23. At a film festival, $\frac{9}{15}$ of the judges gave the movie *The Last Bicycle* the highest rating. Which decimal tells what part of the group of judges gave the movie the highest rating?

A 0.9 C 0.45
B 0.6 D 0.3

24. For the class picnic, $\frac{1}{3}$ of the class voted for vanilla ice cream, $\frac{2}{5}$ voted for chocolate, $\frac{1}{5}$ voted for peach, and $\frac{1}{15}$ voted for strawberry. Which flavor received the least part of the votes?

F strawberry H chocolate
G vanilla J peach

For 25, use the table below.

ARTURO'S BOOKS	
Type	**Number**
Mystery	7
Science Fiction	6
Romance	3
Nonfiction	4

25. Which fraction tells what part of Arturo's books are science fiction?

A $\frac{6}{7}$ C $\frac{3}{10}$
B $\frac{3}{5}$ D $\frac{3}{20}$

Stop

Name ______________________

Write the correct answer.

For 1–3, complete the equation.

1. $\frac{3}{5} = \frac{■}{20}$

____

2. $\frac{8}{40} = \frac{1}{■}$

____

3. $\frac{4}{■} = \frac{8}{14}$

____

4. Write $\frac{15}{18}$ in simplest form.

____

5. Write $\frac{10}{30}$ in simplest form.

____

6. Write $\frac{24}{32}$ in simplest form.

____

7. Write $\frac{23}{4}$ as a mixed number or a whole number.

____

8. Write a fraction with a divisor of 3 that is equal to 6.

____

9. Write $4\frac{3}{4}$ as a fraction.

____

10. Write $2\frac{7}{10}$ as a fraction.

____

11. Write a fraction equivalent to $\frac{2}{3}$.

____

For 12–14, compare. Write <, >, or = for each ●.

12. $\frac{8}{12}$ ● $\frac{1}{3}$

____

13. $\frac{3}{12}$ ● 0.25

____

14. $\frac{4}{5}$ ● 0.75

____

15. Write 0.7 as a fraction.

____

Go On

16. Complete.

$2\frac{1}{9} = \frac{\blacksquare}{9}$

______

17. Write $\frac{4}{5}$ as a decimal. Tell whether the decimal terminates or repeats.

______

18. Write $\frac{1}{6}$ as a decimal. Tell whether the decimal terminates or repeats.

______

19. Write $\frac{1}{4}$ as a percent.

______

20. Write $\frac{83}{100}$ as a percent.

______

21. For the class trip, $\frac{1}{3}$ of the class voted to go to a museum, and $\frac{1}{6}$ voted to go to a theme park. Another $\frac{7}{30}$ voted to go to a concert, and $\frac{4}{15}$ voted to go to the airport. Which trip got the greatest part of the votes?

______

22. In a sixth-grade class, $\frac{19}{20}$ of the students passed the quiz on fractions. What percent of the students passed the quiz?

______

23. In Mr. Chen's class, $\frac{20}{25}$ of the students have tried in-line skating and liked it. What decimal tells what part of the class tried in-line skating and liked it?

______

24. In Mrs. Driscoll's class, $\frac{3}{20}$ of the students have track practice after school. Another $\frac{1}{5}$ practice in the marching band, $\frac{3}{10}$ have gymnastics, and $\frac{7}{20}$ attend the computer lab after school. In which after-school activity do the fewest of Mrs. Driscoll's students participate?

______

For 25, use the table below.

JOSÉ'S ALBUMS	
Type of Music	**Number**
Rock	9
Country	4
Latin	5
Jazz	2

25. What fraction in simplest form tells what part of José's collection is country music albums?

______

Stop

Name ______________________________

Choose the best answer.

For 1–4, estimate the sum or difference.

1. $2\frac{4}{5} + 3\frac{7}{8}$

A 8
B 7
C 6
D 5

2. $5\frac{1}{8} - 3\frac{6}{7}$

F 3
G 2
H 1
J 0

3. $1\frac{5}{6} + 3\frac{1}{5}$

A 4
B 5
C 6
D 7

4. $\frac{5}{7} - \frac{2}{3}$

F 0
G $\frac{1}{2}$
H 1
J 2

5. Kyle spent $2\frac{1}{5}$ hr mowing the lawn, $1\frac{9}{10}$ hr raking, and $\frac{5}{6}$ hr pruning the rose bushes. Estimate the time he spent doing yard work.

A 3 hr
B 4 hr
C 5 hr
D 6 hr

For 6–11, find the sum or difference in simplest form.

6. $\frac{1}{3} + \frac{1}{4}$

F $\frac{1}{7}$
G $\frac{2}{7}$
H $\frac{2}{5}$
J $\frac{7}{12}$

7. $\frac{5}{8} - \frac{1}{4}$

A $\frac{1}{4}$
B $\frac{3}{8}$
C $\frac{1}{2}$
D $\frac{7}{8}$

8. $\frac{2}{3} + \frac{1}{8}$

F $\frac{3}{11}$
G $\frac{13}{24}$
H $\frac{19}{24}$
J $1\frac{5}{24}$

9. $\frac{8}{9} - \frac{5}{6}$

A 1
B $\frac{1}{3}$
C $\frac{1}{18}$
D $\frac{1}{36}$

10. $\frac{3}{5} - \frac{3}{10}$

F 0
G $\frac{1}{10}$
H $\frac{1}{5}$
J $\frac{3}{10}$

11. $\frac{5}{12} + \frac{5}{6}$

A $\frac{5}{9}$
B $\frac{5}{6}$
C $1\frac{1}{6}$
D $1\frac{1}{4}$

12. Mrs. Nelson drove $\frac{2}{3}$ mi to take Manny to school, $\frac{1}{4}$ mi to the grocery store, and $\frac{5}{6}$ mi to her office. How far did she drive?

F $\frac{11}{12}$ mi
G $1\frac{3}{4}$ mi
H $1\frac{11}{12}$ mi
J $2\frac{1}{3}$ mi

13. Mark lives $\frac{3}{4}$ mi north of Ann. Leo lives $2\frac{1}{4}$ mi north of Ann. Draw a diagram to find how far Mark lives from Leo.

A 3 mi
B $2\frac{1}{2}$ mi
C $1\frac{3}{4}$ mi
D $1\frac{1}{2}$ mi

Go On

For 14–19, find the sum or difference in simplest form.

14. $7\frac{4}{5} - 5\frac{1}{2}$

F 2 H $2\frac{7}{10}$

G $2\frac{3}{10}$ J $13\frac{3}{10}$

15. $3\frac{5}{7} + 4\frac{1}{3}$

A $7\frac{1}{21}$ C $8\frac{1}{21}$

B $7\frac{3}{5}$ D $8\frac{3}{5}$

16. $5\frac{1}{4} - 3\frac{2}{3}$

F $1\frac{7}{12}$ H $1\frac{1}{4}$

G $1\frac{5}{12}$ J $\frac{3}{4}$

17. $1\frac{1}{2} + 3\frac{3}{4}$

A $5\frac{1}{4}$ C $4\frac{2}{3}$

B 5 D $4\frac{3}{8}$

18. $8\frac{1}{5} - 5\frac{1}{3}$

F $3\frac{1}{2}$ H $2\frac{13}{15}$

G 3 J $2\frac{2}{15}$

19. $1\frac{2}{3} + 5\frac{1}{6}$

A $6\frac{5}{6}$ C $6\frac{1}{3}$

B $6\frac{4}{9}$ D 6

20. Polly is planting a vegetable garden. She wants $\frac{2}{5}$ of her garden to be corn and $\frac{1}{6}$ to be zucchini. What fraction of the garden will be left?

F $\frac{3}{11}$ H $\frac{13}{30}$

G $\frac{11}{30}$ J $\frac{17}{30}$

For 21–23, find the sum or difference in simplest form.

21. $4\frac{3}{4} - 2\frac{1}{2}$

A $2\frac{1}{4}$ C $1\frac{1}{2}$

B 2 D $1\frac{1}{4}$

22. $3\frac{5}{6} + 1\frac{1}{3}$

F $5\frac{1}{6}$ H $4\frac{2}{3}$

G 5 J $4\frac{1}{2}$

23. $2\frac{1}{2} + 3\frac{1}{4}$

A $6\frac{1}{4}$ C $5\frac{1}{4}$

B $5\frac{3}{4}$ D $\frac{3}{4}$

24. Four friends live along a straight road. Sue lives $\frac{2}{3}$ mi from Ali and $\frac{2}{3}$ mi from Carlos. Ali lives between Sue and Tim. Carlos lives $1\frac{7}{8}$ mi from Tim. How far does Ali live from Tim?

F $\frac{13}{24}$ mi H $2\frac{13}{14}$ mi

G $1\frac{5}{24}$ mi J $3\frac{5}{24}$ mi

25. Martina drives $1\frac{1}{2}$ mi north from her office. Next, she drives $2\frac{3}{4}$ mi east. Then she drives $1\frac{1}{2}$ mi south. Tell how far and in what direction she must drive to get back to her office.

A $4\frac{1}{4}$ mi north C $2\frac{3}{4}$ mi east

B $4\frac{1}{4}$ mi west D $2\frac{3}{4}$ mi west

Stop

Name ______________________

Write the correct answer.

For 1–4, estimate the sum or difference.

1. $2\frac{3}{7} + 3\frac{4}{5}$

____

2. $7\frac{1}{8} - 2\frac{4}{5}$

____

3. $3\frac{1}{5} + 4\frac{9}{16}$

____

4. $\frac{7}{8} - \frac{4}{5}$

____

5. On Tuesday, Keith spent $1\frac{7}{8}$ hr studying for his history test. He studied again for $1\frac{1}{5}$ hr on Wednesday and for $\frac{5}{6}$ hr on Thursday. Estimate the time Keith spent studying for his history test this week.

____

For 6–11, write the sum or difference in simplest form. Estimate to check.

6. $\frac{1}{4} + \frac{2}{3}$

____

7. $\frac{6}{7} - \frac{1}{2}$

____

8. $\frac{3}{5} + \frac{1}{4}$

____

9. $\frac{7}{8} - \frac{5}{6}$

____

10. $\frac{7}{10} - \frac{1}{6}$

____

11. $\frac{7}{16} + \frac{7}{8}$

____

12. Noriko drives $\frac{2}{3}$ mile to pick up Mary, $\frac{3}{4}$ mile to get Marcus, and then $\frac{5}{6}$ mile to the movies. How far does she drive?

____

13. Kim lives $1\frac{3}{4}$ mi south of Patrick. Kara lives $1\frac{1}{2}$ mi south of Kim. Draw a diagram to find out how far Patrick lives from Kara.

____

Go On

Name ______________________

For 14–19, write the sum or difference in simplest form.

14. $1\frac{2}{7} + 3\frac{9}{14}$

____

15. $5\frac{3}{4} - 3\frac{1}{3}$

____

16. $3\frac{4}{5} + 2\frac{1}{4}$

____

17. $4\frac{1}{2} - 2\frac{7}{8}$

____

18. $1\frac{5}{6} + 3\frac{1}{3}$

____

19. $6\frac{1}{5} - 2\frac{1}{3}$

____

20. Jamie is a partner in a bookstore. He owns $\frac{1}{5}$ of the business. His sister, Lila, owns $\frac{1}{4}$, and their friend Jared owns the rest. What fraction of the business does Jared own?

____

For 21–23, draw a diagram to help you find the sum or difference. Write the answer in simplest form.

21. $5\frac{2}{3} - 3\frac{7}{12}$

____

22. $3\frac{5}{8} + 1\frac{1}{4}$

____

23. $7\frac{1}{3} - 4\frac{1}{2}$

____

24. Sarah bikes $\frac{3}{4}$ mi north. Next, she bikes $1\frac{1}{2}$ mi west. Then, she bikes $2\frac{1}{3}$ mi south. In which directions must she bike to return to her starting place?

____

25. Oliver has a piece of cardboard that is 12 in. long. He needs to cut it into $2\frac{2}{5}$-in. strips. How many cuts will he make?

____

Stop

Name ______________________________

Choose the best answer.

For 1–4, estimate the product or quotient.

1. $1\frac{3}{4} \times 4\frac{1}{3}$

A 10
B 8
C 6
D 4

2. $11\frac{2}{3} \times 8\frac{1}{8}$

F 1,200
G 120
H 96
J 88

3. $10\frac{1}{7} \div 1\frac{5}{6}$

A 2
B 5
C 10
D 20

4. $\frac{7}{8} \div \frac{12}{13}$

F 4
G 3
H 2
J 1

For 5–16, find the product or quotient in simplest form.

5. $\frac{3}{5} \times \frac{1}{2}$

A $\frac{3}{10}$
B $\frac{4}{10}$
C $\frac{3}{7}$
D $1\frac{1}{5}$

6. $\frac{3}{8} \times \frac{2}{9}$

F $\frac{6}{17}$
G $\frac{5}{17}$
H $\frac{6}{63}$
J $\frac{1}{12}$

7. $15 \times \frac{1}{3}$

A $\frac{16}{3}$
B 5
C $\frac{45}{3}$
D 45

8. $\frac{3}{4} \times 2\frac{1}{2}$

F $\frac{3}{10}$
G $1\frac{1}{3}$
H $1\frac{7}{8}$
J $3\frac{3}{4}$

9. $1\frac{2}{5} \times 2\frac{2}{3}$

A $2\frac{4}{15}$
B $2\frac{1}{2}$
C $3\frac{11}{15}$
D $4\frac{1}{2}$

10. $4\frac{1}{6} \times 5\frac{3}{5}$

F $20\frac{1}{10}$
G $20\frac{4}{11}$
H $22\frac{7}{30}$
J $23\frac{1}{3}$

11. $8 \div \frac{1}{2}$

A 4
B 10
C 16
D 24

12. $\frac{2}{5} \div \frac{8}{15}$

F $\frac{3}{4}$
G $\frac{30}{40}$
H $\frac{1}{2}$
J $\frac{16}{75}$

13. $\frac{4}{5} \div \frac{1}{4}$

A $\frac{1}{5}$
B $\frac{5}{16}$
C $3\frac{1}{5}$
D 5

Go On

14. $2\frac{1}{4} \div 1\frac{2}{3}$

F $1\frac{7}{20}$ H $3\frac{3}{4}$

G $2\frac{3}{8}$ J $3\frac{11}{12}$

15. $5 \div 3\frac{1}{2}$

A $17\frac{1}{2}$ C $3\frac{5}{2}$

B $8\frac{1}{2}$ D $1\frac{3}{7}$

16. $2\frac{3}{4} \div 1\frac{1}{4}$

F $1\frac{1}{2}$ H $3\frac{7}{16}$

G $2\frac{1}{5}$ J 4

17. Over a 5-day period, it took Ed $8\frac{3}{4}$ hr to read a book. He read for the same amount of time each day. How many hours did he read each day?

A $8\frac{3}{4}$ hr C $1\frac{1}{4}$ hr

B $1\frac{3}{4}$ hr D $\frac{3}{4}$ hr

18. Solve.

$30m = 3$

F $m = \frac{1}{10}$ H $m = 10$

G $m = \frac{1}{3}$ J $m = 90$

19. Jane drank $\frac{1}{3}$ of a carton of milk. Cliff drank $\frac{3}{8}$ of the carton. What fraction of the carton did they drink?

A $\frac{1}{24}$ carton C $\frac{15}{24}$ carton

B $\frac{1}{2}$ carton D $\frac{17}{24}$ carton

20. Felix grew $1\frac{1}{2}$ in. last year. This year he has grown $\frac{3}{4}$ as much as last year. How much has he grown this year?

F $2\frac{1}{4}$ in. H $\frac{3}{4}$ in.

G $1\frac{1}{8}$ in. J $\frac{1}{2}$ in.

21. Evaluate $30 \times g$ for $g = 1\frac{2}{9}$.

A $36\frac{2}{3}$ C $30\frac{2}{9}$

B $31\frac{2}{9}$ D $24\frac{6}{11}$

22. Solve.

$r \div \frac{1}{5} = 15$

F $r = 75$ H $r = \frac{3}{5}$

G $r = 3$ J $r = \frac{1}{3}$

23. Hai completed his science project in $3\frac{1}{3}$ hr. Mai-Ling took $2\frac{3}{4}$ hr. How much longer did it take Hai?

A $\frac{7}{12}$ hr C $6\frac{1}{12}$ hr

B $1\frac{5}{2}$ hr D $9\frac{1}{6}$ hr

24. It takes $1\frac{3}{4}$ cups of flour to make a cake. How many cups of flour does it take to make 3 cakes?

F $\frac{7}{12}$ c H $4\frac{3}{4}$ c

G $1\frac{1}{4}$ c J $5\frac{1}{4}$ c

25. Evaluate $x \div 4\frac{1}{5}$ for $x = \frac{4}{5}$.

A 5 C $\frac{4}{21}$

B $3\frac{2}{5}$ D $\frac{20}{120}$

Stop

Write the correct answer.

For 1–4, estimate the product or quotient.

1. $3\frac{7}{8} \times 2\frac{1}{4}$

2. $12\frac{1}{8} \div 1\frac{15}{16}$

3. $\frac{13}{16} \times \frac{4}{5}$

4. $15\frac{8}{9} \div 7\frac{7}{8}$

For 5–16, find the product or quotient in simplest form.

5. $\frac{5}{8} \times \frac{2}{3}$

6. $\frac{7}{16} \times \frac{8}{9}$

7. $28 \times \frac{3}{7}$

8. $\frac{2}{3} \times 5\frac{1}{2}$

9. $1\frac{3}{4} \times 2\frac{1}{2}$

10. $5\frac{1}{5} \times 4\frac{3}{8}$

11. $12 \div \frac{1}{3}$

12. $\frac{3}{5} \div \frac{9}{10}$

13. $\frac{5}{6} \div \frac{1}{5}$

Go On

14. $3\frac{1}{5} \div 2\frac{2}{7}$

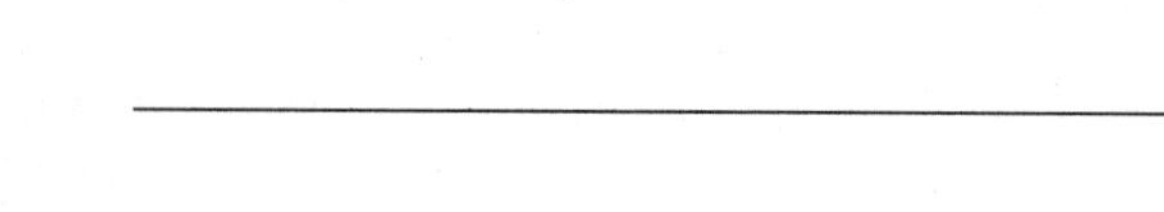

____

15. $8 \div 2\frac{1}{4}$

____

16. $2\frac{4}{5} \div 1\frac{1}{6}$

____

17. Over a 3-day period, it took Mr. Edwards $10\frac{1}{2}$hr to paint his house. He painted the same number of hours each day. How many hours did he paint each day?

____

18. Solve.

$\frac{2}{7}d = 4$

____

19. Carol does $\frac{1}{6}$ of the puzzle, and Doug does an additional $\frac{3}{5}$. What fraction of the puzzle still needs to be done?

____

20. Miguel caught a fish that weighed $2\frac{3}{4}$lb. His mother caught a fish that weighed $1\frac{1}{4}$ times as much as Miguel's fish. How much did his mother's fish weigh?

____

21. Evaluate $20j$ for $j = 2\frac{3}{5}$.

____

22. Solve.

$n \times \frac{1}{8} = 4$

____

23. Nguyen completes her book report in $3\frac{3}{4}$hr. Ben only took $2\frac{1}{3}$ hr to do the same project. How much longer did Nguyen take?

____

24. A batch of cookies takes $1\frac{1}{4}$ cups of sugar. How many cups of sugar are needed for 5 batches of cookies?

____

25. Evaluate $s \div 5\frac{1}{4}$ for $s = \frac{7}{8}$.

____

Stop

Name ______________________________

Choose the best answer.

1. Choose the group of numbers below by which 96 is evenly divisible.

   A 2, 3, 4, 5
   B 2, 3, 4, 6, 8
   C 2, 3, 4, 8, 9
   D 2, 3, 6, 8, 9

2. Andrew has a small library of music CDs. It includes 8 jazz, 12 rock, 5 rap, and 5 classical CDs. What fraction of Andrew's collection is rock music?

   F $\frac{3}{5}$
   G $\frac{2}{5}$
   H $\frac{1}{6}$
   J $\frac{1}{8}$

3. Estimate the sum. $3\frac{7}{8} + 2\frac{1}{4}$

   A 4
   B 5
   C 6
   D 7

4. $2\frac{2}{5} \times \frac{5}{6}$

   F $3\frac{7}{30}$
   G $2\frac{1}{3}$
   H 2
   J $1\frac{5}{6}$

5. Which pair of numbers is divisible by both 3 and 4?

   A 132 and 456
   B 234 and 459
   C 136 and 596
   D 258 and 336

6. Which is $\frac{9}{4}$ written as a mixed number?

   F $\frac{1}{4}$
   G 2
   H $2\frac{1}{9}$
   J $2\frac{1}{4}$

7. Erin spent $\frac{3}{8}$ hr practicing piano, $1\frac{1}{2}$ hr on homework, and $\frac{3}{4}$ hr preparing dinner. In all, how much time did these things take?

   A $2\frac{1}{4}$ hr
   B $2\frac{3}{8}$ hr
   C $2\frac{5}{8}$ hr
   D $2\frac{3}{4}$ hr

8. Yesterday Jim read $\frac{3}{8}$ of a new book. He read only $\frac{1}{2}$ that much today. What part of the book is left to read?

   F $\frac{9}{16}$
   G $\frac{1}{2}$
   H $\frac{7}{16}$
   J $\frac{3}{16}$

9. Which are the first five multiples of 60?

   A 1, 2, 3, 4, 5
   B 3, 4, 5, 10, 30
   C 60, 90, 120, 150, 180
   D 60, 120, 180, 240, 300

10. Which fraction is in simplest form?

    F $\frac{9}{18}$
    G $\frac{7}{18}$
    H $\frac{3}{18}$
    J $\frac{2}{18}$

11. $\frac{7}{9} - \frac{3}{4}$

    A $\frac{4}{5}$
    B $\frac{1}{4}$
    C $\frac{1}{9}$
    D $\frac{1}{36}$

12. $\frac{3}{5} \div \frac{5}{8}$

    F $\frac{3}{8}$
    G $\frac{1}{2}$
    H $\frac{24}{25}$
    J $\frac{39}{40}$

13. Find the GCF of 48 and 64.

    A 4
    B 16
    C 192
    D 3,072

14. Which is 0.7 written as a fraction?

    F $\frac{70}{10}$
    G $\frac{7}{10}$
    H $\frac{7}{100}$
    J $\frac{7}{1,000}$

Go On

15. About $\frac{9}{10}$ of a golf course is made up of fairways. Another $\frac{1}{18}$ is made up of greens, and the rest is made up of tees. What fraction of a golf course is made up of tees?

A $\frac{1}{10}$
B $\frac{1}{18}$
C $\frac{2}{45}$
D $\frac{1}{90}$

16. $5\frac{1}{3} \times 3\frac{3}{4}$

F 20
G $18\frac{3}{12}$
H $16\frac{1}{12}$
J $15\frac{1}{4}$

17. $\frac{2}{3} \div 3$

A $\frac{2}{9}$
B $\frac{1}{3}$
C $\frac{3}{5}$
D $\frac{1}{2}$

18. Which fraction is equal to 8?

F $\frac{56}{6}$
G $\frac{34}{4}$
H $\frac{40}{5}$
J $\frac{32}{8}$

19. Bob lives between Al and Chad on a straight road, $\frac{3}{4}$ mi from Al and $\frac{1}{3}$ mi from Chad. Chad lives between Bob and Dan on the same road. Bob lives $\frac{5}{6}$ mi from Dan. How far does Chad live from Dan?

A $\frac{1}{6}$ mi
B $\frac{1}{3}$ mi
C $\frac{1}{2}$ mi
D $\frac{2}{3}$ mi

20. Estimate.

$5\frac{1}{6} \times 3\frac{7}{8}$

F 24
G 22
H 20
J 15

21. James goes to the playground every 3 days and Natalie goes every 5 days. They meet on March 9 for the first time. How many more times will they meet at the playground by May 12?

A 15 times
B 10 times
C 5 times
D 4 times

22. Which is $\frac{27}{100}$ written as a percent?

F 270%
G 27%
H 2.7%
J 0.27%

23. $5\frac{1}{2} + 3\frac{7}{8}$

A $9\frac{3}{8}$
B $9\frac{1}{4}$
C $8\frac{4}{5}$
D $8\frac{3}{8}$

24. Estimate.

$\frac{9}{10} \div \frac{5}{6}$

F 1
G $1\frac{1}{2}$
H 2
J $2\frac{1}{2}$

25. Machine bolts are sold in boxes of 25. Nuts come in packages of 10 and washers are sold by the dozen. What is the least number of each item you can buy to have an equal number of each with none left over?

A 150
B 250
C 300
D 3,000

26. Which number completes the equation?

$\frac{3}{5} = \frac{■}{25}$

F 20
G 15
H 12
J 9

Go On

Name ______________________

27. Kerry, Kim, and Karin buy a new computer together. Kerry contributes $\frac{1}{2}$ the money and Kim contributes $\frac{1}{5}$. What fraction does Karin contribute?

A $\frac{1}{5}$ C $\frac{1}{3}$

B $\frac{3}{10}$ D $\frac{4}{5}$

28. Selina worked on a science project for 7 days. She spent a total of $15\frac{3}{4}$ hr on the project. She worked the same amount of time each day. How much time did she spend on the project each day?

F $2\frac{1}{4}$ hr H $2\frac{3}{7}$ hr

G $2\frac{1}{3}$ hr J 3 hr

29. The prime factorization of 504 is $2^3 \times 3^2 \times n$. What is the value of n?

A 11 C 7

B 9 D 2

30. Which fraction is equal to 0.8?

F $\frac{80}{10}$ H $\frac{19}{8}$

G $\frac{40}{5}$ J $\frac{4}{5}$

31. $\frac{3}{7} - \frac{1}{4}$

A 0 C $\frac{3}{14}$

B $\frac{5}{28}$ D $\frac{3}{7}$

32. How many ribbons $1\frac{2}{3}$ ft long can you cut from a roll that has 20 ft of ribbon?

F 33 ribbons H 15 ribbons

G 20 ribbons J 12 ribbons

33. Which number is prime?

A 1 C 87

B 53 D 91

34. When the sixth-grade class voted for class president, Nathan received $\frac{12}{30}$ of the votes. Which decimal tells what part of the class voted for Nathan?

F 0.6 H 0.4

G 0.5 J 0.2

35. $\frac{1}{2} + \frac{1}{3} + \frac{1}{6}$

A $\frac{3}{11}$ C $\frac{11}{12}$

B $\frac{1}{2}$ D 1

36. $3\frac{4}{5} \times 5\frac{1}{2}$

F $20\frac{9}{10}$ H $15\frac{5}{7}$

G $20\frac{5}{7}$ J $15\frac{4}{10}$

37. Which list contains factors of 24,570?

A 3 and 9 C 2, 3, and 4

B 3, 5, and 8 D 4 and 10

38. Which fraction is equal to $\frac{5}{12}$?

F $\frac{10}{30}$ H $\frac{15}{24}$

G $\frac{15}{36}$ J $\frac{2}{3}$

Go On

39. Mary lives $\frac{3}{8}$ mi north of Juan. Juan lives $1\frac{3}{4}$ mi south of Noel. Tom lives $\frac{7}{8}$ mi east of Noel. Karl lives due south of Tom and due east of Mary. How far does Karl live from Tom?

A $\frac{7}{8}$ mi
C $1\frac{1}{4}$ mi
B 1 mi
D $1\frac{3}{8}$ mi

40. $25\frac{3}{5} \div 4\frac{4}{15}$

F $6\frac{3}{5}$
H $6\frac{4}{25}$
G $6\frac{1}{2}$
J 6

41. Which shows the prime factorization of 363.

A $3 \times 11 \times 11$
C $2 \times 3 \times 11 \times 11$
B $3 \times 3 \times 11$
D $3 \times 7 \times 13$

42. Which number completes $5\frac{8}{15} = \frac{■}{15}$?

F 128
H 58
G 83
J 13

43. Kris jogged $2\frac{1}{8}$ km Monday, $1\frac{5}{6}$ km Tuesday, and $3\frac{1}{4}$ km today. Estimate the total distance she jogged on these 3 days.

A 8 km
C 6 km
B 7 km
D 5 km

44. A box of breakfast cereal contains 45 ounces. If each serving is $2\frac{1}{4}$ ounces, how many servings are contained in the box?

F 20 servings
H 22.5 servings
G 21 servings
J 24 servings

45. The calculators for Patty's store are packaged 15 to a box, and batteries are 144 to a box. Each calculator requires 4 batteries. What is the least number of boxes of calculators she will need if she wants no calculators or batteries left over?

A 4 boxes
C 12 boxes
B 6 boxes
D 180 boxes

46. What is $\frac{12}{36}$ in simplest form?

F $\frac{1}{3}$
H $\frac{3}{9}$
G $\frac{2}{6}$
J $\frac{1}{6}$

47. $5\frac{2}{3} + 3\frac{1}{8}$

A $8\frac{1}{4}$
C $8\frac{1}{2}$
B $8\frac{3}{11}$
D $8\frac{19}{24}$

48. Solve. $p \div \frac{1}{4} = 24$

F $p = 96$
H $p = 6$
G $p = 48$
J $p = 4$

49. Find the LCM of 12 and 30.

A 60
C 180
B 120
D 360

50. Mr. Watson divides his coin collection so that he has $\frac{1}{4}$ of the coins. He gives each of his three children $\frac{1}{8}$ of the coins, each of his 5 grandchildren $\frac{1}{16}$ of the coins and the rest are given to his brother. Who receives the greatest part of Mr. Watson's coin collection?

F each child
G each grandchild
H Mr. Watson's brother
J Mr. Watson

Stop

Name ______________________

Write the correct answer.

1. Write which of the numbers 2, 3, 4, 5, 6, 8, 9, or 10 are factors of 120.

____

2. Chris has a small library of novels. It includes 10 mystery, 12 science fiction, 6 biography, and 2 technical novels. What fraction of Chris' collection is biography?

____

3. Estimate. $5\frac{2}{9} + 8\frac{7}{8}$.

____

4. $3\frac{1}{8} \times \frac{4}{5}$

____

5. Write which of the numbers 3, 4, 5, 6, 8, 9, or 10 are factors of both 96 and 324.

____

6. Write $\frac{17}{5}$ as a mixed number.

____

7. Winnie spent $\frac{1}{3}$ hour showering, $\frac{1}{4}$ hour getting dressed, and $\frac{1}{2}$ hour eating breakfast. How much total time did she spend in these activities?

____

8. Yesterday, Phillip cleaned $\frac{3}{5}$ of his room. He cleaned only $\frac{1}{3}$ that much today. What part of the room is left to clean?

____

9. Write the first five multiples of 45.

____

10. Write $\frac{3}{12}$ in simplest form.

____

11. $\frac{8}{11} - \frac{2}{3}$

____

12. $\frac{2}{7} \div \frac{7}{8}$

____

13. Find the GCF of 32 and 56.

____

14. Write 0.09 as a fraction.

____

Go On

15. About $\frac{2}{3}$ of a golf course is made up of par 4 holes. Another $\frac{1}{9}$ is made up of par 5 holes, and the rest is par 3 holes. What fraction of a golf course is made up of par 3 holes?

____

16. $4\frac{2}{5} \times 2\frac{1}{4}$

____

17. What is the 15th number in the sequence? 83, 80, 77, 74, 71, . . .

____

18. $\frac{63}{9}$ is equal to what integer?

____

19. Bill lives between Art and Carl on a straight road, $\frac{2}{5}$ mi from Art and $\frac{1}{4}$ mi from Carl. Carl lives between Bill and Don on the same road. Bill lives $\frac{5}{8}$ mi from Don. Draw a diagram to help find how far Carl lives from Don.

____

20. Estimate. $4\frac{1}{8} \times 5\frac{7}{9}$

____

21. Joshua swims every 2 days and Nicole swims every 3 days. They swim together on May 9. How many more times will they meet at the pool by July 4?

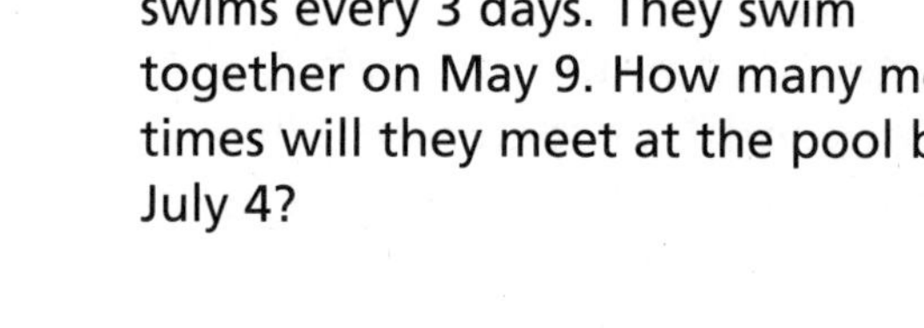

____

22. Write $\frac{53}{100}$ as a percent.

____

23. $7\frac{1}{3} + 4\frac{2}{5}$

____

24. Estimate. $\frac{11}{12} \div \frac{7}{8}$

____

25. Sheet metal screws are sold in boxes of 35. Washers come in packages of 10, and anchors are sold by the dozen. What is the least number of each you can buy to have an equal number of each?

____

26. Solve for x.

$\frac{5}{9} = \frac{x}{36}$

____

Go On

Name ______________________________

27. Michael, Susan, and Pauline bought a new computer game by pooling their resources. Michael contributed $\frac{2}{5}$ of the money and Pauline contributed $\frac{1}{3}$. What fraction did Susan contribute?

____

28. Sebastian worked on painting his sailboat for 9 days. He spent a total of $43\frac{1}{2}$ hours painting. If he painted the same length of time each day, how much time did he spend per day painting?

____

29. Write the prime factorization of 756.

____

30. Write a fraction equivalent to 0.65.

____

31. $\frac{5}{9} - \frac{5}{18}$

____

32. You need to cut $2\frac{3}{4}$ in. pieces of string from a larger piece which is 50 in. long. How many full pieces can you get?

____

33. Which of the numbers 1, 39, 57, 83, 123 is prime?

____

34. The bill received $\frac{37}{50}$ of the votes from the state senate for passage. Write a decimal that tells what part of the senate voted for the bill.

____

35. $\frac{1}{3} + \frac{1}{4} + \frac{1}{9}$

____

36. $4\frac{2}{5} \times 5\frac{2}{3}$

____

37. What are the three smallest prime factors of 24,310?

____

38. Write an equivalent fraction for $\frac{7}{9}$.

____

Go On

Name ______________________

39. Arthur lives $\frac{2}{5}$ mi. north of Jeffrey. Jeffrey lives $2\frac{1}{2}$ mi. south of Jason. Chris lives $\frac{2}{3}$ mi. east of Jason. Andy lives due south of Chris and due east of Arthur. Draw a diagram to help find out how far Andy lives from Chris.

____

40. 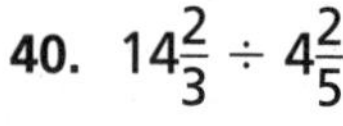 $14\frac{2}{3} \div 4\frac{2}{5}$

____

41. Write the prime factorization of 924.

____

42. Solve for *c*.

$4\frac{3}{8} = \frac{c}{8}$

____

43. Louisa walked $3\frac{1}{4}$ mile on Monday, $2\frac{4}{5}$ mile on Tuesday, and $1\frac{1}{8}$ mile today. Estimate the total distance she walked on these 3 days.

____

44. A box of macaroni & cheese contains 14 ounces. If each serving is 3 ounces, how many servings are contained in the box?

____

45. Tomato plants are grown 6 in a flat, and fertilizer stakes are packaged 10 in a bag. Each plant needs 3 fertilizer stakes when transplanted. What is the fewest number of flats of tomatoes needed if there are to be no tomato plants or fertilizer stakes left over?

____

46. Write $\frac{24}{28}$ in simplest form.

____

47. $2\frac{3}{4} + 4\frac{5}{8}$

____

48. Solve for k.

$k \div \frac{2}{5} = 25$

____

49. Find the LCM of 18 and 24.

____

50. Of the total money raised for charity, the police department raised $\frac{1}{5}$, three schools each raised $\frac{1}{10}$, and five clubs each raised $\frac{1}{20}$. The fire department raised the rest of the money. What fraction of the total did the fire department raise?

____

Stop

Name ______________________________

Choose the best answer.

For 1–4, name the integer that represents each situation.

1. An increase in altitude of 2,547 ft

A $^{+}2,574$　　C $^{-}2,547$
B $^{+}2,547$　　D $^{-}2,574$

2. A drop in temperature of 16°F

F $^{-}32$　　H $^{+}16$
G $^{-}16$　　J $^{+}32$

3. The absolute value of 65

A 65　　C $^{-}130$
B $^{-}65$　　D 0

4. The opposite of 19

F 91　　H $^{-}19$
G 19　　J $^{-}91$

5. Which number is between $3\frac{1}{4}$ and $3\frac{3}{4}$?

A $3\frac{1}{8}$　　C $3\frac{7}{8}$
B $3\frac{1}{2}$　　D $3\frac{13}{16}$

6. Which number is between $^{-}\frac{3}{5}$ and $^{-}\frac{3}{8}$?

F $\frac{-8}{5}$　　H $\frac{-5}{8}$
G $\frac{-4}{5}$　　J $\frac{-2}{5}$

For 7–8, find the rational number written in the form $\frac{a}{b}$.

7. $4\frac{5}{7}$

A $\frac{45}{7}$　　C $\frac{20}{7}$
B $\frac{33}{7}$　　D $\frac{9}{7}$

8. 2.718

F $\frac{2,718}{1,000}$　　H $27\frac{18}{100}$
G $2\frac{178}{1,000}$　　J $271\frac{8}{1000}$

9. What is the value of $|^{-}3.14|$?

A 3.14　　C $^{-}3\frac{14}{1,000}$
B $3\frac{14}{1,000}$　　D $^{-}3.14$

10. Which rational number is between $^{-}\frac{5}{8}$ and $\frac{5}{8}$?

F $\frac{-13}{16}$　　H $\frac{-10}{16}$
G $\frac{-11}{16}$　　J $\frac{-9}{16}$

11. Order $2\frac{3}{7}$, $2\frac{5}{11}$, and 2.5 from *least* to *greatest*.

A $2\frac{5}{11}$, $2\frac{3}{7}$, 2.5
B $2\frac{3}{7}$, 2.5, $2\frac{5}{11}$
C $2\frac{3}{7}$, $2\frac{5}{11}$, 2.5
D 2.5, $2\frac{5}{11}$, $2\frac{3}{7}$

12. Four friends have CD collections that contain 15, 20, 30, and 35 CDs. Mike and Taylor together have 10 fewer CDs than Al and Jeff. Taylor has more CDs than Al. Who has 30 CDs?

F Jeff　　H Taylor
G Al　　J Mike

Go On

13. Sam, Ann, and Jay play the guitar. One practices at 4:00, one at 6:00, and one at 9:00. Jay does not practice at 9:00. Ann practices 2 hours before Jay. Who practices at 4:00?

A Sam
B Ann
C Jay
D Cannot tell

14. In a race, the three fastest times were 20.3 min, $20\frac{1}{6}$ min, and 20.2 min. Order the times from *least* to *greatest*.

F 20.3 min, $20\frac{1}{6}$ min, 20.2 min

G $20\frac{1}{6}$ min, 20.2 min, 20.3 min

H 20.2 min, $20\frac{1}{6}$ min, 20.3 min

J 20.2 min, 20.3 min, $20\frac{1}{6}$ min

15. Which shows a correct comparison of two numbers?

A $0 > {}^{-}7.5$
B ${}^{-}7.5 > 7.5$
C ${}^{-}7.5 > 0$
D $7.5 = {}^{-}7.5$

16. Four students live in four different houses on the same block of the same street. Bob and Ceil live next door to Art. Doug lives closer to Ceil than to Art. Which two students live farthest apart?

F Bob and Ceil
G Ceil and Doug
H Art and Doug
J Bob and Doug

17. Gail, May, and Cara each bought a pop, rock, or jazz CD. No two girls bought the same kind of music. Gail did not buy pop music. May bought rock music. What kind of CD did each girl buy?

A Gail, pop; May, rock, Cara, jazz
B Gail, rock; May, rock; Cara, pop
C Gail, rock; May, jazz; Cara, pop
D Gail, jazz; May, rock; Cara, pop

18. What is the correct order from least to greatest for 1.1, ${}^{-}1\frac{3}{8}$, and $\frac{-9}{8}$?

F ${}^{-}1\frac{3}{8}$, $\frac{-9}{8}$, 1.1

G $\frac{-9}{8}$, ${}^{-}1\frac{3}{8}$, 1.1

H $\frac{-9}{8}$, 1.1, ${}^{-}1\frac{3}{8}$

J 1.1, $\frac{-9}{8}$, ${}^{-}1\frac{3}{8}$

19. Temperatures on the ski slope were recorded as 17°F, ⁻8°F, ⁻2°F, and 0°F during the day. Choose the order of these temperatures from least to greatest.

A 17°F, 0°F, ⁻2°F, ⁻8°F
B 0°F, ⁻2°F, ⁻8°F, 17°F
C ⁻8°F, ⁻2°F, 0°F, 17°F
D 17°F, ⁻8°F, ⁻2°F, 0°F

20. *P, Q, R,* and *S* are integers. *S* is greater than *Q*. *P* is the opposite of *S*. *R* is the opposite of *Q*. *R* is to the right of 0 on the number line. *Q* is less than *P*. Which represents the greatest integer?

F *P*
G *Q*
H *R*
J *S*

Stop

Name ________________________________

Write the correct answer.

For 1–4, write an integer to represent each situation.

1. An increase in altitude of 1,345 ft

____

2. A drop in temperature of 8°F

____

3. The absolute value of 37

____

4. The opposite of 10

____

5. Write a rational number between 4 and $4\frac{1}{4}$.

____

6. Write a rational number between $^-\frac{5}{8}$ and $^-\frac{5}{12}$.

____

For 7–8, write a rational number in the form $\frac{a}{b}$.

7. $6\frac{1}{3}$

____

8. 1.608

____

9. Write the value of $|^-4.18|$.

____

10. Write a rational number between $^-\frac{1}{4}$ and $\frac{1}{4}$.

____

11. Order $3\frac{2}{5}$, $3\frac{3}{8}$, and 3.1 from *least* to *greatest*.

____

12. Mandy's neighbors are 25, 50, 60, and 75 years old. Mr. Botwell's and Ms. Cantor's combined ages are 10 years older than Ms. Axel's and Mrs. Drew 's combined ages. Mr. Botwell is younger than Ms. Cantor and Mrs. Drew. How old is each neighbor?

____

____

Go On

13. Willa, Mi Sook, and Juan take piano lessons at 4:30, 7:00, and 8:00, though not necessarily in that order. Neither Willa's lesson nor Mi Sook's lesson is at 7:00. Juan's lesson is before Willa's lesson. What time is each student's lesson?

____

____

14. The three tallest basketball players on the team are $76\frac{1}{4}$ in., 76.2 in., and $76\frac{3}{8}$ in. tall. Order their heights from shortest to tallest.

____

15. Compare the numbers. Write $<$, $>$, or $=$ for ◯.

0 ◯ $^{-}0.2$

16. Four students are in line for movie tickets. Bo and Celia both are standing next to Anna. Darryl is closer to Celia than to Anna. Which two students are the farthest apart in line?

____

17. Mr. Jones, Mr. Roddy, and Mr. Sims are the manager, waiter, and cashier in a restaurant. Mr. Jones is not the manager or waiter. Mr. Sims is not the manager. What job does each person have? Explain your method.

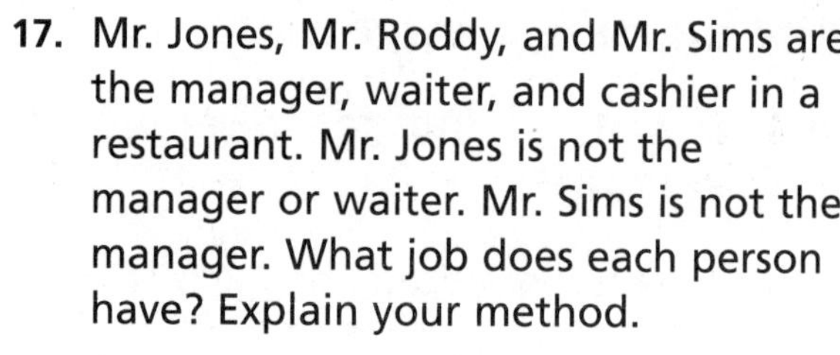

____

____

18. Write the numbers in order from least to greatest.

0.1, $^{-}1\frac{1}{4}$, and $^{-}1\frac{3}{8}$

____

19. The low temperatures for the last four days were recorded as 1°F, $^{-}1$°F, $^{-}2$°F, and 0°F. Order these temperatures from least to greatest.

____

20. Tom, Marta, Joseph, and Beth have these math averages: 99.2, 98.8, 98.1, and 96.9. The difference between Tom's and Marta's averages is less than $\frac{1}{2}$ point. Tom's average is not the highest. A girl does not have the lowest average. What are the averages of the four students?

____

____

Stop

Name ______________________

Choose the best answer.

1. What addition problem is modeled on the number line below?

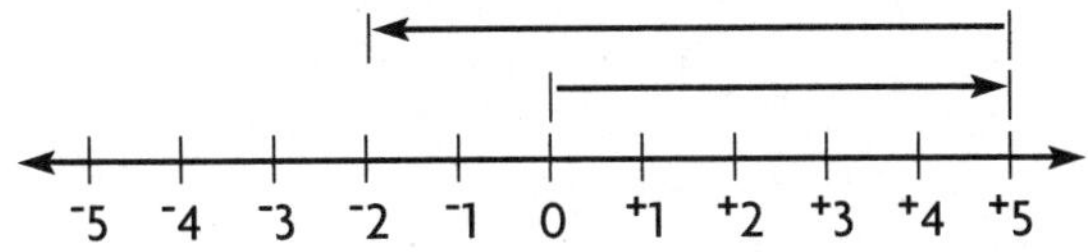

A $^{-}2 + {}^{+}7 = {}^{+}5$
B $^{-}5 + {}^{-}2 = {}^{-}7$
C $^{+}5 + {}^{-}7 = {}^{-}2$
D $^{+}5 - {}^{+}7 = {}^{+}12$

2. What addition problem is modeled on the number line below?

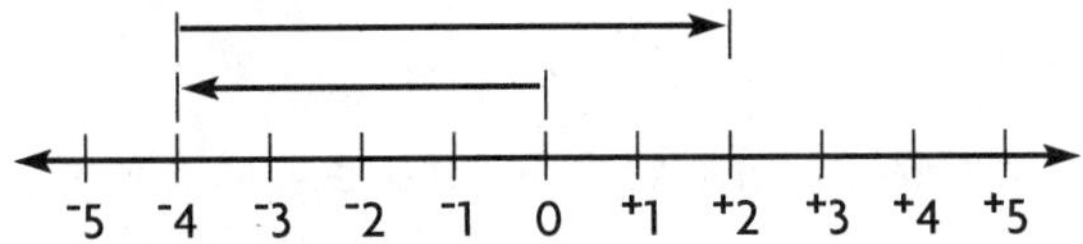

F $^{-}4 + {}^{+}6 = {}^{+}2$
G $^{-}4 + {}^{-}2 = {}^{-}6$
H $^{+}6 + {}^{-}4 = {}^{+}2$
J $^{-}2 + {}^{-}4 = {}^{-}6$

For 3–10, find the sum or difference.

3. $^{-}38 + {}^{+}25$

A $^{-}63$ C $^{+}13$
B $^{-}13$ D $^{+}63$

4. $^{+}3 + {}^{-}5$

F $^{-}8$ H $^{+}2$
G $^{-}2$ J $^{+}8$

5. $^{-}4 + {}^{-}6$

A $^{-}10$ C $^{+}2$
B $^{-}2$ D $^{+}10$

6. $^{-}3 - {}^{-}17$

F $^{-}20$ H $^{+}14$
G $^{-}14$ J $^{+}20$

7. $^{-}16 - {}^{+}42$

A $^{-}58$ C $^{+}34$
B $^{-}34$ D $^{+}58$

8. $^{+}33 - {}^{-}12$

F $^{-}45$ H $^{+}21$
G $^{-}21$ J $^{+}45$

9. $^{-}54 - {}^{-}78$

A $^{-}132$ C 24
B $^{-}24$ D 132

10. $^{+}144 - {}^{-}25$

F $^{-}169$ H 119
G $^{-}119$ J 169

For 11–16, find the product or quotient.

11. $8 \times {}^{-}12$

A 96 C $^{-}4$
B 20 D $^{-}96$

12. $^{-}9 \times 0$

F $^{-}90$ H 0
G 29 J 9

Go On

Name ______________________________

13. $^{-}54 \div {}^{-}9$

A 45 | C $^{-}6$
B 6 | D $^{-}45$

14. $35 \div {}^{-}7$

F 28 | H $^{-}5$
G 5 | J $^{-}28$

15. $^{-}156 \div 4$

A $^{-}624$ | C $^{-}39$
B $^{-}160$ | D 160

16. $360 \div {}^{-}12$

F $^{-}348$ | H 3
G $^{-}30$ | J 372

For 17–18, use mental math to find the value of *y*.

17. $^{-}4 + y = {}^{+}10$

A $y = {}^{-}14$ | C $y = {}^{+}6$
B $y = {}^{-}6$ | D $y = {}^{+}14$

18. $y + {}^{-}5 = {}^{-}12$

F $y = {}^{-}17$ | H $y = {}^{+}7$
G $y = {}^{-}7$ | J $y = {}^{+}17$

For 19–22, evaluate the expression.

19. $^{-}6\frac{1}{2} + 2\frac{3}{4}$

A $^{-}4\frac{3}{4}$ | C $3\frac{3}{4}$
B $^{-}3\frac{3}{4}$ | D $^{+}9\frac{1}{4}$

20. $^{-}3.9 - {}^{-}5.1$

F $^{-}9.0$ | H $^{+}1.2$
G $^{-}1.2$ | J $^{+}9.0$

21. $^{-}7 \times {}^{-}8 \div ({}^{-}3 + 31)$

A $^{-}56$ | C 2
B $^{-}2$ | D 90

22. $8 \times {}^{-}1.5 \div (^{-}\frac{2}{3} + \frac{1}{6})$

F $^{-}24$ | H 24
G $^{-}6$ | J 144

23. At noon, the temperature was 2°F. The temperature at 8:00 P.M. was –11°F. What is the range of the temperatures?

A $^{-}11$°F | C 9°F
B 2°F | D 13°F

24. The change in the water level of a lake over 8 years has been $^{-}24$ in. What is the average yearly change in the water level?

F 16 in. | H $^{-}16$ in.
G $^{-}3$ in. | J $^{-}32$ in.

25. The temperature rose 6°F each hour for 3 hours. What was the total temperature change over the 3-hour period?

A 18°F | C $^{-}9$°F
B 9°F | D $^{-}18$°F

Stop

Name ______________________________

Write the correct answer.

1. What addition problem is modeled on the number line below?

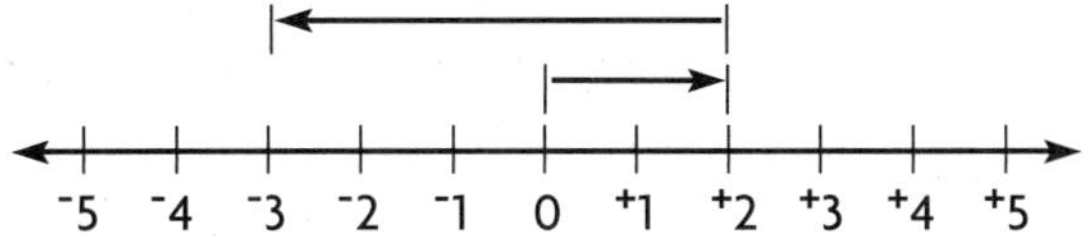

____

2. What addition problem is modeled on the number line below?

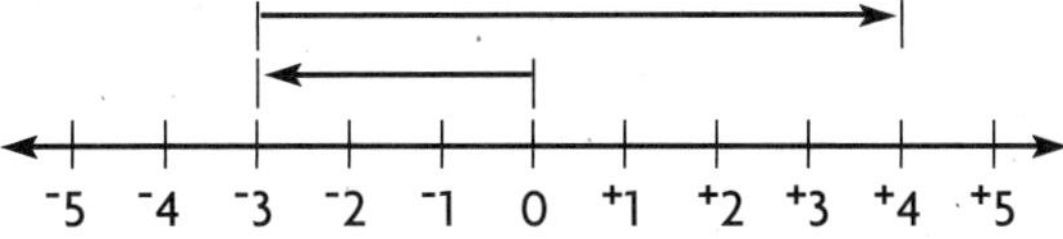

____

For 3–10, find the sum or difference.

3. $^{-}7 + {}^{+}2$

____

4. $^{-}25 + {}^{+}12$

____

5. $^{+}9 + {}^{-}2$

____

6. $^{+}7 - {}^{+}8$

____

7. $^{-}20 - {}^{+}35$

____

8. $^{+}19 - {}^{-}22$

____

9. $^{-}62 - {}^{-}74$

____

10. $124 - {}^{-}27$

____

For 11–16, find the product or quotient.

11. $7 \times {}^{-}10$

____

12. $^{-}4 \times 0$

____

Go On

13. $^{-}48 \div {}^{-}8$

____

14. $28 \div {}^{-}7$

____

15. $^{-}162 \div 6$

____

16. $450 \div {}^{-}15$

____

For 17–18, use mental math to find the value of *y*.

17. $^{-}5 + y = {}^{+}7$

____

18. $y + {}^{-}8 = {}^{-}16$

____

For 19–22, evaluate the expression.

19. $^{-}2.5 + 4.7$

____

20. $6\frac{1}{2} - {}^{-}10\frac{1}{2}$

____

21. $2.3 + 18.6 \div {}^{-}2.0$

____

22. $^{-}2.5 \times 4 \div ({}^{-}\frac{5}{6} + \frac{1}{3})$

____

23. On Wednesday, the low temperature was $^{-}3$°F. The low temperature on Thursday was 11° higher. What was the low temperature on Thursday?

____

24. Due to evaporation, the change in water level in a swimming pool over the last 7 weeks has been $^{-}14$ cm. What is the average weekly change in the water level?

____

25. The Lions football team gained 15 yd on each of 3 plays. What was the total change in yards for the 3 plays?

____

Stop

Name ______________________________

Choose the best answer.

1. What integer represents a decrease in weight of 14 pounds?

   A $^{-}41$ pounds C 14 pounds
   B $^{-}14$ pounds D 41 pounds

2. What equation is modeled on the number line below?

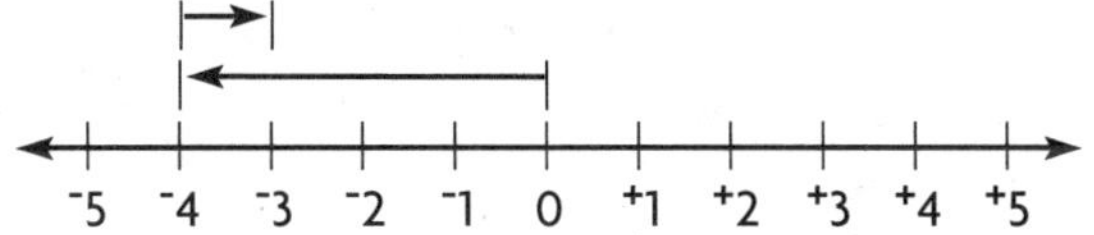

   F $^{-}4 + 1 = {}^{-}3$ H $^{-}4 - 1 = {}^{-}5$
   G $^{-}4 + {}^{-}1 = {}^{-}5$ J $4 - 1 = 3$

3. $^{-}3 \times {}^{-}9$

   A 243 C 12
   B 27 D $^{-}27$

4. Which rational number is between $5\frac{1}{8}$ and $5\frac{3}{5}$?

   F $5\frac{7}{9}$ H $5\frac{1}{2}$
   G $5\frac{4}{5}$ J $5\frac{1}{16}$

5. $4 + {}^{-}6$

   A -2 C 2
   B 0 D 10

6. $24 \div {}^{-}8$

   F 192 H 3
   G 16 J $^{-}3$

7. Order $4\frac{1}{4}$, 4.2, and $4\frac{5}{24}$ from *least* to *greatest*.

   A $4\frac{1}{4}$, 4.2, $4\frac{5}{24}$
   B 4.2, $4\frac{1}{4}$, $4\frac{5}{24}$
   C 4.2, $4\frac{5}{24}$, $4\frac{1}{4}$
   D $4\frac{5}{24}$, $4\frac{1}{4}$, 4.2

8. In January the price of new skis was \$259. In May the price was \$199. How much did the price change?

   F \$199 H $^{-}$\$60
   G \$60 J $^{-}$\$100

9. Use a property to simplify the expression. Then evaluate the expression and identify the property you used.

   $(245 \times 5) \times 2$

   A 1,450; Commutative
   B 2,450; Distributive
   C 1,715; Associative
   D 2,450; Associative

10. Which is the absolute value of $^{-}1.62$?

    F $1\frac{62}{10}$ H $^{-}1.62$
    G 1.62 J $^{-}1\frac{62}{100}$

11. $25 - {}^{-}12$

    A $^{-}37$ C 13
    B $^{-}13$ D 37

12. $^{-}\frac{1}{2} \times {}^{-}16$

    F $^{-}8$ H $\frac{1}{8}$
    G $\frac{-1}{8}$ J 8

13. What is $3\frac{5}{7}$ written in the form $\frac{a}{b}$?

    A $\frac{35}{7}$ C $\frac{22}{7}$
    B $\frac{26}{7}$ D $\frac{8}{7}$

14. Use mental math to find the value of *x*.

    $x + {}^{-}4 = 8$

    F 12 H 4
    G 6 J $^{-}24$

Go On

15. $4.2 + {}^{-}8.5$

A 12.7
B 4.3
C $^{-}12.7$
D $^{-}4.3$

16. What is 3.269 written in the form $\frac{a}{b}$?

F $\frac{3,269}{1,000}$
G $32\frac{69}{1,000}$
H $32\frac{69}{100}$
J $326\frac{9}{10}$

17. An airplane climbed to an altitude of 18,000 ft. Bad weather then forced it to descend 5,000 ft. What was the altitude of the plane then?

A 5,000 ft
B 13,000 ft
C 18,000 ft
D 23,000 ft

18. $^{-}12 \times 15$

F 180
G 27
H $^{-}27$
J $^{-}180$

19. Ian, Mei, and Ana have different hobbies: art, music, and games. Ian does not like art, and Mei does not like games. Ian plays the piano. What hobby does each have?

A Ian, music; Mei, games; Ana, art
B Ian, art; Mei, music; Ana, games
C Ian, music; Mei, art; Ana, games
D Ian, games; Mei, art; Ana, music

20. $^{-}7 + 8$

F $^{-}15$
G $^{-}1$
H 1
J 15

21. Find $10 - (1 - 6)^2$.

A 225
B 35
C 9
D $^{-}15$

22. Positive whole numbers, their opposites, and zero make up the set of __?__ .

F integers
G rational numbers
H fractions
J decimals

23. Today, Naomi walked 2 mi to school, then 3 mi to a friend's house, and 4 mi back home. How far did she walk today?

A 9 mi
B 7 mi
C 6 mi
D 5 mi

24. $36 \div {}^{-}9$

F $^{-}27$
G $^{-}4$
H 4
J 36

25. The letters *a*, *b*, *c*, *d*, and *e* represent the numbers 2.1, $^{-}1\frac{3}{4}$, 1.83, $^{-}2\frac{8}{9}$, and $1\frac{3}{4}$, but not necessarily in that order. The value of *d* is greater than *e* but less than *a*. The values of *b* and *c* are opposites and both are greater than *e*, and *a* is the greatest. Which number is represented by *e*?

A 2.1
B 1.83
C $^{-}1\frac{3}{4}$
D $^{-}2\frac{8}{9}$

26. Solve. $x - 3 = {}^{-}5$

F $x = 5$
G $x = 2$
H $x = {}^{-}2$
J $x = {}^{-}25$

Go On

27. $^{-}7.2 \div 2.4$

A $^{-}3$ C 3
B $^{-}0.3$ D 30

28. Which rational number is between $^{-}1\frac{1}{4}$ and $\frac{1}{2}$?

F $^{-}1\frac{2}{3}$ H $\frac{1}{4}$
G $^{-}1\frac{1}{3}$ J $\frac{5}{8}$

29. $^{-}8 - 5$

A $^{-}13$ C 3
B $^{-}3$ D 13

30. Evaluate $x \bullet y$ if $x = 21$ and $y = {}^{-}7$.

F 147 H $^{-}3$
G 3 J $^{-}147$

31. What is the absolute value of $23\frac{1}{2}$?

A $23\frac{1}{2}$ C $^{-}23$
B 0 D $^{-}23\frac{1}{2}$

32. $^{-}7 + 5$

F $^{-}12$ H 2
G $^{-}2$ J 12

33. Each month you deposit $8 of your earnings in a savings account. How much will you have deposited in this account after 2 years?

A $256 C $16
B $192 D $3

34. In a trout fishing contest, the three winning fish measured $21\frac{7}{8}$ in., 21.6 in., and $21\frac{3}{4}$ in. Order these lengths from *least* to *greatest*.

F $21\frac{3}{4}$ in., $21\frac{7}{8}$ in., 21.6 in.

G 21.6 in., $21\frac{3}{4}$ in., $21\frac{7}{8}$ in.

H 21.6 in., $21\frac{7}{8}$ in., $21\frac{3}{4}$ in.

J $21\frac{3}{4}$ in., 21.6 in., $21\frac{7}{8}$ in.

35. $^{-}12 + {}^{-}20$

A 32 C $^{-}8$
B 8 D $^{-}32$

36. Evaluate $r \div s$ if $r = {}^{-}16$ and $s = 4$.

F $^{-}4$ H 12
G 4 J 64

37. What number is the opposite of $\frac{5}{8}$?

A $\frac{8}{5}$ C $\frac{-5}{8}$
B $\frac{5}{8}$ D $\frac{-8}{5}$

38. An observer in Death Valley at $^{-}200$ ft spots an airplane flying at an altitude of 3,600 ft. What is the altitude difference between the observer and the airplane?

F $^{-}3,800$ ft H 2,800 ft
G $^{-}2,800$ ft J 3,800 ft

Go On

39. On Monday you earned \$17. On Tuesday you spent \$5. Wednesday and Thursday you earned \$11 each day, and Friday you spent \$25. Since Monday, how much do you have left?

A \$69
B \$58
C \$19
D \$9

40. What integer represents an increase of 6 points in a grade average?

F $^{-}6$
G $^{-}3$
H 3
J 6

41. Evaluate $p + q$ for $p = {}^{-}12$ and $q = 18$.

A $^{-}30$
B $^{-}6$
C 6
D 30

42. $^{-}50 \times 0$

F $^{-}50$
G 0
H 50
J 100

43. *a*, *b*, *c*, and *d* represent rational numbers. *c* is between *d* and *a*, and *c* is greater than *b*. *d* and *c* are opposites, and *d* is negative. Which number is the greatest?

A a B b C c D d

44. Dennis got on an elevator and went up 7 floors, and then went down 12 floors. In relation to where Dennis got on, what integer describes where he got off?

F $^{-}5$ G 3 H 5 J 19

45. During any 5-day week, the stock market could both rise and fall. If the market lost 315 points, what was the average change per day?

A 1,575 points
B 630 points
C $^{-}63$ points
D $^{-}1{,}575$ points

46. Which rational number is between $^{-}1\frac{3}{4}$ and $\frac{5}{8}$?

F $^{-}1\frac{7}{8}$
G 0
H $1\frac{1}{4}$
J $2\frac{1}{6}$

47. Evaluate $^{-}m - n$ for $m = {}^{-}8$ and $n = {}^{-}13$.

A $^{-}21$
B $^{-}5$
C 5
D 21

48. Solve. $p \div 3 = 24$

F $p = 8$
G $p = 21$
H $p = 72$
J $p = 96$

49. Paul, Liz and Amy belong to the math, chess, and art clubs. Each belongs to only one club. Paul does not play chess, and the art club is all girls. Liz does not care for art. Which student is in which club?

A Paul, math; Amy, chess; Liz, art
B Paul, math; Liz, chess; Amy, art
C Amy, math; Liz, chess; Paul, art
D Liz, math; Paul, chess, Amy, art

50. On Saturday Josette earned \$8 baby-sitting, \$5 raking leaves, and \$12 washing windows. How much did she earn on Saturday?

F \$13
G \$17
H \$20
J \$25

Stop

Name ______________________

Write the correct answer.

1. Write an integer to represent an increase in length of 21 inches.

____

2. Write the equation that is modeled on the number line below.

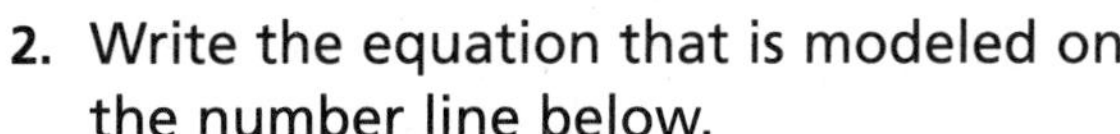

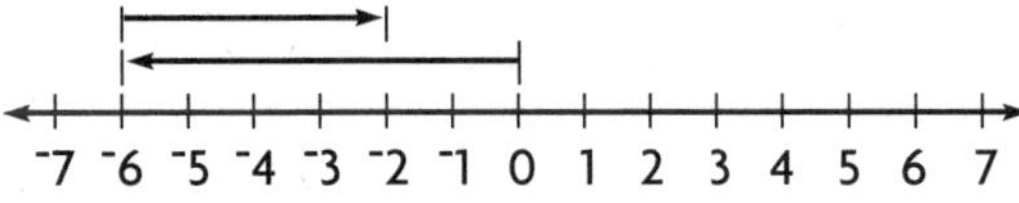

____

3. $^{-}5 \times {}^{-}7$

____

4. Write a rational number between $4\frac{2}{3}$ and $4\frac{4}{5}$.

____

5. $3 + {}^{-}8$

____

6. $27 \div {}^{-}9$

____

7. Order $5\frac{1}{6}$, 5.2, 5.15, and $5\frac{1}{8}$ from *least* to *greatest*.

____

8. In May, the price of a kayak was $1,075. In October the price was $899. What was the price change?

____

9. Use a property to simplify the expression. Then evaluate the expression and identify the property you used.

$25 \times 7 \times 4$

____

10. What is the value of $^{-}|{}^{-}2.57|$?

____

11. $32 - {}^{-}25$

____

12. $\frac{-1}{3} \times {}^{-}27$

____

13. Write $4\frac{4}{9}$ in the form $\frac{a}{b}$.

____

14. Solve for x using mental math.

$x + {}^{-}7 = 15.$

____

Go On

Name ______________________________

15. $3.6 + {}^{-}4.5$

____

16. Write 5.384 in the form $\frac{a}{b}$.

____

17. A submarine dove from the surface to a level of $^{-}284$ fathoms, then rose 57 fathoms. How deep was it then?

____

18. $^{-}8 \times 24$

____

19. Claudia, Doria, and Emily have different interests: movies, music, and math. Claudia does not like movies, and Doria does not enjoy math. Claudia plays the oboe. What interest does each have?

____

20. $^{-}9 + 12$

____

21. $8 + (3 - 7)^2$

____

22. The set of integers is made up of the positive whole numbers, their __?__, and __?__.

____

23. L.J. rode his bicycle 3 mi to the movie theater, then 4 mi to a friend's house, and 5 mi back home. How far did he ride his bicycle?

____

24. $^{-}48 \div {}^{-}8$

____

25. The letters p, q, r, s, and t represent the numbers 3.2, $^{-}2\frac{4}{5}$, 2.94, $^{-}3\frac{7}{8}$, and $2\frac{4}{5}$, but not necessarily in that order. The value of s is greater than t but less than p. The values of q and r are opposites, and p is the greatest. Which number is represented by t?

____

26. Solve for x.

$x - 5 = {}^{-}3$

____

Go On

Name ______________________

27. $^{-}6.4 \div 1.6$

____

28. Write a rational number between $^{-}1\frac{5}{6}$ and $^{-}1\frac{3}{4}$.

____

29. $12 - 7$

____

30. Evaluate $k \times m$ for $k = 18$ and $m = {}^{-}6$.

____

31. What is the absolute value of $^{-}31\frac{7}{8}$?

____

32. $^{-}9 + 6$

____

33. Each week you deposit $12 of your earnings in a savings account. How much will you have deposited in this account after 3 years?

____

34. In the 100 yard dash, the top three times were 11.4 sec, $11\frac{3}{8}$ sec, and $11\frac{4}{7}$ sec. Order these times from *least* to *greatest*.

____

35. $^{-}8 + {}^{-}14$

____

36. Evaluate $w \div z$ for $w = {}^{-}24$ and $z = 8$.

____

37. Write the opposite of $1\frac{5}{7}$.

____

38. An airplane pilot flying at 5,600 feet above sea level spots a submarine sailing beneath him at a depth of 160 feet. What is the vertical distance between the plane and the submarine?

____

Go On

39. On Monday you earned \$23. On Tuesday you spent \$15 of your earnings. On Wednesday and Thursday you earned \$14 each day, and on Friday you spent \$35. Since Monday, how much do you have left?

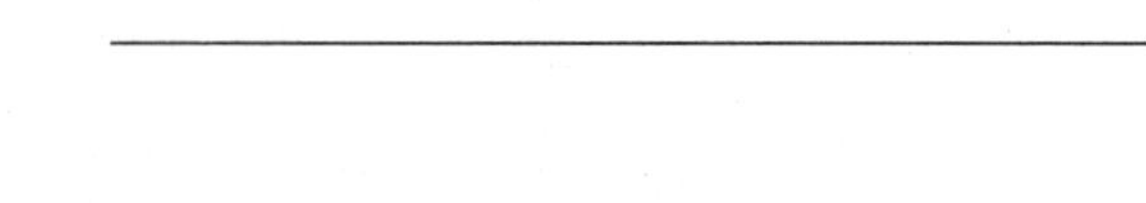

40. What integer represents a decrease of 37°F?

41. Evaluate $p - q$ for $p = {}^{-}14$ and $q = 12$.

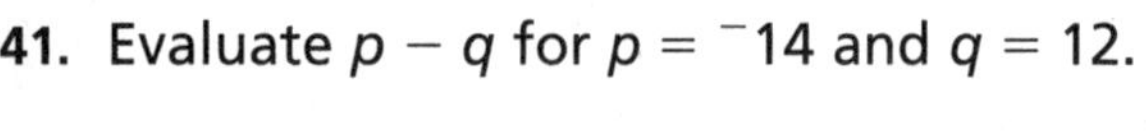

42. ${}^{-}37.5 \times 0$

43. *a*, *b*, *c*, and *d* represent rational numbers. *c* is between *d* and *a*, and *c* is less than *b*. *d* and *c* are opposites, and *d* is the only negative number. Which number is the least?

44. Doris got on an elevator and went up 9 floors, then went down 14 floors to the second floor. On what floor did Doris start?

45. If the price of gas rose \$0.35 a gallon during a 5 week period, what was the average change per week?

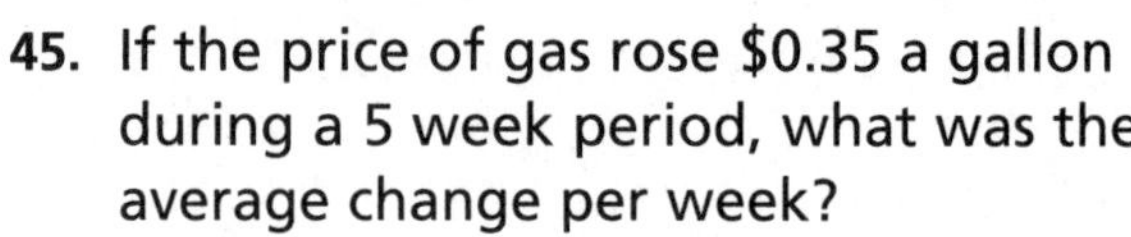

46. Write a rational number between 3.8 and $3\frac{3}{4}$.

47. Evaluate ${}^{-}m + n$ for $m = {}^{-}16$ and $n = {}^{-}12$.

48. Solve for *p*.

$p \div 5 = 15$

49. Lisa, Christopher, and David belong to the karate, jogging, and swimming clubs. Each belongs to only one club. Christopher does not jog, and the swim club is all girls. Which student is in which club?

50. On Sunday, Louisa earned \$12 for child care, \$18 planting flowers, and \$6 sweeping the garage. How much did she earn in all?

Stop

Name ______________________________

Choose the best answer.

For 1–5, find an algebraic expression for the word expression.

1. 12 less than n

A $n - 12$ C $n \div 12$
B $12 - n$ D $12 \div n$

2. 5 more than $3q$

F $5 - 3q$ H $5 \times 3q$
G $5 + 3q$ J $5 \div 3q$

3. The product of $12r$ and $3s$

A $12r \times 3s$ C $12r + 3s$
B $12s \times 3s$ D $3r - 12s$

4. The quotient of $5d$ divided by $3d$

F $3d \times 5d$ H $3d \div 5d$
G $5d \times 3d$ J $5d \div 3d$

5. 18 decreased by p

A $p \div 18$ C $p - 18$
B $18 \div p$ D $18 - p$

For 6–8, evaluate the expression for $k = 6$.

6. $3k + 7$

F 43 H 25
G 39 J 16

7. $\frac{18}{k} - 5$

A 18 C $^{-}2$
B 2 D $^{-}3$

8. $9 + (^{-}2 + 3k)$

F $^{-}11$ H 20
G 15 J 25

For 9–11, evaluate the expression for $r = 3$, $s = {}^{-}4$, and $t = 5$.

9. $(r + s)^2 - t$

A $^{-}6$ C 6
B $^{-}4$ D 44

10. $r + s - t$

F $^{-}6$ H $^{-}2$
G $^{-}4$ J 2

11. $2s + 10 \cdot (r - t)$

A 20 C $^{-}20$
B $^{-}12$ D $^{-}28$

12. Which expression can you evaluate by using the array?

F 25^2 H $\sqrt{5}$
G 2^5 J $\sqrt{25}$

13. Evaluate $^{-}2m^2 + 9$ for $m = {}^{-}3$.

A $^{-}9$ C 18
B 9 D 45

14. Evaluate $8x + 3x - 4$ for $x = 5$.

F 17 H 51
G 49 J 59

Go On

Name ______________________________

15. Which expression can you evaluate by using the array?

A 9^2 C 2^3
B 3^2 D $\sqrt{3}$

16. Evaluate $1 - (5c - 7c)$ for $c = {}^-4$.

F $^-7$ H 8
G 7 J 9

17. Evaluate $3 \bullet \sqrt{x} - 4$ for $x = 25$.

A 4 C 19
B 11 D 71

18. Which expression can you evaluate by using the array?

F $\sqrt{6}$ H 2^6
G 6^2 J 36^2

For questions 19–22, evaluate the expression.

19. $5 \bullet \sqrt{16} + 3$

A 83 C 35
B 43 D 23

20. $2 \bullet \sqrt{81} \div \sqrt{36}$

F 9 H 3
G 6 J $\frac{3}{2}$

21. $4 \bullet \sqrt{25} \div \sqrt{100} - 1$

A 4 C 1
B 2 D 0

22. $\sqrt{100} - \sqrt{36} - 3^2$

F 5 H $^-2$
G 2 J $^-5$

23. Henri starts the week with $23. He earns *d* dollars each day and buys lunch for *l* dollars on some days. Which expression represents the amount of money Henri has at the end of the week if he works 5 days and buys lunch 3 days?

A $23 + d - 3l$ C $23 + 5d - 3l$
B $23 + 5d - l$ D $23 - 5d + 3l$

24. In a contest, everyone starts with 50 points. Contestants get 8 points for every correct answer. They lose 2 points for every wrong answer. Which expression represents the total for a contestant who has *c* correct answers and *w* wrong answers?

F $50 + 8c - 2w$ H $50 + c - w$
G $50 + 8c - 2$ J $50 + 8 - 2w$

25. You have three square pictures that you want to frame. The areas of the pictures are 144 in.^{2}, 64 in.^{2}, and 49 in.^{2} How many inches of framing material are needed?

A 257 in. C 54 in.
B 108 in. D 27 in.

Stop

Name ______________________

Write the correct answer.

For 1–5, write an algebraic expression for the word expression.

1. 6 less than p

____

2. 7 more than $5n$

____

3. The product of $15x$ and $10y$

____

4. The quotient of $2t$ and $8t$

____

5. 12 decreased by n

____

For 6–8, evaluate the expression for $n = 8$.

6. $4n + 3$

____

7. $\frac{40}{n} - 6$

____

8. $4 + (^{-}7 + 2n)$

____

For 9–11, evaluate the expression for $x = 2$, $y = {}^{-}2$, and $z = 4$.

9. $(x + y)^2 - 2z$

____

10. $x + 3z - y$

____

11. $z + 8 \bullet (y - z)$

____

12. Use the array to help you evaluate the expression.

$\sqrt{64}$

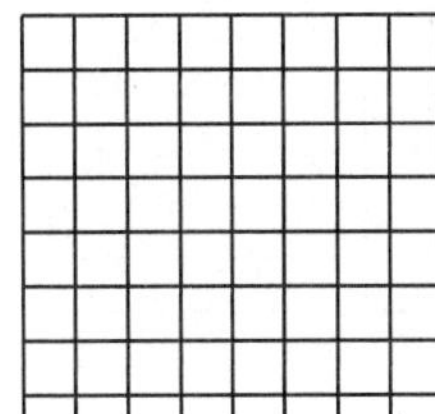

____

13. Evaluate $^{-}5m^2 + 3$ for $m = {}^{-}5$.

____

14. Evaluate $5n - 2n + 10$ for $n = 6$.

____

Go On

Name ______________________

15. Use the array to help you evaluate the expression.

$\sqrt{16}$

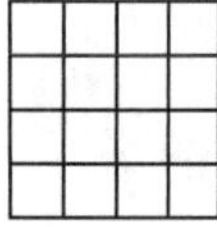

____

16. Evaluate $12 - (2t - t)$ for $t = {}^{-}5$.

____

17. Evaluate $5 \cdot \sqrt{b} - 7$ for $b = 4$.

____

18. Use the array below to help you evaluate the expression.

7^2

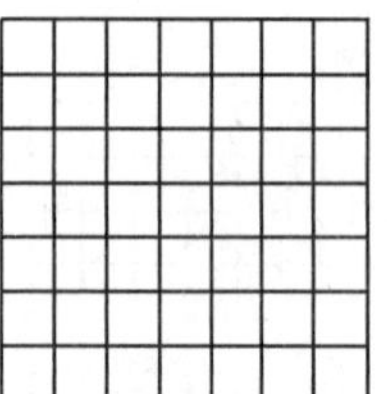

____

For 19–22, evaluate the expression.

19. $4 \cdot \sqrt{36} + 12$

____

20. $3 \cdot \sqrt{49} \div \sqrt{9}$

____

21. $5 \cdot \sqrt{100} \div \sqrt{25} - 5$

____

22. $\sqrt{64} - \sqrt{16} - 4^2$

____

23. Jemma opened a bank account with \$35. Each week she deposits *n* dollars from her paycheck. Some weeks she takes out *p* dollars to pay her share of the phone bill. Write an expression to show the amount of money Jemma has after working 6 weeks and paying for the phone bill for 2 weeks.

____

24. Hector charges \$5 per hour to baby-sit. He also charges a fee of \$2 for each child. Write an expression to show how much Hector charges to baby-sit *c* children for *h* hours.

____

25. Mr. Winslow bought 50 yd of fencing. Does he have enough fencing to enclose a square garden that has an area of 121 sq yd? Explain why or why not.

____

____

Stop

Name ______________________________

Choose the best answer.

For 1–6, choose the correct equation for each word sentence.

1. A number increased by 7 is 12.

A $x = 7 + 12$ C $x - 7 = 12$
B $7x = 12$ D $x + 7 = 12$

2. The price less a $2 discount is $15.

F $p \div 2 = 15$ H $p + 2 = 15$
G $p - 2 = 15$ J $2p = 15$

3. Three times a number is 24.

A $3 \div n = 24$ C $n = 3 \times 24$
B $3 + n = 24$ D $3n = 24$

4. The quotient of 320 and a number is 16.

F $320 \times 16 = r$ H $r \times 320 = 16$
G $320 \div 16 = r$ J $320 \div r = 16$

5. The product of 7 and a number is 63.

A $7z = 63$ C $7 + z = 63$
B $7 = 63z$ D $7 \div z = 63$

6. Nineteen is 7 less than a number.

F $19 = 7 - y$ H $19 - 7 = y$
G $19 = y - 7$ J $19 = y \div 7$

For 7–10, find an equation that is represented by the given model.

7. [long bar] □□ = □□□□□

A $x + 2 = 5$ C $x - 2 = 5$
B $2x = 5$ D $x \div 2 = 5$

8. [long bar] □□□ = □□□□

F $x - 3 = 4$ H $x \div 3 = 4$
G $3x = 4$ J $x + 3 = 4$

9. [long bar] □□□□□ = □□□□□□

A $x \div 5 = 6$ C $x + 6 = 5$
B $x + 5 = 6$ D $x - 5 = 6$

10. [long bar] □ = □

F $1x = 1$ H $x + 1 = 1$
G $x \div 1 = 1$ J $x - 1 = 1$

For 11–20, solve each equation.

11. $8 + y = {}^{-}12$

A $y = {}^{-}20$ C $y = 4$
B $y = {}^{-}4$ D $y = 20$

12. $x + 5 = 15$

F $x = 10$ H $x = 20$
G $x = 15$ J $x = 75$

13. $r - 35 = {}^{-}53$

A $r = 88$ C $r = 18$
B $r = 22$ D $r = {}^{-}18$

14. $2\frac{1}{2} + v = 5\frac{1}{3}$

F $v = 7\frac{5}{6}$ H $v = 2\frac{1}{6}$
G $v = 2\frac{5}{6}$ J $v = 2$

15. $57 = q + 79$

A $q = 136$ C $q = {}^{-}22$
B $q = 22$ D $q = {}^{-}136$

16. $w - 19 = {}^{-}22$

F $w = {}^{-}41$ H $w = 3$
G $w = {}^{-}3$ J $w = 41$

Go On

17. $k - 9 = {}^{-}12$

A $k = {}^{-}21$
B $k = {}^{-}3$
C $k = 3$
D $2k = 1$

18. $13 + n = 17$

F $n = 4$
G $n = {}^{-}4$
H $n = {}^{-}20$
J $n = {}^{-}30$

19. $12.3 + d = 15.45$

A $d = {}^{-}27.75$
B $d = {}^{-}3.15$
C $d = 3.15$
D $d = 27.75$

20. $c - 72 = 82$

F $c = {}^{-}154$
G $c = {}^{-}10$
H $c = 154$
J $c = 164$

For 21–25, choose the correct equation and solution.

21. Joshua has climbed 87 of the 143 steps to the top of Avalanche Mountain. How many more steps, *s*, does he have to climb?

A $87 + 143 = s$; 230 steps
B $s - 87 = 143$; 220 steps
C $87 - 143 = s$; ${}^{-}56$ steps
D $87 + s = 143$; 56 steps

22. Mr. James has another 15 mi to drive to get to his destination. He has already gone 147 mi. How many miles, *m*, is the total trip?

F $147 - 15 = m$; 122 mi
G $m + 15 = 147$; 132 mi
H $m + 147 = 15$; ${}^{-}132$ mi
J $m - 15 = 147$; 162 mi

23. The perimeter of a quadrilateral is 97 in. Three of the sides have lengths 27 in., 30 in., and 32 in. What is the length of the fourth side, *s*?

A $s = 97 + 32 + 30 + 27$; 186 in.
B $97 = 27 + 30 + 32 + s$; 8 in.
C $97 = s - 32 - 30 - 27$; 186 in.
D $s + 97 = 32 + 30 + 27$; ${}^{-}8$ in.

24. Sumi had 27 yd of fabric when she started a craft project. She used 12 yd for quilt blocks and 6 yd for doll clothes. How many yards, *y*, of fabric does she have left?

F $27 + 12 + 6 = y$; 45 yd
G $27 + 12 = y + 6$; 33 yd
H $27 = 12 + 6 + y$; 9 yd
J $27 + 6 = 12 + y$; 21 yd

25. During the final game of a basketball tournament, the winning team scored a total of 97 points. The team scored 81 points by shooting field goals. The balance of the points was made by shooting free throws. How many points, *p*, did the team score by shooting free throws?

A $97 + 81 = p$; 188 points
B $97 = 81 + p$; 16 points
C $81 = 97 + p$; ${}^{-}16$ points
D $97 = p - 81$; 178 points

Stop

Name ______________________________

Write the correct answer.

For 1–6, write an equation for each word sentence. Use *n* as the variable.

1. A number increased by 6 is 15.

____

2. The travel time, less 10 minutes to wait for the bus, is 45 minutes.

____

3. Six times a number is 72.

____

4. 12 is the quotient of 132 and a number.

____

5. The product of a number and 8 is 64.

____

6. Twenty is 4 less than a number.

____

For 7–10, write the equation that is represented by the given model. Use *n* as the variable.

7.

____

8.

____

9.

____

10.

____

For 11–20, solve each equation.

11. $5 + n = {}^{-}7$

____

12. $t + 3 = 30$

____

13. $m - 12 = {}^{-}20$

____

14. $1\frac{1}{2} + w = 2\frac{1}{2}$

____

15. $33 = r + 45$

____

16. $x + 21 = {}^{-}2$

____

Go On

17. $y - 5 = {}^{-}2$

____

18. $1.5 + p = 12$

____

19. $11 + n = 11.45$

____

20. $b - 45 = 62$

____

For 21–25, write an equation and solve it.

21. Randall has saved \$120 toward a new DVD player. If the DVD player costs \$200, how much more must Randall save?

____

22. Giorgio must practice his guitar for another 15 minutes. He has already practiced for 20 minutes. How long does Giorgio practice his guitar?

____

23. In 4 days, Keisha ran a total of 27 miles. She ran 5 miles on the first day, 6 miles on the second day, and 7 miles on the third day. How many miles did she run on the fourth day?

____

24. Tom had \$35. He bought a pair of sunglasses. Now he has \$13 left. How much were the sunglasses?

____

25. Tara lives 85 miles from her cousin. How many more miles must she drive to reach her cousin's house if she has driven 24 miles so far?

____

Stop

Name ______________________________

Choose the best answer.

For 1–8, solve the equation.

1. $9x = 45$

A $x = 405$ C $x = 5$
B $x = 36$ D $x = {}^-5$

2. $24 = 6a$

F $a = {}^-18$ H $a = 18$
G $a = 4$ J $a = 144$

3. $\frac{y}{5} = 15$

A $y = 75$ C $y = 10$
B $y = 20$ D $y = 3$

4. $2.4 = \frac{n}{4}$

F $n = 0.6$ H $n = 2.8$
G $n = 2.0$ J $n = 9.6$

5. $2.5z = 10$

A $z = 4$ C $z = 12.5$
B $z = 7.5$ D $z = 25$

6. $\frac{d}{3} = {}^-9$

F $d = 27$ H $d = {}^-6$
G $d = {}^-3$ J $d = {}^-27$

7. $8c = {}^-24$

A $c = {}^-192$ C $c = 3$
B $c = {}^-3$ D $c = 16$

8. ${}^-8 = \frac{r}{2}$

F $r = {}^-16$ H $r = {}^-4$
G $r = {}^-6$ J $r = 16$

For 9–12, choose the equation that is represented by the model.

9. 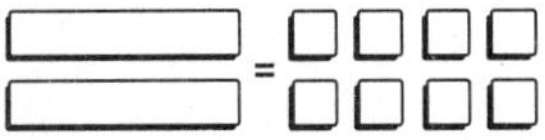

A $x = 4$ C $x = 8$
B $2x = 8$ D $8x = 2$

10. 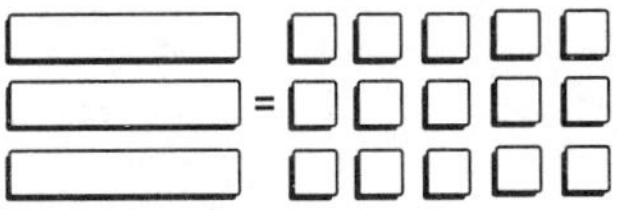

F $x = 5$ H $3x = 15$
G $3x = 5$ J $15x = 3$

11. 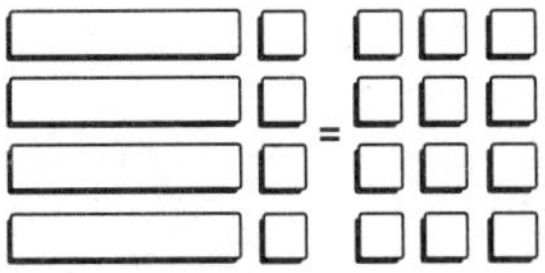

A $x = 2$ C $x = 12$
B $12x = 4x + 4$ D $4x + 4 = 12$

12. 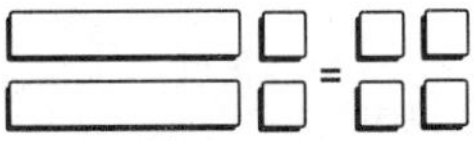

F $2x + 2 = 4$ H $x = 1$
G $4x = 2x + 2$ J $x = 2$

For 13–15, use the formula $d = rt$ to find the unknown value.

13. $d = 455$ mi, $r = 65$ mi per hr; $t = ■$ hr

A $t = 29{,}575$ C $t = 8$
B $t = 360$ D $t = 7$

14. $r = 88$ ft per sec, $t = 44$ sec; $d = ■$ ft

F $d = 4{,}400$ H $d = 44$
G $d = 3{,}872$ J $d = 2$

15. $d = 200$ km, $t = 2.5$ hr; $r = ■$ km per hr

A $r = 500$
B $r = 202.5$
C $r = 100$
D $r = 80$

Go On

For 16–18, convert the temperature to degrees Fahrenheit. Use the formula $F = (\frac{9}{5} \times C) + 32$.

16. 20°C

F 95°F
G 68°F
H 43°F
J 4°F

17. 15°C

A 167°F
B 135°F
C 59°F
D 27°F

18. 27°C

F 112.6°F
G 80.6°F
H 47°F
J 16.6°F

19. Mrs. Randall paid a total of $195.75, before tax, for 3 radial tires. This included a $30 discount. How much did each tire cost before the discount?

A $146.44
B $97.88
C $75.25
D $55.25

20. A national car rental company charges $25.50 per day and $0.35 per mile to rent a car. If the total bill, before tax, for a 3-day rental was $133.55, about how many miles were driven?

F 309 mi
G 236 mi
H 163 mi
J 90 mi

For 21–23, convert the temperature to degrees Celsius. Use the formula $C = \frac{5}{9} \times (F - 32)$. When necessary, round to the nearest tenth of a degree.

21. 41°F

A 5°C
B 9°C
C 45°C
D 81°C

22. 75°F

F 9.7°C
G 15.4°C
H 23.9°C
J 103°C

23. 104°F

A 40°C
B 72°C
C 350°C
D 360°C

24. Ed bought 4 shirts and a $12 belt. All the shirts were the same price. The total cost before tax was $64. How much did each shirt cost?

F $13
G $16
H $17
J $52

25. The admission charge to the state fair is $8.70. Groups larger than 20 people receive a $2.25 discount per person. One group paid a total of $290.25 before tax. How many people were in the group?

A 130
B 85
C 45
D 25

Stop

Name ____________________

Write the correct answer.

For 1–8, solve the equation.

1. $4x = 32$

____

2. $18 = 3n$

____

3. $\frac{p}{8} = 7$

____

4. $8.5 = \frac{t}{5}$

____

5. $1.2x = 72$

____

6. $\frac{a}{6} = {}^{-}7$

____

7. $9b = {}^{-}45$

____

8. ${}^{-}3 = \frac{m}{3}$

____

For 9–12, write the equation that represents the model shown. Then solve the equation. Use *n* as the variable.

9. ▭ ▭ ▭ = □□ □□ □□

____

10. ▭ ▭ ▭ ▭ = □□□ □□□ □□□ □□□

____

11. ▭ ▭ □□□ = □□□ □□□□

____

12. ▭ □□ ▭ □□ ▭ □□ = □□□ □□□ □□□

____

For 13–15, use the formula $d = rt$ to complete.

13. $d = 330$ mi, $r = 55$ mi per hr

$t = ■$ hr

____

Go On

14. $r = 64$ ft per sec, $t = 8$ sec

$d = ■$ ft

____

15. $d = 266$ km, $t = 3.5$ hr

$r = ■$ km per hr

____

For 16–18, convert the temperature to degrees Fahrenheit. Use the formula $F = (\frac{9}{5} \times C) + 32$.

16. 5°C

____

17. 45°C

____

18. 32°C

____

19. Sara paid a total of $22.98 for 2 videos. This included a $12 rebate. How much did each video cost before the rebate?

____

20. A telephone company charges $39.50 per month for basic local phone calls and $0.15 per minute for all long-distance calls. Tiffany's phone bills for the last 3 months totaled $128.25 before tax. For how many minutes did she talk long distance over the 3 months?

____

For 21–23, convert the temperature to degrees Celsius. Use the formula $C = \frac{5}{9} \times (F - 32)$.

21. 77°F

____

22. 50°F

____

23. 113°F

____

24. The Wallaces' bill for 4 dinners was $69.96, which included $3.96 for tax. How much was each dinner if each cost the same amount?

____

25. Movie tickets cost $7.75 for adults and $3.25 for children under 12. Mr. and Mrs. Harrison took their children to the movies. They paid a total of $28.50 for tickets. If all of the Harrisons' children are under 12, how many children do they have? Explain how you arrived at your answer.

____

____

Stop

Name ______________________________

Choose the best answer.

1. What expression represents the product of $3r$ and $2s$?

   A $3r \times 2s$ C $3r \times 2r$
   B $3s \times 2r$ D $3r \div 2s$

2. What is the equation for the word sentence?

   The quotient of 84 and a number is 6.

   F $84 \times n = 6$ H $6 \div n = 84$
   G $84 \div n = 6$ J $n \div 84 = 6$

3. Solve. ${}^{-}12 = \frac{a}{6}$

   A $a = 72$ C $a = {}^{-}2$
   B $a = 2$ D $a = {}^{-}72$

4. Evaluate. $5k - 12$ for $k = 6$

   F 42 H 18
   G 30 J ${}^{-}7$

5. What equation is modeled below?

   A $x + 3 = 6$ C $x - 3 = 6$
   B $3x = 6$ D $x \div 3 = 6$

6. What equation is modeled below?

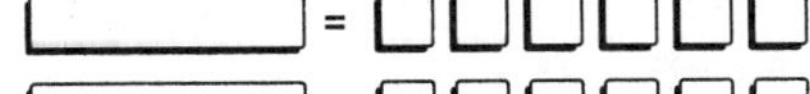

   F $x = 18$ H $3 = 18x$
   G $3 + x = 18$ J $3x = 18$

7. Find $3 \bullet \sqrt{9} - 3$.

   A 24 C $\sqrt{9}$
   B 6 D 3

8. Solve. $r - 7 = {}^{-}3$

   F $r = 4$ H $r = {}^{-}4$
   G $r = 0$ J $r = {}^{-}10$

9. Solve for y.

   $3y = 27$

   A 81 B 31 C 27 D 9

10. What numerical expression represents 5 increased by twice a number?

    F $5 + n$ H $2 \times 5 + n$
    G $5 + 2n$ J $2 \times (5 + n)$

11. John is taking a trip of 257 mi. He has only gone 15 mi. How far does he still have to go?

    A 192 mi C 242 mi
    B 200 mi D 272 mi

12. Convert 68°F to degrees Celsius. Use the formula $C = \frac{5}{9} \times (F - 32)$.

    F ${}^{-}20$°C H 20°C
    G 6°C J 65°C

13. Evaluate $c^2 + 4$ for $c = 2$.

    A 4 B 6 C 8 D 16

14. Which model represents $2 + x = 5$?

    F

    G

    H

    J

Go On

15. Emily purchased 3 pairs of shoes that all cost the same amount, and a pair of \$15 sandals. The bill before tax was \$78. How much was each pair of shoes?

A \$15 C \$21
B \$20 D \$26

16. Three separate square plots of land have areas of 64 sq. ft, 256 sq. ft, and 36 sq. ft. How much fencing is needed to fence in these plots?

F 120 ft H 60 ft
G 90 ft J 30 ft

17. Solve. $1\frac{3}{4} + f = 5\frac{1}{2}$

A $f = 2\frac{3}{4}$ C $f = 3\frac{3}{4}$
B $f = 3\frac{1}{4}$ D $f = 4\frac{1}{4}$

18. Solve. $^{-}12q = {}^{-}60$

F $q = 720$ H $q = {}^{-}5$
G $q = 5$ J $q = {}^{-}720$

19. A game show contestant starts the show with \$100. Each loss costs him c dollars, and each win earns him w dollars. Which expression tells how much money he has after 1 loss and 1 win?

A $\$100 - c + w$ C $\$100c - w$
B $\$100 + c - w$ D $\$100cw$

20. Which equation shows that the product of a number and 9 is 72?

F $n + 9 = 72$ H $n - 9 = 72$
G $n \times 9 = 72$ J $n \div 9 = 72$

21. How long will it take Jill to go 225 miles if her average speed is 50 miles per hour? Use the formula $d = rt$.

A 45 hr C 6 hr
B 11.25 hr D $4\frac{1}{2}$ hr

22. Which does the array model?

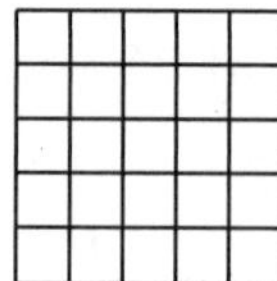

F $5^2 = 25$ H $4^2 = 16$
G $5 + 5 = 10$ J $5 \times 5 = 10$

23. What number decreased by 5 equals $^{-}7$?

A 12 C $^{-}2$
B 2 D $^{-}12$

24. Solve. $\frac{t}{^{-}4} = 16$

F $t = 64$ H $t = {}^{-}4$
G $t = 4$ J $t = {}^{-}64$

25. A car rental agency charges \$25 per day plus m dollars per mile and g dollars for each gallon of gas. Which expression represents the cost of renting a car for one day and driving 120 mi using 5 gal of gas?

A $\$25 + m + g$
B $\$25 + 5m + 120g$
C $\$25 + 120m + 5g$
D $\$25 \times 120m \times 5g$

26. Solve. $43 = h - 12$

F $h = 67$ H $h = {}^{-}31$
G $h = 55$ J $h = {}^{-}55$

Go On

Name ______________________________

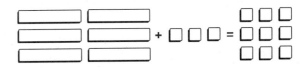

27. Randy purchased 4 new radial tires and 2 seat covers for his car. The total was \$290 before tax. If the seat covers cost \$15 each, how much did each of the tires cost?

A \$57.50 C \$72.50
B \$65 D \$130

28. Which expression represents 23 decreased by d?

F $23 \div d$ H $23 - d$
G $d \div 23$ J $d - 23$

29. Which equation is modeled below?

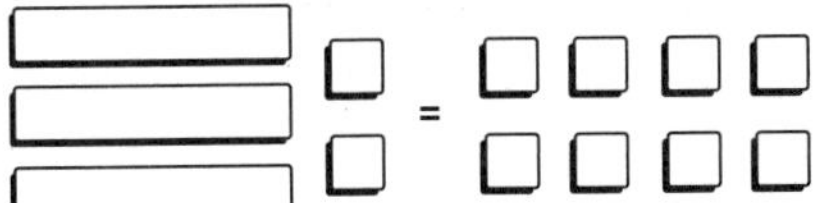

A $3 + x = 8$ C $3x + 2 = 8$
B $x + 8 = 3$ D $2x + 3 = 8$

30. Use the formula $d = rt$ to find r for $d = 540$ and $t = 12$.

F $r = 6{,}480$ H $r = 180$
G $r = 528$ J $r = 45$

31. Find $4 \bullet \sqrt{64} \div \sqrt{16}$.

A 8 C 32
B 16 D 64

32. Which equation represents the word sentence?

27 is 3 less than a number.

F $27 = b - 3$ H $27 = 3 - b$
G $^{-}27 = b - 3$ J $3 = b - 27$

33. Which equation is modeled below?

A $6x = 9$
B $6x + 3 = 9$
C $6x + 9 = 3$
D $x + 3 = 9$

34. Evaluate $5a + \frac{6b}{2}$ for $a = 5$ and $b = 7$.

F 67 H 32
G 46 J 13

35. Sam purchased items costing \$5.25, \$4, and \$3.25. If he started with \$25, how much does Sam have left?

A \$37.50 C \$14.50
B \$25.00 D \$12.50

36. Convert $^{-}10$°C into degrees Fahrenheit. Use the formula $F = (\frac{9}{5} \times C) + 32$.

F 40°F H $^{-}14$°F
G 14°F J $^{-}40$°F

37. How many tiles are needed to make a 6×6 array?

A 6 C 36
B 12 D 216

38. Ed has dug 27 fence post holes. He has 33 more to dig. How many post holes will there be in all?

F 6 post holes H 33 post holes
G 18 post holes J 60 post holes

Go On

39. The football team scored 43 points in the game last night. Field goals are worth 3 points and touchdowns are worth 7 points. If the team scored 5 field goals, how many touchdowns did they score?

A 43   C 7
B 28   D 4

40. Evaluate. $\sqrt{144} + \sqrt{81} - 5^2$

F 46   G 16   H 4   J $^-4$

41. Which equation represents the word sentence?

6 times a number is 22.

A $22 \times 6 = d$ C $6 \times d = 22$
B $6 + d = 22$ D $6 \div d = 22$

42. Which equation can be used to find a number multiplied by 6 and increased by 4 that equals 34.

F $(p \times 6) + 4 = 34$
G $(p \div 6) + 4 = 34$
H $p \times (6 + 4) = 34$
J $(p \times 6) + 4 = 34$

43. Two square arrays have a total of 41 tiles. What could be the sizes of the arrays?

A 4×4 and 5×5
B 3×3 and 5×5
C 3×3 and 6×6
D 2×2 and 7×7

44. Solve the equation represented by the model.

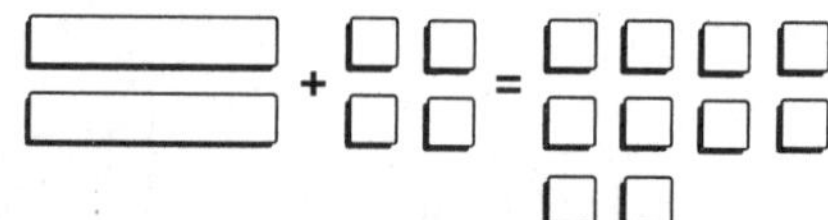

F $2x + 4 = 10, x = 3$
G $2x + 4 = 10, x = 7$
H $2x + 4 = 10, x = {^-3}$
J $2x + 4 = 10, x = {^-7}$

45. Which model represents $3x + 1 = 7$?

A

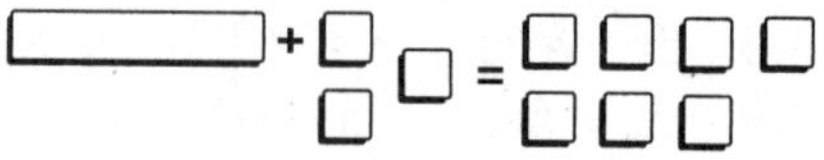

B

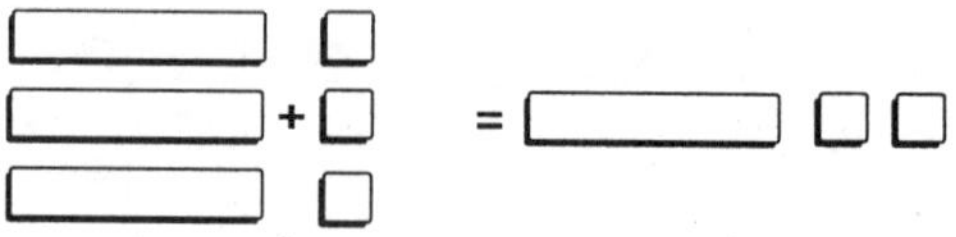

C

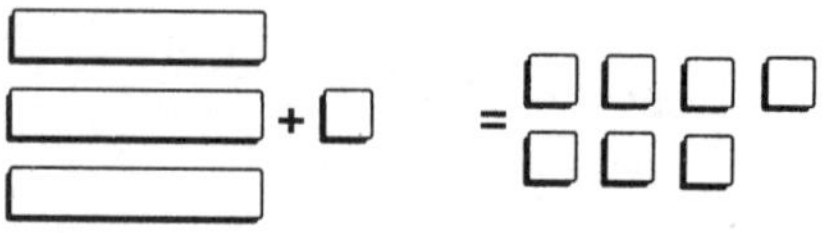

D

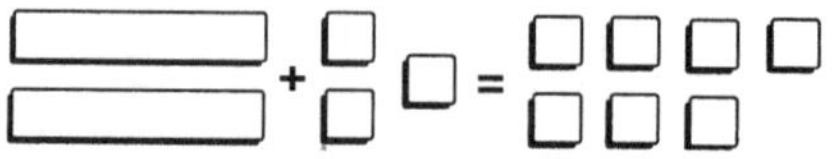

46. Evaluate $50 + 5c + c^2$ for $c = {^-4}$.

F 86   G 46   H 14   J 5

47. Solve. $f - 3\frac{2}{3} = {^-5}\frac{1}{2}$.

A $f = {^-2}$ C $f = 2$
B $f = {^-1}\frac{5}{6}$ D $f = 1\frac{5}{6}$

48. The quotient of a number and the difference $(2 - 4)$ is 5. What is the number?

F -10 H 9
G 412   J 14

49. Sixteen more than the square root of a number is 24. What is the number?

A 100   B 64   C 20   D 8

50. Stefan started the school year with 24 pencils. He has already used 18. How many pencils does he have left?

F 42   H 18
G 24   J 6

Stop

Name ______________________

Write the correct answer.

1. Write an expression to represent the product of $6n$ and $4p$.

____

2. Write an equation for the word sentence, 15 is the quotient of 90 and a number.

____

3. Solve for t.

$^{-}21 = \frac{t}{3}$

____

4. Evaluate $3x + 4$ for $x = 4$.

____

5. Write and solve the equation that is modeled below.

____

6. Write and solve the equation that is modeled below.

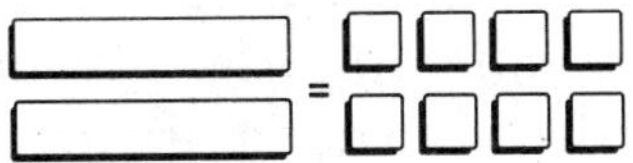

____

7. $2\sqrt{36} - 15$

____

8. Solve for x.

$x - 12 = {}^{-}7$

____

9. Draw a model to represent and solve the equation $5x + 1 = 46$.

____

10. Write a numerical expression for the word expression, twelve less than twice a number.

____

11. Ari is reading a book that has 316 pages. He has read 28 pages so far. How many more pages does he have to read to finish the book? Write an equation to model this situation, and solve.

____

12. Convert 86°F to degrees Celsius. Use the formula $C = \frac{5}{9} \times (F - 32)$.

____

13. Evaluate $5a^2 - 8$ for $a = 3$.

____

14. Draw a model to represent and solve the equation $5 + n = 8$.

____

Go On

Name ____________________

15. Rod bought 3 children's tickets to the movies. He also bought one adult ticket for $8. The total cost for the tickets was $23. How much is a children's ticket for the movies?

____

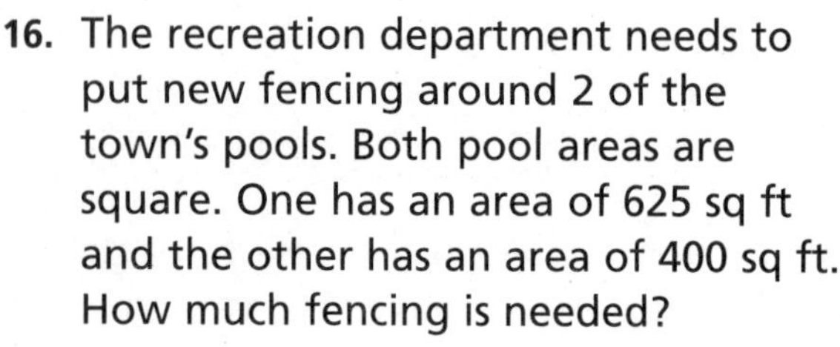

16. The recreation department needs to put new fencing around 2 of the town's pools. Both pool areas are square. One has an area of 625 sq ft and the other has an area of 400 sq ft. How much fencing is needed?

____

17. Solve for x. $2\frac{7}{8} + x = 8$

____

18. Solve for x. ${}^{-}15x = {}^{-}90$

____

19. Scott's math average is 87. Each extra credit paper he does earns him e points toward his average. Each missed homework assignment costs him m points. Write an expression to tell what his average is after he has done one extra credit page, but has missed one homework assignment.

____

20. Write an equation for the word sentence: 63 is the product of 7 and a number.

____

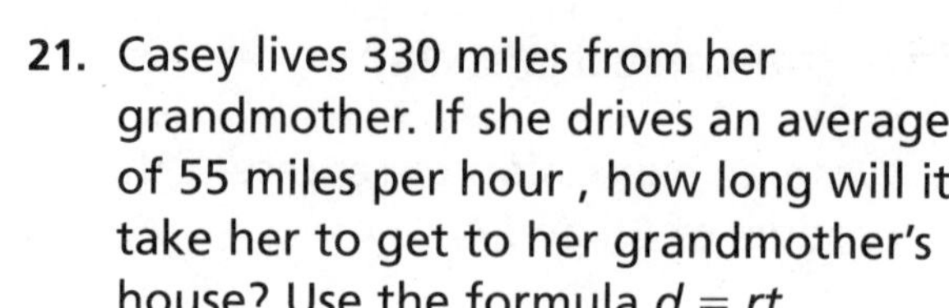

21. Casey lives 330 miles from her grandmother. If she drives an average of 55 miles per hour , how long will it take her to get to her grandmother's house? Use the formula $d = rt$.

____

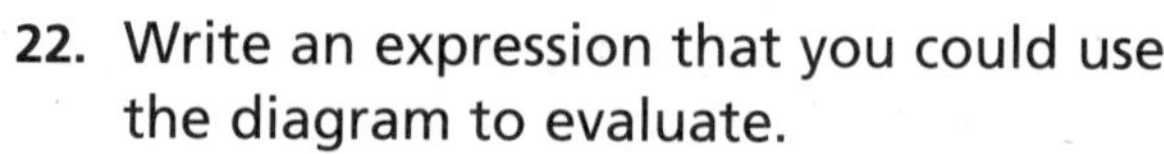

22. Write an expression that you could use the diagram to evaluate.

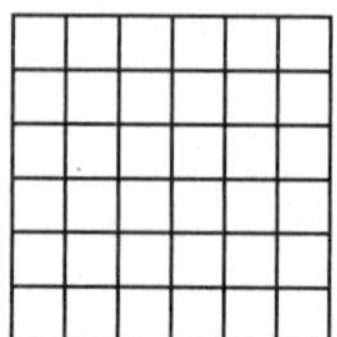

____

23. What number increased by 4 equals ${}^{-}2$?

____

24. Solve for x. $\frac{x}{{}^{-}5} = 7$

____

25. A bank charges a fee of $3 per month for a checking account. In addition they charge d dollars for each check written plus x dollars for each returned check. Write an expression that represents the cost of a checking account for one month after writing 6 checks and having 2 checks returned.

____

26. Solve for x. $54 = x - 22$

____

Go On

Name ______________________

27. Corey bought 4 video games and 2 new controllers for a total of \$210 before tax. If the games cost \$40 each, how much did each of the controllers cost?

____

28. Write an expression to represent 15 decreased by m.

____

29. Write and solve the equation that is modeled below.

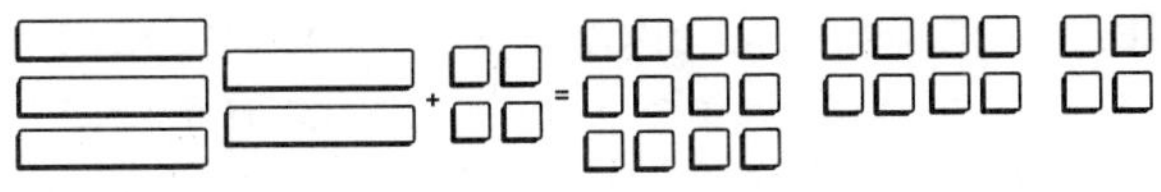

____

30. Use the formula $d = rt$ to find r for $d = 570$ and $t = 15$.

____

31. Find $3 \times \frac{\sqrt{81}}{\sqrt{9}}$.

____

32. Write an equation to represent the word sentence, 46 is 5 less than a number.

____

33. Write and solve the equation shown by the model.

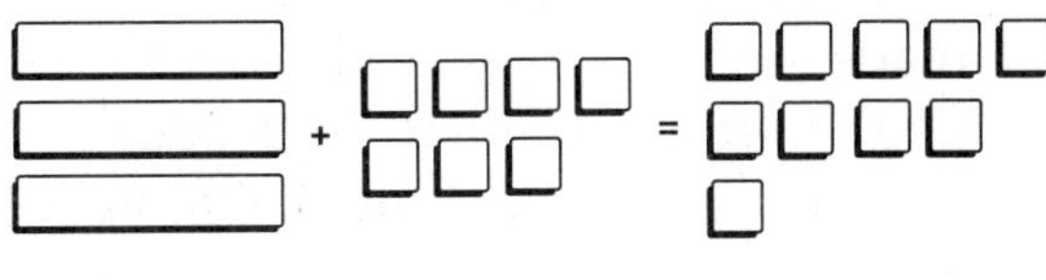

____

34. Evaluate $2x + \frac{5y}{3}$ for $x = 4$ and $y = 3$.

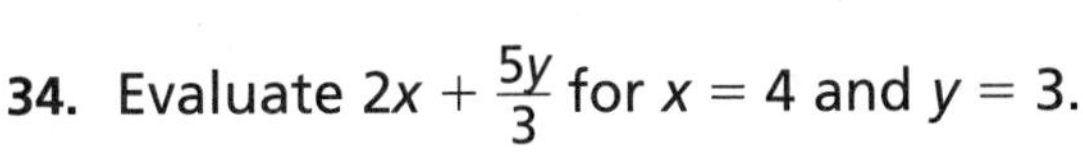

____

35. For lunch Moira bought a sandwich for \$3.75, a drink for \$1.50, and dessert for \$2.25. She paid with a \$20 bill. How much change did she receive?

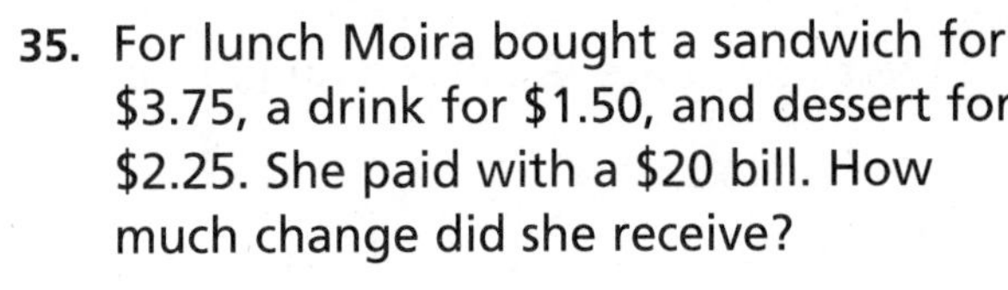

____

36. Convert $^{-}35$°C into degrees Fahrenheit. Use the formula

$F = (\frac{9}{5} \times C) + 32$.

____

37. How many tiles are needed to make an 8×8 array?

____

38. Mr. Saunders has collected 12 permission slips from the students in his class. He needs to collect 16 more. How many students are in his class?

____

Go On

39. Reba scored 21 points in a basketball game. Field goals are 2 points each, and free throws are 1 point each. If she made 7 of her points from free throws, and the rest were from field goals, how many field goals did Reba make?

____

40. Find $\sqrt{121} + \sqrt{81} - 4^2$.

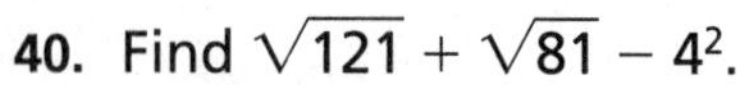

____

41. Write an equation to represent the word sentence, 8 times a number is 40.

____

42. Write and solve the equation that is modeled below.

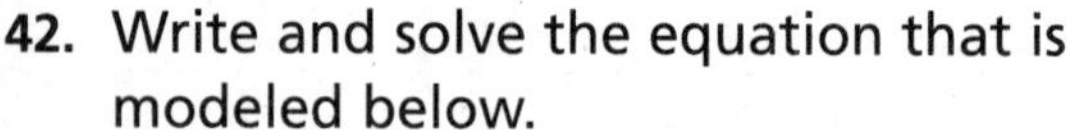

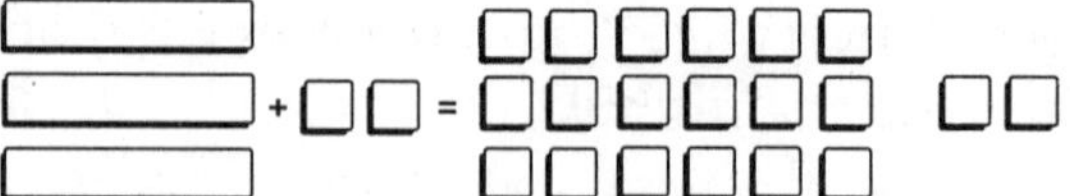

____

43. Two square arrays have a total of 45 squares. What size are the arrays?

____

44. Write and solve the equation represented by the model.

____

45. Draw a model to represent and solve the equation $3x + 4 = 13$.

____

46. Evaluate $15 + 3n + n^2$ for $n = {}^{-}5$.

____

47. Solve. $x - 1\frac{1}{2} = 10$.

____

48. Evan uses his allowance to buy school lunch 5 days per week. Lunch is \$2.50 per day. After buying lunch, he has \$5 left from his allowance each week. How much is Evan's weekly allowance?

____

49. Megan uses 2 eggs for each batch of cookies. She made 3 batches of cookies and now has 5 eggs left. How many eggs did she start out with?

____

50. Max bought 32 quarts of fruit punch for his party. So far his guests drank 14 quarts of punch. How many quarts does he have left?

____

Stop

Name ____________________

Choose the best answer.

For 1–4, name the geometric figure.

1. H K

A ray *HK*
B line segment *HK*
C line *HK*
D ray *KH*

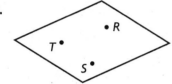

2. P Q

F line segment *PQ*
G ray *PQ*
H line *PQ*
J ray *QP*

3. R T S

A line *RS*
B ∠*RST*
C ray *TS*
D plane *RST*

4.

F line *MN*
G line segment *MN*
H ray *MN*
J ray *NM*

5. Which of the following is the measure of a straight angle?

A 0°
B 90°
C 140°
D 180°

For 6–7, use the figures below.

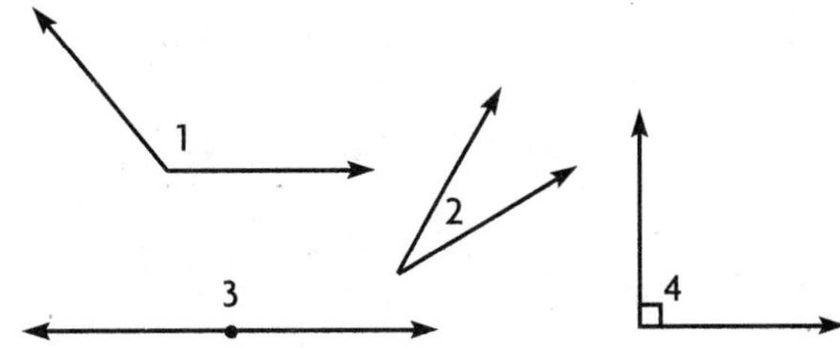

6. Which angle is a right angle?

F ∠1
G ∠2
H ∠3
J ∠4

7. Which angle is an acute angle?

A ∠4
B ∠3
C ∠2
D ∠1

8. What kind of angle has a measure of 135°?

F acute
G obtuse
H right
J straight

9. Which describes ∠1 and ∠3?

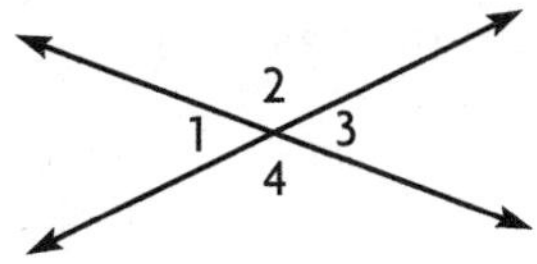

A complementary
B supplementary
C vertical
D perpendicular

10. Which describes two lines that meet at exactly one point?

F intersecting
G supplementary
H parallel
J vertical

Go On

Name ______________________________

For 11–13, use the following figure.

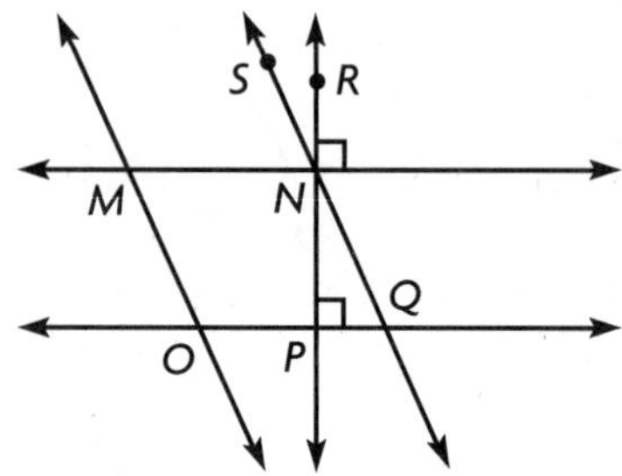

11. Which line is perpendicular to line *MN*?

A line *OQ** **C** line *MO*
B line *NP* **D** line *NQ*

12. Which line is parallel to line *OP*?

F line *MN* **H** line *NQ*
G line *MO* **J** line *NP*

13. Which angle is complementary to $\angle SNR$?

A $\angle SNM$ **C** $\angle PNQ$
B $\angle MNR$ **D** $\angle MNP$

14. Which describes two lines in the same plane that never cross?

F perpendicular **H** parallel
G intersecting **J** right

15. Which pair names adjacent angles?

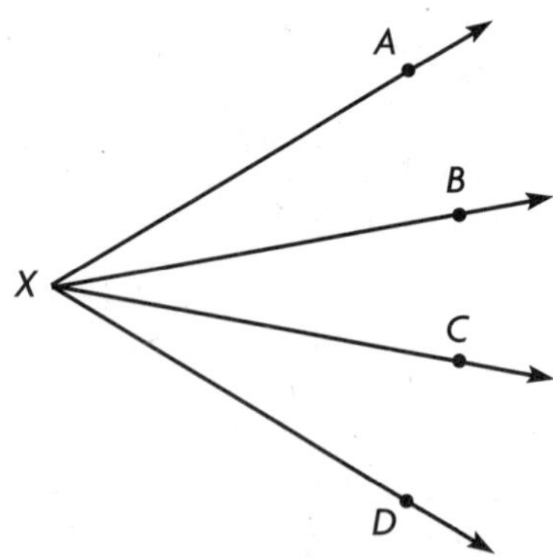

A $\angle AXB$ and $\angle AXC$
B $\angle AXB$ and $\angle BXC$
C $\angle BXC$ and $\angle BXD$
D $\angle AXD$ and $\angle BXC$

For 16–20, use the following figure.

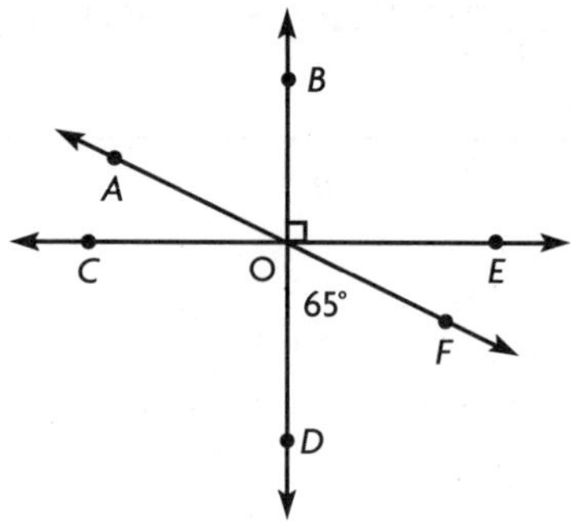

16. What is the measure of $\angle FOC$?

F 90° **H** 165°
G 155° **J** 180°

17. What is the measure of $\angle AOC$?

A 25° **C** 65°
B 35° **D** 115°

18. What is the measure of $\angle AOB$?

F 25° **H** 65°
G 35° **J** 90°

19. Which angle is supplementary to $\angle BOF$?

A $\angle COD$ **C** $\angle COF$
B $\angle BOE$ **D** $\angle AOB$

20. Which two rays are perpendicular?

F $\overrightarrow{OC}$ and $\overrightarrow{OA}$
G $\overrightarrow{OC}$ and $\overrightarrow{OE}$
H $\overrightarrow{OF}$ and $\overrightarrow{OB}$
J $\overrightarrow{OE}$ and $\overrightarrow{OD}$

Stop

Name ______________________

Write the correct answer.

For 1–4, name the geometric figure.

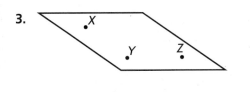

1. A C (line through points A and C)

____

2. D E (ray from D through E)

____

3. X Y Z (plane containing points X, Y, Z)

____

4. A B (segment from A to B)

____

5. What is the measure of a right angle?

____

For 6–7, use the figures below. Write *acute, obtuse,* or *straight*.

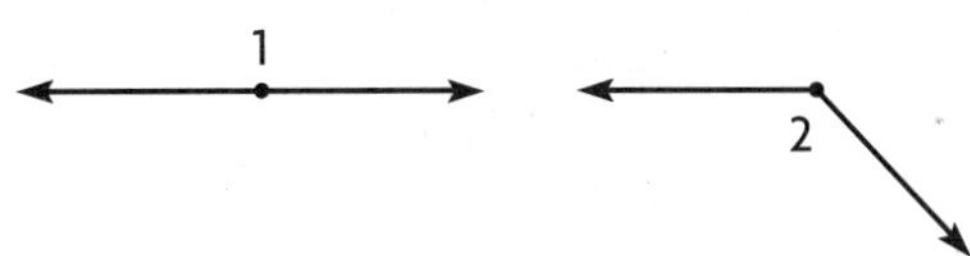

6. ∠1 can be classified as a(n) ___ angle.

____

7. ∠2 can be classified as a(n) ___ angle.

____

8. What kind of angle has a measure of 35°?

____

9. Which two angles in the figure are supplementary angles?

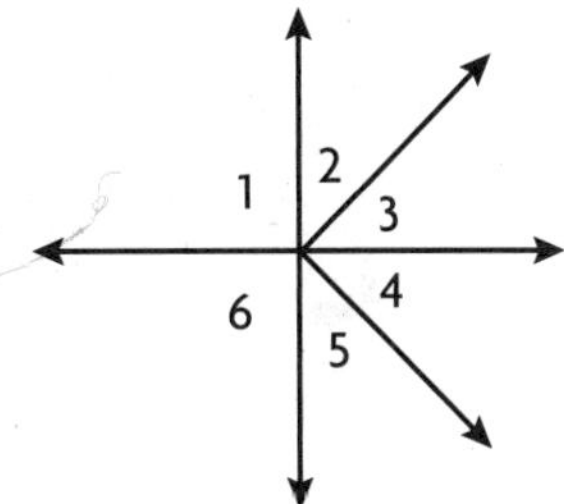

____

10. Draw 3 parallel lines.

____

Go On

Name ______________________

For 11–13, use the following figure.

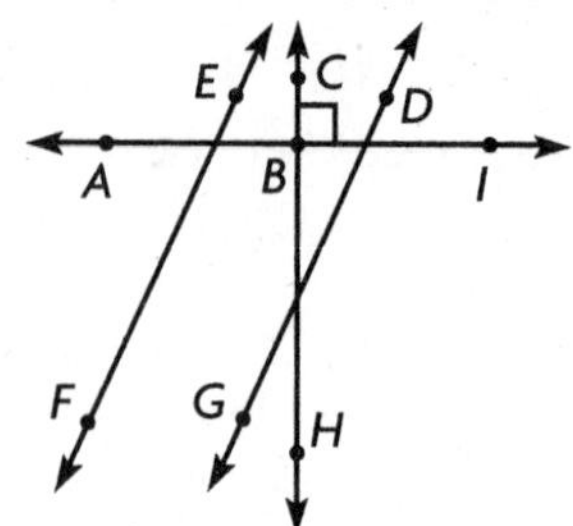

11. Which line is perpendicular to $\overleftrightarrow{AB}$?

____

12. Which line intersects $\overleftrightarrow{EF}$?

____

13. Which angle is a vertical angle with $\angle ABH$?

____

14. What word describes two lines that form a right angle?

____

15. Name a pair of angles that are not adjacent.

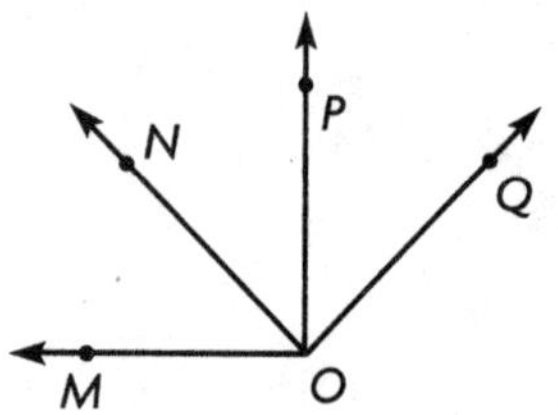

____

For 16–20, use the following figure.

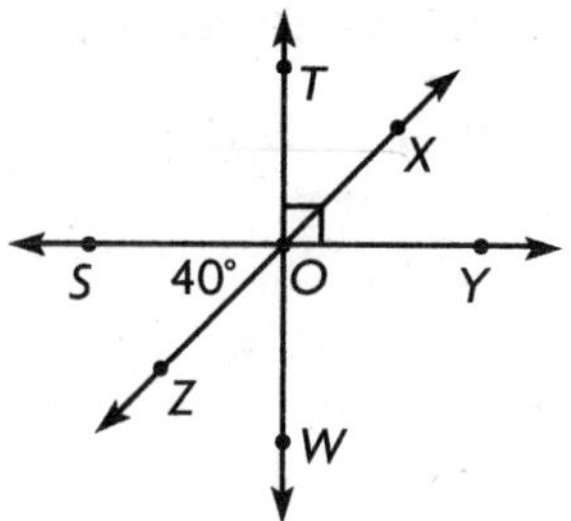

16. What is the measure of $\angle XOT$?

____

17. What is the measure of $\angle SOW$?

____

18. What is the measure of $\angle XOY$?

____

19. Which angle is a complement of $\angle XOY$?

____

20. Tell whether $\overline{TW}$ is perpendicular to $\overline{XZ}$. Explain your answer.

____

Stop

Name ______________________________

Choose the best answer.

For 1–4, complete the sentence.

1. Every trapezoid is also a ______.

A rectangle C quadrilateral
B rhombus D parallelogram

2. The sum of the angle measures in a triangle is ______.

F 90° H 270°
G 180° J 360°

3. Every rhombus is a ______.

A parallelogram C square
B rectangle D trapezoid

4. A triangle that contains an angle of 130° is a(*n*) ______ triangle.

F acute H obtuse
G right J isosceles

5. How many angles in a right triangle are acute angles?

A 0 C 2
B 1 D 3

6. Two angles of a triangle have measures of 35° and 55°. Which word best describes the triangle?

F acute H obtuse
G isosceles J right

7. Find the unknown angle measure.

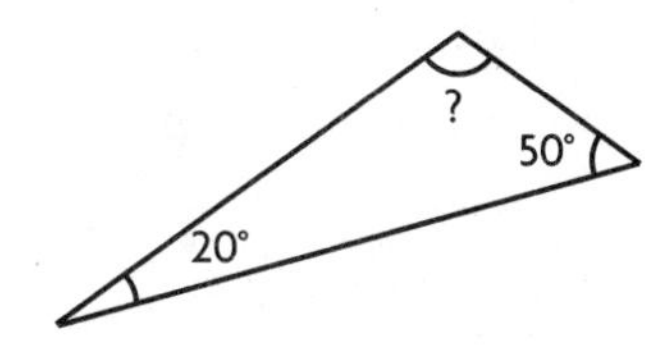

A 110° C 90°
B 100° D 70°

8. What is the measure of each angle of a regular triangle?

F 60° H 100°
G 90° J 120°

For 9–15, give the most exact name for the figure.

9. 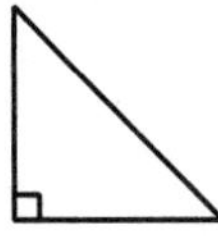

A acute triangle C obtuse triangle
B right triangle D triangle

10. 

F quadrilateral H trapezoid
G parallelogram J rectangle

11. 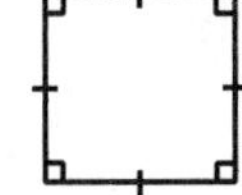

A rhombus C rectangle
B trapezoid D square

12. 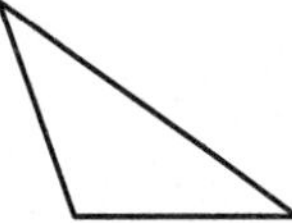

F obtuse triangle H acute triangle
G right triangle J triangle

13. 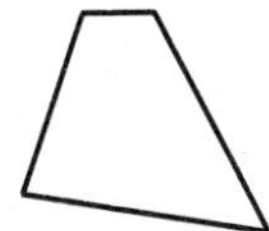

A trapezoid C rhombus
B parallelogram D quadrilateral

Go On

14. 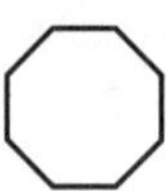

F decagon
G heptagon
H octagon
J hexagon

15. 

A scalene triangle
B isosceles triangle
C equilateral triangle
D obtuse triangle

For 16–20, use the figure below.

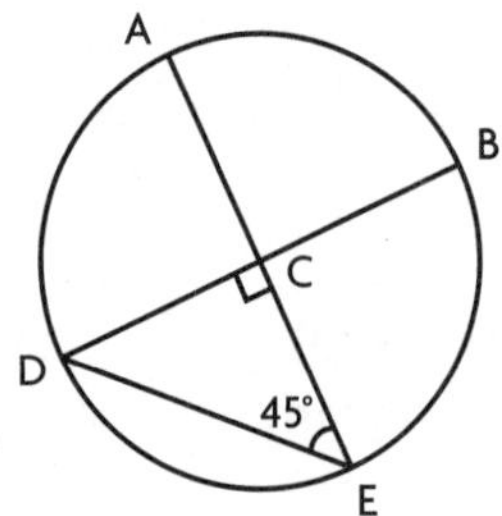

16. Name a diameter of the circle.

F $\overline{AC}$
G $\overline{DB}$
H $\overline{DE}$
J $\overline{CE}$

17. Which of these is **not** a chord of the circle?

A $\overline{AE}$
B $\overline{BC}$
C $\overline{BD}$
D $\overline{DE}$

18. Which of these is **not** a radius?

F $\overline{AC}$
G $\overline{AE}$
H $\overline{BC}$
J $\overline{CD}$

19. Give the most exact name for triangle *CDE*.

A isosceles triangle
B isosceles right triangle
C right triangle
D acute triangle

20. Name two arcs of the circle.

F $\overset{\frown}{AB}$ and $\overset{\frown}{CE}$
G $\overset{\frown}{BE}$ and $\overset{\frown}{CD}$
H $\overset{\frown}{DE}$ and $\overset{\frown}{BC}$
J $\overset{\frown}{AD}$ and $\overset{\frown}{BE}$

For 21–23, use the figure below.

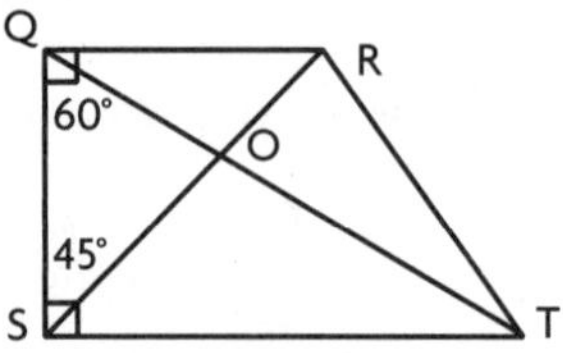

21. Find the measure of angle *STO*.

A 30°
B 60°
C 75°
D 120°

22. What kind of angle is *QOS*?

F obtuse
G right
H acute
J equilateral

23. Give the most exact name for the figure *QRTS*.

A quadrilateral
B rhombus
C parallelogram
D trapezoid

24. Sue is tiling a floor with tiles in the shape of hexagons. What is the measure of each angle in her tiles?

F 120°
G 90°
H 30°
J 60°

25. Find the measure of $\angle ABC$.

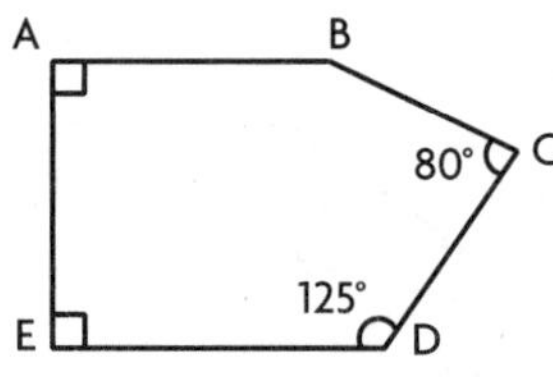

A 335°
B 155°
C 65°
D 60°

Stop

Name ____________________

Write the correct answer.

1. A quadrilateral with both pairs of opposite sides parallel is a ___.

____

2. The sum of the angle measures in a rectangle is ___.

____

3. A parallelogram with 4 congruent sides is called a ___.

____

4. A triangle whose angles are all less than 90° is a(n) ___ triangle.

____

5. A triangle with angles of 60° and 30° is a(n) ___ triangle.

____

6. What is the measure of the largest angle in an obtuse triangle?

____

7. Find the unknown angle measure.

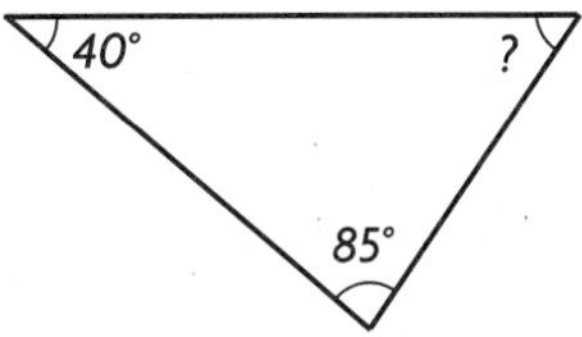

____

8. How can the measure of each angle of a regular quadrilateral be determined?

____

____

____

For 9–14, write the most exact name for the figure shown.

9.  ____________________

10. 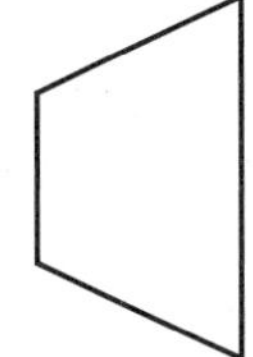 ____________________

11. 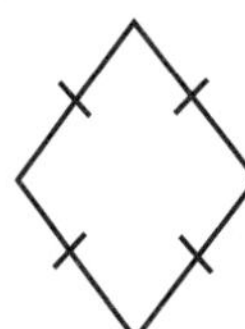 ____________________

12. 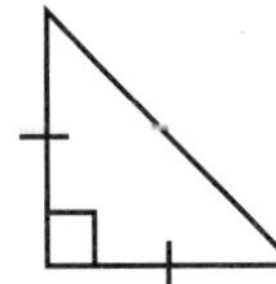 ____________________

13. 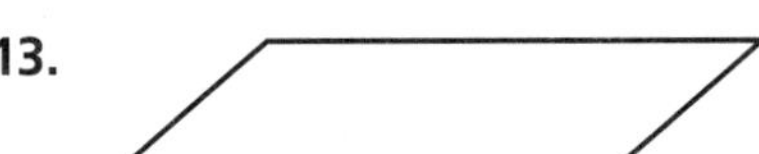 ____________________

Go On

14. 

____

15. Classify the triangle.

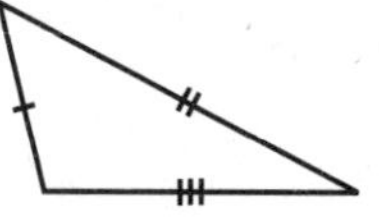

____

For 16–20, use the figure below. Point *O* is the center of the circle.

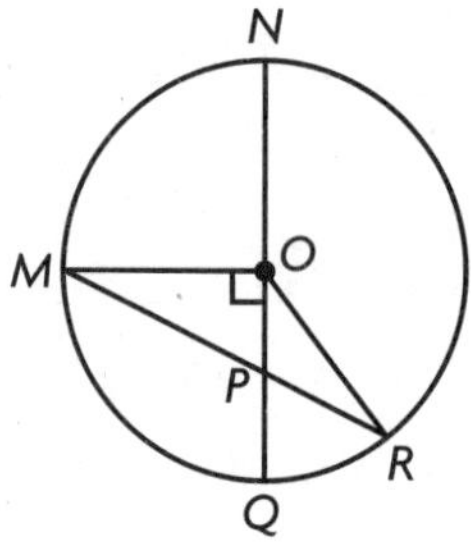

16. Name a diameter of the circle.

____

17. Name two chords of the circle.

____

18. Name four radii of the circle.

____

19. Name a right triangle.

____

20. Name two arcs of the circle that include point *Q*.

____

For 21–23, use the figure below. *STVR* is a parallelogram.

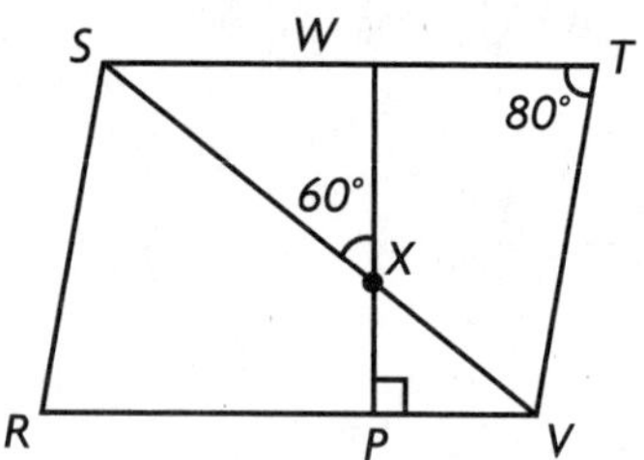

21. Find the measure of angle *PVX* and classify triangle *PVX*.

____

22. Find the measure of angle *RSV* and classify triangle *RSV*.

____

23. Identify a trapezoid in the figure.

____

24. On a math test, Hector must draw a regular pentagon. What is the measure of each interior angle?

____

25. What is the measure of $\angle XYZ$?

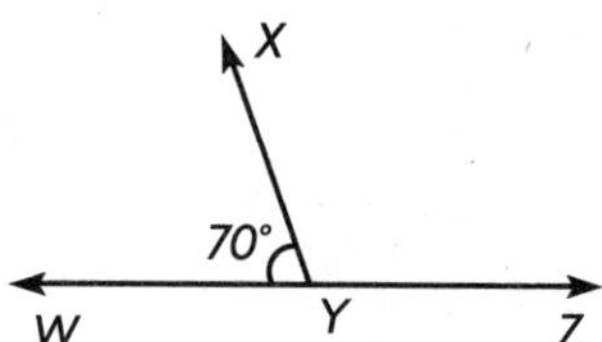

____

Stop

Name ____________________

Choose the best answer.

For 1–3, complete each sentence.

1. A prism is named for the shape of its ________.

   A lateral faces C polyhedron
   B bases D solid

2. A pyramid is related to a prism as a ________ is related to a cylinder.

   F base H cone
   G solid J polyhedron

3. A ________ is a polyhedron with two flat parallel bases.

   A cylinder C polygon
   B solid D prism

For 4–7, name the figure.

4. F pentagonal prism
   G hexagonal prism
   H hexagonal cylinder
   J hexagonal pyramid

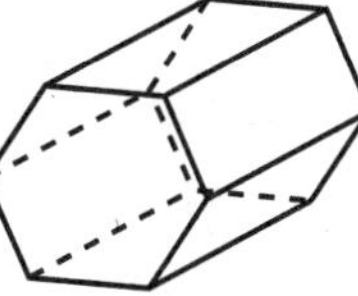

5. A cone
   B pyramid
   C cylinder
   D triangular prism

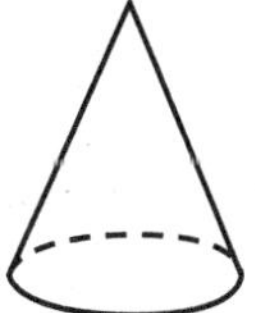

6. F pentagonal prism
   G cylinder
   H rectangular prism
   J triangular prism

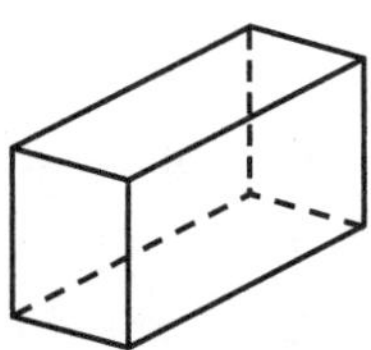

7. 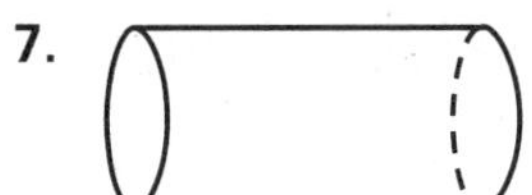

   A cone C sphere
   B cylinder D octagonal prism

8. Rick made a prism with a hexagonal base. How many edges does his prism have?

   F 6 edges H 18 edges
   G 12 edges J 24 edges

For 9–10, name the solid figure that has the given views.

9. 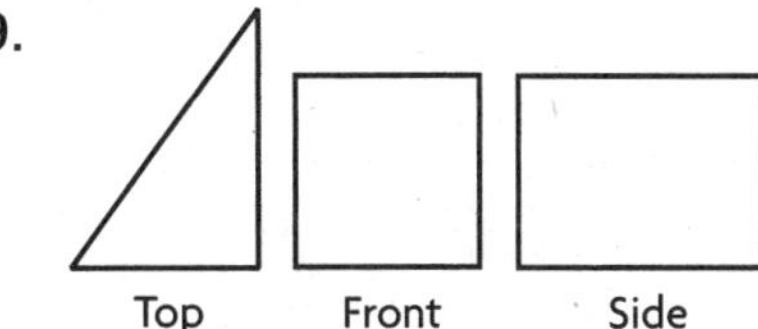

   A triangular prism
   B rectangular pyramid
   C triangular pyramid
   D cone

10. 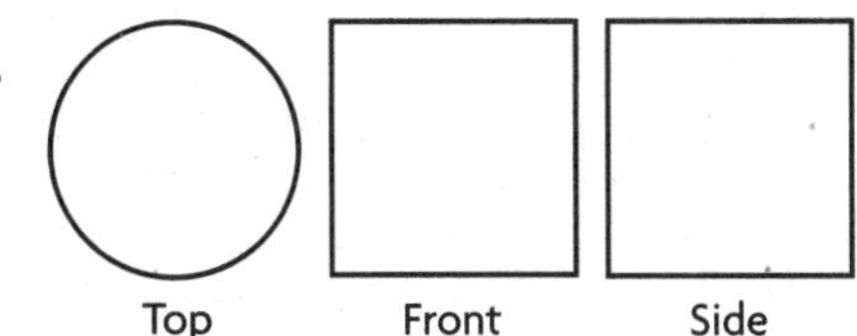

   F cylinder
   G circular prism
   H rectangular cone
   J cone

11. Cereal boxes are stacked for a store display. There are 2 boxes in the top row, 4 boxes in the second row, 6 boxes in the third row, and so on. How many boxes will there be in an entire 8-row display?

   A 16 boxes C 20 boxes
   B 56 boxes D 72 boxes

Go On

For 12–14, identify the top, front, and side views of each solid.

12.

F

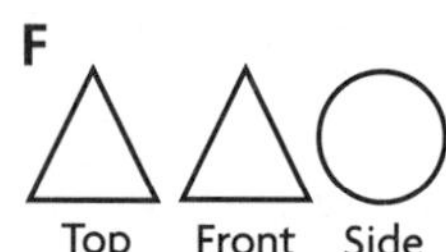

H

G

J

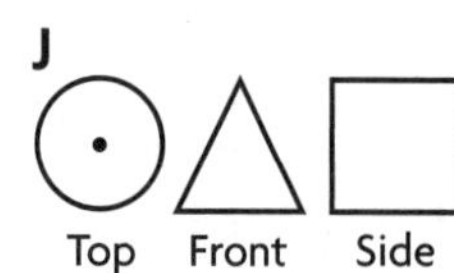

13.

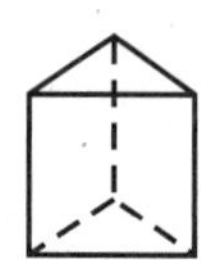

A

Top Front Side

C

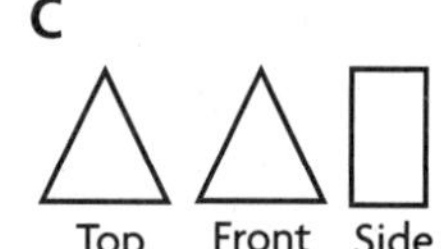

B

D

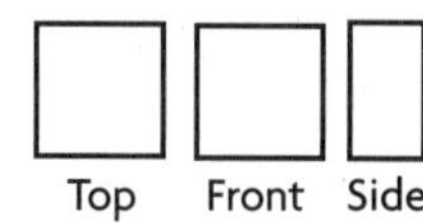

14.

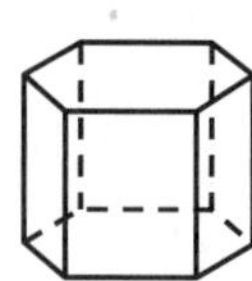

F

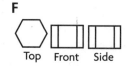

Top Front Side

H

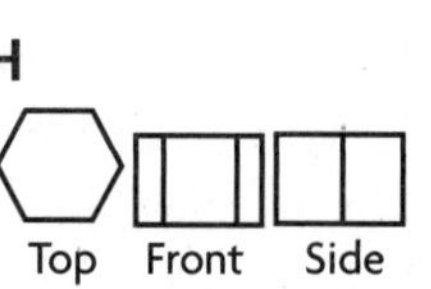

G

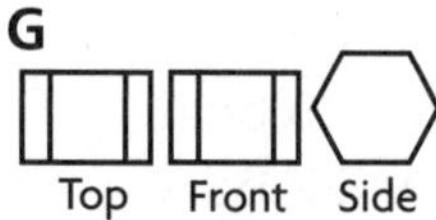

J

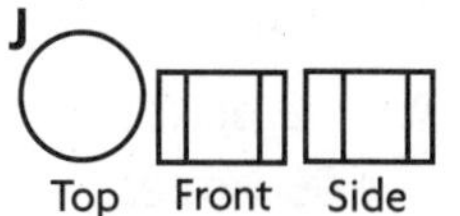

15. Emily wants to make a model of a pyramid with a base that has 12 sides. She will use foam balls for the vertices and straws for the edges. How many straws will she need?

A 12 straws **C** 24 straws
B 14 straws **D** 36 straws

16. This net will fold into which of the following?

F triangular pyramid
G rectangular pyramid
H triangular prism
J rectangular prism

17. How many vertices does a pentagonal pyramid have?

A 5 vertices **C** 8 vertices
B 6 vertices **D** 10 vertices

For 18–19, tell whether the net will fold to form a cube.

18.

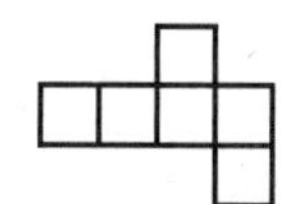

F yes **G** no

19.

A yes **B** no

20. Lee made a model of a pyramid with a base that has 7 sides. How many edges and faces does his model have?

F 14 edges, 8 faces
G 14 edges, 7 faces
H 7 edges, 8 faces
J 8 edges, 14 faces

Stop

Name ______________________

Write the correct answer.

1. The lateral faces of a prism are __?__.

2. A figure that has two flat, parallel, congruent circular bases and a curved lateral surface is a __?__.

3. A solid figure with flat faces that are polygons is a __?__.

For 4–7, name the figure.

4. 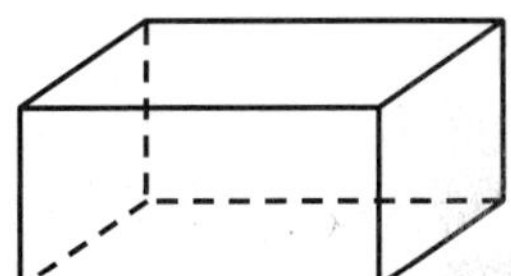

5. 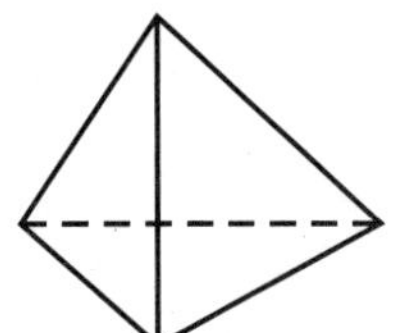

6. 

7. 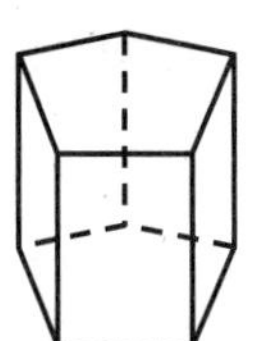

8. Rick made a prism with an octagonal base. How many edges does his prism have?

For 9–10, name the solid figure that has the given views.

9. 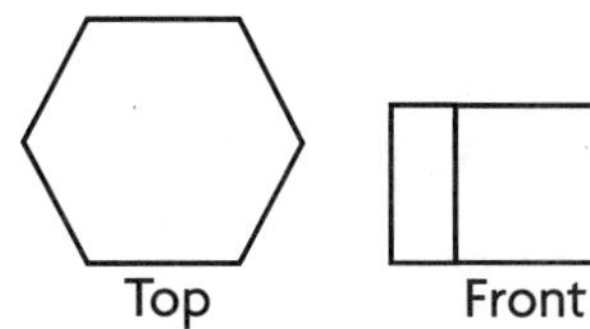 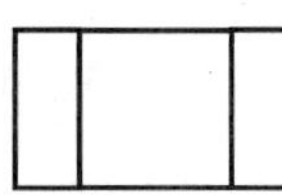 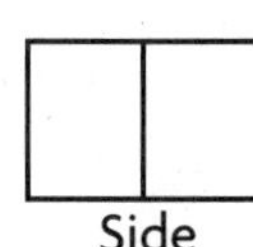

Top Front Side

10. 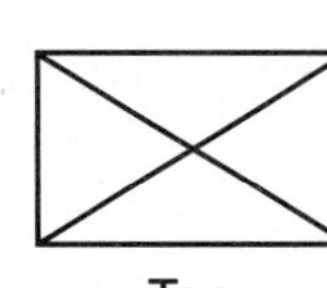  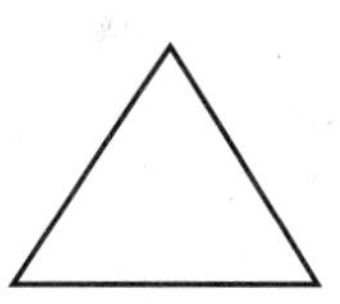

Top Front Side

11. Cat food cans are stacked for a store display. There is 1 can in the top row, 5 cans in the second row, 9 cans in the third row, and so on. How many cans will there be in a 7-row display? Explain how to find the answer.

Go On

For 12–13, identify the solid from its top, front, and side views.

12. 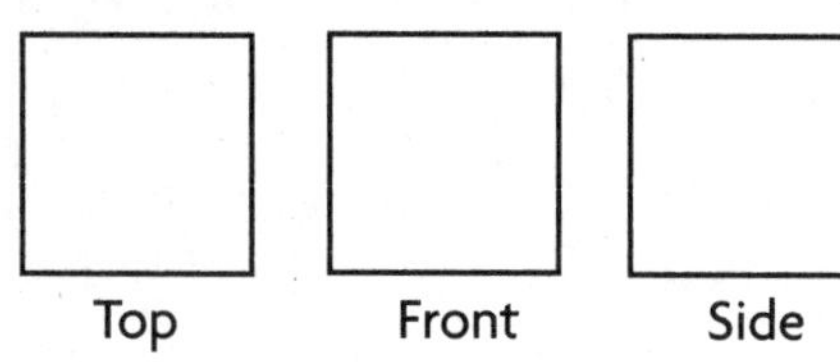

____

13. 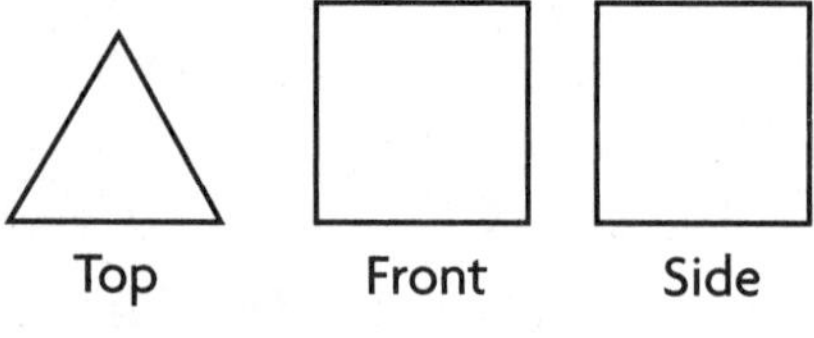

____

14. Draw the top, front, and side views of the solid.

15. Zahora wants to make a model of a pyramid with a base that has 8 sides. She will use foam balls for the vertices and straws for the edges. How many straws and balls will she need? Explain how to find the answer.

____

____

____

16. What shape will this net fold into?

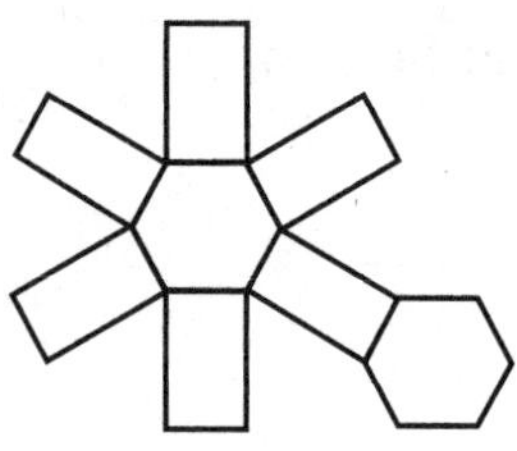

____

17. How many vertices does a hexagonal pyramid have?

____

For 18–19, tell whether the net will fold to form a cube. Write yes or no.

18. 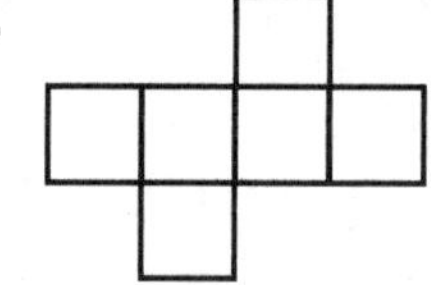

____

19. 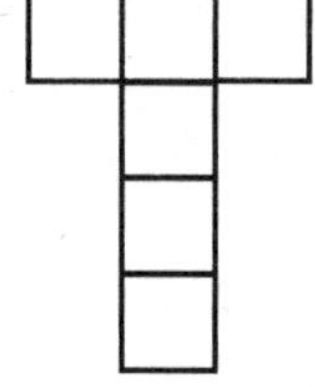

____

20. Yoshio made a model of a pyramid with a base that has 5 sides. How many edges and faces does his model have?

____

Stop

Name ___________________________

Choose the best answer.

1. What does $\overline{AB} \cong \overline{CD}$ mean?

   A $\overline{AB}$ is not equal to $\overline{CD}$.
   B $\overline{AB}$ is greater than $\overline{CD}$.
   C $\overline{AB}$ is congruent to $\overline{CD}$.
   D $\overline{AB}$ is less than $\overline{CD}$.

2. What tools are needed to construct congruent line segments?

   F protractor and compass
   G compass and straightedge
   H straightedge and protractor
   J Not here

3. Use a compass. Which line segments are congruent?

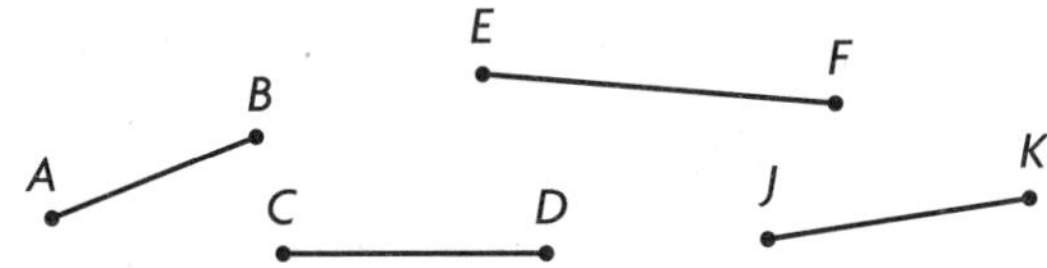

   A $\overline{AB}$ is congruent to $\overline{JK}$.
   B $\overline{CD}$ is congruent to $\overline{JK}$.
   C $\overline{CD}$ is congruent to $\overline{EF}$.
   D $\overline{AB}$ is congruent to $\overline{CD}$.

4. Use a protractor. Which angle is congruent to ∠ABC?

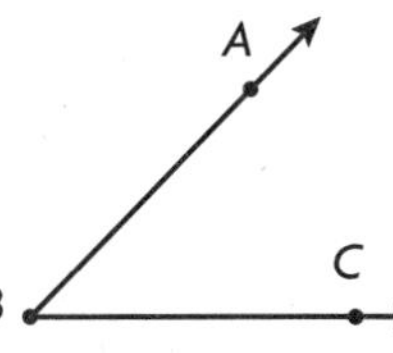

F
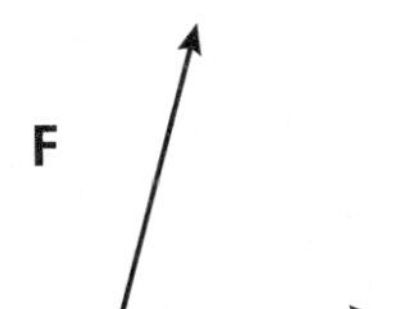

H
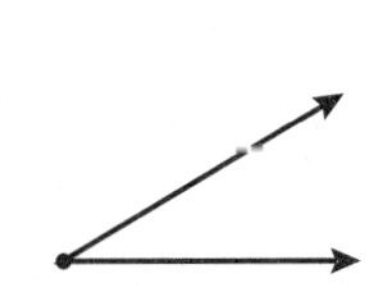

G J
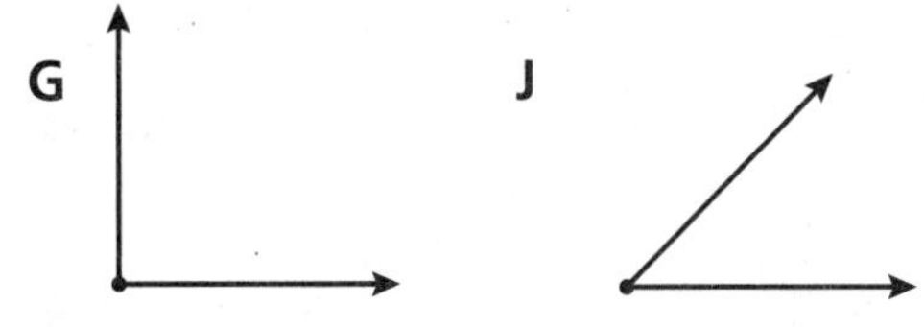

5. What construction is shown in Figure 2 below?

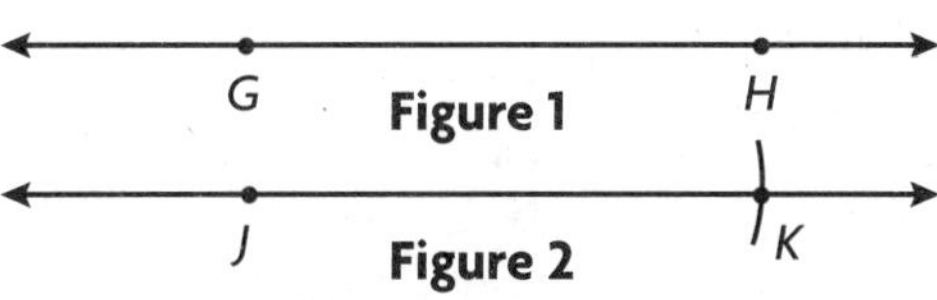

   A congruent line segment
   B congruent angle
   C bisected line segment
   D bisected angle

6. If you construct an angle congruent to ∠*MNP* less ∠*MNO*, what angle would the new angle be congruent to?

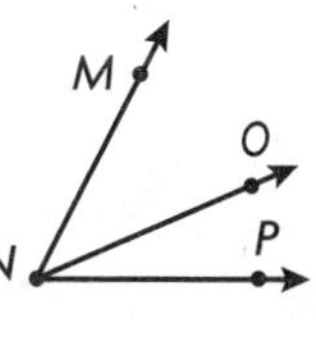

   F ∠*MNO* H ∠*MNP*
   G ∠*ONP* J ∠*OMN*

For questions 7–9, use the figure.

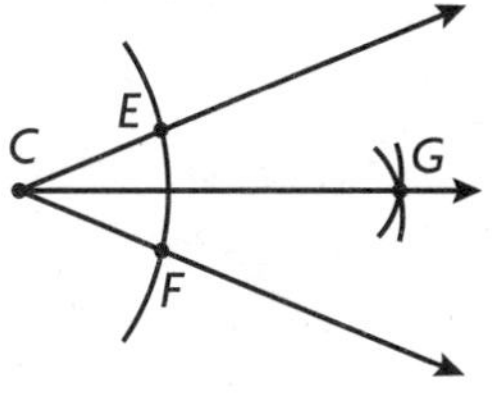

7. What construction does the figure represent?

   A bisected angle
   B congruent line segments
   C parallel lines
   D bisected line segment

8. Which angle is congruent to ∠*GCD*?

   F ∠*ACG* H ∠*ACD*
   G ∠*AEC* J ∠*CFD*

9. Which ray bisects ∠*ACD*?

   A $\overrightarrow{CF}$ C $\overrightarrow{CE}$
   B $\overrightarrow{CG}$ D $\overrightarrow{CA}$

10. If a 96° angle is bisected, what is the measure of each of the new angles that are formed?

   F 96° H 32°
   G 48° J 0°

Go On

Use the figures below for questions 11 and 12.

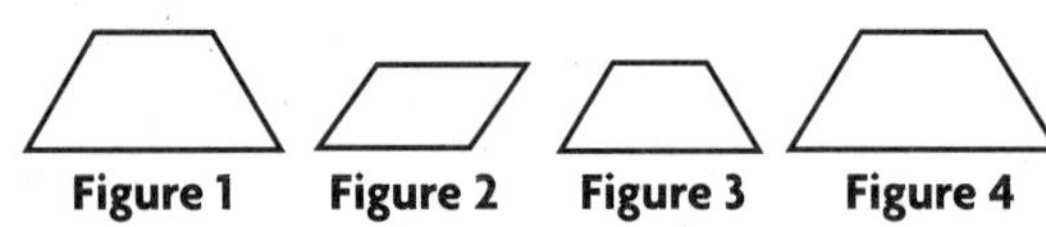

11. Which figures appear to be congruent?

A Figure 1 and Figure 2
B Figure 2 and Figure 3
C Figure 3 and Figure 4
D Figure 1 and Figure 4

12. Which figures appear to be similar, but not congruent?

F Figure 1 and Figure 2
G Figure 3 and Figure 4
H Figure 2 and Figure 3
J Figure 1 and Figure 4

13. Which statement is true about pairs of figures?

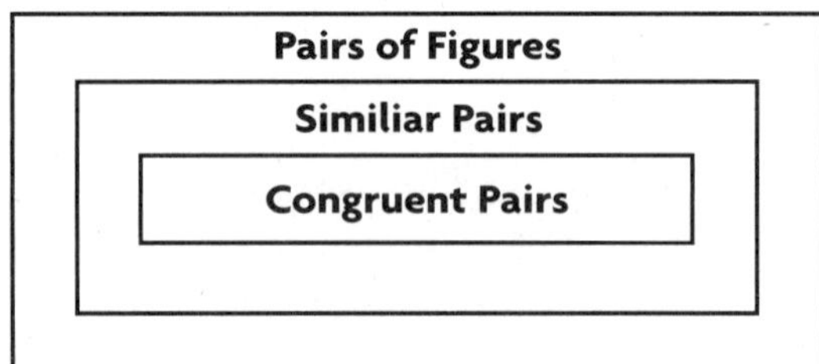

A All similar pairs of figures are congruent.
B All pairs of figures are similar.
C All pairs of figures are congruent.
D All congruent pairs are similar.

14. Tell whether the figures below appear to be *similar, congruent, both* or *neither*.

F similar
G congruent
H neither
J both

15. Tell which statement is true.

A All circles are similar.
B All circles are congruent.
C All circles are not similar.
D All circles are similar and congruent.

16. Robin constructed $\angle MNP$ which is congruent to $\angle ABC$ plus $\angle EFG$. What is the measure of the $\angle MNP$?

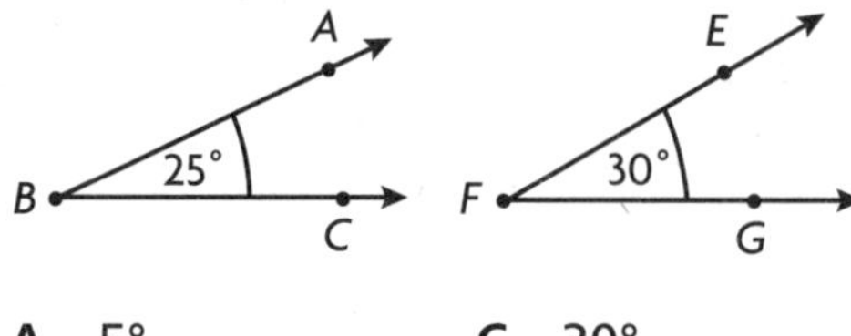

A 5° C 30°
B 25° D 55°

17. Marty bisected a line segment that was 240 cm long. How long is each of the smaller segments?

A 60 cm C 120 cm
B 80 cm D 240 cm

18. The measures of two angles of a triangle are 73° and 41°. If the third angle is bisected, what would be the measure of each of the angles that are formed?

A 33° C 114°
B 66° D 180°

19. Shaun bisected $\angle JKL$ which measured 140°. He then bisected each of the new angles. What is the measure of the smallest angle?

A 17.5° C 70°
B 35° D 140°

20. Pedro bisected an angle that was 112°. What is the measure of each of the new angles?

F 224° H 56°
G 112° J 28°

Stop

Write the correct answer.

1. What does $\overline{CD} \cong \overline{FG}$ mean?

____

2. What tools are needed to construct congruent angles?

____

3. Use a protractor. Which angle is congruent to $\angle XYZ$?

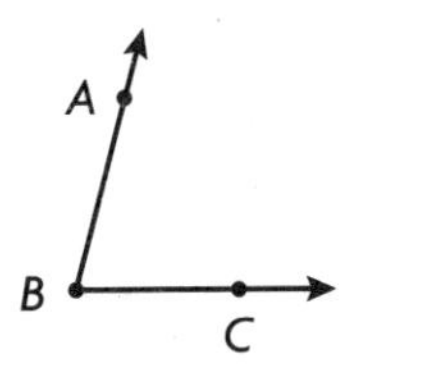

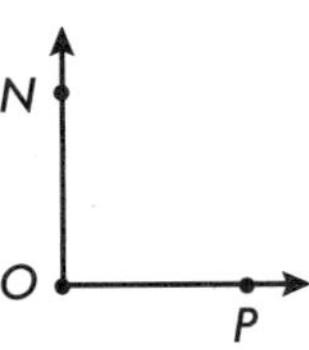

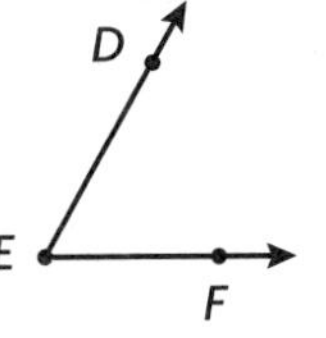

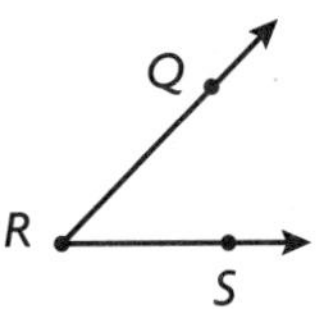

____

4. Use a compass. Which line segments are congruent?

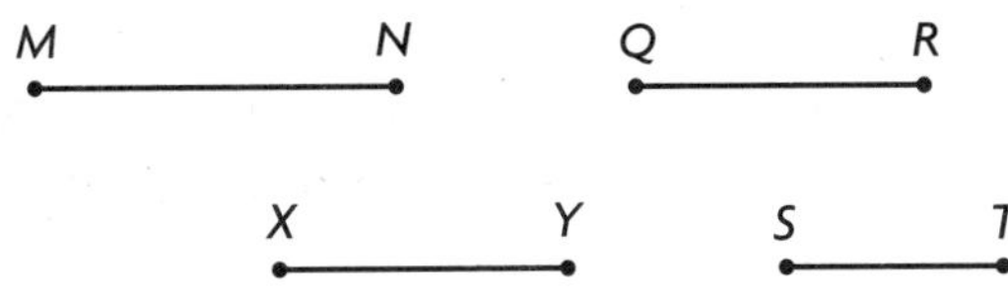

____

5. What construction is shown in Figure 2

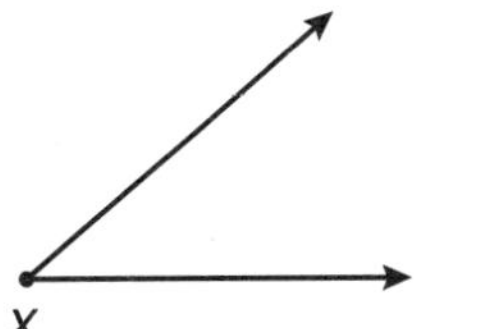

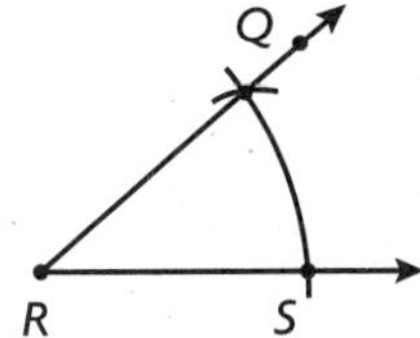

____

6. If you construct an angle congruent to $\angle QRT$ less $\angle QRS$, what angle is the new angle congruent to?

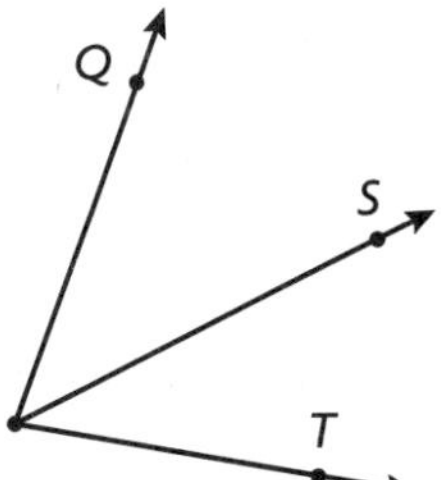

____

For questions 7–9, use the figure below.

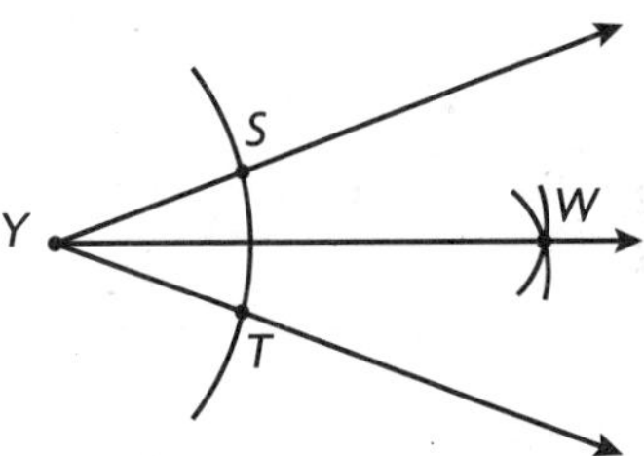

7. What construction does the figure represent?

____

8. Which angle is congruent to $\angle WYS$?

____

9. Which ray bisects $\angle SYT$?

____

Go On

10. If a 118° angle is bisected, what is the measure of each of the new angles that are formed?

____

Use the figures below for questions 11 and 12.

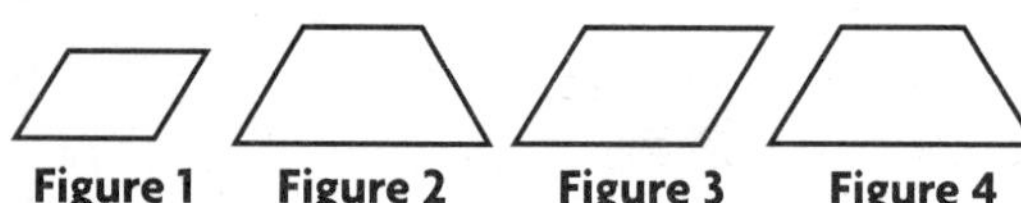

11. Which figures appear to be congruent?

____

12. Which figures appear to be similar, but not congruent?

____

13. Use the Venn diagram to write a true statement about pairs of figures.

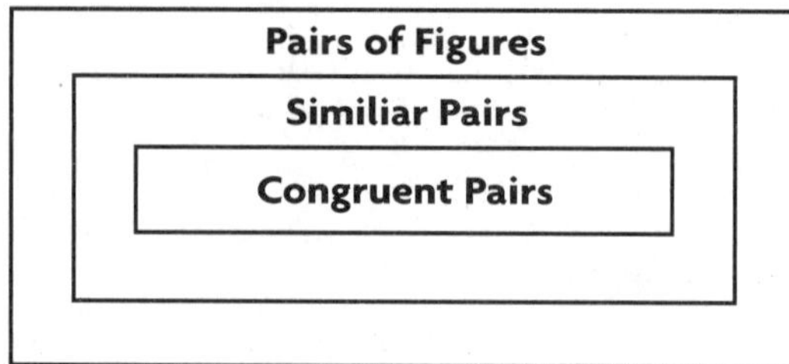

____

____

14. Tell whether the figures appear to be *similar, congruent, both* or *neither.*

____

15. Write a true statement about squares using the words *similar* and *congruent.*

____

16. Melanie constructed $\angle QRS$ which is congruent to $\angle JKL$ plus $\angle MNO$. What is the measure of the $\angle QRS$?

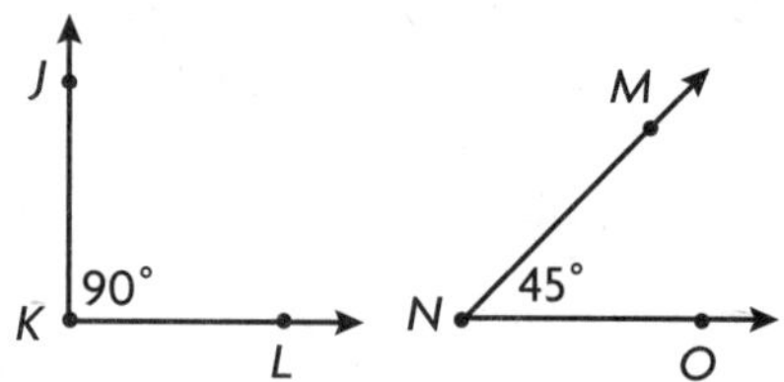

____

17. Marty bisected a line segment that was 130 cm long. How long is each of the smaller segments?

____

18. The measure of two angles of a triangle are 57° and 67°. If the third angle is bisected, what would be the measure of each of the angles that are formed?

____

19. Niccoli bisected $\angle ABC$ which measures 60°. She then bisected each of the new angles. What is the measure of the smallest angle?

____

20. Magali bisected an angle that was 94°. What is the measure of each of the new angles?

____

Stop

Name ______________________________

Choose the best answer.

1. Two rays with a common endpoint form a(n) __?__.

   A line segment C angle
   B line D polygon

2. A regular quadrilateral is called a __?__.

   F rectangle H trapezoid
   G square J rhombus

3. A polyhedron is a solid figure with faces that are __?__.

   A rectangles C triangles
   B rhombuses D polygons

4. Name the geometric figure.

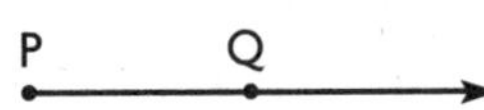

   F line H angle
   G line segment J ray

5. What construction is shown in Figure 2 below?

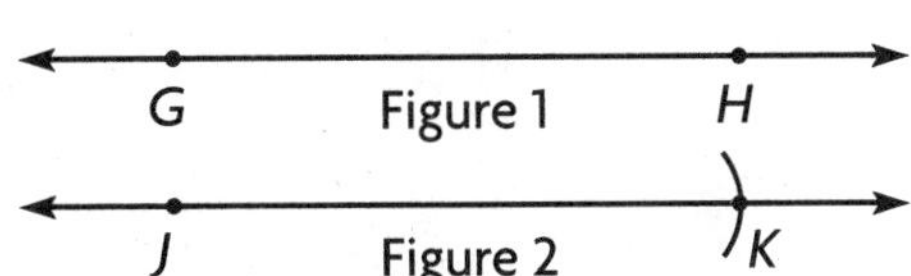

   A congruent angle
   B congruent line segment
   C bisected line segment
   D bisected angle

6. If a 150° angle is bisected, what is the measure of each of the new angles that are formed?

   F 75° H 225°
   G 90° J 300°

7. Shavon bisected a line segment that was 92 cm long. How long is each of the line segments that are formed?

   A 184 cm C 46 cm
   B 92 cm D 23 cm

8. Name the solid that has these views.

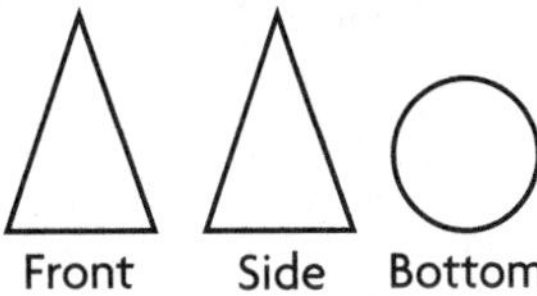

   F prism H cylinder
   G pyramid J cone

9. Find the measure of $\angle CBD$.

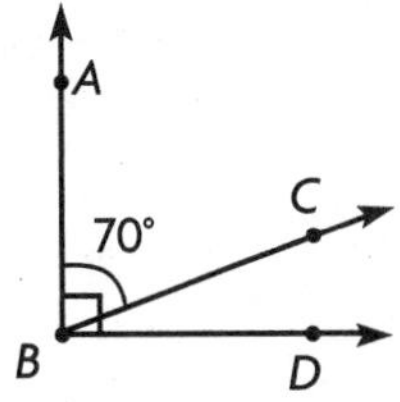

   A 10° C 70°
   B 20° D 110°

10. Give the most exact name for the figure.

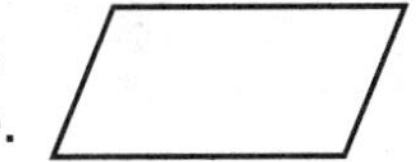

   F parallelogram H quadrilateral
   G rhombus J trapezoid

11. Can this arrangement of squares be folded to form a cube?

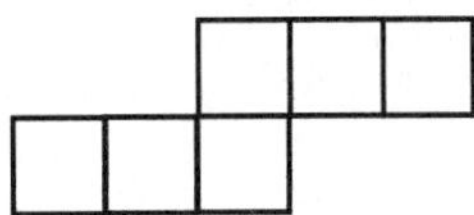

   A yes B no

12. Two angles whose measures have a sum of 180° are __?__.

   F complementary H adjacent
   G supplementary J vertical

Go On

13. In quadrilateral $ABCD$, $\angle A$ and $\angle B$ measure 90°, and $\angle C$ measures 65°. Classify the quadrilateral.

A rectangle
B square
C trapezoid
D rhombus

For 14–16, use the figure to find the measure of each angle.

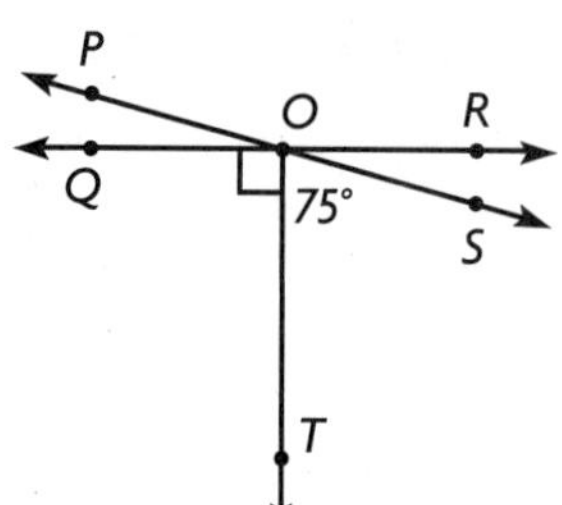

14. $\angle POQ$

F 90°
G 75°
H 15°
J 5°

15. $\angle QOS$

A 175°
B 165°
C 75°
D 15°

16. $\angle ROT$

F 15°
G 60°
H 75°
J 90°

17. Identify the top, front, and side views of this solid.

A

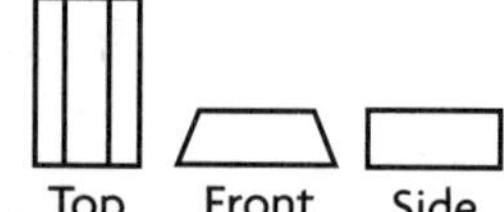

B

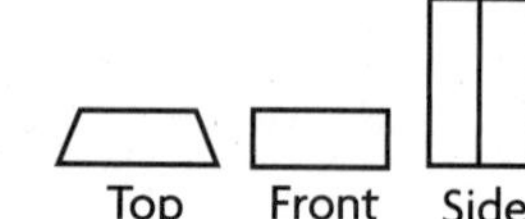

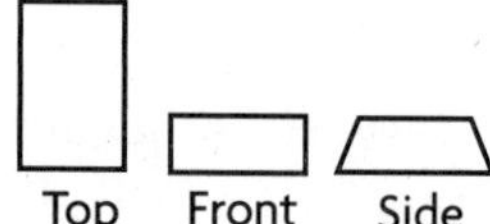

18. What does $\overline{FG} \cong \overline{MN}$ mean?

F $\overline{FG}$ is greater than $\overline{MN}$.
G $\overline{FG}$ is not equal to $\overline{MN}$.
H $\overline{FG}$ is less than $\overline{MN}$.
J $\overline{FG}$ is congruent to $\overline{MN}$.

For 19–21, use the circle.

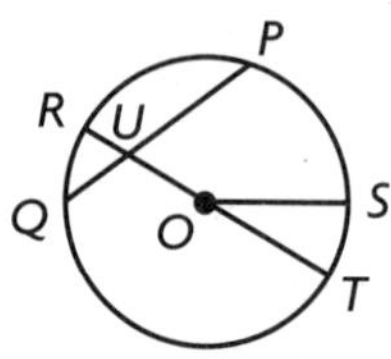

19. Name a radius.

A $\overline{RT}$
B $\overline{QP}$
C $\overline{ST}$
D $\overline{OT}$

20. Name a chord.

F $\overline{QP}$
G $\overline{RO}$
H $\overline{UP}$
J $\overline{UT}$

21. Name a diameter.

A $\overline{RT}$
B $\overline{QP}$
C $\overline{OS}$
D $\overline{UR}$

22. Name the figure.

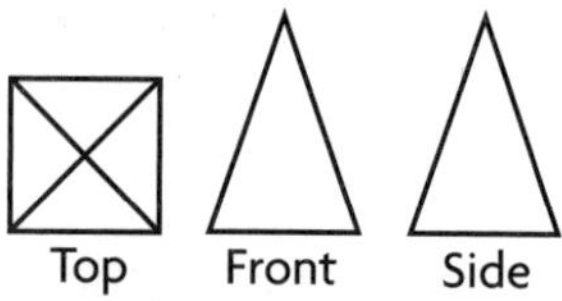

F triangular pyramid
G square pyramid
H square prism
J triangular prism

Go On

Name ______________________

23. What is the least number of points needed to name a plane?

A 5 points
B 4 points
C 3 points
D 2 points

24. What is the measure of each angle in a regular hexagon?

F 150°
G 120°
H 105°
J 60°

25. A prism is made with a 7-sided base. How many edges and faces does it have?

A 21 edges; 7 faces
B 14 edges; 9 faces
C 14 edges; 7 faces
D 21 edges; 9 faces

For 26–27, use the figures below.

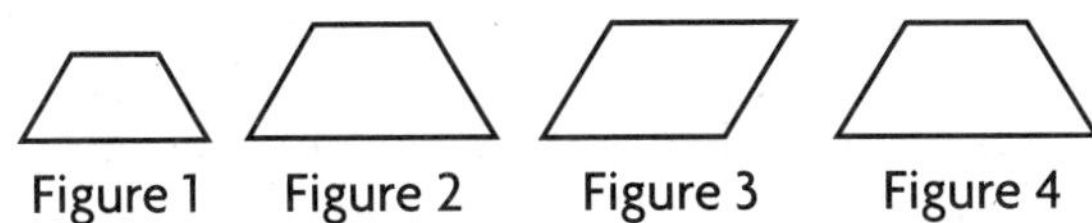

26. Which figures are congruent?

F Figure 1 and Figure 3
G Figure 2 and Figure 3
H Figure 3 and Figure 4
J Figure 2 and Figure 4

27. Which figures are similar, but not congruent?

A Figure 1 and Figure 3
B Figure 3 and Figure 4
C Figure 2 and Figure 3
D Figure 1 and Figure 4

28. Two angles in a triangle measure 38° and 52°. Classify the triangle.

F isosceles
G acute
H obtuse
J right

29. How many vertices are there in a pyramid with a base of 15 sides?

A 30 vertices
B 16 vertices
C 15 vertices
D 1 vertex

30. What is another name for ray *MO*?

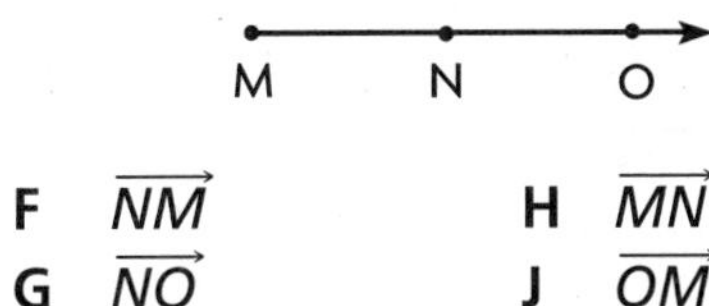

F $\overrightarrow{NM}$
G $\overrightarrow{NO}$
H $\overrightarrow{MN}$
J $\overrightarrow{OM}$

31. A solid figure with 4 triangular sides and a square base is a __?__.

A pyramid
B prism
C cylinder
D cone

32. If a quadrilateral has four congruent sides, then it must be a __?__.

F trapezoid
G parallelogram
H rhombus
J rectangle

Go On

Name ______________________

33. Can this net be folded to form a solid? If so, what kind?

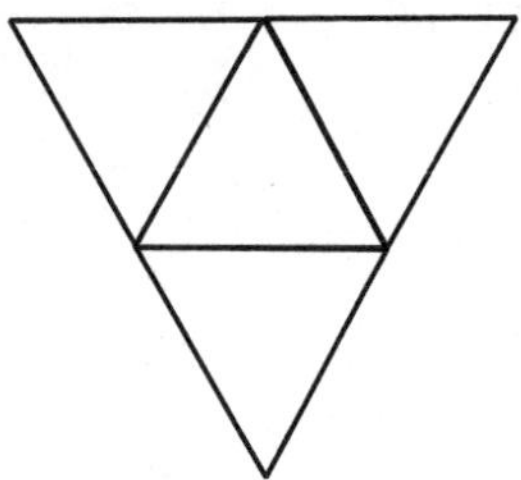

A yes; cone
B yes; prism
C yes; pyramid
D no

For 34–35, use the figure below.

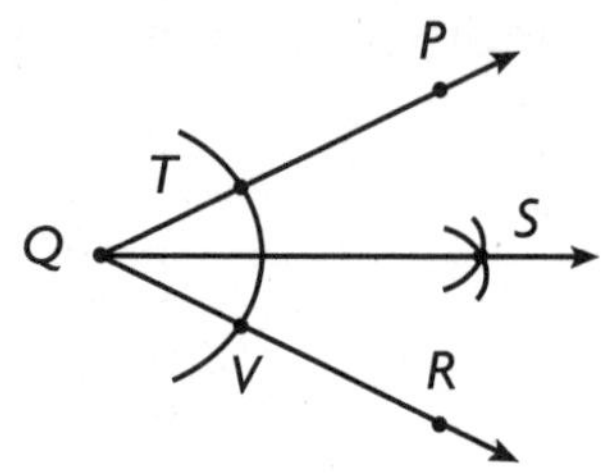

34. What construction does the figure represent?

F congruent line segments
G parallel lines
H bisected angle
J bisected line segment

35. Which angle is congruent to ∠*PQS*

A ∠*PQR*
B ∠*SQR*
C ∠*RQP*
D ∠*RST*

36. How many edges does a triangular prism have?

F 12 edges
G 9 edges
H 6 edges
J 3 edges

37. Name the geometric figure formed by perpendicular rays that have a common endpoint.

A triangle
B parallel lines
C straight angle
D right angle

38. Tell whether the figures below are *similar*, *congruent*, *both* or *neither*.

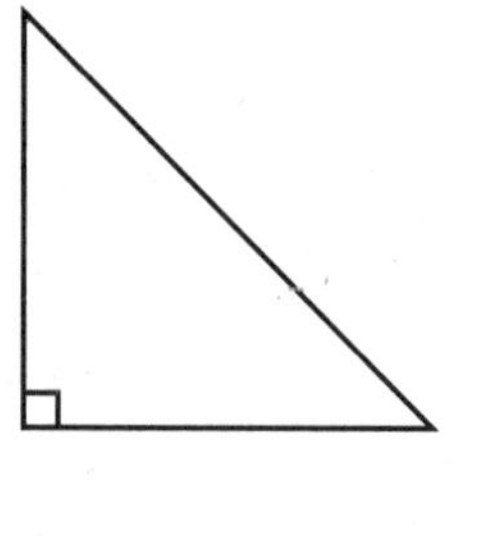

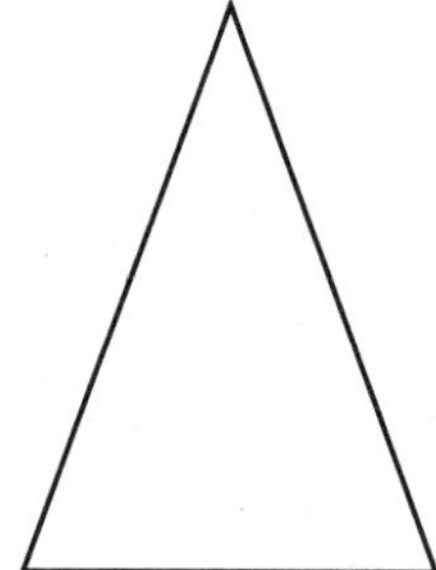

F similiar
G congruent
H neither
J both

39. One angle formed by two intersecting lines measures 65°. What are the measures of the other three angles?

A 25°, 90°, 90°
B 65°, 115°, 115°
C 65°, 65°, 115°
D 25°, 65°, 115°

40. If the number of sides of the bases of a prism is increased by 1, how many more edges will the new prism have?

F 1 more
G 2 more
H 3 more
J 4 more

Stop

Write the correct answer.

1. An angle is formed by two rays with a common endpoint called a(n) __?__.

____

2. A polygon with all sides equal and all angles equal is called __?__.

____

3. A pattern that can be folded to form a solid figure is called a(n) __?__.

____

4. Identify the geometric figure.

____

5. What construction is shown in Figure 2?

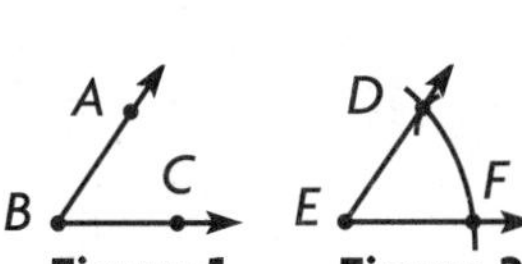

____

6. If a 46° angle is bisected, what is the measure of each of the new angles that are formed?

____

7. Balinda bisected a line segment that was 78 cm long. How long is each of the line segments that are formed?

____

8. Name the solid that has these views.

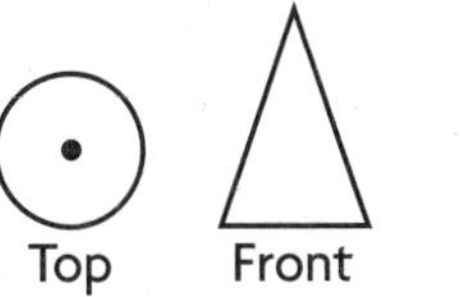

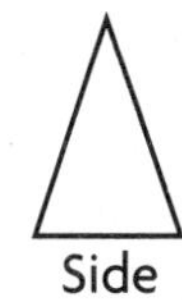

____

9. Find the measure of $\angle ACB$.

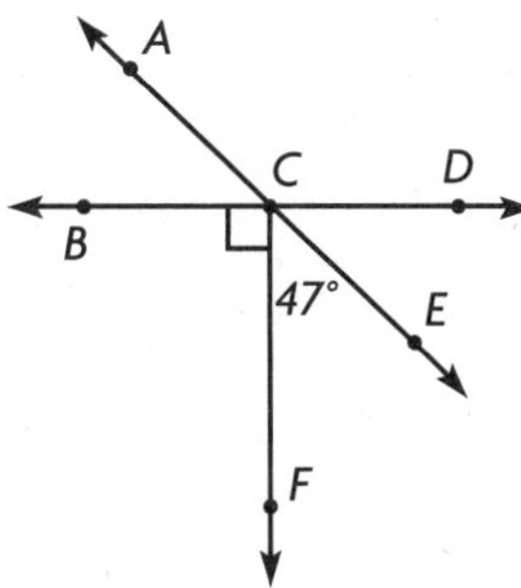

____

10. Give the most exact name for the figure.

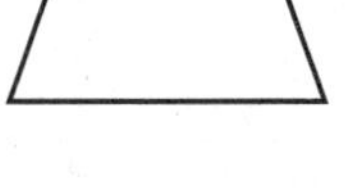

____

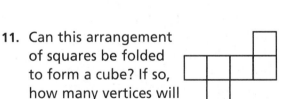

11. Can this arrangement of squares be folded to form a cube? If so, how many vertices will it have?

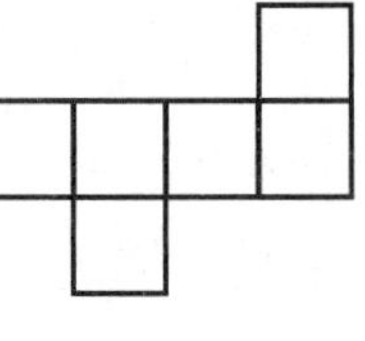

____

12. Two angles with measures that have a sum of 90° are __?__.

____

Go On

Name ______________________

13. In quadrilateral *ABCD*, $\angle A$ and $\angle C$ measure 110°, and $\angle B$ measures 70°. Classify the quadrilateral.

____

For 14–16, use the figure to find the measure of each angle.

14. $\angle ACG$

____

15. $\angle DCE$

____

16. $\angle ACB$

____

17. Draw the top, front, and side views of this solid.

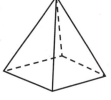

18. What does $\angle ABC \cong \angle JKL$ mean?

____

For 19–21, use the circle.

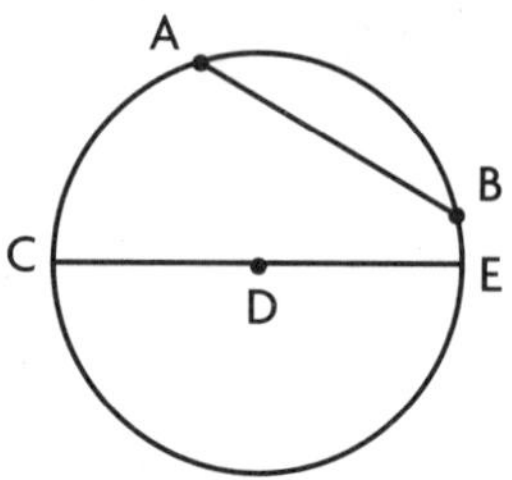

19. Name a radius.

____

20. Name a chord.

____

21. Name a diameter.

____

22. Identify the figure.

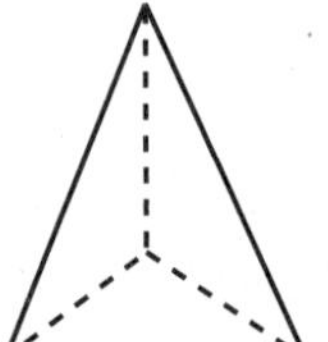

____

Go On

Name ______________________________

23. How many non-collinear points are needed to define a plane?

____

24. What is the measure of each angle in a regular pentagon?

____

25. A prism has a 6-sided base. How many edges and faces does it have?

____

For 26–27, use the figures below.

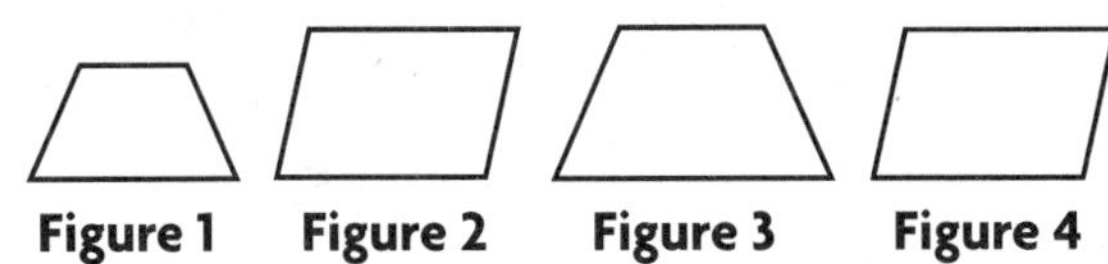

26. Which figures appear to be congruent?

____

27. Which figures appear to be similar, but not congruent?

____

28. Two angles in a triangle measure 48° and 84°. Classify the triangle.

____

29. How many vertices are there in a pyramid with a base of 12 sides?

____

30. What is another name for ray *RT*?

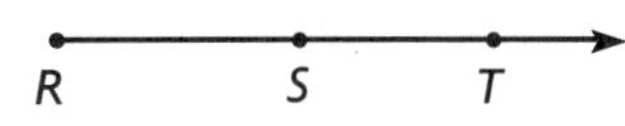

____

31. A solid figure with 6 rectangular sides and 2 hexagonal bases is called a(n) __?__.

____

32. If a quadrilateral has four congruent sides and four congruent angles, then it must be a(n) __?__.

____

Go On

Name ______________________________

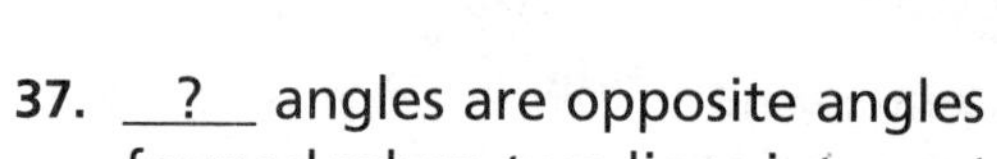

33. Can this net be folded to form a solid? If so, what kind?

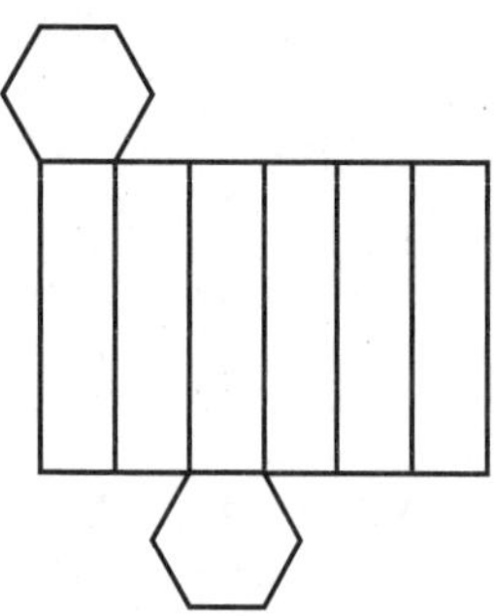

____

For 34-35, use the figure below. $\overline{TU}$ bisects $\overline{XY}$

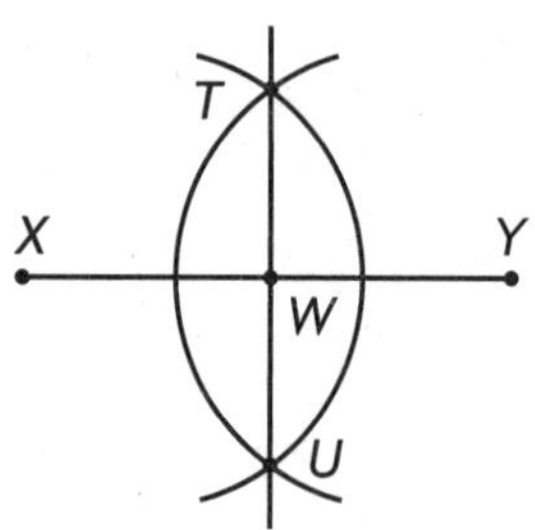

34. What segment is congruent to $\overline{XW}$?

____

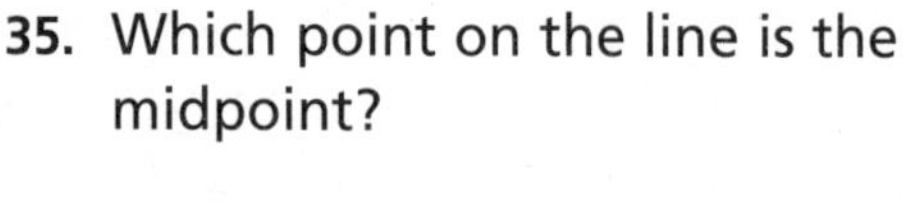

35. Which point on the line is the midpoint?

____

36. How many edges does a pentagonal prism have?

____

37. __?__ angles are opposite angles formed when two lines intersect.

____

38. Tell whether the figures below are *similar, congruent, both* or *neither.*

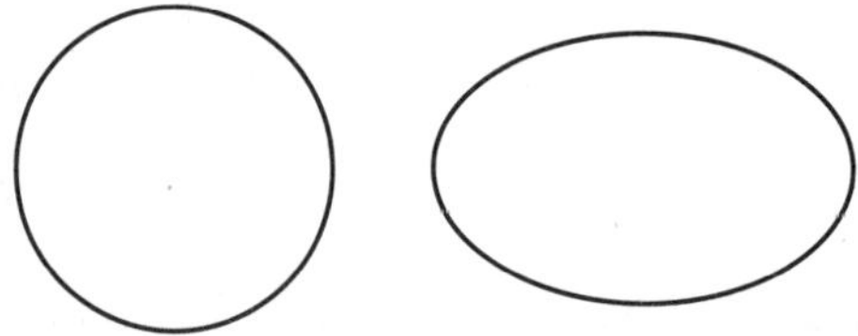

____

39. One angle formed by two intersecting lines measures 70°. What are the measures of the other three angles?

____

40. If the number of sides of the base of a prism is increased by 1, how many more vertices will the new prism have?

____

Stop

Name ______________________________

Choose the best answer.

For 1–2, use the figure.

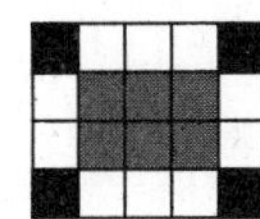

1. What is the ratio of black sections to gray sections?

   A $\frac{2}{3}$ C $\frac{20}{6}$

   B $\frac{6}{4}$ D $\frac{20}{4}$

2. What is the ratio of all sections to white sections?

   F $\frac{5}{1}$ H $\frac{1}{2}$

   G $\frac{10}{3}$ J $\frac{2}{1}$

For 3–4, find the unit rate.

3. 64 mi on 4 gal of gas

   A 64 mi per gal
   B 32 mi per gal
   C 30 mi per gal
   D 16 mi per gal

4. 117 songs on 9 CDs

   F 13 CDs per song

   G 13 songs per CD

   H $\frac{1}{13}$ song per CD

   J $\frac{1}{13}$ CD per song

5. Corn is on sale at $2.00 for 8 ears. Find the cost of 14 ears.

   A $5.60 C $3.00
   B $3.50 D $2.75

6. The scale for a map is 1 in. = 20 mi. Find the map distance for 160 mi.

   F 160 in. H 8 in.

   G 80 in. J $\frac{1}{8}$ in.

7. Bobbi needs 1 cup of flour to make a batch of 32 cookies. How much flour is needed to make 48 cookies?

   A $\frac{2}{3}$ c C $1\frac{1}{2}$ c

   B $1\frac{1}{3}$ c D 7 c

8. The rectangles are similar. Find the unknown length.

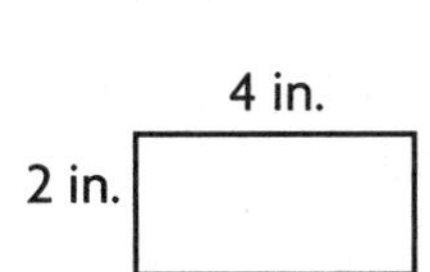

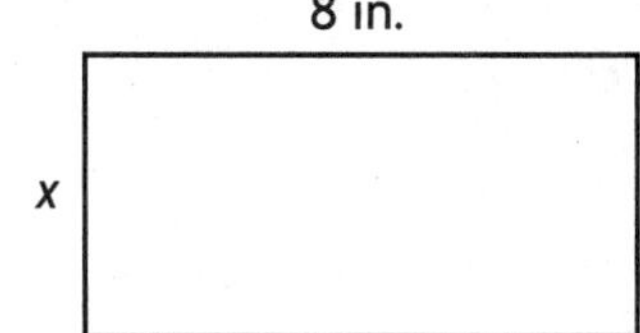

   F $x = 4$ in. H $x = 8$ in.
   G $x = 6$ in. J $x = 16$ in.

9. A scale of 3 in. = 8 ft is used on a house plan drawing. The length of a room on the drawing is 9 in. How long is the actual room?

   A 72 ft C 24 ft

   B 27 ft D $3\frac{3}{8}$ ft

10. The triangles are similar. Find the unknown length.

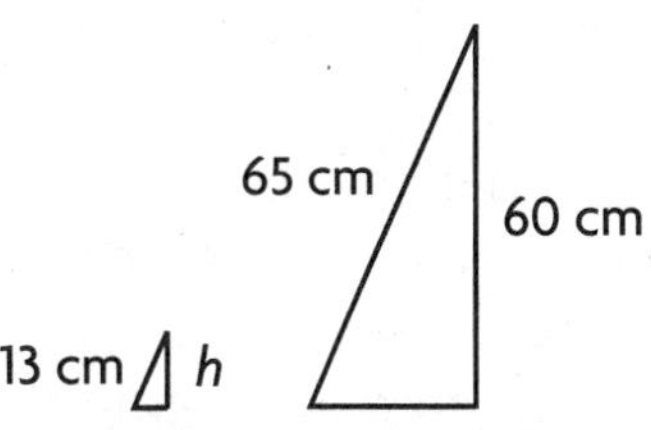

   F $h = 18$ cm H $h = 8$ cm
   G $h = 12$ cm J $h = 6$ cm

Go On

11. The scale for a map is 1 in. = 30 mi. What is the actual distance between two towns that are $1\frac{1}{2}$ in. apart on the map?

A 15 mi C 45 mi
B 40 mi D 90 mi

12. Marianna made 3 quarts of tomato sauce from 2 baskets of tomatoes. How much tomato sauce could she make from 5 baskets of tomatoes?

F $3\frac{1}{3}$ qt H 6 qt
G 4 qt J $7\frac{1}{2}$ qt

13. Which dimensions describe a rectangle similar to the rectangle shown?

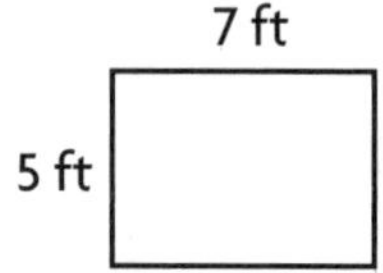

A 6 ft by 8 ft C 10 ft by 6 ft
B 8 ft by 10 ft D 15 ft by 21 ft

14. The figures are similar. Find the unknown length.

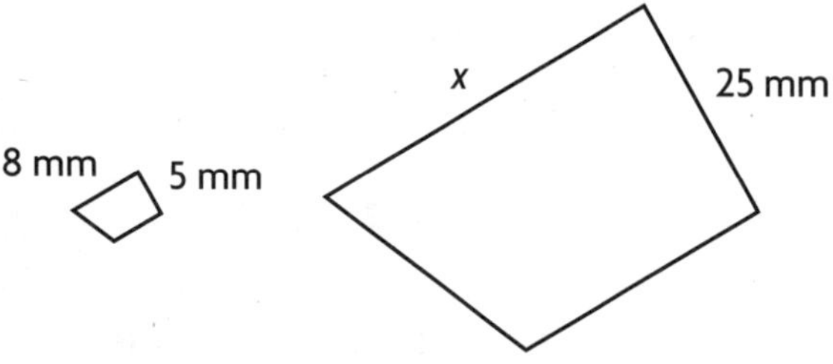

F $x = 40$ mm H $x = 28$ mm
G $x = 35$ mm J $x = 22$ mm

15. All the commercials on a radio station are the same length. Playing 20 commercials takes 15 min. How long does it take to play 80 commercials?

A 60 min C 75 min
B 65 min D 80 min

16. What is the unit rate for driving 120 mi in 2 hr?

F 1 hr for 240 mi
G 60 mi in 1 hr
H 240 mi in 1 hr
J $\frac{1}{60}$ hr for 2 mi

17. The boxes that Ed is painting are all the same size and shape. He can paint 8 boxes in 20 min. How many boxes can he paint in 90 min?

A 30 C 36
B 32 D 40

18. The triangles are similar. Find the unknown length.

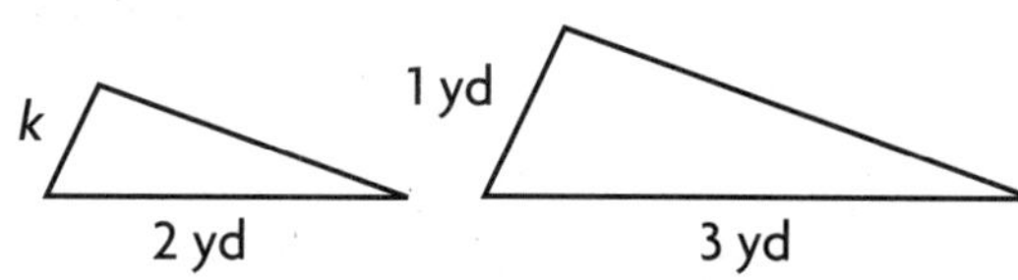

F $k = \frac{1}{2}$ yd H $k = 1$ yd
G $k = \frac{2}{3}$ yd J $k = 1\frac{1}{2}$ yd

19. The sides of a triangle have lengths 5 cm, 6 cm, and 2 cm. Which of the following lengths could be sides of a similar triangle?

A 10 cm, 12 cm, 4 cm
B 12 cm, 8 cm, 9 cm
C 3 cm, 4 cm, 1 cm
D 8 cm, 10 cm, 4 cm

20. The measures of the angles of a triangle are 90°, 50°, and 40°. What are the measures of the angles of a similar triangle?

F 45°, 25°, 20° H 90°, 25°, 20°
G 45°, 50°, 40° J 90°, 50°, 40°

Stop

Name ______________________

Write the correct answer.

For 1–2, use the figure.

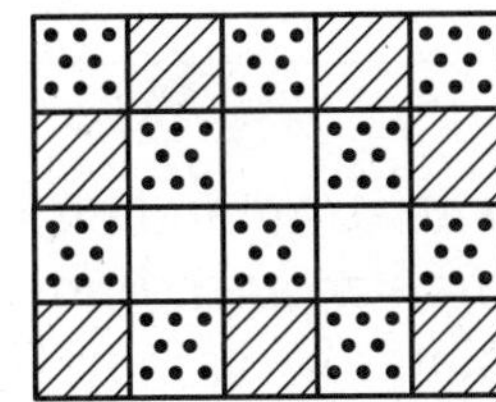

1. What is the ratio of solid white sections to striped sections?

____

2. What is the ratio of all sections to dotted sections?

____

For 3–4, find the unit rate.

3. 80 people in 5 buses

____

4. 153 melons in 9 crates

____

5. Socks are on sale for $9.50 for 5 pairs. Find the cost of 12 pairs. Explain how to find the answer.

____

____

6. The scale for a map is 1 cm = 25 km. Find the map distance for 175 km.

____

7. Cruz needs 1 cup of onions to make 24 tacos. How many cups of onions does he need to make 36 tacos? Explain how to find the answer.

____

8. The rectangles are similar. Find the unknown length.

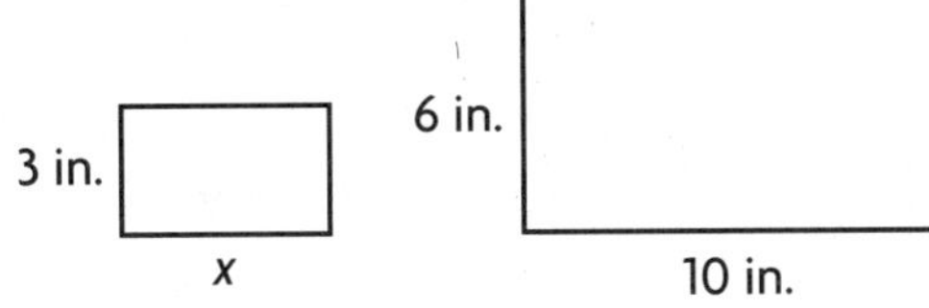

____

9. A scale of 2 in. = 9 ft is used on a building plan drawing. The length of a room on the drawing is 8 in. How long is the actual room?

____

10. The triangles are similar. Find the unknown length.

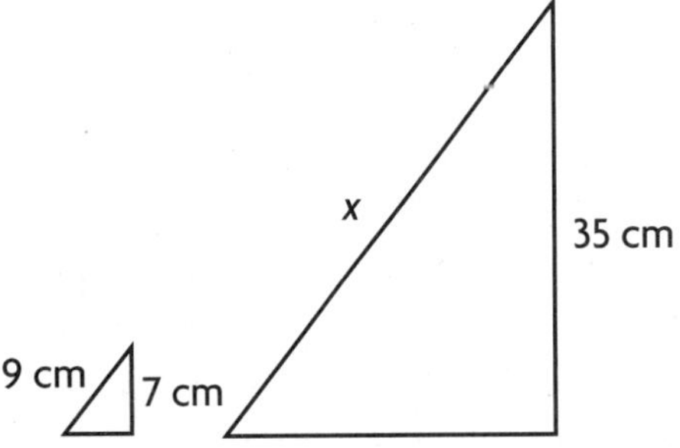

____

Go On

Name ________________________

11. The scale for a map is 1 cm = 50 km. What is the actual distance between two towns that are $2\frac{1}{2}$ cm apart on the map?

____

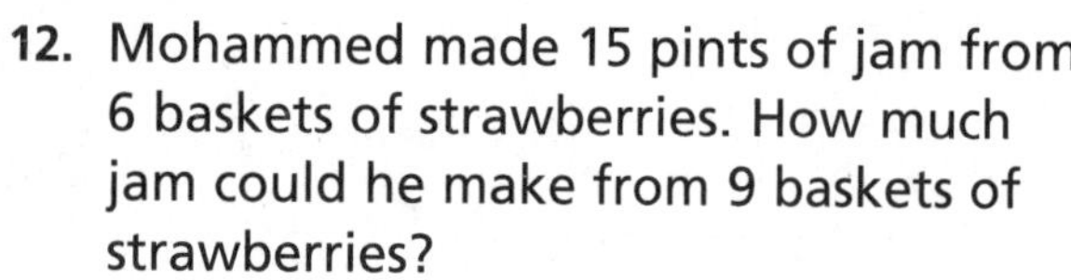

12. Mohammed made 15 pints of jam from 6 baskets of strawberries. How much jam could he make from 9 baskets of strawberries?

____

13. What dimensions describe a rectangle similar to the rectangle shown?

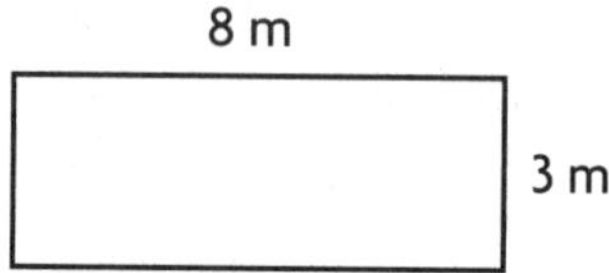

____

14. The figures are similar. Find the missing length.

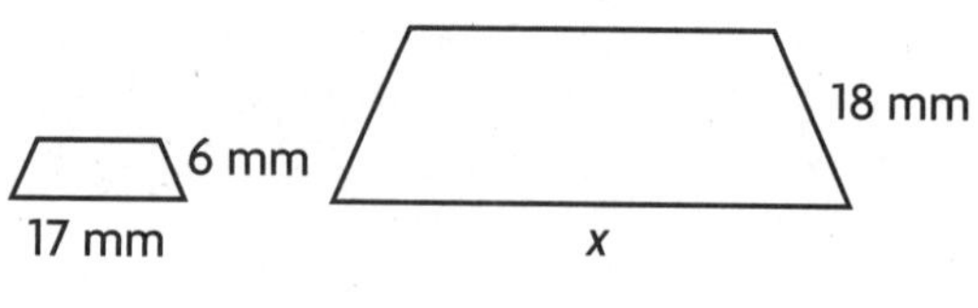

____

15. At the copy shop, it takes 18 minutes to copy 300 flyers. How long does it take to copy 900 flyers?

____

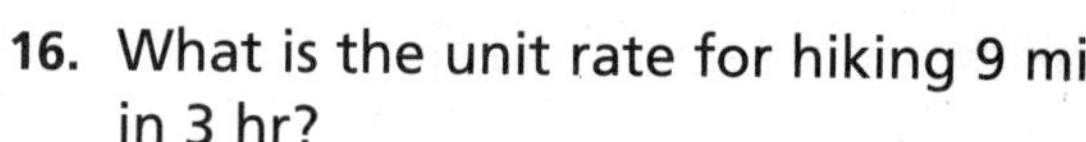

16. What is the unit rate for hiking 9 mi in 3 hr?

____

17. The plates that Amanda is painting are all the same size and shape. She can paint 12 plates in 30 min. How many plates can she paint in 75 min?

____

18. The triangles are similar. Find the missing length.

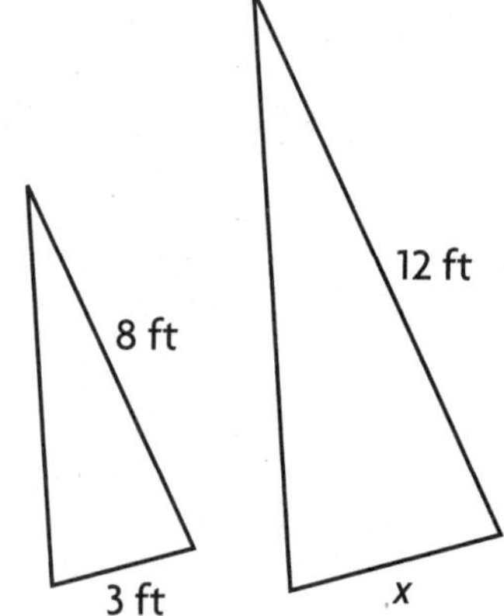

____

19. The sides of a triangle have lengths of 8 cm, 5 cm, and 6 cm. What dimensions could describe a similar triangle?

____

20. The measures of the angles of a triangle are 100°, 60°, and 20°. What are the measures of the angles of a similar triangle?

____

Stop

Name ________________________________

Choose the best answer.

For 1–2, tell the percent of the figure that is shaded.

1. 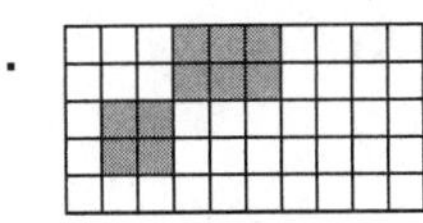

A 90%
B 80%
C 20%
D 10%

2. 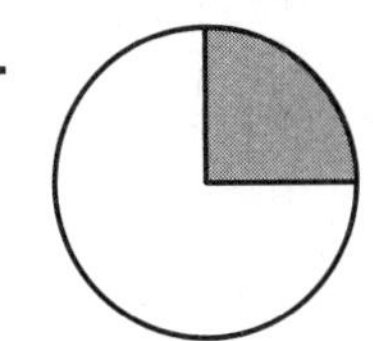

F 75%
G 50%
H $33\frac{1}{3}\%$
J 25%

3. What is the decimal 0.38 as a percent?

A 38%
B 3.8%
C 0.38%
D 0.0038%

4. What is the fraction $\frac{5}{8}$ as a percent?

F 625%
G 62.5%
H 58%
J 0.625%

5. What is 24% as a decimal and as a fraction in simplest form?

A 0.024; $\frac{24}{100}$
B 24; $\frac{6}{25}$
C 0.24; $\frac{6}{25}$
D 24; $\frac{24}{100}$

For 6–10, find the percent of the number.

6. 22% of 50 = __?__

F 39
G 16.5
H 11
J 5.5

7. 200% of 120 = __?__

A 600
B 360
C 240
D 60

8. 5% of 20 = __?__

F 1
G 5
H 10
J 19

9. 95% of 400 = __?__

A 20
B 95
C 360
D 380

10. 25% of 240 = __?__

F 180
G 60
H 50
J 40

11. Find the sale price of a shirt if the regular price is $21.00 and it is on sale at 20% off.

A $1.00
B $4.20
C $16.80
D $20.00

12. How much sales tax is added to the cost of a dress priced at $35.00 if the sales tax rate is 4%?

F $14.00
G $1.40
H $0.40
J $0.35

Go On

13. The regular price of a blanket was discounted 30%. The sale price was $22.40. What was the regular price?

A $15.68
B $29.12
C $32.00
D $35.00

14. What is the total cost of a $120.00 suit on sale at 15% off with 8% sales tax added?

F $129.60
G $110.16
H $102.00
J $93.84

For 15–16, you are investing money in a savings account that earns 6.5% simple interest.

15. Calculate how much interest will be earned if $2,500 is invested for a period of 7 years.

A $1,137.50
B $162.50
C $12.50
D $6.50

16. How much time will it take to earn $468.00 if you invest $1,200.00 in this savings account?

F 6 years
G 5 years
H 4.68 years
J 1.2 years

For 17–19, use the circle graph. Dollar figures are in thousands of dollars.

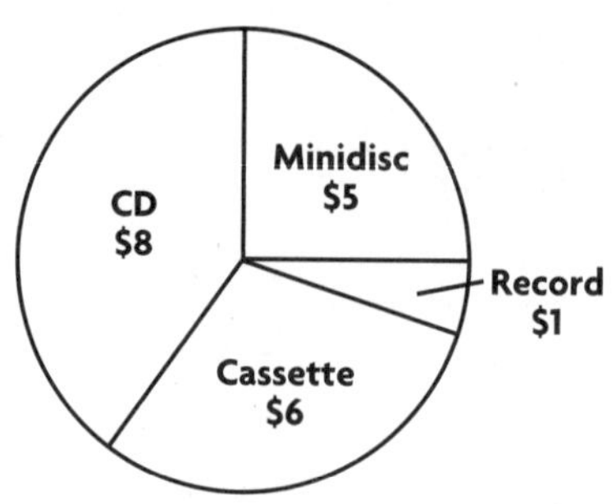

17. Sales of CDs at this music store made up what percent of total sales?

A 60%
B 50%
C 55%
D 40%

18. If the manager decided not to sell records anymore, what percent of sales would he lose?

F 5%
G 10%
H 15%
J 20%

19. Sales of CDs and minidiscs make up what percent of total sales?

A 13%
B 26%
C 50%
D 65%

20. Rob's Clothing is having a sale and has discounts as shown on the sign below.

Regular Price: $140.00
Discounted Price: 30% off Regular Price
Sale Price: 20% off Discounted Price
Bonus Buy: 10% off Sale Price

Calculate the bonus buy price of this item.

F $56.00
G $70.00
H $70.56
J $77.00

Stop

Name ______________________________

Write the correct answer.

For 1–2, write the percent of the figure that is shaded.

1. 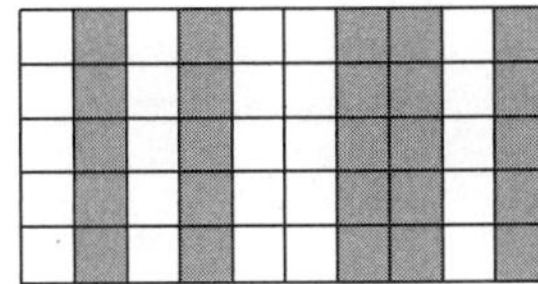

____

2. 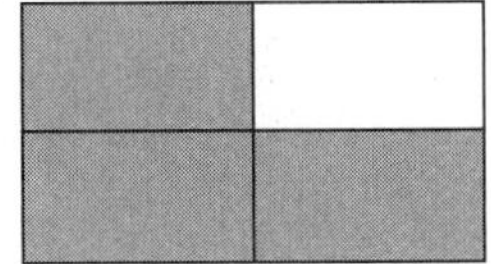

____

3. Write the decimal 0.15 as a percent.

____

4. Write the fraction $\frac{3}{8}$ as a percent.

____

5. Write 12% as a decimal and as a fraction in simplest form.

____

6. 35% of 70 = __?__

____

7. 150% of 150 = __?__

____

8. 8% of 50 = __?__

____

9. 85% of 200 = __?__

____

10. 15% of 640 = __?__

____

11. What is the sale price of a $38.00 video game on sale at 15% off?

____

12. How much sales tax is added to the cost of a shirt priced at $28.00 if the sales tax rate is 5%?

____

Go On

13. The regular price of a coat was discounted 25%. The sale price was $131.25. What was the regular price?

____

14. What is the total cost of a $200.00 television set on sale at 10% off with 6% sales tax added?

____

For 15–16, you are investing money in a money market fund that earns 4.5% simple interest.

15. How much interest will be earned if $5,500 is invested for a period of 8 years?

____

16. How much time will it take to earn $607.50 if you invest $1,500.00 in this fund?

____

For 17–19, use the circle graph. The circle graph shows how Sam spends his weekly earnings from his part-time job.

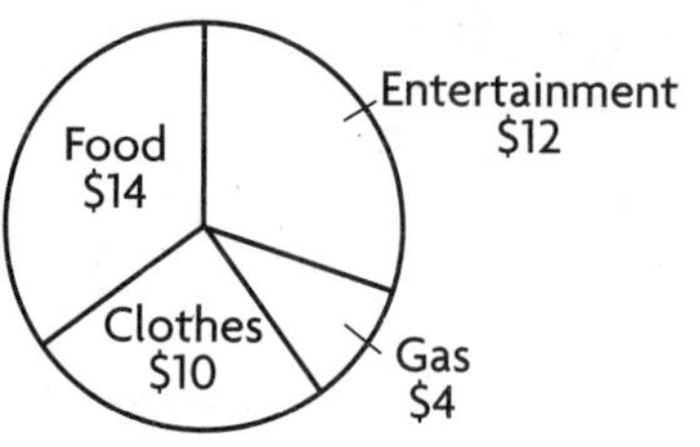

17. What percent of his earnings does Sam spend on food?

____

18. What percent of his total salary does Sam spend on clothes and entertainment?

____

19. If Sam got a ride to work and used his gas money for entertainment, what percent of his salary would he spend on entertainment each week?

____

20. Greg saw the sign shown below in the window of a bike store.

FINAL SALE ON ALL MOUNTAIN BIKES		
Regular Price	$200	
Discount	10%	Off Regular Price
Winter Sale	20%	Off Discounted Price
Final Sale	15%	Off Winter Sale Price

What is the final price of a mountain bike?

____

Stop

Choose the best answer.

For 1–4, use the following situation:

A spinner with 10 equal sections has 1 green section, 4 blue sections, 3 red sections, and 2 yellow sections.

1. Express *P* (red or yellow) as a fraction.

   A $\frac{1}{10}$ C $\frac{1}{2}$
   B $\frac{1}{5}$ D $\frac{7}{10}$

2. Express *P* (not yellow) as a decimal and a percent.

   F 0.9, 90%   H 0.75, 75%
   G 0.8, 80%   J 0.25, 25%

3. Find *P* (blue).

   A $\frac{1}{10}$ C $\frac{2}{5}$
   B $\frac{3}{10}$ D $\frac{3}{5}$

4. Find *P* (red or not red).

   F 1   H $\frac{1}{2}$
   G $\frac{7}{10}$ J $\frac{3}{10}$

For 5–8, use the following situation:

The names of the days of the week are on 7 pieces of paper in a bowl. One piece is drawn.

5. Find *P* (begins with S).

   A $\frac{1}{7}$ C $\frac{2}{5}$
   B $\frac{2}{7}$ D 1

6. Find *P* (begins with T or F).

   F $\frac{3}{4}$ H $\frac{3}{7}$
   G $\frac{4}{7}$ J $\frac{2}{7}$

7. Find *P* (does not contain Y).

   A 1   C $\frac{1}{7}$
   B $\frac{6}{7}$ D 0

8. Which of the following describes drawing a day that has a letter A?

   F certain   H not likely
   G likely   J impossible

For 9–10, use the following situation:

A spinner has red, blue and yellow sections. With 100 spins, Jane got the following results.

COLOR	RED	BLUE	YELLOW
Number of times	20	50	30

9. With 20 spins, how many times can she expect to get yellow?

   A 2 times   C 6 times
   B 3 times   D 12 times

10. With 200 spins, how many times can she expect to get blue?

   F 150 times   H 120 times
   G 130 times   J 100 times

Go On

For 11–13, use the results from the following experiment to make predictions.

Manuel tossed a quarter and a penny 50 times each and recorded the results.

QUARTER		PENNY	
Heads	Tails	Heads	Tails
20	30	35	15

11. How many heads can he expect if he tosses the quarter 100 times?

A 30 B 40 C 60 D 80

12. How many tails can he expect if he tosses the penny 80 times?

F 56 G 45 H 24 J 12

13. How many heads can he expect if he tosses each coin 20 times?

A 22 B 14 C 11 D 8

For 14–16, use the following situation.

A box was filled with marbles of 3 colors. Jan took 20 marbles from the box and recorded the number of each color.

BLACK	BLUE	RED
2	5	13

14. How many black marbles can she expect if she takes 30 marbles from the box?

F 1 G 3 H 5 J 6

15. How many blue marbles can she expect if she takes 44 marbles from the box?

A 38 C 12
B 20 D 11

16. How many red marbles can she expect if she takes 40 marbles from the box?

F 10 G 16 H 26 J 39

For 17–20, use the following situation. Decide whether there is *too much, too little,* or the *right amount* of information to answer each question. Solve, if possible.

A spinner has 10 equal sections. There are 3 blue sections and 2 yellow sections. One yellow section is between 2 red sections.

17. What is the probability that the spinner will land on blue or yellow?

A too much; $\frac{3}{10}$ C too much; $\frac{1}{2}$

B right amount; $\frac{2}{5}$ D too little

18. What is the probability that the spinner will land on red?

F too much; $\frac{1}{5}$

G right amount; $\frac{1}{5}$

H right amount; $\frac{2}{5}$

J too little

19. What is the probability that the spinner will land on yellow?

A too much; $\frac{2}{5}$ C right amount; $\frac{3}{5}$

B too much; $\frac{1}{5}$ D too little

20. What is the probability that the spinner will land on blue?

F too much; $\frac{3}{10}$

G right amount; $\frac{3}{5}$

H too much; $\frac{3}{5}$

J too little

Stop

Name ______________________

Write the correct answer.

For 1–4, use the following situation.

A spinner with 12 equal sections has 2 red sections, 2 yellow sections, 3 white sections, 1 blue section, and 4 black sections.

1. Write *P*(red or black) as a fraction, a decimal, and a percent.

____

2. Write *P*(not black) as a fraction, a decimal to the nearest hundredth, and a percent.

____

3. Find *P*(white) expressed as a fraction.

____

4. Find *P*(white or not white) expressed as a percent.

____

For 5–8, use the following situation.

The names of the first 6 months of the year are on 6 pieces of paper in a box. One piece is drawn.

5. Find *P*(begins with *J*) expressed as a fraction.

____

6. Find *P*(does not begin with *M*) expressed as a fraction.

____

7. Find *P*(does not contain A or E) expressed as a percent.

____

8. Is it likely that you will draw a piece of paper that contains the letter *R*? Explain why or why not?

____

For 9–10, use the following situation.

A spinner has the numbers 1, 2, 3, and 4 on it. With 100 spins, Juan got the following results.

Number	1	2	3	4
Number of times	10	30	40	20

9. With 50 spins, how many times can he expect to land on 2?

____

10. With 300 spins, how many times can he expect to land on 3?

____

Go On

For 11–13, use the results from the following experiment to make predictions.

Rita flipped a nickel and a dime 40 times each and recorded the results.

NICKEL		DIME	
Heads	Tails	Heads	Tails
15	25	24	16

11. Predict how many heads she can expect if she flips the nickel 120 times.

____

12. Predict how many tails she can expect if she flips the dime 10 times?

____

13. How many tails can she expect if she tosses both coins 80 times?

____

For 14–16, use the following situation.

A box was filled with red, blue, and orange crayons. Sara took 15 crayons from the box and recorded the number of each color.

RED	BLUE	ORANGE
5	3	7

14. How many red crayons can she expect if she takes 30 crayons from the box?

____

15. How many blue crayons can she expect if she takes 20 crayons from the box?

____

16. If she takes out 60 crayons, how many can she expect to be orange?

____

For 17–20, use the following situation. Write whether there is *too much*, *too little*, or the *right amount* of information to answer each question. Solve if possible, or describe what information is needed to solve it.

Eight cards are face down on a table. Two cards are blue and 3 are red. There is 1 white card between the 2 blue cards. You pick 1 card.

17. What is the probability that you will pick a blue card or a red card?

____

18. What is the probability that you will pick a blue card?

____

19. What is the probability that you will pick a white card?

____

20. What is the probability that you will pick a red card?

____

Stop

Choose the best answer.

1. Sasha had a choice of 5 shirts and 3 pairs of slacks. How many different outfits could he have made?

   A 5 outfits C 15 outfits
   B 8 outfits D 243 outfits

2. This weekend there are 5 different movies at the theater. How many different ways could you see a movie choosing one day (Saturday or Sunday) and one movie?

   F 2 H 7
   G 5 J 10

3. A license plate for a bicycle has 1 letter followed by 2 digits. How many different license plates are possible?

   A 5,200 plates C 1,000 plates
   B 2,600 plates D 260 plates

For 4–7, use this information.

In a bag of 20 marbles, 10 are red, 8 are green, and 2 are blue.

4. A marble will be selected at random. What is the probability that it will be green?

   F $\frac{2}{5}$ G $\frac{1}{5}$ H $\frac{1}{8}$ J $\frac{1}{20}$

5. A marble is selected, its color noted, and the marble is replaced. Then a second marble is selected. What is the probability both are green?

   A $\frac{4}{5}$ B $\frac{2}{5}$ C $\frac{4}{25}$ D $\frac{1}{25}$

6. If a red marble is chosen and not replaced, what is the probability that a second marble chosen will be blue?

   F $\frac{1}{3}$ G $\frac{1}{5}$ H $\frac{1}{10}$ J $\frac{1}{19}$

7. A marble will be selected, its color noted, and then it will be replaced. A second marble will be chosen. What is the probability that the first one will be red and the second blue?

   A $\frac{1}{20}$ B $\frac{1}{10}$ C $\frac{1}{5}$ D $\frac{1}{2}$

For 8–11, use this information.

In a survey, two hundred high school seniors were randomly selected and asked their choice of college major. Their responses are shown in the table below.

Math	25
Science	40
Business	70
Pre-medicine	40
Pre-law	25

8. What is the probability that a randomly selected senior will choose math?

   F $\frac{1}{25}$ G $\frac{1}{10}$ H $\frac{1}{8}$ J $\frac{1}{4}$

9. What is the probability that a randomly selected senior will choose business?

   A $\frac{3}{5}$ B $\frac{7}{20}$ C $\frac{1}{5}$ D $\frac{1}{70}$

10. What is the probability that a randomly selected senior will choose pre-medicine or pre-law?

    F $\frac{1}{65}$ G $\frac{13}{40}$ H $\frac{1}{2}$ J $\frac{13}{20}$

11. What is the probability that a randomly selected senior will **not** choose math or science?

    A $\frac{1}{65}$ B $\frac{11}{35}$ C $\frac{13}{40}$ D $\frac{27}{40}$

Go On

Name ______________________________

12. At the cafeteria, Sharon has a choice of 2 sandwiches, 4 salads, and 3 desserts. How many different lunches could she purchase if she gets 1 sandwich, 1 salad and 1 dessert?

F 24
G 12
H 9
J 8

13. How many outcomes are possible for tossing a nickel, a dime, and a quarter?

A 8 outcomes
B 6 outcomes
C 3 outcomes
D 2 outcomes

For 14–16, use the spinner and cards shown below.

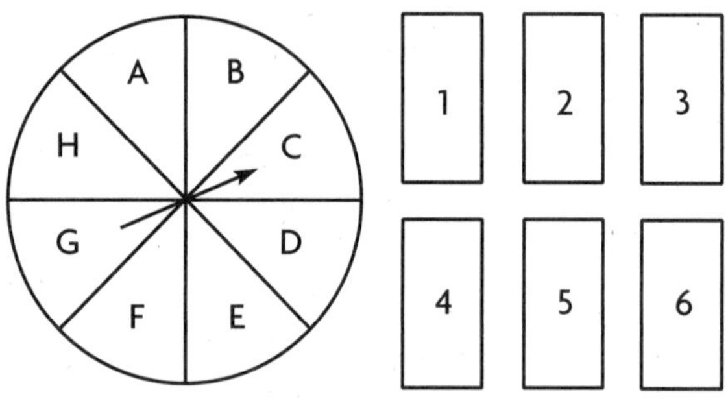

14. How many possible outcomes are there for spinning the pointer on the spinner and randomly choosing one card?

F 120 outcomes
G 48 outcomes
H 24 outcomes
J 14 outcomes

15. What is the probability of spinning a C and drawing a card that has an even number?

A $\frac{1}{16}$ B $\frac{1}{10}$ C $\frac{1}{8}$ D $\frac{1}{2}$

16. Find the probability of spinning a letter that is a vowel and drawing a card with a multiple of 3 on it.

F $\frac{1}{48}$ G $\frac{1}{12}$ H $\frac{3}{8}$ J $\frac{1}{4}$

17. If the outcome of the second event does not depend on the outcome of the first event, the events are called ________.

A random
B samples
C dependent
D independent

18. If one event has m possibilities and another has n possibilities, then there are a total of ________ ways both can occur.

F $m - n$
G $m + n$
H $m \div n$
J $m \times n$

Use the tree diagram for question 19.

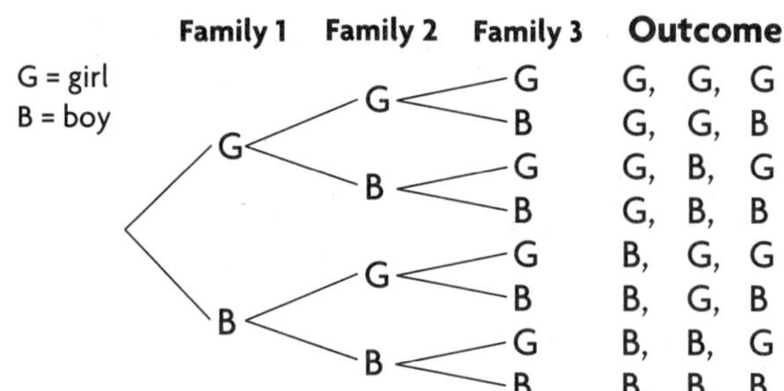

19. Three families each have 1 girl and 1 boy. If you randomly choose a child from each family, what is the probability of choosing all boys or all girls?

A $\frac{1}{12}$ B $\frac{1}{8}$ C $\frac{1}{4}$ D $\frac{1}{2}$

20. An Italian restaurant serves 8 types of pasta and 10 types of sauce. How many weeks can you order one type of pasta with one sauce from the restaurant without repeating a pasta and sauce combination?

F 15 weeks
G 40 weeks
H 60 weeks
J 80 weeks

Stop

Name ______________________________

Write the correct answer.

1. To make a sandwich, Maya has a choice of ham, turkey, or cheese on white or wheat bread. How many different kinds of sandwiches consisting of one meat and one type of bread can she make?

____

2. The sixth, seventh, and eighth grades will study Spanish, French, or Italian next year. How many different language classes are possible if only one grade is in each class?

____

3. In her journal, Alice always writes the month and the day of the week as her heading. How many different headings are possible?

____

For 4–7, use this information.

In a box of 40 coins, 10 are quarters, 5 are dimes, 20 are nickels, and 5 are pennies.

4. A coin will be selected at random. What is the probability that it will be a quarter?

____

5. A coin will be selected and replaced. Then a second coin will be selected. What is the probability that both will be pennies?

____

6. If a dime is chosen and not replaced, what is the probability that a second coin chosen will be a quarter?

____

7. A coin will be selected at random and replaced. Then a second coin will be selected at random. What is the probability that the first coin will be a quarter and the second will be a dime?

____

For 8–11, use the following information.

In a survey, three hundred sixth graders were randomly selected and asked about their favorite type of movie. Their responses are shown in the chart below.

Action	75
Cartoon	30
Romance	50
Science Fiction	90
Comedy	55

8. What is the probability that a randomly selected sixth grader will choose science fiction movies?

____

9. What is the probability that a randomly selected sixth grader will choose action movies?

____

10. What is the probability that a randomly selected sixth grader will choose cartoons or romance movies?

____

Go On

11. What is the probability that a randomly selected sixth grader will **not** choose comedies or action movies?

___

12. Jason has 3 T-shirts, 4 pairs of pants, and 3 pairs of socks to choose from. How many different outfits consisting of 1 shirt, 1 pair of pants, and 1 pair of socks are possible?

___

13. How many different outcomes are possible when you toss a coin and roll a number cube labeled 1–6?

___

For 14–16, use the two spinners shown below.

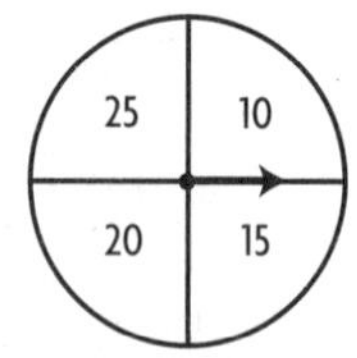

14. How many possible outcomes are there for spinning both pointers once?

___

15. What is the probability of spinning green and an odd number?

___

16. What is the probability of spinning red or yellow and a number divisible by 5?

___

17. If the outcome of the second event depends on the outcome of the first event, what are the events called?

___

18. If there are *a* choices for one category and *b* choices for another, what expression can be used to represent the total number of choices?

___

For 19, use the tree diagram.

Size	Color	Type	Outcome
24	Silver (S)	Mountain (M)	24, S, M
		Racing (R)	24, S, R
	Black (B)	Mountain (M)	24, B, M
		Racing (R)	24, B, R
26	Silver (S)	Mountain (M)	26, S, M
		Racing (R)	26, S, R
	Black (B)	Mountain (M)	26, B, M
		Racing (R)	26, B, R

19. A bike shop has a sale on 24-inch and 26-inch mountain and racing bikes in either silver or black. Jack needs a 26-inch bike. He does not care what color he gets, but he does want a mountain bike. What is the probability Jack can get the bike he wants?

___

20. At a buffet there are 12 different salads and 6 different soups to choose from. How many different combinations of soup and salad are possible?

___

Stop

Name ____________________

Choose the best answer.

1. An item costs $24.50. The sales tax rate is 6%. What is the sales tax?

   A $0.75 C $2.45
   B $1.47 D $4.70

2. Find the unit rate.

   208 miles on 8 gallons of gas

   F 104 mi per gal H 26 mi per gal
   G 54 mi per gal J 16 mi per gal

3. The sides of a rectangle are 18 in. wide and 24 in. long. Which of the following are side lengths for a similar rectangle?

   A 9 in. wide, 12 in. long
   B 9 in. wide, 18 in. long
   C 32 in. wide, 36 in. long
   D 36 in. wide, 36 in. long

4. In a bag of 15 tiles, 9 are blue, 3 are green, and 3 are red. A tile is selected at random. What is the probability that it is red?

   F 20% H 33%
   G 30% J 66%

5. In a class election, 3 people are running for president, 2 for vice president, and 4 for treasurer. How many different choices consisting of one president, one vice president, and one treasurer are possible?

   A 24 C 9
   B 12 D 3

6. What is $\frac{3}{8}$ expressed as a percent?

   F 3.8% H 37.5%
   G 8% J 40%

7. If the outcome of the second event depends on the outcome of the first event, the events are called __?__.

   A samples C independent
   B random D dependent

8. Malcolm tossed a penny 40 times. He tossed 30 heads. Based on these data, how many heads can he expect in 60 tosses?

   F 60 heads H 40 heads
   G 45 heads J 35 heads

9. When you flip four different coins, how many outcomes are possible?

   A 4 outcomes C 12 outcomes
   B 8 outcomes D 16 outcomes

10. Mandy puts $800 in a savings account with a yearly simple interest rate of 2.5%. How much will be in her account after 5 years?

    F $1,800 H $900
    G $1,100 J $100

11. The scale for a map is 1 in. = 80 mi. What is the actual distance between two towns that are $2\frac{1}{4}$ in. apart on the map?

    A 200 mi C 160 mi
    B 180 mi D 140 mi

12. The names of the first five months of the year are on slips of paper in a bowl. One slip is randomly drawn. Find *P*(day does not begin with *M*).

    F $\frac{1}{5}$ H $\frac{3}{5}$
    G $\frac{2}{5}$ J $\frac{4}{5}$

Go On

For 13–15, use the following information.

Five hundred members of a recreation center were asked which addition to the center they would most prefer. Here are the results.

Swimming pool	140
Jogging track	80
Tennis Court	50
Basketball Court	230

13. What is the probability that a randomly selected member will choose the tennis court?

A $\frac{1}{50}$ B $\frac{1}{20}$ C $\frac{1}{10}$ D $\frac{5}{10}$

14. What is the probability that a randomly selected member will choose the swimming pool or the jogging track?

F $\frac{11}{25}$ G $\frac{11}{50}$ H $\frac{1}{22}$ J $\frac{1}{220}$

15. Suppose an additional 100 members are surveyed. What is a reasonable prediction of the number of those members who will choose the basketball court?

A 23 B 38 C 46 D 50

16. Leo needs 1 cup of raisins to make 18 muffins. How many cups of raisins does he need to make 45 muffins?

F $\frac{2}{5}$ c H $2\frac{1}{2}$ c
G $2\frac{2}{5}$ c J $2\frac{2}{3}$ c

17. What is the total cost of a $60 jacket on sale for 25% off with 8% sales tax added on?

A $45.00 C $49.80
B $48.60 D $64.80

For 18–20, use the circle graph. The graph shows the amount of money raised at a charity fair.

18. Sales of books at the charity fair made up what percent of the money raised?

F 30% H 20%
G 25% J 10%

19. What percent of the money raised came from the sale of food and beverages?

A 10% B 20% C 25% D 30%

20. Suppose one half of all the food sales were baked goods. What percent of the money raised came from the sale of baked goods?

F 5% G 10% H 15% J 20%

21. If Mitch types 280 words in 5 min, how many words would you expect him to type in 3 min?

A 56 words C 136 words
B 84 words D 168 words

22. Mangoes are on sale at 5 for $2.00. Find the cost of 8 mangoes.

F $2.80 H $3.50
G $3.20 J $3.80

Go On

Name ______________________________

23. The triangles are similar. Find the unknown length.

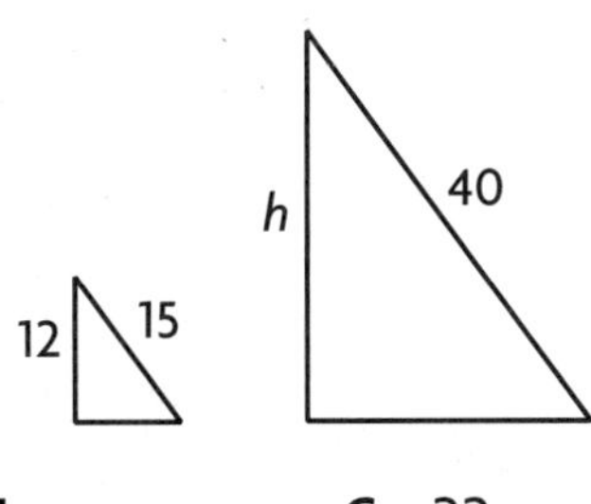

A 24
B 30
C 32
D 36

For 24–25, use the following information.

A bag is filled with cards with 4 different letters. Wanda randomly selected 20 cards from the bag and recorded the number of each letter.

A	B	C	D
8	2	4	6

24. Based on her results how many cards with the letter A can Wanda expect in her next 30 selections?

F 4 cards
G 10 cards
H 12 cards
J 15 cards

25. Based on her results how many cards with the letter C can Wanda expect in her next 45 selections?

A 8 cards
B 9 cards
C 10 cards
D 12 cards

26. A scale drawing for a deck uses a scale of 2 in. = 5 ft. The length of the deck on the drawing is 8 in. How long is the actual deck?

F 40 ft
G 25 ft
H 20 ft
J 10 ft

27. A dressmaker has a choice of 3 fabrics, 5 colors, and 2 patterns. How many different dresses made with 1 fabric, one color, and 1 pattern can she make?

A 30 dresses
B 25 dresses
C 15 dresses
D 10 dresses

For 28–29, use the following information. Write whether there is too much, too little, or the right amount of information to solve the problem. Solve, if possible.

A spinner has 8 equal sections. There are 3 yellow sections, one blue section, and 2 green sections. The blue section is between the green sections.

28. What is the probability that the spinner will land on purple or blue?

F too much; $\frac{1}{4}$

G right amount; $\frac{1}{4}$

H right amount; $\frac{1}{8}$

J too little

29. What is the probability that the spinner will **not** land on yellow?

A too much; $\frac{5}{8}$

B right amount; $\frac{1}{2}$

C too much; $\frac{3}{8}$

D too little

30. Diego travels 1,500 miles in 6 days. If he continues at this rate, how far will he travel in 9 days?

F 1,750 miles
G 2,000 miles
H 2,100 miles
J 2,250 miles

Go On

Name ______________________________

For 31–32, use the following information.

A spinner with 5 equal sections has 1 blue section, 2 red sections, and 2 yellow sections.

31. Express *P*(red or yellow) as a fraction, a decimal, and a percent.

A $\frac{4}{10}$, 0.4, 40%
C $\frac{3}{5}$, 0.6, 60%
B $\frac{1}{2}$, 0.5, 50%
D $\frac{4}{5}$, 0.8, 80%

32. Find *P*(not yellow).

F $\frac{1}{5}$
H $\frac{3}{5}$
G $\frac{2}{5}$
J 1

33. To make 4 dozen tortillas, 3 cups of water are used. How many cups of water are needed to make 72 tortillas?

A $4\frac{1}{2}$ cups
C 9 cups
B 6 cups
D 54 cups

34. What is 38% of 60?

F 40.8
H 24.8
G 32.8
J 22.8

35. Jason wants to leave a 15% tip on a restaurant bill of $28. What is a reasonable estimate for a 15% tip?

A $2.80
C $3.50
B $3.00
D $4.50

36. There are 12 boys and 20 girls in the choir. What is the ratio of boys to girls written as a percent?

F 60%
H 12%
G 40%
J 8%

37. Write 84% both as a decimal and as a fraction in simplest form.

A 0.84; $\frac{84}{100}$
C 0.84; $\frac{21}{25}$
B 0.84; $\frac{48}{50}$
D 84; $\frac{84}{100}$

38. What is 210% of 400?

F 880
H 820
G 840
J 800

For 39–40, use the spinners shown below.

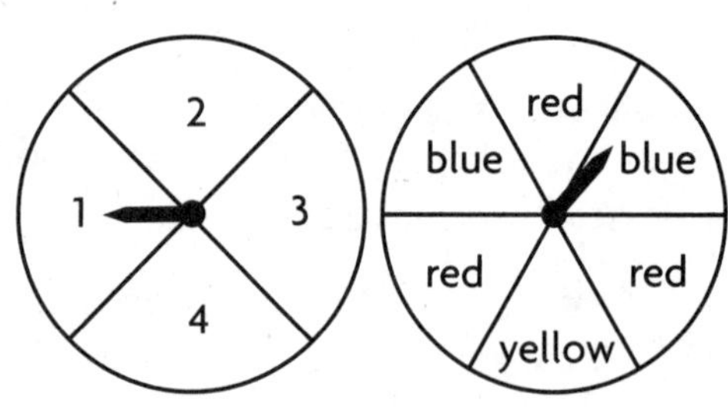

39. What is the probability of the pointers landing on 3 and blue?

A $\frac{1}{2}$
C $\frac{1}{12}$
B $\frac{1}{5}$
D $\frac{1}{24}$

40. What is the probability of the pointers landing on an even number and **not** red?

F $\frac{1}{2}$
H $\frac{1}{5}$
G $\frac{1}{4}$
J $\frac{1}{8}$

Stop

Name ______________________________

Write the correct answer.

1. An item costs $26.50. The sales tax rate is 8%. What is the sales tax?

____

2. Find the unit rate.

   392 miles on 14 gallons of gas

____

3. A rectangle measures 10 in. wide and 24 in. long. A similar rectangle has a width of 17.5 in. What is its length?

____

4. In a group of 25 students, 9 are 7 years old, 11 are 8 years old, and 5 are 9 years old. A student is selected at random. What is the probability that he or she is 8 years old?

____

5. For a class play, 4 students are auditioning for the lead actor, 5 for the lead actress, and 3 for the director. How many different choices of one actor, one actress, and one director are possible?

____

6. Write $\frac{5}{8}$ as a percent.

____

7. If the outcome of the second event does not depend on the outcome of the first event, the events are called __?__.

____

8. Maggie tossed a thumbtack 50 times and the point landed up 30 times. Based on these data, how many times can she expect the thumbtack to land with the point up in 75 tosses?

____

9. When you roll 3 number cubes, each labeled 1 to 6, how many outcomes are possible?

____

10. Maureen puts $500 in a savings account with a yearly simple interest rate of 3.5%. How much will be in her account after 4 years?

____

11. The scale for a map is 1 in. = 150 mi. What is the actual distance between two towns that are $3\frac{1}{2}$ in. apart on the map?

____

12. The names of the days of the week are on slips of paper in a bowl. One slip is randomly drawn. Find *P*(day begins with the letter *T*).

____

Go On

For 13–15, use the following information.

Six hundred members of a community organization were asked which fund-raiser they would prefer. Here are the results.

rummage sale	180
bake sale	105
magazine drive	130
walk-a-thon	185

13. What is the probability that a randomly selected member will choose the bake sale?

____

14. What is the probability that a randomly selected member will choose the rummage sale or the walk-a-thon?

____

15. Suppose an additional 100 members are surveyed. What is a reasonable prediction of the number of those members who will prefer a magazine drive?

____

16. Louise needs 1 cup of flour to make 24 pancakes. How many cups of flour does she need to make 40 pancakes?

____

17. What is the total cost of a $45 skirt on sale for 20% off with 6% sales tax added on?

____

For 18–20, use the circle graph. The graph shows the amount of money spent by a family.

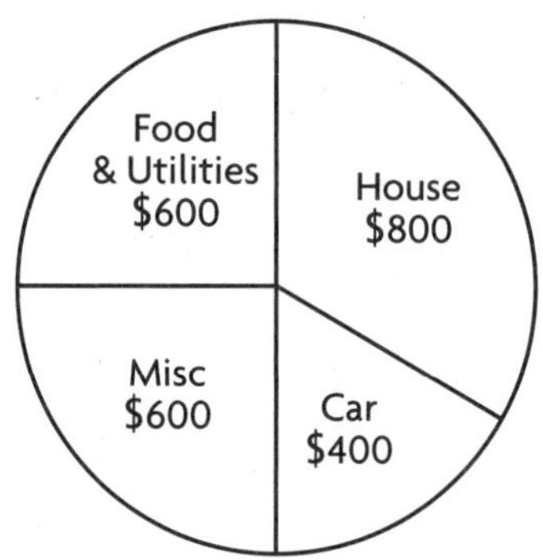

18. House payment expenses made up what percent of the money spent?

____

19. What percent of the money spent is for food and utilities, and miscellaneous?

____

20. Suppose the family increases its car payment by $100. What percent of expenditures would the car payment be?

____

21. If Miguel can go 12 blocks in 8 min on his in-line skates, how many blocks would you expect him to be able to go in 6 min?

____

22. Kiwi fruit are on sale at 4 for $0.88. Find the cost of 7 kiwi fruit.

____

Go On

Name ______________________________

23. The triangles are similar. Find the unknown length.

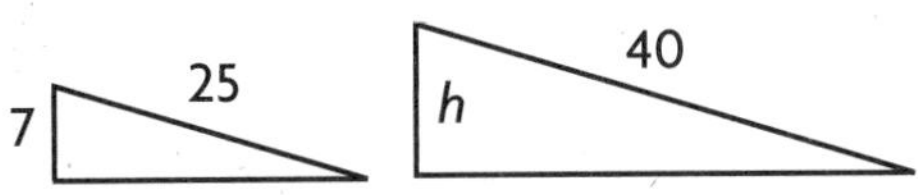

____

For 24–25, use the following information.

A bag is filled with marbles of 4 different colors. Willie randomly selected 20 marbles from the bag and recorded the color of each marble.

BLUE	RED	GREEN	YELLOW
7	4	3	6

24. Based on his results, how many yellow marbles can Willie expect in his next 30 selections?

____

25. Based on his results, how many red marbles can Willie expect in his next 45 selections?

____

26. A scale drawing for a sailboat uses a scale of 2 in. = 15 ft. The length of the sailboat on the drawing is 11 in. How long is the actual sailboat?

____

27. A hair stylist has a choice of 3 hair lengths, 5 hair colors, and 2 hair types. How many different styles based on 1 length, 1 color, and 1 type can she make?

____

For 28–29, use the following information. Write whether there is *too much*, *too little*, or the *right amount* of information to solve the problem. Solve, if possible.

A spinner has 12 equal sections. There are 4 blue sections, 5 yellow sections, 2 green sections and 1 red section. The red section is between the two green sections.

28. What is the probability that the spinner will land on purple or blue?

____

29. What is the probability that the spinner will **not** land on blue?

____

30. Dana travels 1,200 miles in 5 days. If she continues at this rate, how far will she travel in 8 days?

____

Go On

Name ______________________

For 31–32, use the following information.

A six-sided cube with 1 red side, 2 green sides, and 3 yellow sides is tossed, and the color showing is noted.

31. Express P(red or yellow) as a fraction.

____

32. Find P(not yellow).

____

33. To make 5 dozen donuts, 4 cups of milk are used. How many cups of milk are needed to make 96 donuts?

____

34. What is 46% of 80?

____

35. Joy wants to leave a 15% tip on a restaurant bill of $42.25. What is a reasonable estimate for a 15% tip?

____

36. There are 8 motorcycles and 32 cars in the parking lot. What is the ratio of motorcycles to cars written as a percent?

____

37. Write 72% both as a decimal and as a fraction in simplest form.

____

38. What is 305% of 200?

____

For 39–40, use the spinners shown below.

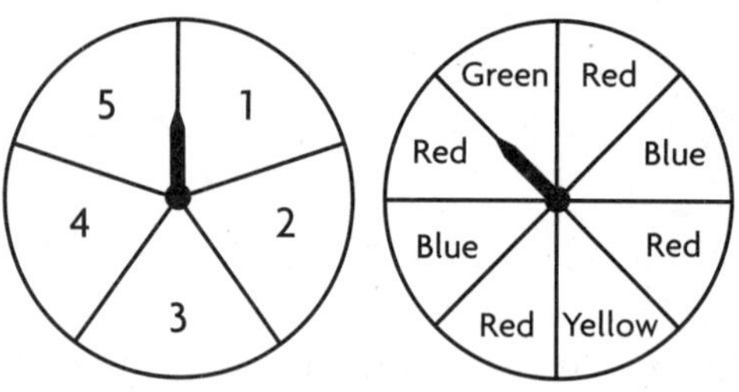

39. What is the probability of the pointers landing on 4 and red?

____

40. What is the probability the pointers landing on an odd number and a color that is **not** blue?

____

Stop

Name ______________________

Choose the best answer.

For 1–7, use a proportion to convert to the given unit.

1. 8 qt = ■ gal

A 1 gal
B 2 gal
C 4 gal
D 32 gal

2. 30 cm = ■ mm

F 30,000 mm
G 3,000 mm
H 300 mm
J 3 mm

3. 5 lb = ■ oz

A 160 oz
B 80 oz
C 40 oz
D 20 oz

4. 400 m = ■ km

F 0.04 km
G 0.4 km
H 4 km
J 40 km

5. 7 L = ■ mL

A 7,000 mL
B 70 mL
C 0.7 mL
D 0.007 mL

6. 27,000 mg = ■ g

F 2,700 g
G 270 g
H 27 g
J 2.7 g

7. 108 in. = ■ yd

A 38 yd
B 36 yd
C 9 yd
D 3 yd

8. A balance shows a mass of 38 kg. What is this amount in grams?

F 380 g
G 3,800 g
H 38,000 g
J 380,000 g

For 9–12, use a proportion to convert to the given unit.

9. 23 in. ≈ ■ cm (1 in. ≈ 2.54 cm)

A 0.58 cm
B 5.84 cm
C 9.06 cm
D 58.42 cm

10. 35 L ≈ ■ gal (1 gal ≈ 3.79 L)

F 1,326.5 gal
G 132.65 gal
H 92.34 gal
J 9.23 gal

11. 50 mi ≈ ■ km (1 mi ≈ 1.61 km)

A 3.11 km
B 31.06 km
C 80.5 km
D 805 km

12. 14 lb ≈ ■ kg (1 lb ≈ 0.45 kg)

F 3.11 kg
G 6.3 kg
H 31.1 kg
J 63 kg

13. Which is an appropriate unit of measure for a person's weight?

A foot
B ounce
C pound
D ton

Go On

Name ______________________________

For 14–15, measure the line segment as described.

14. to the nearest quarter inch

F 1 in.
H $1\frac{1}{2}$ in.
G $1\frac{1}{4}$ in.
J $1\frac{3}{4}$ in.

15. to the nearest centimeter

A 2 cm
C 4 cm
B 3 cm
D 5 cm

For 16–19, choose the measurement which is most precise.

16. F 7 pt. G 3 qt

17. A 8,020 lb B 4 T

18. F 2 kg G 2,200 g

19. A $5\frac{1}{2}$ ft B $5\frac{1}{4}$ ft

20. Which is an appropriate unit of measure for telling how much water a cat drinks in a day?

F kiloliter
H centimeter
G millimeter
J milliliter

21. A scientist is measuring the amount of liquid in a bottle. Which unit will result in the most precise measurement?

A milliliter
C kiloliter
B liter
D centiliter

For 22–25, answer each question. Tell whether an estimate or an exact answer is needed.

22. Bismarck, North Dakota, had 46 inches of snow in January, 58 inches in February, and 33 inches in March. Did this total exceed the previous year's record of 12 feet?

F no; exact
H yes; exact
G yes; estimate
J no; estimate

23. Rita has 250 ft of fencing to enclose a rectangular garden measuring 42 ft by 58 ft. Does she have enough fencing?

A no; exact
C yes; exact
B no; estimate
D yes; estimate

24. Roland has $25. He buys an oil filter for $4.75, spark plugs for $9.60, and 5 qt of oil for $6.95. How much money does he have left?

F $3.70; estimate
H $10.65; estimate
G $3.70; exact
J $8.45; exact

25. Four students each need 11 in. of string for a project. If they have 4 ft of string, do they have enough?

A yes; estimate
C yes; exact
B no; estimate
D no; exact

Stop

Name ______________________________

Write the correct answer.

For 1–7, use a proportion to convert to the given unit.

1. 3 gal = ■ qt

____

2. 1,500 m = ■ km

____

3. ■ lb = 176 oz

____

4. 780 mm = ■ cm

____

5. ■ mL = 0.5 L

____

6. 14 g = ■ mg

____

7. 12 ft = ■ in.

____

8. The height of a room from floor to ceiling is 15 ft. What is the height in yards?

____

For 9–12, use a proportion to convert to the given unit. Round to the nearest tenth.

9. 15 in. ≈ ■ cm (1 in. ≈ 2.54 cm)

____

10. 20 L ≈ ■ gal (1 gal ≈ 3.79 L)

____

11. 86 km ≈ ■ mi (1 mi ≈ 1.61 km)

____

12. 45 lb ≈ ■ kg (1 lb ≈ 0.45 kg)

____

13. Which is an appropriate unit of measure for the capacity of a bathtub?

____

Go On

Name ______________________________

For 14–15, measure the line segment to the given length.

14. nearest half inch; nearest quarter inch

____

15. nearest centimeter; nearest millimeter

____

For 16–20, name an appropriate unit of measure for each item.

16. weight of your dog

____

17. amount a can of soup holds

____

18. length of a car

____

19. weight of a paper clip

____

20. distance from one city to another

____

21. Which unit of measurement is more precise, an inch or a foot? Why?

____

For 22–25, answer each question. Tell whether an estimate or an exact answer is needed.

22. Mr. Wells has 6 pints of grape juice, 8 pints of apple juice, and 2 pints of orange juice. He will mix the juices together to make punch. Does he have enough juice to make 10 quarts of punch?

____

23. The bedroom is a square room with an area of 144 sq ft. Will a rug that is 11 ft long by 10 ft wide fit in the room?

____

24. Jenna has 15 ft of wood for framing. She makes a frame that is 24 in. wide and 36 in. long. How much wood will she have left?

____

25. Anna has $5.00. She needs a gallon of milk. The store has only quarts of milk for $1.50 per quart. Does she have enough money to buy a gallon of milk?

____

Stop

Choose the best answer.

For 1–3, find the perimeter of the polygon.

1.

6 in.

2 in.

A 20 in.
B 16 in.
C 12 in.
D 8 in.

2.

10 cm
14 cm
10 cm

F 10 cm
G 20 cm
H 24 cm
J 34 cm

3.

w w w w w w

A 6*w*
B 5*w*
C 4*w*
D 2*w*

4. Find the circumference of the circle. (Use 3.14 for the value of π.)

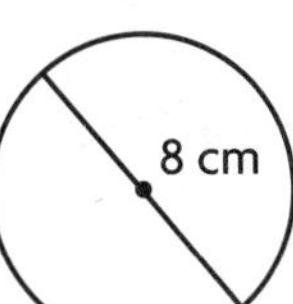

F 50.24 cm
G 25.12 cm
H 12.56 cm
J 8 cm

5. Find the circumference of the circle. (Use 3.14 for the value of π.)

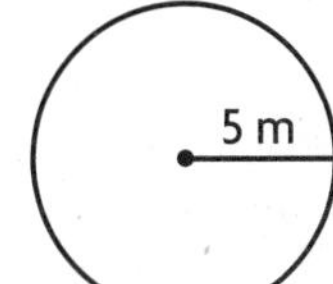

A 8.14 m
B 15.7 m
C 31.4 m
D 78.5 m

6. The perimeter is given. Find the unknown length.

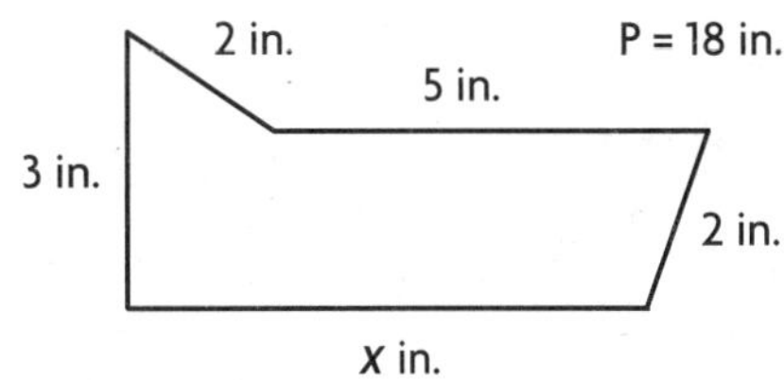

F 18 in.
G 12 in.
H 7 in.
J 6 in.

7. The perimeter is 20 mm. Find the unknown length.

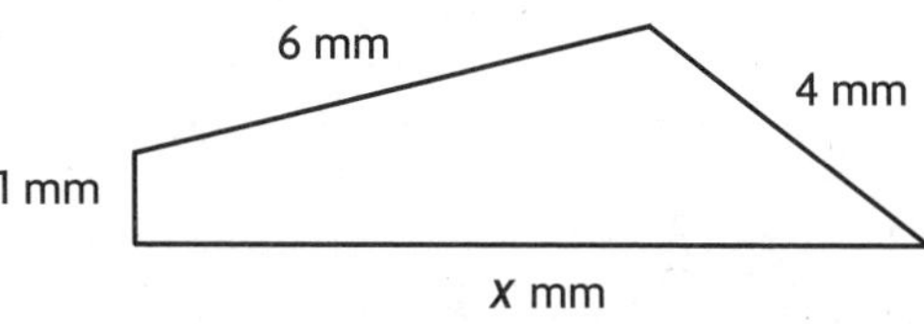

A 5 mm
B 9 mm
C 11 mm
D 20 mm

8. Find the circumference of the circle. (Use 3.14 for the value of π.)

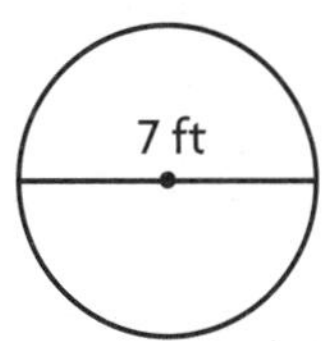

F 10.99 ft
G 21.98 ft
H 43.96 ft
J 49 ft

9. Find the circumference of the circle. (Use 3.14 for the value of π.)

A 18.84 in.
B 37.68 in.
C 75.36 in.
D 452.16 in.

Go On

10. A four-sided polygon has two sides of length 6 cm and two sides of length 8 cm. What is the perimeter of the polygon?

F 28 cm H 20 cm
G 22 cm J 14 cm

11. A baseball diamond is a square with a perimeter of 360 ft. What is the length of one side?

A 80 ft C 120 ft
B 90 ft D 180 ft

12. A kite is made with two isosceles triangles. One of the triangles has side lengths 2 ft, 2 ft, and $2\frac{1}{2}$ ft. The other triangle has side lengths 3 ft, 3 ft, and $2\frac{1}{2}$ ft. What is the perimeter of the kite?

F 10 ft H 15 ft
G $12\frac{1}{2}$ ft J 18 ft

13. A circular window has a radius of 3 ft. How much molding is needed to trim the edge of it? (Use 3.14 for the value of π.)

A 4.71 ft C 18.84 ft
B 9.42 ft D 37.68 ft

14. A swimming pool has a diameter of 30 ft. What is its circumference? (Use 3.14 for the value of π.)

F 23.55 ft H 94.20 ft
G 47.10 ft J 1, 000 ft

15. The perimeter of a rectangle is 54 yd. The length of the rectangle is twice the width. What is the width of the rectangle?

A 36 yd C 18 yd
B 27 yd D 9 yd

16. The diameter of a circle is $4\frac{2}{3}$ ft. What is the circumference? (Use $\frac{22}{7}$ for the value of π.)

F $14\frac{2}{3}$ ft H $18\frac{6}{7}$ ft
G $17\frac{6}{7}$ ft J 44 ft

17. The radius of a circle is $5\frac{1}{4}$ in. What is the circumference? (Use $\frac{22}{7}$ for the value of π.)

A 462 in. C 66 in.
B 231 in. D 33 in.

18. The shortest side of an isosceles triangle with perimeter 240 m is 60 m. What are the other two sides?

F 60 m H 90 m
G 80 m J 180 m

19. Two sides of a rectangle have lengths of 5 m and 3 m. What is the perimeter of the rectangle?

A 16 m C 8 m
B 15 m D 2 m

20. A picture is 21 in. by 36 in. It is in a frame that is 4 in. wide. What is the outside perimeter of the frame?

F 114 in. H 136 in.
G 130 in. J 146 in.

Stop

Write the correct answer.

For 1–3, find the perimeter of the polygon.

1. 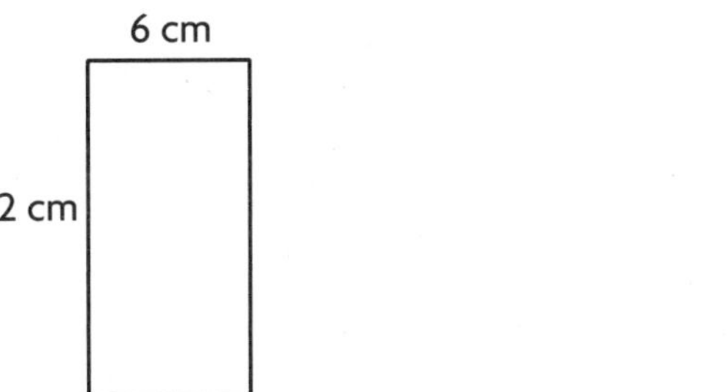

______

2. 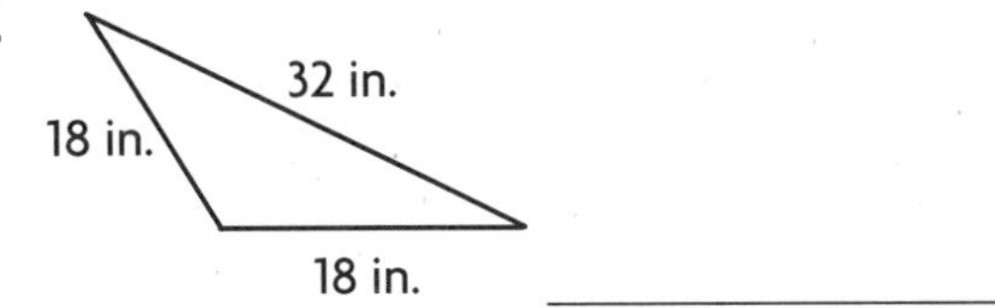

______

3. 

______

4. Find the circumference of the circle. (Use 3.14 for the value of π.)

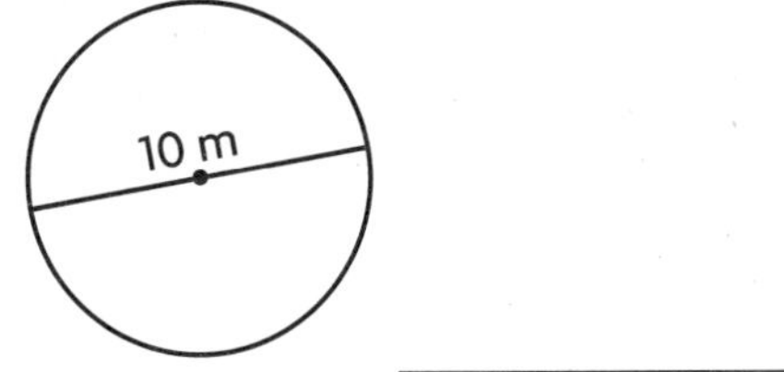

______

5. Find the circumference of the circle. (Use 3.14 for the value of π.)

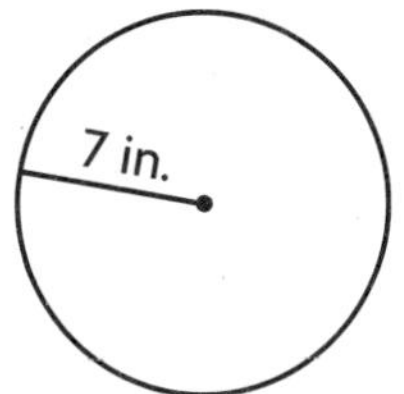

______

6. The perimeter of the figure is 46 cm. Find the unknown length.

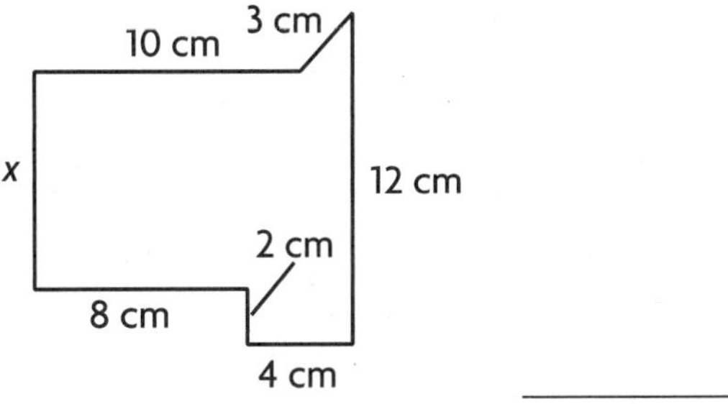

______

7. The perimeter of the figure is 29 in. Find the unknown length.

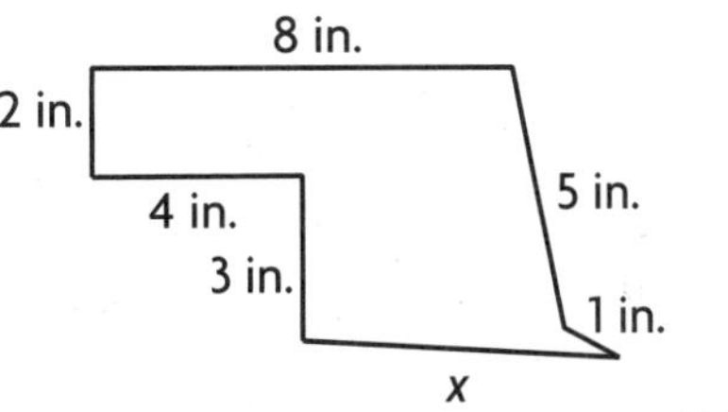

______

8. Find the circumference of the circle. (Use 3.14 for the value of π.)

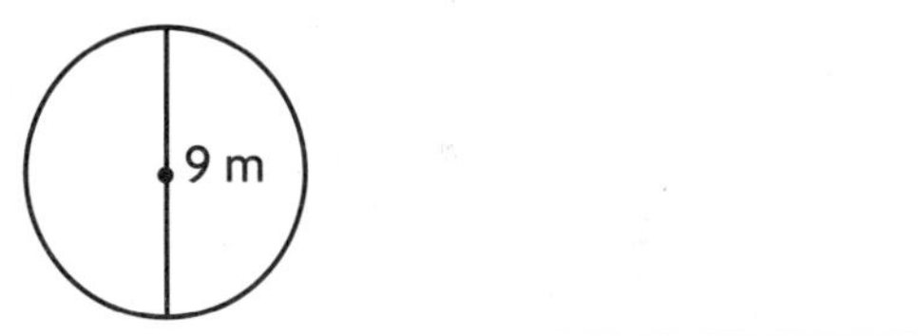

______

9. Find the circumference of the circle. (Use 3.14 for the value of π.)

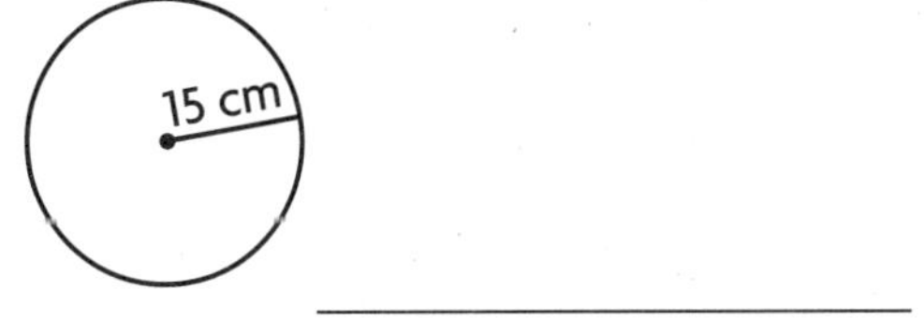

______

10. A six-sided polygon has four sides of length 4 in. and two sides of length 10 in. What is the perimeter of the polygon?

______

Go On

11. A square classroom has a perimeter of 144 ft. How long is one of the sides of the classroom?

____

12. Two equilateral triangular puzzle pieces are put together to make a diamond. Each triangle has a side with a length of 4 cm. What is the perimeter of the diamond?

____

13. A circular garden has a radius of 4 m. How much fencing is needed to enclose it? (Use 3.14 for the value of π.)

____

14. The top of a juice can has a diameter of 6 in. What is the circumference of the can? (Use 3.14 for the value of π.)

____

15. Jared ran twice around a rectangular field. He ran a total of 660 ft. The length of the longer side of the field is 90 ft. What is the length of the shorter side?

____

16. The diameter of a circle is $5\frac{1}{4}$ in. What is the circumference? (Use $\frac{22}{7}$ for the value of π.)

____

17. The radius of a circle is $2\frac{11}{12}$ ft. What is the circumference? (Use $\frac{22}{7}$ for the value of π.)

____

18. The longest side of an isosceles triangle is 20 in. The perimeter is 52 in. What are the lengths of the other two sides of the triangle?

____

19. A rectangular garden measures 32 ft by 15 ft. What is the least amount of fencing you need to enclose the garden?

____

20. A rectangular floor tile is 6 in. by 9 in. The next size tile is 2 in. longer and wider. What is the perimeter of the next size tile?

____

Stop

Name ______________________________

Choose the best answer.

1. Estimate the area of the figure. Each square on the grid represents 1 cm^2.

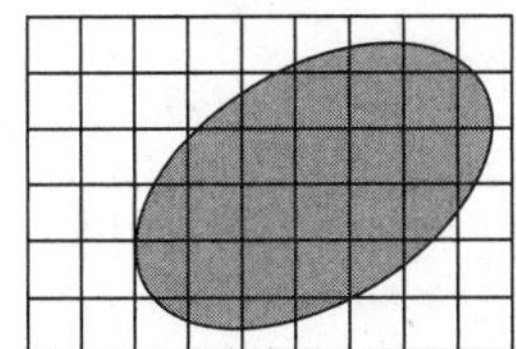

A $15\ cm^2$ C $20\ cm^2$
B $18\ cm^2$ D $23\ cm^2$

2. Find the area of the circle to the nearest whole number. Use 3.14 for π.

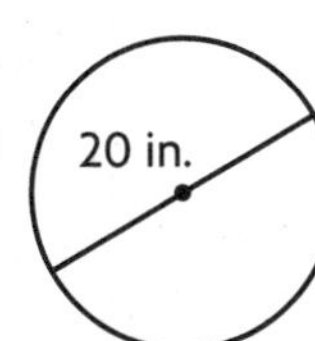

F $63\ in.^2$ H $157\ in.^2$
G $126\ in.^2$ J $314\ in.^2$

For 3–6, find the area.

3. A $6\ in.^2$
B $10\ in.^2$
C $12\ in.^2$
D $15\ in.^2$

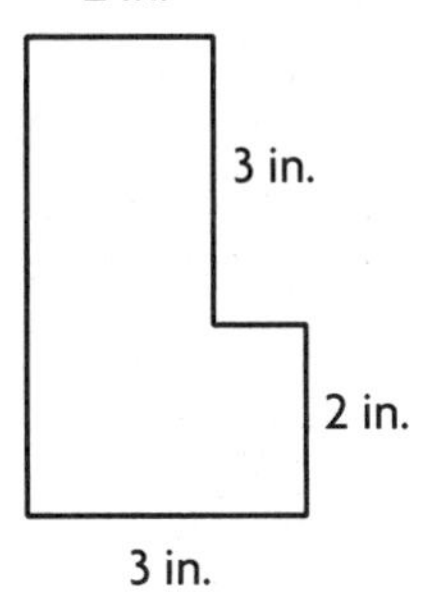

4. F $15\ m^2$
G $25\ m^2$
H $30\ m^2$
J $50\ m^2$

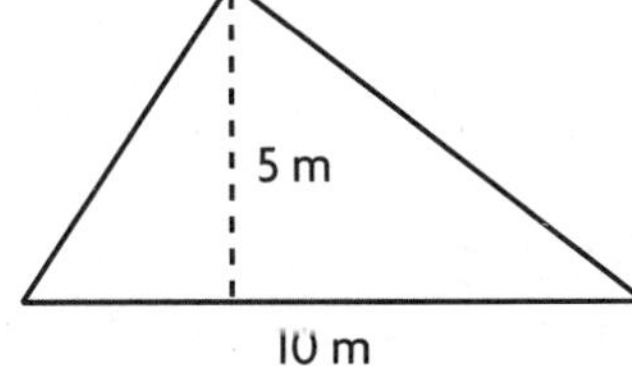

5. A $54\ ft^2$
B $27\ ft^2$
C $15\ ft^2$
D $7.5\ ft^2$

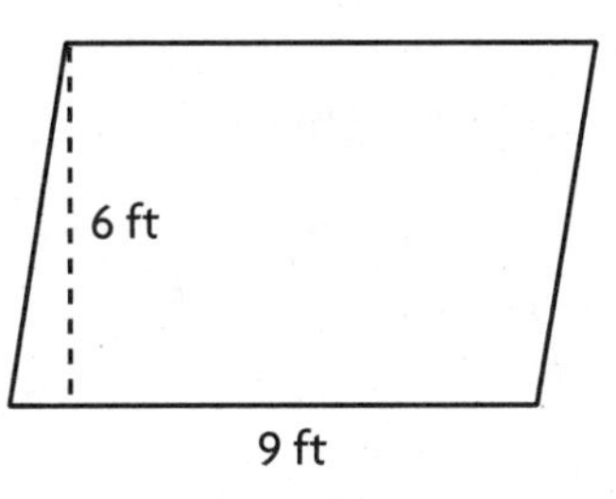

6. F $19\ yd^2$
G $38\ yd^2$
H $44\ yd^2$
J $88\ yd^2$

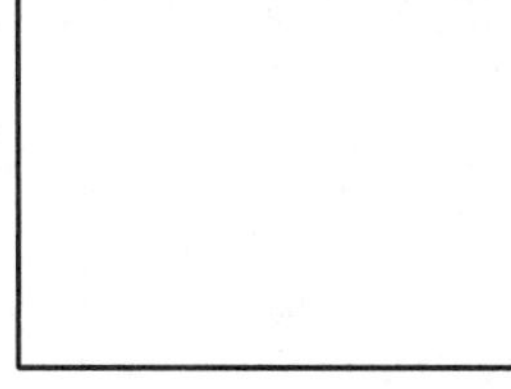

7. Find the surface area.

A $48\ m^2$
B $24\ m^2$
C $16\ m^2$
D $8\ m^2$

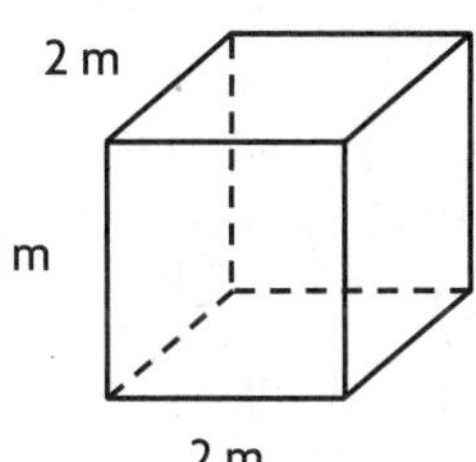

8. The top of a circular table has a radius of 30 in. What is the area of the top of the table to the nearest whole number? (Use 3.14 for π.)

F $94\ in.^2$ H $2,826\ in.^2$
G $188\ in.^2$ J $5,652\ in.^2$

9. Find the area.

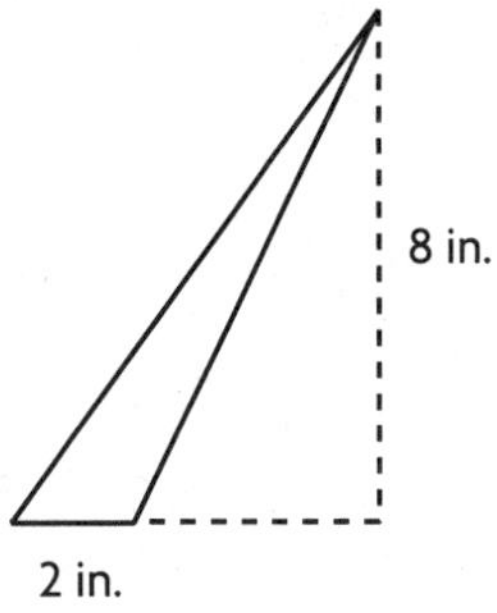

A $8\ in.^2$ C $16\ in.^2$
B $10\ in.^2$ D $32\ in.^2$

10. A rectangular box is 3 ft long, 2 ft wide, and 2 ft tall. How many square feet of paper are needed to cover the outside of the box?

F $32\ ft^2$ H $16\ ft^2$
G $24\ ft^2$ J $12\ ft^2$

Go On

Name ______________________

For 11–14, find the area.

11. A $8\ ft^2$
B $16\ ft^2$
C $24\ ft^2$
D $32\ ft^2$

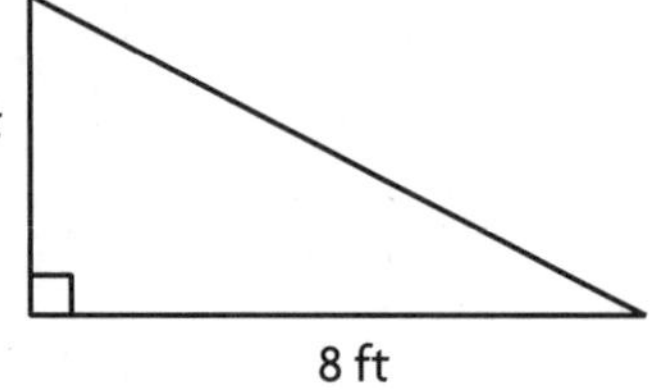

12. F $192\ cm^2$
G $136\ cm^2$
H $112\ cm^2$
J $96\ cm^2$

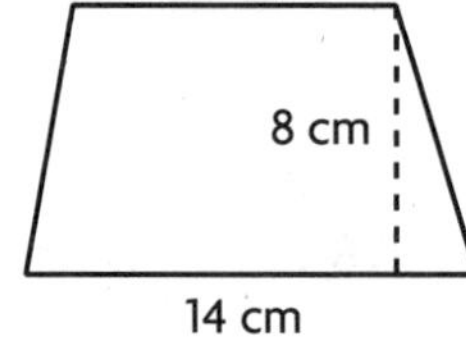

13. A $34\ yd^2$
B $68\ yd^2$
C $140\ yd^2$
D $280\ yd^2$

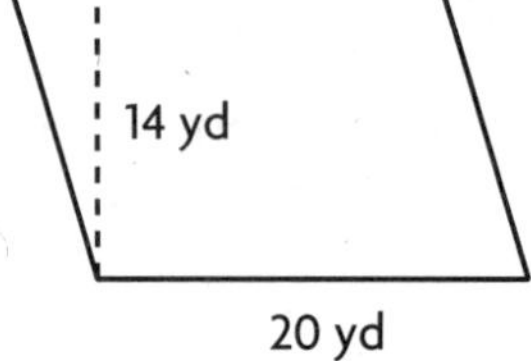

14. F $20\ cm^2$
G $28\ cm^2$
H $40\ cm^2$
J $84\ cm^2$

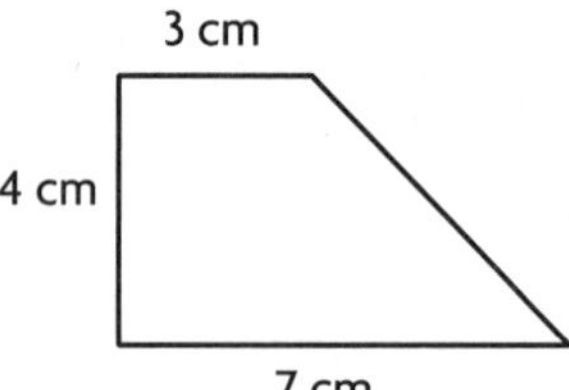

For 15–16, find the area of each circle to the nearest whole number. Use 3.14 for π.

15. $r = 3.5$ cm

A $11\ cm^2$
B $22\ cm^2$
C $38\ cm^2$
D $154\ cm^2$

16. $d = 16$ in.

F $50\ in.^2$
G $100\ in.^2$
H $201\ in.^2$
J $804\ in.^2$

For 17–19, find the surface area.

17.

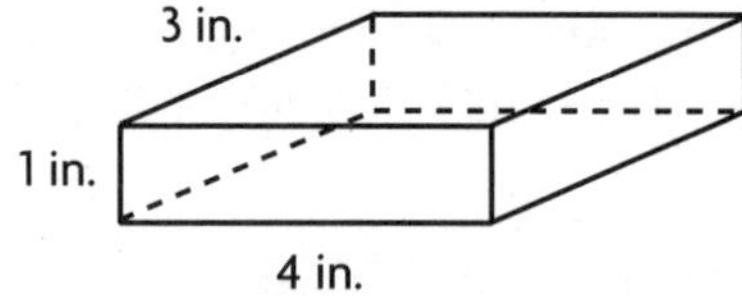

A $72\ in.^2$
B $38\ in.^2$
C $26\ in.^2$
D $12\ in.^2$

18.

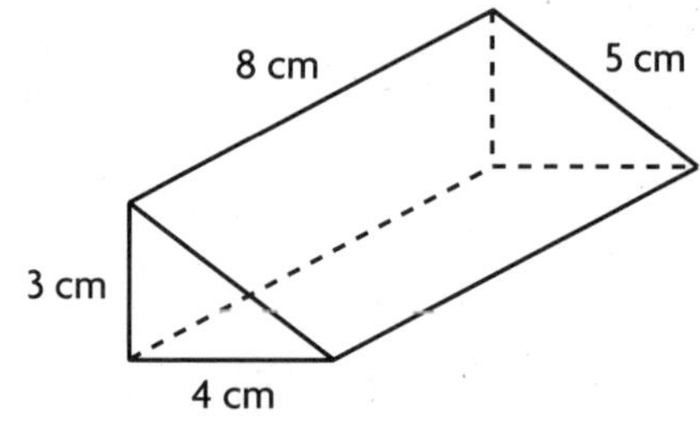

F $240\ cm^2$
G $108\ cm^2$
H $102\ cm^2$
J $96\ cm^2$

19.

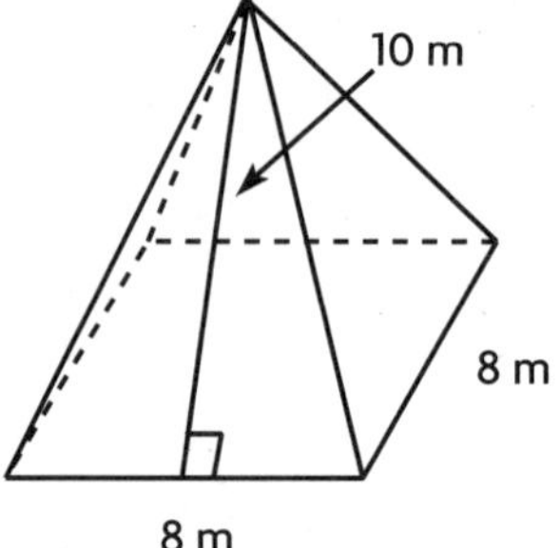

A $64\ m^2$
B $160\ m^2$
C $224\ m^2$
D $640\ m^2$

20. Leona has a rectangular herb garden that is 2.5 m long and 1.2 m wide. What is the area of the herb garden?

F $1.5\ m^2$
G $3.0\ m^2$
H $3.7\ m^2$
J $7.4\ m^2$

Stop

Name ____________________

Write the correct answer.

1. Estimate the area of the figure. Each square on the grid represents 1 cm^2.

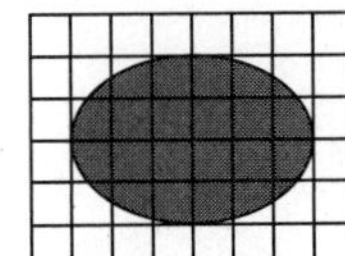

____

2. Find the area of the circle to the nearest whole number. Use 3.14 for π.

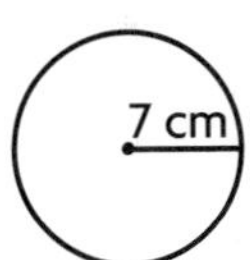

____

For 3–6, find the area.

3. 5 cm; 3 cm; 2 cm; 6 cm

____

4.

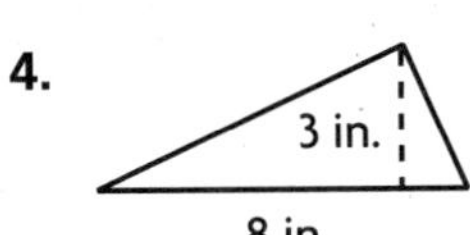

____

5.

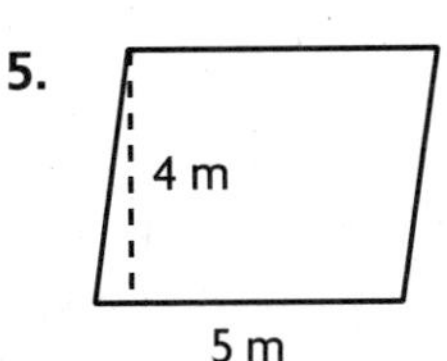

____

6. 5 ft; 9 ft

____

7. Find the surface area.

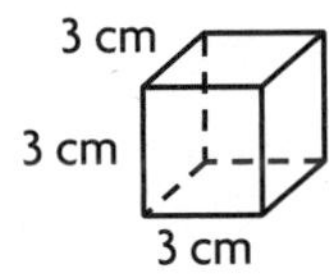

____

8. A circular patio has a radius of 9 ft. What is the area of the patio to the nearest whole number? (Use 3.14 for π.)

____

9. Find the area.

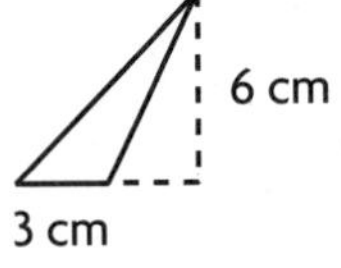

____

10. A rectangular box is 4 ft long, 5 ft wide, and 3 ft tall. How many square feet of paper are needed to cover the outside of the box?

____

Go On

Name ____________________

For 11–14, find the area.

11.

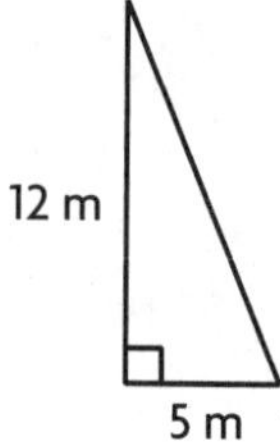

____

12.

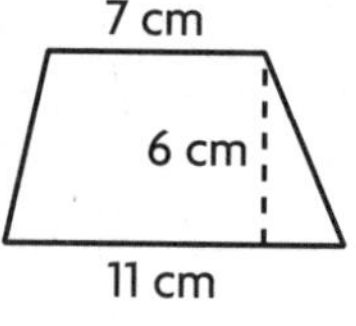

____

13.

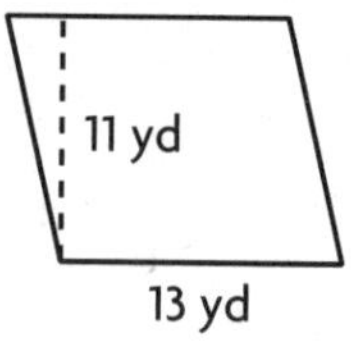

____

14.

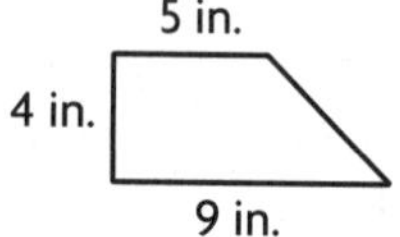

____

For 15–16, find the area of each circle to the nearest whole number. Use 3.14 for π.

15. $r = 2.6$ cm

____

16. $d = 11$ in.

____

For 17–19, find the surface area.

17.

2 in.
6 in.
5 in.

____

18.

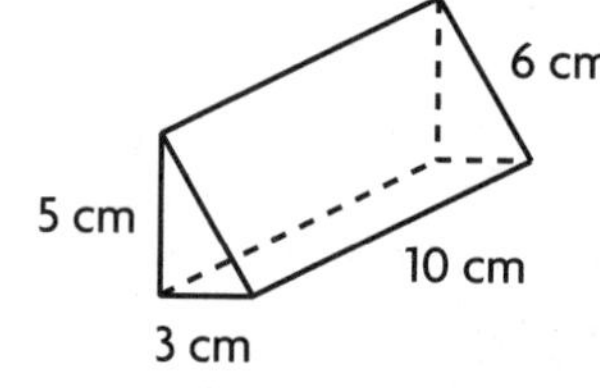

____

19.

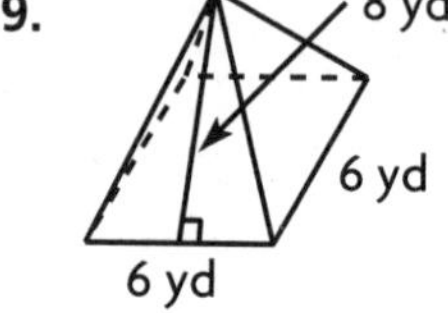

____

20. Ron has a circular vegetable garden that has a 2.6 m diameter. What is the area of the garden to the nearest whole number? (Use 3.14 for π.)

____

Stop

Name ______________________________

Choose the best answer.

For 1–10, find the volume of the solid.

1. A 1,500 m^3
   B 750 m^3
   C 475 m^3
   D 40 m^3

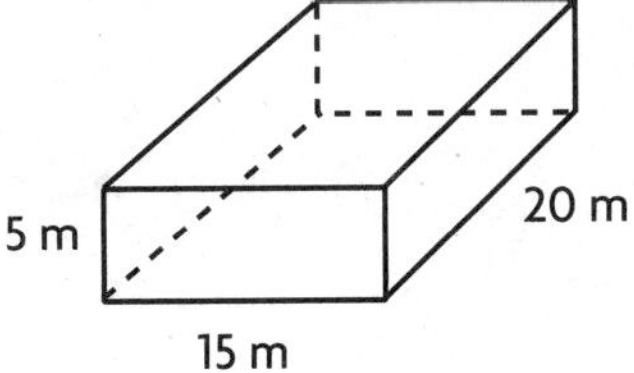

2. F 81 $in.^3$
   G 108 $in.^3$
   H 162 $in.^3$
   J 324 $in.^3$

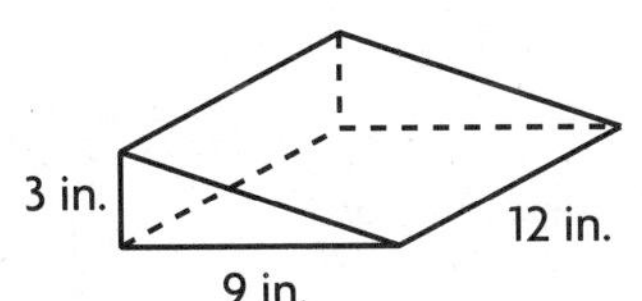

3. A 6 yd^3
   B 3 yd^3
   C 1 yd^3
   D $\frac{1}{3}$ yd^3

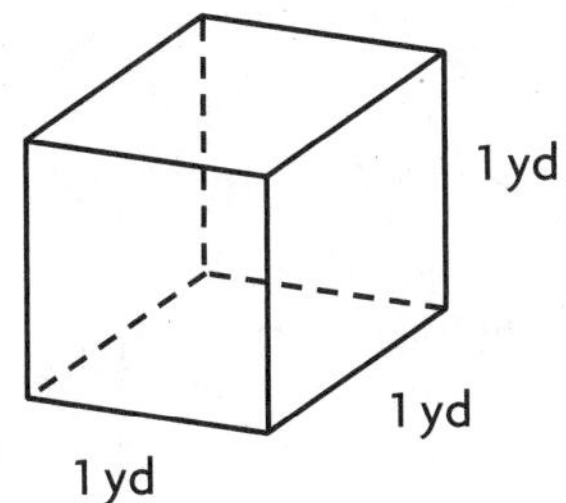

4. F 1,800 ft^3
   G 1,200 ft^3
   H 900 ft^3
   J 600 ft^3

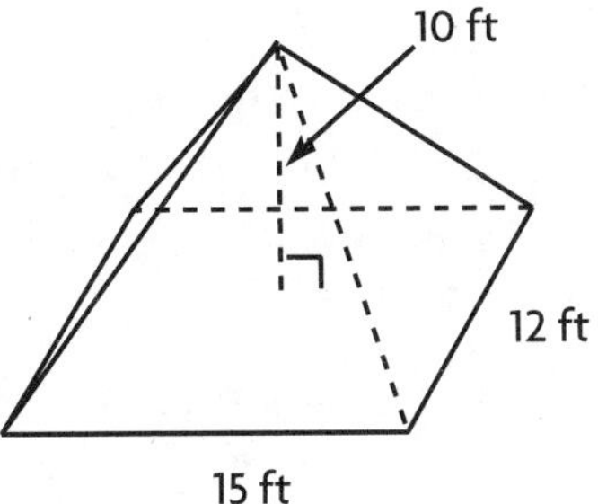

5. A rectangular pyramid with the following dimensions:

   length = 8 cm
   width = 12 cm
   height = 9 cm

   A 288 cm^3
   B 432 cm^3
   C 864 cm^3
   D 2,592 cm^3

6. F $12\frac{1}{2}$ ft^3
   G $8\frac{3}{4}$ ft^3
   H $7\frac{1}{2}$ ft^3
   J $4\frac{3}{8}$ ft^3

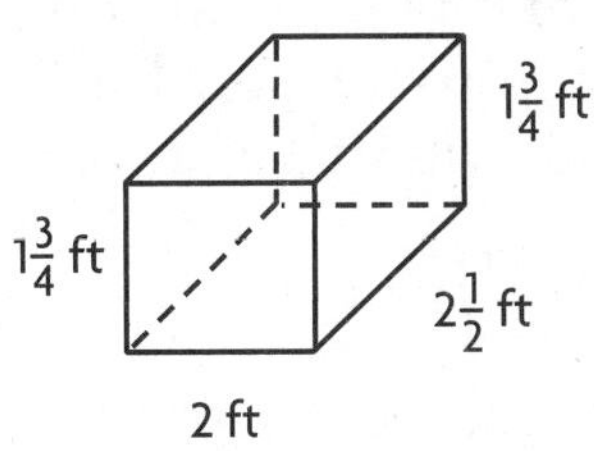

7. A 69.12 m^3
   B 43.24 m^3
   C 34.56 m^3
   D 17.28 m^3

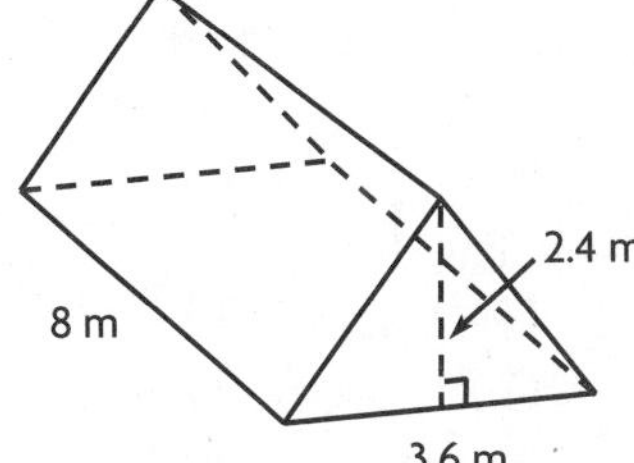

8. F 4.8 $in.^3$
   G 1.44 $in.^3$
   H 0.72 $in.^3$
   J 0.48 $in.^3$

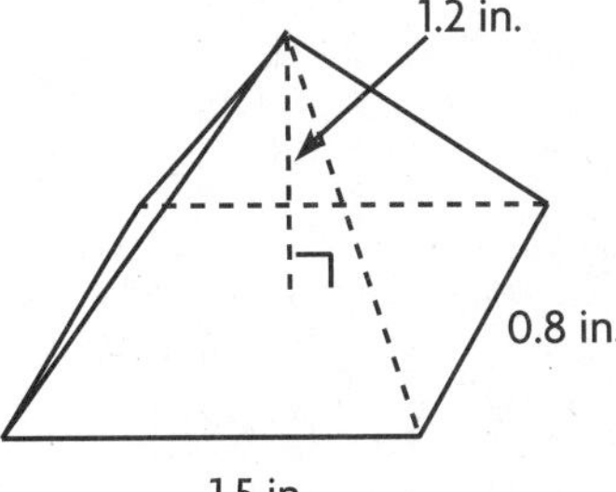

9. A 400 mm^3
   B 40 mm^3
   C 20 mm^3
   D 15 mm^3

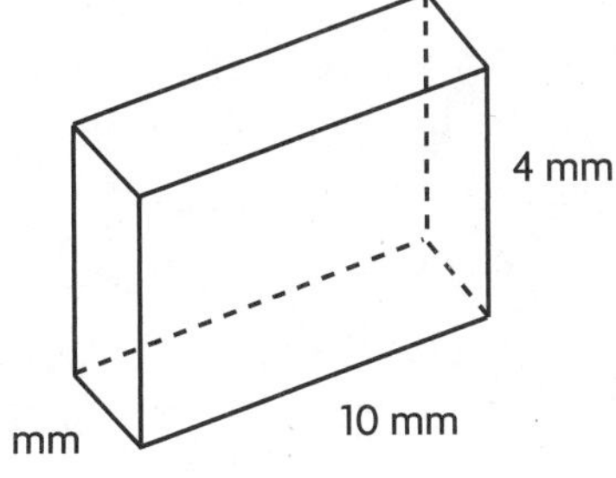

10. A pyramid with the following dimensions:

    base = 36 $in.^2$
    height =5 in.

    F 180 $in.^3$
    G 90 $in.^3$
    H 60 $in.^3$
    J 41 $in.^3$

Go On

Name ______________________________

For 11–13, find the volume of the cylinder. Round to the nearest whole number. (Use 3.14 for the value of π).

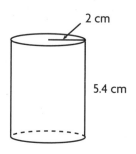

2 cm

5.4 cm

11. A about 34 cm^3
    B about 68 cm^3
    C about 108 cm^3
    D about 271 cm^3

12. F about 353 $in.^3$
    G about 177 $in.^3$
    H about 143 $in.^3$
    J about 88 $in.^3$

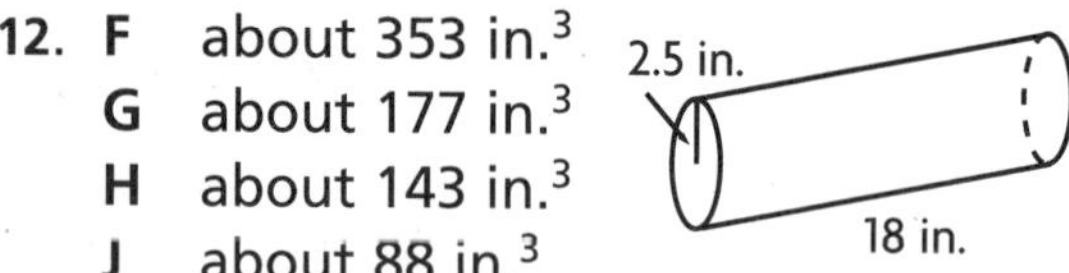

13. A about 345 ft^3
    B about 550 ft^3
    C about 950 ft^3
    D about 1,727 ft^3

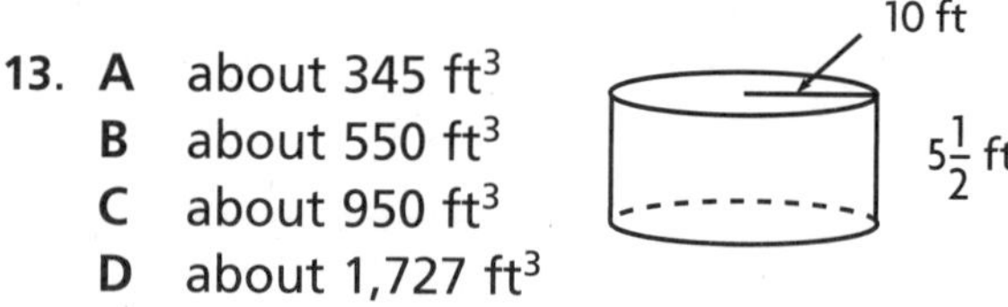

14. A rectangular carton for packaging oranges is 18 in. wide, 24 in. long, and 12 in. high. What is the volume of the carton?

    F 10,368 $in.^3$ H 1,728 $in.^3$
    G 5,184 $in.^3$ J 432 $in.^3$

15. A cylindrical metal drum for shipping coffee beans has a radius of 1.5 ft and a height of 4 ft. Find the volume of the drum to the nearest cubic foot. (Use 3.14 for the value of π).

    A 4,069 ft^3 C 28 ft^3
    B 113 ft^3 D 19 ft^3

For questions 16–18, find the volume of the inside cylinder. Round to the nearest whole number. (Use 3.14 for the value of π).

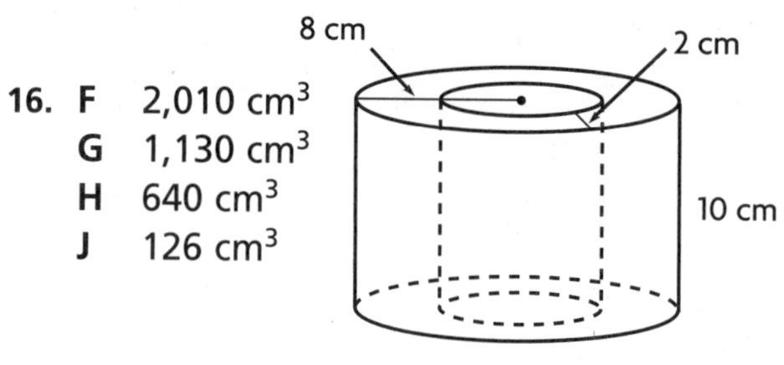

16. F 2,010 cm^3
    G 1,130 cm^3
    H 640 cm^3
    J 126 cm^3

2 yd

3 yd

3 yd

17. A 126 yd^3
    B 85 yd^3
    C 38 yd^3
    D 9 yd^3

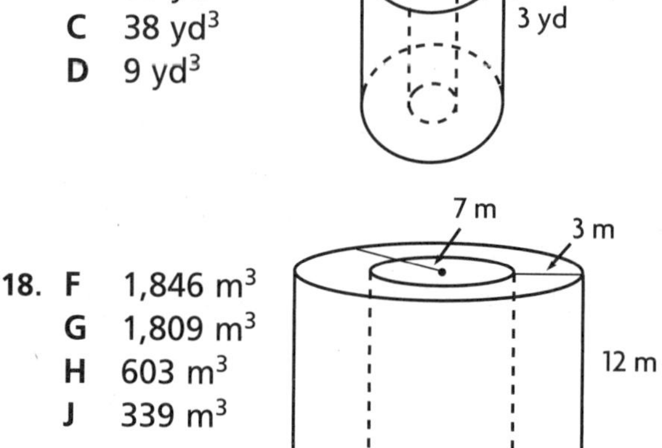

18. F 1,846 m^3
    G 1,809 m^3
    H 603 m^3
    J 339 m^3

19. A box measures 10 cm high, 8 cm wide, and 12 cm long. If the length and width are tripled, what happens to the volume?

    A It becomes 3 times larger.
    B It becomes 6 times larger.
    C It becomes 9 times larger.
    D It becomes 27 times larger.

20. The radius of a cylinder is doubled. How does this affect the volume?

    F The volume is quadrupled.
    G The volume is tripled.
    H The volume is doubled.
    J The volume remains the same.

Stop

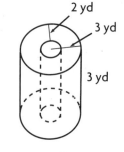

Name ______________________

Write the correct answer.

For 1–10, find the volume. Round to the nearest whole number.

1. 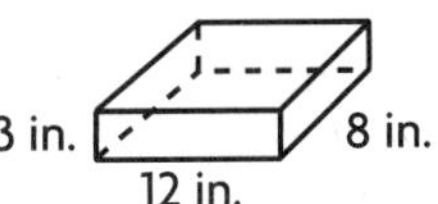

____

2. 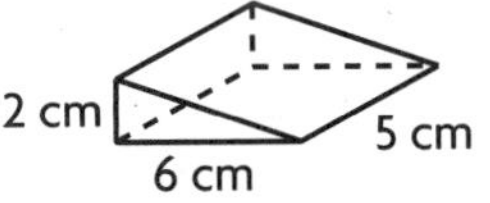

____

3. 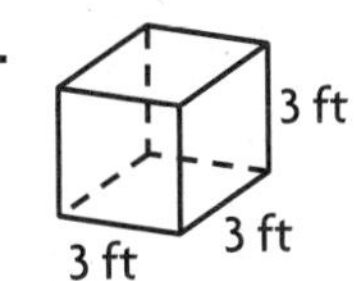

____

4. 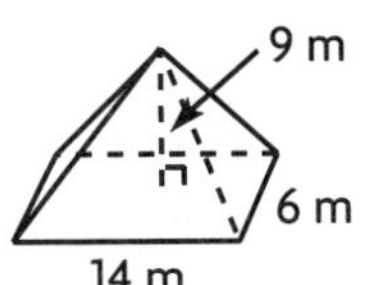

____

5. A rectangular pyramid with the following dimensions:

length = 7 cm
width = 2 cm
height = 12 cm

____

6. 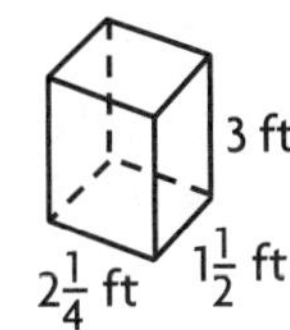

____

7. 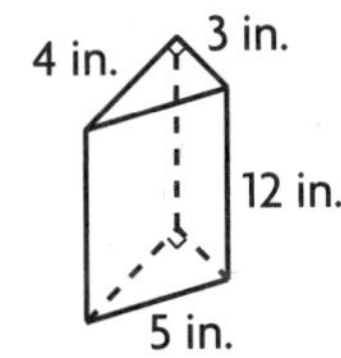

____

8. 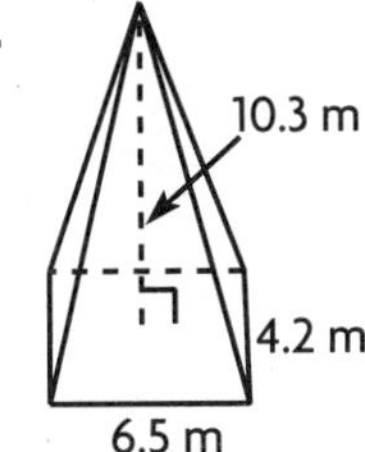

____

9. 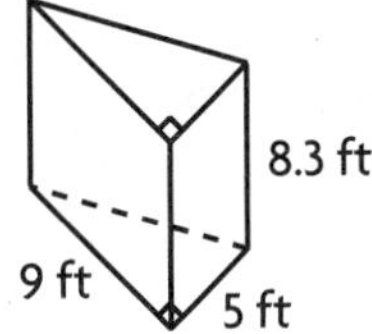

____

10. A pyramid with the following dimensions:

base = 64 in.^{2}
height = 3 in.

____

Go On

For 11–13, find the volume of the cylinder. Round to the nearest whole number. (Use 3.14 for the value of π.)

11. 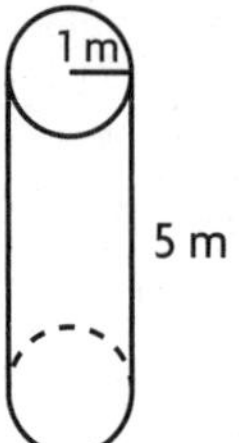

____

12. 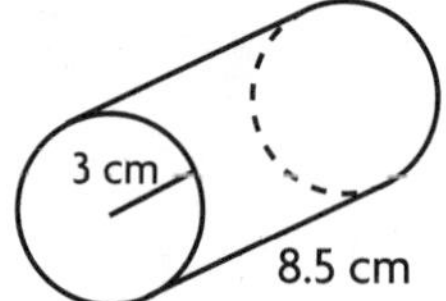

____

13. 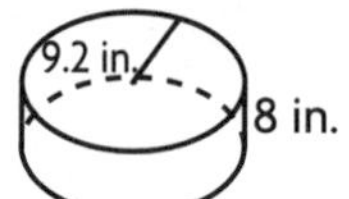

____

14. A rectangular carton for shipping T-shirts is 36 in. wide, 18 in. long, and 18 in. high. What is the volume of the carton?

____

15. A cylindrical metal tank for shipping chemicals has a radius of 0.5 m and a height of 5 m. Find the volume of the drum to the nearest cubic meter. (Use 3.14 for the value of π.)

____

For 16–18, find the volume of the inside cylinder. Round to the nearest whole number. (Use 3.14 for the value of π.)

16. 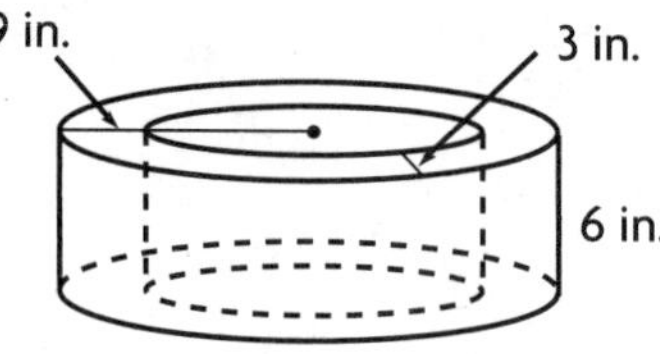

____

17. 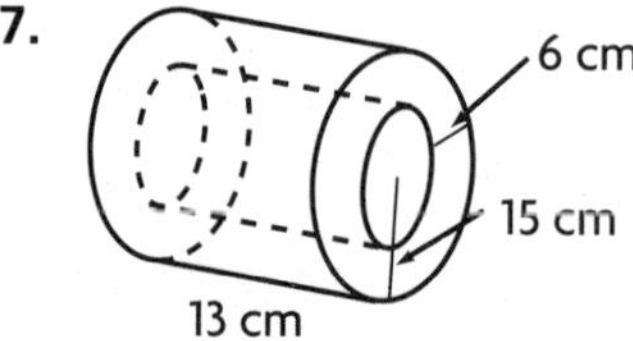

____

18. 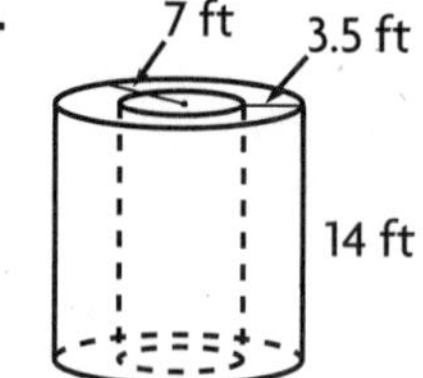

____

19. A box measures 8 cm high, 6 cm wide, and 10 cm long. If the length and width are doubled, what happens to the volume?

____

20. The radius of a cylinder is tripled. How does this affect the volume?

____

Stop

Name ______________________________

Choose the best answer.

1. Which is the most appropriate unit of measurement for the amount of fuel an automobile gas tank can hold?

   A kilogram
   B milliliter
   C centimeter
   D liter

2. The distance around a circle is called the __?__ .

   F diameter
   G circumference
   H perimeter
   J radius

3. Find the area.

   A 100 yd^2
   B 75 yd^2
   C 50 yd^2
   D 25 yd^2

4. The number of cubic units needed to occupy a given space is the __?__ .

   F area
   G circumference
   H volume
   J perimeter

5. Use a proportion to convert to the given unit.

   5.9 L = ■ mL

   A 5,900
   B 590
   C 0.059
   D 0.0059

6. Find the perimeter.

   8 m, 10 m, 6 m, 2 m, 14 m

   F 20 m
   G 30 m
   H 36 m
   J 40 m

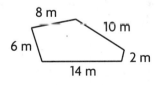

7. Find the area.

   8 mm, 2 mm, 16 mm

   A 48 mm^2
   B 36 mm^2
   C 26 mm^2
   D 24 mm^2

8. Find the volume of the cylinder. Use 3.14 for π.

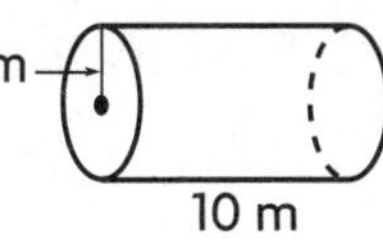

   F 283 m^3
   G 270 m^3
   H 188 m^3
   J 94 m

9. Use a proportion to convert to the given unit.

   $3\frac{1}{2}$ yd = ■ in.

   A 144
   B 126
   C 108
   D 42

10. Find the diameter of a circle with a circumference of 190.9 in. Use 3.14 for π.

    F 121.6 in.
    G 60.8 in.
    H 30.4 in.
    J 5.5 in.

11. Find the area of a circle with a radius of 2 in. Use 3.14 for π.

    A 3.14 in.^{2}
    B 6.28 in.^{2}
    C 12.56 in.^{2}
    D 25.12 in.^{2}

12. A rectangular box has sides that measure 4, 5, and 6 inches. What is the volume?

    F 15 in.^{3}
    G 77 in.^{3}
    H 120 in.^{3}
    J 225 in.^{3}

13. To make pillows for a couch, Dan needs 4 lengths of fabric, each $14\frac{1}{2}$ in. long. He has 2 yd of fabric. Does he have enough? Does he need an exact measurement or an estimate?

    A no; estimate
    B yes; estimate
    C yes; exact
    D no; exact

14. The perimeter is 28.5 cm. Find the unknown length.

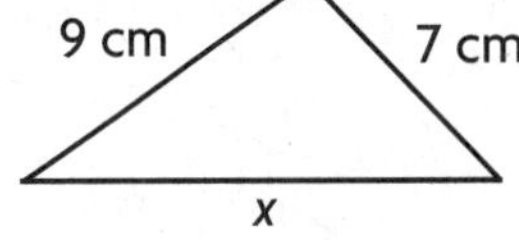

    F $x = 12.5$ cm
    G $x = 11.5$ cm
    H $x = 10.5$ cm
    J $x = 9.5$ cm

Go On

15. Find the surface area of the box.

A $9\ ft^2$
B $27\ ft^2$
C $54\ ft^2$
D $81\ ft^2$

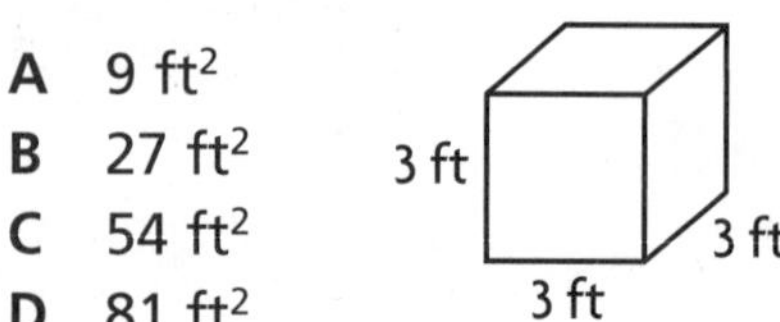

16. Find the volume of the inside cylinder to the nearest whole number. Use 3.14 for π.

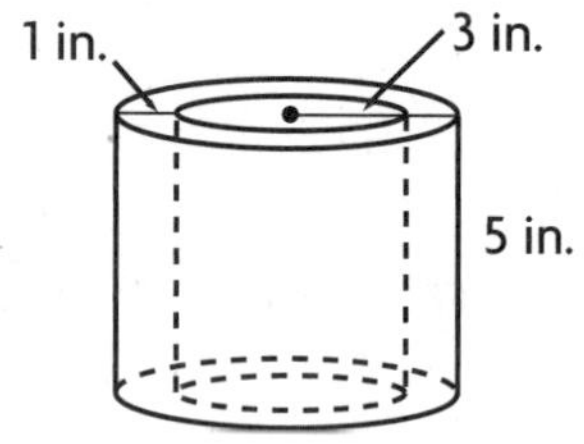

F about 63 $in.^3$ H about 31 $in.^3$
G about 47 $in.^3$ J about 16 $in.^3$

17. Choose the most precise measurement for an individual's weight.

A 0.6 kg C 604 g
B 60,045 cg D 600,402 mg

18. Ken wants to use a wallpaper border for a room that is 8 ft. × 10 ft. How many feet of wallpaper border will he need to buy?

F 80 ft H 18 ft
G 36 ft J 10 ft

19. Noah needs to paint a rectangular box with dimensions 5 in. × 7 in. × 9 in. How many square inches will he paint?

A 286 $in.^2$ C 572 $in.^2$
B 315 $in.^2$ D 630 $in.^2$

20. Find the volume.

F 15,000 ft^3
G 10,000 ft^3
H 7,500 ft^3
J 5,000 ft^3

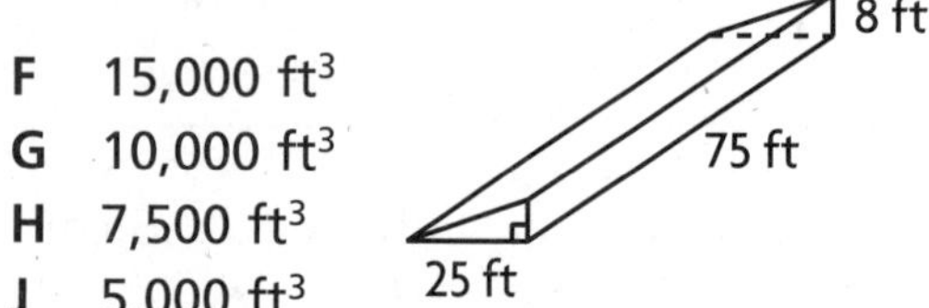

21. Faye is buying molding to make several picture frames. Which will give the most precise measurement?

A kilometer C centimeter
B decimeter D millimeter

22. Find the circumference of the circle. Use 3.14 for π.

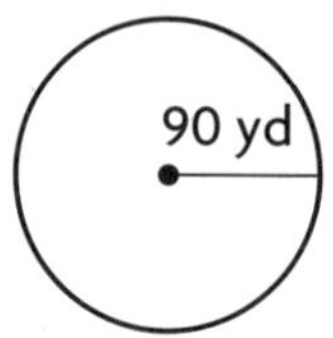

F 565.2 yd H 270 yd
G 282.6 yd J 93.14 yd

23. Find the area.

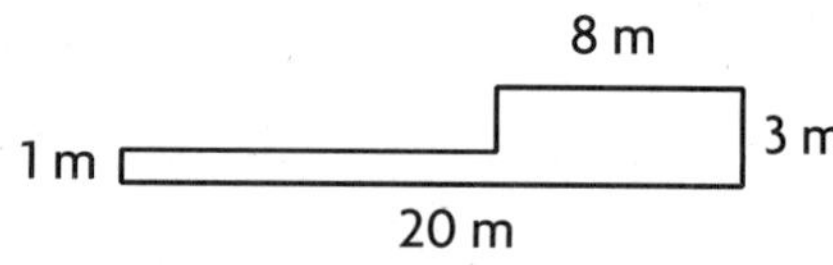

A $36\ m^2$ C $60\ m^2$
B $44\ m^2$ D $84\ m^2$

24. The diameter of a cylinder is tripled. How does this affect the volume?

F It becomes 2 times as large.
G It becomes 3 times as large.
H It becomes 6 times as large.
J It becomes 9 times as large.

25. You purchase an 18 ft tall flagpole for your house. What is the height of the flagpole in meters? (1 in. ≈ 2.54 cm)

A 54 m C 5.5 m
B 6 m D 0.0055 m

26. A regular pentagon has sides that measure 10 cm each. Find the perimeter of the pentagon.

F 60 cm H 31.4 cm
G 50 cm J 10 cm

Go On

27. A circle has area 50.24 ft^2. What is its diameter? (Use 3.14 for π.)

A 4 ft
B 8 ft
C 16 ft
D 256 ft

28. Find the volume.

F 1,152 ft^3
G 1,728 ft^3
H 2,304 ft^3
J 4,608 ft^3

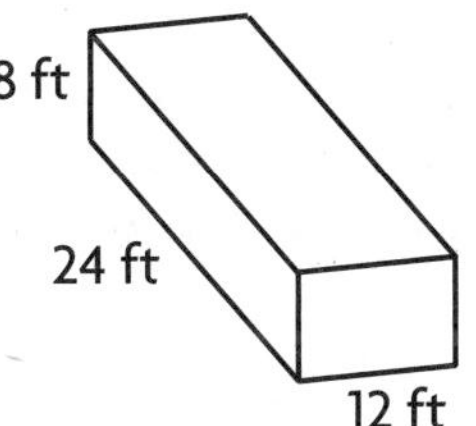

29. Marian has \$14.25. She needs to purchase 2 gal milk for \$2.59 each, 3 dozen eggs at \$1.09 a dozen, and 1 large bag flour for \$4.59. Does she have enough money? Does she need an estimate or exact value?

A no; estimate
B yes; estimate
C no; exact
D yes; exact

30. Leticia wants to build a 10 ft × 25 ft rectangular pen for her pet. She will use the barn as one of the long sides. How much fencing will she need?

F 250 ft
G 70 ft
H 60 ft
J 45 ft

31. Find the surface area.

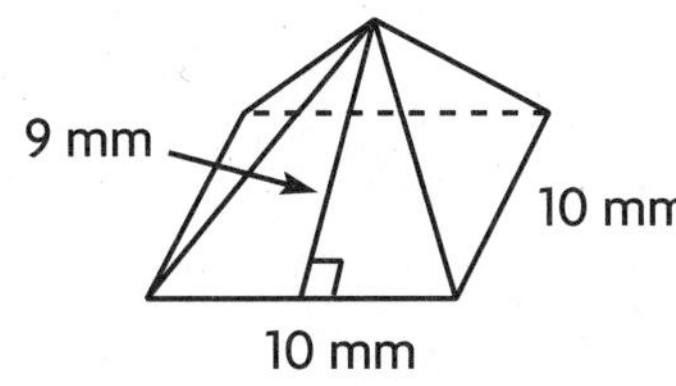

A 280 mm^2
B 190 mm^2
C 180 mm^2
D 145 mm^2

32. Find the volume.

F 1,458 m^3
G 1,944 m^3
H 2,916 m^3
J 5,184 m^3

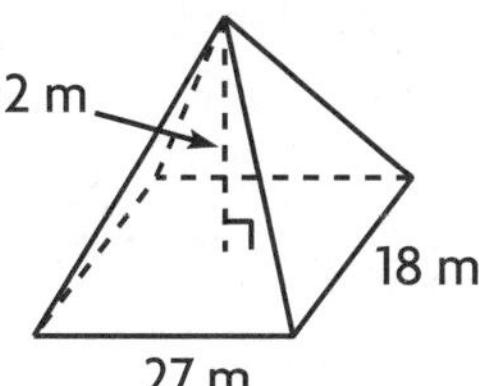

33. Which unit of measurement is most appropriate to measure the length of a canoe?

A inch
B foot
C quart
D ton

34. A square field has a perimeter of 6,400 yd. How long is each side of the field?

F 3,200 yd
G 1,600 yd
H 800 yd
J 80 yd

35. Find the area of the figure shown below. The ends are semicircles. Use 3.14 for π.

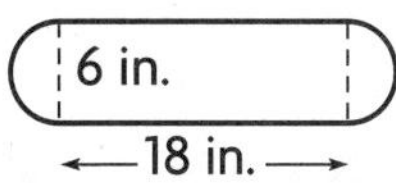

A 108 $in.^2$
B 113.04 $in.^2$
C 120 $in.^2$
D 136.26 $in.^2$

36. What is the volume of a pyramid with a height of 9 m and a base area of 25 m^2?

F 75 m^3
G 112.5 m^3
H 225 m^3
J 450 m^3

37. Use a proportion to convert to the given unit. (1 mi ≈ 1.61 km)

172 mi ≈ ■ km

A 107
B 172
C 277
D 333

38. A circular trampoline has a 15 ft diameter. What is its circumference? (Use 3.14 for π.)

F 15 ft
G 23.55 ft
H 30 ft
J 47.10 ft

Go On

Name ______________________________

39. A pyramid has a square base with sides that measure 8 in. The height of each of the triangular faces is 10 in. Find the surface area of the pyramid.

A 144 in.^2 C 176 in.^2
B 160 in.^2 D 224 in.^2

40. Crude oil is shipped in barrels 30 in. in diameter and 48 in. high. What is the volume of one of these barrels? (Use 3.14 for π.)

F $135{,}648 \text{ in.}^3$ H $56{,}790 \text{ in.}^3$
G $67{,}824 \text{ in.}^3$ J $33{,}912 \text{ in.}^3$

41. Marge and Reuben have a 75-gal fuel oil tank at their home. Convert this into liters. (1 gal $\approx$ 3.79 L)

A 20 L C 284 L
B 75 L D 300 L

42. The shorter sides of a rectangle are 24 cm long. The perimeter is 114 cm. How long are the longer sides?

F 28.5 cm H 57 cm
G 33 cm J 66 cm

43. Find the area.

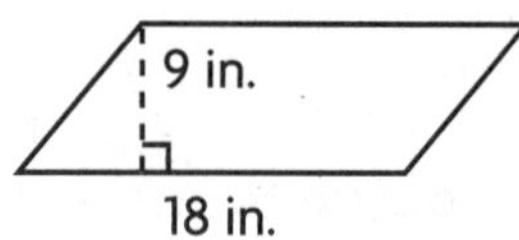

A 108 in.^2 C 162 in.^2
B 144 in.^2 D 270 in.^2

44. The length of a box is doubled, but the width and height remain the same. What happens to the volume?

F It doubles. H It quadruples.
G It triples. J It doesn't change.

45. José needs to cut 47 in. of wire for one project, 23 in. for another, and 130 in. for a third. He has 6 yd of wire. Does he have enough? Did he need an estimate or exact answer?

A yes; exact C yes; estimate
B no; exact D no; estimate

46. The radius of a circle is $4\frac{1}{5}$ in. What is its circumference? (Use $\frac{22}{7}$ for π.)

F $52\frac{4}{5}$ in. H $13\frac{1}{5}$ in.
G $26\frac{2}{5}$ in. J $12\frac{1}{35}$ in.

47. Mrs. Grant wants to irrigate 3 circular fields of radius 50 ft, 65 ft, and 80 ft. To the nearest hundred, how many square feet should she plan to water? (Use 3.14 for the value of π.)

A $41{,}200 \text{ ft}^2$ C $119{,}400 \text{ ft}^2$
B $114{,}100 \text{ ft}^2$ D $164{,}900 \text{ ft}^2$

48. Find the volume.

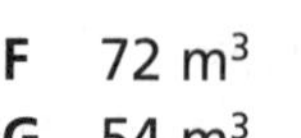

F 72 m^3
G 54 m^3
H 36 m^3
J 24 m^3

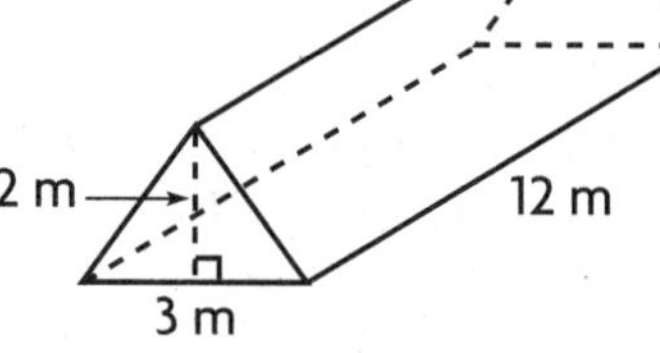

49. Marcus won the long-jump event at the school Olympics. Which measurement is most reasonable for his jump?

A 2 mi C 4 km
B 6 ft D 548 in.

50. The distance around a polygon is called the __?__ .

F length H diameter
G circumference J perimeter

Stop

Name ______________________

Write the correct answer.

1. What is the most appropriate metric unit of measurement for the amount of soda a can holds?

____

2. A line segment that passes through the center of a circle and has both endpoints on the circle is called a __?__ .

____

3. Find the area.

4 m

12 m

____

4. The sum of the areas of the faces of a solid figure is the __?__ .

____

5. Use a proportion to convert to the given unit.

   3.8 L = ■ mL

____

6. Find the perimeter.

3 in.

7 in.

____

7. Find the area.

5 cm

14 cm

____

8. Find the volume of the cylinder. Use 3.14 for π.

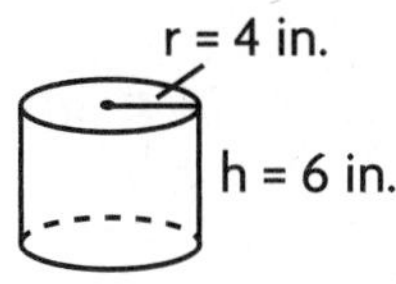

____

9. Use a proportion to convert $4\frac{1}{2}$ yd to inches.

____

10. Find the diameter of a circle with a circumference of 50.24 m. Use 3.14 for π.

____

11. Find the area of a circle with a radius of 8 in. Use 3.14 for π.

____

12. A rectangular box has sides of 3, 6, and 7 inches. What is the volume?

____

13. To set up her stereo Pat needs 4 pieces of speaker wire, each $5\frac{1}{2}$ ft long. Pat has 8 yd of wire. Does she have enough? Does she need an exact measurement or an estimate?

____

14. The perimeter is 16.9 cm. Find the unknown length.

3 cm

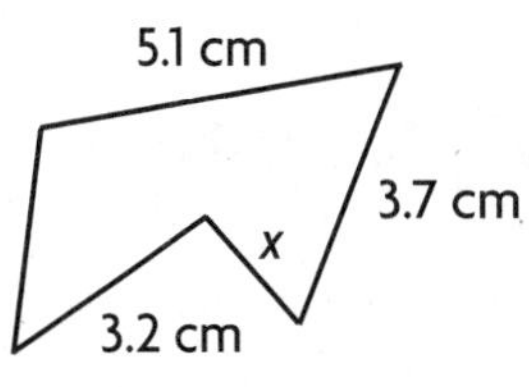

____

Go On

15. Find the surface area of the box.

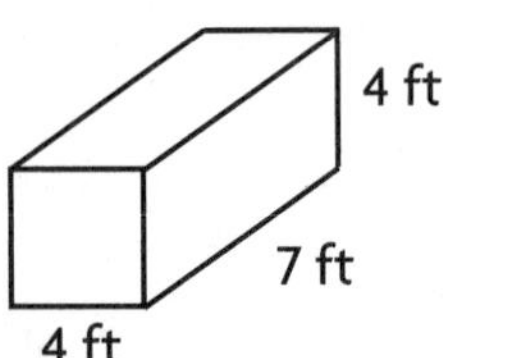

______

16. Find the volume of the inside cylinder to the nearest whole number. Use 3.14 for π.

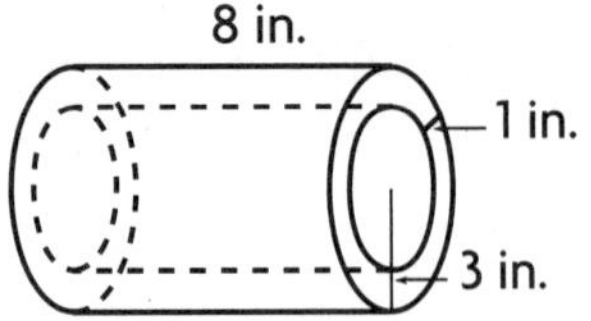

______

17. What is the most common customary measurement for an individual's weight?

______

18. Cinzia wants to put a decorative fence around a garden that is 6 ft $\times$ 12 ft. How many feet of fencing will she need?

______

19. Chris needs to wrap a rectangular box with dimensions 4 in. $\times$ 5 in. $\times$ 13 in. How many square inches of wrapping paper will he use if there is no overlap?

______

20. Find the volume.

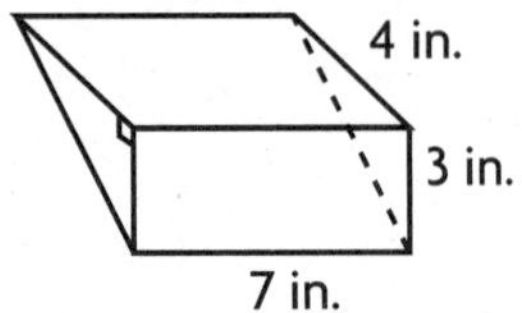

______

21. Faye is going to put fringe around several pillows. Which customary measurement will give her a more precise measurement, inches or feet?

______

22. Find the circumference of the circle. Use 3.14 for π.

______

23. Find the area.

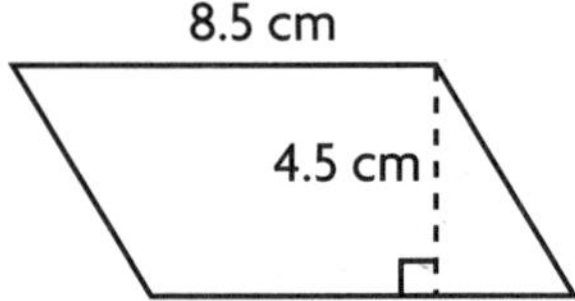

______

24. The radius of a circle is tripled. How does this affect its area?

______

25. A tree in Kim's back yard is 22 ft tall. What is its height in meters? (1 in. $\approx$ 2.54 cm)

______

26. A regular pentagon has sides that measure 18 cm. Find the perimeter of the pentagon.

______

Go On

Name ______________________________

27. A circle has a circumference of 43.96 ft. What is its diameter? Use 3.14 for the value of π.

____

28. Find the volume.

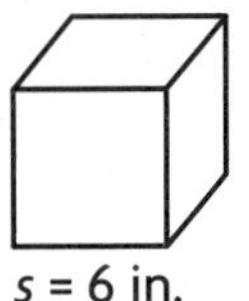

$s = 6$ in.

____

29. Lisa has $50 and wants to purchase a game for $24.95, 2 packs of batteries at $2.59 each, and 3 rolls of film at $3.39 each. Does she have enough money? Does she need an estimate or exact value?

____

30. Stephen wants to fence in his backyard, which measures 15 yd × 25 yd. He will use his house as one of the short sides. How much fencing does he need?

____

31. Find the surface area.

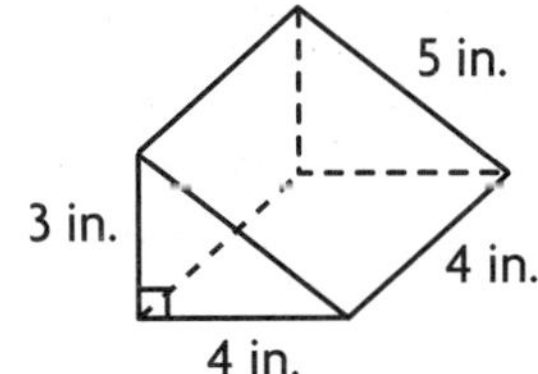

____

32. What is the volume of a pyramid with a height of 5 m and a base area of 36 m^2?

____

33. What metric unit of measurement is appropriate to measure the length of a paper clip?

____

34. A square courtyard has a perimeter of 120 yd. How long is each side of the courtyard?

____

35. Find the area of the figure shown below. Use 3.14 for π.

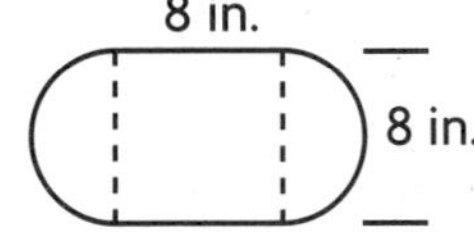

____

36. Find the volume.

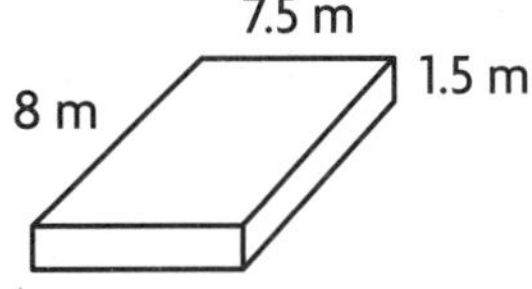

____

37. Use a proportion to convert to the given unit. (1 mi ≈ 1.61 km)

203 mi ≈ ■ km

____

38. A circular parachute has an 18 ft diameter. What is its circumference? (Use 3.14 for π.)

____

Go On

Name ______________________________

39. A pyramid has a square base with sides that measure 6 in. The height of the triangular faces is 12 in. Find the surface area of the pyramid.

____

40. What is the volume of a barrel that has a diameter of 20 in. and a height of 36 in.? Use 3.14 for π.

____

41. Ms. Catalanello's car used 120 gallons of gas last month. Convert this into liters. (1 gal $\approx$ 3.79 L)

____

42. The shorter sides of a rectangle are 14 m long. The perimeter is 100 m. How long are the longer sides?

____

43. Find the area.

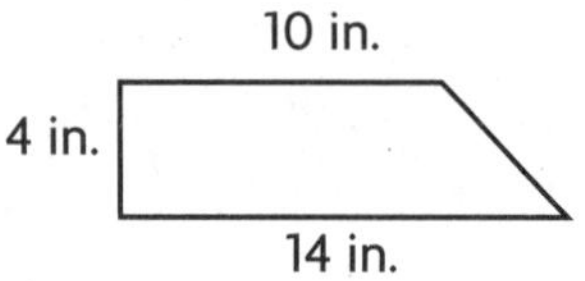

____

44. The length of a box is tripled, but the width and height remain the same. What happens to the volume?

____

45. André needs to cut 38 in. of tubing for one science project, 18 in. for another, and 155 in. for a third. He has $5\frac{1}{2}$ yd of tubing. Does he have enough? Does he need an exact answer or an estimate?

____

46. The radius of a circle is $5\frac{3}{5}$ in. What is its circumference? (Use $\frac{22}{7}$ for π.)

____

47. Pauline cut 3 fabric circles with radii of 34 cm, 54 cm, and 84 cm. Find the total area of the three fabric cirles to the nearest hundred centimeters. (Use 3.14 for π.)

____

48. Find the volume.

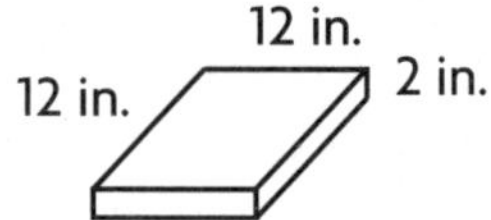

____

49. Melanie is expecting to complete the New York City Marathon in about 4 hours. What customary unit of measurement is most appropriate to measure the distance of the run?

____

50. The distance around a circle is called the __?__ .

____

Stop

Name ___________________________________

Choose the best answer.

1. A(n) ________ has a repeating pattern containing shapes that are like the whole, but of different sizes.

   A term C function
   B sequence D fractal

For 2–6, tell which is the rule for the sequence.

2. 73, 67, 61, . . .

   F add 7 H subtract 6
   G divide by 7 J subtract 7

3. 3, 24, 192, . . .

   A divide by 8 C multiply by 9
   B add 21 D multiply by 8

4. 21, 7, $2\frac{1}{3}$, . . .

   F subtract 14 H multiply by 3
   G divide by 3 J divide by $\frac{1}{3}$

5. 2.56, 12.8, 64, . . .

   A multiply by 5 C multiply by 2
   B divide by 5 D divide by 2

6. 5.8, 7.9, 10.0, . . .

   F add 2.1 H multiply by 1.4
   G subtract 2.1 J add 1.1

For 7–10, find the next three possible terms in each sequence

7. 6, 3, $1\frac{1}{2}$, . . .

   A $\frac{1}{4}, \frac{1}{8}, \frac{1}{16}$ C $\frac{3}{4}, \frac{3}{8}, \frac{3}{16}$
   B $\frac{3}{2}, \frac{3}{4}, \frac{3}{8}$ D 0, $^-3$, $^-6$

8. 12, 17, 22, . . .

   F 22, 27, 32 H 17, 12, 7
   G 32, 37, 42 J 27, 32, 37

9. 1, $^-2$, 4, . . .

   A 8, 16, 32 C 8, $^-16$, 32
   B $^-8$, 16, $^-32$ D $^-6$, 8, $^-10$

10. $^-8$, $^-14$, $^-20$, . . .

   F $^-26$, $^-32$, $^-38$ H $^-26$, 32, $^-38$
   G $^-24$, $^-30$, $^-34$ J $^-25$, $^-33$, $^-40$

11. Mr. Reese received 49 e-mails in July, 60 in August, and 71 in September. If this pattern continues, how many e-mails will he receive in December?

   A 82 e-mails C 104 e-mails
   B 93 e-mails D 213 e-mails

12. An elevator started down from the 75th floor. Five seconds later, it was at the 71st floor. Five seconds after that, it was at the 67th floor. If this pattern continues, at what floor will it be 60 seconds after it started down?

   F 31st floor H 23rd floor
   G 27th floor J 15th floor

Go On

Name ______________________________________

For 13–16, tell which equation represents the function.

13.

x	1	2	3	4	5
y	7	14	21	28	35

A $y = x + 7$ C $y = x \div 7$
B $y = 7x$ D $y = x + 6$

14.

x	0	5	10	15	20
y	7	12	17	22	27

F $y = x + 7$ H $y = 7x$
G $y = x - 7$ J $y = 5x$

15.

x	$^{-}2$	$^{-}1$	0	1	2
y	$^{-}5$	$^{-}4$	$^{-}3$	$^{-}2$	$^{-}1$

A $y = x - 3$ C $y = x + 5$
B $y = x + 3$ D $y = x \div 1$

16.

x	128	64	32	16	8
y	32	16	8	4	2

F $y = x + 8$ H $y = 4x$
G $y = 8x$ J $y = x \div 4$

For 17–19, identify the next two figures in the pattern.

17. 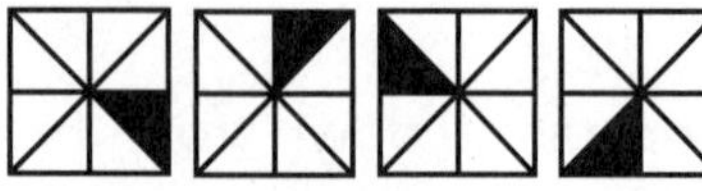

A 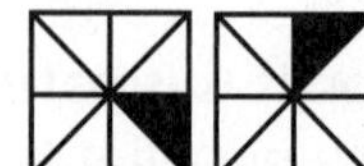

C 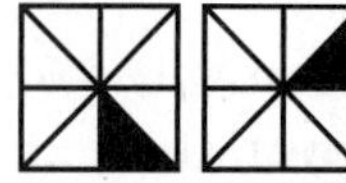

B 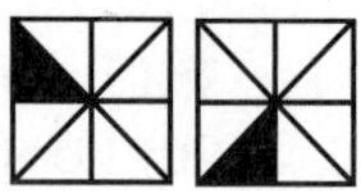

D 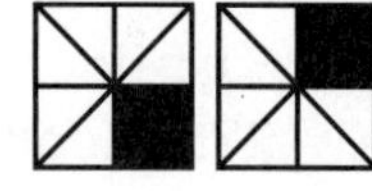

18. 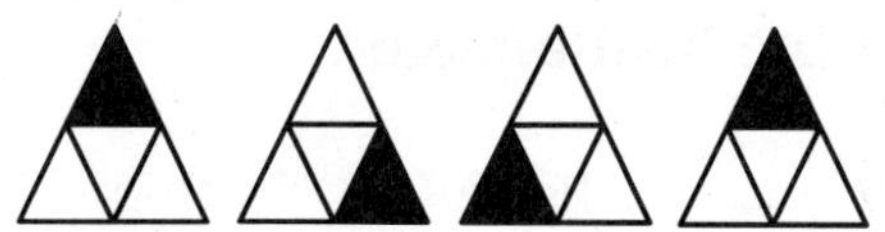

F 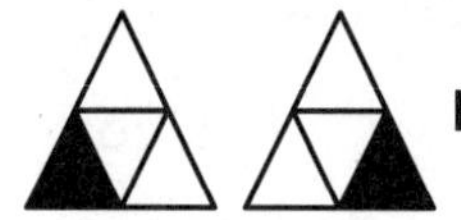

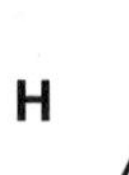

H 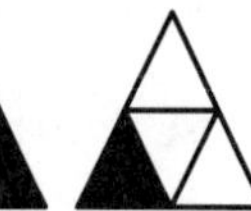

G 

J 

19. 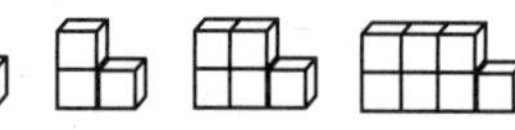

A 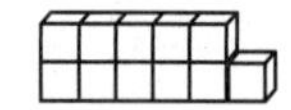

B 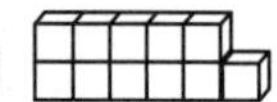

C 

D 

20. Look at the following pattern. How many small squares are in the seventh figure?

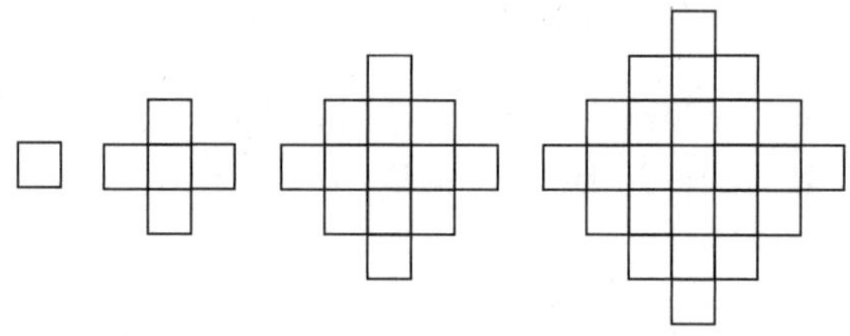

F 7 squares
G 61 squares
H 85 squares
J 113 squares

Stop

Name ______________________________

Write the correct answer.

1. What has a repeating pattern containing shapes that are like the whole, but of different sizes?

____

For 2–6, write the rule for the sequence.

2. 60, 54, 48, . . .

____

3. 392, 56, 8, . . .

____

4. $\frac{1}{3}$, 1, 3,. . .

____

5. 1.87, 3, 4.13 . . .

____

6. 5, 2, $\frac{4}{5}$ . . .

____

For 7–10, write the next three possible terms in each sequence.

7. 9, $4\frac{1}{2}$, $2\frac{1}{4}$, . . .

____

8. 76, 84, 92, . . .

____

9. 4, $^{-}16$, 64, . . .

____

10. $^{-}32$, $^{-}23$, $^{-}14$, . . .

____

11. The Snack Shop had a total of $245 in sales receipts on Monday, a total of $286 on Tuesday, and a total of $327 on Wednesday. If this pattern continues, what will be the total of the sales receipts for Friday?

____

12. Marty is driving 540 mi to visit his cousin. After 15 min, Marty is 527 mi from his cousin's house. Fifteen minutes later he is 514 mi away. Fifteen minutes after that, he is 501 mi away. If this pattern continues, how far away will Marty be 2 hr after he began driving?

____

Go On

Name ______________________________

For 13–16, complete the equation that represents the function.

13.

x	1	2	3	4	5
y	9	18	27	36	45

____

14.

x	2	4	6	8	10
y	$^{-}2$	0	2	4	6

____

15.

x	$^{-}5$	$^{-}3$	$^{-}1$	1	3
y	1	3	5	7	9

____

16.

x	100	90	80	70	60
y	20	18	16	14	12

____

For 17–19, draw the next two figures in the pattern.

17. 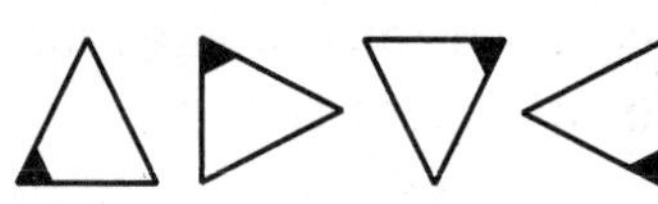

____

18. 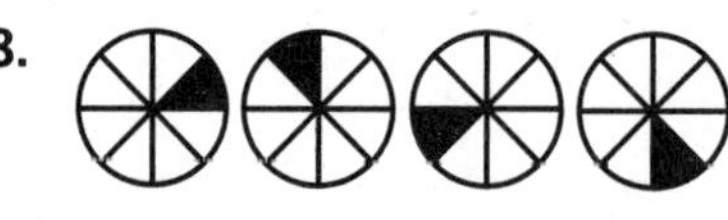

____

19. 

____

20. Examine the following pattern. How many small squares will be in the tenth figure?

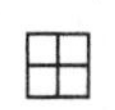 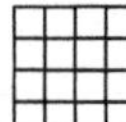

____

Stop

Choose the best answer.

For 1–4, tell which type of transformation the second figure is of the first figure.

1. A rotation
   B reflection
   C translation
   D symmetry

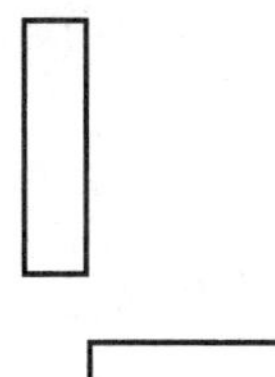

2. F rotation
   G reflection
   H symmetry
   J translation

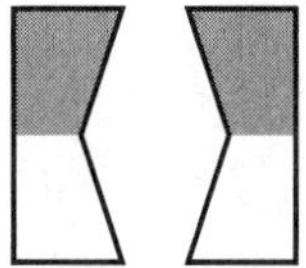

3. A rotation
   B translation
   C symmetry
   D reflection

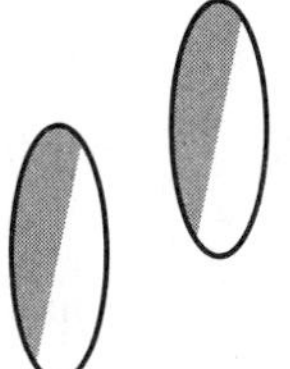

4. F symmetry
   G reflection
   H translation
   J rotation

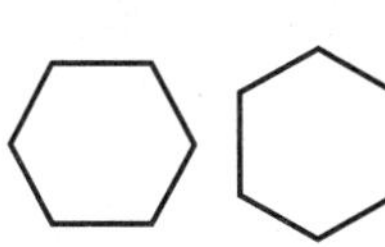

For 5–8, identify which of the figures can be used to form a tessellation.

5.

A 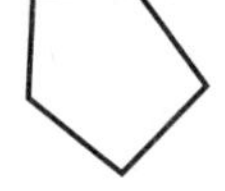

C 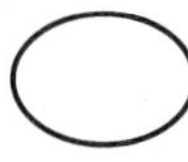

B 

D 

6.

F 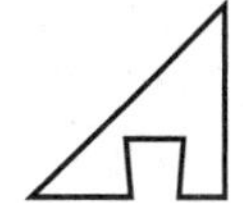

H 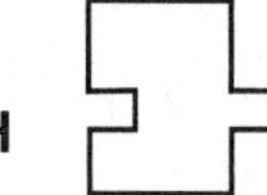

G 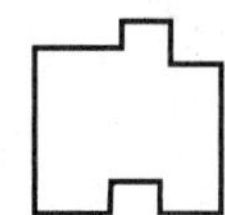

J 

7.

A 

C 

B 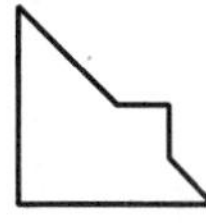

D 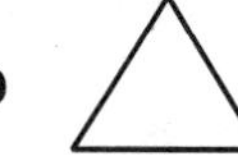

8.

F 

H 

G 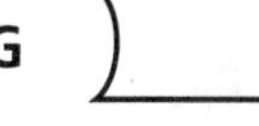

J

For 9–12, tell how many ways you can place the solid figure on the outline.

9.

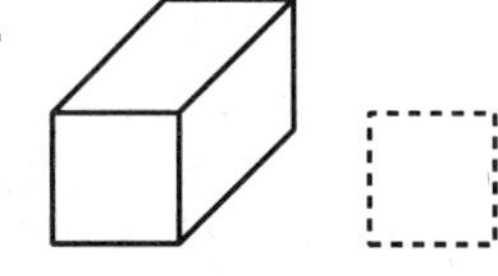

A 2 ways
B 4 ways
C 6 ways
D 8 ways

10.

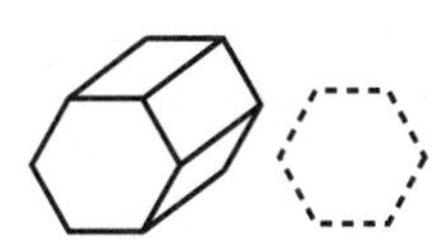

F 2 ways
G 6 ways
H 12 ways
J 20 ways

Go On

Name ______________________________

11. A unlimited
    B 8 ways
    C 4 ways
    D 2 ways

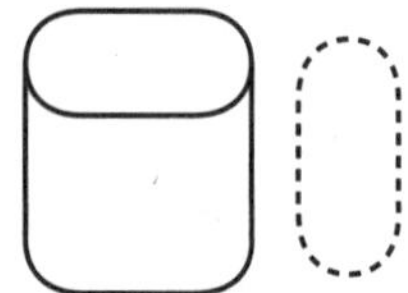

12. F 6 ways
    G 4 ways
    H 3 ways
    J 2 ways

For 13–15, tell how many lines of symmetry the figure has.

13. A 3 lines
    B 4 lines
    C 6 lines
    D 9 lines

14. F 8 lines
    G 4 lines
    H 2 lines
    J 1 lines

15. A 6 lines
    B 4 lines
    C 2 lines
    D 1 lines

16. A solid yellow circle is placed exactly in the center of a blue cardboard square. You want to put a hook on the outer rim of the square so that the figure will have a vertical line of symmetry when hung on a wall. For how many locations is this possible, and where are they?

    F 8, on any of the four corners or in the middle of any side
    G 4, on any of the four corners
    H 4, in the middle of any side
    J 1, in the middle of the top side

For 17–19, tell whether each figure has rotational symmetry, and, if so, identify the symmetry as a fraction of a turn and in degrees.

17. A Yes, $\frac{1}{2}$, 180°
    B Yes, $\frac{1}{3}$, 120°
    C Yes, $\frac{1}{4}$, 90°
    D No

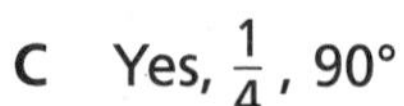

18. F Yes, $\frac{1}{4}$, 90°
    G Yes, $\frac{1}{3}$, 120°
    H Yes, $\frac{1}{2}$, 180°
    J No

19. A Yes, $\frac{1}{8}$, 45°
    B Yes, $\frac{1}{5}$, 108°
    C Yes, $\frac{1}{3}$, 120°
    D No

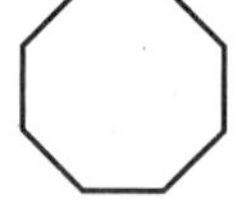

20. Which kind of figure can always be used to form a tessellation?

    F 10-sided polygon
    G octagon
    H pentagon
    J triangle

Stop

Name ______________________________

Write the correct answer.

For 1–4, tell which type of transformation the second figure is of the first. Write *translation*, *rotation*, or *reflection*.

1. 

____

2. 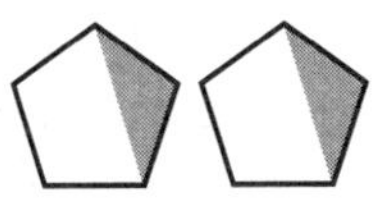

____

3. 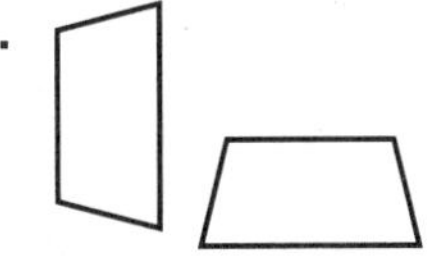

____

4. 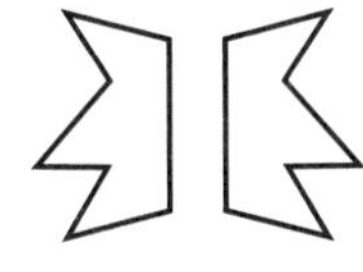

____

For 5–8, tell whether each figure can be used to form a tessellation. Write *yes* or *no*.

5. 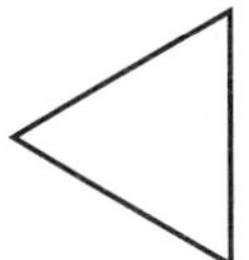

____

6. 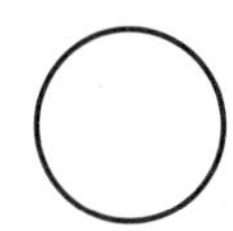

____

7. 

____

8. 

____

For 9–12, tell how many ways you can place the solid figure on the outline.

9. 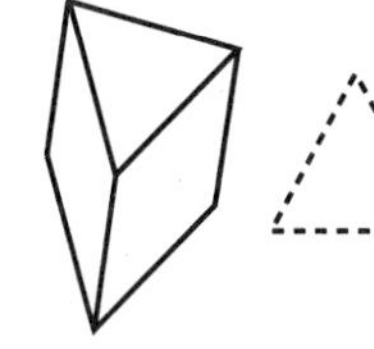

____

10. 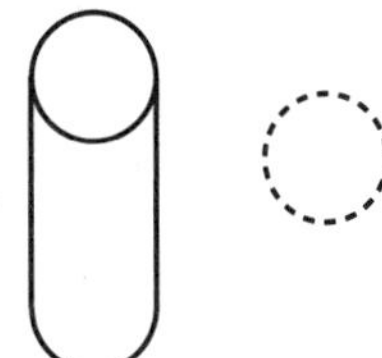

____

Go On

11. 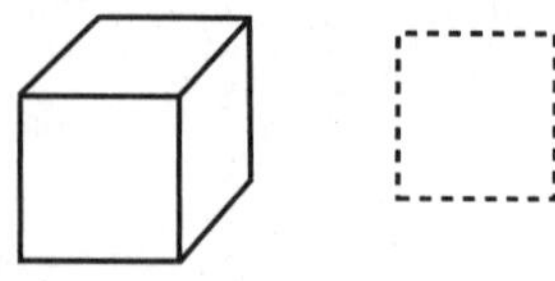

____

12. 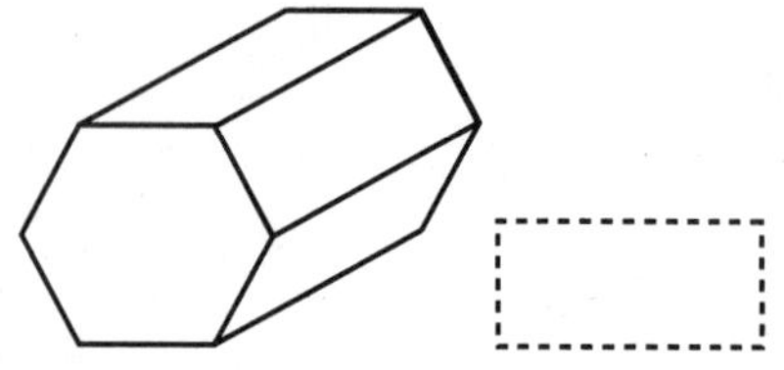

____

For 13–15, tell how many lines of symmetry the figure has.

13. 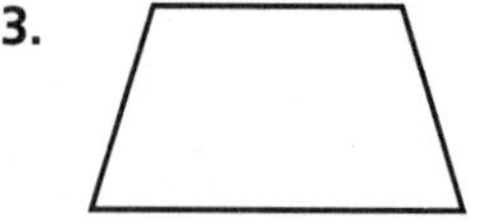

____

14. 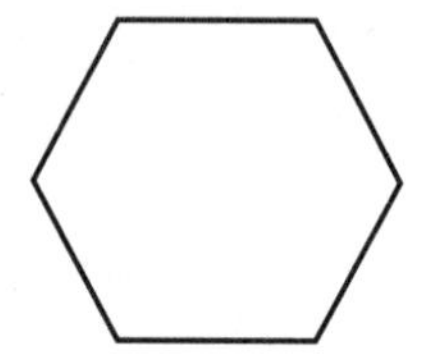

____

15. 

____

16. A solid green circle is placed exactly in the center of an orange cardboard regular hexagon. You want to put a hook on the outer rim of the hexagon so that the figure will have a vertical line of symmetry when hung on a wall. For how many locations is this possible, and where are they?

____

____

For 17–19, tell whether each figure has rotational symmetry. Write *yes* or *no*. If it does, identify the symmetry as a fraction of a turn and in degrees.

17. □

____

18. ⬠

____

19. 

____

20. Draw a figure that can be used to form a tessellation.

____

Stop

Choose the best answer.

1. Using a(n) __________, you can locate any point on the coordinate plane.

   A relation C function
   B ordered pair D quadrant

2. A(n) __________ contains one of the symbols $>$, $<$, $\geq$, $\leq$, or $\neq$.

   F inequality H equation
   G relation J translation

3. The coordinate plane is divided by a vertical line called the _______.

   A quadrant C *x*-axis
   B *y*-axis D origin

4. The point whose coordinates are (0,0) is called the _________.

   F *x*-axis H relation
   G *y*-axis J origin

For 5–6, find the graph of the solutions of the inequality.

5. $x > 5$

A 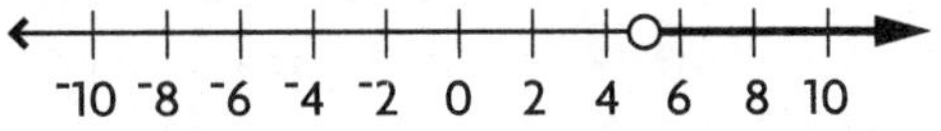

B 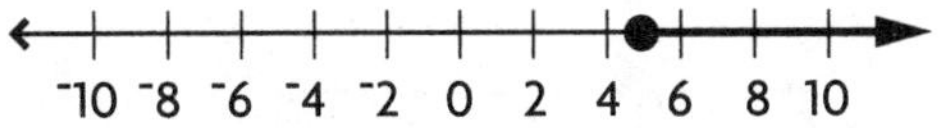

C 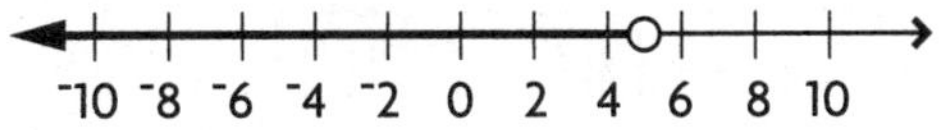

D 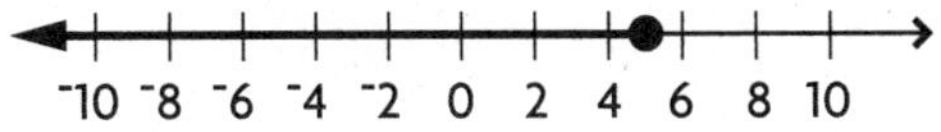

6. $x \leq\ 2$

F 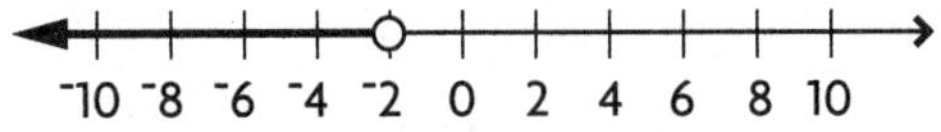

G 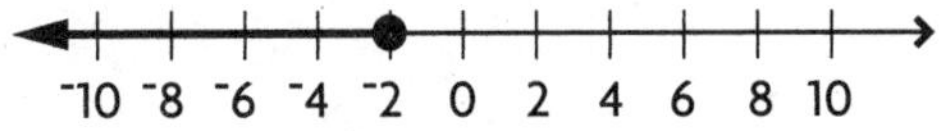

H 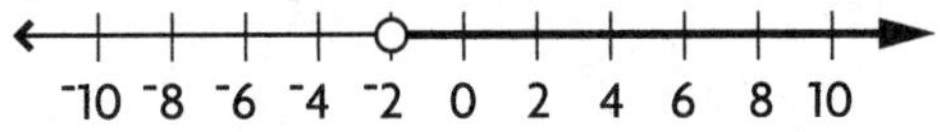

J 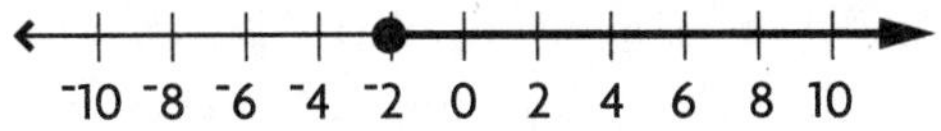

For 7–10, solve the inequality.

7. $n + 3 > 5$

   A $n > 8$ C $n > 2$
   B $n < 8$ D $n < 2$

8. $x - 1 < 3$

   F $x > 2$ H $x > 4$
   G $x < 2$ J $x < 4$

9. $p + 5 \leq 7$

   A $p \geq 2$ C $p \geq {}^-2$
   B $p \leq 2$ D $p \leq {}^-2$

10. $4c \geq 20$

   F $c \geq 15$ H $c \geq 5$
   G $c \leq 5$ J $c \leq 80$

For 11–12, describe how to locate the point for the ordered pair on the coordinate plane.

11. Locate the point $(5, {}^-9)$, starting at (0,0).

   A Go right 5 and up 9.
   B Go left 5 and up 9.
   C Go left 5 and up 9.
   D Go right 5 and down 9.

12. Locate the point $({}^-2, {}^-7)$, starting at (0,0).

   F Go left 2 and up 7.
   G Go right 2 and up 7.
   H Go left 2 and down 7.
   J Go right 2 and down 7.

Go On

For 13–14, use the table below.

x	0	1	2	3	4
y	7	10	13	16	19

13. List the ordered pairs from the table.

A (7,0), (10,1), (13,2), (16,3), (19,4)
B (7,4), (10,3), (13,2), (16,2), (19,1)
C (4,7), (3,10), (2,13), (1,16), (0,19)
D (0,7), (1,10), (2,13), (3,16), (4,19)

14. Which equation relates *y* to *x*?

F $y = x + 7$
G $y = 3x + 7$
H $x = y - 7$
J $x = 3y - 7$

15. Parallelogram *ABCD* has coordinates *A*(2, 5), *B*(2, 11),*C*($^-1$, 7), and *D*($^-1$, 1). It is translated 3 units up and 4 units to the left. What are the new coordinates?

A A'($^-1$, 1), B'($^-1$, 7), C'($^-4$, 3), D'($^-4$, $^-3$)
B A'(2, 8), B'(2, 14), C'($^-1$, 10), D'($^-1$, 4)
C A'($^-2$, 8), B'($^-2$, 14), C'($^-5$, 10), D'($^-5$, 4)
D A'(5, 1), B'(5, 7), C'(2, 3), D'(2, $^-3$)

16. Triangle *QRS* has coordinates *Q*(4,4), *R*(4,7), and *S*(7,7). It is reflected across the x- axis and then the y-axis. What are the new coordinates?

F Q'($^-4$,$^-4$), R'($^-4$,$^-7$), S'($^-7$,$^-7$)
G Q'($^-4$, 4), R'($^-4$, 7), S'($^-7$, 7)
H Q'(4,$^-4$), R'(4,$^-7$), S'(7,$^-7$)
J Q'(4,$^-4$), R'($^-4$, 7), S'(7,$^-7$)

For 17–18, use the table below.

x	$^-2$	$^-1$	0	1	2
y	25	20	15	10	5

17. Which equation relates *y* to *x*?

A $y = {}^-5x + 15$
B $y = 5x + 15$
C $y = 5x - 15$
D $y = {}^-5x - 15$

18. The points in the table above are rotated 90° clockwise around the origin. What are the coordinates of the point that corresponds to (1, 10) after the rotation?

F ($^-1$,$^-10$)
G (10,$^-1$)
H ($^-10$,1)
J ($^-10$,–1)

For 19–20, use the table below, which shows the cost *c* (in dollars) for Lucy to make *n* necklaces.

n	5	10	15	20
c	25	50	75	100

19. Which equation relates *c* to *n*?

A $c = 5 + n$
B $c = n \div 5$
C $c = 5n$
D $c = n - 25$

20. How much will it cost Lucy to make 50 necklaces?

F $250
G $200
H $150
J $10

Stop

Name ______________________________

Write the correct answer.

1. You can use an ordered pair to locate any __?__ .

____

2. Write five symbols that can be contained in an inequality.

____

3. The horizontal axis of a coordinate plane is also called the __?__ .

____

4. Identify the ordered pair that names the origin.

____

For 5–6, draw the graph of the solutions of the inequality.

5. $x < {}^{-}1$

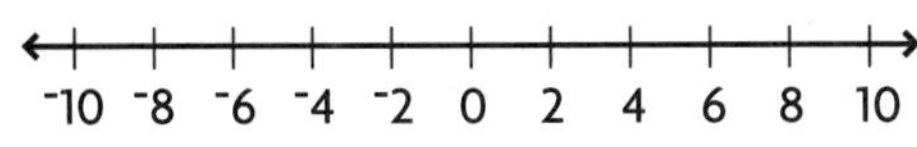

6. $x > {}^{-}4$

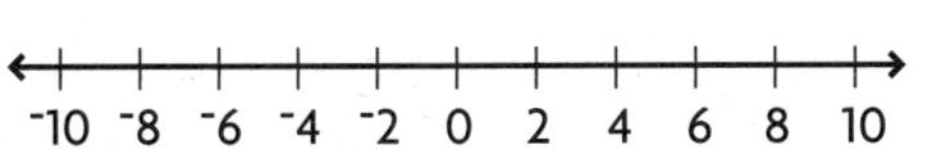

For 7–10, solve the inequality.

7. $x + 6 > 8$

____

8. $a - 2 < 2$

____

9. $m + 4 \leq 10$

____

10. $2n \geq 14$

____

For 11–12, describe how to locate the point for the ordered pair on the coordinate plane.

11. Locate the point $(3, {}^{-}3)$, starting at $(0,0)$.

____

____

12. Locate the point $({}^{-}3, 4)$, starting at $(0,0)$.

____

____

Go On

For 13–14, use the table below.

x	0	1	2	3	4
y	$^-1$	1	3	5	7

13. List the ordered pairs from the table.

____

14. Write an equation that relates *y* to *x*.

____

15. Rectangle *MNOP* has coordinates *M*($^-2$,1), *N*(2, 1), *O*(2,3) and *P*($^-2$,3). It is translated 4 units down and 3 units to the right. What are the new coordinates?

____

____

16. Triangle *ABC* has coordinates *A*(2,3), *B*(2,6), and *C*(6,3). It is reflected across the *x*-axis and then the *y*-axis. What are the new coordinates?

____

For 17–18, use the table below.

x	$^-2$	$^-1$	0	1	2
y	9	7	5	3	1

17. Write an equation that relates *y* to *x*.

____

18. The points in the table above are rotated 180° clockwise around the origin. What are the coordinates of the point that corresponds to (1,3) after the rotation?

____

For 19–20, use the table below, which shows the time *h* (in hours) that Jason works in *d* days.

d	2	4	6	8
h	12	24	36	48

19. Write an equation that relates *h* to *d*.

____

20. If Jason works 15 days this month, how many hours will he work?

____

Stop

Name ______________________________

Choose the best answer.

1. Describe how to locate the point $(^-6, 3)$ starting from the origin.

   A Go left 6 and up 3.
   B Go right 6 and up 3.
   C Go left 6 and down 3.
   D Go right 6 and down 3.

2. What is the rule for the sequence?

   20, 4, 0.8, 0.16, …

   F divide by 5 H multiply by 5
   G divide by 0.2 J multiply by 0.4

3. A repeating arrangement of shapes that completely covers a plane with no overlaps is called a __?__.

   A reflection C tessellation
   B rotation D transformation

4. Which graph is a solution of the inequality $x \geq {}^-1$?

   F
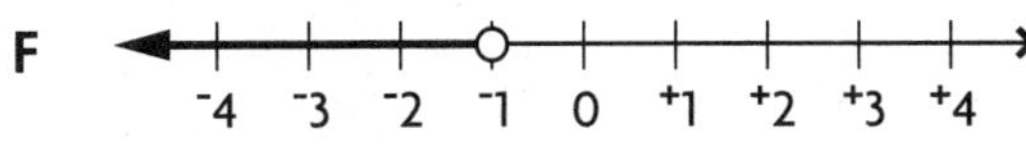

   G

   H
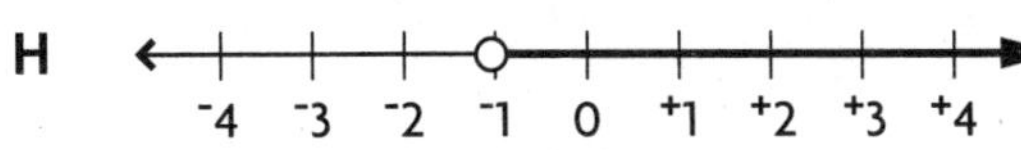

   J
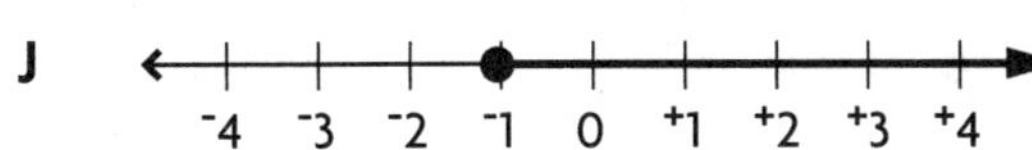

5. Which word describes the transformation that moves the first figure to the second?

   A rotation C translation
   B reflection D symmetry

6. Solve the inequality. $x + 3 < 5$

   F $x < 8$ H $x < 2$
   G $x > 8$ J $x > 2$

7. Which equation relates c to d?

c	1	2	3	4
d	4	8	12	16

   A $c = 4d$ C $c = 8d$
   B $d = 4c$ D $d = 8c$

8. Bennett wants to make a walkway using a shape that will tessellate. Which shape should he not choose?

   F  H

   G  J

9. How many lines of symmetry does the figure have?

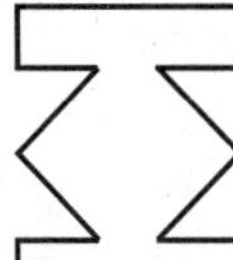

   A 1 line
   B 2 lines
   C 3 lines
   D 4 lines

10. What are the next two figures in the pattern?

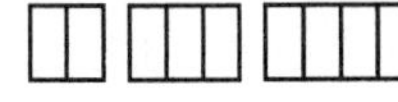

   F

   G

   H

   J

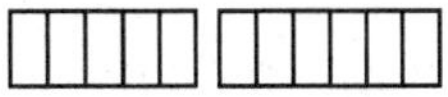

Go On

Name ___________________________

11. At 8 A.M., the temperature was 48°F. At 10 A.M., the temperature was 52°F. At noon, the temperature was 56°F. If this pattern continues, what will the temperature be at 5 P.M.?

A 64°F C 68°F
B 66°F D 70°F

12. Which equation represents the function?

x	0	3	6	9	12
y	0	24	48	72	96

F $y = x$ H $y = 3x$
G $y = x + 3$ J $y = 8x$

13. Triangle *QRS* has coordinates *Q*(0,⁻1), *R*(0,⁻3), and *S*(4,⁻2). It is translated 1 unit down and 2 units to the right. What are the new coordinates?

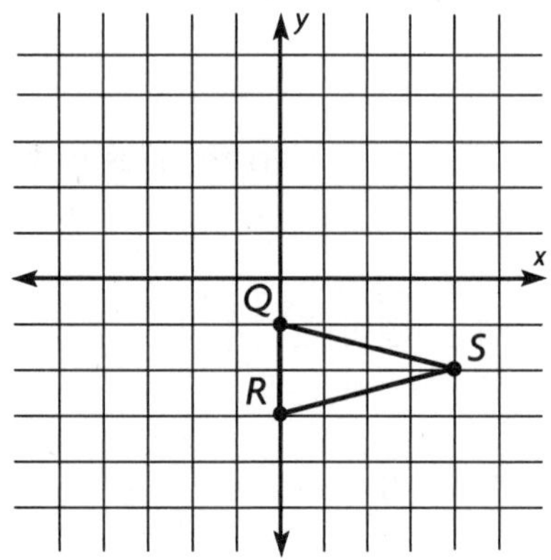

A *Q*'(1,0), *R*'(1,⁻2), *S*'(5,⁻3)
B *Q*'(2,0), *R*'(2,⁻2), *S*'(3,0)
C *Q*'(2,⁻2), *R*'(2,⁻4), *S*'(6,⁻3)
D *Q*'(2,0), *R*'(2,⁻4), *S*'(6,⁻1)

14. Eric sold 28 candles the first week, 40 the second week, and 52 the third week. If this pattern continues, how many candles will he sell the eighth week?

F 112 candles H 88 candles
G 104 candles J 64 candles

15. How many ways can you place the solid figure on the black plane figure?

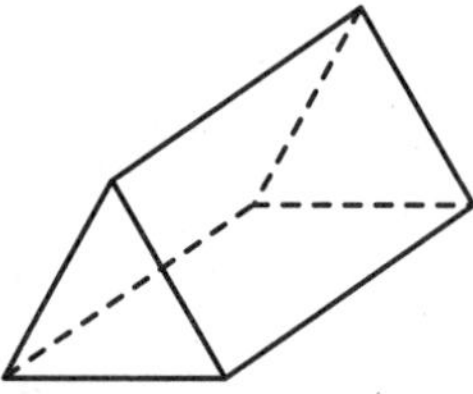

A 2 ways C 6 ways
B 3 ways D 8 ways

16. Identify the rotational symmetry as a fraction of a turn and in degrees.

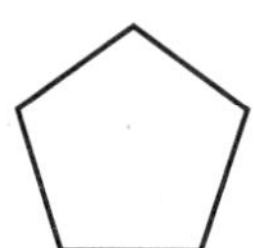

F $\frac{1}{4}$; 90° H $\frac{1}{6}$; 60°
G $\frac{1}{5}$; 72° J $\frac{1}{2}$; 180°

17. What are the next three terms in the sequence?

⁻2, 4, ⁻8, …

A 10, ⁻12, 14 C ⁻16, 32, ⁻64
B ⁻16, ⁻32, ⁻64 D 16, ⁻32, 64

18. How many parts are there in the eighth circle in the following pattern?

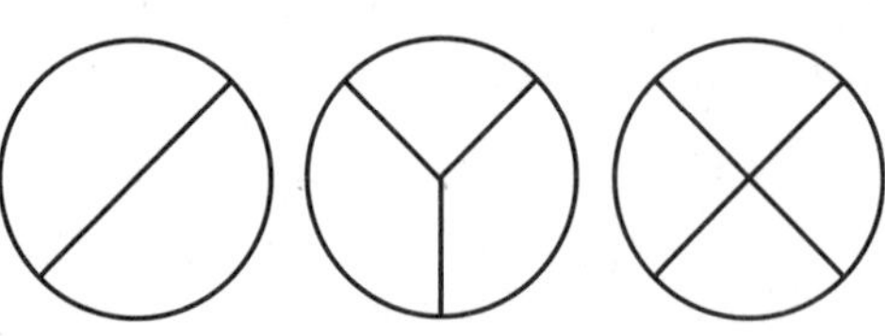

F 7 parts H 9 parts
G 8 parts J 10 parts

Go On

Name ______________________________

For questions 19–21, use the table below.

x	$^-2$	$^-1$	0	1	2
y	7	5	3	1	$^-1$

19. List the ordered pairs from the table.

A $(7,^-2), (5,^-1), (3, 0), (1,1), (^-1,2)$
B $(7,2), (5,1), (3,0), (1,^-1), (^-1,^-2)$
C $(^-2,7), (^-1,5), (0,3), (1, 1), (2,^-1)$
D $(^-2,^-1), (^-1,1), (0,3), (1,5), (2,7)$

20. Which equation relates x to y?

F $y = 2x - 3$ **H** $y = {}^-2x - 3$
G $y = 2x + 3$ **J** $y = {}^-2x + 3$

21. The points in the table are rotated 180° clockwise around the origin. What are the coordinates of the first point in the table after the rotation?

A $(^-2,^-7)$ **C** $(7,^-2)$
B $(2,^-7)$ **D** $(7,2)$

22. Each number in a sequence is called a __?__.

F term **H** relation
G function **J** reflection

23. Which symbol does not show an inequality?

A $>$ **C** $\leq$
B $\neq$ **D** $=$

24. What moves were made to transform each figure into its next position?

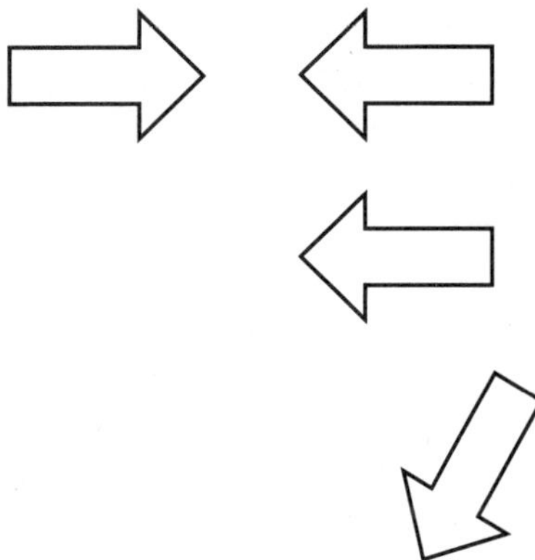

F translation, reflection, rotation
G rotation, translation, reflection
H reflection, translation, rotation
J rotation, reflection, translation

25. The table shows the total profit, p, for the number of magazines sold, m. Which equation shows the total profit?

m	1	2	3	4
p	\$6	\$12	\$18	\$24

A $p = 6m$ **C** $p = m + 5$
B $m = 6p$ **D** $m = p + 5$

26. Meryl walked 1.5 miles the first week, 2.25 miles the second week, and 3 miles the third week. If this pattern continues, how many miles will she walk the tenth week?

F 6.75 mi **H** 10.25 mi
G 8.25 mi **J** 15 mi

Go On

27. A supermarket display is set up on 4 shelves that are 18 cm apart. The bottom shelf of the display is 6 cm from the floor. How far from the floor is the top shelf?

A 36 cm
B 42 cm
C 60 cm
D 78 cm

28. Which equation represents the function?

x	$^-10$	$^-5$	0	5	10
y	$^-7$	$^-2$	3	8	13

F $y = x + 3$
G $y = x - 3$
H $y = 3x$
J $y = {}^-3x$

29. Identify which of the figures forms a tessellation.

A 

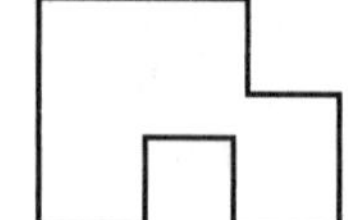

B 

C 

D 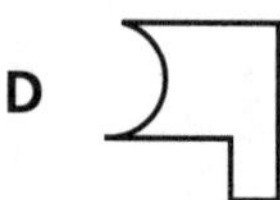

30. Which word describes the transformation that moves the first figure to the second?

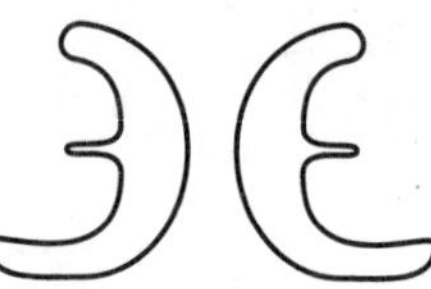

F rotation
G reflection
H translation
J symmetry

For questions 31–32, use the table below which shows how the length *l* of a rectangle is related to its width, *w*.

w	2	4	6	8
l	7	13	19	25

31. Which equation relates l to w?

A $l = w + 5$
B $l = w - 5$
C $l = 4w - 1$
D $l = 3w + 1$

32. If the width of the rectangle is 15 ft, how long is the rectangle?

F 46 ft
G 45 ft
H 31 ft
J 30 ft

33. Examine the following pattern. How many small triangles are in the ninth figure?

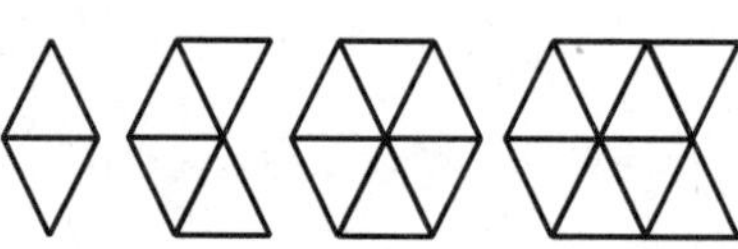

A 10 triangles
B 15 triangles
C 18 triangles
D 20 triangles

Stop

Name ______________________________

Write the correct answer.

1. Describe how to locate the point ($^-4$, 5) starting at the origin.

____

2. What is a possible rule for the sequence?

   24, 6, 1.5, 0.375, …

____

3. A repeating arrangement of shapes that completely covers a plane with no overlaps is called a __?__ .

____

4. Graph the solution of the inequality $x \leq 2$.

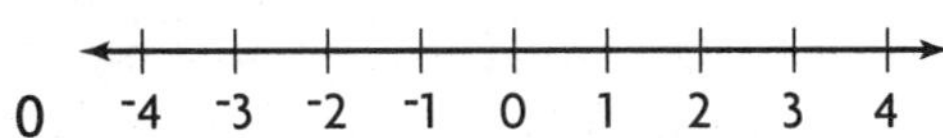

5. Which word describes the transformation that moves the first figure to the second?

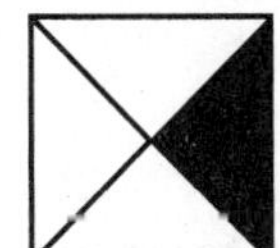
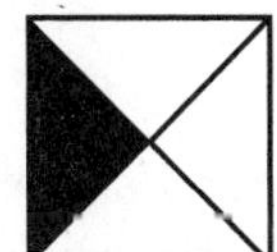

____

6. Solve the inequality. $x + 4 > 6$

____

7. Write an equation that relates *c* to *d*.

c	1	2	3	4
d	3	6	9	12

____

8. Bennett wants to make a walkway using a shape that will tessellate. Name a regular polygon that he should not choose.

____

9. How many lines of symmetry does the figure have?

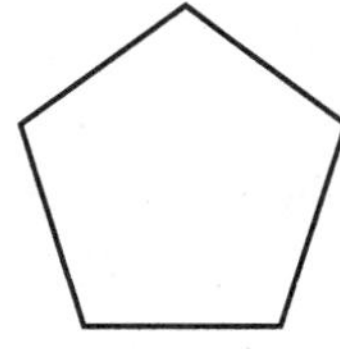

____

10. What are the next two figures in the pattern?

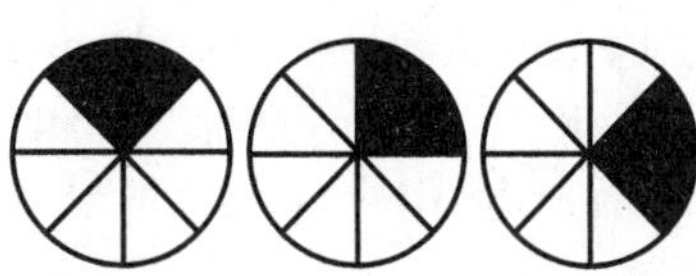

____

Go On

Name ______________________________

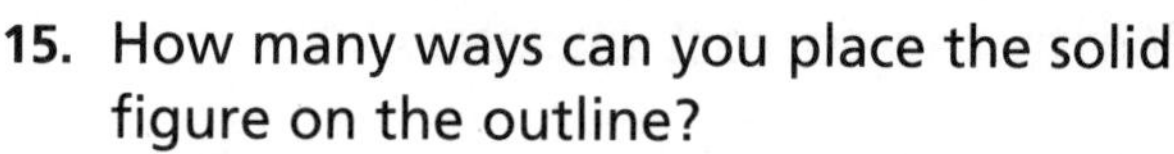

11. At 5 P.M., the temperature was 64°F. At 7 P.M., the temperature was 61°F. At 9 P.M., the temperature was 58°F. If this pattern continues, what will the temperature be at 1 A.M.?

____

12. Write an equation to relate x to y.

x	0	2	4	6	8
y	0	14	28	42	56

____

13. Triangle QRS has coordinates $Q(1,0)$, $R(1,^{-}2)$, and $S(5,^{-}1)$. It is translated 3 units up and 1 unit to the left. What are the new coordinates?

____

14. Allison's Nursery sold 30 plants the first week, 44 the second week, and 58 the third week. If this pattern continues, how many plants will it sell the eighth week?

____

15. How many ways can you place the solid figure on the outline?

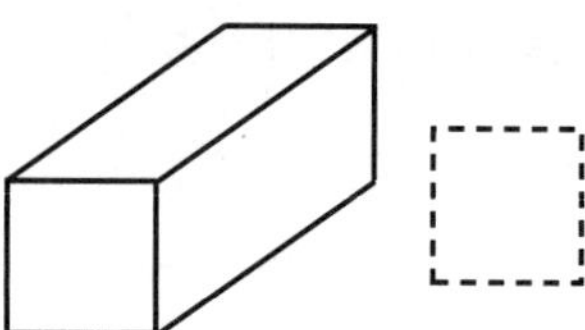

____

16. Does the figure have rotational symmetry? If so, identify the symmetry as a fraction of a turn and in degrees.

____

17. What are the next three possible terms in the sequence?

64, $^{-}32$, 16, . . .

____

18. How many squares are shaded in the seventh figure in the following pattern?

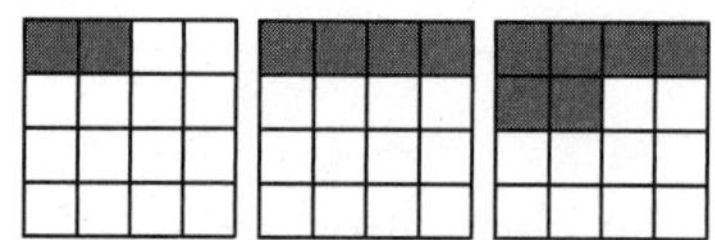

____

Go On

Name ______________________________

For questions 19–21, use the table below.

x	$^-2$	$^-1$	0	1	2
y	$^-7$	$^-4$	$^-1$	2	5

19. List the ordered pairs from the table.

____

20. Write an equation that relates x to y.

____

21. The points in the table are rotated 180° clockwise around the origin. What are the coordinates of the first point in the table after the rotation?

____

22. A set of terms that follows a pattern from one term to the next is called a __?__ .

____

23. Write three symbols that show an inequality.

____

24. What moves were made to transform each figure into its next position?

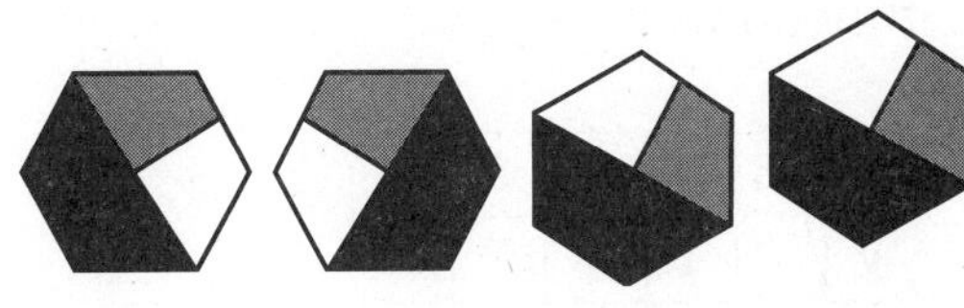

____

25. The table shows the number of cups of apple cider, c, needed per gallon of fruit punch, p. Write an equation relating p and c.

p	1	2	3	4
c	4	8	12	16

____

26. Chris jogged 1.3 miles the first week, 1.7 miles the second week, and 2.1 miles the third week. If this pattern continues, how many miles will he jog the tenth week?

____

Go On

27. Five layers of boxes are stacked on a shelf 10 cm from the floor. Each box is 16 cm tall. How far from the floor is the top of the highest layer?

____

28. Write an equation that represents the function.

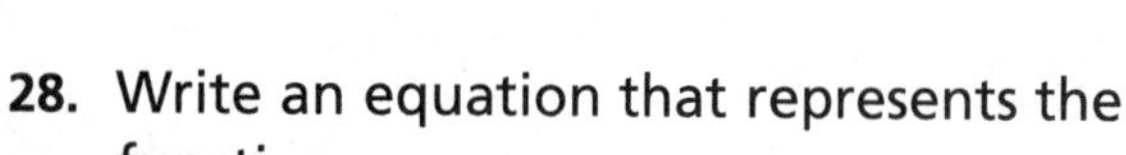

x	$^{-}6$	$^{-}3$	0	3	6
y	$^{-}2$	1	4	7	10

____

29. Identify which of the figures can be used to form a tessellation.

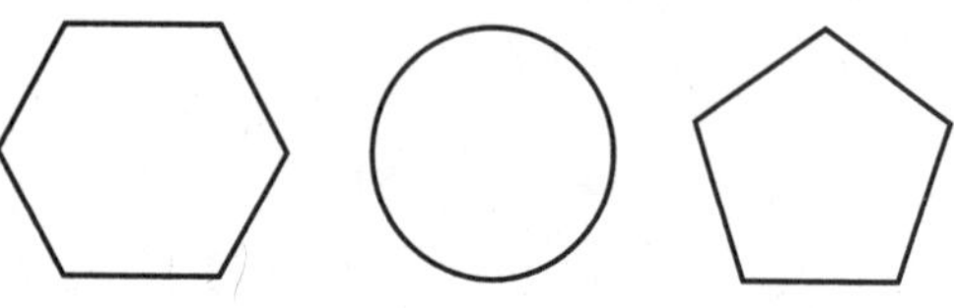

____

30. What transformation moves the first figure to the second?

____

For questions 31–32, use the table below which shows how the length, *l*, of a rectangle is related to its width, *w*.

w	1	2	3	4
l	4	6	8	10

31. Which equation relates *l* to *w*?

____

32. If the width of the rectangle is 12 m, how long is the rectangle?

____

33. Examine the following pattern. How many small black triangles are in the sixth figure?

____

Stop

Name ________________________________

Choose the best answer.

1. $6\overline{)3{,}290}$

   A 548 C 548 r3
   B 548 r2 D 549

2. Which number should be in the box so that the numbers are in order from *least* to *greatest*?

   2.496, ■, 2.502, 2.514

   F 2.52 H 2.5
   G 2.511 J 2.49

3. Of the 100 students in Mr. Brill's science classes, 20 have not yet decided on a project. What percent of the students have already chosen a project?

   A 2% B 8% C 20% D 80%

4. Between them, Roberto and Jerry shared $1\frac{1}{2}$ pizzas. Which shows how much pizza each boy could have eaten?

   F $\frac{3}{4}$ and $\frac{3}{4}$ H $\frac{5}{8}$ and $\frac{3}{4}$
   G $\frac{7}{8}$ and $\frac{1}{2}$ J $1\frac{1}{8}$ and $\frac{3}{4}$

5. Solve. $a - 6 = 10$

   A $a = {}^{-}16$ C $a = 4$
   B $a = {}^{-}4$ D $a = 16$

6. The difference in length between two shelves is $\frac{5}{6}$ ft. If the longer shelf is $5\frac{3}{4}$ ft long, how long is the shorter shelf?

   F $4\frac{1}{2}$ ft H $5\frac{1}{2}$ ft
   G $4\frac{11}{12}$ ft J $5\frac{3}{4}$ ft

7. There were 17 people in a restaurant. Three groups of 4 came in before anyone left. After that, two groups of 3 finished dinner and left. Which expression tells how many people remained in the restaurant?

   A $17 + 3 \times 4 - 2 \times 3$
   B $(17 + 3) \times 4 - 2 \times 3$
   C $17 + 3 \times (4 - 2) \times 3$
   D $17 - 3 \times 4 + 2 \times 3$

8. Peter, Charles, Joann, and Linda all began a race at the same time. The table shows the distances they had run after 9 minutes. Who was leading the race?

RUNNER	DISTANCE
Peter	$\frac{3}{4}$ mi
Charles	$\frac{1}{2}$ mi
Joann	$\frac{5}{6}$ mi
Linda	$\frac{7}{8}$ mi

   F Peter H Joann
   G Charles J Linda

9. Which expression represents the square root of 64, times the difference between the squares of 5 and 3?

   A $64^2 \times 5^2 - 3^2$
   B $\sqrt{64} \times 5^2 - 3^2$
   C $\sqrt{64} \times (5^2 - 3^2)$
   D $(\sqrt{64} \times 5^2) - 3^2$

10. What is the probability that a card selected at random will be a multiple of 4?

30	20	14	16	4

   F $\frac{2}{5}$ G $\frac{3}{5}$ H $\frac{2}{3}$ J $\frac{3}{2}$

Go On

11. What is the probability that if you choose a marble, do not replace it, and then choose a second marble, they will both be red?

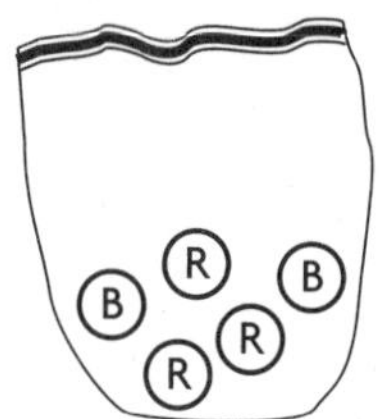

Key
R = Red Marble
B = Blue Marble

A $\frac{3}{10}$ B $\frac{6}{25}$ C $\frac{1}{4}$ D $\frac{1}{10}$

12. Which equation represents the function shown in the table?

x	$^{-}1$	0	1	2	3
y	6	7	8	9	10

F $y = x + 7$ H $y = x + 6$
G $y = x - 7$ J $y = x - 6$

13. How many degrees of rotational symmetry does the figure have?

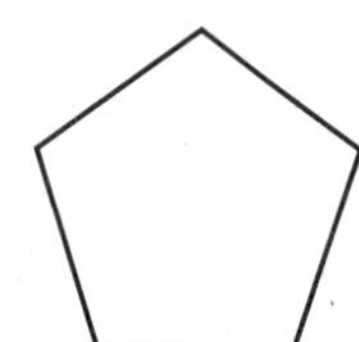

A 70° B 72° C 90° D 140°

14. Which inequality describes the graph?

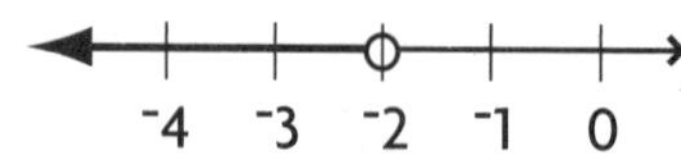

F $x \geq {}^{-}2$ H $x > {}^{-}2$
G $x \leq {}^{-}2$ J $x < {}^{-}2$

15. Which expression is equivalent to 27.18 ÷ 0.14

A 2,718 ÷ 0.14 C 271.8 ÷ 14
B 2,718 ÷ 14 D 2.718 ÷ 14

16. For the set of data, which are the same?

SCORES ON A TEST									
82	86	80	90	75	87	74	86	98	86

F mode and median
G mean and mode
H median and mean
J mean, median, and mode

17. What type of graph would best show how a teenager divided her money among her expenses?

A bar graph C circle graph
B line graph D histogram

18. The graph shows the change in the price of a gallon of gasoline over 4 months. If the trend continues, estimate the price of gasoline in the next month.

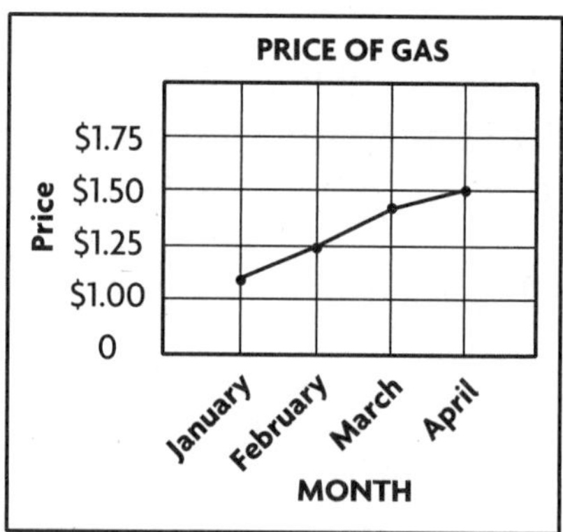

F $1.45 H $1.60
G $1.50 J $1.85

19. Aaron is building a frame for a rectangular picture that measures 18 in. by 26 in. He has cut the wood for two adjacent sides. What is the least length of wood he still needs in order to complete the frame?

A 18 in. C 35 in.
B 26 in. D 44 in.

Go On

For 20–21, use the following information.

A large tree has a circumference of 25 ft.

20. To the nearest foot, what is the length of the tree's diameter? Use 3.14 for the value of π.

F 8 ft G 12 ft H 16 ft J 20 ft

21. To the nearest whole number, what would be the area of the cut surface of the tree if the tree was cut parallel to the ground? Use 3.14 for the value of π.

A 25 ft^2 C 50 ft^2
B 48 ft^2 D 96 ft^2

22. Three friends won some money in a contest. They were able to share the money equally. How much could they have won?

F $949 H $1,333
G $1,025 J $1,407

23. A line segment is 40 cm long. If it is bisected, how long will each of the smaller segments be?

A 40cm B 20cm C 10cm D 5cm

24. Callers from a research company asked every 8th person they phoned about their favorite TV show. They asked every 12th person about their favorite newspaper. Which was the first person they asked about both?

F 16th person H 24th person
G 20th person J 96th person

25. After one week of work, Antonio recorded his earnings as $^{+}$\$45. The next week he did not work, but spent \$60. What integer describes the change in Antonio's wealth over the two weeks?

A $^{-}$\$15 C $^{+}$\$15
B $^{-}$\$5 D $^{+}$\$105

26. Use the figure to find the unknown angle measure.

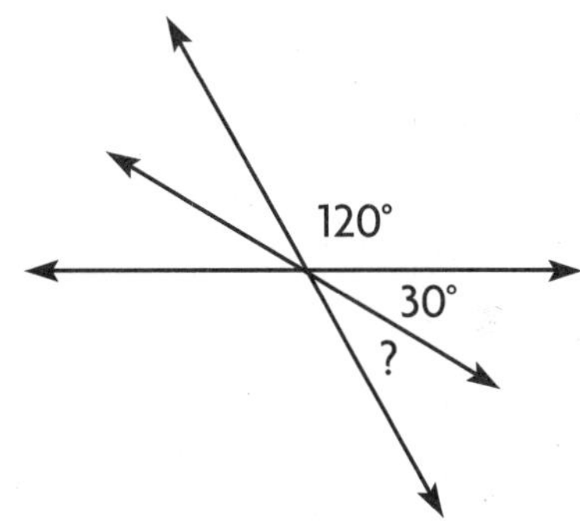

F 30° H 50°
G 40° J 60°

27. A quadrilateral that has 4 congruent sides must be a _____ .

A trapezoid C rectangle
B rhombus D parallelogram

28. The side view of a solid figure is a rectangle. Which of the following could the figure be?

F cone
G cylinder
H rectangular pyramid
J triangular pyramid

29. The formula $h = \frac{m}{60}$ relates the number of hours, h, to the number of minutes, m. How many hours are there in 150 minutes?

A 2 hr C 3 hr
B 2.5 hr D 3.5 hr

Go On

Name ______________________________

30. $-\frac{3}{4} \times 1\frac{1}{5}$

F $-\frac{10}{9}$ H $\frac{9}{10}$

G $-\frac{9}{10}$ J $\frac{10}{9}$

31. The scale of a map is 1 cm equals 40 km. On the map, two cities are 3.5 cm apart. What is the actual distance between the cities?

A 40 km C 140 km

B 120 km D 1,400 km

32. A factory found that 4% of its TVs had defects. Out of 2,000, how many TVs would be expected to have defects?

F 8 TVs H 80 TVs

G 40 TVs J 800 TVs

33. A spinner has 8 equal sections. If 2 of them are red, what percent of the spinner is **not** red?

A 2% B 25% C 75% D 80%

34. Which measurement is the most precise?

F 270 mm H 6 m

G 14 cm J 2 km

35. Find the volume.

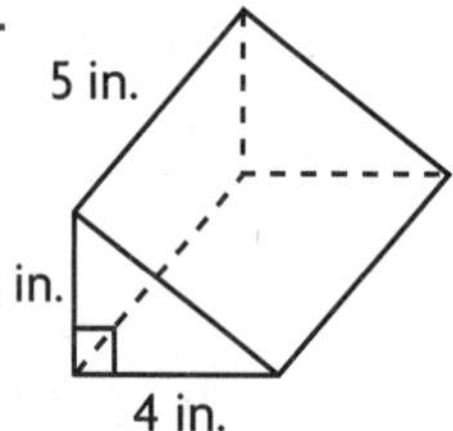

A 15 in.^{3}

B 20 in.^{3}

C 30 in.^{3}

D 60 in.^{3}

36. Annie waits by the entrance to her school and asks the first 50 students that come in a question. What type of sample is she using?

F random H structured

G systematic J convenience

37. Which measure is equivalent to 56 oz?

A $3\frac{1}{2}$ lb C $4\frac{1}{2}$ lb

B 4 lb D 7 lb

38. The line plot shows the number of people living in each house on one street. What is the median number of people living in the houses on this street?

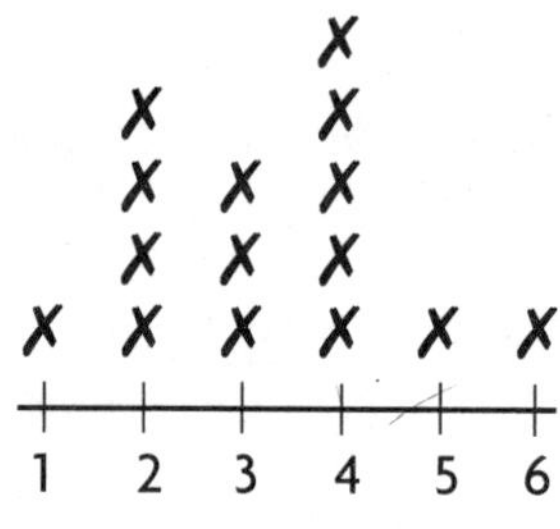

F 2 G 3 H 4 J 5

39. Which set shows three numbers in order from *least* to *greatest*?

A $1\frac{5}{8}$, $1\frac{2}{3}$, 1.42

B 1.24, $1\frac{2}{5}$, 1.55

C $3\frac{1}{4}$, 3.14, 3.24

D 2.65, $2\frac{5}{6}$, $2\frac{3}{5}$

40. The square field has an area of 1,600 ft^2. The owner of the field wants to put a fence around it. How many feet of fencing will be needed to completely enclose the field?

F 40 ft H 120 ft

G 80 ft J 160 ft

Stop

Name ______________________

Write the correct answer.

1. $5\overline{)2,741}$

____

2. Order 3.895, 3.905, 3.985, and 3.899 from *least* to *greatest*.

____

3. Ken has completed 65 of the 100 questions on his science test. What percent of the questions does he still have to finish?

____

4. Stephen and Leticia shared $1\frac{1}{2}$ pizzas. If Stephen ate $\frac{7}{8}$ of a pizza, could Leticia have eaten $\frac{3}{4}$ of a pizza? Explain.

____

5. Solve.

   $d - 9 = 12$

____

6. The difference in length between two ropes is $\frac{3}{8}$ ft. If the shorter rope is $4\frac{3}{4}$ ft long, how long is the longer rope?

____

7. There were 23 people on the bus. Three couples got on before anyone got off. After that, groups of 4 people got off at each of the next two stops. Write an expression you could evaluate to find out how many people remained on the bus.

____

8. Ed, Shelley, Hank, and David all walk to school. The table shows the distance each lives from the school. Who lives nearest the school?

Ed	$\frac{2}{3}$ mi
Shelley	$\frac{3}{4}$ mi
Hank	$\frac{5}{6}$ mi
David	$\frac{3}{8}$ mi

____

9. Write the expression that represents the square root of 49 times the sum of the squares of 9 and 4.

____

10. What is the probability, expressed as a percent, that if one card is drawn from a stack of cards numbered 1 to 100, it will be a multiple of 5?

____

Go On

Name ______________________

11. What is the probability that if you choose a marble from a bag containing 5 red and 5 black marbles, do not replace it, and then choose a second marble, they will both be red?

____

12. Write an equation that represents the function shown in the table.

x	$^-2$	0	2	4	6
y	3	5	7	9	11

____

13. How many degrees of rotational symmetry does the figure have?

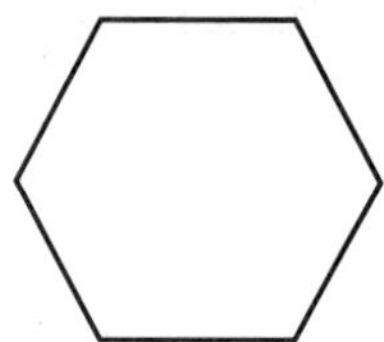

____

14. Write an inequality that describes the graph.

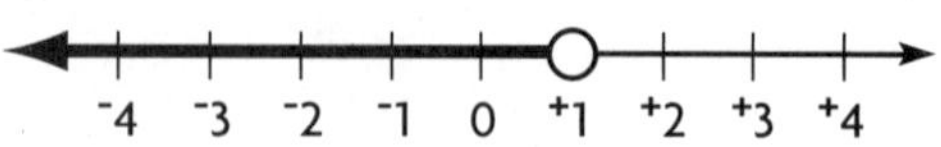

____

15. Write an equivalent expression.
47.61 ÷ 0.23

____

16. For the set of data, give the mean, median, and mode.

77, 81, 75, 85, 70, 82, 69, 81, 93, 81

____

17. What type of graph would best show how the student council divided the money it spent on the school dance among the expenses?

____

18. The graph shows the change in the price of a movie ticket over 4 years. If the trend continues, estimate the price of a movie ticket in the fifth year.

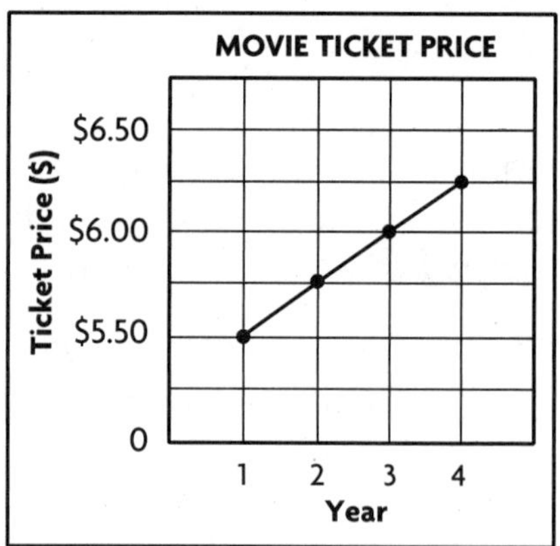

____

19. Felicia is building the sides of a rectangular sandbox that will measure 6 ft by $4\frac{1}{2}$ ft. She has cut the wood for two adjacent sides. How much wood does she still need to complete the sides?

____

Go On

For 20–21, use the information below.

A giant sequoia tree has a circumference at its base of 90 ft.

20. To the nearest foot, what is the tree's diameter? Use 3.14 for π.

____

21. To the nearest foot, what is the area of the base of the tree? Use 3.14 for π..

____

22. Andrea wants to donate a total of \$50.00 to three of her favorite charities. Will she be able to give each of the charities an equal amount? Explain.

____

23. A line segment is 6 in. long. If it is bisected, how long wil each of the smaller segments be?

____

24. Researchers asked every 6th person entering the mall about their favorite radio stations. They asked every 8th person about their favorite television stations. Which was the first person they asked about both?

____

25. Last week, Erik deposited \$55 in his bank account. This week, he withdrew \$65. What integer describes the change in Erik's bank account balance over these two weeks?

____

26. What is the measure of the unknown angle?

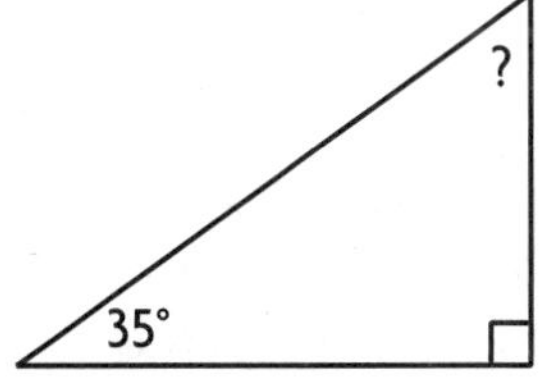

____

27. A quadrilateral that has 4 congruent sides and congruent opposite angles is a ___?___ .

____

28. Identify the solid that has these views.

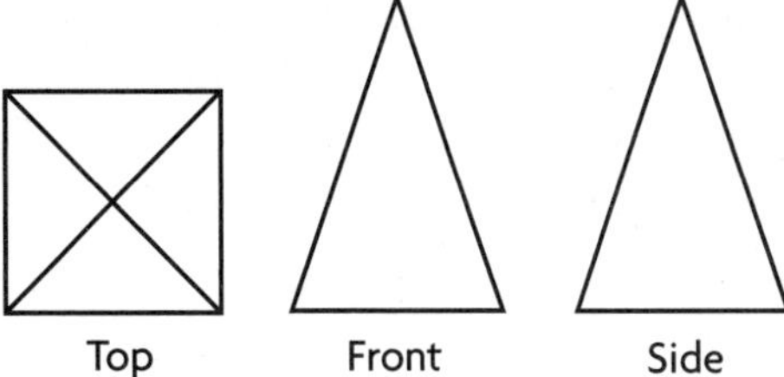

____

29. The formula $h = 24d$ relates the number of days, d, to the number of hours, h. How many days are there in 80 hours?

____

Go On

30. $-\frac{2}{3} \times 2\frac{1}{4}$

____

31. The scale of a map is 1 in. equals 30 mi. On the map, two mountains are 4.5 in. apart. What is the actual distance between the mountains?

____

32. A prize is included in 3% of the boxes of a certain cereal. Out of 3,000 boxes, how many are expected to contain a prize?

____

33. A spinner has 8 equal sections. If 6 of them are blue, what percent of the spinner is **not** blue?

____

34. Which metric measurement is generally used to measure the distance between two cities?

____

35. Find the volume.

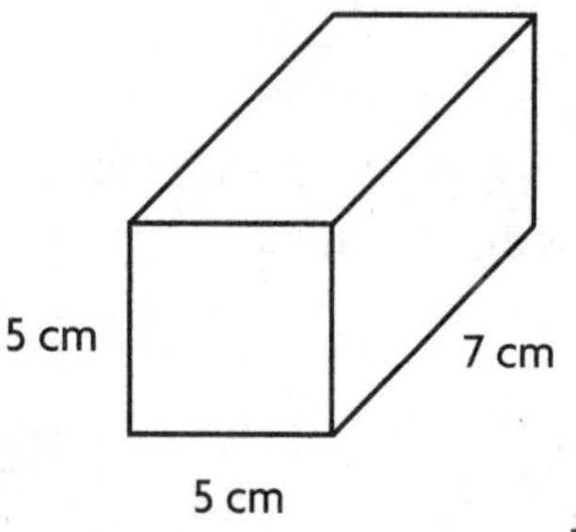

____

36. Chris conducts a survey at his school by questioning every third person who walks into the cafeteria at lunch time. What type of sample is he using?

____

37. How many pounds are in 72 oz?

____

38. The line plot shows the age of ten kids at the roller skating rink. What is the median age of those ten kids?

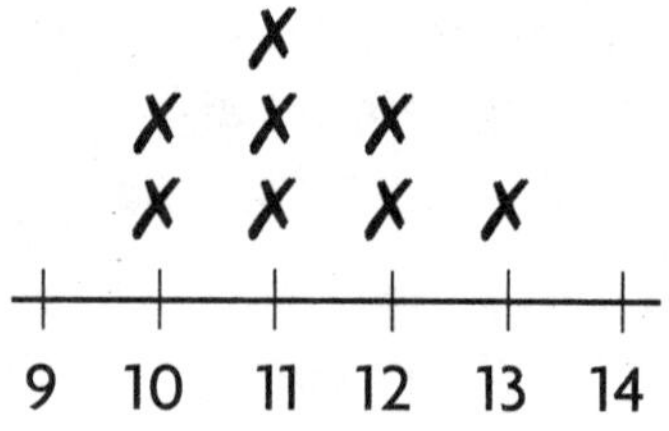

____

39. Order $5\frac{2}{3}$, 5.23, and 5.32 from *least* to *greatest*.

____

40. A square field has an area of 2,500 ft^2. The owner of the field wants to put a fence around it. How many feet of fencing will be needed to enclose the field completely?

____

Stop

Name ______________________ **INVENTORY TEST • PAGE 1**

Choose the best answer.

1. In which number does the 6 have the greatest value?
   A 26,834 Ⓒ 612,099
   B 62,872 D 763,988

2. Which number should go in the ■ so that the numbers are in order from *least* to *greatest*?
   199,153; ■; 203,471
   F 199,089 Ⓗ 200,865
   G 199,149 J 204,003

3. Chris bought gasoline and paid $1.499 per gal. Which is the best estimate of how much she paid for 10 gal?
   A $149 C $14.00
   Ⓑ $15.00 D $10.00

4. Choose the best estimate for 391 ÷ 8.
   F 30 Ⓗ 50
   G 40 J 60

5. For which set of data do the mean and mode have the same value?
   A 7, 7, 7, 9, 10 C 5, 8, 9, 9, 9
   B 3, 8, 9, 10, 10 Ⓓ 4, 8, 8, 9, 11

6. Mike earns $24.00 per week mowing lawns. Which expression represents the amount he earns in *n* weeks?
   Ⓕ $24 \times n$ H $n + 24$
   G $n \div 24$ J $24 \div n$

7. The population of a city is 550,000 when rounded to the nearest ten thousand. Which city could it be?
   A Boston: 555,447
   Ⓑ Austin: 552,434
   C Seattle: 536,978
   D Washington, DC: 523,124

8. The table shows the batting averages of 4 baseball players. Who has the highest average?

PLAYER	BATTING AVERAGE
Cruz	0.274
Gomez	0.302
Li	0.249
Jackson	0.310

   F Cruz H Gomez
   G Li Ⓙ Jackson

9. Kevin wants to use a graph to compare the heights of five buildings. Which type of graph should he use?
   Ⓐ bar graph C circle graph
   B line plot D line graph

10. The rainfall for two years was 42.71 in. and 54.38 in. Which is the best estimate of the total rainfall for these two years?
    F 107 in. H 87 in.
    Ⓖ 97 in. J 80 in.

11. Which figure has all of its sides equal in length?
    Ⓐ rhombus C trapezoid
    B rectangle D parallelogram

Go On

Name ______________________ **INVENTORY TEST • PAGE 2**

12. The sides of a number cube are numbered from 1 to 6. What is the probability of rolling a number greater than 4?
    Ⓕ $\frac{2}{6}$ H $\frac{4}{6}$
    G $\frac{3}{6}$ J $\frac{5}{6}$

13. $0.5\overline{)0.35}$
    A 70 Ⓒ 0.7
    B 7 D 0.07

14. Which number sentence is true?
    F $\frac{1}{2} < \frac{3}{7}$ Ⓗ $\frac{5}{6} = \frac{10}{12}$
    G $\frac{3}{4} = \frac{10}{12}$ J $\frac{2}{5} > \frac{2}{3}$

15. $53\overline{)409}$
    Ⓐ 7 r38 C 7 r59
    B 7 r49 D 8 r5

16. One winter morning, the temperature was $^{-}4$°F. By the afternoon, the temperature was $^{+}7$°F. What was the temperature change from morning to afternoon?
    F $^{-}11$°F H $^{+}3$°F
    G $^{-}3$°F Ⓙ $^{+}11$°F

17. What are the coordinates of point *K*?
    A (5,0) C (4,0)
    B (5,4) Ⓓ (4,5)

18. What is the rule for the table below?

x	3	6	9	12	15
y	6	12	18	24	30

    F $y = x + 3$ Ⓗ $y = 2x$
    G $x = y + 3$ J $x = 2y$

19. During a song, Diana claps every third note and Matthew taps his foot every fourth note. Which is the first note when they will both participate?
    A 6th note C 18th note
    Ⓑ 12th note D 24th note

20. Which sum is closest to 1?
    F $\frac{7}{8} + \frac{5}{6}$ H $\frac{2}{7} + \frac{1}{4}$
    Ⓖ $\frac{3}{5} + \frac{1}{2}$ J $\frac{1}{8} + \frac{1}{8}$

21. Find $24 \times \frac{3}{8}$ in simplest form.
    A $\frac{3}{4}$ Ⓒ 9
    B $1\frac{1}{8}$ D 64

22. Carol estimated a product to be 12,000. For which multiplication problem was she estimating the product?
    F 63×19 H 163×19
    G 193×16 Ⓙ 603×19

23. 2.79×1.3
    A 0.3627
    Ⓑ 3.627
    C 36.27
    D 362.724

Go On

Name ______________________ **INVENTORY TEST • PAGE 3**

24. Twenty-four students in a class equally shared the $38.40 cost of 3 pizzas. How much did each student pay?
    Ⓕ $1.60 H $12.30
    G $1.80 J $12.80

25. During the school year, Crystal's height increased by $2\frac{3}{8}$ in. Choose an equivalent way to name the change in Crystal's height.
    A 0.238 in. C 2.38 in.
    Ⓑ 2.375 in. D 2.5 in.

26. The radius of a circle measures 8 cm. Which expression gives the length of the diameter?
    Ⓕ 8×2 cm H $8 \div 2$ cm
    G $8 \times \pi$ cm J $8 \div \pi$ cm

27. On Monday, the high temperature was 8°F less than on Wednesday. If the high temperature on Wednesday was 23°F, which equation can be used to find the high temperature on Monday?
    A $t - 8 = 23$ C $t - 23 = 8$
    Ⓑ $t = 23 - 8$ D $23 + t = 8$

28. Rachel ordered 3 medium pizzas for a party. Each was sliced into eighths. If $2\frac{3}{8}$ pizzas were eaten, how much was left?
    F $\frac{3}{8}$ of a pizza H $1\frac{3}{8}$ pizzas
    Ⓖ $\frac{5}{8}$ of a pizza J $1\frac{5}{8}$ pizzas

29. Divide. Write the answer in simplest form.
    $\frac{2}{3} \div \frac{4}{5}$
    A $\frac{5}{12}$ Ⓒ $\frac{5}{6}$
    B $\frac{8}{15}$ D $1\frac{1}{5}$

30. Add. Write the answer in simplest form.
    $\frac{2}{5} + \frac{1}{10}$
    F $\frac{3}{15}$ H $\frac{3}{10}$
    G $\frac{1}{5}$ Ⓙ $\frac{1}{2}$

31. The length of George's desk is 85 cm, and the width is 40 cm. What is the perimeter of his desk?
    A 125 cm Ⓒ 250 cm
    B 210 cm D 3,400 cm

32. A pencil is 5 in. long. What is the approximate length of the pencil in centimeters? (1 in. ≈ 2.54 cm)
    Ⓕ 12.7 cm H 1.27 cm
    G 12.5 cm J 1.25 cm

33. Choose the ratio that compares the number of squares to the number of circles.
    A 6 : 4 Ⓒ 2 : 3
    B 4 : 10 D 3 : 2

Go On

Name ______________________ **INVENTORY TEST • PAGE 4**

34. Which rectangles are congruent?
    F
    Ⓖ
    H
    J

35. How many ways can you make 40 cents using only dimes and nickels?
    Ⓐ 5 ways C 3 ways
    B 4 ways D 2 ways

36. How many of the small cubes make up the larger solid figure?
    F 6 H 18
    G 12 Ⓙ 24

37. Which set shows three forms of the same number?
    A $\frac{1}{4}$, 0.25, 2.5% Ⓒ $\frac{3}{4}$, 0.75, 75%
    B $\frac{3}{8}$, 0.38, 38% D $\frac{1}{2}$, 0.5, 5%

38. What is 30% of 90?
    F 3 H 30
    Ⓖ 27 J 270

39. What is the probability that the pointer will land on the red section in this spinner?

    A $\frac{7}{8}$ C $\frac{1}{7}$
    B $\frac{6}{7}$ Ⓓ $\frac{1}{8}$

40. The table shows the number of blocks from school that students in one class live.

NUMBER OF BLOCKS	NUMBER OF STUDENTS
1	3
2	2
3	6
4	4
more than 4	7

    How many students live at least 3 blocks from school?
    F 5 students H 11 students
    G 6 students Ⓙ 17 students

Stop

Name ______________________ **INVENTORY TEST • PAGE 1**

Write the correct answer.

1. What is the value of the 8 in 678,253?

 8,000

2. Order the numbers from *greatest* to *least*.

 199,417; 201,416; 200,415

 201,416; 200,415; 199,417

3. Dennis paid $1.359 per gallon for gasoline. Estimate, to the nearest tenth of a dollar, how much he paid for 10 gal.

 $13.60

4. Estimate. 447 ÷ 9

 Possible estimate: 50

5. Give the mean and mode for the set of data.

 8, 6, 9, 7, 7, 6, 5, 7, 8

 mean 7 mode 7

6. Delaney earns $18.00 per week delivering papers. Write an expression that represents the amount she earns in *d* weeks.

 $18 \times d$

7. Round 345,012 to the nearest ten thousand.

 350,000

8. The table shows the amount of rainfall for four days last week. On which day did the most rain fall?

DAY	RAIN (IN INCHES)
Monday	0.304
Tuesday	0.282
Wednesday	0.309
Thursday	0.299

 Wednesday

9. Carly wants to use a graph to compare the lengths of six bridges. What type of graph should she use?

 bar graph

10. James bicycled 52.81 mi one week, and 47.28 mi the next week. Estimate, to the nearest whole number, the total distance he bicycled in those two weeks.

 100 mi

11. Which quadrilateral must have all sides equal in length, but does not have four equal angles?

 rhombus

Go On

Name ______________________ **INVENTORY TEST • PAGE 2**

12. The sides of a cube are numbered from 1 to 6. Express the probability of rolling a number greater than 2 as a fraction?

 $\frac{2}{3}$

13. $0.6\overline{)0.42}$

 0.7

14. Write an equivalent fraction for $\frac{3}{5}$.

 Possible answer: $\frac{6}{10}$

15. $43\overline{)341}$

 7 r40

16. One afternoon, the temperature was $^-8$°F. By the evening, the temperature was $^-13$°F. What was the temperature change from afternoon to evening?

 $^-5$°F

17. What are the coordinates of point *C*?

 (1, $^-2$)

18. What is the rule for the table below?

x	3	6	9	12	15
y	4.5	9	13.5	18	22.5

 $y = 1.5x$

19. During a song, David claps every second note and Matthew taps his foot every sixth note. Which is the first note when they will both participate?

 the sixth note

20. Add. Write the answer in simplest form.

 $\frac{1}{4} + \frac{3}{8}$

 $\frac{5}{8}$

21. Multiply. Write the answer in simplest form.

 $30 \times \frac{2}{5}$

 12

22. Estimate. 702×21

 about 14,000

23.
$$\begin{array}{r} 3.28 \\ \times\ 1.7 \\ \hline \end{array}$$

 5.576

Go On

Name ______________________ **INVENTORY TEST • PAGE 3**

24. Twenty-eight students equally shared the $50.40 cost of supplies for a class party. How much did each student pay?

 $1.80

25. Name a decimal equivalent to $3\frac{5}{8}$.

 3.625

26. The radius of a circle measures 7 in. Write an expression that gives the length of the diameter.

 7×2 in.

27. A share of stock in CMG Company sold for $7.00 more on Wednesday than it did on Monday. The price of the share on Wednesday was $65.00. Write an equation to find the price of the share on Monday.

 $m = 65 - 7$

28. Ms. Manning's class ordered 5 pizzas for a class picnic. The students ate $4\frac{1}{3}$ pizzas. How much was left?

 $\frac{2}{3}$ of a pizza

29. Divide. Write the answer in simplest form.

 $\frac{3}{4} \div \frac{1}{2}$

 $\frac{3}{2}$, or $1\frac{1}{2}$

30. Add. Write the answer in simplest form.

 $\frac{3}{8} + \frac{3}{4}$

 $\frac{9}{8}$, or $1\frac{1}{8}$

31. The length of Bernie's beach towel is 205 cm, and the width is 80 cm. What is the perimeter of the towel?

 570 cm

32. A blackboard eraser is 6 in. long. What is the approximate length of the eraser in centimeters? (1 in. ≈ 2.54 cm)

 15.24 cm

33. Write a ratio that compares the number of triangles to the number of circles.

 2:3

Go On

Name ______________________ **INVENTORY TEST • PAGE 4**

34. Circle two rectangles that are congruent.

35. How many ways can you make 35¢, using only nickels and dimes?

 4 ways

36. How many small cubes make up the larger solid figure?

 12 cubes

37. Name a decimal and fraction equivalent to 43%.

 0.43, $\frac{43}{100}$

38. What is 40% of 80?

 32

39. A spinner that is divided into 8 equal sections, has 2 blue, 3 orange, and 3 white sections. What is the probability that the pointer will land on a blue section?

 25% or $\frac{1}{4}$

40. The table shows the number of books that students in Mr. Brockelman's class read over the summer.

NUMBER OF BOOKS	NUMBER OF STUDENTS
1	2
2	5
3	6
4	7
more than 4	4

 How many students read at least 3 books over the summer?

 17 students

Stop

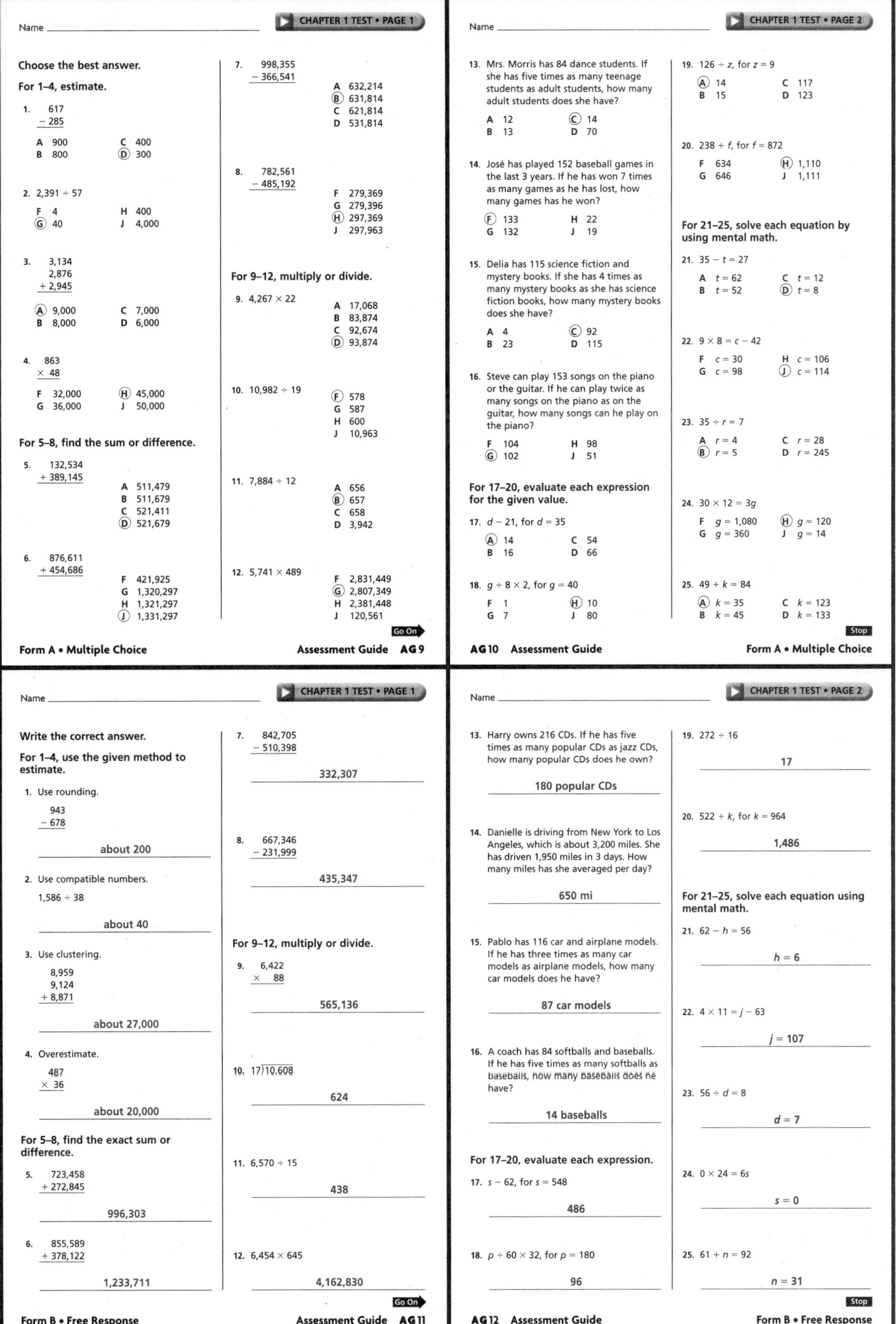

Name ______________________ CHAPTER 1 TEST • PAGE 1

Choose the best answer.

For 1–4, estimate.

1. 617 − 285
   - A 900
   - B 800
   - C 400
   - (D) 300

2. 2,391 ÷ 57
   - F 4
   - (G) 40
   - H 400
   - J 4,000

3. 3,134 + 2,876 + 2,945
   - (A) 9,000
   - B 8,000
   - C 7,000
   - D 6,000

4. 863 × 48
   - F 32,000
   - G 36,000
   - (H) 45,000
   - J 50,000

For 5–8, find the sum or difference.

5. 132,534 + 389,145
   - A 511,479
   - B 511,679
   - C 521,411
   - (D) 521,679

6. 876,611 + 454,686
   - F 421,925
   - G 1,320,297
   - H 1,321,297
   - (J) 1,331,297

7. 998,355 − 366,541
   - A 632,214
   - (B) 631,814
   - C 621,814
   - D 531,814

8. 782,561 − 485,192
   - F 279,369
   - G 279,396
   - (H) 297,369
   - J 297,963

For 9–12, multiply or divide.

9. 4,267 × 22
   - A 17,068
   - B 83,874
   - C 92,674
   - (D) 93,874

10. 10,982 ÷ 19
    - (F) 578
    - G 587
    - H 600
    - J 10,963

11. 7,884 ÷ 12
    - A 656
    - (B) 657
    - C 658
    - D 3,942

12. 5,741 × 489
    - F 2,831,449
    - (G) 2,807,349
    - H 2,381,448
    - J 120,561

Go On

Form A • Multiple Choice — Assessment Guide AG 9

Name ______________________ CHAPTER 1 TEST • PAGE 2

13. Mrs. Morris has 84 dance students. If she has five times as many teenage students as adult students, how many adult students does she have?
    - A 12
    - B 13
    - (C) 14
    - D 70

14. José has played 152 baseball games in the last 3 years. If he has won 7 times as many games as he has lost, how many games has he won?
    - (F) 133
    - G 132
    - H 22
    - J 19

15. Delia has 115 science fiction and mystery books. If she has 4 times as many mystery books as she has science fiction books, how many mystery books does she have?
    - A 4
    - B 23
    - (C) 92
    - D 115

16. Steve can play 153 songs on the piano or the guitar. If he can play twice as many songs on the piano as on the guitar, how many songs can he play on the piano?
    - F 104
    - (G) 102
    - H 98
    - J 51

For 17–20, evaluate each expression for the given value.

17. $d - 21$, for $d = 35$
    - (A) 14
    - B 16
    - C 54
    - D 66

18. $g \div 8 \times 2$, for $g = 40$
    - F 1
    - G 7
    - (H) 10
    - J 80

19. $126 \div z$, for $z = 9$
    - (A) 14
    - B 15
    - C 117
    - D 123

20. $238 + f$, for $f = 872$
    - F 634
    - G 646
    - (H) 1,110
    - J 1,111

For 21–25, solve each equation by using mental math.

21. $35 - t = 27$
    - A $t = 62$
    - B $t = 52$
    - C $t = 12$
    - (D) $t = 8$

22. $9 \times 8 = c - 42$
    - F $c = 30$
    - G $c = 98$
    - H $c = 106$
    - (J) $c = 114$

23. $35 \div r = 7$
    - A $r = 4$
    - (B) $r = 5$
    - C $r = 28$
    - D $r = 245$

24. $30 \times 12 = 3g$
    - F $g = 1{,}080$
    - G $g = 360$
    - (H) $g = 120$
    - J $g = 14$

25. $49 + k = 84$
    - (A) $k = 35$
    - B $k = 45$
    - C $k = 123$
    - D $k = 133$

Stop

AG 10 Assessment Guide — Form A • Multiple Choice

Name ______________________ CHAPTER 1 TEST • PAGE 1

Write the correct answer.

For 1–4, use the given method to estimate.

1. Use rounding.
   943 − 678
   about 200

2. Use compatible numbers.
   1,586 ÷ 38
   about 40

3. Use clustering.
   8,959 + 9,124 + 8,871
   about 27,000

4. Overestimate.
   487 × 36
   about 20,000

For 5–8, find the exact sum or difference.

5. 723,458 + 272,845
   996,303

6. 855,589 + 378,122
   1,233,711

7. 842,705 − 510,398
   332,307

8. 667,346 − 231,999
   435,347

For 9–12, multiply or divide.

9. 6,422 × 88
   565,136

10. $17\overline{)10{,}608}$
    624

11. 6,570 ÷ 15
    438

12. 6,454 × 645
    4,162,830

Go On

Form B • Free Response — Assessment Guide AG 11

Name ______________________ CHAPTER 1 TEST • PAGE 2

13. Harry owns 216 CDs. If he has five times as many popular CDs as jazz CDs, how many popular CDs does he own?
    180 popular CDs

14. Danielle is driving from New York to Los Angeles, which is about 3,200 miles. She has driven 1,950 miles in 3 days. How many miles has she averaged per day?
    650 mi

15. Pablo has 116 car and airplane models. If he has three times as many car models as airplane models, how many car models does he have?
    87 car models

16. A coach has 84 softballs and baseballs. If he has five times as many softballs as baseballs, how many baseballs does he have?
    14 baseballs

For 17–20, evaluate each expression.

17. $s - 62$, for $s = 548$
    486

18. $p \div 60 \times 32$, for $p = 180$
    96

19. 272 ÷ 16
    17

20. $522 + k$, for $k = 964$
    1,486

For 21–25, solve each equation using mental math.

21. $62 - h = 56$
    $h = 6$

22. $4 \times 11 = j - 63$
    $j = 107$

23. $56 \div d = 8$
    $d = 7$

24. $0 \times 24 = 6s$
    $s = 0$

25. $61 + n = 92$
    $n = 31$

Stop

AG 12 Assessment Guide — Form B • Free Response

Name ______________________

Choose the best answer.

For 1–6, use mental math to find the value.

1. 19 + 254

A 263 (C) 273
B 265 D 275

2. $2 \times 7 \times 40$

F 280 (H) 560
G 360 J 650

3. 395 − 87

A 318 C 306
(B) 308 D 288

4. $225 \div 5$

(F) 45 H 35
G 41 J 31

5. $6,784 \times 1$

A 6,785 C 1
(B) 6,784 D 0

6. $20 \times 37 \times 5$

F 137 H 925
G 185 (J) 3,700

For 7–10, find the value.

7. 8^5

A 390,625 (C) 32,768
B 262,144 D 4,096

8. 5^6

(F) 15,625 H 3,125
G 5,600 J 25

9. 7^5

A 49 C 7,500
B 2,401 (D) 16,807

10. 6^4

F 216 H 7,776
(G) 1,296 J 46,656

For 11–15, evaluate the expression.

11. $3^3 + 4 \times 5$

A 29 C 155
(B) 47 D 180

12. $42 - (6 \div 3) \times (5 + 3)$

F 320 H 168
G 312 (J) 26

13. $33 \times (4 - 2) - 4^2$

(A) 50 C 82
B 58 D 560

14. $(44 \div 4) \times (2 + 3^2)$

F 39 H 110
G 55 (J) 121

15. $(72 \div 9) + 13^2 - 8$

A 22 (C) 169
B 42 D 433

Go On

Name ______________________

16. Ling has written 8 pages each day for the last 30 days. If she has to write a total of 400 pages in 46 days, how many pages will she have to write per day during the remaining time in order to meet her goal?

(F) 10 pages H 25 pages
G 15 pages J 50 pages

17. Robin baby-sits 5 hours a week for $6 per hour. He mows lawns for $10 each twice a week. How much will he make in 12 weeks?

A $6,000 C $480
(B) $600 D $380

For 18–21, evaluate the expression for $a = 8$ and $b = 3$.

18. $9 + a^2 \div (12 - 4)$

F 64 H 11
(G) 17 J 3

19. $b \times 5 + 43$

(A) 58 C 144
B 88 D 645

20. $80 \div a \times (28 - 23)$

F 450 H 15
(G) 50 J 2

21. $48 \div b - 7$

A 23 C 10
B 11 (D) 9

22. Deborah's train ride takes 8 hours. She reads 30 pages per hour. How many pages will she read if she sleeps for 2 hours and reads the rest of the time?

F 300 pages (H) 180 pages
G 240 pages J 38 pages

For 23–25, use the following chart.

GUIDED TOUR TIMES	
1 Expressionists	10 A.M., 4 P.M.
2 American Painters	10 A.M., 3 P.M.
3 Dutch Painters	12 P.M., 3 P.M.
4 Sculpture	1 P.M, 4 P.M.
5 Impressionists	2 P.M., 4 P.M.

Each tour lasts 50 minutes.

23. Miranda wants to take the Sculpture tour at 1 P.M. If she arrives at the museum at 10 A.M. and leaves at 4 P.M., in which order could she take all of the tours?

A 1, 2, 3, 4, 5 C 2, 5, 4, 3, 1
(B) 1, 3, 4, 5, 2 D 5, 4, 3, 2, 1

24. Ivan wants to take the 12 P.M. Dutch Painters tour. If he takes the tour and then eats for 45 minutes, what other tour could he take before he leaves the museum at 3:00 P.M.?

F 1 H 4
G 3 (J) 5

25. Susan wants to take the 10 A.M. Expressionists tour. If she plans to leave the museum by 2 P.M., which other tours could she take?

(A) 3, 4 C 2, 3
B 1, 2 D 5, 4

Stop

Name ______________________

Write the correct answer.

For 1–6, use mental math to find the value of each expression.

1. 64 + 319

383

2. $6 \times 4 \times 30$

720

3. 487 − 242

245

4. $342 \div 6$

57

5. $9,208 \times 1$

9,208

6. $20 \times 64 \times 5$

6,400

For 7–15, evaluate the expression.

7. 7^5

16,807

8. 16^2

256

9. 4^8

65,536

10. 6^4

1,296

11. $42 + 8 \times 2$

58

12. $97 - 8^2 + (10 \times 5)$

83

13. $(13 \times 5 + 1) \div (4^2 - 5)$

6

14. $(72 \div 6) \times (3 + 1^2)$

48

15. $5^3 \div 25 \times (14 - 12)$

10

Go On

Name ______________________

16. Bernardo has sold an average of 9 pairs of shoes per day for the last 20 days. He has to sell a total of 260 pairs of shoes in 30 days to get a bonus. How many pairs of shoes will he have to sell per day during the remaining time in order to get a bonus?

8 pairs

17. Martha weeds gardens 7 hours a week for $8 per hour. She washes three cars a week for $12 each. How much will she be able to make in the next 14 weeks?

$1,288

For 18–21, evaluate the expression for $a = 6$ and $b = 4$.

18. $(6 + a^2) \div (10 - 3)$

6

19. $b \times 9 + 35$

71

20. $90 \div a \times (42 - 37)$

75

21. $64 \div b - 6$

10

22. Rick plants 15 bushes per hour. He is at work for 8 hours per day, but he gets 1 hour off for lunch and 2 half-hour breaks. How many bushes can Rick plant in a day?

90 bushes

For 23–25, use the following chart.

ACTIVITY SESSION TIMES	
Dancing	12 P.M., 3 P.M.
Gymnastics	10 A.M., 4 P.M.
Yoga	11 A.M., 4 P.M.
Volleyball	2 P.M.
Basketball	3 P.M., 4 P.M.

Each activity lasts 50 minutes.

23. Cyril wants to do yoga at 11 A.M. If he arrives at the sports center at 10 A.M. and leaves at 4 P.M., in what order could he do all the activities?

Gymnastics, Yoga, Dancing

Volleyball, Basketball

24. If Marina goes to the dancing class at noon and then takes a 1 hour 15 minute break for lunch, what other activity could she do before she leaves the sports center at 4 P.M.?

Basketball

25. Amy plans to take gymnastics at 10 A.M. If she plans to leave the sports center by 12:30, what other activity could she do?

Yoga

Stop

Name ______________________

CHAPTER 3 TEST • PAGE 1

Choose the best answer.

1. Compare the numbers in each pair. For which pair is > the correct symbol?
   (A) 43.27 ● 43.22
   B 43.77 ● 43.77
   C 3.22 ● 3.27
   D 43.22 ● 43.22

2. Compare the numbers in each pair. For which pair is < the correct symbol?
   F 188.3 ● 188.03
   (G) 188.03 ● 188.3
   H 188.03 ● 188.03
   J 88.3 ● 88.3

3. Which is equal to 0.834?
   (A) 0.8340 C 0.84
   B 0.843 D 8.8340

4. Which is greater than 92.05?
   F 1.0005
   G 92.005
   H 92.05
   (J) 92.5

For 5–8, order the numbers from *least* to *greatest*.

5. 5.22, 5.81, 5.27, 5.041
   A 5.81, 5.27, 5.22, 5.041
   B 5.81, 5.041, 5.27, 5.22
   C 5.041, 5.27, 5.22, 5.81
   (D) 5.041, 5.22, 5.27, 5.81

6. 22.1, 22.7, 22.09, 22.078
   F 22.7, 22.1, 22.09, 22.078
   G 22.09, 22.7, 22.078, 22.1
   (H) 22.078, 22.09, 22.1, 22.7
   J 22.09, 22.078, 22.7, 22.1

7. 18.87, 18.45, 18.03, 18.30
   A 18.87, 18.45, 18.30, 18.03
   B 18.03, 18.87, 18.45, 18.30
   C 18.30, 18.45, 18.87, 18.03
   (D) 18.03, 18.30, 18.45, 18.87

8. 25.05, 25.80, 25.40, 25.99
   F 25.99, 25.80, 25.40, 25.05
   (G) 25.05, 25.40, 25.80, 25.99
   H 25.80, 25.40, 25.99, 25.05
   J 25.40, 25.80, 25.99, 25.05

For 9–11, find the value of the underlined digit.

9. 5.2394
   A 3 ones
   B 3 tens
   (C) 3 hundredths
   D 3 thousandths

10. 37.66257
   (F) 2 thousandths
   G 2 hundredths
   H 2 tenths
   J 2 ones

11. 0.30809
   A 3 ones
   (B) 3 tenths
   C 3 hundredths
   D 3 thousandths

Go On

Name ______________________

CHAPTER 3 TEST • PAGE 2

For 12–13, find the percent and the decimal for the shaded part.

12. F 0.66%, 66
   G 66%, 0.66
   (H) 34%, 0.34
   J 0.34%, 34

13. A 0.27%, 27
   (B) 27%, 0.27
   C 0.73%, 73
   D 73%, 0.73

For 14–16, find the corresponding percent or decimal.

14. 0.07
   F 700% (H) 7%
   G 70% J 0.7%

15. 5%
   A 5.0 (C) 0.05
   B 0.5 D 0.005

16. 0.9
   F 900% H 9%
   (G) 90% J 0.9%

For 17–20, use the data in the chart below. The greater the number, the stronger the earthquake.

STRENGTH OF RECENT EARTHQUAKES (MAGNITUDE ON THE RICHTER SCALE)	
Los Angeles	3.4
Tokyo	3.1
San Francisco	4.1
Mexico City	4.2
New Delhi	3.6
Hong Kong	3.9

17. Which of these cities had the weakest earthquake?
   A Hong Kong C San Francisco
   (B) Tokyo D New Delhi

18. Which of these cities had the strongest earthquake?
   (F) Mexico City H Hong Kong
   G San Francisco J New Delhi

19. Which of these cities had the second weakest earthquake?
   (A) Los Angeles C Mexico City
   B Tokyo D Hong Kong

20. Which city had the second strongest earthquake?
   F Tokyo H Mexico City
   G New Delhi (J) San Francisco

For 21–25, estimate.

21. 4.8 × 7.2
   A 28 C 40
   (B) 35 D 3,500

22. 64.3 ÷ 8.1
   F 0.7 H 7
   G 0.8 (J) 8

23. 38.9 + 162.3
   A 20 C 150
   B 130 (D) 200

24. 5.13 + 4.97 + 4.88 + 5.04
   F 21 H 19
   (G) 20 J 16

25. 80.7 − 2.5
   A 94 (C) 78
   B 83 D 75

Stop

Name ______________________

CHAPTER 3 TEST • PAGE 1

Write the correct answer.

For 1–4, compare the numbers in each pair. Write >, <, or =.

1. 83.09 ● 83.9
   <

2. 3.0984 ● 3.0849
   >

3. 8.80 ● 8.800
   =

4. 48.75 ● 48.5
   >

For 5–8, order the numbers from *least* to *greatest*.

5. 4.53, 4.091, 4.58, 4.12
   4.091, 4.12, 4.53, 4.58

6. 25.802, 25.8, 25.08, 25.818
   25.08, 25.8, 25.802, 25.818

7. 1.50, 1.05, 1.04, 1.45, 1.40
   1.04, 1.05, 1.40, 1.45, 1.50

8. 7.54, 7.53, 7.08, 7.58
   7.08, 7.53, 7.54, 7.58

For 9–11, write the value of the underlined digit.

9. 8.09346
   3 thousandths

10. 9.68723
   6 tenths

11. 8.28706
   8 hundredths

Go On

Name ______________________

CHAPTER 3 TEST • PAGE 2

For 12–13, write the percent and the decimal for the shaded part.

12. 46%; 0.46

13. 50%; 0.50 or 0.5

For 14–16, write the corresponding percent or decimal.

14. 0.03
   3%

15. 6%
   0.06

16. 0.2
   20%

For 17–20, use the data in the chart below.

AVERAGE WIND SPEED (MILES PER HOUR)	
Boston, MA	12.5
Chicago, IL	10.4
Houston, TX	7.8
Mobile, AL	8.9
St. Louis, MO	9.7
San Diego, CA	7.0

17. Which city had the lowest average wind speed?
   San Diego

18. Which city had the highest average wind speed?
   Boston

19. Which city had the second lowest average wind speed?
   Houston

20. Which city had the second highest average wind speed?
   Chicago

For 21–25, estimate. Possible estimates are given.

21. 6.3 × 8.2
   about 48

22. 78.2 ÷ 8.5
   about 9

23. 62.5 + 127.7
   about 190

24. 3.25 + 4.08 + 7.62 + 9.13
   about 24

25. 43.8 − 6.1
   about 38

Stop

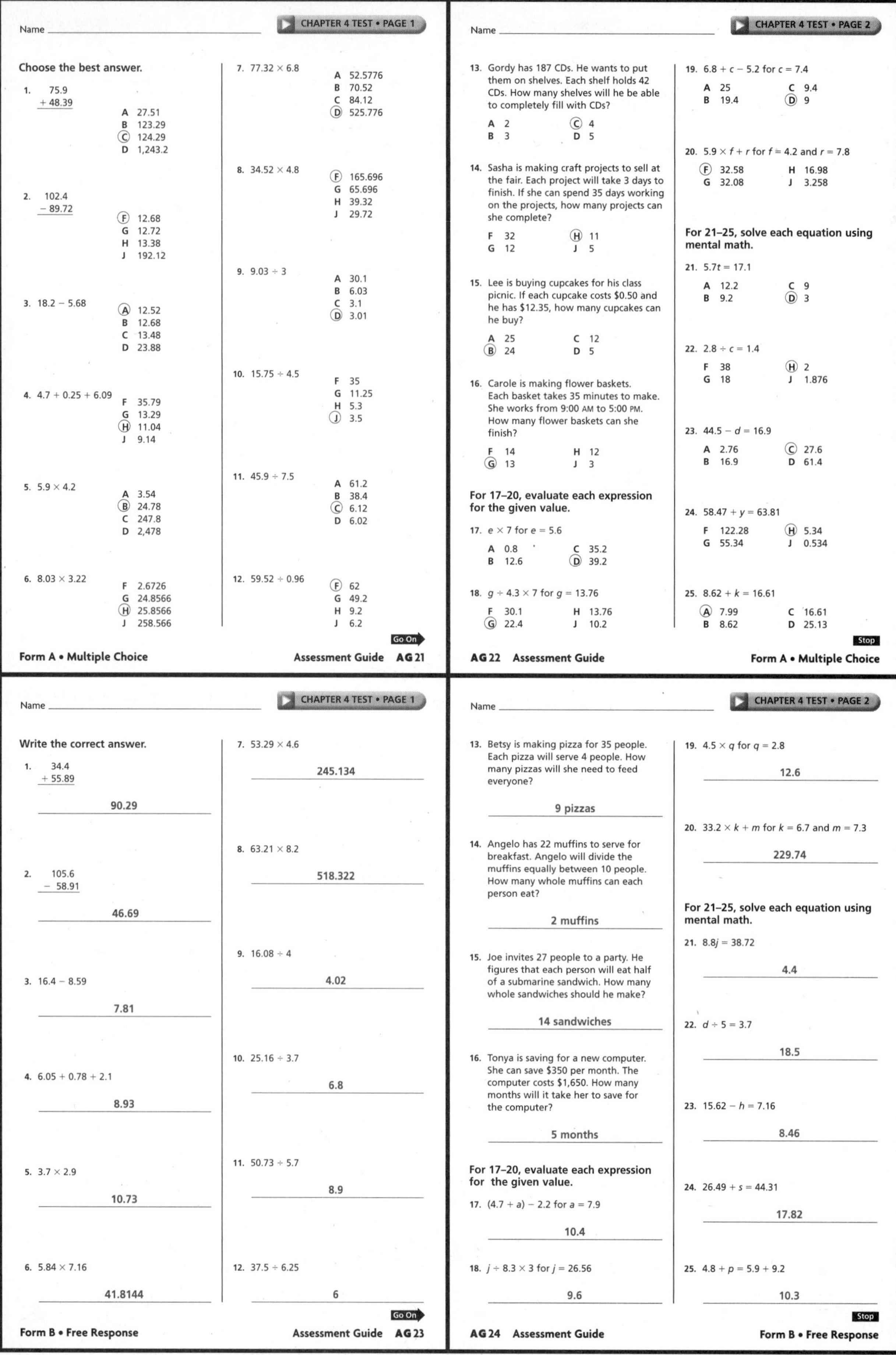

Name ____________________

CHAPTER 4 TEST • PAGE 1

Choose the best answer.

1. 75.9 + 48.39
   A 27.51
   B 123.29
   (C) 124.29
   D 1,243.2

2. 102.4 − 89.72
   (F) 12.68
   G 12.72
   H 13.38
   J 192.12

3. 18.2 − 5.68
   (A) 12.52
   B 12.68
   C 13.48
   D 23.88

4. 4.7 + 0.25 + 6.09
   F 35.79
   G 13.29
   (H) 11.04
   J 9.14

5. 5.9 × 4.2
   A 3.54
   (B) 24.78
   C 247.8
   D 2,478

6. 8.03 × 3.22
   F 2.6726
   G 24.8566
   (H) 25.8566
   J 258.566

7. 77.32 × 6.8
   A 52.5776
   B 70.52
   C 84.12
   (D) 525.776

8. 34.52 × 4.8
   (F) 165.696
   G 65.696
   H 39.32
   J 29.72

9. 9.03 ÷ 3
   A 30.1
   B 6.03
   C 3.1
   (D) 3.01

10. 15.75 ÷ 4.5
    F 35
    G 11.25
    H 5.3
    (J) 3.5

11. 45.9 ÷ 7.5
    A 61.2
    B 38.4
    (C) 6.12
    D 6.02

12. 59.52 ÷ 0.96
    (F) 62
    G 49.2
    H 9.2
    J 6.2

Go On

Form A • Multiple Choice — Assessment Guide AG 21

Name ____________________

CHAPTER 4 TEST • PAGE 2

13. Gordy has 187 CDs. He wants to put them on shelves. Each shelf holds 42 CDs. How many shelves will he be able to completely fill with CDs?
    A 2 (C) 4
    B 3 D 5

14. Sasha is making craft projects to sell at the fair. Each project will take 3 days to finish. If she can spend 35 days working on the projects, how many projects can she complete?
    F 32 (H) 11
    G 12 J 5

15. Lee is buying cupcakes for his class picnic. If each cupcake costs $0.50 and he has $12.35, how many cupcakes can he buy?
    A 25 C 12
    (B) 24 D 5

16. Carole is making flower baskets. Each basket takes 35 minutes to make. She works from 9:00 AM to 5:00 PM. How many flower baskets can she finish?
    F 14 H 12
    (G) 13 J 3

For 17–20, evaluate each expression for the given value.

17. $e \times 7$ for $e = 5.6$
    A 0.8 C 35.2
    B 12.6 (D) 39.2

18. $g \div 4.3 \times 7$ for $g = 13.76$
    F 30.1 H 13.76
    (G) 22.4 J 10.2

19. $6.8 + c - 5.2$ for $c = 7.4$
    A 25 C 9.4
    B 19.4 (D) 9

20. $5.9 \times f + r$ for $f = 4.2$ and $r = 7.8$
    (F) 32.58 H 16.98
    G 32.08 J 3.258

For 21–25, solve each equation using mental math.

21. $5.7t = 17.1$
    A 12.2 C 9
    B 9.2 (D) 3

22. $2.8 \div c = 1.4$
    F 38 (H) 2
    G 18 J 1.876

23. $44.5 - d = 16.9$
    A 2.76 (C) 27.6
    B 16.9 D 61.4

24. $58.47 + y = 63.81$
    F 122.28 (H) 5.34
    G 55.34 J 0.534

25. $8.62 + k = 16.61$
    (A) 7.99 C 16.61
    B 8.62 D 25.13

Stop

AG 22 Assessment Guide — Form A • Multiple Choice

Name ____________________

CHAPTER 4 TEST • PAGE 1

Write the correct answer.

1. 34.4 + 55.89 — 90.29
2. 105.6 − 58.91 — 46.69
3. 16.4 − 8.59 — 7.81
4. 6.05 + 0.78 + 2.1 — 8.93
5. 3.7 × 2.9 — 10.73
6. 5.84 × 7.16 — 41.8144
7. 53.29 × 4.6 — 245.134
8. 63.21 × 8.2 — 518.322
9. 16.08 ÷ 4 — 4.02
10. 25.16 ÷ 3.7 — 6.8
11. 50.73 ÷ 5.7 — 8.9
12. 37.5 ÷ 6.25 — 6

Go On

Form B • Free Response — Assessment Guide AG 23

Name ____________________

CHAPTER 4 TEST • PAGE 2

13. Betsy is making pizza for 35 people. Each pizza will serve 4 people. How many pizzas will she need to feed everyone? — 9 pizzas

14. Angelo has 22 muffins to serve for breakfast. Angelo will divide the muffins equally between 10 people. How many whole muffins can each person eat? — 2 muffins

15. Joe invites 27 people to a party. He figures that each person will eat half of a submarine sandwich. How many whole sandwiches should he make? — 14 sandwiches

16. Tonya is saving for a new computer. She can save $350 per month. The computer costs $1,650. How many months will it take her to save for the computer? — 5 months

For 17–20, evaluate each expression for the given value.

17. $(4.7 + a) - 2.2$ for $a = 7.9$ — 10.4

18. $j \div 8.3 \times 3$ for $j = 26.56$ — 9.6

19. $4.5 \times q$ for $q = 2.8$ — 12.6

20. $33.2 \times k + m$ for $k = 6.7$ and $m = 7.3$ — 229.74

For 21–25, solve each equation using mental math.

21. $8.8j = 38.72$ — 4.4

22. $d \div 5 = 3.7$ — 18.5

23. $15.62 - h = 7.16$ — 8.46

24. $26.49 + s = 44.31$ — 17.82

25. $4.8 + p = 5.9 + 9.2$ — 10.3

Stop

AG 24 Assessment Guide — Form B • Free Response

Choose the best answer.

1. An estimate that is greater than the exact answer is called a(n) __?__.

A underestimate C error
Ⓑ overestimate D prediction

2. In the expression 4^7, the number 7 is called the __?__.

Ⓕ exponent H base
G remainder J power

3. What is the value of the 5 in 3.1415926?

A 5 millionths
B 5 hundred-thousandths
Ⓒ 5 ten-thousandths
D 5 thousandths

4. $2.7\overline{)72.9}$

F 0.27
G 2.7
Ⓗ 27
J 270

5. Estimate.

$$\begin{array}{r} 2,497 \\ +\ 1,723 \\ \hline \end{array}$$

A 5,000 C 3,500
Ⓑ 4,200 D 3,000

6. Find the value of $6 + 12 \div 3 - 2$.

F 18 H 4
Ⓖ 8 J 2

7. Which list shows the numbers written in order from *least* to *greatest*?

A 2.71, 2.7, 2.72, 2.718
B 2.718, 2.7, 2.72, 2.71
Ⓒ 2.7, 2.71, 2.718, 2.72
D 2.7, 2.71, 2.72, 2.718

8. 16.2×314.16

F 5,089,392 H 50,893.92
G 509,839.2 Ⓙ 5,089.392

9. 125×25

A 15,625 C 150
Ⓑ 3,125 D 5

10. Find the value of 6^6.

F 279,936 H 7,776
Ⓖ 46,656 J 36

11. Estimate.

$35.1 \div 6.85$

A 9 C 7
B 8 Ⓓ 5

12. Evaluate $r \times (8.35 - t)$ for $r = 2.5$ and $t = 5.84$.

F 15.035 H 8.775
G 12.25 Ⓙ 6.275

13. Estimate.

$3{,}542 \div 72$

Ⓐ 50 C 60
B 55 D 70

14. Evaluate $x^4 - y \bullet x$ for $x = 3$ and $y = 4$.

F 756 Ⓗ 69
G 231 J 0

Go On

15. Which list shows the numbers in order from *least* to *greatest*?

0.240, 0.229, 0.251

A 0.251, 0.229, 0.240
B 0.251, 0.240, 0.229
Ⓒ 0.229, 0.240, 0.251
D 0.240, 0.251, 0.229

16. Solve the equation by using mental math.

$p = 52.8 \div 5.28$

Ⓕ $p = 10$ H $p = 110$
G $p = 100$ J $p = 1{,}000$

17. Juanita read a book in two weeks. She read for a total of 15 hr. She read twice as many hours the second week as the first week. How many hours did she read the second week?

Ⓐ 10 hr C 3 hr
B 5 hr D 2 hr

18. Huang has $50 from delivering papers. He wants to buy 3 books at $7.95 each, a new pen for $5.49, and 2 maps for $3.75 each. How much money will he have left?

F $11.42 H $32.81
Ⓖ $13.16 J $36.84

19. Which percent is equivalent to 0.28?

A 280% C 2.8%
Ⓑ 28% D 0.28%

20. Kris finished a ski race in 53.27 sec. Tim finished in 51.84 sec. Who was faster and by how much?

F Kris; 2.43 sec Ⓗ Tim; 1.43 sec
G Kris; 1.43 sec J Tim; 1.34 sec

21. Solve the equation using mental math.

$20x = 240$

A $x = 4{,}800$ C $x = 48$
B $x = 120$ Ⓓ $x = 12$

22. Find the value of $25 \times (6 - 2)^2 + 4$.

F 10,004 Ⓗ 404
G 804 J 204

23. Find a decimal and percent for the shaded area.

Ⓐ 0.24, 24% C 0.28, 28%
B 0.25, 25% D 0.76, 76%

24. Jim can make one poster every 4.3 minutes. If he works non-stop from 8:00 A.M. to noon, how many posters can he finish?

F 240 H 56
G 60 Ⓙ 55

25. Evaluate $a + b - 27$ for $a = 50$ and $b = 40$.

A 43 Ⓒ 63
B 53 D 117

26. Find the value of $(3 + 4)^2$.

F 144 H 19
Ⓖ 49 J 14

Go On

27. In a track event, Carl's time was 16.1 sec, Evan's was 16.13 sec, Ed's was 16.02 sec, and Phil's was 16.09 sec. Who came in third?

Ⓐ Carl C Ed
B Evan D Phil

28. Notebooks cost $0.79 each, colored pencils are $0.29 each, and erasers are $0.24 each. Ms. Johnston wants to purchase 1 notebook, 2 colored pencils, and 1 eraser for each of the 33 students in her sixth-grade class. How much money will she need?

Ⓕ $53.13 H $18.48
G $36.63 J $10.51

29. $$\begin{array}{r} 321,456 \\ -\ 56,814 \\ \hline \end{array}$$

A 378,270
B 335,442
Ⓒ 264,642
D 264,462

30. Use mental math to find the value of $42 - (26 + 4)$.

F 74 H 64
G 66 Ⓙ 12

31. Estimate.

597.993×48.817

Ⓐ 30,000 C 25,000
B 29,192 D 20,000

32. Evaluate $k + 67.89$ for $k = 12.3$.

F 88.12 H 79.19
Ⓖ 80.19 J 55.59

33. Kirk sold a total of 48 magazines in the last two days. He sold 12 more today than yesterday. How many magazines did he sell yesterday?

Ⓐ 18 C 24
B 20 D 30

34. Jill, Sue, Fred, and Walt are going to a movie after they do their chores. The time it takes for each chore is shown below. To finish at the same time, in what order should they start?

Jill	Cleaning house	2 hr
Sue	Mowing lawn	3 hr
Fred	Washing dishes	1 hr
Walt	Washing clothes	4 hr

F Fred, Jill, Sue, Walt
G Sue, Walt, Jill, Fred
H Sue, Walt, Fred, Jill
Ⓙ Walt, Sue, Jill, Fred

35. What is the value of 1 in 2.71828?

A 1 hundred C 1 tenth
B 1 ten Ⓓ 1 hundredth

36. How many boxes of 12 calculators are needed for 369 students?

F 30 H 37
Ⓖ 31 J 50

37. Use mental math to solve.

$360 = 12h$

A $h = 240$ C $h = 40$
B $h = 140$ Ⓓ $h = 30$

38. Find the value of $(60 \div 5) + (8 - 5)^2$.

F 15 Ⓗ 21
G 18 J 225

Go On

39. Liam learns that the first bus arrives at his bus stop at 7:27 A.M. Buses then come every 17 min. When will the sixth bus arrive?

A 9:09 A.M. C 8:50 A.M.
Ⓑ 8:52 A.M. D 8:35 A.M.

40. $2.31 + 12.5 + 0.284$

F 64.0
G 17.65
Ⓗ 15.094
J 15.0

41. Dorothy has 84 apples. She has three times as many red apples as she has green apples. How many red apples does she have?

A 84 C 42
Ⓑ 63 D 21

42. Which of the following is the first step to evaluate $2 \times 3^4 - 18 \div 8$?

Ⓕ 3^4 H 2×3
G $4 - 18$ J $18 \div 8$

43. Which is a decimal equivalent of 40%?

A 40.0 Ⓒ 0.4
B 4.0 D 0.04

44. How many decimal places will be in the product 8.24×9.56?

F 2 H 5
Ⓖ 4 J 6

45. Evaluate $21 \div a - b + 4$ for $a = 7$ and $b = 3$.

A 0 C 8
Ⓑ 4 D 10

46. Find the value of $16 - 4^2$.

Ⓕ 0 H 24
G 8 J 144

47. Zachary earned $9.75 raking leaves, $15.25 mowing lawns, $11.20 pruning shrubs, and $21.80 washing windows. Which is a reasonable estimate of his total earnings?

A $40 C $50
B $45 Ⓓ $55

48. Jessica has to stack vegetable cans on shelves. She has 247 cans and each shelf holds 14 cans. How many complete shelves can she fill?

F 24 Ⓗ 17
G 18 J 15

49. Find the value of $12 \times 12 \times 12$.

Ⓐ 1,728 C 144
B 324 D 36

50. Pablo earns $3 for each car he washes and $7 for each car he waxes. If he washes 8 cars this month and waxes 5, how much will he earn?

F $10 H $39
G $31 Ⓙ $59

Stop

Name

UNIT 1 TEST • PAGE 1

Write the correct answer.

1. An estimate that is less than the exact answer is called a(n) __?__ .

underestimate

2. In the expression 3^2, the number 3 is called the __?__ .

base

3. What is the value of the 5 in 8.675309?

5 thousandths

4. $3.1\overline{)58.9}$

19

5. Estimate the sum.

 3,807
+ 1,288

Possible estimate: 5,000

6. $9 - 16 \div 4 + 8$

13

7. Order the numbers from *greatest* to *least*.

3.417, 3.471, 3.447, 3.474

3.474, 3.471, 3.447, 3.417

8. 18.7×407.52

7,620.624

9. 250×15

3,750

10. Find the value of 4^5.

1,024

11. Estimate.

$28.1 \div 7.35$

Possible estimate: 4

12. Evaluate $d \times (6.94 + g)$ for $d = 4.2$ and $g = 3.14$.

42.336

13. Estimate the quotient.

$4,777 \div 81$

Possible estimate: 60

14. Evaluate $c^3 + m \times c$ for $c = 4$ and $m = 7$.

92

Go On

Name

UNIT 1 TEST • PAGE 2

15. Order the numbers from *greatest* to *least*.

0.880, 0.804, 0.808

0.880, 0.808, 0.804

16. Solve the equation using mental math.

$c = 417 \div 4.17$

$c = 100$

17. Chris collected a total of 60 shells during a weekend at the beach. He collected three times as many shells on Saturday as he did on Sunday. How many shells did he collect on Sunday?

15 shells

18. Lynda began a craft project with a piece of copper wire 36 in. long. From this she cut 2 pieces that were each 3.5 in. long, 3 pieces that were each 4.75 in. long, and 1 piece that was 11.5 in. long. How much wire did she have left?

3.25 in. of wire

19. Write a percent that is equivalent to 0.54.

54%

20. Maggie bought two CDs at the mall. One was priced \$11.98, and the other was \$13.45. What was the difference in their prices?

\$1.47

21. Solve the equation using mental math.

$30y = 360$

$y = 12$

22. Evaluate the expression.

$48 \div (8 - 6)^2 + 11$

23

23. Write the decimal and percent for the shaded area.

0.40, 40%

24. A pool is losing water through a leak at a constant rate of one gallon every 2.5 days. How much water does the pool lose in 4 weeks?

11.2 gallons of water

25. Evaluate $t - w + 31$ for $t = 47$ and $w = 18$.

60

26. $(4 + 2)^3$

216

Go On

Name

UNIT 1 TEST • PAGE 3

27. At a gymnastics meet, Katherine scored 9.15 on the balance beam, 9.06 on the vault, and 9.10 on the uneven parallel bars. In which event did she receive the lowest score?

vault

28. Michael's father made bags of party favors for the 12 friends that came to Michael's party. For each bag he bought 2 packs of baseball cards for \$1.59 each, 1 pack of bubblegum for \$0.49, and a kazoo for \$0.25. How much did he spend on party favors?

\$47.04

29.
 456,391
− 88,012

368,379

30. Use mental math to find the value of $28 + (41 - 9)$.

60

31. Estimate the product.

389.896×24.502

Possible estimate: 10,000

32. Evaluate $c + 56.78$ for $c = 23.4$.

80.18

33. It rained a total of 46 days in March and April. It rained 8 more days in April than in March. How many days did it rain in March?

19 days

34. David, Gary, Susan, and Walter are meeting at the mall. The time it takes for each to ride to the mall is shown below. To arrive at the same time, in what order should they leave their homes?

David	25 minutes
Gary	15 minutes
Susan	30 minutes
Walter	10 minutes

Susan, David, Gary, Walter

35. Write the value of the 2 in 8.32971.

2 hundredths

36. How many complete rows of 15 parking spaces are needed to park 280 cars?

19 rows

37. Use mental math to solve.

$440 = 11g$

$g = 40$

38. $(56 \div 4) + (9 - 3)^2$

50

Go On

Name

UNIT 1 TEST • PAGE 4

39. Diane saw on a schedule that the first tram leaving the parking lot departs at 8:42 A.M. Trams then depart every 12 min. When will the sixth tram depart?

9:42 A.M.

40. $3.65 + 20.1 + 0.197$

23.947

41. Richard has 64 comic books in his collection. He has three times as many superhero comics as he has humor comics. How many superhero comic books does he have?

48 superhero comic books

42. Which operation is the first step to evaluate $3 \times 2^4 + 25 \div 5$?

clear exponents - 2^4

43. Write the decimal equivalent of 65%.

0.65

44. How many decimal places will be in the product 6.97×8.42?

4

45. Evaluate $42 \div d + g - 3$ for $d = 6$ and $g = 6$.

10

46. $36 - 6^2$

0

47. Vi spent \$8.15 on Monday, \$13.45 on Tuesday, \$9.90 on Wednesday, and \$18.65 on Thursday. What is a reasonable estimate of the amount of money he spent on these four days?

\$50

48. Wally has to pack his rock collection in cases. He has 165 rocks and each case holds 12 rocks. How many cases can he fill completely?

13 cases

49. $11 \times 11 \times 11$

1,331

50. Bill earns \$12 for each lawn he mows and \$8 for each garden he weeds. If he mows 6 lawns this month and weeds 3 gardens, how much will he earn?

\$96

Stop

Name ______________________

Choose the best answer.

For 1–2, determine the type of sample used.

1. John randomly selected a student from his class and then every fifth student after that to determine the number of videos watched each week.

   A convenience C random
   B voluntary Ⓓ systematic

2. Samantha randomly surveys 1 out of every 6 people in the movie theater to find the brand of popcorn most often eaten at home.

   F convenience Ⓗ random
   G voluntary J systematic

For 3–7, use the table below, which shows the ages of teachers at Martin Luther King, Jr. School.

AGES OF TEACHERS				
24	53	32	48	28
35	41	29	33	51
40	29	31	25	28
38	47	52	29	27

3. What is the range of ages?

   A 3 Ⓒ 29
   B 24 D 53

4. What is the mode?

   F 28 H 31
   Ⓖ 29 J 53

5. What is the median?

   A 32 C 33
   Ⓑ 32.5 D 53

6. What is the mean?

   F 24 Ⓗ 36
   G 32.5 J 53

7. What is the sample size?

   Ⓐ 20 C 63
   B 24 D 66

8. Which measure is best for describing the following data?

   2, 4, 3, 1, 4, 1, 87, 2, 3, 4, 3, 1, 2

   Ⓕ median H mean
   G mode J range

9. Juanita wants to find out how much time sixth-grade students spend studying math. Which method of sampling is unbiased?

   A Survey her 2 best friends in the class.
   B Randomly survey the girls in her sixth-grade gym class.
   C Randomly survey 5 students from grades 3 through 6.
   Ⓓ Randomly survey 40 sixth-grade students.

10. Find the mean of the data in the line plot.

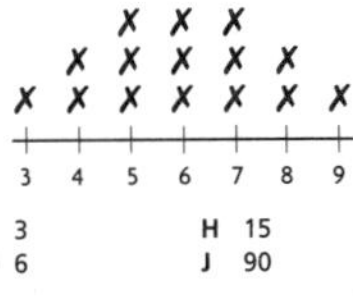

   F 3 H 15
   Ⓖ 6 J 90

Go On

11. Meghan sells magazines. She sold 10 magazines the first week, 8 the second, and then had sales of 12, 14, 9, and 14 the following weeks. In the final week of sales, she sold 32 magazines. Which measure was most affected by the final week's sales?

   Ⓐ mean
   B mode
   C median
   D mean and mode

12. Music can be purchased on CDs, cassettes, mini-discs, and CD-singles. From a survey of 500 randomly chosen teenagers, the following results were obtained.

   Which is a possible conclusion?

   F Cassettes were the most popular.
   G Mini-discs were more popular than CD-singles.
   H CD-singles were more popular than cassettes.
   Ⓙ CDs were the most popular.

13. The following frequency table lists the ratings given to a new science fiction movie.

SCIENCE FICTION MOVIE RATING		
Rating	Frequency	Cumulative Frequency
Excellent	25	25
Good	■	65
Fair	20	85
Poor	10	■
Disaster	5	100

   What numbers are missing from the frequency column and the cumulative frequency column?

   A 40, 85 C 65, 10
   Ⓑ 40, 95 D 65, 95

For 14–15, use the chart below. Jason recorded the kinds of cars parked in the school parking lot.

van	sports car	
sedan	SUV	sedan
sports car	sedan	mini-van
sedan	sedan	mini-van

14. How many rows would be needed to make a table that shows all the different kinds of cars?

   F 2 rows H 4 rows
   G 3 rows Ⓙ 5 rows

15. How many of the cars were sports cars?

   A 5 cars C 3 cars
   B 4 cars Ⓓ 2 cars

Stop

Name ______________________

Write the correct answer.

1. Fifty students are randomly selected from the 378 students at George Washington School for a survey. What are the 50 chosen students called?

   a sample

2. A survey was conducted at a mall to determine how many families would consider buying a DVD player for their home. One shopper was selected and then every tenth shopper that entered the mall after her was surveyed. What type of sample was used?

   systematic

3. Sales of special pizzas at a small pizza shop were recorded for the past two weeks. Find the mean, median, and mode for this data set.

NUMBER OF PIZZAS SOLD						
7	9	8	6	7	8	12
8	7	14	7	9	10	14

   mean 9 median 8 mode 7

4. The annual wages in thousands of dollars for the owner and six workers at a small manufacturing company are:

   $25, $25, $20, $25, $25, $25, $100.

   What measure(s) of central tendency are most useful to describe this set of data?

   median and mode

5. The mean of two numbers is 15. When a third number is included, the mean increases to 20. What is the third number?

   30

For 6–7, use this chart that lists the age of automobiles driven by counselors at the Community Center.

AGE OF AUTOMOBILE (IN YEARS)									
5	9	2	6	4	7	1	5	3	10
8	12	3	6	7	1	7	14	7	3

6. What is the range of ages for these automobiles?

   14 years

7. What is the sample size?

   20

8. What measure of central tendency best describes the data set below?

   5, 3, 7, 2, 6, 4, 75, 5, 3, 6, 2, 4, 2

   median

9. José wants to know if students at his school spend as much time playing soccer as he does. He asks his three best friends how much time they spend playing soccer. Is this sampling method biased or unbiased? Explain.

   Biased; the sample is not large enough; his friends probably have the same interests

Go On

Name ______________________

10. Find the mean of the data in the following line plot.

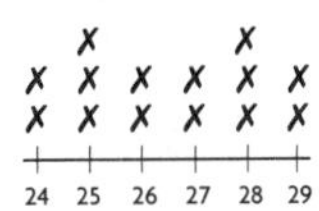

   26.5

11. Cups and Cones sold 10 gal of ice cream the first day of summer, 8 gal the second day, and had sales of 12, 14, 9, and 14 gal the following days. On the seventh day, the store sold 32 gal of ice cream. What measure of central tendency was most affected by the seventh day's sales?

   the mean

12. Popular movie rentals include VHS tapes, laser discs, and DVDs. The results of a survey of randomly chosen teens at the local video store are shown in the bar graph. What is a possible conclusion about the popularity of different ways to rent movies?

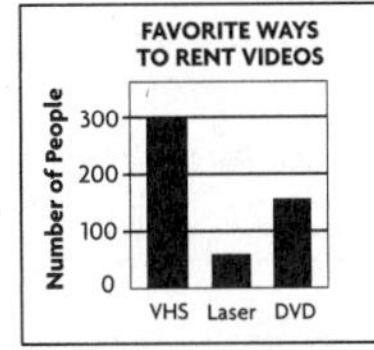

   Possible answer: The most popular movie rental is VHS tapes.

13. The following frequency table lists the ratings given to cafeteria food by sixth grade students. What numbers are missing from the frequency column and the cumulative frequency column?

CAFETERIA FOOD RATING		
Rating	Frequency	Cumulative Frequency
Excellent	5	5
Good	■	30
Fair	35	65
Poor	20	■
Disaster	15	100

   frequency, 25; cumulative frequency, 85

For 14–15, use the chart below. It lists the music format most often listened to by the students in the music club.

CD	cassette	CD
mini-disc	CD	CD single
cassette	CD	mini-disc
CD single	cassette	CD

14. Make a table for this data.

   Possible table:

Music Format	Number of Students
CD	卌
CD single	II
Mini-disc	II
Cassette	III

15. How many students listened to cassettes?

   3 students

Stop

Name ______________________

Choose the best answer.

For 1–8, choose the best type of graph to show the given situation.

1. a stock price changing over time
   A histogram C bar graph
   (B) line graph D circle graph

2. the lengths of five different rivers
   F box-and-whisker (H) bar graph
   G line graph J circle graph

3. the number of visitors to a museum grouped by intervals
   (A) histogram C bar graph
   B box-and-whisker D circle graph

4. favorite music choices by percent
   F histogram H stem-and-leaf
   G line graph (J) circle graph

5. the season scores of a basketball team
   A histogram (C) stem-and-leaf
   B line graph D circle graph

6. how the extreme numbers are related to the median numbers
   F stem-and-leaf H bar graph
   (G) box-and-whisker J circle graph

7. to compare parts to the whole or to other parts
   A histogram C bar graph
   B box-and-whisker (D) circle graph

8. to show how data change over time
   (F) line graph H circle graph
   G histogram J bar graph

For 9–13, use the graph below.

TOURISTS SINCE HOTEL OPENED

Number of Tourists (in thousands): 15, 16, 17, 18, 19, 20, 21, 22

Jan, Feb, Mar, Apr, May

9. Which month had the most tourists?
   (A) January C March
   B February D April

10. How many tourists would be a good prediction for July, if the trend continues?
   F 17,000 (H) 15,000
   G 16,000 J 14,000

11. How many tourists came in April?
   A 17 C 17,000
   B 18 (D) 18,000

12. Which other type of graph could be used to show the same data?
   F circle (H) bar
   G multiple-line J stem-and-leaf

13. Which of these changes could cause the graph to be misleading?
   A Use larger numbers.
   (B) Make the intervals unequal.
   C Double the intervals.
   D Start the scale at zero.

Go On

Name ______________________

14. Choose the least biased question.
   F Do you think that vanilla is the favorite flavor, or is it chocolate?
   G Do you think chocolate is the favorite flavor, or is it vanilla?
   (H) Which do you think is the favorite flavor, chocolate or vanilla?
   J Isn't vanilla the favorite flavor, or is it chocolate?

15. Choose the least biased question.
   (A) Who is correct, Karen, Lars, or David?
   B Is Lars correct, or is it Karen or David?
   C Karen is correct, isn't she? Or is it Lars or David?
   D Do you think that David is correct, or is it Lars or Karen?

For 16–19, use the graph below.

250 270 290 310 330 350 370 390 410 430 450

16. What is the lower quartile?
   (F) 290 H 450
   G 330 J 590

17. What is the median?
   A 33 C 290
   B 270 (D) 330

18. What is the lower extreme?
   F 170 H 390
   (G) 270 J 450

19. What is the upper quartile?
   (A) 390 C 290
   B 330 D 120

For 20–23, make a stem-and-leaf plot of the following scores.

87, 88, 94, 77, 98, 68, 72, 96, 80, 90, 79, 81, 69, 93, 92, 85, 99, 92, 83, 74

20. Which list shows the leaves for the stem 6?
   F 9, 8, 0 H 2, 4, 7, 9
   G 0, 1, 3, 5, 7, 8 (J) 8, 9

21. Which list shows the leaves for the stem 7?
   A 8, 9 C 0, 1, 3, 5, 7, 8
   (B) 2, 4, 7, 9 D 9, 7, 4, 2, 0

22. Which list shows the leaves for the stem 8?
   F 2, 4, 7, 9 H 8, 9
   (G) 0, 1, 3, 5, 7, 8 J 1, 3, 5, 7, 8

23. Which list shows the leaves for the stem 9?
   (A) 0, 2, 2, 3, 4, 6, 8, 9 C 8, 9
   B 0, 1, 3, 5, 7, 8 D 2, 4, 7, 9

For 24–25, use the table below.

DISTANCE ALLIE BICYCLED					
Week	1	2	3	4	5
Miles	65	80	95	115	135

24. If Allie continues her trend, estimate how far she will bike in week 6.
   F 95 miles (H) 160 miles
   G 130 miles J 240 miles

25. If the trend continues, in which week will Allie bike more than 200 miles?
   (A) week 8 C week 10
   B week 9 D week 11

Stop

Name ______________________

Write the correct answer.

1. Which type of graph is best to show temperature changing over time?
   line graph

2. Which type of graph is best to show the lengths of time cars were parked in a parking lot grouped by hourly intervals?
   histogram

3. Which type of graph is best to show a family budget by percent?
   circle graph

4. Which type of graph is best to show every student's grade on a quiz?
   stem-and-leaf plot

5. Which type of graph is best to show how the amount of a person's savings changed over time?
   line graph

6. Which type of graph is best to show the percentages of people surveyed who chose different candidates?
   circle graph

7. Which type of graph is best to show how the high and low test scores relate to the median?
   box-and-whisker graph

8. Which type of graph is best to show how well different brands of orange juice sell?
   bar graph

For 9–13, use the graph below.

AREA CONCERT TICKET SALES

Number of Tickets in thousands: 110, 120, 130, 140, 150, 160

Sept, Oct, Nov, Dec, Jan

MONTH

9. In which month were the most tickets sold?
   January

10. How many tickets would be expected to be sold in February if the trend continued?
   155,000

11. How many tickets were sold in October?
   130,000

12. What other type of graph could be used to show the same data?
   bar graph

13. Explain why the graph would be less misleading if the scale started at 0?
   Answers may vary. Possible answer: The monthly changes would appear to be smaller and truer to size.

Go On

Name ______________________

For 14–15, rewrite the statement so that it is less biased.

14. Do you think that the Zebra is the best car ever made, or is it the Antelope or the Gazelle?
   Possible answer: Which do you think is the best car ever made, the Zebra, the Antelope, or the Gazelle?

15. Is Saul the best athlete, or is it Mia or Andrew?
   Possible answer: Who do you think is the best athlete, Saul, Mia, or Andrew?

For 16–19, use the box-and-whisker graph below.

60 65 70 75 80 85 90 95 100

16. What is the upper extreme?
   100

17. What is the lower quartile?
   72

18. What is the median?
   88

19. What is the upper quartile?
   96

20. Make a stem-and-leaf plot for the following scores.

   78, 56, 95, 48, 99, 87, 92, 79, 32, 94, 86, 85, 81, 76, 84, 55, 88, 88, 99, 68

Stem	Leaves
3	2
4	8
5	5 6
6	8
7	6 8 9
8	1 4 5 6 7 8 8
9	2 4 5 9 9

For 21–23, use the stem-and-leaf plot you drew.

21. What are the leaves for the stem 9?
   2, 4, 5, 9, 9

22. Which stem has the most leaves? List the leaves for that stem.
   8; 1, 4, 5, 6, 7, 8, 8

23. Which stem has only two leaves? List the leaves for that stem.
   5; 5, 6

For 24–25, use the table below.

DISTANCE JOHN DROVE					
Week	1	2	3	4	5
Miles	280	300	330	370	420

24. Estimate how far John will drive in week 6 if he continues his trend.
   480 miles

25. In which week should John drive more than 600 miles if the trend continues?
   week 8

Stop

Name ______________________

Choose the best answer.

1. The entire group of individuals or objects for which data is collected is called the _?_.
   A sample C survey
   Ⓑ population D cluster

2. The graph shows the price of a share of stock each day last week.

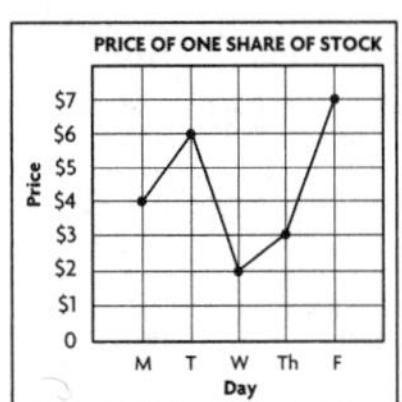

   What was the greatest price increase on any one day?
   Ⓕ $4 G $2
   H $3 J $1

3. Which type of graph or plot would best show heights of students in a math class?
   A histogram Ⓒ stem-and-leaf
   B line graph D circle graph

4. The best graph to show two or more sets of data on the same graph is a _?_ graph.
   Ⓕ multiple-bar H line
   G bar J circle

5. Josh asked, "Do you agree that math teachers assign too much homework?" is _?_.
   A random Ⓒ biased
   B unbiased D unclear

For 6–7, use the table showing how many nights a week some people eat out.

Number of Nights Eating Out	
1	卌 |||
2	卌 卌 |||
3	卌 |||
4	||||
5 or more	||

6. How many eat out 3 nights a week?
   F 14 H 5
   Ⓖ 8 J 3

7. How many eat out at least 4 nights a week?
   A 9 C 4
   Ⓑ 6 D 2

8. Which is the mean of this data?
   5, 5, 7, 15, 28
   F 5 H 10
   G 7 Ⓙ 12

For 9–10, use the box-and-whisker graph below.

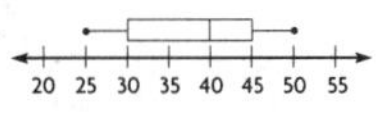

9. Which is the median?
   A 30 Ⓒ 40
   B 37.5 D 45

10. Which is the upper extreme?
   F 30 H 45
   G 40 Ⓙ 50

Go On

Name ______________________

11. Which is the median number of fish caught?

NUMBER OF FISH CAUGHT
4, 2, 9, 3, 2, 2, 9, 4, 1

   A 1 Ⓒ 3
   B 2 D 4

12. The median of the upper half of a set of data is called the _?_.
   Ⓕ upper quartile H lower quartile
   G upper extreme J lower extreme

13. For the following set of data, what word describes the data value 15?
   1, 1, 1, 2, 3, 3, 4, 5, 6, 6, 8, 15
   Ⓐ outlier C sample
   B data D mode

14. Which type of graph shows all values in the set of data?
   F histogram H circle
   G bar Ⓙ stem-and-leaf

15. Nine out of ten teenagers prefer action movies to dramas. Which conclusion is valid?
   Ⓐ Teenagers prefer action movies.
   B Teenagers do not like dramas.
   C A tenth of Linda's friends prefer action movies.
   D Nine tenths of Linda's friends never watch dramas.

16. Which type of graph would be best to show a family's monthly budget?
   F histogram
   Ⓖ circle graph
   H line graph
   J stem-and-leaf

For 17–18, use the circle graph below.

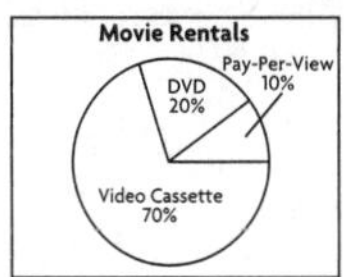

17. Which percent of people rented DVDs?
   A 10% C 30%
   Ⓑ 20% D 70%

18. Which way to rent a movie was most preferred?
   F DVD Ⓗ Video Cassette
   G Pay-Per-View J no preferred way

For 19–20, use the cumulative frequency table showing how people rated a new bike.

Rating	Frequency	Cumulative Frequency
Excellent	6	6
Good	?	14
Fair	5	?
Poor	3	22

19. How many people gave the bike a "Good" rating?
   A 6 C 14
   Ⓑ 8 D 19

20. Which conclusion is valid for the data?
   F Few gave an "Excellent" rating.
   G 22 people gave a "Poor" rating.
   Ⓗ Most people liked the bike.
   J No conclusion is possible.

Go On

Name ______________________

21. Every fourth person entering a store is asked to name their favorite brand of jeans. What kind of sample is this?
   A convenience C random
   Ⓑ systematic D cluster

For questions 22–24, use the bar graph showing this year's rainfall.

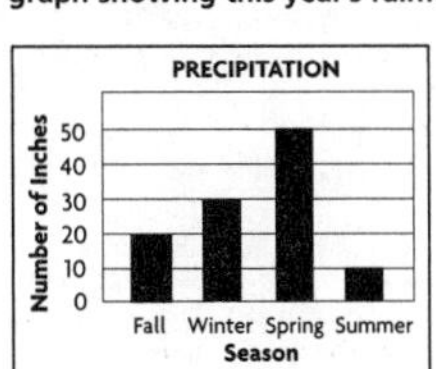

22. Which season had the most rainfall?
   Ⓕ spring H winter
   G summer J fall

23. If next year is like this year, how much precipitation would be predicted for next summer?
   A 50 in. C 20 in.
   B 30 in. Ⓓ 10 in.

24. Which change would make the graph misleading?
   F Use larger numbers.
   G Start the scale at zero.
   H Double the intervals.
   Ⓙ Make the intervals unequal.

25. The mean age of 10 people is 20 years. When Mr. Wax's age is included, the mean age increases to 25. How old is Mr. Wax?
   A 25 years C 50 years
   B 30 years Ⓓ 75 years

26. From her school of 285 students, Kim sampled 5 students and concluded that most students prefer beef. Why is her conclusion not valid?
   F The sample is too random.
   Ⓖ The sample is too small.
   H The sample is biased.
   J The sample is not systematic.

For 27–29, make a stem-and-leaf plot of the following scores.

41, 34, 45, 22, 18, 28, 22, 34, 36,
22, 33, 25, 17, 26, 27, 46, 21, 32,
23, 14, 22, 25, 39, 39, 11, 16, 28

27. How many stems are in the stem-and-leaf plot?
   A 5 C 3
   Ⓑ 4 D 2

28. Which are the leaves for the stem 3?
   F 1, 4, 6, 7, 8
   G 1, 2, 2, 2, 2, 3, 5, 5, 6, 7, 8, 8
   Ⓗ 2, 3, 4, 4, 6, 9, 9
   J 1, 5, 6

29. Which is the median for the data?
   A 22 C 27.6
   Ⓑ 26 D 28.5

30. Find the mode(s) for the data in the line plot.

```
    X        X
    X     X  X  X
 X  X  X  X  X  X  X
 22 23 24 25 26 27 28
```

   F 3 Ⓗ 23 and 26
   G 23 J 24.5

Go On

Name ______________________

For 31–33, use the following stem-and-leaf plot of test score data.

Stem	Leaf
7	0 0 2 5 5 8 8 8 9
8	0 0 4 6 6 6 6 8
9	2 4 6 6 8

31. Which is the median?
   A 78 C 80
   B 79 Ⓓ 82

32. Which is the range?
   F 19 H 82
   Ⓖ 28 J 86

33. What other type of graph could be used to show the same data?
   Ⓐ line plot C circle graph
   B line graph D bar graph

34. Which of the following should **not** be used to describe typical values in a set of data?
   Ⓕ outlier H mode
   G median J mean

35. Which type of graph best shows how data is distributed?
   A stem-and-leaf
   Ⓑ box-and-whisker
   C circle bar
   D line graph

36. In the first month of swimming class, Jordan swam 2 km. If she doubles her distance each month, how far will she swim in the fourth month?
   F 4 km Ⓗ 16 km
   G 8 km J 32 km

37. Larry's savings deposits for the first 6 weeks of the new year were $3, $2, $3, $2, $3, and $2. If this trend continues, how much money will he have saved by the end of the 10th week?
   A $50 C $45
   B $47 Ⓓ $25

38. Which is the upper quartile?

25 30 35 40 45 50 55

   F 30 Ⓗ 45
   G 35 J 55

39. Which is the range of the data?
   12, 19, 15, 22, 14
   Ⓐ 10 C 7
   B 8 D 2

40. Which type of sample is most likely to give results that lead to invalid conclusions?
   F convenience H systematic
   G random Ⓙ biased

Stop

Name ______

UNIT 2 TEST • PAGE 1

Write the correct answer.

1. A __?__ is a method of gathering information about a group.

survey

2. The graph shows the average temperature for each day last week. What was the greatest average temperature increase between any two days?

AVERAGE DAILY TEMPERATURE (Temperature in Degrees: 0, 1°, 2°, 3°, 4°, 5°, 6°, 7°; Day: M T W T F)

4°

3. What type of graph would best show the number of visitors, grouped by age, to a theme park?

histogram

4. What type of graph would best show the numbers of points scored by players in a basketball game?

stem and leaf

5. Rewrite the question so that it is less biased.

Is Ms. Nathan the best teacher, or is it Mr. Gold or Mrs. Cone?

Possible answer: Who is the best teacher, Ms. Nathan, Mr. Gold, or Mrs. Cone?

Use the data for 6–8. It shows the number of brothers and sisters each student in Mrs. Yokoi's class has.

0, 3, 2, 4, 0, 1, 1, 2, 5, 4, 6, 2, 3, 1, 0, 2, 5, 2, 1, 2, 0, 7, 4, 2, 1

6. Complete the tally table.

Number of Brothers and Sisters	
0	IIII
1	~~IIII~~
2	~~IIII~~ II
3	II
4	III
5 or more	IIII

7. How many students have at least 4 brothers and sisters?

7 students

8. What is the mean of the data?

2.4

For 9–10, use the box-and-whisker graph.

55 60 65 70 75 80 85 90 95

9. What is the median?

75

10. What is the lower extreme?

60

Go On

Name ______

UNIT 2 TEST • PAGE 2

11. What is the median price for a pair of jeans?

PRICE OF JEANS								
$11	$12	$13	$13	$15	$16	$19	$22	$24

$15

12. What is the median of the lower half of a set of data called?

the lower quartile

13. For the following set of data, what word describes the value 13?

13, 20, 21, 23, 23, 25, 26, 28

outlier

14. Which type of graph would best show how the high and low scores of a soccer team relate to the median?

box and whisker graph

15. A random sample from one basketball team shows that the players prefer to wear two pairs of socks. Fati decides that all basketball players on the team prefer to wear two pairs of socks. Is the conclusion valid? Explain.

Possible answer: yes; the sample is random and representative of the population.

16. Which type of graph would best show how a baby gorilla's weight changed over time?

line graph

For 17–18, use the circle graph.

BIKE HELMET COLORS (sixth graders)

Blue 40%, Black 15%, Red 35%, White 10%

17. What percent of sixth graders have red bike helmets?

35%

18. Which color of helmet is the most popular?

blue

For 19–20, use the cumulative frequency table showing how people rated a new VCR.

19. Complete the table.

Rating	Frequency	Cumulative Frequency
Outstanding	3	3
Above Average	4	■
Average	■	12
Below Average	2	14

7, 5

20. How many people rated the new VCR?

14 people

Go On

Name ______

UNIT 2 TEST • PAGE 3

21. A store surveyed the first 50 customers of the day. What type of sample was this?

convenience

For 22–24, use the bar graph showing this week's absences at Sojourner Truth Middle School.

STUDENT ABSENCES (Number of Students Absent: 0, 5, 10, 15, 20, 25, 30; Day: M T W T F)

22. On which day were the fewest students absent?

Wednesday

23. If next week is similar to this week, how many absences would be predicted for Friday?

15 absences

24. Why would it **not** be good to start the vertical scale at 5 instead of 0?

Possible answer: the graph would be misleading.

25. The mean age of 8 people is 16 years. When Mrs. Hernandez's age is included, the mean age increases to 20. How old is Mrs. Hernandez?

52 years old

26. Andy randomly surveyed 30 children at the pet store to celebrate bird day. He concluded that children prefer birds as pets. Why is Andy's conclusion not valid?

The sample is not representative of the population; it excludes children not at the pet store.

27. Make a stem-and-leaf plot for the following scores.

23, 25, 29, 34, 33, 38, 42, 41, 40, 45, 49, 51, 53, 50, 50, 54, 60, 62, 70, 72, 76, 79, 76, 22, 23, 24, 45

Stem	Leaves
2	2 3 3 4 5 9
3	3 4 8
4	0 1 2 5 5 9
5	0 0 1 3 4
6	0 2
7	0 2 6 6 9

For 28–29, use the stem-and-leaf plot you drew.

28. What is the median for the data?

45

29. What are the modes for the data?

23, 45, 50, and 76

Go On

Name ______

UNIT 2 TEST • PAGE 4

30. What are the modes for the data in the line plot?

48 49 50 51 52 53 54

50, 52

For 31–33, use the stem-and-leaf plot of test score data.

Stem	Leaves
1	0 0 1 3 3 3 4 5
2	0 2 6 6 8 9 9
3	1 2 4 5 7 7 8

31. What is the median score?

26

32. What is the range of the scores?

28

33. Could a histogram be used to show the same data? Explain.

Yes; the histogram would show the number of test scores in each interval.

34. Amy scored 65, 70, 75, 80, and 85 on her first 5 math quizzes. What does she have to score on the next quiz to increase her mean score by 2 points?

87

35. Which type of graph would best show the percent of votes all candidates in an election received?

circle graph

36. In the first week of soccer training, Melissa did 20 crunches. If she doubles the number of crunches each week, how many crunches will she do in the fifth week?

320 crunches

37. Mr. Perez's savings deposits for the first 6 weeks of the year were $25, $20, $25, $20, $25, and $20. If this pattern continues, how much money will he have saved in all by the end of the 10th week?

$225

38. What is the upper quartile of the data?

30 35 40 45 50 55 60

50

39. What is the range of the data?

64, 55, 72, 43, 36

36

40. A store surveyed every tenth customer during the day. What type of sample was this?

systematic

Stop

Name ______________________

Choose the best answer.

For 1–2, choose the list that contains all the numbers from 2 to 10 by which the given number is divisible.

1. 24

   A 2   Ⓒ 2, 3, 4, 6, 8
   B 2, 3, 4   D 2, 3, 4, 6, 8, 9

2. 245

   F 2   H 3, 5
   Ⓖ 5, 7   J 3, 5, 9

3. Which number is divisible by both 5 and 9?

   A 550   C 2,345
   B 801   Ⓓ 4,005

4. Which pair of numbers is divisible by both 6 and 9?

   F 136 and 594   H 270 and 369
   G 234 and 458   Ⓙ 414 and 630

5. What are the first five multiples of 21?

   A 1, 3, 7, 21, 63
   B 3, 7, 21, 63, 147
   Ⓒ 21, 42, 63, 84, 105
   D 21, 42, 84, 168, 336

6. What is the prime factorization of 594 in exponent form?

   F $2^3 \times 3^2 \times 11$ Ⓗ $2 \times 3^3 \times 11$
   G $3^3 \times 4 \times 11$ J $2^2 \times 3^2 \times 11$

7. What is the prime factorization of 936 in exponent form?

   A $2^3 \times 3^2$ C $2^3 \times 3 \times 13$
   Ⓑ $2^3 \times 3^2 \times 13$ D $8 \times 9 \times 13$

8. What is the prime factorization of 52?

   Ⓕ $2^2 \times 13$ H 2×26
   G 4×13 J $2 \times 3 \times 7$

9. Which number is prime?

   Ⓐ 37   C 75
   B 54   D 91

10. Find the GCF of 52 and 195.

   F 780   H 15
   G 26   Ⓙ 13

11. Find the LCM of 70 and 105.

   A 35   Ⓒ 210
   B 42   D 7,350

12. Emily is making treats that need 1 chocolate bar and 1 marshmallow each. Chocolate bars come in packages of 12. Marshmallows come in packages of 30. What is the least number of packages of each she will have to buy in order to have equal numbers of chocolate bars and marshmallows?

   F 2 chocolate, 5 marshmallow
   Ⓖ 5 chocolate, 2 marshmallow
   H 30 chocolate, 10 marshmallow
   J 60 chocolate, 60 marshmallow

13. Find a pair of numbers whose LCM is 360 and whose GCF is 3.

   A 15 and 18   Ⓒ 24 and 45
   B 18 and 24   D 45 and 1,280

14. What is the 25th number in the pattern?

   137, 134, 131, 128, 125, ...

   F 26   Ⓗ 65
   G 62   J 74

Go On

Name ______________________

15. There are 12 cheerleaders and 45 band members. All of the cheerleaders and band members will work in groups at the car wash. Each group will have the same number of cheerleaders and the same number of band members. What is the greatest number of groups that can be formed?

   Ⓐ 3   C 6
   B 5   D 12

16. Five weeks ago, Jules typed 8 words per min. During the next 4 weeks his speed increased to 12 words, 16 words, 20 words, and then 24 words per min. To get a job, Jules must type 60 words per min. If his improvement continues to follow this pattern, in how many more weeks will he reach 60 words per min?

   F 12 weeks   H 6 weeks
   Ⓖ 9 weeks   J 3 weeks

17. If you fold a piece of paper in half once, there are 2 parts. Folding twice gives you 4 parts. Three folds gives you 8 parts, and so on. How many folds would be necessary to get 128 parts?

   A 4   C 24
   Ⓑ 7   D 64

18. Find the LCM of 8, 12, and 18.

   F 1,728   H 96
   G 216   Ⓙ 72

19. By which pair of numbers below is 16,728 divisible?

   A 2 and 9   Ⓒ 3 and 8
   B 3 and 5   D 4 and 7

20. Joshua swims every 4 days and Katarina swims every 7 days. They both swam on July 4. How many more times will they swim on the same day by September 4?

   F 1   H 5
   Ⓖ 2   J 10

21. Hot dogs are sold 12 in a package. Buns are sold 8 in a package. Ketchup packets come 100 in a box. What is the least number of each item you can buy and have the same number of hot dogs, buns, and ketchup packets?

   A 4   C 1,200
   Ⓑ 600   D 9,600

22. Carbon-14 (C-14) has a half-life of about 6,000 yr. If you start with 6,400 g of C-14, there would be 3,200 g left after 6,000 yr, 1,600 g after 12,000 yr, and 800 g after 18,000 yr. How long would it be until only 100 g were left?

   F 17,984 yr   H 30,000 yr
   G 24,000 yr   Ⓙ 36,000 yr

23. Find the GCF of 15, 18, and 54.

   A 2   C 5
   Ⓑ 3   D 270

24. The prime factorization of 378 is $2 \times 3^n \times 7$. What is the value of n?

   Ⓕ 3   H 7
   G 4   J 27

25. Which pair of numbers has 36 as the LCM?

   A 3, 6   C 6, 9
   B 3, 12   Ⓓ 9, 12

Stop

Name ______________________

Write the correct answer.

1. Write the numbers from 2 through 10 by which 36 is divisible.

   2, 3, 4, 6, 9

2. Write the numbers from 2 through 10 by which 495 is divisible.

   3, 5, 9

3. Which numbers between 100 and 200 are divisible by both 5 and 9?

   135, 180

4. Write *true* or *false*.

   Numbers that are even and divisible by 9 are also divisible by 6.

   true

5. List the first five multiples of 17.

   17, 34, 51, 68, 85

6. Write the prime factorization of 150 in exponent form.

   $2 \times 3 \times 5^2$

7. Write the prime factorization of 531 in exponent form.

   $3^2 \times 59$

8. Find the prime factorization of 66.

   $2 \times 3 \times 11$

9. A number c is a prime factor of both 35 and 98. What is the value of c?

   7

10. Find the GCF of the numbers 12 and 20.

   4

11. Find the LCM of the numbers 8 and 50.

   200

12. Dr. Russell has 54 tape strips and 36 gauze pads. What is the greatest number of packages she can make if she puts the same numbers of tape strips and gauze pads in each package and uses all the strips and pads?

   18 packages

13. Find a pair of numbers whose LCM is 75 and whose GCF is 5.

   15 and 25

14. What is the 26th number in the pattern?

   257, 253, 249, 245, 241, ...

   157

Go On

Name ______________________

15. Daniel has 12 quarters and 45 dimes to share among his friends at the arcade. He wants to give each friend the same number of quarters and the same number of dimes and not have any money left over. How many friends can he take to the arcade?

   3 friends

16. Mikael is in a training program assembling robot parts. He will finish the training when he can assemble 100 parts a day. He assembled 16 parts the first day, 22 the second day, 28 the third day, and 34 the fourth day. If he continues this pattern, when will he finish training?

   on the 15th day

17. A single cell amoeba reproduces by splitting into two cells. One cell reproduces to form 2 cells. Those cells split to form 4 cells. Then those cells split to form 8 cells, and so forth. How many times will a single cell have to split until there are more than 1,000 cells?

   10 times

18. Find the LCM of the numbers 9, 18, and 27.

   54

19. 20,202 is divisible by what numbers from 2 through 10?

   2, 3, 6, 7

20. Aaron works out at the gym every third day. Ashley works out only every five days. They meet at the gym for the first time on March 1. When will they meet at the gym for the third time?

   March 31

21. Dimes are packaged 50 in a roll. Quarters come 40 in a roll. Susan B. Anthony dollars come in rolls of 25. How many rolls of each do you need to have an equal number of each coin?

   4 rolls of dimes, 5 rolls of quarters, and 8 rolls of dollars

22. It is possible for the amount of money in a savings account to double every 7 years. If you put $2,500 in a savings account of this type and never take any out, about how long would it take for your balance to be $80,000?

   35 years

23. Find the GCF of the numbers 14, 42, and 63.

   7

24. The prime factorization of 495 is $3^n \times 5 \times 11$. What is the value of n?

   2

25. Find a pair of numbers that has 90 as the LCM and 15 as the GCF.

   30 and 45

Stop

Name ______________________

CHAPTER 8 TEST • PAGE 1

Choose the best answer.

For 1–3, find the number that completes the equation.

1. $\frac{2}{3} = \frac{■}{15}$

A 5   Ⓑ 10   C 12   D 18

2. $\frac{12}{24} = \frac{4}{■}$

F 72   Ⓖ 8   H 6   J 2

3. $\frac{3}{■} = \frac{6}{8}$

A 16   B 5   Ⓒ 4   D 2

4. Which fraction is in simplest form?

Ⓕ $\frac{5}{12}$ G $\frac{6}{12}$ H $\frac{9}{12}$ J $\frac{10}{12}$

5. Which is $\frac{6}{30}$ in simplest form?

A $\frac{6}{5}$ B $\frac{5}{6}$ Ⓒ $\frac{1}{5}$ D $\frac{1}{30}$

6. Which is $\frac{10}{16}$ in simplest form?

F $\frac{20}{32}$ Ⓖ $\frac{5}{8}$ H $\frac{4}{6}$ J $\frac{5}{4}$

7. Which is $\frac{8}{3}$ as a mixed number?

A $\frac{2}{3}$ B 2   C $2\frac{1}{3}$ Ⓓ $2\frac{2}{3}$

8. Which fraction is equal to 4?

Ⓕ $\frac{20}{5}$ G $\frac{22}{4}$ H $\frac{25}{5}$ J $\frac{24}{4}$

9. Which is $2\frac{3}{4}$ as a fraction?

Ⓐ $\frac{11}{4}$ B $\frac{10}{4}$ C $\frac{9}{4}$ D $\frac{8}{4}$

10. Which is $3\frac{5}{8}$ as a fraction?

F $\frac{5}{8}$ G $\frac{16}{8}$ Ⓗ $\frac{29}{8}$ J $\frac{40}{8}$

For 11–14, find the number that makes the number sentence true.

11. $\frac{5}{6} = \frac{■}{12}$

A 2   B 6   Ⓒ 10   D 11

12. $■ < \frac{11}{16}$

F $\frac{14}{16}$ G $\frac{8}{10}$ H $\frac{6}{8}$ Ⓙ $\frac{5}{8}$

13. $■ > \frac{4}{7}$

A 0.3   B 0.4   C 0.5   Ⓓ 0.6

14. $0.6 = ■$

F $\frac{60}{10}$ G $\frac{10}{6}$ Ⓗ $\frac{3}{5}$ J $\frac{3}{50}$

Go On

Name ______________________

CHAPTER 8 TEST • PAGE 2

15. Which is 0.3 as a fraction?

A $\frac{30}{10}$ Ⓑ $\frac{3}{10}$ C $\frac{3}{100}$ D $\frac{3}{1,000}$

16. Which completes the equation?

$6\frac{7}{10} = \frac{670}{■}$

F 1,000   Ⓖ 100   H 10   J 1

17. What is $\frac{3}{4}$ in decimal form? Tell whether the decimal terminates or repeats.

A 0.25; repeats
B 0.25; terminates
C 0.75; repeats
Ⓓ 0.75; terminates

18. What is $\frac{8}{9}$ in decimal form?

F 0.9   Ⓖ $0.\overline{8}$ H 0.8   J $0.\overline{3}$

19. What is $\frac{2}{5}$ written as a percent?

A 2%   B 20%   Ⓒ 40%   D 45%

20. What is $\frac{19}{100}$ written as a percent?

F 190%   Ⓖ 19%   H 1.9%   J 0.19%

21. In gym class, $\frac{1}{4}$ of the students voted to play soccer, $\frac{4}{12}$ voted to play baseball, $\frac{3}{8}$ voted to play volleyball, and $\frac{1}{24}$ voted to play basketball. Which activity got the greatest part of the votes?

Ⓐ volleyball   B soccer   C basketball   D baseball

22. In a sixth-grade class, $\frac{7}{20}$ of the students got 100 on a test. What percent of the students got 100 on the test?

F 3.5%   G 5%   H 21%   Ⓙ 35%

23. At a film festival, $\frac{9}{15}$ of the judges gave the movie *The Last Bicycle* the highest rating. Which decimal tells what part of the group of judges gave the movie the highest rating?

A 0.9   Ⓑ 0.6   C 0.45   D 0.3

24. For the class picnic, $\frac{1}{3}$ of the class voted for vanilla ice cream, $\frac{2}{5}$ voted for chocolate, $\frac{1}{5}$ voted for peach, and $\frac{1}{15}$ voted for strawberry. Which flavor received the least part of the votes?

Ⓕ strawberry   G vanilla   H chocolate   J peach

For 25, use the table below.

ARTURO'S BOOKS

Type	Number
Mystery	7
Science Fiction	6
Romance	3
Nonfiction	4

25. Which fraction tells what part of Arturo's books are science fiction?

A $\frac{6}{7}$ B $\frac{3}{5}$ Ⓒ $\frac{3}{10}$ D $\frac{3}{20}$

Stop

Name ______________________

CHAPTER 8 TEST • PAGE 1

Write the correct answer.

For 1–3, complete the equation.

1. $\frac{3}{5} = \frac{■}{20}$

12

2. $\frac{8}{40} = \frac{1}{■}$

5

3. $\frac{4}{■} = \frac{8}{14}$

7

4. Write $\frac{15}{18}$ in simplest form.

$\frac{5}{6}$

5. Write $\frac{10}{30}$ in simplest form.

$\frac{1}{3}$

6. Write $\frac{24}{32}$ in simplest form.

$\frac{3}{4}$

7. Write $\frac{23}{4}$ as a mixed number or a whole number.

$5\frac{3}{4}$

8. Write a fraction with a divisor of 3 that is equal to 6.

$\frac{18}{3}$

9. Write $4\frac{3}{4}$ as a fraction.

$\frac{19}{4}$

10. Write $2\frac{7}{10}$ as a fraction.

$\frac{27}{10}$

11. Write a fraction equivalent to $\frac{2}{3}$.

Possible answer: $\frac{4}{6}$

For 12–14, compare. Write <, >, or = for each ●.

12. $\frac{8}{12}$ ● $\frac{1}{3}$

>

13. $\frac{3}{12}$ ● 0.25

=

14. $\frac{4}{5}$ ● 0.75

>

15. Write 0.7 as a fraction.

$\frac{7}{10}$

Go On

Name ______________________

CHAPTER 8 TEST • PAGE 2

16. Complete.

$2\frac{1}{9} = \frac{■}{9}$

19

17. Write $\frac{4}{5}$ as a decimal. Tell whether the decimal terminates or repeats.

0.8; terminates

18. Write $\frac{1}{6}$ as a decimal. Tell whether the decimal terminates or repeats.

$0.1\overline{6}$; repeats

19. Write $\frac{1}{4}$ as a percent.

25%

20. Write $\frac{83}{100}$ as a percent.

83%

21. For the class trip, $\frac{1}{3}$ of the class voted to go to a museum, and $\frac{1}{6}$ voted to go to a theme park. Another $\frac{7}{30}$ voted to go to a concert, and $\frac{4}{15}$ voted to go to the airport. Which trip got the greatest part of the votes?

the museum

22. In a sixth-grade class, $\frac{19}{20}$ of the students passed the quiz on fractions. What percent of the students passed the quiz?

95%

23. In Mr. Chen's class, $\frac{20}{25}$ of the students have tried in-line skating and liked it. What decimal tells what part of the class tried in-line skating and liked it?

0.8

24. In Mrs. Driscoll's class, $\frac{3}{20}$ of the students have track practice after school. Another $\frac{1}{5}$ practice in the marching band, $\frac{3}{10}$ have gymnastics, and $\frac{7}{20}$ attend the computer lab after school. In which after-school activity do the fewest of Mrs. Driscoll's students participate?

track practice

For 25, use the table below.

JOSÉ'S ALBUMS

Type of Music	Number
Rock	9
Country	4
Latin	5
Jazz	2

25. What fraction in simplest form tells what part of José's collection is country music albums?

$\frac{1}{5}$

Stop

Name ______________

Choose the best answer.

For 1–4, estimate the sum or difference.

1. $2\frac{4}{5} + 3\frac{7}{8}$
   A 8   (B) 7   C 6   D 5

2. $5\frac{1}{8} - 3\frac{6}{7}$
   F 3   G 2   (H) 1   J 0

3. $1\frac{5}{6} + 3\frac{1}{5}$
   A 4   (B) 5   C 6   D 7

4. $\frac{5}{7} - \frac{2}{3}$
   (F) 0   G $\frac{1}{2}$ H 1   J 2

5. Kyle spent $2\frac{1}{5}$ hr mowing the lawn, $1\frac{9}{10}$ hr raking, and $\frac{5}{6}$ hr pruning the rose bushes. Estimate the time he spent doing yard work.
   A 3 hr   B 4 hr   (C) 5 hr   D 6 hr

For 6–11, find the sum or difference in simplest form.

6. $\frac{1}{3} + \frac{1}{4}$
   F $\frac{1}{7}$ G $\frac{2}{7}$ H $\frac{2}{5}$ (J) $\frac{7}{12}$

7. $\frac{5}{8} - \frac{1}{4}$
   A $\frac{1}{4}$ (B) $\frac{3}{8}$ C $\frac{1}{2}$ D $\frac{7}{8}$

8. $\frac{2}{3} + \frac{1}{8}$
   F $\frac{3}{11}$ G $\frac{13}{24}$ (H) $\frac{19}{24}$ J $1\frac{5}{24}$

9. $\frac{8}{9} - \frac{5}{6}$
   A 1   B $\frac{1}{3}$ (C) $\frac{1}{18}$ D $\frac{1}{36}$

10. $\frac{3}{5} - \frac{3}{10}$
   F 0   G $\frac{1}{10}$ H $\frac{1}{5}$ (J) $\frac{3}{10}$

11. $\frac{5}{12} + \frac{5}{6}$
   A $\frac{5}{9}$ B $\frac{5}{6}$ C $1\frac{1}{6}$ (D) $1\frac{1}{4}$

12. Mrs. Nelson drove $\frac{2}{3}$ mi to take Manny to school, $\frac{1}{4}$ mi to the grocery store, and $\frac{5}{6}$ mi to her office. How far did she drive?
   F $\frac{11}{12}$ mi   (G) $1\frac{3}{4}$ mi   H $1\frac{11}{12}$ mi   J $2\frac{1}{3}$ mi

13. Mark lives $\frac{3}{4}$ mi north of Ann. Leo lives $2\frac{1}{4}$ mi north of Ann. Draw a diagram to find how far Mark lives from Leo.
   A 3 mi   B $2\frac{1}{2}$ mi   C $1\frac{3}{4}$ mi   (D) $1\frac{1}{2}$ mi

Go On

Name ______________

For 14–19, find the sum or difference in simplest form.

14. $7\frac{4}{5} - 5\frac{1}{2}$
   F 2   (G) $2\frac{3}{10}$ H $2\frac{7}{10}$ J $13\frac{3}{10}$

15. $3\frac{5}{7} + 4\frac{1}{3}$
   A $7\frac{1}{21}$ B $7\frac{3}{5}$ (C) $8\frac{1}{21}$ D $8\frac{3}{5}$

16. $5\frac{1}{4} - 3\frac{2}{3}$
   (F) $1\frac{7}{12}$ G $1\frac{5}{12}$ H $1\frac{1}{4}$ J $\frac{3}{4}$

17. $1\frac{1}{2} + 3\frac{3}{4}$
   (A) $5\frac{1}{4}$ B 5   C $4\frac{2}{3}$ D $4\frac{3}{8}$

18. $8\frac{1}{5} - 5\frac{1}{3}$
   F $3\frac{1}{2}$ G 3   (H) $2\frac{13}{15}$ J $2\frac{2}{15}$

19. $1\frac{2}{3} + 5\frac{1}{6}$
   (A) $6\frac{5}{6}$ B $6\frac{4}{9}$ C $6\frac{1}{3}$ D 6

20. Polly is planting a vegetable garden. She wants $\frac{2}{5}$ of her garden to be corn and $\frac{1}{6}$ to be zucchini. What fraction of the garden will be left?
   F $\frac{3}{11}$ G $\frac{11}{30}$ (H) $\frac{13}{30}$ J $\frac{17}{30}$

For 21–23, find the sum or difference in simplest form.

21. $4\frac{3}{4} - 2\frac{1}{2}$
   (A) $2\frac{1}{4}$ B 2   C $1\frac{1}{2}$ D $1\frac{1}{4}$

22. $3\frac{5}{6} + 1\frac{1}{3}$
   (F) $5\frac{1}{6}$ G 5   H $4\frac{2}{3}$ J $4\frac{1}{2}$

23. $2\frac{1}{2} + 3\frac{1}{4}$
   A $6\frac{1}{4}$ (B) $5\frac{3}{4}$ C $5\frac{1}{4}$ D $\frac{3}{4}$

24. Four friends live along a straight road. Sue lives $\frac{2}{3}$ mi from Ali and $\frac{2}{3}$ mi from Carlos. Ali lives between Sue and Tim. Carlos lives $1\frac{7}{8}$ mi from Tim. How far does Ali live from Tim?
   (F) $\frac{13}{24}$ mi   G $1\frac{5}{24}$ mi   H $2\frac{13}{14}$ mi   J $3\frac{5}{24}$ mi

25. Martina drives $1\frac{1}{2}$ mi north from her office. Next, she drives $2\frac{3}{4}$ mi east. Then she drives $1\frac{1}{2}$ mi south. Tell how far and in what direction she must drive to get back to her office.
   A $4\frac{1}{4}$ mi north   B $4\frac{1}{4}$ mi west   C $2\frac{3}{4}$ mi east   (D) $2\frac{3}{4}$ mi west

Stop

Name ______________

Write the correct answer.

For 1–4, estimate the sum or difference.
Possible estimates are given.

1. $2\frac{3}{7} + 3\frac{4}{5}$
   about $6\frac{1}{2}$

2. $7\frac{1}{8} - 2\frac{4}{5}$
   about 4

3. $3\frac{1}{5} + 4\frac{9}{16}$
   about $7\frac{1}{2}$

4. $\frac{7}{8} - \frac{4}{5}$
   about 0

5. On Tuesday, Keith spent $1\frac{7}{8}$ hr studying for his history test. He studied again for $1\frac{1}{3}$ hr on Wednesday and for $\frac{5}{8}$ hr on Thursday. Estimate the time Keith spent studying for his history test this week.
   about 4 hr

For 6–11, write the sum or difference in simplest form. Estimate to check.
Possible estimates are given.

6. $\frac{1}{4} + \frac{2}{3}$
   $\frac{11}{12}$; about 1

7. $\frac{6}{7} - \frac{1}{2}$
   $\frac{5}{14}$; about $\frac{1}{2}$

8. $\frac{3}{5} + \frac{1}{4}$
   $\frac{17}{20}$; about 1

9. $\frac{7}{8} - \frac{5}{6}$
   $\frac{1}{24}$; about 0

10. $\frac{7}{10} - \frac{1}{6}$
   $\frac{8}{15}$; about $\frac{1}{2}$

11. $\frac{7}{16} + \frac{7}{8}$
   $1\frac{5}{16}$; about $1\frac{1}{2}$

12. Noriko drives $\frac{2}{3}$ mile to pick up Mary, $\frac{3}{4}$ mile to get Marcus, and then $\frac{5}{6}$ mile to the movies. How far does she drive?
   $2\frac{1}{4}$ mi

13. Kim lives $1\frac{3}{4}$ mi south of Patrick. Kara lives $1\frac{1}{2}$ mi south of Kim. Draw a diagram to find out how far Patrick lives from Kara.
   Check students' diagrams; $3\frac{1}{4}$ mi

Go On

Name ______________

For 14–19, write the sum or difference in simplest form.

14. $1\frac{2}{7} + 3\frac{9}{14}$
   $4\frac{13}{14}$

15. $5\frac{3}{4} - 3\frac{1}{3}$
   $2\frac{5}{12}$

16. $3\frac{4}{5} + 2\frac{1}{4}$
   $6\frac{1}{20}$

17. $4\frac{1}{2} - 2\frac{7}{8}$
   $1\frac{5}{8}$

18. $1\frac{5}{6} + 3\frac{1}{3}$
   $5\frac{1}{6}$

19. $6\frac{1}{5} - 2\frac{1}{3}$
   $3\frac{13}{15}$

20. Jamie is a partner in a bookstore. He owns $\frac{1}{5}$ of the business. His sister, Lila, owns $\frac{1}{4}$, and their friend Jared owns the rest. What fraction of the business does Jared own?
   $\frac{11}{20}$

For 21–23, draw a diagram to help you find the sum or difference. Write the answer in simplest form.
Check students' diagrams.

21. $5\frac{2}{3} - 3\frac{7}{12}$
   $2\frac{1}{12}$

22. $3\frac{5}{8} + 1\frac{1}{4}$
   $4\frac{7}{8}$

23. $7\frac{1}{3} - 4\frac{1}{2}$
   $2\frac{5}{6}$

24. Sarah bikes $\frac{3}{4}$ mi north. Next, she bikes $1\frac{1}{2}$ mi west. Then, she bikes $2\frac{1}{3}$ mi south. In which directions must she bike to return to her starting place?
   north and east

25. Oliver has a piece of cardboard that is 12 in. long. He needs to cut it into $2\frac{2}{5}$-in. strips. How many cuts will he make?
   4 cuts

Stop

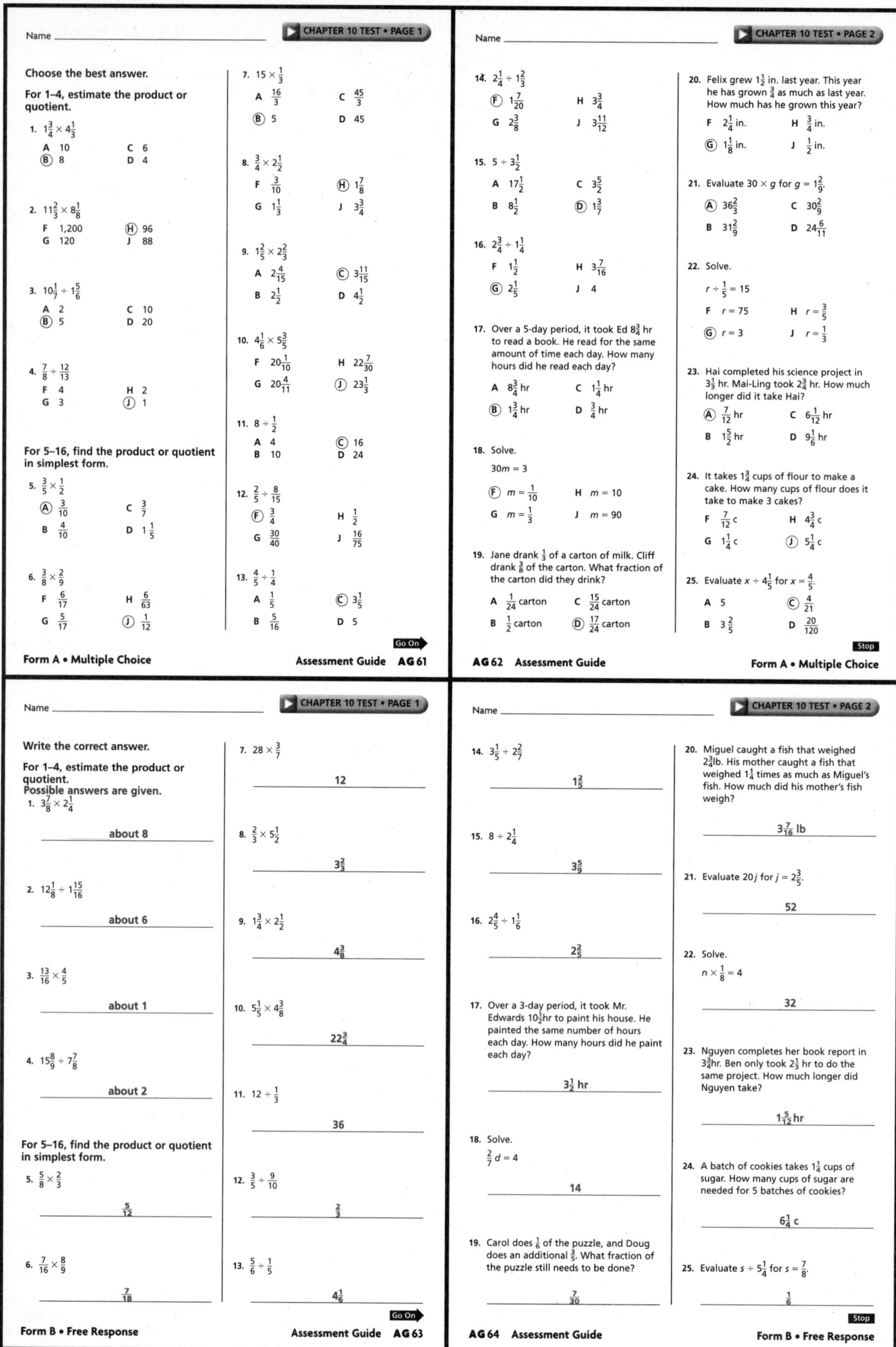

Name ____________ CHAPTER 10 TEST • PAGE 1

Choose the best answer.

For 1–4, estimate the product or quotient.

1. $1\frac{3}{4} \times 4\frac{1}{3}$
   A 10 C 6
   (B) 8 D 4

2. $11\frac{2}{3} \times 8\frac{1}{8}$
   F 1,200 (H) 96
   G 120 J 88

3. $10\frac{1}{7} \div 1\frac{5}{6}$
   A 2 C 10
   (B) 5 D 20

4. $\frac{7}{8} \div \frac{12}{13}$
   F 4 H 2
   G 3 (J) 1

For 5–16, find the product or quotient in simplest form.

5. $\frac{3}{5} \times \frac{1}{2}$
   (A) $\frac{3}{10}$ C $\frac{3}{7}$
   B $\frac{4}{10}$ D $1\frac{1}{5}$

6. $\frac{3}{8} \times \frac{2}{9}$
   F $\frac{6}{17}$ H $\frac{6}{63}$
   G $\frac{5}{17}$ (J) $\frac{1}{12}$

7. $15 \times \frac{1}{3}$
   A $\frac{16}{3}$ C $\frac{45}{3}$
   (B) 5 D 45

8. $\frac{3}{4} \times 2\frac{1}{2}$
   F $\frac{3}{10}$ (H) $1\frac{7}{8}$
   G $1\frac{1}{3}$ J $3\frac{3}{4}$

9. $1\frac{2}{5} \times 2\frac{2}{3}$
   A $2\frac{4}{15}$ (C) $3\frac{11}{15}$
   B $2\frac{1}{2}$ D $4\frac{1}{2}$

10. $4\frac{1}{6} \times 5\frac{3}{5}$
    F $20\frac{1}{10}$ H $22\frac{7}{30}$
    G $20\frac{4}{11}$ (J) $23\frac{1}{3}$

11. $8 \div \frac{1}{2}$
    A 4 (C) 16
    B 10 D 24

12. $\frac{2}{5} \div \frac{8}{15}$
    (F) $\frac{3}{4}$ H $\frac{1}{2}$
    G $\frac{30}{40}$ J $\frac{16}{75}$

13. $\frac{4}{5} \div \frac{1}{4}$
    A $\frac{1}{5}$ (C) $3\frac{1}{5}$
    B $\frac{5}{16}$ D 5

Go On

Form A • Multiple Choice Assessment Guide AG 61

Name ____________ CHAPTER 10 TEST • PAGE 2

14. $2\frac{1}{4} \div 1\frac{2}{3}$
    (F) $1\frac{7}{20}$ H $3\frac{3}{4}$
    G $2\frac{3}{8}$ J $3\frac{11}{12}$

15. $5 \div 3\frac{1}{2}$
    A $17\frac{1}{2}$ C $3\frac{5}{2}$
    B $8\frac{1}{2}$ (D) $1\frac{3}{7}$

16. $2\frac{3}{4} \div 1\frac{1}{4}$
    F $1\frac{1}{2}$ H $3\frac{7}{16}$
    (G) $2\frac{1}{5}$ J 4

17. Over a 5-day period, it took Ed $8\frac{3}{4}$ hr to read a book. He read for the same amount of time each day. How many hours did he read each day?
    A $8\frac{3}{4}$ hr C $1\frac{1}{4}$ hr
    (B) $1\frac{3}{4}$ hr D $\frac{3}{4}$ hr

18. Solve.
    $30m = 3$
    (F) $m = \frac{1}{10}$ H $m = 10$
    G $m = \frac{1}{3}$ J $m = 90$

19. Jane drank $\frac{1}{3}$ of a carton of milk. Cliff drank $\frac{3}{8}$ of the carton. What fraction of the carton did they drink?
    A $\frac{1}{24}$ carton C $\frac{15}{24}$ carton
    B $\frac{1}{2}$ carton (D) $\frac{17}{24}$ carton

20. Felix grew $1\frac{1}{2}$ in. last year. This year he has grown $\frac{3}{4}$ as much as last year. How much has he grown this year?
    F $2\frac{1}{4}$ in. H $\frac{3}{4}$ in.
    (G) $1\frac{1}{8}$ in. J $\frac{1}{2}$ in.

21. Evaluate $30 \times g$ for $g = 1\frac{2}{9}$.
    (A) $36\frac{2}{3}$ C $30\frac{2}{9}$
    B $31\frac{2}{9}$ D $24\frac{6}{11}$

22. Solve.
    $r \div \frac{1}{5} = 15$
    F $r = 75$ H $r = \frac{3}{5}$
    (G) $r = 3$ J $r = \frac{1}{3}$

23. Hai completed his science project in $3\frac{1}{3}$ hr. Mai-Ling took $2\frac{3}{4}$ hr. How much longer did it take Hai?
    (A) $\frac{7}{12}$ hr C $6\frac{1}{12}$ hr
    B $1\frac{5}{2}$ hr D $9\frac{1}{6}$ hr

24. It takes $1\frac{3}{4}$ cups of flour to make a cake. How many cups of flour does it take to make 3 cakes?
    F $\frac{7}{12}$ c H $4\frac{3}{4}$ c
    G $1\frac{1}{4}$ c (J) $5\frac{1}{4}$ c

25. Evaluate $x \div 4\frac{1}{5}$ for $x = \frac{4}{5}$.
    A 5 (C) $\frac{4}{21}$
    B $3\frac{2}{5}$ D $\frac{20}{120}$

Stop

AG 62 Assessment Guide Form A • Multiple Choice

Name ____________ CHAPTER 10 TEST • PAGE 1

Write the correct answer.

For 1–4, estimate the product or quotient.
Possible answers are given.

1. $3\frac{7}{8} \times 2\frac{1}{4}$ — about 8

2. $12\frac{1}{8} \div 1\frac{15}{16}$ — about 6

3. $\frac{13}{16} \times \frac{4}{5}$ — about 1

4. $15\frac{8}{9} \div 7\frac{7}{8}$ — about 2

For 5–16, find the product or quotient in simplest form.

5. $\frac{5}{8} \times \frac{2}{3}$ — $\frac{5}{12}$

6. $\frac{7}{16} \times \frac{8}{9}$ — $\frac{7}{18}$

7. $28 \times \frac{3}{7}$ — 12

8. $\frac{2}{3} \times 5\frac{1}{2}$ — $3\frac{2}{3}$

9. $1\frac{3}{4} \times 2\frac{1}{2}$ — $4\frac{3}{8}$

10. $5\frac{1}{5} \times 4\frac{3}{8}$ — $22\frac{3}{4}$

11. $12 \div \frac{1}{3}$ — 36

12. $\frac{3}{5} \div \frac{9}{10}$ — $\frac{2}{3}$

13. $\frac{5}{6} \div \frac{1}{5}$ — $4\frac{1}{6}$

Go On

Form B • Free Response Assessment Guide AG 63

Name ____________ CHAPTER 10 TEST • PAGE 2

14. $3\frac{1}{5} \div 2\frac{2}{7}$ — $1\frac{2}{5}$

15. $8 \div 2\frac{1}{4}$ — $3\frac{5}{9}$

16. $2\frac{4}{5} \div 1\frac{1}{6}$ — $2\frac{2}{5}$

17. Over a 3-day period, it took Mr. Edwards $10\frac{1}{2}$hr to paint his house. He painted the same number of hours each day. How many hours did he paint each day? — $3\frac{1}{2}$ hr

18. Solve.
    $\frac{2}{7}d = 4$ — 14

19. Carol does $\frac{1}{6}$ of the puzzle, and Doug does an additional $\frac{3}{5}$. What fraction of the puzzle still needs to be done? — $\frac{7}{30}$

20. Miguel caught a fish that weighed $2\frac{3}{4}$lb. His mother caught a fish that weighed $1\frac{1}{4}$ times as much as Miguel's fish. How much did his mother's fish weigh? — $3\frac{7}{16}$ lb

21. Evaluate $20j$ for $j = 2\frac{3}{5}$. — 52

22. Solve.
    $n \times \frac{1}{8} = 4$ — 32

23. Nguyen completes her book report in $3\frac{3}{4}$hr. Ben only took $2\frac{1}{3}$ hr to do the same project. How much longer did Nguyen take? — $1\frac{5}{12}$ hr

24. A batch of cookies takes $1\frac{1}{4}$ cups of sugar. How many cups of sugar are needed for 5 batches of cookies? — $6\frac{1}{4}$ c

25. Evaluate $s \div 5\frac{1}{4}$ for $s = \frac{7}{8}$. — $\frac{1}{6}$

Stop

AG 64 Assessment Guide Form B • Free Response

Name ____________________

Choose the best answer.

1. Choose the group of numbers below by which 96 is evenly divisible.
   - A 2, 3, 4, 5
   - C 2, 3, 4, 8, 9
   - (B) 2, 3, 4, 6, 8
   - D 2, 3, 6, 8, 9

2. Andrew has a small library of music CDs. It includes 8 jazz, 12 rock, 5 rap, and 5 classical CDs. What fraction of Andrew's collection is rock music?
   - F $\frac{3}{5}$
   - H $\frac{1}{6}$
   - (G) $\frac{2}{5}$
   - J $\frac{1}{8}$

3. Estimate the sum. $3\frac{7}{8} + 2\frac{1}{4}$
   - A 4
   - (C) 6
   - B 5
   - D 7

4. $2\frac{2}{5} \times \frac{5}{6}$
   - F $3\frac{7}{30}$
   - (H) 2
   - G $2\frac{1}{3}$
   - J $1\frac{5}{6}$

5. Which pair of numbers is divisible by both 3 and 4?
   - (A) 132 and 456
   - C 136 and 596
   - B 234 and 459
   - D 258 and 336

6. Which is $\frac{9}{4}$ written as a mixed number?
   - F $\frac{1}{4}$
   - H $2\frac{1}{9}$
   - G 2
   - (J) $2\frac{1}{4}$

7. Erin spent $\frac{3}{8}$ hr practicing piano, $1\frac{1}{2}$ hr on homework, and $\frac{3}{4}$ hr preparing dinner. In all, how much time did these things take?
   - A $2\frac{1}{4}$ hr
   - (C) $2\frac{5}{8}$ hr
   - B $2\frac{3}{8}$ hr
   - D $2\frac{3}{4}$ hr

8. Yesterday Jim read $\frac{3}{8}$ of a new book. He read only $\frac{1}{2}$ that much today. What part of the book is left to read?
   - F $\frac{9}{16}$
   - (H) $\frac{7}{16}$
   - G $\frac{1}{2}$
   - J $\frac{3}{16}$

9. Which are the first five multiples of 60?
   - A 1, 2, 3, 4, 5
   - B 3, 4, 5, 10, 30
   - C 60, 90, 120, 150, 180
   - (D) 60, 120, 180, 240, 300

10. Which fraction is in simplest form?
    - F $\frac{9}{18}$
    - H $\frac{3}{18}$
    - (G) $\frac{7}{18}$
    - J $\frac{2}{18}$

11. $\frac{7}{9} - \frac{3}{4}$
    - A $\frac{4}{5}$
    - C $\frac{1}{9}$
    - B $\frac{1}{4}$
    - (D) $\frac{1}{36}$

12. $\frac{3}{5} \div \frac{5}{8}$
    - F $\frac{3}{8}$
    - (H) $\frac{24}{25}$
    - G $\frac{1}{2}$
    - J $\frac{39}{40}$

13. Find the GCF of 48 and 64.
    - A 4
    - C 192
    - (B) 16
    - D 3,072

14. Which is 0.7 written as a fraction?
    - F $\frac{70}{10}$
    - H $\frac{7}{100}$
    - (G) $\frac{7}{10}$
    - J $\frac{7}{1,000}$

Go On

Name ____________________

15. About $\frac{9}{10}$ of a golf course is made up of fairways. Another $\frac{1}{18}$ is made up of greens, and the rest is made up of tees. What fraction of a golf course is made up of tees?
    - A $\frac{1}{10}$
    - (C) $\frac{2}{45}$
    - B $\frac{1}{18}$
    - D $\frac{1}{90}$

16. $5\frac{1}{3} \times 3\frac{3}{4}$
    - (F) 20
    - H $16\frac{1}{12}$
    - G $18\frac{3}{12}$
    - J $15\frac{1}{4}$

17. $\frac{2}{3} \div 3$
    - (A) $\frac{2}{9}$
    - C $\frac{3}{5}$
    - B $\frac{1}{3}$
    - D $\frac{1}{2}$

18. Which fraction is equal to 8?
    - F $\frac{56}{6}$
    - (H) $\frac{40}{5}$
    - G $\frac{34}{4}$
    - J $\frac{32}{8}$

19. Bob lives between Al and Chad on a straight road, $\frac{3}{4}$ mi from Al and $\frac{1}{3}$ mi from Chad. Chad lives between Bob and Dan on the same road. Bob lives $\frac{5}{6}$ mi from Dan. How far does Chad live from Dan?
    - A $\frac{1}{6}$ mi
    - (C) $\frac{1}{2}$ mi
    - B $\frac{1}{3}$ mi
    - D $\frac{2}{3}$ mi

20. Estimate.

    $5\frac{1}{6} \times 3\frac{7}{8}$
    - F 24
    - (H) 20
    - G 22
    - J 15

21. James goes to the playground every 3 days and Natalie goes every 5 days. They meet on March 9 for the first time. How many more times will they meet at the playground by May 12?
    - A 15 times
    - C 5 times
    - B 10 times
    - (D) 4 times

22. Which is $\frac{27}{100}$ written as a percent?
    - F 270%
    - H 2.7%
    - (G) 27%
    - J 0.27%

23. $5\frac{1}{2} + 3\frac{7}{8}$
    - (A) $9\frac{3}{8}$
    - C $8\frac{4}{5}$
    - B $9\frac{1}{4}$
    - D $8\frac{3}{8}$

24. Estimate.

    $\frac{9}{10} \div \frac{5}{6}$
    - (F) 1
    - H 2
    - G $1\frac{1}{2}$
    - J $2\frac{1}{2}$

25. Machine bolts are sold in boxes of 25. Nuts come in packages of 10 and washers are sold by the dozen. What is the least number of each item you can buy to have an equal number of each with none left over?
    - A 150
    - (C) 300
    - B 250
    - D 3,000

26. Which number completes the equation?

    $\frac{3}{5} = \frac{■}{25}$
    - F 20
    - H 12
    - (G) 15
    - J 9

Go On

Name ____________________

27. Kerry, Kim, and Karin buy a new computer together. Kerry contributes $\frac{1}{2}$ the money and Kim contributes $\frac{1}{5}$. What fraction does Karin contribute?
    - A $\frac{1}{5}$
    - C $\frac{1}{3}$
    - (B) $\frac{3}{10}$
    - D $\frac{4}{5}$

28. Selina worked on a science project for 7 days. She spent a total of $15\frac{3}{4}$ hr on the project. She worked the same amount of time each day. How much time did she spend on the project each day?
    - (F) $2\frac{1}{4}$ hr
    - H $2\frac{3}{7}$ hr
    - G $2\frac{1}{3}$ hr
    - J 3 hr

29. The prime factorization of 504 is $2^3 \times 3^2 \times n$. What is the value of n?
    - A 11
    - (C) 7
    - B 9
    - D 2

30. Which fraction is equal to 0.8?
    - F $\frac{80}{10}$
    - H $\frac{19}{8}$
    - G $\frac{40}{5}$
    - (J) $\frac{4}{5}$

31. $\frac{3}{7} - \frac{1}{4}$
    - A 0
    - C $\frac{3}{14}$
    - (B) $\frac{5}{28}$
    - D $\frac{3}{7}$

32. How many ribbons $1\frac{2}{3}$ ft long can you cut from a roll that has 20 ft of ribbon?
    - F 33 ribbons
    - H 15 ribbons
    - G 20 ribbons
    - (J) 12 ribbons

33. Which number is prime?
    - A 1
    - C 87
    - (B) 53
    - D 91

34. When the sixth-grade class voted for class president, Nathan received $\frac{12}{30}$ of the votes. Which decimal tells what part of the class voted for Nathan?
    - F 0.6
    - (H) 0.4
    - G 0.5
    - J 0.2

35. $\frac{1}{2} + \frac{1}{3} + \frac{1}{6}$
    - A $\frac{3}{11}$
    - C $\frac{11}{12}$
    - B $\frac{1}{2}$
    - (D) 1

36. $3\frac{4}{5} \times 5\frac{1}{2}$
    - (F) $20\frac{9}{10}$
    - H $15\frac{5}{7}$
    - G $20\frac{5}{7}$
    - J $15\frac{4}{10}$

37. Which list contains factors of 24,570?
    - (A) 3 and 9
    - C 2, 3, and 4
    - B 3, 5, and 8
    - D 4 and 10

38. Which fraction is equal to $\frac{5}{12}$?
    - F $\frac{10}{30}$
    - H $\frac{15}{24}$
    - (G) $\frac{15}{36}$
    - J $\frac{2}{3}$

Go On

Name ____________________

39. Mary lives $\frac{3}{8}$ mi north of Juan. Juan lives $1\frac{3}{4}$ mi south of Noel. Tom lives $\frac{7}{8}$ mi east of Noel. Karl lives due south of Tom and due east of Mary. How far does Karl live from Tom?
    - A $\frac{7}{8}$ mi
    - C $1\frac{1}{4}$ mi
    - B 1 mi
    - (D) $1\frac{3}{8}$ mi

40. $25\frac{3}{5} \div 4\frac{4}{15}$
    - F $6\frac{3}{5}$
    - H $6\frac{4}{25}$
    - G $6\frac{1}{2}$
    - (J) 6

41. Which shows the prime factorization of 363.
    - (A) $3 \times 11 \times 11$
    - C $2 \times 3 \times 11 \times 11$
    - B $3 \times 3 \times 11$
    - D $3 \times 7 \times 13$

42. Which number completes $5\frac{8}{15} = \frac{■}{15}$?
    - F 128
    - H 58
    - (G) 83
    - J 13

43. Kris jogged $2\frac{1}{8}$ km Monday, $1\frac{5}{6}$ km Tuesday, and $3\frac{1}{4}$ km today. Estimate the total distance she jogged on these 3 days.
    - A 8 km
    - C 6 km
    - (B) 7 km
    - D 5 km

44. A box of breakfast cereal contains 45 ounces. If each serving is $2\frac{1}{4}$ ounces, how many servings are contained in the box?
    - (F) 20 servings
    - H 22.5 servings
    - G 21 servings
    - J 24 servings

45. The calculators for Patty's store are packaged 15 to a box, and batteries are 144 to a box. Each calculator requires 4 batteries. What is the least number of boxes of calculators she will need if she wants no calculators or batteries left over?
    - A 4 boxes
    - (C) 12 boxes
    - B 6 boxes
    - D 180 boxes

46. What is $\frac{12}{36}$ in simplest form?
    - (F) $\frac{1}{3}$
    - H $\frac{3}{9}$
    - G $\frac{2}{6}$
    - J $\frac{1}{6}$

47. $5\frac{2}{3} + 3\frac{1}{8}$
    - A $8\frac{1}{4}$
    - C $8\frac{1}{2}$
    - B $8\frac{3}{11}$
    - (D) $8\frac{19}{24}$

48. Solve. $p \div \frac{1}{4} = 24$
    - F $p = 96$
    - (H) $p = 6$
    - G $p = 48$
    - J $p = 4$

49. Find the LCM of 12 and 30.
    - (A) 60
    - C 180
    - B 120
    - D 360

50. Mr. Watson divides his coin collection so that he has $\frac{1}{4}$ of the coins. He gives each of his three children $\frac{1}{8}$ of the coins, each of his 5 grandchildren $\frac{1}{16}$ of the coins and the rest are given to his brother. Who receives the greatest part of Mr. Watson's coin collection?
    - F each child
    - G each grandchild
    - H Mr. Watson's brother
    - (J) Mr. Watson

Stop

Name ______________________

UNIT 3 TEST • PAGE 1

Write the correct answer.

1. Write which of the numbers 2, 3, 4, 5, 6, 8, 9, or 10 are factors of 120.

   2, 3, 4, 5, 6, 8, 10

2. Chris has a small library of novels. It includes 10 mystery, 12 science fiction, 6 biography, and 2 technical novels. What fraction of Chris' collection is biography?

   $\frac{1}{5}$

3. Estimate. $5\frac{2}{9} + 8\frac{7}{8}$.

   about 14

4. $3\frac{1}{8} \times \frac{4}{5}$

   $2\frac{1}{2}$

5. Write which of the numbers 3, 4, 5, 6, 8, 9, or 10 are factors of both 96 and 324.

   3, 4, and 6

6. Write $\frac{17}{5}$ as a mixed number.

   $3\frac{2}{5}$

7. Winnie spent $\frac{1}{3}$ hour showering, $\frac{1}{4}$ hour getting dressed, and $\frac{1}{2}$ hour eating breakfast. How much total time did she spend in these activities?

   $1\frac{1}{12}$ hours

8. Yesterday, Phillip cleaned $\frac{3}{5}$ of his room. He cleaned only $\frac{1}{3}$ that much today. What part of the room is left to clean?

   $\frac{1}{5}$

9. Write the first five multiples of 45.

   45, 90, 135, 180, 225

10. Write $\frac{3}{12}$ in simplest form.

    $\frac{1}{4}$

11. $\frac{8}{11} - \frac{2}{3}$

    $\frac{2}{33}$

12. $\frac{2}{7} \div \frac{7}{8}$

    $\frac{16}{49}$

13. Find the GCF of 32 and 56.

    8

14. Write 0.09 as a fraction.

    $\frac{9}{100}$

Go On

Name ______________________

UNIT 3 TEST • PAGE 2

15. About $\frac{2}{3}$ of a golf course is made up of par 4 holes. Another $\frac{1}{9}$ is made up of par 5 holes, and the rest is par 3 holes. What fraction of a golf course is made up of par 3 holes?

    $\frac{2}{9}$

16. $4\frac{2}{5} \times 2\frac{1}{4}$

    $9\frac{9}{10}$

17. What is the 15th number in the sequence? 83, 80, 77, 74, 71, . . .

    41

18. $\frac{63}{9}$ is equal to what integer?

    7

19. Bill lives between Art and Carl on a straight road, $\frac{2}{5}$ mi from Art and $\frac{1}{4}$ mi from Carl. Carl lives between Bill and Don on the same road. Bill lives $\frac{5}{8}$ mi from Don. Draw a diagram to help find how far Carl lives from Don.

    $\frac{3}{8}$ mi

20. Estimate. $4\frac{1}{8} \times 5\frac{7}{9}$

    about 24

21. Joshua swims every 2 days and Nicole swims every 3 days. They swim together on May 9. How many more times will they meet at the pool by July 4?

    9 times

22. Write $\frac{53}{100}$ as a percent.

    53%

23. $7\frac{1}{3} + 4\frac{2}{5}$

    $11\frac{11}{15}$

24. Estimate. $\frac{11}{12} \div \frac{7}{8}$

    about 1

25. Sheet metal screws are sold in boxes of 35. Washers come in packages of 10, and anchors are sold by the dozen. What is the least number of each you can buy to have an equal number of each?

    420

26. Solve for x.
    $\frac{5}{9} = \frac{x}{36}$

    $x = 20$

Go On

Name ______________________

UNIT 3 TEST • PAGE 3

27. Michael, Susan, and Pauline bought a new computer game by pooling their resources. Michael contributed $\frac{2}{5}$ of the money and Pauline contributed $\frac{1}{3}$. What fraction did Susan contribute?

    $\frac{4}{15}$

28. Sebastian worked on painting his sailboat for 9 days. He spent a total of $43\frac{1}{2}$ hours painting. If he painted the same length of time each day, how much time did he spend per day painting?

    $4\frac{5}{6}$ hours

29. Write the prime factorization of 756.

    $2^2 \times 3^3 \times 7$

30. Write a fraction equivalent to 0.65.

    Possible answer: $\frac{13}{20}$

31. $\frac{5}{9} - \frac{5}{18}$

    $\frac{5}{18}$

32. You need to cut $2\frac{3}{4}$ in. pieces of string from a larger piece which is 50 in. long. How many full pieces can you get?

    18 pieces

33. Which of the numbers 1, 39, 57, 83, 123 is prime?

    83

34. The bill received $\frac{37}{50}$ of the votes from the state senate for passage. Write a decimal that tells what part of the senate voted for the bill.

    0.74

35. $\frac{1}{3} + \frac{1}{4} + \frac{1}{9}$

    $\frac{25}{36}$

36. $4\frac{2}{5} \times 5\frac{2}{3}$

    $24\frac{14}{15}$

37. What are the three smallest prime factors of 24,310?

    2, 5, and 11

38. Write an equivalent fraction for $\frac{7}{9}$.

    Possible answer: $\frac{21}{27}$

Go On

Name ______________________

UNIT 3 TEST • PAGE 4

39. Arthur lives $\frac{2}{5}$ mi. north of Jeffrey. Jeffrey lives $2\frac{1}{2}$ mi. south of Jason. Chris lives $\frac{3}{5}$ mi. east of Jason. Andy lives due south of Chris and due east of Arthur. Draw a diagram to help find out how far Andy lives from Chris.

    $2\frac{1}{10}$ mile

40. $14\frac{2}{3} \div 4\frac{2}{5}$

    $3\frac{1}{3}$

41. Write the prime factorization of 924.

    $2^2 \times 3 \times 7 \times 11$

42. Solve for c.
    $4\frac{3}{8} = \frac{c}{8}$

    $c = 35$

43. Louisa walked $3\frac{1}{4}$ mile on Monday, $2\frac{4}{5}$ mile on Tuesday, and $1\frac{1}{8}$ mile today. Estimate the total distance she walked on these 3 days.

    about 7 miles

44. A box of macaroni & cheese contains 14 ounces. If each serving is 3 ounces, how many servings are contained in the box?

    $4\frac{2}{3}$ servings

45. Tomato plants are grown 6 in a flat, and fertilizer stakes are packaged 10 in a bag. Each plant needs 3 fertilizer stakes when transplanted. What is the fewest number of flats of tomatoes needed if there are to be no tomato plants or fertilizer stakes left over?

    5 flats

46. Write $\frac{24}{28}$ in simplest form.

    $\frac{6}{7}$

47. $2\frac{3}{4} + 4\frac{5}{8}$

    $7\frac{3}{8}$

48. Solve for k.
    $k \div \frac{2}{5} = 25$

    $k = 10$

49. Find the LCM of 18 and 24.

    72

50. Of the total money raised for charity, the police department raised $\frac{1}{5}$, three schools each raised $\frac{1}{10}$, and five clubs each raised $\frac{1}{20}$. The fire department raised the rest of the money. What fraction of the total did the fire department raise?

    $\frac{1}{4}$

Stop

Name ______________________________

Choose the best answer.

For 1–4, name the integer that represents each situation.

1. An increase in altitude of 2,547 ft

A $^+2,574$ C $^-2,547$
(B) $^+2,547$ D $^-2,574$

2. A drop in temperature of 16°F

F $^-32$ H $^+16$
(G) $^-16$ J $^+32$

3. The absolute value of 65

(A) 65 C $^-130$
B $^-65$ D 0

4. The opposite of 19

F 91 **(H)** $^-19$
G 19 J $^-91$

5. Which number is between $3\frac{1}{4}$ and $3\frac{3}{4}$?

A $3\frac{1}{8}$ C $3\frac{7}{8}$
(B) $3\frac{1}{2}$ D $3\frac{13}{16}$

6. Which number is between $^-\frac{3}{5}$ and $^-\frac{3}{8}$?

F $\frac{-8}{5}$ H $\frac{-5}{8}$
G $\frac{-4}{5}$ **(J)** $\frac{-2}{5}$

For 7–8, find the rational number written in the form $\frac{a}{b}$.

7. $4\frac{5}{7}$

A $\frac{45}{7}$ C $\frac{20}{7}$
(B) $\frac{33}{7}$ D $\frac{9}{7}$

8. 2.718

(F) $\frac{2,718}{1,000}$ H $27\frac{18}{100}$
G $2\frac{178}{1,000}$ J $271\frac{8}{1000}$

9. What is the value of $|^-3.14|$?

(A) 3.14 C $^-3\frac{14}{1,000}$
B $3\frac{14}{1,000}$ D $^-3.14$

10. Which rational number is between $^-\frac{5}{8}$ and $\frac{5}{8}$?

F $\frac{-13}{16}$ H $\frac{-10}{16}$
G $\frac{-11}{16}$ **(J)** $\frac{-9}{16}$

11. Order $2\frac{3}{7}$, $2\frac{5}{11}$, and 2.5 from *least* to *greatest*.

A $2\frac{5}{11}$, $2\frac{3}{7}$, 2.5
B $2\frac{3}{7}$, 2.5, $2\frac{5}{11}$
(C) $2\frac{3}{7}$, $2\frac{5}{11}$, 2.5
D 2.5, $2\frac{5}{11}$, $2\frac{3}{7}$

12. Four friends have CD collections that contain 15, 20, 30, and 35 CDs. Mike and Taylor together have 10 fewer CDs than Al and Jeff. Taylor has more CDs than Al. Who has 30 CDs?

F Jeff **(H)** Taylor
G Al J Mike

Go On

Name ______________________________

13. Sam, Ann, and Jay play the guitar. One practices at 4:00, one at 6:00, and one at 9:00. Jay does not practice at 9:00. Ann practices 2 hours before Jay. Who practices at 4:00?

A Sam
(B) Ann
C Jay
D Cannot tell

14. In a race, the three fastest times were 20.3 min, $20\frac{1}{6}$ min, and 20.2 min. Order the times from *least* to *greatest*.

F 20.3 min, $20\frac{1}{6}$ min, 20.2 min
(G) $20\frac{1}{6}$ min, 20.2 min, 20.3 min
H 20.2 min, $20\frac{1}{6}$ min, 20.3 min
J 20.2 min, 20.3 min, $20\frac{1}{6}$ min

15. Which shows a correct comparison of two numbers?

(A) $0 > {}^-7.5$ C $^-7.5 > 0$
B $^-7.5 > 7.5$ D $7.5 = {}^-7.5$

16. Four students live in four different houses on the same block of the same street. Bob and Ceil live next door to Art. Doug lives closer to Ceil than to Art. Which two students live farthest apart?

F Bob and Ceil H Art and Doug
G Ceil and Doug **(J)** Bob and Doug

17. Gail, May, and Cara each bought a pop, rock, or jazz CD. No two girls bought the same kind of music. Gail did not buy pop music. May bought rock music. What kind of CD did each girl buy?

A Gail, pop; May, rock, Cara, jazz
B Gail, rock; May, rock; Cara, pop
C Gail, rock; May, jazz; Cara, pop
(D) Gail, jazz; May, rock; Cara, pop

18. What is the correct order from least to greatest for 1.1, $^-1\frac{3}{8}$, and $\frac{-9}{8}$?

(F) $^-1\frac{3}{8}$, $\frac{-9}{8}$, 1.1
G $\frac{-9}{8}$, $^-1\frac{3}{8}$, 1.1
H $\frac{-9}{8}$, 1.1, $^-1\frac{3}{8}$
J 1.1, $\frac{-9}{8}$, $^-1\frac{3}{8}$

19. Temperatures on the ski slope were recorded as 17°F, $^-8$°F, $^-2$°F, and 0°F during the day. Choose the order of these temperatures from least to greatest.

A 17°F, 0°F, $^-2$°F, $^-8$°F
B 0°F, $^-2$°F, $^-8$°F, 17°F
(C) $^-8$°F, $^-2$°F, 0°F, 17°F
D 17°F, $^-8$°F, $^-2$°F, 0°F

20. *P, Q, R,* and *S* are integers. *S* is greater than *Q*. *P* is the opposite of *S*. *R* is the opposite of *Q*. *R* is to the right of 0 on the number line. *Q* is less than *P*. Which represents the greatest integer?

F *P* **(H)** *R*
G *Q* J *S*

Stop

Name ______________________________

Write the correct answer.

For 1–4, write an integer to represent each situation.

1. An increase in altitude of 1,345 ft

$^+1,345$

2. A drop in temperature of 8°F

$^-8°$

3. The absolute value of 37

37

4. The opposite of 10

$^-10$

5. Write a rational number between 4 and $4\frac{1}{4}$.

Possible answers: $4\frac{1}{8}$, $4\frac{1}{10}$, $4\frac{1}{12}$, $4\frac{1}{16}$, $4\frac{1}{32}$

6. Write a rational number between $^-\frac{5}{8}$ and $^-\frac{5}{12}$.

Possible answers: $\frac{-4}{8}$, $\frac{-5}{10}$, $\frac{-6}{10}$, $\frac{-7}{12}$, $\frac{-12}{24}$

For 7–8, write a rational number in the form $\frac{a}{b}$.

Possible answers are given.

7. $6\frac{1}{3}$

$\frac{19}{3}$

8. 1.608

$\frac{201}{125}$ or equivalent

9. Write the value of $|^-4.18|$.

4.18

10. Write a rational number between $^-\frac{1}{4}$ and $\frac{1}{4}$.

Possible answers: $\frac{1}{5}$, $\frac{1}{6}$, $\frac{1}{7}$, $\frac{-1}{8}$, $\frac{-1}{10}$

11. Order $3\frac{2}{5}$, $3\frac{3}{8}$, and 3.1 from *least* to *greatest*.

3.1, $3\frac{3}{8}$, $3\frac{2}{5}$

12. Mandy's neighbors are 25, 50, 60, and 75 years old. Mr. Botwell's and Ms. Cantor's combined ages are 10 years older than Ms. Axel's and Mrs. Drew 's combined ages. Mr. Botwell is younger than Ms. Cantor and Mrs. Drew. How old is each neighbor?

Ms. Axel: 25; Mr. Botwell: 50;
Ms. Cantor: 60; Mrs. Drew: 75

Go On

Name ______________________________

13. Willa, Mi Sook, and Juan take piano lessons at 4:30, 7:00, and 8:00, though not necessarily in that order. Neither Willa's lesson nor Mi Sook's lesson is at 7:00. Juan's lesson is before Willa's lesson. What time is each student's lesson?

Mi Sook: 4:30; Juan: 7:00;
Willa: 8:00

14. The three tallest basketball players on the team are $76\frac{1}{4}$ in., 76.2 in., and $76\frac{3}{8}$ in. tall. Order their heights from shortest to tallest.

76.2 in., $76\frac{1}{4}$ in., $76\frac{3}{8}$ in.

15. Compare the numbers. Write <, >, or = for ◯.

0 (>) $^-0.2$

16. Four students are in line for movie tickets. Bo and Celia both are standing next to Anna. Darryl is closer to Celia than to Anna. Which two students are the farthest apart in line?

Bo and Darryl

17. Mr. Jones, Mr. Roddy, and Mr. Sims are the manager, waiter, and cashier in a restaurant. Mr. Jones is not the manager or waiter. Mr. Sims is not the manager. What job does each person have? Explain your method.

	MANAGER	WAITER	CASHIER
Mr. Jones	X	X	✓
Mr. Roddy	✓		
Mr. Sims	X	✓	X

Possible method: make a table
Mr. Jones is the cashier, Mr. Roddy is the manager, Mr. Sims is the waiter

18. Write the numbers in order from least to greatest.

0.1, $^-1\frac{1}{4}$, and $^-1\frac{3}{8}$

$^-1\frac{3}{8}$, $^-1\frac{1}{4}$, 0.1

19. The low temperatures for the last four days were recorded as 1°F, $^-1$°F, $^-2$°F, and 0°F. Order these temperatures from least to greatest.

$^-2$°F, $^-1$°F, 0°F, 1°F

20. Tom, Marta, Joseph, and Beth have these math averages: 99.2, 98.8, 98.1, and 96.9. The difference between Tom's and Marta's averages is less than $\frac{1}{2}$ point. Tom's average is not the highest. A girl does not have the lowest average. What are the averages of the four students?

Tom: 98.8; Marta: 99.2;
Beth: 98.1; Joseph: 96.9

Stop

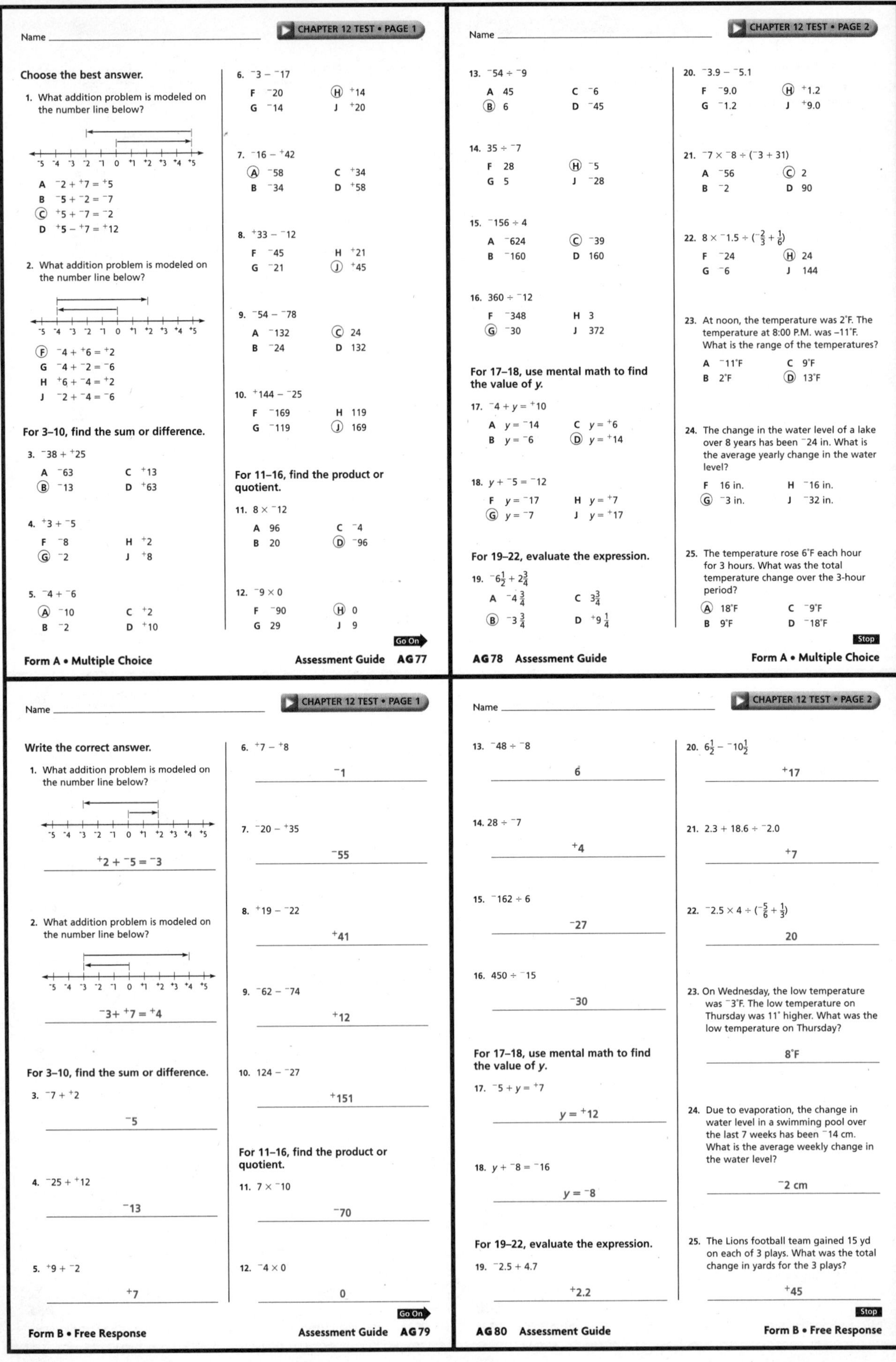

Name

CHAPTER 12 TEST • PAGE 1

Choose the best answer.

1. What addition problem is modeled on the number line below?

$-5\ -4\ -3\ -2\ -1\ 0\ +1\ +2\ +3\ +4\ +5$

A $^{-}2 + {}^{+}7 = {}^{+}5$
B $^{-}5 + {}^{-}2 = {}^{-}7$
Ⓒ $^{+}5 + {}^{-}7 = {}^{-}2$
D $^{+}5 - {}^{+}7 = {}^{+}12$

2. What addition problem is modeled on the number line below?

$-5\ -4\ -3\ -2\ -1\ 0\ +1\ +2\ +3\ +4\ +5$

Ⓕ $^{-}4 + {}^{+}6 = {}^{+}2$
G $^{-}4 + {}^{-}2 = {}^{-}6$
H $^{+}6 + {}^{-}4 = {}^{+}2$
J $^{-}2 + {}^{-}4 = {}^{-}6$

For 3–10, find the sum or difference.

3. $^{-}38 + {}^{+}25$
A $^{-}63$ C $^{+}13$
Ⓑ $^{-}13$ D $^{+}63$

4. $^{+}3 + {}^{-}5$
F $^{-}8$ H $^{+}2$
Ⓖ $^{-}2$ J $^{+}8$

5. $^{-}4 + {}^{-}6$
Ⓐ $^{-}10$ C $^{+}2$
B $^{-}2$ D $^{+}10$

6. $^{-}3 - {}^{-}17$
F $^{-}20$ Ⓗ $^{+}14$
G $^{-}14$ J $^{+}20$

7. $^{-}16 - {}^{+}42$
Ⓐ $^{-}58$ C $^{+}34$
B $^{-}34$ D $^{+}58$

8. $^{+}33 - {}^{-}12$
F $^{-}45$ H $^{+}21$
G $^{-}21$ Ⓙ $^{+}45$

9. $^{-}54 - {}^{-}78$
A $^{-}132$ Ⓒ 24
B $^{-}24$ D 132

10. $^{+}144 - {}^{-}25$
F $^{-}169$ H 119
G $^{-}119$ Ⓙ 169

For 11–16, find the product or quotient.

11. $8 \times {}^{-}12$
A 96 C $^{-}4$
B 20 Ⓓ $^{-}96$

12. $^{-}9 \times 0$
F $^{-}90$ Ⓗ 0
G 29 J 9

Go On

Form A • Multiple Choice Assessment Guide **AG 77**

Name

CHAPTER 12 TEST • PAGE 2

13. $^{-}54 \div {}^{-}9$
A 45 C $^{-}6$
Ⓑ 6 D $^{-}45$

14. $35 \div {}^{-}7$
F 28 Ⓗ $^{-}5$
G 5 J $^{-}28$

15. $^{-}156 \div 4$
A $^{-}624$ Ⓒ $^{-}39$
B $^{-}160$ D 160

16. $360 \div {}^{-}12$
F $^{-}348$ H 3
Ⓖ $^{-}30$ J 372

For 17–18, use mental math to find the value of *y*.

17. $^{-}4 + y = {}^{+}10$
A $y = {}^{-}14$ C $y = {}^{+}6$
B $y = {}^{-}6$ Ⓓ $y = {}^{+}14$

18. $y + {}^{-}5 = {}^{-}12$
F $y = {}^{-}17$ H $y = {}^{+}7$
Ⓖ $y = {}^{-}7$ J $y = {}^{+}17$

For 19–22, evaluate the expression.

19. $^{-}6\frac{1}{2} + 2\frac{3}{4}$
A $^{-}4\frac{3}{4}$ C $3\frac{3}{4}$
Ⓑ $^{-}3\frac{3}{4}$ D $^{+}9\frac{1}{4}$

20. $^{-}3.9 - {}^{-}5.1$
F $^{-}9.0$ Ⓗ $^{+}1.2$
G $^{-}1.2$ J $^{+}9.0$

21. $^{-}7 \times {}^{-}8 \div ({}^{-}3 + 31)$
A $^{-}56$ Ⓒ 2
B $^{-}2$ D 90

22. $8 \times {}^{-}1.5 \div ({}^{-}\frac{2}{3} + \frac{1}{6})$
F $^{-}24$ Ⓗ 24
G $^{-}6$ J 144

23. At noon, the temperature was 2°F. The temperature at 8:00 P.M. was –11°F. What is the range of the temperatures?
A $^{-}11$°F C 9°F
B 2°F Ⓓ 13°F

24. The change in the water level of a lake over 8 years has been $^{-}24$ in. What is the average yearly change in the water level?
F 16 in. H $^{-}16$ in.
Ⓖ $^{-}3$ in. J $^{-}32$ in.

25. The temperature rose 6°F each hour for 3 hours. What was the total temperature change over the 3-hour period?
Ⓐ 18°F C $^{-}9$°F
B 9°F D $^{-}18$°F

Stop

AG 78 Assessment Guide **Form A • Multiple Choice**

Name

CHAPTER 12 TEST • PAGE 1

Write the correct answer.

1. What addition problem is modeled on the number line below?

$-5\ -4\ -3\ -2\ -1\ 0\ +1\ +2\ +3\ +4\ +5$

$^{+}2 + {}^{-}5 = {}^{-}3$

2. What addition problem is modeled on the number line below?

$-5\ -4\ -3\ -2\ -1\ 0\ +1\ +2\ +3\ +4\ +5$

$^{-}3 + {}^{+}7 = {}^{+}4$

For 3–10, find the sum or difference.

3. $^{-}7 + {}^{+}2$

$^{-}5$

4. $^{-}25 + {}^{+}12$

$^{-}13$

5. $^{+}9 + {}^{-}2$

$^{+}7$

6. $^{+}7 - {}^{+}8$

$^{-}1$

7. $^{-}20 - {}^{+}35$

$^{-}55$

8. $^{+}19 - {}^{-}22$

$^{+}41$

9. $^{-}62 - {}^{-}74$

$^{+}12$

10. $124 - {}^{-}27$

$^{+}151$

For 11–16, find the product or quotient.

11. $7 \times {}^{-}10$

$^{-}70$

12. $^{-}4 \times 0$

0

Go On

Form B • Free Response Assessment Guide **AG 79**

Name

CHAPTER 12 TEST • PAGE 2

13. $^{-}48 \div {}^{-}8$

6

14. $28 \div {}^{-}7$

$^{+}4$

15. $^{-}162 \div 6$

$^{-}27$

16. $450 \div {}^{-}15$

$^{-}30$

For 17–18, use mental math to find the value of *y*.

17. $^{-}5 + y = {}^{+}7$

$y = {}^{+}12$

18. $y + {}^{-}8 = {}^{-}16$

$y = {}^{-}8$

For 19–22, evaluate the expression.

19. $^{-}2.5 + 4.7$

$^{+}2.2$

20. $6\frac{1}{2} - {}^{-}10\frac{1}{2}$

$^{+}17$

21. $2.3 + 18.6 \div {}^{-}2.0$

$^{+}7$

22. $^{-}2.5 \times 4 \div ({}^{-}\frac{5}{6} + \frac{1}{3})$

20

23. On Wednesday, the low temperature was $^{-}3$°F. The low temperature on Thursday was 11° higher. What was the low temperature on Thursday?

8°F

24. Due to evaporation, the change in water level in a swimming pool over the last 7 weeks has been $^{-}14$ cm. What is the average weekly change in the water level?

$^{-}2$ cm

25. The Lions football team gained 15 yd on each of 3 plays. What was the total change in yards for the 3 plays?

$^{+}45$

Stop

AG 80 Assessment Guide **Form B • Free Response**

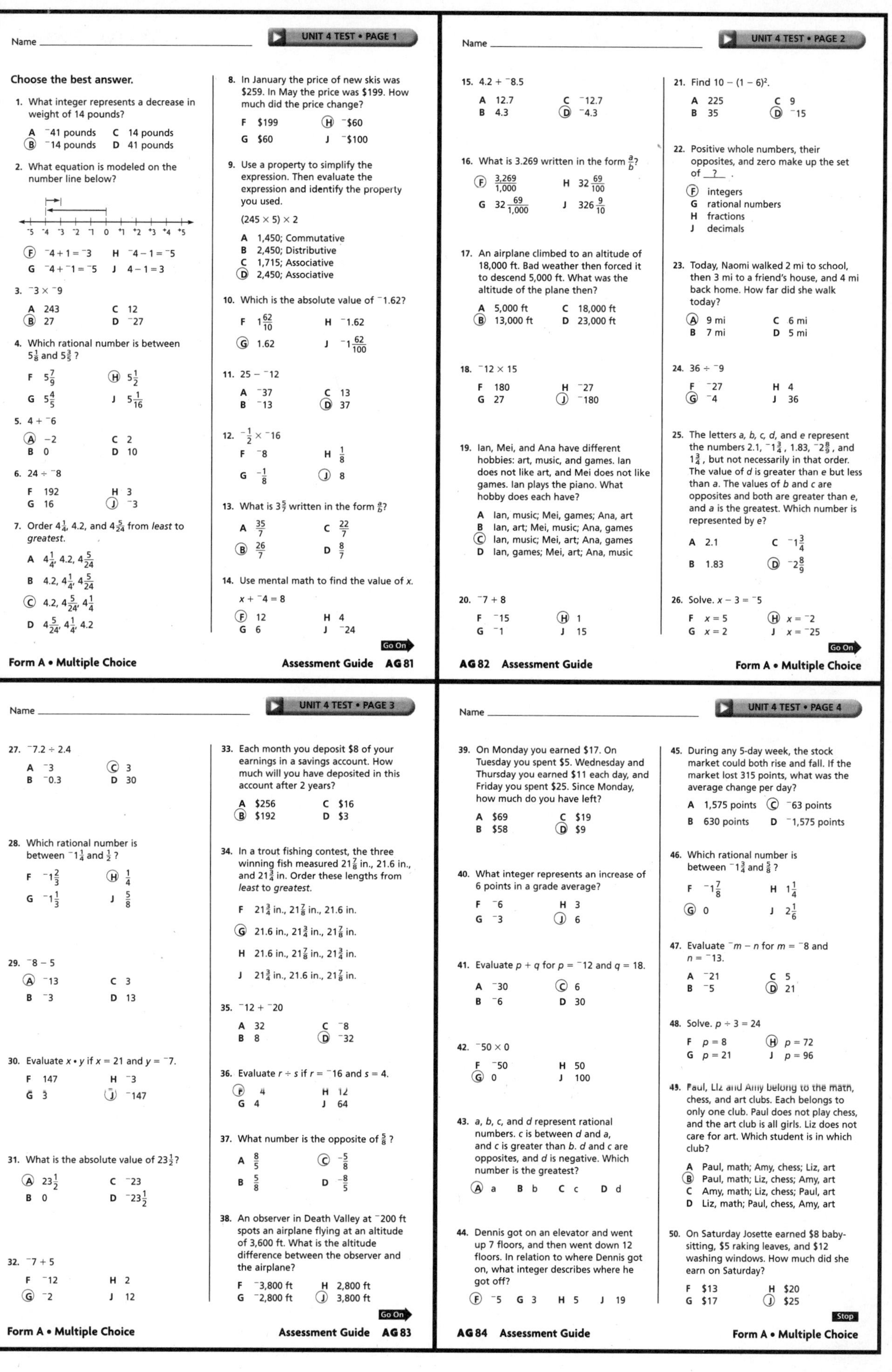

Name ______________________

UNIT 4 TEST • PAGE 1

Choose the best answer.

1. What integer represents a decrease in weight of 14 pounds?
   A $^-41$ pounds   C 14 pounds
   (B) $^-14$ pounds   D 41 pounds

2. What equation is modeled on the number line below?
   (number line from $^-5$ to $^+5$)
   (F) $^-4 + 1 = {}^-3$ H $^-4 - 1 = {}^-5$
   G $^-4 + {}^-1 = {}^-5$ J $4 - 1 = 3$

3. $^-3 \times {}^-9$
   A 243   C 12
   (B) 27   D $^-27$

4. Which rational number is between $5\frac{1}{8}$ and $5\frac{3}{5}$?
   F $5\frac{7}{9}$ (H) $5\frac{1}{2}$
   G $5\frac{4}{5}$ J $5\frac{1}{16}$

5. $4 + {}^-6$
   (A) -2 C 2
   B 0   D 10

6. $24 \div {}^-8$
   F 192   H 3
   G 16   (J) $^-3$

7. Order $4\frac{1}{4}$, 4.2, and $4\frac{5}{24}$ from *least* to *greatest*.
   A $4\frac{1}{4}$, 4.2, $4\frac{5}{24}$
   B 4.2, $4\frac{1}{4}$, $4\frac{5}{24}$
   (C) 4.2, $4\frac{5}{24}$, $4\frac{1}{4}$
   D $4\frac{5}{24}$, $4\frac{1}{4}$, 4.2

8. In January the price of new skis was \$259. In May the price was \$199. How much did the price change?
   F \$199   (H) $^-$\$60
   G \$60   J $^-$\$100

9. Use a property to simplify the expression. Then evaluate the expression and identify the property you used.
   $(245 \times 5) \times 2$
   A 1,450; Commutative
   B 2,450; Distributive
   C 1,715; Associative
   (D) 2,450; Associative

10. Which is the absolute value of $^-1.62$?
   F $1\frac{62}{10}$ H $^-1.62$
   (G) 1.62   J $^-1\frac{62}{100}$

11. $25 - {}^-12$
   A $^-37$ C 13
   B $^-13$ (D) 37

12. $-\frac{1}{2} \times {}^-16$
   F $^-8$ H $\frac{1}{8}$
   G $\frac{-1}{8}$ (J) 8

13. What is $3\frac{5}{7}$ written in the form $\frac{a}{b}$?
   A $\frac{35}{7}$ C $\frac{22}{7}$
   (B) $\frac{26}{7}$ D $\frac{8}{7}$

14. Use mental math to find the value of x.
   $x + {}^-4 = 8$
   (F) 12   H 4
   G 6   J $^-24$

Go On

Name ______________________

UNIT 4 TEST • PAGE 2

15. $4.2 + {}^-8.5$
   A 12.7   C $^-12.7$
   B 4.3   (D) $^-4.3$

16. What is 3.269 written in the form $\frac{a}{b}$?
   (F) $\frac{3{,}269}{1{,}000}$ H $32\frac{69}{100}$
   G $32\frac{69}{1{,}000}$ J $326\frac{9}{10}$

17. An airplane climbed to an altitude of 18,000 ft. Bad weather then forced it to descend 5,000 ft. What was the altitude of the plane then?
   A 5,000 ft   C 18,000 ft
   (B) 13,000 ft   D 23,000 ft

18. $^-12 \times 15$
   F 180   H $^-27$
   G 27   (J) $^-180$

19. Ian, Mei, and Ana have different hobbies: art, music, and games. Ian does not like art, and Mei does not like games. Ian plays the piano. What hobby does each have?
   A Ian, music; Mei, games; Ana, art
   B Ian, art; Mei, music; Ana, games
   (C) Ian, music; Mei, art; Ana, games
   D Ian, games; Mei, art; Ana, music

20. $^-7 + 8$
   F $^-15$ (H) 1
   G $^-1$ J 15

21. Find $10 - (1 - 6)^2$.
   A 225   C 9
   B 35   (D) $^-15$

22. Positive whole numbers, their opposites, and zero make up the set of __?__ .
   (F) integers
   G rational numbers
   H fractions
   J decimals

23. Today, Naomi walked 2 mi to school, then 3 mi to a friend's house, and 4 mi back home. How far did she walk today?
   (A) 9 mi   C 6 mi
   B 7 mi   D 5 mi

24. $36 \div {}^-9$
   F $^-27$ H 4
   (G) $^-4$ J 36

25. The letters *a*, *b*, *c*, *d*, and *e* represent the numbers 2.1, $^-1\frac{3}{4}$, 1.83, $^-2\frac{8}{9}$, and $1\frac{3}{4}$, but not necessarily in that order. The value of *d* is greater than *e* but less than *a*. The values of *b* and *c* are opposites and both are greater than *e*, and *a* is the greatest. Which number is represented by *e*?
   A 2.1   C $^-1\frac{3}{4}$
   B 1.83   (D) $^-2\frac{8}{9}$

26. Solve. $x - 3 = {}^-5$
   F $x = 5$ (H) $x = {}^-2$
   G $x = 2$ J $x = {}^-25$

Go On

Name ______________________

UNIT 4 TEST • PAGE 3

27. $^-7.2 \div 2.4$
   A $^-3$ (C) 3
   B $^-0.3$ D 30

28. Which rational number is between $^-1\frac{1}{4}$ and $\frac{1}{2}$?
   F $^-1\frac{2}{3}$ (H) $\frac{1}{4}$
   G $^-1\frac{1}{3}$ J $\frac{5}{8}$

29. $^-8 - 5$
   (A) $^-13$ C 3
   B $^-3$ D 13

30. Evaluate $x \bullet y$ if $x = 21$ and $y = {}^-7$.
   F 147   H $^-3$
   G 3   (J) $^-147$

31. What is the absolute value of $23\frac{1}{2}$?
   (A) $23\frac{1}{2}$ C $^-23$
   B 0   D $^-23\frac{1}{2}$

32. $^-7 + 5$
   F $^-12$ H 2
   (G) $^-2$ J 12

33. Each month you deposit \$8 of your earnings in a savings account. How much will you have deposited in this account after 2 years?
   A \$256   C \$16
   (B) \$192   D \$3

34. In a trout fishing contest, the three winning fish measured $21\frac{7}{8}$ in., 21.6 in., and $21\frac{3}{4}$ in. Order these lengths from *least* to *greatest*.
   F $21\frac{3}{4}$ in., $21\frac{7}{8}$ in., 21.6 in.
   (G) 21.6 in., $21\frac{3}{4}$ in., $21\frac{7}{8}$ in.
   H 21.6 in., $21\frac{7}{8}$ in., $21\frac{3}{4}$ in.
   J $21\frac{3}{4}$ in., 21.6 in., $21\frac{7}{8}$ in.

35. $^-12 + {}^-20$
   A 32   C $^-8$
   B 8   (D) $^-32$

36. Evaluate $r \div s$ if $r = {}^-16$ and $s = 4$.
   (F) 4   H 12
   G 4   J 64

37. What number is the opposite of $\frac{5}{8}$?
   A $\frac{8}{5}$ (C) $\frac{-5}{8}$
   B $\frac{5}{8}$ D $\frac{-8}{5}$

38. An observer in Death Valley at $^-200$ ft spots an airplane flying at an altitude of 3,600 ft. What is the altitude difference between the observer and the airplane?
   F $^-3{,}800$ ft   H 2,800 ft
   G $^-2{,}800$ ft   (J) 3,800 ft

Go On

Name ______________________

UNIT 4 TEST • PAGE 4

39. On Monday you earned \$17. On Tuesday you spent \$5. Wednesday and Thursday you earned \$11 each day, and Friday you spent \$25. Since Monday, how much do you have left?
   A \$69   C \$19
   B \$58   (D) \$9

40. What integer represents an increase of 6 points in a grade average?
   F $^-6$ H 3
   G $^-3$ (J) 6

41. Evaluate $p + q$ for $p = {}^-12$ and $q = 18$.
   A $^-30$ (C) 6
   B $^-6$ D 30

42. $^-50 \times 0$
   F $^-50$ H 50
   (G) 0   J 100

43. *a*, *b*, *c*, and *d* represent rational numbers. *c* is between *d* and *a*, and *c* is greater than *b*. *d* and *c* are opposites, and *d* is negative. Which number is the greatest?
   (A) a   B b   C c   D d

44. Dennis got on an elevator and went up 7 floors, and then went down 12 floors. In relation to where Dennis got on, what integer describes where he got off?
   (F) $^-5$ G 3   H 5   J 19

45. During any 5-day week, the stock market could both rise and fall. If the market lost 315 points, what was the average change per day?
   A 1,575 points   (C) $^-63$ points
   B 630 points   D $^-1{,}575$ points

46. Which rational number is between $^-1\frac{3}{4}$ and $\frac{5}{8}$?
   F $^-1\frac{7}{8}$ H $1\frac{1}{4}$
   (G) 0   J $2\frac{1}{6}$

47. Evaluate $^-m - n$ for $m = {}^-8$ and $n = {}^-13$.
   A $^-21$ C 5
   B $^-5$ (D) 21

48. Solve. $p \div 3 = 24$
   F $p = 8$ (H) $p = 72$
   G $p = 21$ J $p = 96$

49. Paul, Liz and Amy belong to the math, chess, and art clubs. Each belongs to only one club. Paul does not play chess, and the art club is all girls. Liz does not care for art. Which student is in which club?
   A Paul, math; Amy, chess; Liz, art
   (B) Paul, math; Liz, chess; Amy, art
   C Amy, math; Liz, chess; Paul, art
   D Liz, math; Paul, chess, Amy, art

50. On Saturday Josette earned \$8 babysitting, \$5 raking leaves, and \$12 washing windows. How much did she earn on Saturday?
   F \$13   H \$20
   G \$17   (J) \$25

Stop

Name ______________________

Write the correct answer.

1. Write an integer to represent an increase in length of 21 inches.

   $^{+}21$

2. Write the equation that is modeled on the number line below.

   $^-7$ $^-6$ $^-5$ $^-4$ $^-3$ $^-2$ $^-1$ 0 1 2 3 4 5 6 7

   $^-6 + 4 = {}^-2$

3. $^-5 \times {}^-7$

   35

4. Write a rational number between $4\frac{2}{3}$ and $4\frac{4}{5}$.

   Possible answer: $4\frac{11}{15}$

5. $3 + {}^-8$

   $^-5$

6. $27 \div {}^-9$

   $^-3$

7. Order $5\frac{1}{6}$, 5.2, 5.15, and $5\frac{1}{8}$ from *least* to *greatest*.

   $5\frac{1}{8}$, 5.15, $5\frac{1}{6}$, 5.2

8. In May, the price of a kayak was $1,075. In October the price was $899. What was the price change?

   $^-$$176

9. Use a property to simplify the expression. Then evaluate the expression and identify the property you used.

   $25 \times 7 \times 4$

   700; Associative

10. What is the value of $^-|{}^-2.57|$?

    2.57

11. $32 - {}^-25$

    57

12. $^-\frac{1}{3} \times {}^-27$

    9

13. Write $4\frac{4}{9}$ in the form $\frac{a}{b}$.

    $\frac{40}{9}$

14. Solve for x using mental math.

    $x + {}^-7 = 15.$

    $x = 22$

Go On

Name ______________________

15. $3.6 + {}^-4.5$

    $^-0.9$

16. Write 5.384 in the form $\frac{a}{b}$.

    $\frac{5,384}{1,000}$

17. A submarine dove from the surface to a level of $^-284$ fathoms, then rose 57 fathoms. How deep was it then?

    $^-227$ fathoms

18. $^-8 \times 24$

    $^-192$

19. Claudia, Doria, and Emily have different interests: movies, music, and math. Claudia does not like movies, and Doria does not enjoy math. Claudia plays the oboe. What interest does each have?

    Claudia, music; Doria, movies; Emily, math

20. $^-9 + 12$

    3

21. $8 + (3 - 7)^2$

    24

22. The set of integers is made up of the positive whole numbers, their __?__, and __?__.

    opposites, zero

23. L.J. rode his bicycle 3 mi to the movie theater, then 4 mi to a friend's house, and 5 mi back home. How far did he ride his bicycle?

    12 mi

24. $^-48 \div {}^-8$

    6

25. The letters p, q, r, s, and t represent the numbers 3.2, $^-2\frac{4}{5}$, 2.94, $^-3\frac{7}{8}$, and $2\frac{4}{5}$, but not necessarily in that order. The value of s is greater than t but less than p. The values of q and r are opposites, and p is the greatest. Which number is represented by t?

    $^-3\frac{7}{8}$

26. Solve for x.

    $x - 5 = {}^-3$

    $x = 2$

Go On

Name ______________________

27. $^-6.4 \div 1.6$

    $^-4$

28. Write a rational number between $^-1\frac{5}{6}$ and $^-1\frac{3}{4}$.

    Possible answer: $^-1\frac{19}{24}$

29. $12 - 7$

    5

30. Evaluate $k \times m$ for $k = 18$ and $m = {}^-6$.

    $^-108$

31. What is the absolute value of $^-31\frac{7}{8}$?

    $31\frac{7}{8}$

32. $^-9 + 6$

    $^-3$

33. Each week you deposit $12 of your earnings in a savings account. How much will you have deposited in this account after 3 years?

    $1,872

34. In the 100 yard dash, the top three times were 11.4 sec, $11\frac{3}{8}$ sec, and $11\frac{4}{7}$ sec. Order these times from *least* to *greatest*.

    $11\frac{3}{8}$ sec, 11.4 sec, $11\frac{4}{7}$ sec

35. $^-8 + {}^-14$

    $^-22$

36. Evaluate $w \div z$ for $w = {}^-24$ and $z = 8$.

    $^-3$

37. Write the opposite of $1\frac{5}{7}$.

    $^-1\frac{5}{7}$

38. An airplane pilot flying at 5,600 feet above sea level spots a submarine sailing beneath him at a depth of 160 feet. What is the vertical distance between the plane and the submarine?

    5,760 ft

Go On

Name ______________________

39. On Monday you earned $23. On Tuesday you spent $15 of your earnings. On Wednesday and Thursday you earned $14 each day, and on Friday you spent $35. Since Monday, how much do you have left?

    $1

40. What integer represents a decrease of 37°F?

    $^-37$

41. Evaluate $p - q$ for $p = {}^-14$ and $q = 12$.

    $^-26$

42. $^-37.5 \times 0$

    0

43. a, b, c, and d represent rational numbers. c is between d and a, and c is less than b. d and c are opposites, and d is the only negative number. Which number is the least?

    d

44. Doris got on an elevator and went up 9 floors, then went down 14 floors to the second floor. On what floor did Doris start?

    the seventh floor

45. If the price of gas rose $0.35 a gallon during a 5 week period, what was the average change per week?

    $^{+}$$0.07

46. Write a rational number between 3.8 and $3\frac{3}{4}$.

    Possible answer: $3\frac{31}{40}$

47. Evaluate $^-m + n$ for $m = {}^-16$ and $n = {}^-12$.

    4

48. Solve for p.

    $p \div 5 = 15$

    $p = 75$

49. Lisa, Christopher, and David belong to the karate, jogging, and swimming clubs. Each belongs to only one club. Christopher does not jog, and the swim club is all girls. Which student is in which club?

    Lisa, swim; Christopher, karate; David, jogging

50. On Sunday, Louisa earned $12 for child care, $18 planting flowers, and $6 sweeping the garage. How much did she earn in all?

    $36

Stop

Name ________________

Choose the best answer.

For 1–5, find an algebraic expression for the word expression.

1. 12 less than n

   Ⓐ $n - 12$ C $n \div 12$
   B $12 - n$ D $12 \div n$

2. 5 more than $3q$

   F $5 - 3q$ H $5 \times 3q$
   Ⓖ $5 + 3q$ J $5 \div 3q$

3. The product of $12r$ and $3s$

   Ⓐ $12r \times 3s$ C $12r + 3s$
   B $12s \times 3s$ D $3r - 12s$

4. The quotient of $5d$ divided by $3d$

   F $3d \times 5d$ H $3d \div 5d$
   G $5d \times 3d$ Ⓙ $5d \div 3d$

5. 18 decreased by p

   A $p \div 18$ C $p - 18$
   B $18 \div p$ Ⓓ $18 - p$

For 6–8, evaluate the expression for $k = 6$.

6. $3k + 7$

   F 43 Ⓗ 25
   G 39 J 16

7. $\frac{18}{k} - 5$

   A 18 Ⓒ $^-2$
   B 2 D $^-3$

8. $9 + (^-2 + 3k)$

   F $^-11$ H 20
   G 15 Ⓙ 25

For 9–11, evaluate the expression for $r = 3$, $s = {}^-4$, and $t = 5$.

9. $(r + s)^2 - t$

   A $^-6$ C 6
   Ⓑ $^-4$ D 44

10. $r + s - t$

    Ⓕ $^-6$ H $^-2$
    G $^-4$ J 2

11. $2s + 10 \cdot (r - t)$

    A 20 C $^-20$
    B $^-12$ Ⓓ $^-28$

12. Which expression can you evaluate by using the array?

    F 25^2 H $\sqrt{5}$
    G 2^5 Ⓙ $\sqrt{25}$

13. Evaluate $^-2m^2 + 9$ for $m = {}^-3$.

    Ⓐ $^-9$ C 18
    B 9 D 45

14. Evaluate $8x + 3x - 4$ for $x = 5$.

    F 17 Ⓗ 51
    G 49 J 59

Go On

Name ________________

15. Which expression can you evaluate by using the array?

    A 9^2 C 2^3
    Ⓑ 3^2 D $\sqrt{3}$

16. Evaluate $1 - (5c - 7c)$ for $c = {}^-4$.

    Ⓕ $^-7$ H 8
    G 7 J 9

17. Evaluate $3 \cdot \sqrt{x} - 4$ for $x = 25$.

    A 4 C 19
    Ⓑ 11 D 71

18. Which expression can you evaluate by using the array?

    F $\sqrt{6}$ H 2^6
    Ⓖ 6^2 J 36^2

For questions 19–22, evaluate the expression.

19. $5 \cdot \sqrt{16} + 3$

    A 83 C 35
    B 43 Ⓓ 23

20. $2 \cdot \sqrt{81} \div \sqrt{36}$

    F 9 Ⓗ 3
    G 6 J $\frac{3}{2}$

21. $4 \cdot \sqrt{25} \div \sqrt{100} - 1$

    A 4 Ⓒ 1
    B 2 D 0

22. $\sqrt{100} - \sqrt{36} - 3^2$

    F 5 H $^-2$
    G 2 Ⓙ $^-5$

23. Henri starts the week with \$23. He earns d dollars each day and buys lunch for l dollars on some days. Which expression represents the amount of money Henri has at the end of the week if he works 5 days and buys lunch 3 days?

    A $23 + d - 3l$ Ⓒ $23 + 5d - 3l$
    B $23 + 5d - l$ D $23 - 5d + 3l$

24. In a contest, everyone starts with 50 points. Contestants get 8 points for every correct answer. They lose 2 points for every wrong answer. Which expression represents the total for a contestant who has c correct answers and w wrong answers?

    Ⓕ $50 + 8c - 2w$ H $50 + c - w$
    G $50 + 8c - 2$ J $50 + 8 - 2w$

25. You have three square pictures that you want to frame. The areas of the pictures are 144 in.², 64 in.², and 49 in.² How many inches of framing material are needed?

    A 257 in. C 54 in.
    Ⓑ 108 in. D 27 in.

Stop

Name ________________

Write the correct answer.

For 1–5, write an algebraic expression for the word expression.

1. 6 less than p

   $p - 6$

2. 7 more than $5n$

   $5n + 7$

3. The product of $15x$ and $10y$

   $15x \times 10y$

4. The quotient of $2t$ and $8t$

   $2t \div 8t$

5. 12 decreased by n

   $12 - n$

For 6–8, evaluate the expression for $n = 8$.

6. $4n + 3$

   35

7. $\frac{40}{n} - 6$

   $^-1$

8. $4 + (^-7 + 2n)$

   13

For 9–11, evaluate the expression for $x = 2$, $y = {}^-2$, and $z = 4$.

9. $(x + y)^2 - 2z$

   $^-8$

10. $x + 3z - y$

    16

11. $z + 8 \cdot (y - z)$

    $^-44$

12. Use the array to help you evaluate the expression.

    $\sqrt{64}$

    8

13. Evaluate $^-5m^2 + 3$ for $m = {}^-5$.

    $^-122$

14. Evaluate $5n - 2n + 10$ for $n = 6$.

    28

Go On

Name ________________

15. Use the array to help you evaluate the expression.

    $\sqrt{16}$

    4

16. Evaluate $12 - (2t - t)$ for $t = {}^-5$.

    17

17. Evaluate $5 \cdot \sqrt{b} - 7$ for $b = 4$.

    3

18. Use the array below to help you evaluate the expression.

    7^2

    49

For 19–22, evaluate the expression.

19. $4 \cdot \sqrt{36} + 12$

    36

20. $3 \cdot \sqrt{49} \div \sqrt{9}$

    7

21. $5 \cdot \sqrt{100} \div \sqrt{25} - 5$

    5

22. $\sqrt{64} - \sqrt{16} - 4^2$

    $^-12$

23. Jemma opened a bank account with \$35. Each week she deposits n dollars from her paycheck. Some weeks she takes out p dollars to pay her share of the phone bill. Write an expression to show the amount of money Jemma has after working 6 weeks and paying for the phone bill for 2 weeks.

    $35 + 6n - 2p$

24. Hector charges \$5 per hour to baby-sit. He also charges a fee of \$2 for each child. Write an expression to show how much Hector charges to baby-sit c children for h hours.

    $5h + 2c$

25. Mr. Winslow bought 50 yd of fencing. Does he have enough fencing to enclose a square garden that has an area of 121 sq yd? Explain why or why not.

    Yes, because $\sqrt{121} = 11$. The garden is 11 yd on each side, so the perimeter is 44 yd; $50 > 44$, therefore, he has enough fencing.

Stop

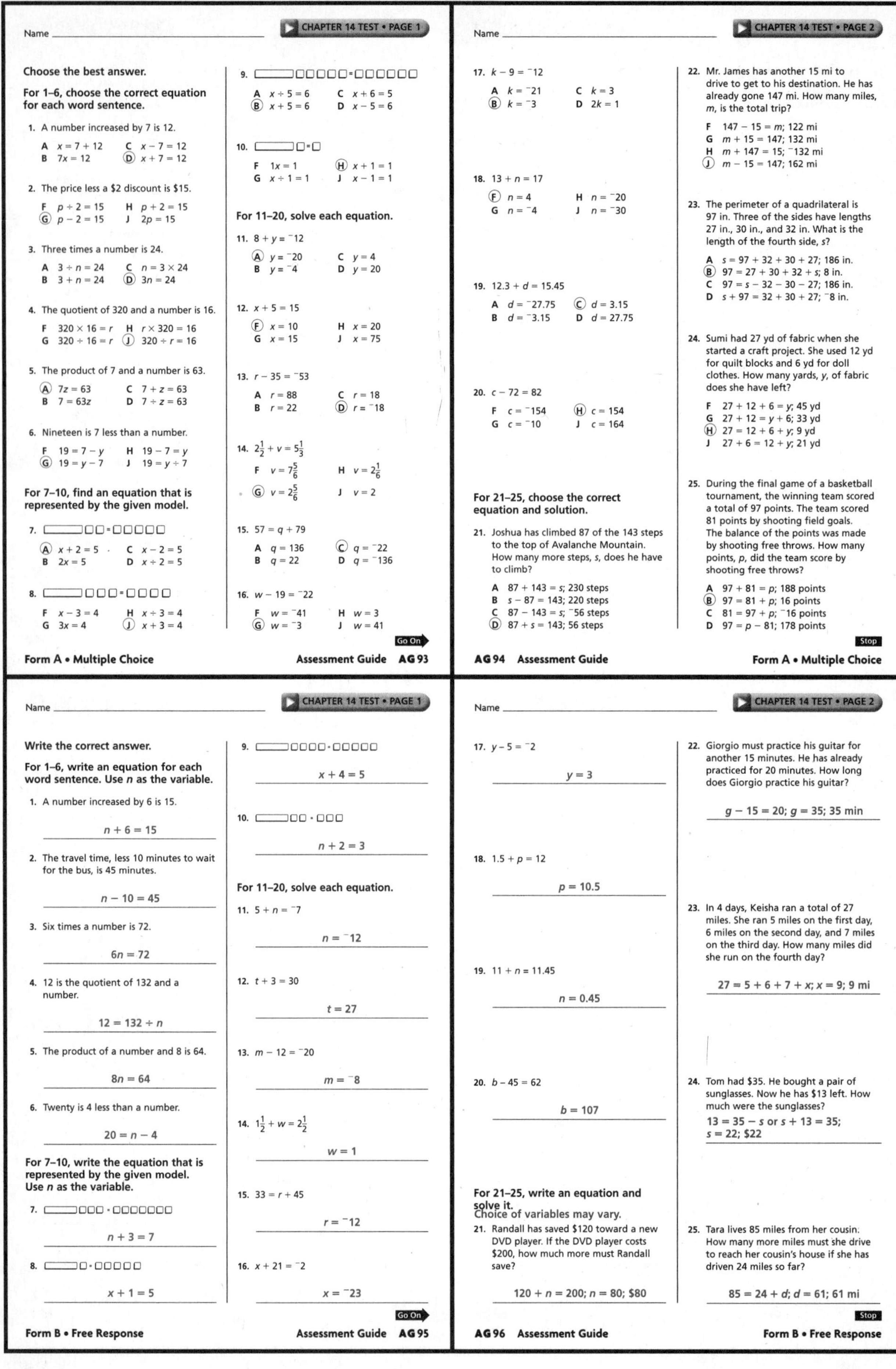

Name ____________________ CHAPTER 14 TEST • PAGE 1

Choose the best answer.

For 1–6, choose the correct equation for each word sentence.

1. A number increased by 7 is 12.
   A $x = 7 + 12$ C $x - 7 = 12$
   B $7x = 12$ (D) $x + 7 = 12$

2. The price less a \$2 discount is \$15.
   F $p \div 2 = 15$ H $p + 2 = 15$
   (G) $p - 2 = 15$ J $2p = 15$

3. Three times a number is 24.
   A $3 \div n = 24$ C $n = 3 \times 24$
   B $3 + n = 24$ (D) $3n = 24$

4. The quotient of 320 and a number is 16.
   F $320 \times 16 = r$ H $r \times 320 = 16$
   G $320 \div 16 = r$ (J) $320 \div r = 16$

5. The product of 7 and a number is 63.
   (A) $7z = 63$ C $7 + z = 63$
   B $7 = 63z$ D $7 \div z = 63$

6. Nineteen is 7 less than a number.
   F $19 = 7 - y$ H $19 - 7 = y$
   (G) $19 = y - 7$ J $19 = y \div 7$

For 7–10, find an equation that is represented by the given model.

7. (A) $x + 2 = 5$ C $x - 2 = 5$
   B $2x = 5$ D $x \div 2 = 5$

8. F $x - 3 = 4$ H $x \div 3 = 4$
   G $3x = 4$ (J) $x + 3 = 4$

9. A $x \div 5 = 6$ C $x + 6 = 5$
   (B) $x + 5 = 6$ D $x - 5 = 6$

10. F $1x = 1$ (H) $x + 1 = 1$
    G $x \div 1 = 1$ J $x - 1 = 1$

For 11–20, solve each equation.

11. $8 + y = {}^{-}12$
    (A) $y = {}^{-}20$ C $y = 4$
    B $y = {}^{-}4$ D $y = 20$

12. $x + 5 = 15$
    (F) $x = 10$ H $x = 20$
    G $x = 15$ J $x = 75$

13. $r - 35 = {}^{-}53$
    A $r = 88$ C $r = 18$
    B $r = 22$ (D) $r = {}^{-}18$

14. $2\frac{1}{2} + v = 5\frac{1}{3}$
    F $v = 7\frac{5}{6}$ H $v = 2\frac{1}{6}$
    (G) $v = 2\frac{5}{6}$ J $v = 2$

15. $57 = q + 79$
    A $q = 136$ (C) $q = {}^{-}22$
    B $q = 22$ D $q = {}^{-}136$

16. $w - 19 = {}^{-}22$
    F $w = {}^{-}41$ H $w = 3$
    (G) $w = {}^{-}3$ J $w = 41$

Go On

Form A • Multiple Choice Assessment Guide AG 93

Name ____________________ CHAPTER 14 TEST • PAGE 2

17. $k - 9 = {}^{-}12$
    A $k = {}^{-}21$ C $k = 3$
    (B) $k = {}^{-}3$ D $2k = 1$

18. $13 + n = 17$
    (F) $n = 4$ H $n = {}^{-}20$
    G $n = {}^{-}4$ J $n = {}^{-}30$

19. $12.3 + d = 15.45$
    A $d = {}^{-}27.75$ (C) $d = 3.15$
    B $d = {}^{-}3.15$ D $d = 27.75$

20. $c - 72 = 82$
    F $c = {}^{-}154$ (H) $c = 154$
    G $c = {}^{-}10$ J $c = 164$

For 21–25, choose the correct equation and solution.

21. Joshua has climbed 87 of the 143 steps to the top of Avalanche Mountain. How many more steps, *s*, does he have to climb?
    A $87 + 143 = s$; 230 steps
    B $s - 87 = 143$; 220 steps
    C $87 - 143 = s$; ${}^{-}56$ steps
    (D) $87 + s = 143$; 56 steps

22. Mr. James has another 15 mi to drive to get to his destination. He has already gone 147 mi. How many miles, *m*, is the total trip?
    F $147 - 15 = m$; 122 mi
    G $m + 15 = 147$; 132 mi
    H $m + 147 = 15$; ${}^{-}132$ mi
    (J) $m - 15 = 147$; 162 mi

23. The perimeter of a quadrilateral is 97 in. Three of the sides have lengths 27 in., 30 in., and 32 in. What is the length of the fourth side, *s*?
    A $s = 97 + 32 + 30 + 27$; 186 in.
    (B) $97 = 27 + 30 + 32 + s$; 8 in.
    C $97 = s - 32 - 30 - 27$; 186 in.
    D $s + 97 = 32 + 30 + 27$; ${}^{-}8$ in.

24. Sumi had 27 yd of fabric when she started a craft project. She used 12 yd for quilt blocks and 6 yd for doll clothes. How many yards, *y*, of fabric does she have left?
    F $27 + 12 + 6 = y$; 45 yd
    G $27 + 12 = y + 6$; 33 yd
    (H) $27 = 12 + 6 + y$; 9 yd
    J $27 + 6 = 12 + y$; 21 yd

25. During the final game of a basketball tournament, the winning team scored a total of 97 points. The team scored 81 points by shooting field goals. The balance of the points was made by shooting free throws. How many points, *p*, did the team score by shooting free throws?
    A $97 + 81 = p$; 188 points
    (B) $97 = 81 + p$; 16 points
    C $81 = 97 + p$; ${}^{-}16$ points
    D $97 = p - 81$; 178 points

Stop

AG 94 Assessment Guide Form A • Multiple Choice

Name ____________________ CHAPTER 14 TEST • PAGE 1

Write the correct answer.

For 1–6, write an equation for each word sentence. Use *n* as the variable.

1. A number increased by 6 is 15.
   $n + 6 = 15$

2. The travel time, less 10 minutes to wait for the bus, is 45 minutes.
   $n - 10 = 45$

3. Six times a number is 72.
   $6n = 72$

4. 12 is the quotient of 132 and a number.
   $12 = 132 \div n$

5. The product of a number and 8 is 64.
   $8n = 64$

6. Twenty is 4 less than a number.
   $20 = n - 4$

For 7–10, write the equation that is represented by the given model. Use *n* as the variable.

7. $n + 3 = 7$

8. $x + 1 = 5$

9. $x + 4 = 5$

10. $n + 2 = 3$

For 11–20, solve each equation.

11. $5 + n = {}^{-}7$
    $n = {}^{-}12$

12. $t + 3 = 30$
    $t = 27$

13. $m - 12 = {}^{-}20$
    $m = {}^{-}8$

14. $1\frac{1}{2} + w = 2\frac{1}{2}$
    $w = 1$

15. $33 = r + 45$
    $r = {}^{-}12$

16. $x + 21 = {}^{-}2$
    $x = {}^{-}23$

Go On

Form B • Free Response Assessment Guide AG 95

Name ____________________ CHAPTER 14 TEST • PAGE 2

17. $y - 5 = {}^{-}2$
    $y = 3$

18. $1.5 + p = 12$
    $p = 10.5$

19. $11 + n = 11.45$
    $n = 0.45$

20. $b - 45 = 62$
    $b = 107$

For 21–25, write an equation and solve it.
Choice of variables may vary.

21. Randall has saved \$120 toward a new DVD player. If the DVD player costs \$200, how much more must Randall save?
    $120 + n = 200$; $n = 80$; \$80

22. Giorgio must practice his guitar for another 15 minutes. He has already practiced for 20 minutes. How long does Giorgio practice his guitar?
    $g - 15 = 20$; $g = 35$; 35 min

23. In 4 days, Keisha ran a total of 27 miles. She ran 5 miles on the first day, 6 miles on the second day, and 7 miles on the third day. How many miles did she run on the fourth day?
    $27 = 5 + 6 + 7 + x$; $x = 9$; 9 mi

24. Tom had \$35. He bought a pair of sunglasses. Now he has \$13 left. How much were the sunglasses?
    $13 = 35 - s$ or $s + 13 = 35$; $s = 22$; \$22

25. Tara lives 85 miles from her cousin. How many more miles must she drive to reach her cousin's house if she has driven 24 miles so far?
    $85 = 24 + d$; $d = 61$; 61 mi

Stop

AG 96 Assessment Guide Form B • Free Response

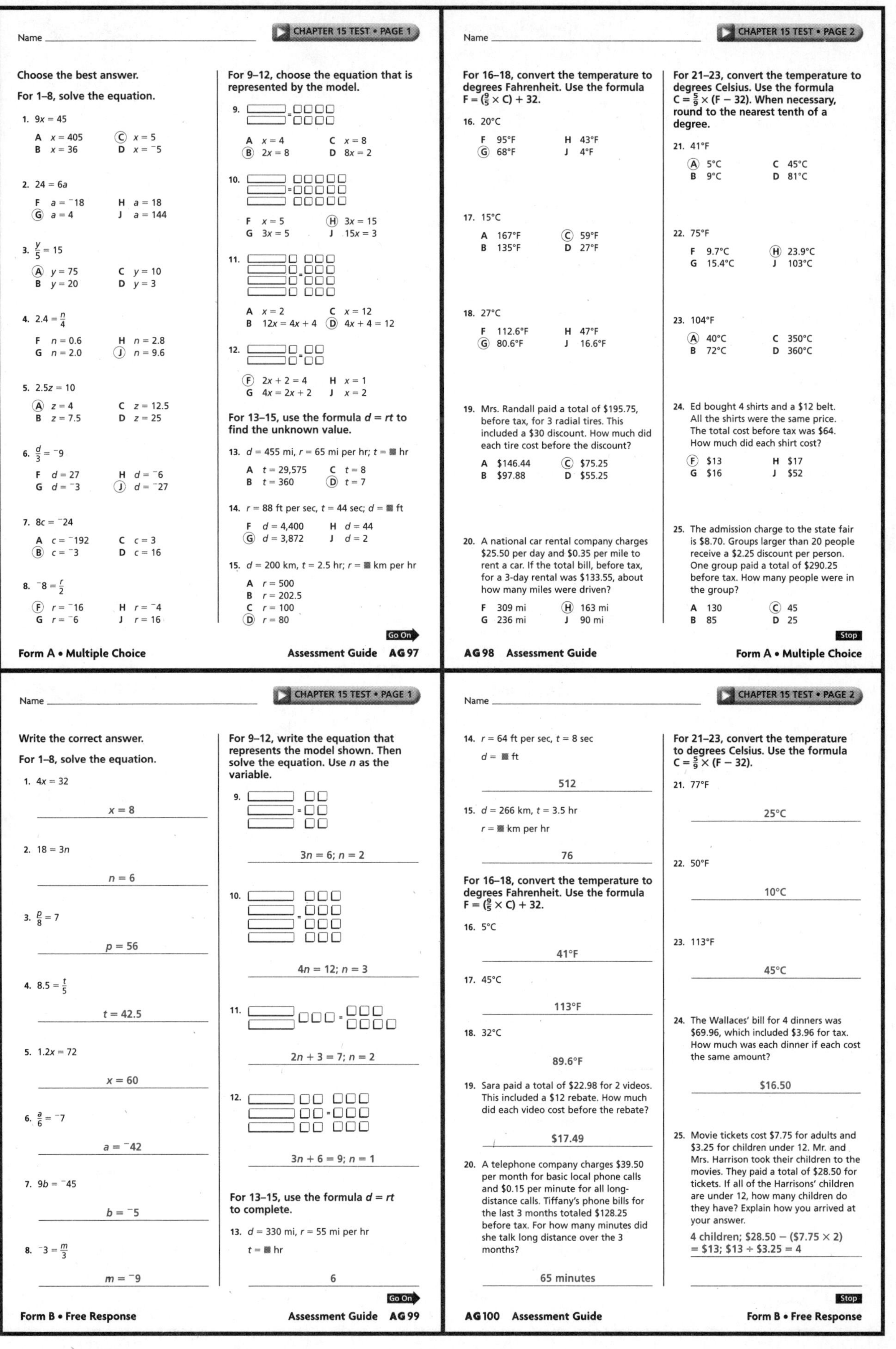

Name ______________________ **CHAPTER 15 TEST • PAGE 1**

Choose the best answer.

For 1–8, solve the equation.

1. $9x = 45$
   - A $x = 405$
   - Ⓒ $x = 5$
   - B $x = 36$
   - D $x = {}^{-}5$

2. $24 = 6a$
   - F $a = {}^{-}18$
   - H $a = 18$
   - Ⓖ $a = 4$
   - J $a = 144$

3. $\frac{y}{5} = 15$
   - Ⓐ $y = 75$
   - C $y = 10$
   - B $y = 20$
   - D $y = 3$

4. $2.4 = \frac{n}{4}$
   - F $n = 0.6$
   - H $n = 2.8$
   - G $n = 2.0$
   - Ⓙ $n = 9.6$

5. $2.5z = 10$
   - Ⓐ $z = 4$
   - C $z = 12.5$
   - B $z = 7.5$
   - D $z = 25$

6. $\frac{d}{3} = {}^{-}9$
   - F $d = 27$
   - H $d = {}^{-}6$
   - G $d = {}^{-}3$
   - Ⓙ $d = {}^{-}27$

7. $8c = {}^{-}24$
   - A $c = {}^{-}192$
   - C $c = 3$
   - Ⓑ $c = {}^{-}3$
   - D $c = 16$

8. ${}^{-}8 = \frac{r}{2}$
   - Ⓕ $r = {}^{-}16$
   - H $r = {}^{-}4$
   - G $r = {}^{-}6$
   - J $r = 16$

For 9–12, choose the equation that is represented by the model.

9. [model]
   - A $x = 4$
   - C $x = 8$
   - Ⓑ $2x = 8$
   - D $8x = 2$

10. [model]
    - F $x = 5$
    - Ⓗ $3x = 15$
    - G $3x = 5$
    - J $15x = 3$

11. [model]
    - A $x = 2$
    - C $x = 12$
    - B $12x = 4x + 4$
    - Ⓓ $4x + 4 = 12$

12. [model]
    - Ⓕ $2x + 2 = 4$
    - H $x = 1$
    - G $4x = 2x + 2$
    - J $x = 2$

For 13–15, use the formula $d = rt$ to find the unknown value.

13. $d = 455$ mi, $r = 65$ mi per hr; $t = ■$ hr
    - A $t = 29{,}575$
    - C $t = 8$
    - B $t = 360$
    - Ⓓ $t = 7$

14. $r = 88$ ft per sec, $t = 44$ sec; $d = ■$ ft
    - F $d = 4{,}400$
    - H $d = 44$
    - Ⓖ $d = 3{,}872$
    - J $d = 2$

15. $d = 200$ km, $t = 2.5$ hr; $r = ■$ km per hr
    - A $r = 500$
    - B $r = 202.5$
    - C $r = 100$
    - Ⓓ $r = 80$

Go On

Form A • Multiple Choice **Assessment Guide AG 97**

Name ______________________ **CHAPTER 15 TEST • PAGE 2**

For 16–18, convert the temperature to degrees Fahrenheit. Use the formula $F = (\frac{9}{5} \times C) + 32$.

16. 20°C
    - F 95°F
    - H 43°F
    - Ⓖ 68°F
    - J 4°F

17. 15°C
    - A 167°F
    - Ⓒ 59°F
    - B 135°F
    - D 27°F

18. 27°C
    - F 112.6°F
    - H 47°F
    - Ⓖ 80.6°F
    - J 16.6°F

19. Mrs. Randall paid a total of $195.75, before tax, for 3 radial tires. This included a $30 discount. How much did each tire cost before the discount?
    - A $146.44
    - Ⓒ $75.25
    - B $97.88
    - D $55.25

20. A national car rental company charges $25.50 per day and $0.35 per mile to rent a car. If the total bill, before tax, for a 3-day rental was $133.55, about how many miles were driven?
    - F 309 mi
    - Ⓗ 163 mi
    - G 236 mi
    - J 90 mi

For 21–23, convert the temperature to degrees Celsius. Use the formula $C = \frac{5}{9} \times (F - 32)$. When necessary, round to the nearest tenth of a degree.

21. 41°F
    - Ⓐ 5°C
    - C 45°C
    - B 9°C
    - D 81°C

22. 75°F
    - F 9.7°C
    - Ⓗ 23.9°C
    - G 15.4°C
    - J 103°C

23. 104°F
    - Ⓐ 40°C
    - C 350°C
    - B 72°C
    - D 360°C

24. Ed bought 4 shirts and a $12 belt. All the shirts were the same price. The total cost before tax was $64. How much did each shirt cost?
    - Ⓕ $13
    - H $17
    - G $16
    - J $52

25. The admission charge to the state fair is $8.70. Groups larger than 20 people receive a $2.25 discount per person. One group paid a total of $290.25 before tax. How many people were in the group?
    - A 130
    - Ⓒ 45
    - B 85
    - D 25

Stop

AG 98 Assessment Guide **Form A • Multiple Choice**

Name ______________________ **CHAPTER 15 TEST • PAGE 1**

Write the correct answer.

For 1–8, solve the equation.

1. $4x = 32$ — $x = 8$
2. $18 = 3n$ — $n = 6$
3. $\frac{p}{8} = 7$ — $p = 56$
4. $8.5 = \frac{t}{5}$ — $t = 42.5$
5. $1.2x = 72$ — $x = 60$
6. $\frac{a}{6} = {}^{-}7$ — $a = {}^{-}42$
7. $9b = {}^{-}45$ — $b = {}^{-}5$
8. ${}^{-}3 = \frac{m}{3}$ — $m = {}^{-}9$

For 9–12, write the equation that represents the model shown. Then solve the equation. Use n as the variable.

9. [model] — $3n = 6$; $n = 2$
10. [model] — $4n = 12$; $n = 3$
11. [model] — $2n + 3 = 7$; $n = 2$
12. [model] — $3n + 6 = 9$; $n = 1$

For 13–15, use the formula $d = rt$ to complete.

13. $d = 330$ mi, $r = 55$ mi per hr
    $t = ■$ hr — 6

Go On

Form B • Free Response **Assessment Guide AG 99**

Name ______________________ **CHAPTER 15 TEST • PAGE 2**

14. $r = 64$ ft per sec, $t = 8$ sec
    $d = ■$ ft — 512
15. $d = 266$ km, $t = 3.5$ hr
    $r = ■$ km per hr — 76

For 16–18, convert the temperature to degrees Fahrenheit. Use the formula $F = (\frac{9}{5} \times C) + 32$.

16. 5°C — 41°F
17. 45°C — 113°F
18. 32°C — 89.6°F
19. Sara paid a total of $22.98 for 2 videos. This included a $12 rebate. How much did each video cost before the rebate? — $17.49
20. A telephone company charges $39.50 per month for basic local phone calls and $0.15 per minute for all long-distance calls. Tiffany's phone bills for the last 3 months totaled $128.25 before tax. For how many minutes did she talk long distance over the 3 months? — 65 minutes

For 21–23, convert the temperature to degrees Celsius. Use the formula $C = \frac{5}{9} \times (F - 32)$.

21. 77°F — 25°C
22. 50°F — 10°C
23. 113°F — 45°C
24. The Wallaces' bill for 4 dinners was $69.96, which included $3.96 for tax. How much was each dinner if each cost the same amount? — $16.50
25. Movie tickets cost $7.75 for adults and $3.25 for children under 12. Mr. and Mrs. Harrison took their children to the movies. They paid a total of $28.50 for tickets. If all of the Harrisons' children are under 12, how many children do they have? Explain how you arrived at your answer.
    4 children; $28.50 − ($7.75 × 2) = $13; $13 ÷ $3.25 = 4

Stop

AG 100 Assessment Guide **Form B • Free Response**

Name ________________ UNIT 5 TEST • PAGE 1

Choose the best answer.

1. What expression represents the product of $3r$ and $2s$?
Ⓐ $3r \times 2s$ C $3r \times 2r$
B $3s \times 2r$ D $3r \div 2s$

2. What is the equation for the word sentence?
The quotient of 84 and a number is 6.
F $84 \times n = 6$ H $6 \div n = 84$
Ⓖ $84 \div n = 6$ J $n \div 84 = 6$

3. Solve. $^{-}12 = \frac{a}{6}$
A $a = 72$ C $a = {}^{-}2$
B $a = 2$ Ⓓ $a = {}^{-}72$

4. Evaluate. $5k - 12$ for $k = 6$
F 42 Ⓗ 18
G 30 J $^{-}7$

5. What equation is modeled below?
Ⓐ $x + 3 = 6$ C $x - 3 = 6$
B $3x = 6$ D $x \div 3 = 6$

6. What equation is modeled below? 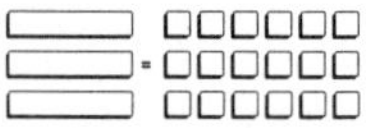
F $x = 18$ H $3 = 18x$
G $3 + x = 18$ Ⓙ $3x = 18$

7. Find $3 \cdot \sqrt{9} - 3$.
A 24 C $\sqrt{9}$
Ⓑ 6 D 3

8. Solve. $r - 7 = {}^{-}3$
Ⓕ $r = 4$ H $r = {}^{-}4$
G $r = 0$ J $r = {}^{-}10$

9. Solve for y.
$3y = 27$
A 81 B 31 C 27 Ⓓ 9

10. What numerical expression represents 5 increased by twice a number?
F $5 + n$ H $2 \times 5 + n$
Ⓖ $5 + 2n$ J $2 \times (5 + n)$

11. John is taking a trip of 257 mi. He has only gone 15 mi. How far does he still have to go?
A 192 mi Ⓒ 242 mi
B 200 mi D 272 mi

12. Convert 68°F to degrees Celsius. Use the formula $C = \frac{5}{9} \times (F - 32)$.
F $^{-}20$°C Ⓗ 20°C
G 6°C J 65°C

13. Evaluate $c^2 + 4$ for $c = 2$.
A 4 B 6 Ⓒ 8 D 16

14. Which model represents $2 + x = 5$?
F
Ⓖ
H 
J

Go On

Name ________________ UNIT 5 TEST • PAGE 2

15. Emily purchased 3 pairs of shoes that all cost the same amount, and a pair of \$15 sandals. The bill before tax was \$78. How much was each pair of shoes?
A \$15 Ⓒ \$21
B \$20 D \$26

16. Three separate square plots of land have areas of 64 sq. ft, 256 sq. ft, and 36 sq. ft. How much fencing is needed to fence in these plots?
Ⓕ 120 ft H 60 ft
G 90 ft J 30 ft

17. Solve. $1\frac{3}{4} + f = 5\frac{1}{2}$
A $f = 2\frac{3}{4}$ Ⓒ $f = 3\frac{3}{4}$
B $f = 3\frac{1}{4}$ D $f = 4\frac{1}{4}$

18. Solve. $^{-}12q = {}^{-}60$
F $q = 720$ H $q = {}^{-}5$
Ⓖ $q = 5$ J $q = {}^{-}720$

19. A game show contestant starts the show with \$100. Each loss costs him c dollars, and each win earns him w dollars. Which expression tells how much money he has after 1 loss and 1 win?
Ⓐ $\$100 - c + w$ C $\$100c - w$
B $\$100 + c - w$ D $\$100cw$

20. Which equation shows that the product of a number and 9 is 72?
F $n + 9 = 72$ H $n - 9 = 72$
Ⓖ $n \times 9 = 72$ J $n \div 9 = 72$

21. How long will it take Jill to go 225 miles if her average speed is 50 miles per hour? Use the formula $d = rt$.
A 45 hr C 6 hr
B 11.25 hr Ⓓ $4\frac{1}{2}$ hr

22. Which does the array model?
Ⓕ $5^2 = 25$ H $4^2 = 16$
G $5 + 5 = 10$ J $5 \times 5 = 10$

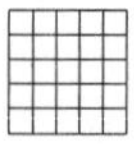

23. What number decreased by 5 equals $^{-}7$?
A 12 Ⓒ $^{-}2$
B 2 D $^{-}12$

24. Solve. $\frac{t}{^{-}4} = 16$
F $t = 64$ H $t = {}^{-}4$
G $t = 4$ Ⓙ $t = {}^{-}64$

25. A car rental agency charges \$25 per day plus m dollars per mile and g dollars for each gallon of gas. Which expression represents the cost of renting a car for one day and driving 120 mi using 5 gal of gas?
A $\$25 + m + g$
B $\$25 + 5m + 120g$
Ⓒ $\$25 + 120m + 5g$
D $\$25 \times 120m \times 5g$

26. Solve. $43 = h - 12$
F $h = 67$ H $h = {}^{-}31$
Ⓖ $h = 55$ J $h = {}^{-}55$

Go On

Name ________________ UNIT 5 TEST • PAGE 3

27. Randy purchased 4 new radial tires and 2 seat covers for his car. The total was \$290 before tax. If the seat covers cost \$15 each, how much did each of the tires cost?
A \$57.50 C \$72.50
Ⓑ \$65 D \$130

28. Which expression represents 23 decreased by d?
F $23 \div d$ Ⓗ $23 - d$
G $d \div 23$ J $d - 23$

29. Which equation is modeled below? 
A $3 + x = 8$ Ⓒ $3x + 2 = 8$
B $x + 8 = 3$ D $2x + 3 = 8$

30. Use the formula $d = rt$ to find r for $d = 540$ and $t = 12$.
F $r = 6{,}480$ H $r = 180$
G $r = 528$ Ⓙ $r = 45$

31. Find $4 \cdot \sqrt{64} \div \sqrt{16}$.
Ⓐ 8 C 32
B 16 D 64

32. Which equation represents the word sentence?
27 is 3 less than a number.
Ⓕ $27 = b - 3$ H $27 = 3 - b$
G $^{-}27 = b - 3$ J $3 = b - 27$

33. Which equation is modeled below? 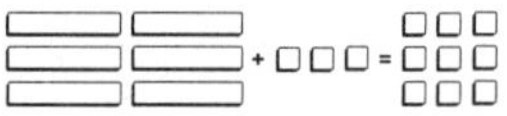
A $6x = 9$
Ⓑ $6x + 3 = 9$
C $6x + 9 = 3$
D $x + 3 = 9$

34. Evaluate $5a + \frac{6b}{2}$ for $a = 5$ and $b = 7$.
F 67 H 32
Ⓖ 46 J 13

35. Sam purchased items costing \$5.25, \$4, and \$3.25. If he started with \$25, how much does Sam have left?
A \$37.50 C \$14.50
B \$25.00 Ⓓ \$12.50

36. Convert $^{-}10$°C into degrees Fahrenheit. Use the formula $F = (\frac{9}{5} \times C) + 32$.
F 40°F H $^{-}14$°F
Ⓖ 14°F J $^{-}40$°F

37. How many tiles are needed to make a 6×6 array?
A 6 Ⓒ 36
B 12 D 216

38. Ed has dug 27 fence post holes. He has 33 more to dig. How many post holes will there be in all?
F 6 post holes H 33 post holes
G 18 post holes Ⓙ 60 post holes

Go On

Name ________________ UNIT 5 TEST • PAGE 4

39. The football team scored 43 points in the game last night. Field goals are worth 3 points and touchdowns are worth 7 points. If the team scored 5 field goals, how many touchdowns did they score?
A 43 C 7
B 28 Ⓓ 4

40. Evaluate. $\sqrt{144} + \sqrt{81} - 5^2$
F 46 G 16 H 4 Ⓙ $^{-}4$

41. Which equation represents the word sentence?
6 times a number is 22.
A $22 \times 6 = d$ Ⓒ $6 \times d = 22$
B $6 + d = 22$ D $6 \div d = 22$

42. Which equation can be used to find a number multiplied by 6 and increased by 4 that equals 34.
Ⓕ $(p \times 6) + 4 = 34$
G $(p \div 6) + 4 = 34$
H $p \times (6 + 4) = 34$
J $(p \times 6) + 4 = 34$

43. Two square arrays have a total of 41 tiles. What could be the sizes of the arrays?
Ⓐ 4×4 and 5×5
B 3×3 and 5×5
C 3×3 and 6×6
D 2×2 and 7×7

44. Solve the equation represented by the model.
Ⓕ $2x + 4 = 10, x = 3$
G $2x + 4 = 10, x = 7$
H $2x + 4 = 10, x = {}^{-}3$
J $2x + 4 = 10, x = {}^{-}7$

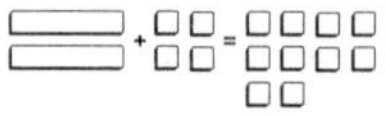

45. Which model represents $3x + 1 = 7$?
A 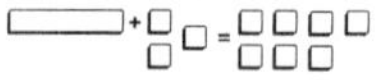
B
Ⓒ
D

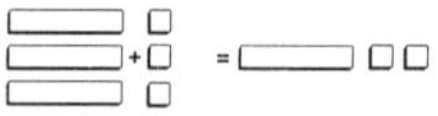

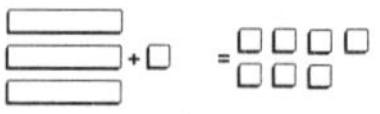

46. Evaluate $50 + 5c + c^2$ for $c = {}^{-}4$.
F 86 Ⓖ 46 H 14 J 5

47. Solve. $f - 3\frac{2}{3} = {}^{-}5\frac{1}{2}$.
A $f = {}^{-}2$ C $f = 2$
Ⓑ $f = {}^{-}1\frac{5}{6}$ D $f = 1\frac{5}{6}$

48. The quotient of a number and the difference $(2 - 4)$ is 5. What is the number?
Ⓕ -10 H 9
G 412 J 14

49. Sixteen more than the square root of a number is 24. What is the number?
A 100 Ⓑ 64 C 20 D 8

50. Stefan started the school year with 24 pencils. He has already used 18. How many pencils does he have left?
F 42 H 18
G 24 Ⓙ 6

Stop

Name ______________________

UNIT 5 TEST • PAGE 1

Write the correct answer.

1. Write an expression to represent the product of $6n$ and $4p$.

   $6n \times 4p$

2. Write an equation for the word sentence, 15 is the quotient of 90 and a number.

   $15 = 90 \div x$; choice of variable may vary.

3. Solve for t.

   $^{-}21 = \frac{t}{3}$

   $t = {}^{-}63$

4. Evaluate $3x + 4$ for $x = 4$.

   16

5. Write and solve the equation that is modeled below.

   $x + 2 = 5$; $x = 3$; choice of variable may vary.

6. Write and solve the equation that is modeled below.

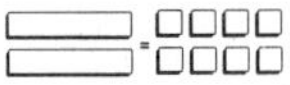

   $2x = 8$; $x = 4$; choice of variable may vary.

7. $2\sqrt{36} - 15$

   $^{-}3$

8. Solve for x.

   $x - 12 = {}^{-}7$

   $x = 5$

9. Draw a model to represent and solve the equation $5x + 1 = 46$.

   Check students' models; $x = 9$

10. Write a numerical expression for the word expression, twelve less than twice a number.

    $2x - 12$; choice of variable may vary.

11. Ari is reading a book that has 316 pages. He has read 28 pages so far. How many more pages does he have to read to finish the book? Write an equation to model this situation, and solve.

    $28 + p = 316$; $p = 288$ pages

12. Convert 86°F to degrees Celsius. Use the formula $C = \frac{5}{9} \times (F - 32)$.

    30°C

13. Evaluate $5a^2 - 8$ for $a = 3$.

    37

14. Draw a model to represent and solve the equation $5 + n = 8$.

    Check students' models; $n = 3$

Go On

Form B • Free Response   Assessment Guide AG 105

Name ______________________

UNIT 5 TEST • PAGE 2

15. Rod bought 3 children's tickets to the movies. He also bought one adult ticket for $8. The total cost for the tickets was $23. How much is a children's ticket for the movies?

    $5

16. The recreation department needs to put new fencing around 2 of the town's pools. Both pool areas are square. One has an area of 625 sq ft and the other has an area of 400 sq ft. How much fencing is needed?

    180 ft

17. Solve for x. $2\frac{7}{8} + x = 8$

    $x = 5\frac{1}{8}$

18. Solve for x. $^{-}15x = {}^{-}90$

    $x = 6$

19. Scott's math average is 87. Each extra credit paper he does earns him e points toward his average. Each missed homework assignment costs him m points. Write an expression to tell what his average is after he has done one extra credit page, but has missed one homework assignment.

    $87 + e - m$

20. Write an equation for the word sentence: 63 is the product of 7 and a number.

    $63 = 7x$; choice of variable may vary.

21. Casey lives 330 miles from her grandmother. If she drives an average of 55 miles per hour, how long will it take her to get to her grandmother's house? Use the formula $d = rt$.

    6 hours

22. Write an expression that you could use the diagram to evaluate.

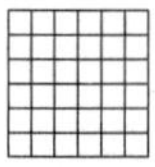

    Possible answers: $\sqrt{36}$, 6^2

23. What number increased by 4 equals $^{-}2$?

    $^{-}6$

24. Solve for x. $\frac{x}{5} = 7$

    $^{-}35$

25. A bank charges a fee of $3 per month for a checking account. In addition they charge d dollars for each check written plus x dollars for each returned check. Write an expression that represents the cost of a checking account for one month after writing 6 checks and having 2 checks returned.

    $3 + 6d + 2x$

26. Solve for x. $54 = x - 22$

    $x = 76$

Go On

AG 106 Assessment Guide   Form B • Free Response

Name ______________________

UNIT 5 TEST • PAGE 3

27. Corey bought 4 video games and 2 new controllers for a total of $210 before tax. If the games cost $40 each, how much did each of the controllers cost?

    $25

28. Write an expression to represent 15 decreased by m.

    $15 - m$

29. Write and solve the equation that is modeled below.

    $5x + 4 = 24$; $x = 4$; choice of variable may vary.

30. Use the formula $d = rt$ to find r for $d = 570$ and $t = 15$.

    $r = 38$

31. Find $3 \times \frac{\sqrt{81}}{\sqrt{9}}$.

    9

32. Write an equation to represent the word sentence, 46 is 5 less than a number.

    $46 = x - 5$; choice of variable may vary.

33. Write and solve the equation shown by the model.

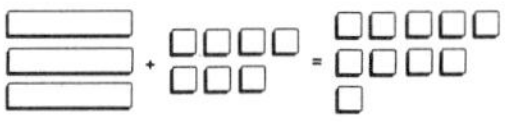

    $3x + 7 = 10$; $x = 1$; choice of variable may vary.

34. Evaluate $2x + \frac{5y}{3}$ for $x = 4$ and $y = 3$.

    13

35. For lunch Moira bought a sandwich for $3.75, a drink for $1.50, and dessert for $2.25. She paid with a $20 bill. How much change did she receive?

    $12.50

36. Convert $^{-}35$°C into degrees Fahrenheit. Use the formula $F = (\frac{9}{5} \times C) + 32$.

    $^{-}31$ °F

37. How many tiles are needed to make an 8×8 array?

    64

38. Mr. Saunders has collected 12 permission slips from the students in his class. He needs to collect 16 more. How many students are in his class?

    28 students

Go On

Form B • Free Response   Assessment Guide AG 107

Name ______________________

UNIT 5 TEST • PAGE 4

39. Reba scored 21 points in a basketball game. Field goals are 2 points each, and free throws are 1 point each. If she made 7 of her points from free throws, and the rest were from field goals, how many field goals did Reba make?

    7 field goals

40. Find $\sqrt{121} + \sqrt{81} - 4^2$.

    4

41. Write an equation to represent the word sentence, 8 times a number is 40.

    $8x = 40$; choice of variable may vary.

42. Write and solve the equation that is modeled below.

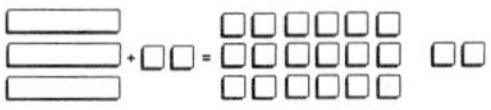

    $3x + 2 = 20$; $x = 6$; choice of variable may vary.

43. Two square arrays have a total of 45 squares. What size are the arrays?

    3×3 and 6×6

44. Write and solve the equation represented by the model.

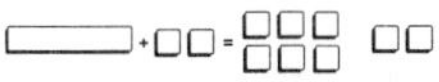

    $x + 2 = 8$; $x = 6$; choice of variable may vary.

45. Draw a model to represent and solve the equation $3x + 4 = 13$.

    Check students' models; $x = 3$

46. Evaluate $15 + 3n + n^2$ for $n = {}^{-}5$.

    25

47. Solve. $x - 1\frac{1}{2} = 10$.

    $x = 11\frac{1}{2}$

48. Evan uses his allowance to buy school lunch 5 days per week. Lunch is $2.50 per day. After buying lunch, he has $5 left from his allowance each week. How much is Evan's weekly allowance?

    $17.50 per week

49. Megan uses 2 eggs for each batch of cookies. She made 3 batches of cookies and now has 5 eggs left. How many eggs did she start out with?

    11 eggs

50. Max bought 32 quarts of fruit punch for his party. So far his guests drank 14 quarts of punch. How many quarts does he have left?

    18 quarts

Stop

AG 108 Assessment Guide   Form B • Free Response

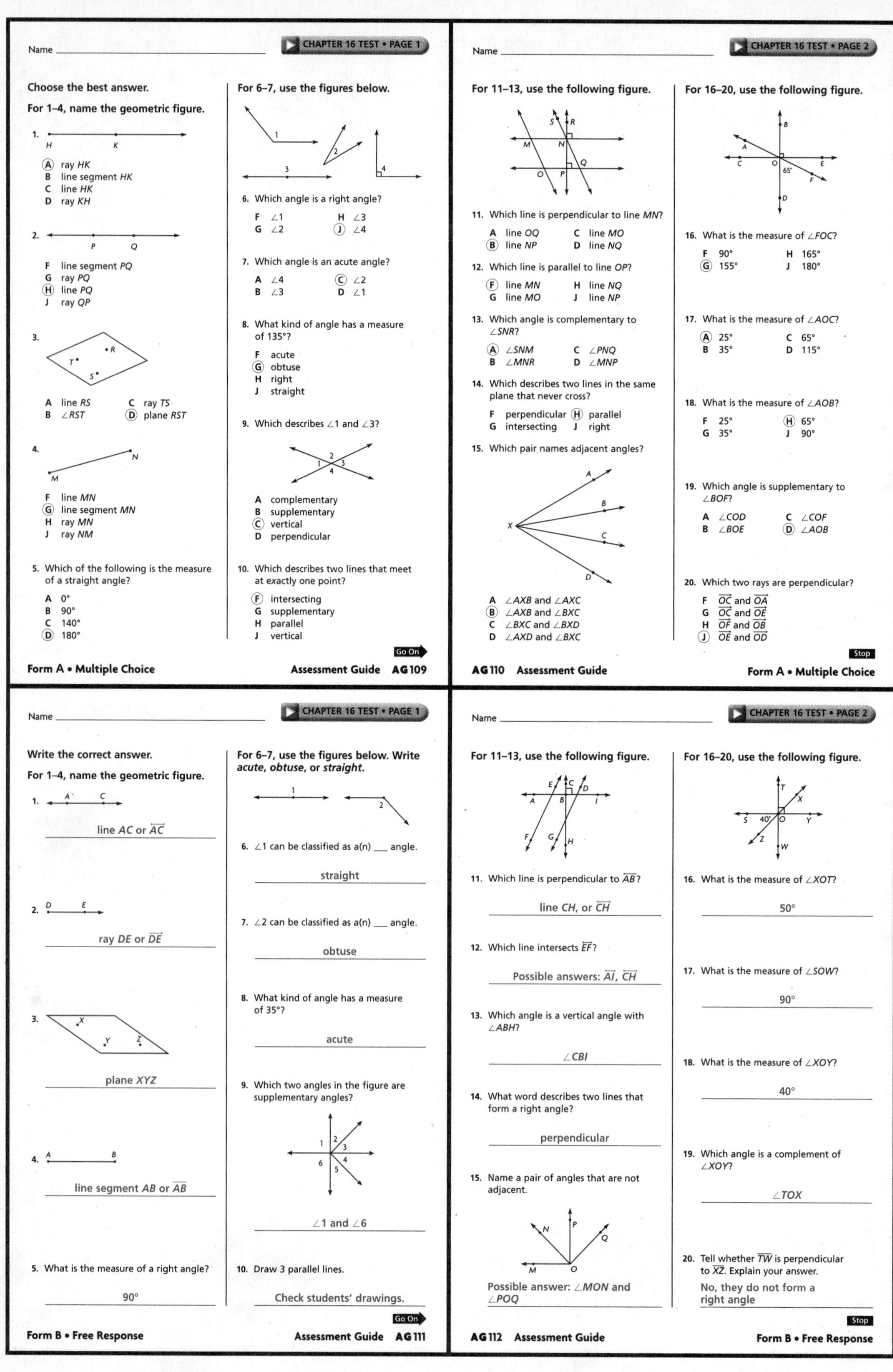

Name ______________________ CHAPTER 16 TEST • PAGE 1

Choose the best answer.

For 1–4, name the geometric figure.

1. H K
   - **(A) ray HK**
   - B line segment HK
   - C line HK
   - D ray KH

2. P Q
   - F line segment PQ
   - G ray PQ
   - **(H) line PQ**
   - J ray QP

3. T R S
   - A line RS
   - B $\angle RST$
   - C ray TS
   - **(D) plane RST**

4. M N
   - F line MN
   - **(G) line segment MN**
   - H ray MN
   - J ray NM

5. Which of the following is the measure of a straight angle?
   - A 0°
   - B 90°
   - C 140°
   - **(D) 180°**

For 6–7, use the figures below.

6. Which angle is a right angle?
   - F $\angle 1$
   - G $\angle 2$
   - H $\angle 3$
   - **(J) $\angle 4$**

7. Which angle is an acute angle?
   - A $\angle 4$
   - B $\angle 3$
   - **(C) $\angle 2$**
   - D $\angle 1$

8. What kind of angle has a measure of 135°?
   - F acute
   - **(G) obtuse**
   - H right
   - J straight

9. Which describes $\angle 1$ and $\angle 3$?
   - A complementary
   - B supplementary
   - **(C) vertical**
   - D perpendicular

10. Which describes two lines that meet at exactly one point?
    - **(F) intersecting**
    - G supplementary
    - H parallel
    - J vertical

Go On

Form A • Multiple Choice Assessment Guide AG 109

Name ______________________ CHAPTER 16 TEST • PAGE 2

For 11–13, use the following figure.

11. Which line is perpendicular to line MN?
    - A line OQ
    - **(B) line NP**
    - C line MO
    - D line NQ

12. Which line is parallel to line OP?
    - **(F) line MN**
    - G line MO
    - H line NQ
    - J line NP

13. Which angle is complementary to $\angle SNR$?
    - **(A) $\angle SNM$**
    - B $\angle MNR$
    - C $\angle PNQ$
    - D $\angle MNP$

14. Which describes two lines in the same plane that never cross?
    - F perpendicular
    - G intersecting
    - **(H) parallel**
    - J right

15. Which pair names adjacent angles?
    - A $\angle AXB$ and $\angle AXC$
    - **(B) $\angle AXB$ and $\angle BXC$**
    - C $\angle BXC$ and $\angle BXD$
    - D $\angle AXD$ and $\angle BXC$

For 16–20, use the following figure.

16. What is the measure of $\angle FOC$?
    - F 90°
    - **(G) 155°**
    - H 165°
    - J 180°

17. What is the measure of $\angle AOC$?
    - **(A) 25°**
    - B 35°
    - C 65°
    - D 115°

18. What is the measure of $\angle AOB$?
    - F 25°
    - G 35°
    - **(H) 65°**
    - J 90°

19. Which angle is supplementary to $\angle BOF$?
    - A $\angle COD$
    - B $\angle BOE$
    - C $\angle COF$
    - **(D) $\angle AOB$**

20. Which two rays are perpendicular?
    - F $\overrightarrow{OC}$ and $\overrightarrow{OA}$
    - G $\overrightarrow{OC}$ and $\overrightarrow{OE}$
    - H $\overrightarrow{OF}$ and $\overrightarrow{OB}$
    - **(J) $\overrightarrow{OE}$ and $\overrightarrow{OD}$**

Stop

AG 110 Assessment Guide Form A • Multiple Choice

Name ______________________ CHAPTER 16 TEST • PAGE 1

Write the correct answer.

For 1–4, name the geometric figure.

1. A C

   line AC or $\overleftrightarrow{AC}$

2. D E

   ray DE or $\overrightarrow{DE}$

3. X Y Z

   plane XYZ

4. A B

   line segment AB or $\overline{AB}$

5. What is the measure of a right angle?

   90°

For 6–7, use the figures below. Write *acute*, *obtuse*, or *straight*.

6. $\angle 1$ can be classified as a(n) ___ angle.

   straight

7. $\angle 2$ can be classified as a(n) ___ angle.

   obtuse

8. What kind of angle has a measure of 35°?

   acute

9. Which two angles in the figure are supplementary angles?

   $\angle 1$ and $\angle 6$

10. Draw 3 parallel lines.

    Check students' drawings.

Go On

Form B • Free Response Assessment Guide AG 111

Name ______________________ CHAPTER 16 TEST • PAGE 2

For 11–13, use the following figure.

11. Which line is perpendicular to $\overleftrightarrow{AB}$?

    line CH, or $\overleftrightarrow{CH}$

12. Which line intersects $\overleftrightarrow{EF}$?

    Possible answers: $\overleftrightarrow{AI}$, $\overleftrightarrow{CH}$

13. Which angle is a vertical angle with $\angle ABH$?

    $\angle CBI$

14. What word describes two lines that form a right angle?

    perpendicular

15. Name a pair of angles that are not adjacent.

    Possible answer: $\angle MON$ and $\angle POQ$

For 16–20, use the following figure.

16. What is the measure of $\angle XOT$?

    50°

17. What is the measure of $\angle SOW$?

    90°

18. What is the measure of $\angle XOY$?

    40°

19. Which angle is a complement of $\angle XOY$?

    $\angle TOX$

20. Tell whether $\overleftrightarrow{TW}$ is perpendicular to $\overleftrightarrow{XZ}$. Explain your answer.

    No, they do not form a right angle

Stop

AG 112 Assessment Guide Form B • Free Response

Name ______________

Choose the best answer.

For 1–4, complete the sentence.

1. Every trapezoid is also a ______.

A rectangle (C) quadrilateral
B rhombus D parallelogram

2. The sum of the angle measures in a triangle is ______.

F 90° H 270°
(G) 180° J 360°

3. Every rhombus is a ______.

(A) parallelogram C square
B rectangle D trapezoid

4. A triangle that contains an angle of 130° is a(n) ______ triangle.

F acute (H) obtuse
G right J isosceles

5. How many angles in a right triangle are acute angles?

A 0 (C) 2
B 1 D 3

6. Two angles of a triangle have measures of 35° and 55°. Which word best describes the triangle?

F acute H obtuse
G isosceles (J) right

7. Find the unknown angle measure.

?, 50°, 20°

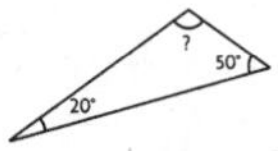

(A) 110° C 90°
B 100° D 70°

8. What is the measure of each angle of a regular triangle?

(F) 60° H 100°
G 90° J 120°

For 9–15, give the most exact name for the figure.

9.

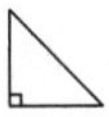

A acute triangle C obtuse triangle
(B) right triangle D triangle

10.

F quadrilateral (H) trapezoid
G parallelogram J rectangle

11.

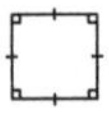

A rhombus C rectangle
B trapezoid (D) square

12.

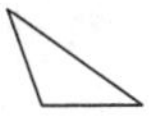

(F) obtuse triangle H acute triangle
G right triangle J triangle

13.

A trapezoid C rhombus
B parallelogram (D) quadrilateral

Go On

Name ______________

14.

F decagon (H) octagon
G heptagon J hexagon

15.

A scalene triangle
B isosceles triangle
(C) equilateral triangle
D obtuse triangle

For 16–20, use the figure below.

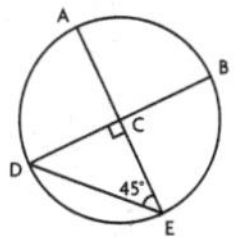

A, B, C, D, E, 45°

16. Name a diameter of the circle.

F $\overline{AC}$ H $\overline{DE}$
(G) $\overline{DB}$ J $\overline{CE}$

17. Which of these is **not** a chord of the circle?

A $\overline{AE}$ C $\overline{BD}$
(B) $\overline{BC}$ D $\overline{DE}$

18. Which of these is **not** a radius?

F $\overline{AC}$ H $\overline{BC}$
(G) $\overline{AE}$ J $\overline{CD}$

19. Give the most exact name for triangle *CDE*.

A isosceles triangle
(B) isosceles right triangle
C right triangle
D acute triangle

20. Name two arcs of the circle.

F $\overset{\frown}{AB}$ and $\overset{\frown}{CE}$ H $\overset{\frown}{DE}$ and $\overset{\frown}{BC}$
G $\overset{\frown}{BE}$ and $\overset{\frown}{CD}$ (J) $\overset{\frown}{AD}$ and $\overset{\frown}{BE}$

For 21–23, use the figure below.

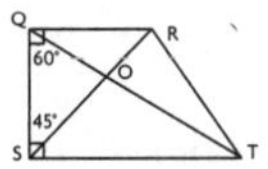

Q, R, O, S, T, 60°, 45°

21. Find the measure of angle *STO*.

(A) 30° C 75°
B 60° D 120°

22. What kind of angle is *QOS*?

F obtuse (H) acute
G right J equilateral

23. Give the most exact name for the figure *QRTS*.

A quadrilateral C parallelogram
B rhombus (D) trapezoid

24. Sue is tiling a floor with tiles in the shape of hexagons. What is the measure of each angle in her tiles?

(F) 120° H 30°
G 90° J 60°

25. Find the measure of ∠*ABC*.

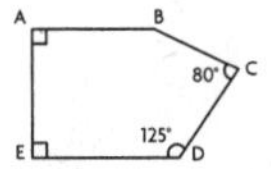

A, B, C, D, E, 80°, 125°

A 335° C 65°
(B) 155° D 60°

Stop

Name ______________

Write the correct answer.

1. A quadrilateral with both pairs of opposite sides parallel is a ___.

parallelogram

2. The sum of the angle measures in a rectangle is ___.

360°

3. A parallelogram with 4 congruent sides is called a ___.

Possible answers: rhombus, square

4. A triangle whose angles are all less than 90° is a(n) ___ triangle.

acute

5. A triangle with angles of 60° and 30° is a(n) ___ triangle.

right

6. What is the measure of the largest angle in an obtuse triangle?

Possible answers: any measure greater than 90° and less than 180°

7. Find the unknown angle measure.

40°, ?, 85°

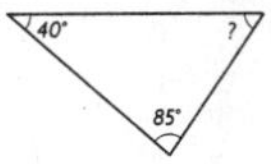

55°

8. How can the measure of each angle of a regular quadrilateral be determined?

Since all angles are equal, and the sum of the angles of a quadrilateral is 360°, the measure of each angle of a regular quadrilateral is 360° ÷ 4, or 90°.

For 9–14, write the most exact name for the figure shown.

9.  acute isosceles triangle

10. 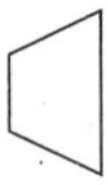 trapezoid

11.  rhombus

12. 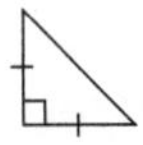 right isosceles triangle

13. 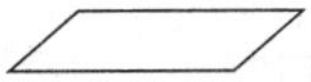 parallelogram

Go On

Name ______________

14.  hexagon

15. Classify the triangle.

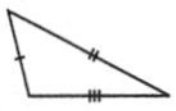

scalene, obtuse, or obtuse scalene

For 16–20, use the figure below. Point *O* is the center of the circle.

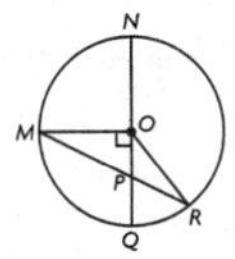

N, M, O, P, R, Q

16. Name a diameter of the circle.

$\overline{NQ}$

17. Name two chords of the circle.

$\overline{MR}$, $\overline{NQ}$

18. Name four radii of the circle.

$\overline{MO}$, $\overline{NO}$, $\overline{OQ}$, $\overline{OR}$

19. Name a right triangle.

triangle *MOP*

20. Name two arcs of the circle that include point *Q*.

Possible answers: $\overset{\frown}{MQ}$, $\overset{\frown}{QR}$, $\overset{\frown}{QN}$

For 21–23, use the figure below. *STVR* is a parallelogram.

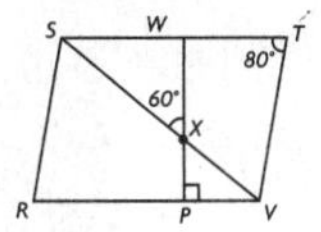

S, W, T, 80°, 60°, X, R, P, V

21. Find the measure of angle *PVX* and classify triangle *PVX*.

30°; right triangle

22. Find the measure of angle *RSV* and classify triangle *RSV*.

70°; acute triangle

23. Identify a trapezoid in the figure.

Possible answers: *WPRS* or *WTVP*

24. On a math test, Hector must draw a regular pentagon. What is the measure of each interior angle?

108°

25. What is the measure of ∠*XYZ*?

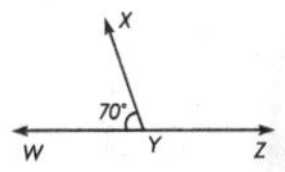

X, 70°, W, Y, Z

110°

Stop

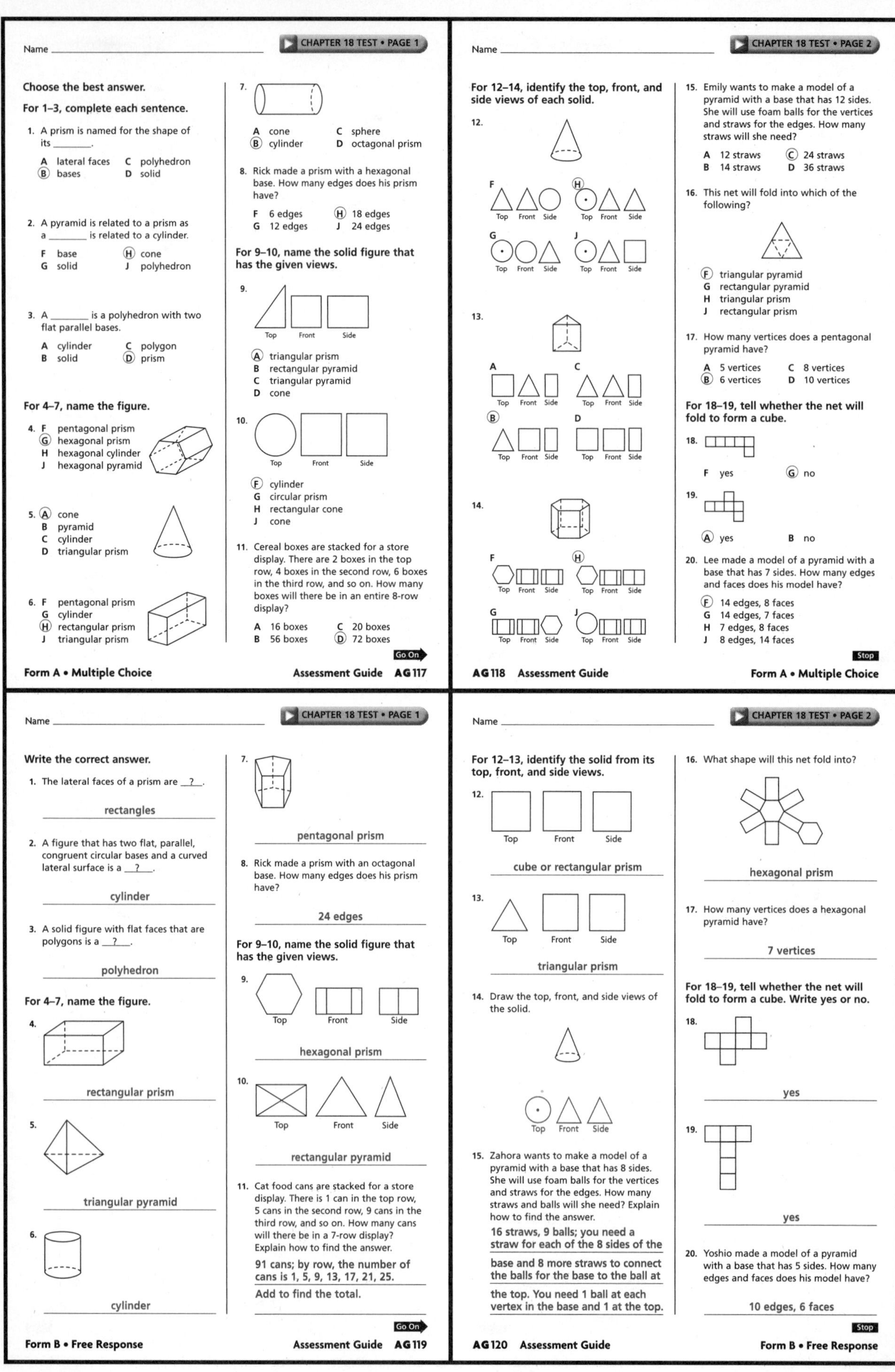

Name ______________________ CHAPTER 18 TEST • PAGE 1

Choose the best answer.

For 1–3, complete each sentence.

1. A prism is named for the shape of its ________.

   A lateral faces (B) bases C polyhedron D solid

2. A pyramid is related to a prism as a ________ is related to a cylinder.

   F base G solid (H) cone J polyhedron

3. A ________ is a polyhedron with two flat parallel bases.

   A cylinder B solid C polygon (D) prism

For 4–7, name the figure.

4. F pentagonal prism (G) hexagonal prism H hexagonal cylinder J hexagonal pyramid

5. (A) cone B pyramid C cylinder D triangular prism

6. F pentagonal prism G cylinder (H) rectangular prism J triangular prism

7. A cone (B) cylinder C sphere D octagonal prism

8. Rick made a prism with a hexagonal base. How many edges does his prism have?

   F 6 edges G 12 edges (H) 18 edges J 24 edges

For 9–10, name the solid figure that has the given views.

9. Top Front Side

   (A) triangular prism B rectangular pyramid C triangular pyramid D cone

10. Top Front Side

   (F) cylinder G circular prism H rectangular cone J cone

11. Cereal boxes are stacked for a store display. There are 2 boxes in the top row, 4 boxes in the second row, 6 boxes in the third row, and so on. How many boxes will there be in an entire 8-row display?

   A 16 boxes B 56 boxes C 20 boxes (D) 72 boxes

Go On

Form A • Multiple Choice Assessment Guide AG 117

Name ______________________ CHAPTER 18 TEST • PAGE 2

For 12–14, identify the top, front, and side views of each solid.

12. F Top Front Side (H) Top Front Side G Top Front Side J Top Front Side

13. A Top Front Side C Top Front Side (B) Top Front Side D Top Front Side

14. F Top Front Side (H) Top Front Side G Top Front Side J Top Front Side

15. Emily wants to make a model of a pyramid with a base that has 12 sides. She will use foam balls for the vertices and straws for the edges. How many straws will she need?

   A 12 straws B 14 straws (C) 24 straws D 36 straws

16. This net will fold into which of the following?

   (F) triangular pyramid G rectangular pyramid H triangular prism J rectangular prism

17. How many vertices does a pentagonal pyramid have?

   A 5 vertices (B) 6 vertices C 8 vertices D 10 vertices

For 18–19, tell whether the net will fold to form a cube.

18. F yes (G) no

19. (A) yes B no

20. Lee made a model of a pyramid with a base that has 7 sides. How many edges and faces does his model have?

   (F) 14 edges, 8 faces G 14 edges, 7 faces H 7 edges, 8 faces J 8 edges, 14 faces

Stop

AG 118 Assessment Guide Form A • Multiple Choice

Name ______________________ CHAPTER 18 TEST • PAGE 1

Write the correct answer.

1. The lateral faces of a prism are __?__.

   rectangles

2. A figure that has two flat, parallel, congruent circular bases and a curved lateral surface is a __?__.

   cylinder

3. A solid figure with flat faces that are polygons is a __?__.

   polyhedron

For 4–7, name the figure.

4. rectangular prism

5. triangular pyramid

6. cylinder

7. pentagonal prism

8. Rick made a prism with an octagonal base. How many edges does his prism have?

   24 edges

For 9–10, name the solid figure that has the given views.

9. Top Front Side

   hexagonal prism

10. Top Front Side

   rectangular pyramid

11. Cat food cans are stacked for a store display. There is 1 can in the top row, 5 cans in the second row, 9 cans in the third row, and so on. How many cans will there be in a 7-row display? Explain how to find the answer.

   91 cans; by row, the number of cans is 1, 5, 9, 13, 17, 21, 25. Add to find the total.

Go On

Form B • Free Response Assessment Guide AG 119

Name ______________________ CHAPTER 18 TEST • PAGE 2

For 12–13, identify the solid from its top, front, and side views.

12. Top Front Side

   cube or rectangular prism

13. Top Front Side

   triangular prism

14. Draw the top, front, and side views of the solid.

   Top Front Side

15. Zahora wants to make a model of a pyramid with a base that has 8 sides. She will use foam balls for the vertices and straws for the edges. How many straws and balls will she need? Explain how to find the answer.

   16 straws, 9 balls; you need a straw for each of the 8 sides of the base and 8 more straws to connect the balls for the base to the ball at the top. You need 1 ball at each vertex in the base and 1 at the top.

16. What shape will this net fold into?

   hexagonal prism

17. How many vertices does a hexagonal pyramid have?

   7 vertices

For 18–19, tell whether the net will fold to form a cube. Write yes or no.

18. yes

19. yes

20. Yoshio made a model of a pyramid with a base that has 5 sides. How many edges and faces does his model have?

   10 edges, 6 faces

Stop

AG 120 Assessment Guide Form B • Free Response

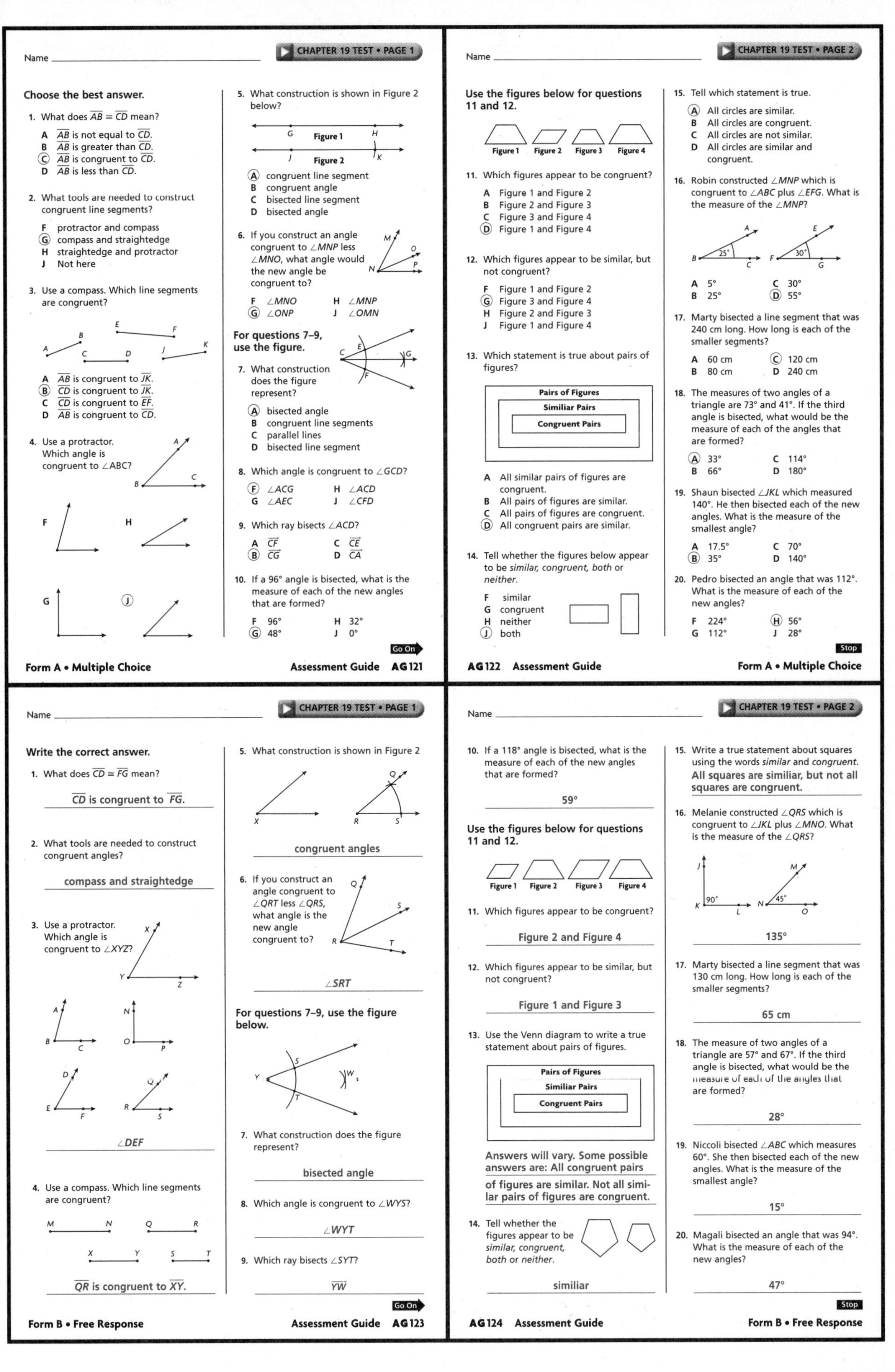

Name ____________________ CHAPTER 19 TEST • PAGE 1

Choose the best answer.

1. What does $\overline{AB} \cong \overline{CD}$ mean?
   A $\overline{AB}$ is not equal to $\overline{CD}$.
   B $\overline{AB}$ is greater than $\overline{CD}$.
   (C) $\overline{AB}$ is congruent to $\overline{CD}$.
   D $\overline{AB}$ is less than $\overline{CD}$.

2. What tools are needed to construct congruent line segments?
   F protractor and compass
   (G) compass and straightedge
   H straightedge and protractor
   J Not here

3. Use a compass. Which line segments are congruent?
   A $\overline{AB}$ is congruent to $\overline{JK}$.
   (B) $\overline{CD}$ is congruent to $\overline{JK}$.
   C $\overline{CD}$ is congruent to $\overline{EF}$.
   D $\overline{AB}$ is congruent to $\overline{CD}$.

4. Use a protractor. Which angle is congruent to $\angle ABC$?
   F   H   G   (J)

5. What construction is shown in Figure 2 below?
   Figure 1   Figure 2
   (A) congruent line segment
   B congruent angle
   C bisected line segment
   D bisected angle

6. If you construct an angle congruent to $\angle MNP$ less $\angle MNO$, what angle would the new angle be congruent to?
   F $\angle MNO$ H $\angle MNP$
   (G) $\angle ONP$ J $\angle OMN$

For questions 7–9, use the figure.

7. What construction does the figure represent?
   (A) bisected angle
   B congruent line segments
   C parallel lines
   D bisected line segment

8. Which angle is congruent to $\angle GCD$?
   (F) $\angle ACG$ H $\angle ACD$
   G $\angle AEC$ J $\angle CFD$

9. Which ray bisects $\angle ACD$?
   A $\overrightarrow{CF}$ C $\overrightarrow{CE}$
   (B) $\overrightarrow{CG}$ D $\overrightarrow{CA}$

10. If a 96° angle is bisected, what is the measure of each of the new angles that are formed?
   F 96°   H 32°
   (G) 48°   J 0°

Go On

Form A • Multiple Choice   Assessment Guide AG121

Name ____________________ CHAPTER 19 TEST • PAGE 2

Use the figures below for questions 11 and 12.

Figure 1   Figure 2   Figure 3   Figure 4

11. Which figures appear to be congruent?
   A Figure 1 and Figure 2
   B Figure 2 and Figure 3
   C Figure 3 and Figure 4
   (D) Figure 1 and Figure 4

12. Which figures appear to be similar, but not congruent?
   F Figure 1 and Figure 2
   (G) Figure 3 and Figure 4
   H Figure 2 and Figure 3
   J Figure 1 and Figure 4

13. Which statement is true about pairs of figures?
   Pairs of Figures / Similiar Pairs / Congruent Pairs
   A All similar pairs of figures are congruent.
   B All pairs of figures are similar.
   C All pairs of figures are congruent.
   (D) All congruent pairs are similar.

14. Tell whether the figures below appear to be *similar, congruent, both* or *neither.*
   F similar
   G congruent
   H neither
   (J) both

15. Tell which statement is true.
   (A) All circles are similar.
   B All circles are congruent.
   C All circles are not similar.
   D All circles are similar and congruent.

16. Robin constructed $\angle MNP$ which is congruent to $\angle ABC$ plus $\angle EFG$. What is the measure of the $\angle MNP$?
   A 5°   C 30°
   B 25°   (D) 55°

17. Marty bisected a line segment that was 240 cm long. How long is each of the smaller segments?
   A 60 cm   (C) 120 cm
   B 80 cm   D 240 cm

18. The measures of two angles of a triangle are 73° and 41°. If the third angle is bisected, what would be the measure of each of the angles that are formed?
   (A) 33°   C 114°
   B 66°   D 180°

19. Shaun bisected $\angle JKL$ which measured 140°. He then bisected each of the new angles. What is the measure of the smallest angle?
   A 17.5°   C 70°
   (B) 35°   D 140°

20. Pedro bisected an angle that was 112°. What is the measure of each of the new angles?
   F 224°   (H) 56°
   G 112°   J 28°

Stop

AG122 Assessment Guide   Form A • Multiple Choice

Name ____________________ CHAPTER 19 TEST • PAGE 1

Write the correct answer.

1. What does $\overline{CD} \cong \overline{FG}$ mean?
   $\overline{CD}$ is congruent to $\overline{FG}$.

2. What tools are needed to construct congruent angles?
   compass and straightedge

3. Use a protractor. Which angle is congruent to $\angle XYZ$?
   $\angle DEF$

4. Use a compass. Which line segments are congruent?
   $\overline{QR}$ is congruent to $\overline{XY}$.

5. What construction is shown in Figure 2
   congruent angles

6. If you construct an angle congruent to $\angle QRT$ less $\angle QRS$, what angle is the new angle congruent to?
   $\angle SRT$

For questions 7–9, use the figure below.

7. What construction does the figure represent?
   bisected angle

8. Which angle is congruent to $\angle WYS$?
   $\angle WYT$

9. Which ray bisects $\angle SYT$?
   $\overrightarrow{YW}$

Go On

Form B • Free Response   Assessment Guide AG123

Name ____________________ CHAPTER 19 TEST • PAGE 2

10. If a 118° angle is bisected, what is the measure of each of the new angles that are formed?
   59°

Use the figures below for questions 11 and 12.

Figure 1   Figure 2   Figure 3   Figure 4

11. Which figures appear to be congruent?
   Figure 2 and Figure 4

12. Which figures appear to be similar, but not congruent?
   Figure 1 and Figure 3

13. Use the Venn diagram to write a true statement about pairs of figures.
   Pairs of Figures / Similiar Pairs / Congruent Pairs
   Answers will vary. Some possible answers are: All congruent pairs of figures are similar. Not all similar pairs of figures are congruent.

14. Tell whether the figures appear to be *similar, congruent, both* or *neither.*
   similiar

15. Write a true statement about squares using the words *similar* and *congruent.*
   All squares are similiar, but not all squares are congruent.

16. Melanie constructed $\angle QRS$ which is congruent to $\angle JKL$ plus $\angle MNO$. What is the measure of the $\angle QRS$?
   135°

17. Marty bisected a line segment that was 130 cm long. How long is each of the smaller segments?
   65 cm

18. The measure of two angles of a triangle are 57° and 67°. If the third angle is bisected, what would be the measure of each of the angles that are formed?
   28°

19. Niccoli bisected $\angle ABC$ which measures 60°. She then bisected each of the new angles. What is the measure of the smallest angle?
   15°

20. Magali bisected an angle that was 94°. What is the measure of each of the new angles?
   47°

Stop

AG124 Assessment Guide   Form B • Free Response

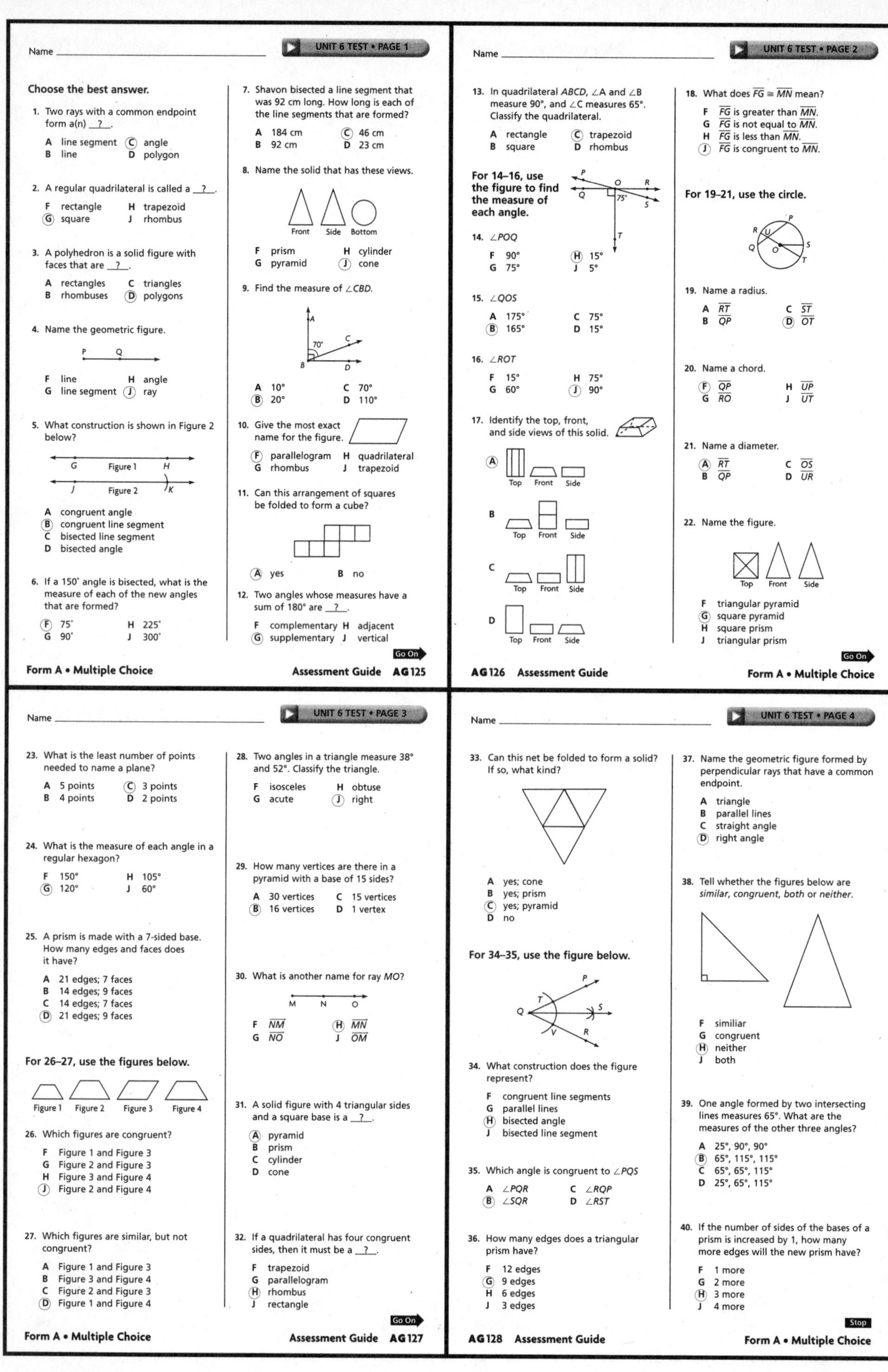

Name ____________________

UNIT 6 TEST • PAGE 1

Choose the best answer.

1. Two rays with a common endpoint form a(n) __?__.
   A line segment **C** angle
   B line D polygon

2. A regular quadrilateral is called a __?__.
   F rectangle H trapezoid
   G square J rhombus

3. A polyhedron is a solid figure with faces that are __?__.
   A rectangles C triangles
   B rhombuses **D** polygons

4. Name the geometric figure.
   P Q
   F line H angle
   G line segment **J** ray

5. What construction is shown in Figure 2 below?
   G Figure 1 H
   J Figure 2 K
   A congruent angle
   B congruent line segment
   C bisected line segment
   D bisected angle

6. If a 150° angle is bisected, what is the measure of each of the new angles that are formed?
   F 75° H 225°
   G 90° J 300°

7. Shavon bisected a line segment that was 92 cm long. How long is each of the line segments that are formed?
   A 184 cm **C** 46 cm
   B 92 cm D 23 cm

8. Name the solid that has these views.
   Front Side Bottom
   F prism H cylinder
   G pyramid **J** cone

9. Find the measure of ∠CBD.
   A 70° C B D
   A 10° C 70°
   B 20° D 110°

10. Give the most exact name for the figure.
   F parallelogram H quadrilateral
   G rhombus J trapezoid

11. Can this arrangement of squares be folded to form a cube?
   A yes B no

12. Two angles whose measures have a sum of 180° are __?__.
   F complementary H adjacent
   G supplementary J vertical

Go On

Form A • Multiple Choice Assessment Guide AG125

Name ____________________

UNIT 6 TEST • PAGE 2

13. In quadrilateral ABCD, ∠A and ∠B measure 90°, and ∠C measures 65°. Classify the quadrilateral.
   A rectangle **C** trapezoid
   B square D rhombus

For 14–16, use the figure to find the measure of each angle.

P O R Q 75° S T

14. ∠POQ
   F 90° **H** 15°
   G 75° J 5°

15. ∠QOS
   A 175° C 75°
   B 165° D 15°

16. ∠ROT
   F 15° H 75°
   G 60° **J** 90°

17. Identify the top, front, and side views of this solid.
   A Top Front Side
   B Top Front Side
   C Top Front Side
   D Top Front Side

18. What does $\overline{FG} \cong \overline{MN}$ mean?
   F $\overline{FG}$ is greater than $\overline{MN}$.
   G $\overline{FG}$ is not equal to $\overline{MN}$.
   H $\overline{FG}$ is less than $\overline{MN}$.
   J $\overline{FG}$ is congruent to $\overline{MN}$.

For 19–21, use the circle.

P R U Q O S T

19. Name a radius.
   A $\overline{RT}$ C $\overline{ST}$
   B $\overline{QP}$ **D** $\overline{OT}$

20. Name a chord.
   F $\overline{QP}$ H $\overline{UP}$
   G $\overline{RO}$ J $\overline{UT}$

21. Name a diameter.
   A $\overline{RT}$ C $\overline{OS}$
   B $\overline{QP}$ D $\overline{UR}$

22. Name the figure.
   Top Front Side
   F triangular pyramid
   G square pyramid
   H square prism
   J triangular prism

Go On

AG126 Assessment Guide Form A • Multiple Choice

Name ____________________

UNIT 6 TEST • PAGE 3

23. What is the least number of points needed to name a plane?
   A 5 points **C** 3 points
   B 4 points D 2 points

24. What is the measure of each angle in a regular hexagon?
   F 150° H 105°
   G 120° J 60°

25. A prism is made with a 7-sided base. How many edges and faces does it have?
   A 21 edges; 7 faces
   B 14 edges; 9 faces
   C 14 edges; 7 faces
   D 21 edges; 9 faces

For 26–27, use the figures below.

Figure 1 Figure 2 Figure 3 Figure 4

26. Which figures are congruent?
   F Figure 1 and Figure 3
   G Figure 2 and Figure 3
   H Figure 3 and Figure 4
   J Figure 2 and Figure 4

27. Which figures are similar, but not congruent?
   A Figure 1 and Figure 3
   B Figure 3 and Figure 4
   C Figure 2 and Figure 3
   D Figure 1 and Figure 4

28. Two angles in a triangle measure 38° and 52°. Classify the triangle.
   F isosceles H obtuse
   G acute **J** right

29. How many vertices are there in a pyramid with a base of 15 sides?
   A 30 vertices C 15 vertices
   B 16 vertices D 1 vertex

30. What is another name for ray MO?
   M N O
   F $\overrightarrow{NM}$ **H** $\overrightarrow{MN}$
   G $\overrightarrow{NO}$ J $\overrightarrow{OM}$

31. A solid figure with 4 triangular sides and a square base is a __?__.
   A pyramid
   B prism
   C cylinder
   D cone

32. If a quadrilateral has four congruent sides, then it must be a __?__.
   F trapezoid
   G parallelogram
   H rhombus
   J rectangle

Go On

Form A • Multiple Choice Assessment Guide AG127

Name ____________________

UNIT 6 TEST • PAGE 4

33. Can this net be folded to form a solid? If so, what kind?
   A yes; cone
   B yes; prism
   C yes; pyramid
   D no

For 34–35, use the figure below.

P T S Q V R

34. What construction does the figure represent?
   F congruent line segments
   G parallel lines
   H bisected angle
   J bisected line segment

35. Which angle is congruent to ∠PQS
   A ∠PQR C ∠RQP
   B ∠SQR D ∠RST

36. How many edges does a triangular prism have?
   F 12 edges
   G 9 edges
   H 6 edges
   J 3 edges

37. Name the geometric figure formed by perpendicular rays that have a common endpoint.
   A triangle
   B parallel lines
   C straight angle
   D right angle

38. Tell whether the figures below are *similar, congruent, both* or *neither.*
   F similiar
   G congruent
   H neither
   J both

39. One angle formed by two intersecting lines measures 65°. What are the measures of the other three angles?
   A 25°, 90°, 90°
   B 65°, 115°, 115°
   C 65°, 65°, 115°
   D 25°, 65°, 115°

40. If the number of sides of the bases of a prism is increased by 1, how many more edges will the new prism have?
   F 1 more
   G 2 more
   H 3 more
   J 4 more

Stop

AG128 Assessment Guide Form A • Multiple Choice

Name

UNIT 6 TEST • PAGE 1

Write the correct answer.

1. An angle is formed by two rays with a common endpoint called a(n) __?__.

vertex

2. A polygon with all sides equal and all angles equal is called __?__.

regular

3. A pattern that can be folded to form a solid figure is called a(n) __?__.

net

4. Identify the geometric figure.

line

5. What construction is shown in Figure 2?

Figure 1 Figure 2

congruent angles

6. If a 46° angle is bisected, what is the measure of each of the new angles that are formed?

23°

7. Balinda bisected a line segment that was 78 cm long. How long is each of the line segments that are formed?

39 cm

8. Name the solid that has these views.

Top Front Side

cone

9. Find the measure of ∠ACB.

43°

10. Give the most exact name for the figure.

trapezoid

11. Can this arrangement of squares be folded to form a cube? If so, how many vertices will it have?

yes; 8 vertices

12. Two angles with measures that have a sum of 90° are __?__.

complementary

Go On

Name

UNIT 6 TEST • PAGE 2

13. In quadrilateral *ABCD*, ∠*A* and ∠*C* measure 110°, and ∠*B* measures 70°. Classify the quadrilateral.

parallelogram

For 14–16, use the figure to find the measure of each angle.

14. ∠*ACG*

48°

15. ∠*DCE*

42°

16. ∠*ACB*

42°

17. Draw the top, front, and side views of this solid.

Top Front Side

18. What does ∠*ABC* ≅ ∠*JKL* mean?

∠*ABC* is congruent to ∠*JKL*

For 19–21, use the circle.

19. Name a radius.

Possible answers: $\overline{DE}$, $\overline{DC}$

20. Name a chord.

Possible answers: $\overline{AB}$, $\overline{CE}$

21. Name a diameter.

$\overline{CE}$

22. Identify the figure.

triangular pyramid

Go On

Name

UNIT 6 TEST • PAGE 3

23. How many non-collinear points are needed to define a plane?

at least 3

24. What is the measure of each angle in a regular pentagon?

108°

25. A prism has a 6-sided base. How many edges and faces does it have?

18 edges, 8 faces

For 26–27, use the figures below.

Figure 1 Figure 2 Figure 3 Figure 4

26. Which figures appear to be congruent?

Figure 2 and Figure 4

27. Which figures appear to be similar, but not congruent?

Figure 1 and Figure 3

28. Two angles in a triangle measure 48° and 84°. Classify the triangle.

isosceles

29. How many vertices are there in a pyramid with a base of 12 sides?

13 vertices

30. What is another name for ray *RT*?

$\overrightarrow{RS}$

31. A solid figure with 6 rectangular sides and 2 hexagonal bases is called a(n) __?__.

hexagonal prism

32. If a quadrilateral has four congruent sides and four congruent angles, then it must be a(n) __?__.

square

Go On

Name

UNIT 6 TEST • PAGE 4

33. Can this net be folded to form a solid? If so, what kind?

yes; hexagonal prism

For 34-35, use the figure below. $\overline{TU}$ bisects $\overline{XY}$

34. What segment is congruent to $\overline{XW}$?

$\overline{WY}$

35. Which point on the line is the midpoint?

Point *W*

36. How many edges does a pentagonal prism have?

15 edges

37. __?__ angles are opposite angles formed when two lines intersect.

vertical

38. Tell whether the figures below are *similar, congruent, both* or *neither.*

neither

39. One angle formed by two intersecting lines measures 70°. What are the measures of the other three angles?

70°, 110°, 110°

40. If the number of sides of the base of a prism is increased by 1, how many more vertices will the new prism have?

2 vertices

Stop

Name ______________________ CHAPTER 20 TEST • PAGE 1

Choose the best answer.

For 1–2, use the figure.

1. What is the ratio of black sections to gray sections?

A $\frac{2}{3}$ C $\frac{20}{6}$
B $\frac{6}{4}$ D $\frac{20}{4}$

2. What is the ratio of all sections to white sections?

F $\frac{5}{1}$ H $\frac{1}{2}$
G $\frac{10}{3}$ **J** $\frac{2}{1}$

For 3–4, find the unit rate.

3. 64 mi on 4 gal of gas

A 64 mi per gal
B 32 mi per gal
C 30 mi per gal
D 16 mi per gal

4. 117 songs on 9 CDs

F 13 CDs per song
G 13 songs per CD
H $\frac{1}{13}$ song per CD
J $\frac{1}{13}$ CD per song

5. Corn is on sale at \$2.00 for 8 ears. Find the cost of 14 ears.

A \$5.60 C \$3.00
B \$3.50 D \$2.75

6. The scale for a map is 1 in. = 20 mi. Find the map distance for 160 mi.

F 160 in. **H** 8 in.
G 80 in. J $\frac{1}{8}$ in.

7. Bobbi needs 1 cup of flour to make a batch of 32 cookies. How much flour is needed to make 48 cookies?

A $\frac{2}{3}$ c **C** $1\frac{1}{2}$ c
B $1\frac{1}{3}$ c D 7 c

8. The rectangles are similar. Find the unknown length.

4 in.
2 in.
8 in.
x

F $x = 4$ in. H $x = 8$ in.
G $x = 6$ in. J $x = 16$ in.

9. A scale of 3 in. = 8 ft is used on a house plan drawing. The length of a room on the drawing is 9 in. How long is the actual room?

A 72 ft **C** 24 ft
B 27 ft D $3\frac{3}{8}$ ft

10. The triangles are similar. Find the unknown length.

65 cm
60 cm
13 cm
h

F $h = 18$ cm H $h = 8$ cm
G $h = 12$ cm J $h = 6$ cm

Go On

Name ______________________ CHAPTER 20 TEST • PAGE 2

11. The scale for a map is 1 in. = 30 mi. What is the actual distance between two towns that are $1\frac{1}{2}$ in. apart on the map?

A 15 mi **C** 45 mi
B 40 mi D 90 mi

12. Marianna made 3 quarts of tomato sauce from 2 baskets of tomatoes. How much tomato sauce could she make from 5 baskets of tomatoes?

F $3\frac{1}{3}$ qt H 6 qt
G 4 qt **J** $7\frac{1}{2}$ qt

13. Which dimensions describe a rectangle similar to the rectangle shown?

7 ft
5 ft

A 6 ft by 8 ft C 10 ft by 6 ft
B 8 ft by 10 ft **D** 15 ft by 21 ft

14. The figures are similar. Find the unknown length.

8 mm
5 mm
x
25 mm

F $x = 40$ mm H $x = 28$ mm
G $x = 35$ mm J $x = 22$ mm

15. All the commercials on a radio station are the same length. Playing 20 commercials takes 15 min. How long does it take to play 80 commercials?

A 60 min C 75 min
B 65 min D 80 min

16. What is the unit rate for driving 120 mi in 2 hr?

F 1 hr for 240 mi
G 60 mi in 1 hr
H 240 mi in 1 hr
J $\frac{1}{60}$ hr for 2 mi

17. The boxes that Ed is painting are all the same size and shape. He can paint 8 boxes in 20 min. How many boxes can he paint in 90 min?

A 30 **C** 36
B 32 D 40

18. The triangles are similar. Find the unknown length.

k
2 yd
1 yd
3 yd

F $k = \frac{1}{2}$ yd H $k = 1$ yd
G $k = \frac{2}{3}$ yd J $k = 1\frac{1}{2}$ yd

19. The sides of a triangle have lengths 5 cm, 6 cm, and 2 cm. Which of the following lengths could be sides of a similar triangle?

A 10 cm, 12 cm, 4 cm
B 12 cm, 8 cm, 9 cm
C 3 cm, 4 cm, 1 cm
D 8 cm, 10 cm, 4 cm

20. The measures of the angles of a triangle are 90°, 50°, and 40°. What are the measures of the angles of a similar triangle?

F 45°, 25°, 20° H 90°, 25°, 20°
G 45°, 50°, 40° **J** 90°, 50°, 40°

Stop

Name ______________________ CHAPTER 20 TEST • PAGE 1

Write the correct answer.

For 1–2, use the figure.

1. What is the ratio of solid white sections to striped sections?

$\frac{3}{7}$

2. What is the ratio of all sections to dotted sections?

$\frac{20}{10}$ or $\frac{2}{1}$

For 3–4, find the unit rate.

3. 80 people in 5 buses

16 people per bus

4. 153 melons in 9 crates

17 melons per crate

5. Socks are on sale for \$9.50 for 5 pairs. Find the cost of 12 pairs. Explain how to find the answer.

\$22.80; Possible answer: The unit rate is \$1.90 per pair; multiply 12 × \$1.90 = \$22.80.

6. The scale for a map is 1 cm = 25 km. Find the map distance for 175 km.

7 cm

7. Cruz needs 1 cup of onions to make 24 tacos. How many cups of onions does he need to make 36 tacos? Explain how to find the answer.

$1\frac{1}{2}$ c; Possible answer: Write and solve a proportion: $\frac{1}{24} = \frac{n}{36}$.

8. The rectangles are similar. Find the unknown length.

3 in.
x
6 in.
10 in.

$x = 5$ in.

9. A scale of 2 in. = 9 ft is used on a building plan drawing. The length of a room on the drawing is 8 in. How long is the actual room?

36 ft

10. The triangles are similar. Find the unknown length.

9 cm
7 cm
x
35 cm

$x = 45$ cm

Go On

Name ______________________ CHAPTER 20 TEST • PAGE 2

11. The scale for a map is 1 cm = 50 km. What is the actual distance between two towns that are $2\frac{1}{2}$ cm apart on the map?

125 km

12. Mohammed made 15 pints of jam from 6 baskets of strawberries. How much jam could he make from 9 baskets of strawberries?

$22\frac{1}{2}$ pt

13. What dimensions describe a rectangle similar to the rectangle shown?

8 m
3 m

Possible answer: 6 m by 16 m

14. The figures are similar. Find the missing length.

6 mm
17 mm
18 mm
x

$x = 51$ mm

15. At the copy shop, it takes 18 minutes to copy 300 flyers. How long does it take to copy 900 flyers?

54 min

16. What is the unit rate for hiking 9 mi in 3 hr?

3 mi per hr

17. The plates that Amanda is painting are all the same size and shape. She can paint 12 plates in 30 min. How many plates can she paint in 75 min?

30 plates

18. The triangles are similar. Find the missing length.

8 ft
3 ft
12 ft
x

$x = 4\frac{1}{2}$ ft

19. The sides of a triangle have lengths of 8 cm, 5 cm, and 6 cm. What dimensions could describe a similar triangle?

Possible answer: 16 cm, 10 cm, and 12 cm

20. The measures of the angles of a triangle are 100°, 60°, and 20°. What are the measures of the angles of a similar triangle?

100°, 60°, 20°

Stop

Name ____________________

Choose the best answer.

For 1–2, tell the percent of the figure that is shaded.

1\. 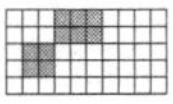 [grid figure]

A 90% (C) 20%
B 80% D 10%

2\. 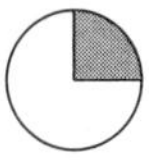 [circle figure]

F 75% H $33\frac{1}{3}$%
G 50% (J) 25%

3\. What is the decimal 0.38 as a percent?

(A) 38% C 0.38%
B 3.8% D 0.0038%

4\. What is the fraction $\frac{5}{8}$ as a percent?

F 625% H 58%
(G) 62.5% J 0.625%

5\. What is 24% as a decimal and as a fraction in simplest form?

A 0.024; $\frac{24}{100}$ (C) 0.24; $\frac{6}{25}$
B 24; $\frac{6}{25}$ D 24; $\frac{24}{100}$

For 6–10, find the percent of the number.

6\. 22% of 50 = _?_

F 39 (H) 11
G 16.5 J 5.5

7\. 200% of 120 = _?_

A 600 (C) 240
B 360 D 60

8\. 5% of 20 = _?_

(F) 1 H 10
G 5 J 19

9\. 95% of 400 = _?_

A 20 C 360
B 95 (D) 380

10\. 25% of 240 = _?_

F 180 H 50
(G) 60 J 40

11\. Find the sale price of a shirt if the regular price is $21.00 and it is on sale at 20% off.

A $1.00 (C) $16.80
B $4.20 D $20.00

12\. How much sales tax is added to the cost of a dress priced at $35.00 if the sales tax rate is 4%?

F $14.00 H $0.40
(G) $1.40 J $0.35

Go On

Name ____________________

13\. The regular price of a blanket was discounted 30%. The sale price was $22.40. What was the regular price?

A $15.68 (C) $32.00
B $29.12 D $35.00

14\. What is the total cost of a $120.00 suit on sale at 15% off with 8% sales tax added?

F $129.60 H $102.00
(G) $110.16 J $93.84

For 15–16, you are investing money in a savings account that earns 6.5% simple interest.

15\. Calculate how much interest will be earned if $2,500 is invested for a period of 7 years.

(A) $1,137.50
B $162.50
C $12.50
D $6.50

16\. How much time will it take to earn $468.00 if you invest $1,200.00 in this savings account?

(F) 6 years H 4.68 years
G 5 years J 1.2 years

For 17–19, use the circle graph. Dollar figures are in thousands of dollars.

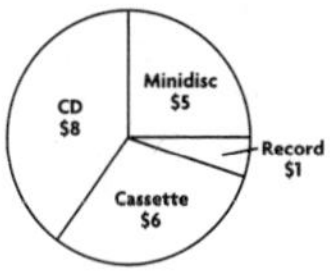

CD $8
Minidisc $5
Record $1
Cassette $6

17\. Sales of CDs at this music store made up what percent of total sales?

A 60% C 55%
B 50% (D) 40%

18\. If the manager decided not to sell records anymore, what percent of sales would he lose?

(F) 5% H 15%
G 10% J 20%

19\. Sales of CDs and minidiscs make up what percent of total sales?

A 13% C 50%
B 26% (D) 65%

20\. Rob's Clothing is having a sale and has discounts as shown on the sign below.

Regular Price: $140.00
Discounted Price: 30% off Regular Price
Sale Price: 20% off Discounted Price
Bonus Buy: 10% off Sale Price

Calculate the bonus buy price of this item.

F $56.00
G $70.00
(H) $70.56
J $77.00

Stop

Name ____________________

Write the correct answer.

For 1–2, write the percent of the figure that is shaded.

1\. 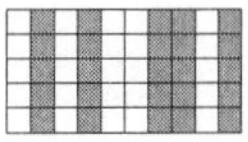 [grid figure]

50%

2\. [rectangle figure]

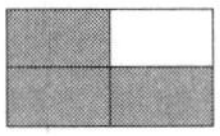

75%

3\. Write the decimal 0.15 as a percent.

15%

4\. Write the fraction $\frac{3}{8}$ as a percent.

37.5%

5\. Write 12% as a decimal and as a fraction in simplest form.

0.12; $\frac{3}{25}$

6\. 35% of 70 = _?_

24.5

7\. 150% of 150 = _?_

225

8\. 8% of 50 = _?_

4

9\. 85% of 200 = _?_

170

10\. 15% of 640 = _?_

96

11\. What is the sale price of a $38.00 video game on sale at 15% off?

$32.30

12\. How much sales tax is added to the cost of a shirt priced at $28.00 if the sales tax rate is 5%?

$1.40

Go On

Name ____________________

13\. The regular price of a coat was discounted 25%. The sale price was $131.25. What was the regular price?

$175.00

14\. What is the total cost of a $200.00 television set on sale at 10% off with 6% sales tax added?

$190.80

For 15–16, you are investing money in a money market fund that earns 4.5% simple interest.

15\. How much interest will be earned if $5,500 is invested for a period of 8 years?

$1,980

16\. How much time will it take to earn $607.50 if you invest $1,500.00 in this fund?

9 years

For 17–19, use the circle graph. The circle graph shows how Sam spends his weekly earnings from his part-time job.

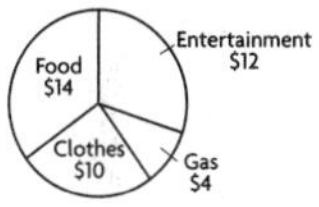

Food $14
Entertainment $12
Clothes $10
Gas $4

17\. What percent of his earnings does Sam spend on food?

35%

18\. What percent of his total salary does Sam spend on clothes and entertainment?

55%

19\. If Sam got a ride to work and used his gas money for entertainment, what percent of his salary would he spend on entertainment each week?

40%

20\. Greg saw the sign shown below in the window of a bike store.

FINAL SALE ON ALL MOUNTAIN BIKES		
Regular Price	$200	
Discount	10%	Off Regular Price
Winter Sale	20%	Off Discounted Price
Final Sale	15%	Off Winter Sale Price

What is the final price of a mountain bike?

$122.40

Stop

Choose the best answer.

For 1–4, use the following situation:

A spinner with 10 equal sections has 1 green section, 4 blue sections, 3 red sections, and 2 yellow sections.

1. Express *P* (red or yellow) as a fraction.

   A $\frac{1}{10}$ (C) $\frac{1}{2}$
   B $\frac{1}{5}$ D $\frac{7}{10}$

2. Express *P* (not yellow) as a decimal and a percent.

   F 0.9, 90% H 0.75, 75%
   (G) 0.8, 80% J 0.25, 25%

3. Find *P* (blue).

   A $\frac{1}{10}$ (C) $\frac{2}{5}$
   B $\frac{3}{10}$ D $\frac{3}{5}$

4. Find *P* (red or not red).

   (F) 1 H $\frac{1}{2}$
   G $\frac{7}{10}$ J $\frac{3}{10}$

For 5–8, use the following situation:

The names of the days of the week are on 7 pieces of paper in a bowl. One piece is drawn.

5. Find *P* (begins with S).

   A $\frac{1}{7}$ C $\frac{2}{5}$
   (B) $\frac{2}{7}$ D 1

6. Find *P* (begins with T or F).

   F $\frac{3}{4}$ (H) $\frac{3}{7}$
   G $\frac{4}{7}$ J $\frac{2}{7}$

7. Find *P* (does not contain Y).

   A 1 C $\frac{1}{7}$
   B $\frac{6}{7}$ (D) 0

8. Which of the following describes drawing a day that has a letter A?

   (F) certain H not likely
   G likely J impossible

For 9–10, use the following situation:

A spinner has red, blue and yellow sections. With 100 spins, Jane got the following results.

COLOR	RED	BLUE	YELLOW
Number of times	20	50	30

9. With 20 spins, how many times can she expect to get yellow?

   A 2 times (C) 6 times
   B 3 times D 12 times

10. With 200 spins, how many times can she expect to get blue?

    F 150 times H 120 times
    G 130 times (J) 100 times

Go On

For 11–13, use the results from the following experiment to make predictions.

Manuel tossed a quarter and a penny 50 times each and recorded the results.

QUARTER		PENNY	
Heads	Tails	Heads	Tails
20	30	35	15

11. How many heads can he expect if he tosses the quarter 100 times?

    A 30 (B) 40 C 60 D 80

12. How many tails can he expect if he tosses the penny 80 times?

    F 56 G 45 (H) 24 J 12

13. How many heads can he expect if he tosses each coin 20 times?

    (A) 22 B 14 C 11 D 8

For 14–16, use the following situation.

A box was filled with marbles of 3 colors. Jan took 20 marbles from the box and recorded the number of each color.

BLACK	BLUE	RED
2	5	13

14. How many black marbles can she expect if she takes 30 marbles from the box?

    F 1 (G) 3 H 5 J 6

15. How many blue marbles can she expect if she takes 44 marbles from the box?

    A 38 C 12
    B 20 (D) 11

16. How many red marbles can she expect if she takes 40 marbles from the box?

    F 10 G 16 (H) 26 J 39

For 17–20, use the following situation. Decide whether there is *too much, too little*, or the *right amount* of information to answer each question. Solve, if possible.

A spinner has 10 equal sections. There are 3 blue sections and 2 yellow sections. One yellow section is between 2 red sections.

17. What is the probability that the spinner will land on blue or yellow?

    A too much; $\frac{3}{10}$ (C) too much; $\frac{1}{2}$
    B right amount; $\frac{2}{5}$ D too little

18. What is the probability that the spinner will land on red?

    F too much; $\frac{1}{5}$
    G right amount; $\frac{1}{5}$
    H right amount; $\frac{2}{5}$
    (J) too little

19. What is the probability that the spinner will land on yellow?

    A too much; $\frac{2}{5}$ C right amount; $\frac{3}{5}$
    (B) too much; $\frac{1}{5}$ D too little

20. What is the probability that the spinner will land on blue?

    (F) too much; $\frac{3}{10}$
    G right amount; $\frac{3}{5}$
    H too much; $\frac{3}{5}$
    J too little

Stop

Write the correct answer.

For 1–4, use the following situation.

A spinner with 12 equal sections has 2 red sections, 2 yellow sections, 3 white sections, 1 blue section, and 4 black sections.

1. Write *P*(red or black) as a fraction, a decimal, and a percent.

   $\frac{1}{2}$, 0.5, 50%

2. Write *P*(not black) as a fraction, a decimal to the nearest hundredth, and a percent.

   $\frac{2}{3}$, 0.67, 67%

3. Find *P*(white) expressed as a fraction.

   $\frac{1}{4}$

4. Find *P*(white or not white) expressed as a percent.

   100%

For 5–8, use the following situation.

The names of the first 6 months of the year are on 6 pieces of paper in a box. One piece is drawn.

5. Find *P*(begins with *J*) expressed as a fraction.

   $\frac{1}{3}$

6. Find *P*(does not begin with *M*) expressed as a fraction.

   $\frac{2}{3}$

7. Find *P*(does not contain A or E) expressed as a percent.

   0%

8. Is it likely that you will draw a piece of paper that contains the letter *R*? Explain why or why not.

   yes, the probability is $\frac{2}{3}$, which is more likely than not likely

For 9–10, use the following situation.

A spinner has the numbers 1, 2, 3, and 4 on it. With 100 spins, Juan got the following results.

Number	1	2	3	4
Number of times	10	30	40	20

9. With 50 spins, how many times can he expect to land on 2?

   15 times

10. With 300 spins, how many times can he expect to land on 3?

    120 times

Go On

For 11–13, use the results from the following experiment to make predictions.

Rita flipped a nickel and a dime 40 times each and recorded the results.

NICKEL		DIME	
Heads	Tails	Heads	Tails
15	25	24	16

11. Predict how many heads she can expect if she flips the nickel 120 times.

    45 heads

12. Predict how many tails she can expect if she flips the dime 10 times?

    4 tails

13. How many tails can she expect if she tosses both coins 80 times?

    82 tails

For 14–16, use the following situation.

A box was filled with red, blue, and orange crayons. Sara took 15 crayons from the box and recorded the number of each color.

RED	BLUE	ORANGE
5	3	7

14. How many red crayons can she expect if she takes 30 crayons from the box?

    10 red crayons

15. How many blue crayons can she expect if she takes 20 crayons from the box?

    4 blue crayons

16. If she takes out 60 crayons, how many can she expect to be orange?

    28 orange crayons

For 17–20, use the following situation. Write whether there is *too much, too little*, or the *right amount* of information to answer each question. Solve if possible, or describe what information is needed to solve it.

Eight cards are face down on a table. Two cards are blue and 3 are red. There is 1 white card between the 2 blue cards. You pick 1 card.

17. What is the probability that you will pick a blue card or a red card?

    too much; $\frac{5}{8}$

18. What is the probability that you will pick a blue card?

    too much; $\frac{1}{4}$

19. What is the probability that you will pick a white card?

    too little; need to know how many cards are white

20. What is the probability that you will pick a red card?

    too much; $\frac{3}{8}$

Stop

Name ______________________

Choose the best answer.

1. Sasha had a choice of 5 shirts and 3 pairs of slacks. How many different outfits could he have made?

   A 5 outfits Ⓒ 15 outfits
   B 8 outfits D 243 outfits

2. This weekend there are 5 different movies at the theater. How many different ways could you see a movie choosing one day (Saturday or Sunday) and one movie?

   F 2 H 7
   G 5 Ⓙ 10

3. A license plate for a bicycle has 1 letter followed by 2 digits. How many different license plates are possible?

   A 5,200 plates C 1,000 plates
   Ⓑ 2,600 plates D 260 plates

For 4–7, use this information.

In a bag of 20 marbles, 10 are red, 8 are green, and 2 are blue.

4. A marble will be selected at random. What is the probability that it will be green?

   Ⓕ $\frac{2}{5}$ G $\frac{1}{5}$ H $\frac{1}{8}$ J $\frac{1}{20}$

5. A marble is selected, its color noted, and the marble is replaced. Then a second marble is selected. What is the probability both are green?

   A $\frac{4}{5}$ B $\frac{2}{5}$ Ⓒ $\frac{4}{25}$ D $\frac{1}{25}$

6. If a red marble is chosen and not replaced, what is the probability that a second marble chosen will be blue?

   F $\frac{1}{3}$ G $\frac{1}{5}$ H $\frac{1}{10}$ Ⓙ $\frac{1}{19}$

7. A marble will be selected, its color noted, and then it will be replaced. A second marble will be chosen. What is the probability that the first one will be red and the second blue?

   Ⓐ $\frac{1}{20}$ B $\frac{1}{10}$ C $\frac{1}{5}$ D $\frac{1}{2}$

For 8–11, use this information.

In a survey, two hundred high school seniors were randomly selected and asked their choice of college major. Their responses are shown in the table below.

Math	25
Science	40
Business	70
Pre-medicine	40
Pre-law	25

8. What is the probability that a randomly selected senior will choose math?

   F $\frac{1}{25}$ G $\frac{1}{10}$ Ⓗ $\frac{1}{8}$ J $\frac{1}{4}$

9. What is the probability that a randomly selected senior will choose business?

   A $\frac{3}{5}$ Ⓑ $\frac{7}{20}$ C $\frac{1}{5}$ D $\frac{1}{70}$

10. What is the probability that a randomly selected senior will choose pre-medicine or pre-law?

    F $\frac{1}{65}$ Ⓖ $\frac{13}{40}$ H $\frac{1}{2}$ J $\frac{13}{20}$

11. What is the probability that a randomly selected senior will **not** choose math or science?

    A $\frac{1}{65}$ B $\frac{11}{35}$ C $\frac{13}{40}$ Ⓓ $\frac{27}{40}$

Go On

Name ______________________

12. At the cafeteria, Sharon has a choice of 2 sandwiches, 4 salads, and 3 desserts. How many different lunches could she purchase if she gets 1 sandwich, 1 salad and 1 dessert?

    Ⓕ 24 H 9
    G 12 J 8

13. How many outcomes are possible for tossing a nickel, a dime, and a quarter?

    Ⓐ 8 outcomes C 3 outcomes
    B 6 outcomes D 2 outcomes

For 14–16, use the spinner and cards shown below.

14. How many possible outcomes are there for spinning the pointer on the spinner and randomly choosing one card?

    F 120 outcomes H 24 outcomes
    Ⓖ 48 outcomes J 14 outcomes

15. What is the probability of spinning a C and drawing a card that has an even number?

    Ⓐ $\frac{1}{16}$ B $\frac{1}{10}$ C $\frac{1}{8}$ D $\frac{1}{2}$

16. Find the probability of spinning a letter that is a vowel and drawing a card with a multiple of 3 on it.

    F $\frac{1}{48}$ Ⓖ $\frac{1}{12}$ H $\frac{3}{8}$ J $\frac{1}{4}$

17. If the outcome of the second event does not depend on the outcome of the first event, the events are called ______.

    A random C dependent
    B samples Ⓓ independent

18. If one event has *m* possibilities and another has *n* possibilities, then there are a total of ______ ways both can occur.

    F $m - n$ H $m \div n$
    G $m + n$ Ⓙ $m \times n$

Use the tree diagram for question 19.

19. Three families each have 1 girl and 1 boy. If you randomly choose a child from each family, what is the probability of choosing all boys or all girls?

    A $\frac{1}{12}$ B $\frac{1}{8}$ Ⓒ $\frac{1}{4}$ D $\frac{1}{2}$

20. An Italian restaurant serves 8 types of pasta and 10 types of sauce. How many weeks can you order one type of pasta with one sauce from the restaurant without repeating a pasta and sauce combination?

    F 15 weeks
    G 40 weeks
    H 60 weeks
    Ⓙ 80 weeks

Stop

Name ______________________

Write the correct answer.

1. To make a sandwich, Maya has a choice of ham, turkey, or cheese on white or wheat bread. How many different kinds of sandwiches consisting of one meat and one type of bread can she make?

   6 different sandwiches

2. The sixth, seventh, and eighth grades will study Spanish, French, or Italian next year. How many different language classes are possible if only one grade is in each class?

   9 classes

3. In her journal, Alice always writes the month and the day of the week as her heading. How many different headings are possible?

   84 headings

For 4–7, use this information.

In a box of 40 coins, 10 are quarters, 5 are dimes, 20 are nickels, and 5 are pennies.

4. A coin will be selected at random. What is the probability that it will be a quarter?

   $\frac{1}{4}$

5. A coin will be selected and replaced. Then a second coin will be selected. What is the probability that both will be pennies?

   $\frac{1}{64}$

6. If a dime is chosen and not replaced, what is the probability that a second coin chosen will be a quarter?

   $\frac{10}{39}$

7. A coin will be selected at random and replaced. Then a second coin will be selected at random. What is the probability that the first coin will be a quarter and the second will be a dime?

   $\frac{1}{32}$

For 8–11, use the following information.

In a survey, three hundred sixth graders were randomly selected and asked about their favorite type of movie. Their responses are shown in the chart below.

Action	75
Cartoon	30
Romance	50
Science Fiction	90
Comedy	55

8. What is the probability that a randomly selected sixth grader will choose science fiction movies?

   $\frac{3}{10}$

9. What is the probability that a randomly selected sixth grader will choose action movies?

   $\frac{1}{4}$

10. What is the probability that a randomly selected sixth grader will choose cartoons or romance movies?

    $\frac{4}{15}$

Go On

Name ______________________

11. What is the probability that a randomly selected sixth grader will **not** choose comedies or action movies?

    $\frac{17}{30}$

12. Jason has 3 T-shirts, 4 pairs of pants, and 3 pairs of socks to choose from. How many different outfits consisting of 1 shirt, 1 pair of pants, and 1 pair of socks are possible?

    36 outfits

13. How many different outcomes are possible when you toss a coin and roll a number cube labeled 1–6?

    12 outcomes

For 14–16, use the two spinners shown below.

14. How many possible outcomes are there for spinning both pointers once?

    32 outcomes

15. What is the probability of spinning green and an odd number?

    $\frac{1}{16}$

16. What is the probability of spinning red or yellow and a number divisible by 5?

    $\frac{1}{4}$

17. If the outcome of the second event depends on the outcome of the first event, what are the events called?

    dependent events

18. If there are *a* choices for one category and *b* choices for another, what expression can be used to represent the total number of choices?

    $a \times b$

For 19, use the tree diagram.

19. A bike shop has a sale on 24-inch and 26-inch mountain and racing bikes in either silver or black. Jack needs a 26-inch bike. He does not care what color he gets, but he needs a mountain bike. What is the probability Jack can get the bike he wants?

    $\frac{1}{4}$

20. At a buffet there are 12 different salads and 6 different soups to choose from. How many different combinations of soup and salad are possible?

    72 combinations

Stop

Name ______________________

Choose the best answer.

1. An item costs \$24.50. The sales tax rate is 6%. What is the sales tax?

A \$0.75 C \$2.45
Ⓑ \$1.47 D \$4.70

2. Find the unit rate.

208 miles on 8 gallons of gas

F 104 mi per gal Ⓗ 26 mi per gal
G 54 mi per gal J 16 mi per gal

3. The sides of a rectangle are 18 in. wide and 24 in. long. Which of the following are side lengths for a similar rectangle?

Ⓐ 9 in. wide, 12 in. long
B 9 in. wide, 18 in. long
C 32 in. wide, 36 in. long
D 36 in. wide, 36 in. long

4. In a bag of 15 tiles, 9 are blue, 3 are green, and 3 are red. A tile is selected at random. What is the probability that it is red?

Ⓕ 20% H 33%
G 30% J 66%

5. In a class election, 3 people are running for president, 2 for vice president, and 4 for treasurer. How many different choices consisting of one president, one vice-president, and one treasurer are possible?

Ⓐ 24 C 9
B 12 D 3

6. What is $\frac{3}{8}$ expressed as a percent?

F 3.8% Ⓗ 37.5%
G 8% J 40%

7. If the outcome of the second event depends on the outcome of the first event, the events are called __?__.

A samples C independent
B random Ⓓ dependent

8. Malcolm tossed a penny 40 times. He tossed 30 heads. Based on these data, how many heads can he expect in 60 tosses?

F 60 heads H 40 heads
Ⓖ 45 heads J 35 heads

9. When you flip four different coins, how many outcomes are possible?

A 4 outcomes C 12 outcomes
B 8 outcomes Ⓓ 16 outcomes

10. Mandy puts \$800 in a savings account with a yearly simple interest rate of 2.5%. How much will be in her account after 5 years?

F \$1,800 Ⓗ \$900
G \$1,100 J \$100

11. The scale for a map is 1 in. = 80 mi. What is the actual distance between two towns that are $2\frac{1}{4}$ in. apart on the map?

A 200 mi C 160 mi
Ⓑ 180 mi D 140 mi

12. The names of the first five months of the year are on slips of paper in a bowl. One slip is randomly drawn. Find *P*(day does not begin with *M*).

F $\frac{1}{5}$ Ⓗ $\frac{3}{5}$
G $\frac{2}{5}$ J $\frac{4}{5}$

Go On

Name ______________________

For 13–15, use the following information.

Five hundred members of a recreation center were asked which addition to the center they would most prefer. Here are the results.

Swimming pool	140
Jogging track	80
Tennis Court	50
Basketball Court	230

13. What is the probability that a randomly selected member will choose the tennis court?

A $\frac{1}{50}$ B $\frac{1}{20}$ Ⓒ $\frac{1}{10}$ D $\frac{5}{10}$

14. What is the probability that a randomly selected member will choose the swimming pool or the jogging track?

Ⓕ $\frac{11}{25}$ G $\frac{11}{50}$ H $\frac{1}{22}$ J $\frac{1}{220}$

15. Suppose an additional 100 members are surveyed. What is a reasonable prediction of the number of those members who will choose the basketball court?

A 23 B 38 Ⓒ 46 D 50

16. Leo needs 1 cup of raisins to make 18 muffins. How many cups of raisins does he need to make 45 muffins?

F $\frac{2}{5}$ c Ⓗ $2\frac{1}{2}$ c
G $2\frac{2}{5}$ c J $2\frac{2}{3}$ c

17. What is the total cost of a \$60 jacket on sale for 25% off with 8% sales tax added on?

A \$45.00 C \$49.80
Ⓑ \$48.60 D \$64.80

For 18–20, use the circle graph. The graph shows the amount of money raised at a charity fair.

18. Sales of books at the charity fair made up what percent of the money raised?

Ⓕ 30% H 20%
G 25% J 10%

19. What percent of the money raised came from the sale of food and beverages?

A 10% B 20% C 25% Ⓓ 30%

20. Suppose one half of all the food sales were baked goods. What percent of the money raised came from the sale of baked goods?

F 5% Ⓖ 10% H 15% J 20%

21. If Mitch types 280 words in 5 min, how many words would you expect him to type in 3 min?

A 56 words C 136 words
B 84 words Ⓓ 168 words

22. Mangoes are on sale at 5 for \$2.00. Find the cost of 8 mangoes.

F \$2.80 H \$3.50
Ⓖ \$3.20 J \$3.80

Go On

Name ______________________

23. The triangles are similar. Find the unknown length.

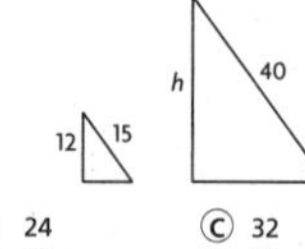

A 24 Ⓒ 32
B 30 D 36

For 24–25, use the following information.

A bag is filled with cards with 4 different letters. Wanda randomly selected 20 cards from the bag and recorded the number of each letter.

A	B	C	D
8	2	4	6

24. Based on her results how many cards with the letter A can Wanda expect in her next 30 selections?

F 4 cards Ⓗ 12 cards
G 10 cards J 15 cards

25. Based on her results how many cards with the letter C can Wanda expect in her next 45 selections?

A 8 cards C 10 cards
Ⓑ 9 cards D 12 cards

26. A scale drawing for a deck uses a scale of 2 in. = 5 ft. The length of the deck on the drawing is 8 in. How long is the actual deck?

F 40 ft Ⓗ 20 ft
G 25 ft J 10 ft

27. A dressmaker has a choice of 3 fabrics, 5 colors, and 2 patterns. How many different dresses made with 1 fabric, one color, and 1 pattern can she make?

Ⓐ 30 dresses C 15 dresses
B 25 dresses D 10 dresses

For 28–29, use the following information. Write whether there is too much, too little, or the right amount of information to solve the problem. Solve, if possible.

A spinner has 8 equal sections. There are 3 yellow sections, one blue section, and 2 green sections. The blue section is between the green sections.

28. What is the probability that the spinner will land on purple or blue?

F too much; $\frac{1}{4}$

G right amount; $\frac{1}{4}$

H right amount; $\frac{1}{8}$

Ⓙ too little

29. What is the probability that the spinner will **not** land on yellow?

Ⓐ too much; $\frac{5}{8}$

B right amount; $\frac{1}{2}$

C too much; $\frac{3}{8}$

D too little

30. Diego travels 1,500 miles in 6 days. If he continues at this rate, how far will he travel in 9 days?

F 1,750 miles H 2,100 miles
G 2,000 miles Ⓙ 2,250 miles

Go On

Name ______________________

For 31–32, use the following information.

A spinner with 5 equal sections has 1 blue section, 2 red sections, and 2 yellow sections.

31. Express *P*(red or yellow) as a fraction, a decimal, and a percent.

A $\frac{4}{10}$, 0.4, 40% C $\frac{3}{5}$, 0.6, 60%
B $\frac{1}{2}$, 0.5, 50% Ⓓ $\frac{4}{5}$, 0.8, 80%

32. Find *P*(not yellow).

F $\frac{1}{5}$ Ⓗ $\frac{3}{5}$
G $\frac{2}{5}$ J 1

33. To make 4 dozen tortillas, 3 cups of water are used. How many cups of water are needed to make 72 tortillas?

Ⓐ $4\frac{1}{2}$ cups C 9 cups
B 6 cups D 54 cups

34. What is 38% of 60?

F 40.8 H 24.8
G 32.8 Ⓙ 22.8

35. Jason wants to leave a 15% tip on a restaurant bill of \$28. What is a reasonable estimate for a 15% tip?

A \$2.80 C \$3.50
B \$3.00 Ⓓ \$4.50

36. There are 12 boys and 20 girls in the choir. What is the ratio of boys to girls written as a percent?

Ⓕ 60% H 12%
G 40% J 8%

37. Write 84% both as a decimal and as a fraction in simplest form.

A 0.84; $\frac{84}{100}$ Ⓒ 0.84; $\frac{21}{25}$
B 0.84; $\frac{48}{50}$ D 84; $\frac{84}{100}$

38. What is 210% of 400?

F 880 H 820
Ⓖ 840 J 800

For 39–40, use the spinners shown below.

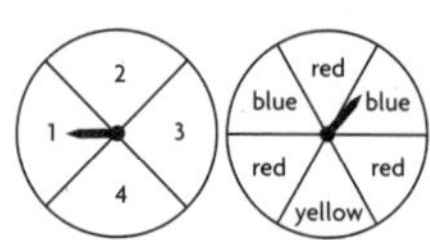

39. What is the probability of the pointers landing on 3 and blue?

A $\frac{1}{2}$ Ⓒ $\frac{1}{12}$
B $\frac{1}{5}$ D $\frac{1}{24}$

40. What is the probability of the pointers landing on an even number and **not** red?

F $\frac{1}{2}$ H $\frac{1}{5}$
Ⓖ $\frac{1}{4}$ J $\frac{1}{8}$

Stop

Name ______

Write the correct answer.

1. An item costs $26.50. The sales tax rate is 8%. What is the sales tax?

$2.12

2. Find the unit rate.

392 miles on 14 gallons of gas

28 miles per gallon

3. A rectangle measures 10 in. wide and 24 in. long. A similar rectangle has a width of 17.5 in. What is its length?

42 in.

4. In a group of 25 students, 9 are 7 years old, 11 are 8 years old, and 5 are 9 years old. A student is selected at random. What is the probability that he or she is 8 years old?

$\frac{11}{25}$ or 44%

5. For a class play, 4 students are auditioning for the lead actor, 5 for the lead actress, and 3 for the director. How many different choices of one actor, one actress, and one director are possible?

60

6. Write $\frac{5}{8}$ as a percent.

62.5%

7. If the outcome of the second event does not depend on the outcome of the first event, the events are called __?__.

independent

8. Maggie tossed a thumbtack 50 times and the point landed up 30 times. Based on these data, how many times can she expect the thumbtack to land with the point up in 75 tosses?

45 times

9. When you roll 3 number cubes, each labeled 1 to 6, how many outcomes are possible?

216 outcomes

10. Maureen puts $500 in a savings account with a yearly simple interest rate of 3.5%. How much will be in her account after 4 years?

$570

11. The scale for a map is 1 in. = 150 mi. What is the actual distance between two towns that are $3\frac{1}{2}$ in. apart on the map?

525 miles

12. The names of the days of the week are on slips of paper in a bowl. One slip is randomly drawn. Find *P*(day begins with the letter *T*).

$\frac{2}{7}$

Go On

Name ______

For 13–15, use the following information.

Six hundred members of a community organization were asked which fund-raiser they would prefer. Here are the results.

rummage sale	180
bake sale	105
magazine drive	130
walk-a-thon	185

13. What is the probability that a randomly selected member will choose the bake sale?

$\frac{105}{600}$, or $\frac{7}{40}$

14. What is the probability that a randomly selected member will choose the rummage sale or the walk-a-thon?

$\frac{365}{600}$, or $\frac{73}{120}$

15. Suppose an additional 100 members are surveyed. What is a reasonable prediction of the number of those members who will prefer a magazine drive?

about 22

16. Louise needs 1 cup of flour to make 24 pancakes. How many cups of flour does she need to make 40 pancakes?

$1\frac{2}{3}$ cup

17. What is the total cost of a $45 skirt on sale for 20% off with 6% sales tax added on?

$38.16

For 18–20, use the circle graph. The graph shows the amount of money spent by a family.

Food & Utilities $600
House $800
Misc $600
Car $400

18. House payment expenses made up what percent of the money spent?

$33\frac{1}{3}$%

19. What percent of the money spent is for food and utilities, and miscellaneous?

50%

20. Suppose the family increases its car payment by $100. What percent of expenditures would the car payment be?

20%

21. If Miguel can go 12 blocks in 8 min on his in-line skates, how many blocks would you expect him to be able to go in 6 min?

9 blocks

22. Kiwi fruit are on sale at 4 for $0.88. Find the cost of 7 kiwi fruit.

$1.54

Go On

Name ______

23. The triangles are similar. Find the unknown length.

7, 25; h, 40

11.2

For 24–25, use the following information.

A bag is filled with marbles of 4 different colors. Willie randomly selected 20 marbles from the bag and recorded the color of each marble.

BLUE	RED	GREEN	YELLOW
7	4	3	6

24. Based on his results, how many yellow marbles can Willie expect in his next 30 selections?

9 yellow marbles

25. Based on his results, how many red marbles can Willie expect in his next 45 selections?

9 red marbles

26. A scale drawing for a sailboat uses a scale of 2 in. = 15 ft. The length of the sailboat on the drawing is 11 in. How long is the actual sailboat?

82.5 feet

27. A hair stylist has a choice of 3 hair lengths, 5 hair colors, and 2 hair types. How many different styles based on 1 length, 1 color, and 1 type can she make?

30 styles

For 28–29, use the following information. Write whether there is *too much*, *too little*, or the *right amount* of information to solve the problem. Solve, if possible.

A spinner has 12 equal sections. There are 4 blue sections, 5 yellow sections, 2 green sections and 1 red section. The red section is between the two green sections.

28. What is the probability that the spinner will land on purple or blue?

too much; $\frac{1}{3}$

29. What is the probability that the spinner will **not** land on blue?

too much; $\frac{2}{3}$

30. Dana travels 1,200 miles in 5 days. If she continues at this rate, how far will she travel in 8 days?

1,920 miles

Go On

Name ______

For 31–32, use the following information.

A six-sided cube with 1 red side, 2 green sides, and 3 yellow sides is tossed, and the color showing is noted.

31. Express P(red or yellow) as a fraction.

$\frac{4}{6}$ or $\frac{2}{3}$

32. Find P(not yellow).

$\frac{3}{6}$ or $\frac{1}{2}$

33. To make 5 dozen donuts, 4 cups of milk are used. How many cups of milk are needed to make 96 donuts?

6.4 cups or $6\frac{2}{5}$ cups

34. What is 46% of 80?

36.8

35. Joy wants to leave a 15% tip on a restaurant bill of $42.25. What is a reasonable estimate for a 15% tip?

$6.00

36. There are 8 motorcycles and 32 cars in the parking lot. What is the ratio of motorcycles to cars written as a percent?

25%

37. Write 72% both as a decimal and as a fraction in simplest form.

0.72, $\frac{18}{25}$

38. What is 305% of 200?

610

For 39–40, use the spinners shown below.

Spinner 1: 5, 1, 2, 3, 4
Spinner 2: Green, Red, Blue, Red, Yellow, Red, Blue, Red

39. What is the probability of the pointers landing on 4 and red?

$\frac{1}{10}$

40. What is the probability the pointers landing on an odd number and a color that is **not** blue?

$\frac{9}{20}$

Stop

Name ____________________

CHAPTER 24 TEST • PAGE 1

Choose the best answer.

For 1–7, use a proportion to convert to the given unit.

1. 8 qt = ■ gal

A 1 gal C 4 gal
(B) 2 gal D 32 gal

2. 30 cm = ■ mm

F 30,000 mm (H) 300 mm
G 3,000 mm J 3 mm

3. 5 lb = ■ oz

A 160 oz C 40 oz
(B) 80 oz D 20 oz

4. 400 m = ■ km

F 0.04 km H 4 km
(G) 0.4 km J 40 km

5. 7 L = ■ mL

(A) 7,000 mL C 0.7 mL
B 70 mL D 0.007 mL

6. 27,000 mg = ■ g

F 2,700 g (H) 27 g
G 270 g J 2.7 g

7. 108 in. = ■ yd

A 38 yd C 9 yd
B 36 yd (D) 3 yd

8. A balance shows a mass of 38 kg. What is this amount in grams?

F 380 g (H) 38,000 g
G 3,800 g J 380,000 g

For 9–12, use a proportion to convert to the given unit.

9. 23 in. ≈ ■ cm (1 in. ≈ 2.54 cm)

A 0.58 cm C 9.06 cm
B 5.84 cm (D) 58.42 cm

10. 35 L ≈ ■ gal (1 gal ≈ 3.79 L)

F 1,326.5 gal H 92.34 gal
G 132.65 gal (J) 9.23 gal

11. 50 mi ≈ ■ km (1 mi ≈ 1.61 km)

A 3.11 km (C) 80.5 km
B 31.06 km D 805 km

12. 14 lb ≈ ■ kg (1 lb ≈ 0.45 kg)

F 3.11 kg H 31.1 kg
(G) 6.3 kg J 63 kg

13. Which is an appropriate unit of measure for a person's weight?

A foot (C) pound
B ounce D ton

Go On

Form A • Multiple Choice   Assessment Guide AG 157

Name ____________________

CHAPTER 24 TEST • PAGE 2

For 14–15, measure the line segment as described.

14. to the nearest quarter inch

F 1 in. H $1\frac{1}{2}$ in.
G $1\frac{1}{4}$ in. (J) $1\frac{3}{4}$ in.

15. to the nearest centimeter

A 2 cm C 4 cm
(B) 3 cm D 5 cm

For 16–19, choose the measurement which is most precise.

16. (F) 7 pt. G 3 qt

17. (A) 8,020 lb B 4 T

18. F 2 kg (G) 2,200 g

19. A $5\frac{1}{2}$ ft (B) $5\frac{1}{4}$ ft

20. Which is an appropriate unit of measure for telling how much water a cat drinks in a day?

F kiloliter H centimeter
G millimeter (J) milliliter

21. A scientist is measuring the amount of liquid in a bottle. Which unit will result in the most precise measurement?

(A) milliliter C kiloliter
B liter D centiliter

For 22–25, answer each question. Tell whether an estimate or an exact answer is needed.

22. Bismarck, North Dakota, had 46 inches of snow in January, 58 inches in February, and 33 inches in March. Did this total exceed the previous year's record of 12 feet?

F no; exact H yes; exact
G yes; estimate (J) no; estimate

23. Rita has 250 ft of fencing to enclose a rectangular garden measuring 42 ft by 58 ft. Does she have enough fencing?

A no; exact C yes; exact
B no; estimate (D) yes; estimate

24. Roland has $25. He buys an oil filter for $4.75, spark plugs for $9.60, and 5 qt of oil for $6.95. How much money does he have left?

F $3.70; estimate H $10.65; estimate
(G) $3.70; exact J $8.45; exact

25. Four students each need 11 in. of string for a project. If they have 4 ft of string, do they have enough?

(A) yes; estimate C yes; exact
B no; estimate D no; exact

Stop

AG 158 Assessment Guide   Form A • Multiple Choice

Name ____________________

CHAPTER 24 TEST • PAGE 1

Write the correct answer.

For 1–7, use a proportion to convert to the given unit.

1. 3 gal = ■ qt

12

2. 1,500 m = ■ km

1.5

3. ■ lb = 176 oz

11

4. 780 mm = ■ cm

78

5. ■ mL = 0.5 L

500

6. 14 g = ■ mg

14,000

7. 12 ft = ■ in.

144

8. The height of a room from floor to ceiling is 15 ft. What is the height in yards?

5 yd

For 9–12, use a proportion to convert to the given unit. Round to the nearest tenth.

9. 15 in. ≈ ■ cm (1 in. ≈ 2.54 cm)

38.1

10. 20 L ≈ ■ gal (1 gal ≈ 3.79 L)

5.3

11. 86 km ≈ ■ mi (1 mi ≈ 1.61 km)

53.4

12. 45 lb ≈ ■ kg (1 lb ≈ 0.45 kg)

20.3

13. Which is an appropriate unit of measure for the capacity of a bathtub?

Possible answers: gallons, liters

Go On

Form B • Free Response   Assessment Guide AG 159

Name ____________________

CHAPTER 24 TEST • PAGE 2

For 14–15, measure the line segment to the given length.

14. nearest half inch; nearest quarter inch

1 in.; $1\frac{1}{4}$ in.

15. nearest centimeter; nearest millimeter

3 cm; 32 mm

For 16–20, name an appropriate unit of measure for each item.

16. weight of your dog

pounds or kilograms

17. amount a can of soup holds

ounces or milliliters

18. length of a car

feet or meters

19. weight of a paper clip

ounces or grams

20. distance from one city to another

miles or kilometers

21. Which unit of measurement is more precise, an inch or a foot? Why?

An inch; the smaller the unit of measure, the more precise it is.

For 22–25, answer each question. Tell whether an estimate or an exact answer is needed.

22. Mr. Wells has 6 pints of grape juice, 8 pints of apple juice, and 2 pints of orange juice. He will mix the juices together to make punch. Does he have enough juice to make 10 quarts of punch?

no; estimate

23. The bedroom is a square room with an area of 144 sq ft. Will a rug that is 11 ft long by 10 ft wide fit in the room?

yes; estimate

24. Jenna has 15 ft of wood for framing. She makes a frame that is 24 in. wide and 36 in. long. How much wood will she have left?

5 ft; exact

25. Anna has $5.00. She needs a gallon of milk. The store has only quarts of milk for $1.50 per quart. Does she have enough money to buy a gallon of milk?

no; estimate

Stop

AG 160 Assessment Guide   Form B • Free Response

Name ______________________

Choose the best answer.

For 1–3, find the perimeter of the polygon.

1. 6 in. 2 in.

A 20 in. C 12 in.
(B) 16 in. D 8 in.

2. 10 cm 14 cm 10 cm

F 10 cm H 24 cm
G 20 cm (J) 34 cm

3. w w w w w w

(A) 6*w* C 4*w*
B 5*w* D 2*w*

4. Find the circumference of the circle. (Use 3.14 for the value of π.)

8 cm

F 50.24 cm
(G) 25.12 cm
H 12.56 cm
J 8 cm

5. Find the circumference of the circle. (Use 3.14 for the value of π.)

5 m

A 8.14 m
B 15.7 m
(C) 31.4 m
D 78.5 m

6. The perimeter is given. Find the unknown length.

2 in. 5 in. P = 18 in. 3 in. 2 in. *x* in.

F 18 in. H 7 in.
G 12 in. (J) 6 in.

7. The perimeter is 20 mm. Find the unknown length.

6 mm 4 mm 1 mm *x* mm

A 5 mm C 11 mm
(B) 9 mm D 20 mm

8. Find the circumference of the circle. (Use 3.14 for the value of π.)

7 ft

F 10.99 ft H 43.96 ft
(G) 21.98 ft J 49 ft

9. Find the circumference of the circle. (Use 3.14 for the value of π.)

12 in.

A 18.84 in. (C) 75.36 in.
B 37.68 in. D 452.16 in.

Go On

Name ______________________

10. A four-sided polygon has two sides of length 6 cm and two sides of length 8 cm. What is the perimeter of the polygon?

(F) 28 cm H 20 cm
G 22 cm J 14 cm

11. A baseball diamond is a square with a perimeter of 360 ft. What is the length of one side?

A 80 ft C 120 ft
(B) 90 ft D 180 ft

12. A kite is made with two isosceles triangles. One of the triangles has side lengths 2 ft, 2 ft, and $2\frac{1}{2}$ ft. The other triangle has side lengths 3 ft, 3 ft, and $2\frac{1}{2}$ ft. What is the perimeter of the kite?

(F) 10 ft H 15 ft
G $12\frac{1}{2}$ ft J 18 ft

13. A circular window has a radius of 3 ft. How much molding is needed to trim the edge of it? (Use 3.14 for the value of π.)

A 4.71 ft (C) 18.84 ft
B 9.42 ft D 37.68 ft

14. A swimming pool has a diameter of 30 ft. What is its circumference? (Use 3.14 for the value of π.)

F 23.55 ft (H) 94.20 ft
G 47.10 ft J 1, 000 ft

15. The perimeter of a rectangle is 54 yd. The length of the rectangle is twice the width. What is the width of the rectangle?

A 36 yd C 18 yd
B 27 yd (D) 9 yd

16. The diameter of a circle is $4\frac{2}{3}$ ft. What is the circumference? (Use $\frac{22}{7}$ for the value of π.)

(F) $14\frac{2}{3}$ ft H $18\frac{6}{7}$ ft
G $17\frac{6}{7}$ ft J 44 ft

17. The radius of a circle is $5\frac{1}{4}$ in. What is the circumference? (Use $\frac{22}{7}$ for the value of π.)

A 462 in. C 66 in.
B 231 in. (D) 33 in.

18. The shortest side of an isosceles triangle with perimeter 240 m is 60 m. What are the other two sides?

F 60 m (H) 90 m
G 80 m J 180 m

19. Two sides of a rectangle have lengths of 5 m and 3 m. What is the perimeter of the rectangle?

(A) 16 m C 8 m
B 15 m D 2 m

20. A picture is 21 in. by 36 in. It is in a frame that is 4 in. wide. What is the outside perimeter of the frame?

F 114 in. H 136 in.
G 130 in. (J) 146 in.

Stop

Name ______________________

Write the correct answer.

For 1–3, find the perimeter of the polygon.

1. 6 cm 12 cm

36 cm

2. 32 in. 18 in. 18 in.

68 in.

3. *a* *a* *a* *a* *a*

5*a* or *a* + *a* + *a* + *a* + *a*

4. Find the circumference of the circle. (Use 3.14 for the value of π.)

10 m

31.4 m

5. Find the circumference of the circle. (Use 3.14 for the value of π.)

7 in.

43.96 in.

6. The perimeter of the figure is 46 cm. Find the unknown length.

10 cm 3 cm *x* 12 cm 2 cm 8 cm 4 cm

7 cm

7. The perimeter of the figure is 29 in. Find the unknown length.

8 in. 2 in. 4 in. 5 in. 3 in. 1 in. *x*

6 in.

8. Find the circumference of the circle. (Use 3.14 for the value of π.)

9 m

28.26 m

9. Find the circumference of the circle. (Use 3.14 for the value of π.)

15 cm

94.2 cm

10. A six-sided polygon has four sides of length 4 in. and two sides of length 10 in. What is the perimeter of the polygon?

36 in.

Go On

Name ______________________

11. A square classroom has a perimeter of 144 ft. How long is one of the sides of the classroom?

36 ft

12. Two equilateral triangular puzzle pieces are put together to make a diamond. Each triangle has a side with a length of 4 cm. What is the perimeter of the diamond?

16 cm

13. A circular garden has a radius of 4 m. How much fencing is needed to enclose it? (Use 3.14 for the value of π.)

25.12 m

14. The top of a juice can has a diameter of 6 in. What is the circumference of the can? (Use 3.14 for the value of π.)

18.84 in.

15. Jared ran twice around a rectangular field. He ran a total of 660 ft. The length of the longer side of the field is 90 ft. What is the length of the shorter side?

75 ft

16. The diameter of a circle is $5\frac{1}{4}$ in. What is the circumference? (Use $\frac{22}{7}$ for the value of π.)

$16\frac{1}{2}$ in.

17. The radius of a circle is $2\frac{11}{12}$ ft. What is the circumference? (Use $\frac{22}{7}$ for the value of π.)

$18\frac{1}{3}$ ft

18. The longest side of an isosceles triangle is 20 in. The perimeter is 52 in. What are the lengths of the other two sides of the triangle?

16 in. each

19. A rectangular garden measures 32 ft by 15 ft. What is the least amount of fencing you need to enclose the garden?

94 ft

20. A rectangular floor tile is 6 in. by 9 in. The next size tile is 2 in. longer and wider. What is the perimeter of the next size tile?

38 in.

Stop

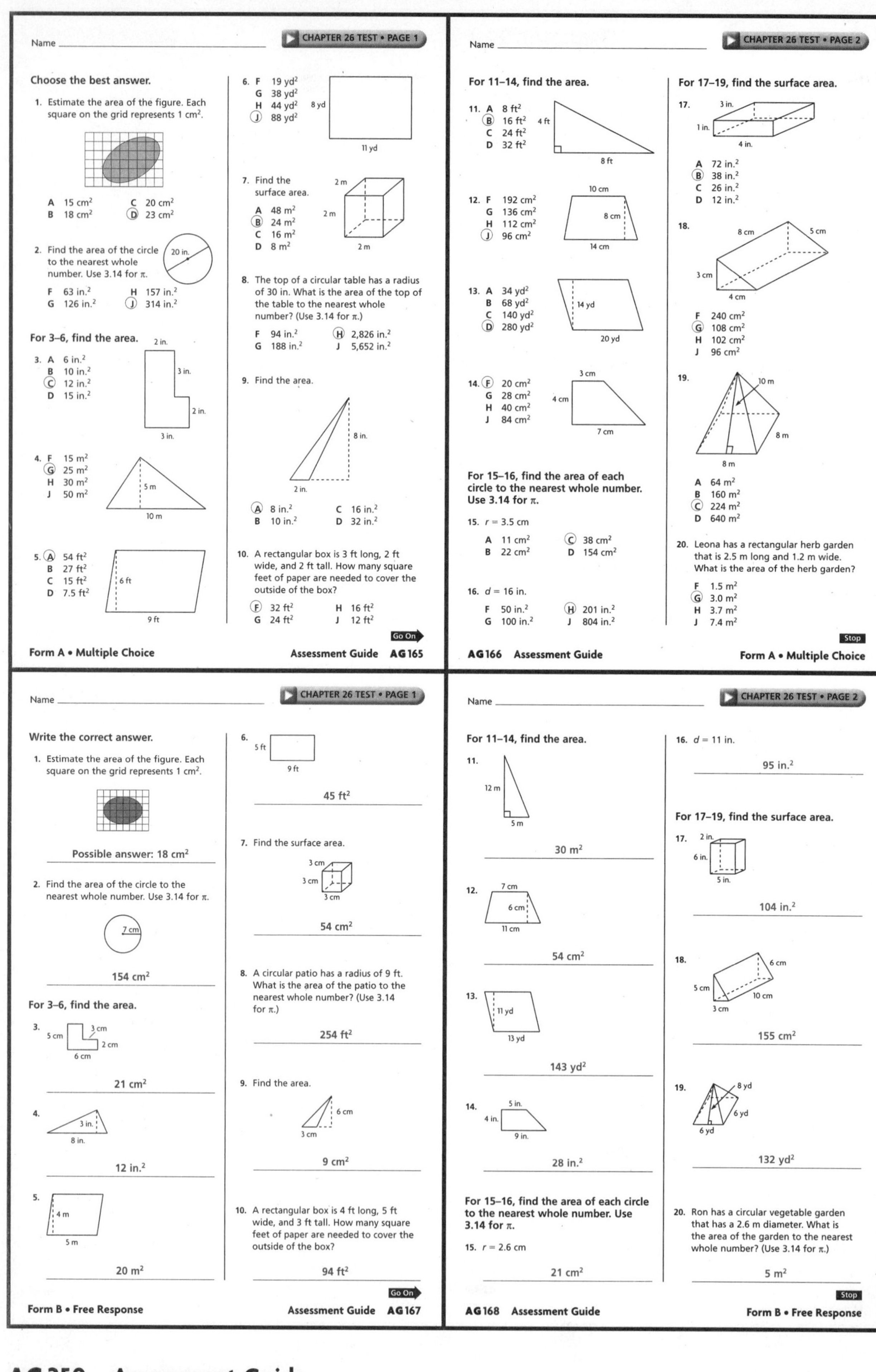

Name ______________________ CHAPTER 26 TEST • PAGE 1

Choose the best answer.

1. Estimate the area of the figure. Each square on the grid represents 1 cm^2.

A 15 cm^2 B 18 cm^2 C 20 cm^2 (D) 23 cm^2

2. Find the area of the circle to the nearest whole number. Use 3.14 for π. (20 in.)

F 63 $in.^2$ G 126 $in.^2$ H 157 $in.^2$ (J) 314 $in.^2$

For 3–6, find the area.

3. (2 in., 3 in., 2 in., 3 in.) A 6 $in.^2$ B 10 $in.^2$ (C) 12 $in.^2$ D 15 $in.^2$

4. (5 m, 10 m) F 15 m^2 (G) 25 m^2 H 30 m^2 J 50 m^2

5. (6 ft, 9 ft) (A) 54 ft^2 B 27 ft^2 C 15 ft^2 D 7.5 ft^2

6. (8 yd, 11 yd) F 19 yd^2 G 38 yd^2 H 44 yd^2 (J) 88 yd^2

7. Find the surface area. (2 m, 2 m, 2 m) A 48 m^2 (B) 24 m^2 C 16 m^2 D 8 m^2

8. The top of a circular table has a radius of 30 in. What is the area of the top of the table to the nearest whole number? (Use 3.14 for π.)

F 94 $in.^2$ G 188 $in.^2$ (H) 2,826 $in.^2$ J 5,652 $in.^2$

9. Find the area. (8 in., 2 in.)

(A) 8 $in.^2$ B 10 $in.^2$ C 16 $in.^2$ D 32 $in.^2$

10. A rectangular box is 3 ft long, 2 ft wide, and 2 ft tall. How many square feet of paper are needed to cover the outside of the box?

(F) 32 ft^2 G 24 ft^2 H 16 ft^2 J 12 ft^2

Go On

Form A • Multiple Choice — Assessment Guide AG 165

Name ______________________ CHAPTER 26 TEST • PAGE 2

For 11–14, find the area.

11. (4 ft, 8 ft) A 8 ft^2 (B) 16 ft^2 C 24 ft^2 D 32 ft^2

12. (10 cm, 8 cm, 14 cm) F 192 cm^2 G 136 cm^2 H 112 cm^2 (J) 96 cm^2

13. (14 yd, 20 yd) A 34 yd^2 B 68 yd^2 C 140 yd^2 (D) 280 yd^2

14. (3 cm, 4 cm, 7 cm) (F) 20 cm^2 G 28 cm^2 H 40 cm^2 J 84 cm^2

For 15–16, find the area of each circle to the nearest whole number. Use 3.14 for π.

15. r = 3.5 cm

A 11 cm^2 B 22 cm^2 (C) 38 cm^2 D 154 cm^2

16. d = 16 in.

F 50 $in.^2$ G 100 $in.^2$ (H) 201 $in.^2$ J 804 $in.^2$

For 17–19, find the surface area.

17. (3 in., 1 in., 4 in.) A 72 $in.^2$ (B) 38 $in.^2$ C 26 $in.^2$ D 12 $in.^2$

18. (8 cm, 5 cm, 3 cm, 4 cm) F 240 cm^2 (G) 108 cm^2 H 102 cm^2 J 96 cm^2

19. (10 m, 8 m, 8 m) A 64 m^2 B 160 m^2 (C) 224 m^2 D 640 m^2

20. Leona has a rectangular herb garden that is 2.5 m long and 1.2 m wide. What is the area of the herb garden?

F 1.5 m^2 (G) 3.0 m^2 H 3.7 m^2 J 7.4 m^2

Stop

AG 166 Assessment Guide — Form A • Multiple Choice

Name ______________________ CHAPTER 26 TEST • PAGE 1

Write the correct answer.

1. Estimate the area of the figure. Each square on the grid represents 1 cm^2.

Possible answer: 18 cm^2

2. Find the area of the circle to the nearest whole number. Use 3.14 for π. (7 cm)

154 cm^2

For 3–6, find the area.

3. (5 cm, 3 cm, 2 cm, 6 cm) 21 cm^2

4. (3 in., 8 in.) 12 $in.^2$

5. (4 m, 5 m) 20 m^2

6. (5 ft, 9 ft) 45 ft^2

7. Find the surface area. (3 cm, 3 cm, 3 cm) 54 cm^2

8. A circular patio has a radius of 9 ft. What is the area of the patio to the nearest whole number? (Use 3.14 for π.)

254 ft^2

9. Find the area. (6 cm, 3 cm) 9 cm^2

10. A rectangular box is 4 ft long, 5 ft wide, and 3 ft tall. How many square feet of paper are needed to cover the outside of the box?

94 ft^2

Go On

Form B • Free Response — Assessment Guide AG 167

Name ______________________ CHAPTER 26 TEST • PAGE 2

For 11–14, find the area.

11. (12 m, 5 m) 30 m^2

12. (7 cm, 6 cm, 11 cm) 54 cm^2

13. (11 yd, 13 yd) 143 yd^2

14. (5 in., 4 in., 9 in.) 28 $in.^2$

For 15–16, find the area of each circle to the nearest whole number. Use 3.14 for π.

15. r = 2.6 cm

21 cm^2

16. d = 11 in.

95 $in.^2$

For 17–19, find the surface area.

17. (2 in., 6 in., 5 in.) 104 $in.^2$

18. (6 cm, 5 cm, 10 cm, 3 cm) 155 cm^2

19. (8 yd, 6 yd, 6 yd) 132 yd^2

20. Ron has a circular vegetable garden that has a 2.6 m diameter. What is the area of the garden to the nearest whole number? (Use 3.14 for π.)

5 m^2

Stop

AG 168 Assessment Guide — Form B • Free Response

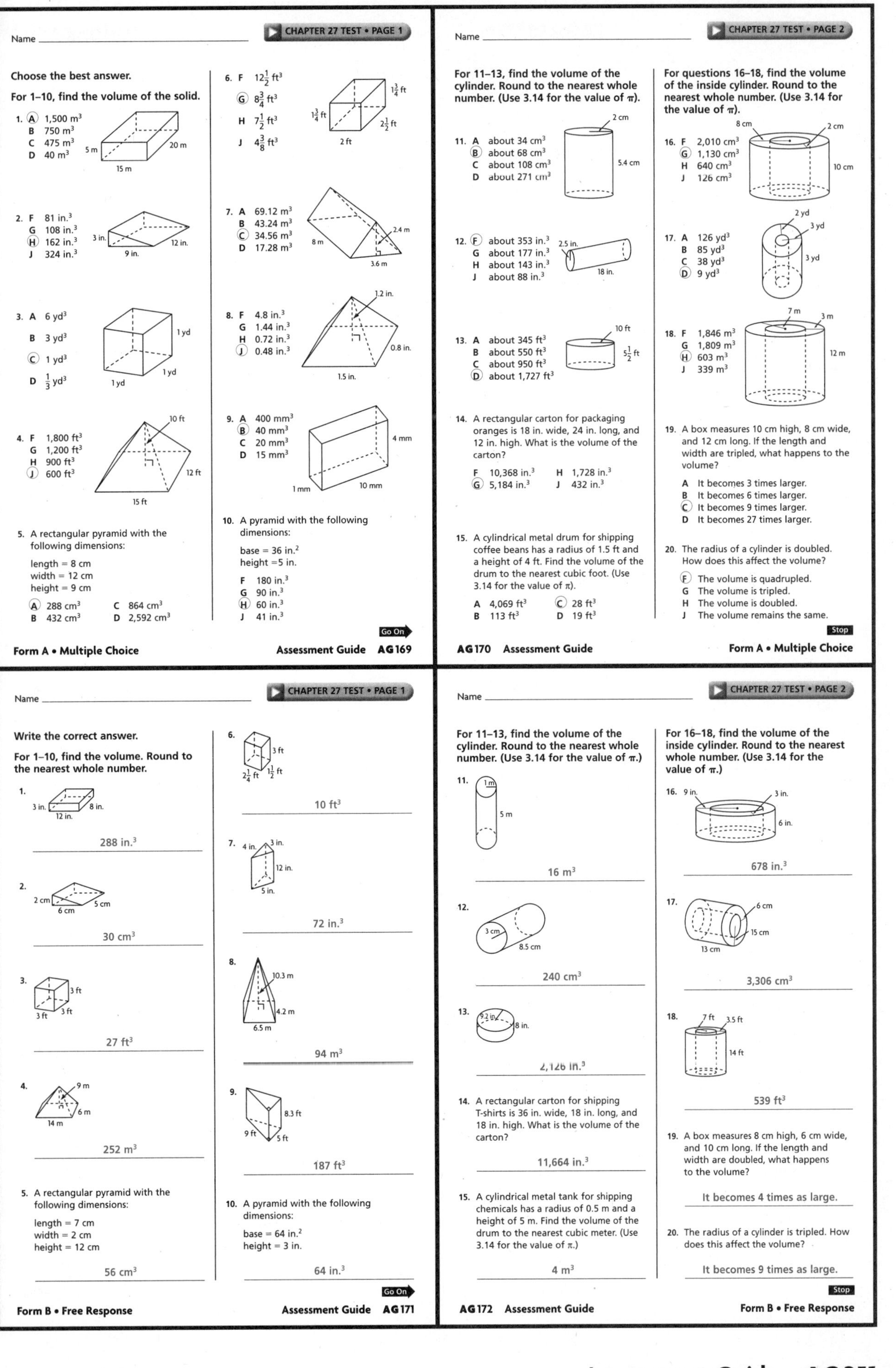

Name

CHAPTER 27 TEST • PAGE 1

Choose the best answer.

For 1–10, find the volume of the solid.

1. A $1,500\ m^3$
   B $750\ m^3$
   C $475\ m^3$
   D $40\ m^3$

2. F $81\ in.^3$
   G $108\ in.^3$
   H $162\ in.^3$
   J $324\ in.^3$

3. A $6\ yd^3$
   B $3\ yd^3$
   C $1\ yd^3$
   D $\frac{1}{3}\ yd^3$

4. F $1,800\ ft^3$
   G $1,200\ ft^3$
   H $900\ ft^3$
   J $600\ ft^3$

5. A rectangular pyramid with the following dimensions:

   length = 8 cm
   width = 12 cm
   height = 9 cm

   A $288\ cm^3$ C $864\ cm^3$
   B $432\ cm^3$ D $2,592\ cm^3$

6. F $12\frac{1}{2}\ ft^3$
   G $8\frac{3}{4}\ ft^3$
   H $7\frac{1}{2}\ ft^3$
   J $4\frac{3}{8}\ ft^3$

7. A $69.12\ m^3$
   B $43.24\ m^3$
   C $34.56\ m^3$
   D $17.28\ m^3$

8. F $4.8\ in.^3$
   G $1.44\ in.^3$
   H $0.72\ in.^3$
   J $0.48\ in.^3$

9. A $400\ mm^3$
   B $40\ mm^3$
   C $20\ mm^3$
   D $15\ mm^3$

10. A pyramid with the following dimensions:

    base = $36\ in.^2$
    height = 5 in.

    F $180\ in.^3$
    G $90\ in.^3$
    H $60\ in.^3$
    J $41\ in.^3$

Go On

Form A • Multiple Choice Assessment Guide AG169

Name

CHAPTER 27 TEST • PAGE 2

For 11–13, find the volume of the cylinder. Round to the nearest whole number. (Use 3.14 for the value of π).

11. A about $34\ cm^3$
    B about $68\ cm^3$
    C about $108\ cm^3$
    D about $271\ cm^3$

12. F about $353\ in.^3$
    G about $177\ in.^3$
    H about $143\ in.^3$
    J about $88\ in.^3$

13. A about $345\ ft^3$
    B about $550\ ft^3$
    C about $950\ ft^3$
    D about $1,727\ ft^3$

14. A rectangular carton for packaging oranges is 18 in. wide, 24 in. long, and 12 in. high. What is the volume of the carton?

    F $10,368\ in.^3$ H $1,728\ in.^3$
    G $5,184\ in.^3$ J $432\ in.^3$

15. A cylindrical metal drum for shipping coffee beans has a radius of 1.5 ft and a height of 4 ft. Find the volume of the drum to the nearest cubic foot. (Use 3.14 for the value of π).

    A $4,069\ ft^3$ C $28\ ft^3$
    B $113\ ft^3$ D $19\ ft^3$

For questions 16–18, find the volume of the inside cylinder. Round to the nearest whole number. (Use 3.14 for the value of π).

16. F $2,010\ cm^3$
    G $1,130\ cm^3$
    H $640\ cm^3$
    J $126\ cm^3$

17. A $126\ yd^3$
    B $85\ yd^3$
    C $38\ yd^3$
    D $9\ yd^3$

18. F $1,846\ m^3$
    G $1,809\ m^3$
    H $603\ m^3$
    J $339\ m^3$

19. A box measures 10 cm high, 8 cm wide, and 12 cm long. If the length and width are tripled, what happens to the volume?

    A It becomes 3 times larger.
    B It becomes 6 times larger.
    C It becomes 9 times larger.
    D It becomes 27 times larger.

20. The radius of a cylinder is doubled. How does this affect the volume?

    F The volume is quadrupled.
    G The volume is tripled.
    H The volume is doubled.
    J The volume remains the same.

Stop

AG170 Assessment Guide Form A • Multiple Choice

Name

CHAPTER 27 TEST • PAGE 1

Write the correct answer.

For 1–10, find the volume. Round to the nearest whole number.

1. $288\ in.^3$
2. $30\ cm^3$
3. $27\ ft^3$
4. $252\ m^3$
5. A rectangular pyramid with the following dimensions:

   length = 7 cm
   width = 2 cm
   height = 12 cm

   $56\ cm^3$

6. $10\ ft^3$
7. $72\ in.^3$
8. $94\ m^3$
9. $187\ ft^3$
10. A pyramid with the following dimensions:

    base = $64\ in.^2$
    height = 3 in.

    $64\ in.^3$

Go On

Form B • Free Response Assessment Guide AG171

Name

CHAPTER 27 TEST • PAGE 2

For 11–13, find the volume of the cylinder. Round to the nearest whole number. (Use 3.14 for the value of π.)

11. $16\ m^3$
12. $240\ cm^3$
13. $2,126\ in.^3$
14. A rectangular carton for shipping T-shirts is 36 in. wide, 18 in. long, and 18 in. high. What is the volume of the carton?

    $11,664\ in.^3$

15. A cylindrical metal tank for shipping chemicals has a radius of 0.5 m and a height of 5 m. Find the volume of the drum to the nearest cubic meter. (Use 3.14 for the value of π.)

    $4\ m^3$

For 16–18, find the volume of the inside cylinder. Round to the nearest whole number. (Use 3.14 for the value of π.)

16. $678\ in.^3$
17. $3,306\ cm^3$
18. $539\ ft^3$
19. A box measures 8 cm high, 6 cm wide, and 10 cm long. If the length and width are doubled, what happens to the volume?

    It becomes 4 times as large.

20. The radius of a cylinder is tripled. How does this affect the volume?

    It becomes 9 times as large.

Stop

AG172 Assessment Guide Form B • Free Response

Name ____________________

Choose the best answer.

1. Which is the most appropriate unit of measurement for the amount of fuel an automobile gas tank can hold?

   A kilogram　　C centimeter
   B milliliter　　Ⓓ liter

2. The distance around a circle is called the __?__ .

   F diameter　　H perimeter
   Ⓖ circumference　　J radius

3. Find the area.

   A 100 yd²
   B 75 yd²
   Ⓒ 50 yd²
   D 25 yd²

   20 yd; 5 yd

4. The number of cubic units needed to occupy a given space is the __?__ .

   F area　　Ⓗ volume
   G circumference　　J perimeter

5. Use a proportion to convert to the given unit.

   5.9 L = ■ mL

   Ⓐ 5,900　　C 0.059
   B 590　　D 0.0059

6. Find the perimeter.

   F 20 m
   G 30 m
   H 36 m
   Ⓙ 40 m

   8 m; 10 m; 6 m; 2 m; 14 m

7. Find the area.

   8 mm; 2 mm; 16 mm

   A 48 mm²　　C 26 mm²
   B 36 mm²　　Ⓓ 24 mm²

8. Find the volume of the cylinder. Use 3.14 for π.

   3 m; 10 m

   Ⓕ 283 m³　　H 188 m³
   G 270 m³　　J 94 m

9. Use a proportion to convert to the given unit.

   $3\frac{1}{2}$ yd = ■ in.

   A 144　　C 108
   Ⓑ 126　　D 42

10. Find the diameter of a circle with a circumference of 190.9 in. Use 3.14 for π.

    F 121.6 in.　　H 30.4 in.
    Ⓖ 60.8 in.　　J 5.5 in.

11. Find the area of a circle with a radius of 2 in. Use 3.14 for π.

    A 3.14 in.²　　Ⓒ 12.56 in.²
    B 6.28 in.²　　D 25.12 in.²

12. A rectangular box has sides that measure 4, 5, and 6 inches. What is the volume?

    F 15 in.³　　Ⓗ 120 in.³
    G 77 in.³　　J 225 in.³

13. To make pillows for a couch, Dan needs 4 lengths of fabric, each $14\frac{1}{2}$ in. long. He has 2 yd of fabric. Does he have enough? Does he need an exact measurement or an estimate?

    A no; estimate　　C yes; exact
    Ⓑ yes; estimate　　D no; exact

14. The perimeter is 28.5 cm. Find the unknown length.

    9 cm; 7 cm; x

    Ⓕ x = 12.5 cm　　H x = 10.5 cm
    G x = 11.5 cm　　J x = 9.5 cm

Go On

Name ____________________

15. Find the surface area of the box.

    A 9 ft²
    B 27 ft²
    Ⓒ 54 ft²
    D 81 ft²

    3 ft; 3 ft; 3 ft

16. Find the volume of the inside cylinder to the nearest whole number. Use 3.14 for π.

    1 in.; 3 in.; 5 in.

    Ⓕ about 63 in.³　　H about 31 in.³
    G about 47 in.³　　J about 16 in.³

17. Choose the most precise measurement for an individual's weight.

    A 0.6 kg　　Ⓒ 604 g
    B 60,045 cg　　D 600,402 mg

18. Ken wants to use a wallpaper border for a room that is 8 ft. × 10 ft. How many feet of wallpaper border will he need to buy?

    F 80 ft　　H 18 ft
    Ⓖ 36 ft　　J 10 ft

19. Noah needs to paint a rectangular box with dimensions 5 in. × 7 in. × 9 in. How many square inches will he paint?

    Ⓐ 286 in.²　　C 572 in.²
    B 315 in.²　　D 630 in.²

20. Find the volume.

    8 ft; 75 ft; 25 ft

    F 15,000 ft³
    G 10,000 ft³
    Ⓗ 7,500 ft³
    J 5,000 ft³

21. Faye is buying molding to make several picture frames. Which will give the most precise measurement?

    A kilometer　　C centimeter
    B decimeter　　Ⓓ millimeter

22. Find the circumference of the circle. Use 3.14 for π.

    90 yd

    Ⓕ 565.2 yd　　H 270 yd
    G 282.6 yd　　J 93.14 yd

23. Find the area.

    8 m; 1 m; 3 m; 20 m

    Ⓐ 36 m²　　C 60 m²
    B 44 m²　　D 84 m²

24. The diameter of a cylinder is tripled. How does this affect the volume?

    F It becomes 2 times as large.
    G It becomes 3 times as large.
    H It becomes 6 times as large.
    Ⓙ It becomes 9 times as large.

25. You purchase an 18 ft tall flagpole for your house. What is the height of the flagpole in meters? (1 in. ≈ 2.54 cm)

    A 54 m　　Ⓒ 5.5 m
    B 6 m　　D 0.0055 m

26. A regular pentagon has sides that measure 10 cm each. Find the perimeter of the pentagon.

    F 60 cm　　H 31.4 cm
    Ⓖ 50 cm　　J 10 cm

Go On

Name ____________________

27. A circle has area 50.24 ft². What is its diameter? (Use 3.14 for π.)

    A 4 ft　　C 16 ft
    Ⓑ 8 ft　　D 256 ft

28. Find the volume.

    8 ft; 24 ft; 12 ft

    F 1,152 ft³
    G 1,728 ft³
    Ⓗ 2,304 ft³
    J 4,608 ft³

29. Marian has $14.25. She needs to purchase 2 gal milk for $2.59 each, 3 dozen eggs at $1.09 a dozen, and 1 large bag flour for $4.59. Does she have enough money? Does she need an estimate or exact value?

    A no; estimate　　C no; exact
    Ⓑ yes; estimate　　D yes; exact

30. Leticia wants to build a 10 ft × 25 ft rectangular pen for her pet. She will use the barn as one of the long sides. How much fencing will she need?

    F 250 ft　　H 60 ft
    G 70 ft　　Ⓙ 45 ft

31. Find the surface area.

    9 mm; 10 mm; 10 mm

    Ⓐ 280 mm²　　C 180 mm²
    B 190 mm²　　D 145 mm²

32. Find the volume.

    12 m; 18 m; 27 m

    F 1,458 m³
    Ⓖ 1,944 m³
    H 2,916 m³
    J 5,184 m³

33. Which unit of measurement is most appropriate to measure the length of a canoe?

    A inch　　C quart
    Ⓑ foot　　D ton

34. A square field has a perimeter of 6,400 yd. How long is each side of the field?

    F 3,200 yd　　H 800 yd
    Ⓖ 1,600 yd　　J 80 yd

35. Find the area of the figure shown below. The ends are semicircles. Use 3.14 for π.

    6 in.; 18 in.

    A 108 in.²　　C 120 in.²
    B 113.04 in.²　　Ⓓ 136.26 in.²

36. What is the volume of a pyramid with a height of 9 m and a base area of 25 m²?

    Ⓕ 75 m³　　H 225 m³
    G 112.5 m³　　J 450 m³

37. Use a proportion to convert to the given unit. (1 mi ≈ 1.61 km)

    172 mi ≈ ■ km

    A 107　　Ⓒ 277
    B 172　　D 333

38. A circular trampoline has a 15 ft diameter. What is its circumference? (Use 3.14 for π.)

    F 15 ft　　H 30 ft
    G 23.55 ft　　Ⓙ 47.10 ft

Go On

Name ____________________

39. A pyramid has a square base with sides that measure 8 in. The height of each of the triangular faces is 10 in. Find the surface area of the pyramid.

    A 144 in.²　　C 176 in.²
    B 160 in.²　　Ⓓ 224 in.²

40. Crude oil is shipped in barrels 30 in. in diameter and 48 in. high. What is the volume of one of these barrels? (Use 3.14 for π.)

    F 135,648 in.³　　H 56,790 in.³
    G 67,824 in.³　　Ⓙ 33,912 in.³

41. Marge and Reuben have a 75-gal fuel oil tank at their home. Convert this into liters. (1 gal ≈ 3.79 L)

    A 20 L　　Ⓒ 284 L
    B 75 L　　D 300 L

42. The shorter sides of a rectangle are 24 cm long. The perimeter is 114 cm. How long are the longer sides?

    F 28.5 cm　　H 57 cm
    Ⓖ 33 cm　　J 66 cm

43. Find the area.

    9 in.; 18 in.

    A 108 in.²　　Ⓒ 162 in.²
    B 144 in.²　　D 270 in.²

44. The length of a box is doubled, but the width and height remain the same. What happens to the volume?

    Ⓕ It doubles.　　H It quadruples.
    G It triples.　　J It doesn't change.

45. José needs to cut 47 in. of wire for one project, 23 in. for another, and 130 in. for a third. He has 6 yd of wire. Does he have enough? Did he need an estimate or exact answer?

    A yes; exact　　Ⓒ yes; estimate
    B no; exact　　D no; estimate

46. The radius of a circle is $4\frac{1}{5}$ in. What is its circumference? (Use $\frac{22}{7}$ for π.)

    F $52\frac{4}{5}$ in.　　H $13\frac{1}{5}$ in.
    Ⓖ $26\frac{2}{5}$ in.　　J $12\frac{1}{35}$ in.

47. Mrs. Grant wants to irrigate 3 circular fields of radius 50 ft, 65 ft, and 80 ft. To the nearest hundred, how many square feet should she plan to water? (Use 3.14 for the value of π.)

    Ⓐ 41,200 ft²　　C 119,400 ft²
    B 114,100 ft²　　D 164,900 ft²

48. Find the volume.

    2 m; 12 m; 3 m

    F 72 m³
    G 54 m³
    Ⓗ 36 m³
    J 24 m³

49. Marcus won the long-jump event at the school Olympics. Which measurement is most reasonable for his jump?

    A 2 mi　　C 4 km
    Ⓑ 6 ft　　D 548 in.

50. The distance around a polygon is called the __?__ .

    F length　　H diameter
    G circumference　　Ⓙ perimeter

Stop

Name ______________________ **UNIT 8 TEST • PAGE 1**

Write the correct answer.

1. What is the most appropriate metric unit of measurement for the amount of soda a can holds?

   milliliter

2. A line segment that passes through the center of a circle and has both endpoints on the circle is called a __?__ .

   diameter

3. Find the area. 4 m, 12 m

   48 m^2

4. The sum of the areas of the faces of a solid figure is the __?__ .

   surface area

5. Use a proportion to convert to the given unit.

   3.8 L = ■ mL

   3,800

6. Find the perimeter. 3 in., 7 in.

   20 in.

7. Find the area. 5 cm, 14 cm

   35 cm^2

8. Find the volume of the cylinder. Use 3.14 for π. r = 4 in., h = 6 in.

   301.44 $in.^3$

9. Use a proportion to convert $4\frac{1}{2}$ yd to inches.

   162 in.

10. Find the diameter of a circle with a circumference of 50.24 m. Use 3.14 for π.

    16 m

11. Find the area of a circle with a radius of 8 in. Use 3.14 for π.

    200.96 $in.^2$

12. A rectangular box has sides of 3, 6, and 7 inches. What is the volume?

    126 $in.^3$

13. To set up her stereo Pat needs 4 pieces of speaker wire, each $5\frac{1}{2}$ ft long. Pat has 8 yd of wire. Does she have enough? Does she need an exact measurement or an estimate?

    estimate; yes

14. The perimeter is 16.9 cm. Find the unknown length. 5.1 cm, 3 cm, 3.7 cm, 3.2 cm, x

    $x = 1.9$ cm

Go On

Form B • Free Response **Assessment Guide AG 177**

Name ______________________ **UNIT 8 TEST • PAGE 2**

15. Find the surface area of the box. 4 ft, 7 ft, 4 ft

    144 ft^2

16. Find the volume of the inside cylinder to the nearest whole number. Use 3.14 for π. 8 in., 1 in., 3 in.

    100 cm^3

17. What is the most common customary measurement for an individual's weight?

    pound

18. Cinzia wants to put a decorative fence around a garden that is 6 ft × 12 ft. How many feet of fencing will she need?

    36 ft

19. Chris needs to wrap a rectangular box with dimensions 4 in. × 5 in. × 13 in. How many square inches of wrapping paper will he use if there is no overlap?

    274 $in.^2$

20. Find the volume. 4 in., 3 in., 7 in.

    42 $in.^3$

21. Faye is going to put fringe around several pillows. Which customary measurement will give her a more precise measurement, inches or feet?

    inches

22. Find the circumference of the circle. Use 3.14 for π. 4.5 in.

    28.26 in.

23. Find the area. 8.5 cm, 4.5 cm

    38.25 cm^2

24. The radius of a circle is tripled. How does this affect its area?

    The area becomes 9 times as large.

25. A tree in Kim's back yard is 22 ft tall. What is its height in meters? (1 in. ≈ 2.54 cm)

    6.71 m

26. A regular pentagon has sides that measure 18 cm. Find the perimeter of the pentagon.

    90 cm

Go On

AG 178 Assessment Guide **Form B • Free Response**

Name ______________________ **UNIT 8 TEST • PAGE 3**

27. A circle has a circumference of 43.96 ft. What is its diameter? Use 3.14 for the value of π.

    14 ft

28. Find the volume. s = 6 in.

    216 $in.^3$

29. Lisa has $50 and wants to purchase a game for $24.95, 2 packs of batteries at $2.59 each, and 3 rolls of film at $3.39 each. Does she have enough money? Does she need an estimate or exact value?

    yes; estimate

30. Stephen wants to fence in his backyard, which measures 15 yd × 25 yd. He will use his house as one of the short sides. How much fencing does he need?

    65 yd of fencing

31. Find the surface area. 5 in., 3 in., 4 in., 4 in.

    60 $in.^2$

32. What is the volume of a pyramid with a height of 5 m and a base area of 36 m^2?

    60 m^3

33. What metric unit of measurement is appropriate to measure the length of a paper clip?

    centimeter

34. A square courtyard has a perimeter of 120 yd. How long is each side of the courtyard?

    30 yd

35. Find the area of the figure shown below. Use 3.14 for π. 8 in., 8 in.

    114.24 $in.^2$

36. Find the volume. 7.5 m, 8 m, 1.5 m

    90 m^3

37. Use a proportion to convert to the given unit. (1 mi ≈ 1.61 km)

    203 mi ≈ ■ km

    326.83

38. A circular parachute has an 18 ft diameter. What is its circumference? (Use 3.14 for π.)

    56.52 ft

Go On

Form B • Free Response **Assessment Guide AG 179**

Name ______________________ **UNIT 8 TEST • PAGE 4**

39. A pyramid has a square base with sides that measure 6 in. The height of the triangular faces is 12 in. Find the surface area of the pyramid.

    180 $in.^2$

40. What is the volume of a barrel that has a diameter of 20 in. and a height of 36 in.? Use 3.14 for π.

    11,304 $in.^3$

41. Ms. Catalanello's car used 120 gallons of gas last month. Convert this into liters. (1 gal ≈ 3.79 L)

    454.8 L

42. The shorter sides of a rectangle are 14 m long. The perimeter is 100 m. How long are the longer sides?

    36 m

43. Find the area. 10 in., 4 in., 14 in.

    48 $in.^2$

44. The length of a box is tripled, but the width and height remain the same. What happens to the volume?

    it triples

45. André needs to cut 38 in. of tubing for one science project, 18 in. for another, and 155 in. for a third. He has $5\frac{1}{2}$ yd of tubing. Does he have enough? Does he need an exact answer or an estimate?

    no; exact

46. The radius of a circle is $5\frac{3}{5}$ in. What is its circumference? (Use $\frac{22}{7}$ for π.)

    $35\frac{1}{5}$ in.

47. Pauline cut 3 fabric circles with radii of 34 cm, 54 cm, and 84 cm. Find the total area of the three fabric cirles to the nearest hundred centimeters. (Use 3.14 for π.)

    34,900 cm^2

48. Find the volume. 12 in., 12 in., 2 in.

    288 $in.^3$

49. Melanie is expecting to complete the New York City Marathon in about 4 hours. What customary unit of measurement is most appropriate to measure the distance of the run?

    mile

50. The distance around a circle is called the __?__ .

    circumference

Stop

AG 180 Assessment Guide **Form B • Free Response**

Name ______________________

Choose the best answer.

1. A(n) ________ has a repeating pattern containing shapes that are like the whole, but of different sizes.

   A term C function
   B sequence (D) fractal

For 2–6, tell which is the rule for the sequence.

2. 73, 67, 61, . . .

   F add 7 (H) subtract 6
   G divide by 7 J subtract 7

3. 3, 24, 192, . . .

   A divide by 8 C multiply by 9
   B add 21 (D) multiply by 8

4. 21, 7, $2\frac{1}{3}$, . . .

   F subtract 14 H multiply by 3
   (G) divide by 3 J divide by $\frac{1}{3}$

5. 2.56, 12.8, 64, . . .

   (A) multiply by 5 C multiply by 2
   B divide by 5 D divide by 2

6. 5.8, 7.9, 10.0, . . .

   (F) add 2.1 H multiply by 1.4
   G subtract 2.1 J add 1.1

For 7–10, find the next three possible terms in each sequence

7. 6, 3, $1\frac{1}{2}$, . . .

   A $\frac{1}{4}, \frac{1}{8}, \frac{1}{16}$ (C) $\frac{3}{4}, \frac{3}{8}, \frac{3}{16}$
   B $\frac{3}{2}, \frac{3}{4}, \frac{3}{8}$ D 0, $^-3$, $^-6$

8. 12, 17, 22, . . .

   F 22, 27, 32 H 17, 12, 7
   G 32, 37, 42 (J) 27, 32, 37

9. 1, $^-2$, 4, . . .

   A 8, 16, 32 C 8, $^-16$, 32
   (B) $^-8$, 16, $^-32$ D $^-6$, 8, $^-10$

10. $^-8$, $^-14$, $^-20$, . . .

   (F) $^-26$, $^-32$, $^-38$ H $^-26$, 32, $^-38$
   G $^-24$, $^-30$, $^-34$ J $^-25$, $^-33$, $^-40$

11. Mr. Reese received 49 e-mails in July, 60 in August, and 71 in September. If this pattern continues, how many e-mails will he receive in December?

   A 82 e-mails (C) 104 e-mails
   B 93 e-mails D 213 e-mails

12. An elevator started down from the 75th floor. Five seconds later, it was at the 71st floor. Five seconds after that, it was at the 67th floor. If this pattern continues, at what floor will it be 60 seconds after it started down?

   F 31st floor H 23rd floor
   (G) 27th floor J 15th floor

Go On

Name ______________________

For 13–16, tell which equation represents the function.

13.

x	1	2	3	4	5
y	7	14	21	28	35

   A $y = x + 7$ C $y = x \div 7$
   (B) $y = 7x$ D $y = x + 6$

14.

x	0	5	10	15	20
y	7	12	17	22	27

   (F) $y = x + 7$ H $y = 7x$
   G $y = x - 7$ J $y = 5x$

15.

x	$^-2$	$^-1$	0	1	2
y	$^-5$	$^-4$	$^-3$	$^-2$	$^-1$

   (A) $y = x - 3$ C $y = x + 5$
   B $y = x + 3$ D $y = x \div 1$

16.

x	128	64	32	16	8
y	32	16	8	4	2

   F $y = x + 8$ H $y = 4x$
   G $y = 8x$ (J) $y = x \div 4$

For 17–19, identify the next two figures in the pattern.

17.

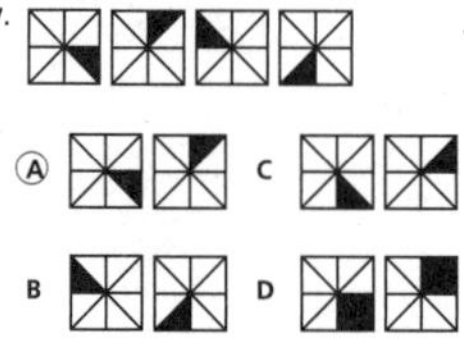

   (A) C
   B D

18.

   F (H)
   G J

19.

   A
   (B)
   C
   D

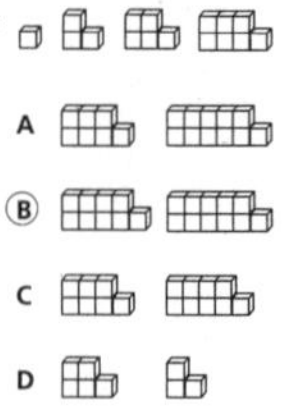

20. Look at the following pattern. How many small squares are in the seventh figure?

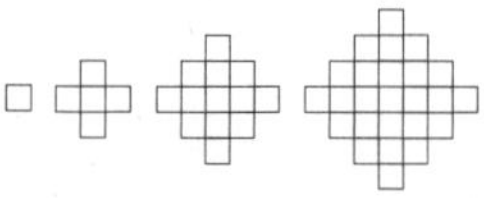

   F 7 squares
   G 61 squares
   (H) 85 squares
   J 113 squares

Stop

Name ______________________

Write the correct answer.

1. What has a repeating pattern containing shapes that are like the whole, but of different sizes?

   fractal

For 2–6, write the rule for the sequence.

2. 60, 54, 48, . . .

   Subtract 6.

3. 392, 56, 8, . . .

   Divide by 7.

4. $\frac{1}{3}$, 1, 3, . . .

   Multiply by 3.

5. 1.87, 3, 4.13 . . .

   Add 1.13.

6. 5, 2, $\frac{4}{5}$ . . .

   Multiply by $\frac{2}{5}$.

For 7–10, write the next three possible terms in each sequence.

7. 9, $4\frac{1}{2}$, $2\frac{1}{4}$, . . .

   $1\frac{1}{8}, \frac{9}{16}, \frac{9}{32}$

8. 76, 84, 92, . . .

   100, 108, 116

9. 4, $^-16$, 64, . . .

   $^-256$, 1,024, $^-4,096$

10. $^-32$, $^-23$, $^-14$, . . .

   $^-5$, 4, 13

11. The Snack Shop had a total of \$245 in sales receipts on Monday, a total of \$286 on Tuesday, and a total of \$327 on Wednesday. If this pattern continues, what will be the total of the sales receipts for Friday?

   \$409

12. Marty is driving 540 mi to visit his cousin. After 15 min, Marty is 527 mi from his cousin's house. Fifteen minutes later he is 514 mi away. Fifteen minutes after that, he is 501 mi away. If this pattern continues, how far away will Marty be 2 hr after he began driving?

   436 mi away

Go On

Name ______________________

For 13–16, complete the equation that represents the function.

13.

x	1	2	3	4	5
y	9	18	27	36	45

   $y = 9x$

14.

x	2	4	6	8	10
y	$^-2$	0	2	4	6

   $y = x - 4$

15.

x	$^-5$	$^-3$	$^-1$	1	3
y	1	3	5	7	9

   $y = x + 6$

16.

x	100	90	80	70	60
y	20	18	16	14	12

   $y = x \div 5$

For 17–19, draw the next two figures in the pattern.

17.

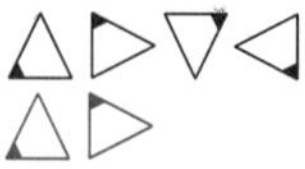

18.

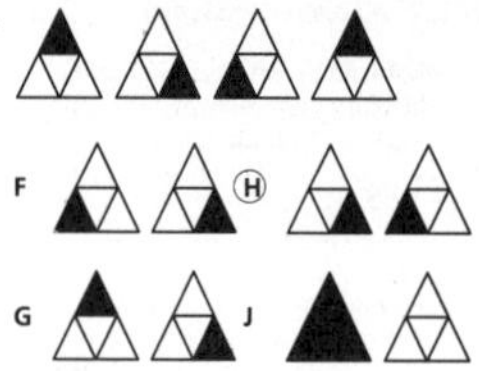

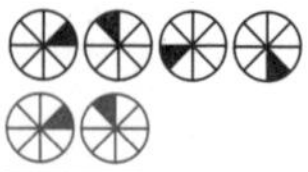

19.

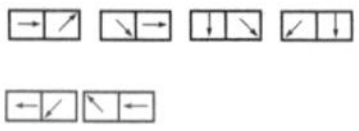

20. Examine the following pattern. How many small squares will be in the tenth figure?

   100 squares

Stop

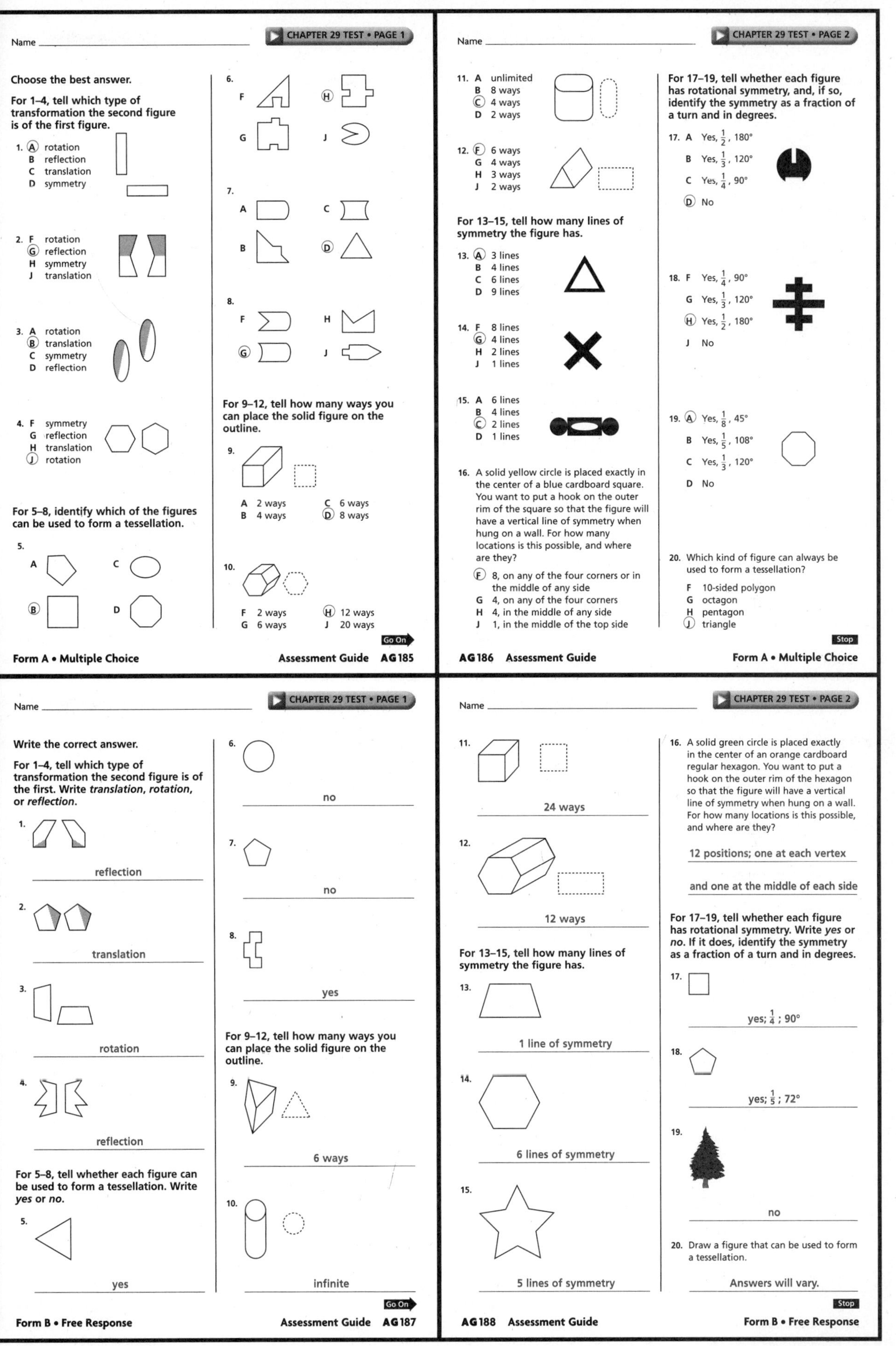

Name ____________________

CHAPTER 29 TEST • PAGE 1

Choose the best answer.

For 1–4, tell which type of transformation the second figure is of the first figure.

1. (A) rotation
   B reflection
   C translation
   D symmetry

2. F rotation
   (G) reflection
   H symmetry
   J translation

3. A rotation
   (B) translation
   C symmetry
   D reflection

4. F symmetry
   G reflection
   H translation
   (J) rotation

For 5–8, identify which of the figures can be used to form a tessellation.

5. A (B) C D

6. F G (H) J

7. A B C (D)

8. F (G) H J

For 9–12, tell how many ways you can place the solid figure on the outline.

9. A 2 ways
   B 4 ways
   C 6 ways
   (D) 8 ways

10. F 2 ways
    G 6 ways
    (H) 12 ways
    J 20 ways

Go On

Form A • Multiple Choice — Assessment Guide AG 185

Name ____________________

CHAPTER 29 TEST • PAGE 2

11. A unlimited
    B 8 ways
    (C) 4 ways
    D 2 ways

12. (F) 6 ways
    G 4 ways
    H 3 ways
    J 2 ways

For 13–15, tell how many lines of symmetry the figure has.

13. (A) 3 lines
    B 4 lines
    C 6 lines
    D 9 lines

14. F 8 lines
    (G) 4 lines
    H 2 lines
    J 1 lines

15. A 6 lines
    B 4 lines
    (C) 2 lines
    D 1 lines

16. A solid yellow circle is placed exactly in the center of a blue cardboard square. You want to put a hook on the outer rim of the square so that the figure will have a vertical line of symmetry when hung on a wall. For how many locations is this possible, and where are they?
    (F) 8, on any of the four corners or in the middle of any side
    G 4, on any of the four corners
    H 4, in the middle of any side
    J 1, in the middle of the top side

For 17–19, tell whether each figure has rotational symmetry, and, if so, identify the symmetry as a fraction of a turn and in degrees.

17. A Yes, $\frac{1}{2}$, 180°
    B Yes, $\frac{1}{3}$, 120°
    C Yes, $\frac{1}{4}$, 90°
    (D) No

18. F Yes, $\frac{1}{4}$, 90°
    G Yes, $\frac{1}{3}$, 120°
    (H) Yes, $\frac{1}{2}$, 180°
    J No

19. (A) Yes, $\frac{1}{8}$, 45°
    B Yes, $\frac{1}{5}$, 108°
    C Yes, $\frac{1}{3}$, 120°
    D No

20. Which kind of figure can always be used to form a tessellation?
    F 10-sided polygon
    G octagon
    H pentagon
    (J) triangle

Stop

AG 186 Assessment Guide — Form A • Multiple Choice

Name ____________________

CHAPTER 29 TEST • PAGE 1

Write the correct answer.

For 1–4, tell which type of transformation the second figure is of the first. Write *translation*, *rotation*, or *reflection*.

1. reflection

2. translation

3. rotation

4. reflection

For 5–8, tell whether each figure can be used to form a tessellation. Write *yes* or *no*.

5. yes

6. no

7. no

8. yes

For 9–12, tell how many ways you can place the solid figure on the outline.

9. 6 ways

10. infinite

Go On

Form B • Free Response — Assessment Guide AG 187

Name ____________________

CHAPTER 29 TEST • PAGE 2

11. 24 ways

12. 12 ways

For 13–15, tell how many lines of symmetry the figure has.

13. 1 line of symmetry

14. 6 lines of symmetry

15. 5 lines of symmetry

16. A solid green circle is placed exactly in the center of an orange cardboard regular hexagon. You want to put a hook on the outer rim of the hexagon so that the figure will have a vertical line of symmetry when hung on a wall. For how many locations is this possible, and where are they?

12 positions; one at each vertex and one at the middle of each side

For 17–19, tell whether each figure has rotational symmetry. Write *yes* or *no*. If it does, identify the symmetry as a fraction of a turn and in degrees.

17. yes; $\frac{1}{4}$; 90°

18. yes; $\frac{1}{5}$; 72°

19. no

20. Draw a figure that can be used to form a tessellation.

Answers will vary.

Stop

AG 188 Assessment Guide — Form B • Free Response

Name ____________________ **CHAPTER 30 TEST • PAGE 1**

Choose the best answer.

1. Using a(n) ________, you can locate any point on the coordinate plane.
   A relation C function
   (B) ordered pair D quadrant

2. A(n) ________ contains one of the symbols $>, <, \geq, \leq$, or $\neq$.
   (F) inequality H equation
   G relation J translation

3. The coordinate plane is divided by a vertical line called the ______.
   A quadrant C *x*-axis
   (B) *y*-axis D origin

4. The point whose coordinates are (0,0) is called the ________.
   F *x*-axis H relation
   G *y*-axis (J) origin

For 5–6, find the graph of the solutions of the inequality.

5. $x > 5$

(A) 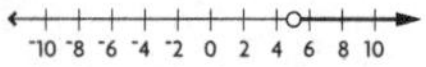

B 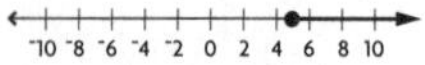

C 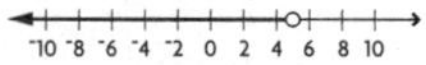

D 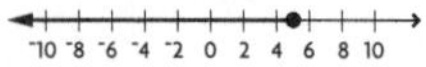

6. $x \leq {}^-2$

F 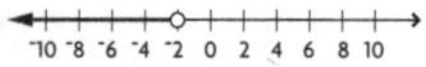

(G) 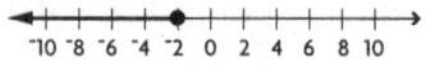

H 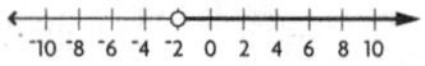

J 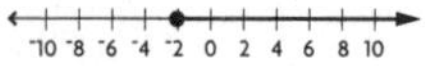

For 7–10, solve the inequality.

7. $n + 3 > 5$
   A $n > 8$ (C) $n > 2$
   B $n < 8$ D $n < 2$

8. $x - 1 < 3$
   F $x > 2$ H $x > 4$
   G $x < 2$ (J) $x < 4$

9. $p + 5 \leq 7$
   A $p \geq 2$ C $p \geq {}^-2$
   (B) $p \leq 2$ D $p \leq {}^-2$

10. $4c \geq 20$
    F $c \geq 15$ (H) $c \geq 5$
    G $c \leq 5$ J $c \leq 80$

For 11–12, describe how to locate the point for the ordered pair on the coordinate plane.

11. Locate the point $(5, {}^-9)$, starting at (0,0).
    A Go right 5 and up 9.
    B Go left 5 and up 9.
    C Go left 5 and up 9.
    (D) Go right 5 and down 9.

12. Locate the point $({}^-2, {}^-7)$, starting at (0,0).
    F Go left 2 and up 7.
    G Go right 2 and up 7.
    (H) Go left 2 and down 7.
    J Go right 2 and down 7.

Go On

Name ____________________ **CHAPTER 30 TEST • PAGE 2**

For 13–14, use the table below.

x	0	1	2	3	4
y	7	10	13	16	19

13. List the ordered pairs from the table.
    A (7,0), (10,1), (13,2), (16,3), (19,4)
    B (7,4), (10,3), (13,2), (16,2), (19,1)
    C (4,7), (3,10), (2,13), (1,16), (0,19)
    (D) (0,7), (1,10), (2,13), (3,16), (4,19)

14. Which equation relates *y* to *x*?
    F $y = x + 7$
    (G) $y = 3x + 7$
    H $x = y - 7$
    J $x = 3y - 7$

15. Parallelogram *ABCD* has coordinates *A*(2, 5), *B*(2, 11), *C*($^-1$, 7), and *D*($^-1$, 1). It is translated 3 units up and 4 units to the left. What are the new coordinates?
    A A'($^-1$, 1), B'($^-1$, 7), C'($^-4$, 3), D'($^-4$, $^-3$)
    B A'(2, 8), B'(2, 14), C'($^-1$, 10), D'($^-1$, 4)
    (C) A'($^-2$, 8), B'($^-2$, 14), C'($^-5$, 10), D'($^-5$, 4)
    D A'(5, 1), B'(5, 7), C'(2, 3), D'(2, $^-3$)

16. Triangle *QRS* has coordinates *Q*(4,4), *R*(4,7), and *S*(7,7). It is reflected across the x- axis and then the y-axis. What are the new coordinates?
    (F) Q'($^-4$,$^-4$), R'($^-4$,$^-7$), S'($^-7$,$^-7$)
    G Q'($^-4$, 4), R'($^-4$, 7), S'($^-7$, 7)
    H Q'(4,$^-4$), R'(4,$^-7$), S'(7,$^-7$)
    J Q'(4,$^-4$), R'($^-4$, 7), S'(7,$^-7$)

For 17–18, use the table below.

x	$^-2$	$^-1$	0	1	2
y	25	20	15	10	5

17. Which equation relates *y* to *x*?
    (A) $y = {}^-5x + 15$
    B $y = 5x + 15$
    C $y = 5x - 15$
    D $y = {}^-5x - 15$

18. The points in the table above are rotated 90° clockwise around the origin. What are the coordinates of the point that corresponds to (1, 10) after the rotation?
    F ($^-1$,$^-10$) H ($^-10$,1)
    (G) (10,$^-1$) J ($^-10$,–1)

For 19–20, use the table below, which shows the cost *c* (in dollars) for Lucy to make *n* necklaces.

n	5	10	15	20
c	25	50	75	100

19. Which equation relates *c* to *n*?
    A $c = 5 + n$ (C) $c = 5n$
    B $c = n \div 5$ D $c = n - 25$

20. How much will it cost Lucy to make 50 necklaces?
    (F) \$250 H \$150
    G \$200 J \$10

Stop

Name ____________________ **CHAPTER 30 TEST • PAGE 1**

Write the correct answer.

1. You can use an ordered pair to locate any __?__.

   point

2. Write five symbols that can be contained in an inequality.

   $>, <, \geq, \leq, \neq$

3. The horizontal axis of a coordinate plane is also called the __?__.

   x-axis

4. Identify the ordered pair that names the origin.

   (0, 0)

For 5–6, draw the graph of the solutions of the inequality.

5. $x < {}^-1$

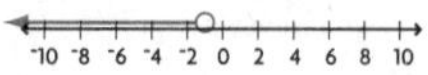

6. $x > {}^-4$

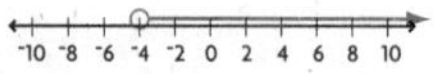

For 7–10, solve the inequality.

7. $x + 6 > 8$

   $x > 2$

8. $a - 2 < 2$

   $a < 4$

9. $m + 4 \leq 10$

   $m \leq 6$

10. $2n \geq 14$

    $n \geq 7$

For 11–12, describe how to locate the point for the ordered pair on the coordinate plane.

11. Locate the point $(3, {}^-3)$, starting at (0,0).

    Start at the origin; go right 3 and down 3.

12. Locate the point $({}^-3, 4)$, starting at (0,0).

    Start at the origin; go left 3 and up 4.

Go On

Name ____________________ **CHAPTER 30 TEST • PAGE 2**

For 13–14, use the table below.

x	0	1	2	3	4
y	$^-1$	1	3	5	7

13. List the ordered pairs from the table.

    (0, $^-1$), (1, 1), (2, 3), (3, 5), (4, 7)

14. Write an equation that relates *y* to *x*.

    $y = 2x - 1$

15. Rectangle *MNOP* has coordinates *M*($^-2$,1), *N*(2, 1), *O*(2,3) and *P*($^-2$,3). It is translated 4 units down and 3 units to the right. What are the new coordinates?

    M'(1, $^-3$), *N*'(5, $^-3$), *O*'(5, $^-1$), *P*'(1, $^-1$)

16. Triangle *ABC* has coordinates *A*(2,3), *B*(2,6), and *C*(6,3). It is reflected across the *x*-axis and then the *y*-axis. What are the new coordinates?

    A'($^-2$, $^-3$), *B*'($^-2$, $^-6$), *C*'($^-6$, $^-3$)

For 17–18, use the table below.

x	$^-2$	$^-1$	0	1	2
y	9	7	5	3	1

17. Write an equation that relates *y* to *x*.

    $y = {}^-2x + 5$

18. The points in the table above are rotated 180° clockwise around the origin. What are the coordinates of the point that corresponds to (1,3) after the rotation?

    ($^-1$, $^-3$)

For 19–20, use the table below, which shows the time *h* (in hours) that Jason works in *d* days.

d	2	4	6	8
h	12	24	36	48

19. Write an equation that relates *h* to *d*.

    $h = 6d$

20. If Jason works 15 days this month, how many hours will he work?

    90 hr

Stop

Name ______________________________ UNIT 9 TEST • PAGE 1

Choose the best answer.

1. Describe how to locate the point ($^{-}6$, 3) starting from the origin.
   Ⓐ Go left 6 and up 3.
   B Go right 6 and up 3.
   C Go left 6 and down 3.
   D Go right 6 and down 3.

2. What is the rule for the sequence?
   20, 4, 0.8, 0.16, …
   Ⓕ divide by 5 H multiply by 5
   G divide by 0.2 J multiply by 0.4

3. A repeating arrangement of shapes that completely covers a plane with no overlaps is called a __?__.
   A reflection Ⓒ tessellation
   B rotation D transformation

4. Which graph is a solution of the inequality $x \geq {}^{-}1$?

F G H Ⓙ
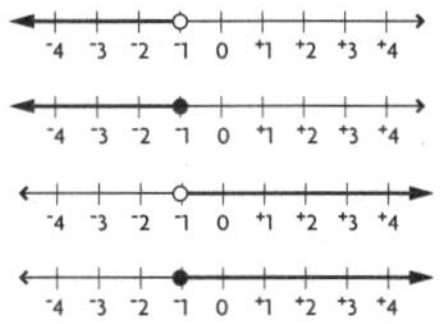

5. Which word describes the transformation that moves the first figure to the second?

   Ⓐ rotation C translation
   B reflection D symmetry

6. Solve the inequality. $x + 3 < 5$
   F $x < 8$ Ⓗ $x < 2$
   G $x > 8$ J $x > 2$

7. Which equation relates c to d?

c	1	2	3	4
d	4	8	12	16

   A $c = 4d$ C $c = 8d$
   Ⓑ $d = 4c$ D $d = 8c$

8. Bennett wants to make a walkway using a shape that will tessellate. Which shape should he not choose?

F  H 

Ⓖ  J 

9. How many lines of symmetry does the figure have?

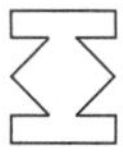

   A 1 line
   Ⓑ 2 lines
   C 3 lines
   D 4 lines

10. What are the next two figures in the pattern?

F 

G 

H 

Ⓙ 

Go On

Name ______________________________ UNIT 9 TEST • PAGE 2

11. At 8 A.M., the temperature was 48°F. At 10 A.M., the temperature was 52°F. At noon, the temperature was 56°F. If this pattern continues, what will the temperature be at 5 P.M.?
   A 64°F C 68°F
   Ⓑ 66°F D 70°F

12. Which equation represents the function?

x	0	3	6	9	12
y	0	24	48	72	96

   F $y = x$ H $y = 3x$
   G $y = x + 3$ Ⓙ $y = 8x$

13. Triangle QRS has coordinates $Q(0, {}^{-}1)$, $R(0, {}^{-}3)$, and $S(4, {}^{-}2)$. It is translated 1 unit down and 2 units to the right. What are the new coordinates?

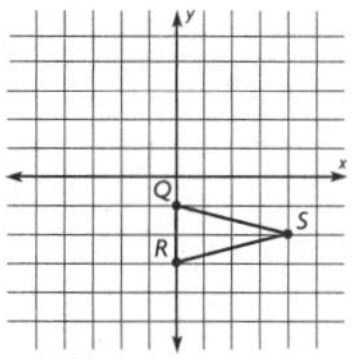

   A $Q'(1,0)$, $R'(1,{}^{-}2)$, $S'(5,{}^{-}3)$
   B $Q'(2,0)$, $R'(2,{}^{-}2)$, $S'(3,0)$
   Ⓒ $Q'(2,{}^{-}2)$, $R'(2,{}^{-}4)$, $S'(6,{}^{-}3)$
   D $Q'(2,0)$, $R'(2,{}^{-}4)$, $S'(6,{}^{-}1)$

14. Eric sold 28 candles the first week, 40 the second week, and 52 the third week. If this pattern continues, how many candles will he sell the eighth week?
   Ⓕ 112 candles H 88 candles
   G 104 candles J 64 candles

15. How many ways can you place the solid figure on the black plane figure?

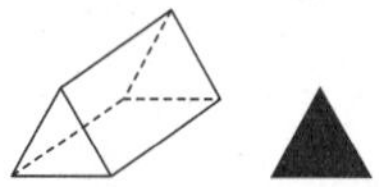

   A 2 ways Ⓒ 6 ways
   B 3 ways D 8 ways

16. Identify the rotational symmetry as a fraction of a turn and in degrees.

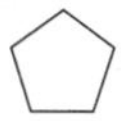

   F $\frac{1}{4}$; 90° H $\frac{1}{6}$; 60°
   Ⓖ $\frac{1}{5}$; 72° J $\frac{1}{2}$; 180°

17. What are the next three terms in the sequence?
   $^{-}2$, 4, $^{-}8$, …
   A 10, $^{-}12$, 14 C $^{-}16$, 32, $^{-}64$
   B $^{-}16$, $^{-}32$, $^{-}64$ Ⓓ 16, $^{-}32$, 64

18. How many parts are there in the eighth circle in the following pattern?

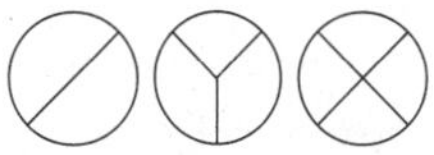

   F 7 parts Ⓗ 9 parts
   G 8 parts J 10 parts

Go On

Name ______________________________ UNIT 9 TEST • PAGE 3

For questions 19–21, use the table below.

x	$^{-}2$	$^{-}1$	0	1	2
y	7	5	3	1	$^{-}1$

19. List the ordered pairs from the table.
   A (7,$^{-}2$), (5,$^{-}1$), (3, 0), (1,1), ($^{-}1$,2)
   B (7,2), (5,1), (3,0), (1,$^{-}1$), ($^{-}1$,$^{-}2$)
   Ⓒ ($^{-}2$,7), ($^{-}1$,5), (0,3), (1, 1), (2,$^{-}1$)
   D ($^{-}2$,$^{-}1$), ($^{-}1$,1), (0,3), (1,5), (2,7)

20. Which equation relates x to y?
   F $y = 2x - 3$ H $y = {}^{-}2x - 3$
   G $y = 2x + 3$ Ⓙ $y = {}^{-}2x + 3$

21. The points in the table are rotated 180° clockwise around the origin. What are the coordinates of the first point in the table after the rotation?
   A ($^{-}2$,$^{-}7$) C (7, 2)
   Ⓑ (2,$^{-}7$) D (7,2)

22. Each number in a sequence is called a __?__.
   Ⓕ term H relation
   G function J reflection

23. Which symbol does not show an inequality?
   A > C ≤
   B ≠ Ⓓ =

24. What moves were made to transform each figure into its next position?

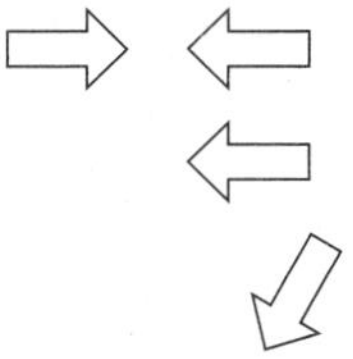

   F translation, reflection, rotation
   G rotation, translation, reflection
   Ⓗ reflection, translation, rotation
   J rotation, reflection, translation

25. The table shows the total profit, p, for the number of magazines sold, m. Which equation shows the total profit?

m	1	2	3	4
p	\$6	\$12	\$18	\$24

   Ⓐ $p = 6m$ C $p = m + 5$
   B $m = 6p$ D $m = p + 5$

26. Meryl walked 1.5 miles the first week, 2.25 miles the second week, and 3 miles the third week. If this pattern continues, how many miles will she walk the tenth week?
   F 6.75 mi H 10.25 mi
   Ⓖ 8.25 mi J 15 mi

Go On

Name ______________________________ UNIT 9 TEST • PAGE 4

27. A supermarket display is set up on 4 shelves that are 18 cm apart. The bottom shelf of the display is 6 cm from the floor. How far from the floor is the top shelf?
   A 36 cm Ⓒ 60 cm
   B 42 cm D 78 cm

28. Which equation represents the function?

x	$^{-}10$	$^{-}5$	0	5	10
y	$^{-}7$	$^{-}2$	3	8	13

   Ⓕ $y = x + 3$ H $y = 3x$
   G $y = x - 3$ J $y = {}^{-}3x$

29. Identify which of the figures forms a tessellation.

A 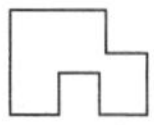

Ⓑ 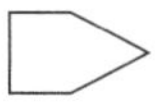

C 

D 

30. Which word describes the transformation that moves the first figure to the second?

   F rotation H translation
   Ⓖ reflection J symmetry

For questions 31–32, use the table below which shows how the length l of a rectangle is related to its width, w.

w	2	4	6	8
l	7	13	19	25

31. Which equation relates l to w?
   A $l = w + 5$ C $l = 4w - 1$
   B $l = w - 5$ Ⓓ $l = 3w + 1$

32. If the width of the rectangle is 15 ft, how long is the rectangle?
   Ⓕ 46 ft H 31 ft
   G 45 ft J 30 ft

33. Examine the following pattern. How many small triangles are in the ninth figure?

   A 10 triangles Ⓒ 18 triangles
   B 15 triangles D 20 triangles

Stop

Name ______

UNIT 9 TEST • PAGE 1

Write the correct answer.

1. Describe how to locate the point ($^-4$, 5) starting at the origin.

Go left 4 and up 5

2. What is a possible rule for the sequence?

24, 6, 1.5, 0.375, ...

divide by 4

3. A repeating arrangement of shapes that completely covers a plane with no overlaps is called a __?__ .

tessellation

4. Graph the solution of the inequality $x \leq 2$.

0 $^-4$ $^-3$ $^-2$ $^-1$ 0 1 2 3 4

5. Which word describes the transformation that moves the first figure to the second?

reflection or rotation

6. Solve the inequality. $x + 4 > 6$

$x > 2$

7. Write an equation that relates c to d.

c	1	2	3	4
d	3	6	9	12

$d = 3c$

8. Bennett wants to make a walkway using a shape that will tessellate. Name a regular polygon that he should not choose.

Possible answer: octagon

9. How many lines of symmetry does the figure have?

5

10. What are the next two figures in the pattern?

Go On

Name ______

UNIT 9 TEST • PAGE 2

11. At 5 P.M., the temperature was 64°F. At 7 P.M., the temperature was 61°F. At 9 P.M., the temperature was 58°F. If this pattern continues, what will the temperature be at 1 A.M.?

52°F

12. Write an equation to relate x to y.

x	0	2	4	6	8
y	0	14	28	42	56

$y = 7x$

13. Triangle QRS has coordinates $Q(1,0)$, $R(1,^-2)$, and $S(5,^-1)$. It is translated 3 units up and 1 unit to the left. What are the new coordinates?

$Q'(0, 3)$, $R'(0, 1)$, $S'(4, 2)$

14. Allison's Nursery sold 30 plants the first week, 44 the second week, and 58 the third week. If this pattern continues, how many plants will it sell the eighth week?

128 plants

15. How many ways can you place the solid figure on the outline?

8 ways

16. Does the figure have rotational symmetry? If so, identify the symmetry as a fraction of a turn and in degrees.

yes; possible answer: $\frac{1}{3}$ turn or 120°

17. What are the next three possible terms in the sequence?

64, $^-32$, 16, . . .

$^-8$, 4, $^-2$

18. How many squares are shaded in the seventh figure in the following pattern?

14

Go On

Name ______

UNIT 9 TEST • PAGE 3

For questions 19–21, use the table below.

x	$^-2$	$^-1$	0	1	2
y	$^-7$	$^-4$	$^-1$	2	5

19. List the ordered pairs from the table.

($^-2$,$^-7$), ($^-1$,$^-4$), (0,$^-1$), (1,2), (2,5)

20. Write an equation that relates x to y.

$y = 3x - 1$

21. The points in the table are rotated 180° clockwise around the origin. What are the coordinates of the first point in the table after the rotation?

(2, 7)

22. A set of terms that follows a pattern from one term to the next is called a __?__ .

sequence

23. Write three symbols that show an inequality.

Possible answers: <, >, ≠, ≤, ≥

24. What moves were made to transform each figure into its next position?

reflection, rotation, translation

25. The table shows the number of cups of apple cider, c, needed per gallon of fruit punch, p. Write an equation relating p and c.

p	1	2	3	4
c	4	8	12	16

$c = 4p$

26. Chris jogged 1.3 miles the first week, 1.7 miles the second week, and 2.1 miles the third week. If this pattern continues, how many miles will he jog the tenth week?

4.9 miles

Go On

Name ______

UNIT 9 TEST • PAGE 4

27. Five layers of boxes are stacked on a shelf 10 cm from the floor. Each box is 16 cm tall. How far from the floor is the top of the highest layer?

90 cm

28. Write an equation that represents the function.

x	$^-6$	$^-3$	0	3	6
y	$^-2$	1	4	7	10

$y = x + 4$

29. Identify which of the figures can be used to form a tessellation.

hexagon

30. What transformation moves the first figure to the second?

rotation

For questions 31–32, use the table below which shows how the length, l, of a rectangle is related to its width, w.

w	1	2	3	4
l	4	6	8	10

31. Which equation relates l to w?

$l = 2w + 2$

32. If the width of the rectangle is 12 m, how long is the rectangle?

26 m

33. Examine the following pattern. How many small black triangles are in the sixth figure?

21 triangles

Stop

Name ______________________________

Choose the best answer.

1. $6\overline{)3,290}$

A 548   C 548 r3
(B) 548 r2   D 549

2. Which number should be in the box so that the numbers are in order from *least* to *greatest*?

2.496, ■, 2.502, 2.514

F 2.52   (H) 2.5
G 2.511   J 2.49

3. Of the 100 students in Mr. Brill's science classes, 20 have not yet decided on a project. What percent of the students have already chosen a project?

A 2%   B 8%   C 20%   (D) 80%

4. Between them, Roberto and Jerry shared $1\frac{1}{2}$ pizzas. Which shows how much pizza each boy could have eaten?

(F) $\frac{3}{4}$ and $\frac{3}{4}$ H $\frac{5}{8}$ and $\frac{3}{4}$
G $\frac{7}{8}$ and $\frac{1}{2}$ J $1\frac{1}{8}$ and $\frac{3}{4}$

5. Solve. $a - 6 = 10$

A $a = {}^-16$ C $a = 4$
B $a = {}^-4$ (D) $a = 16$

6. The difference in length between two shelves is $\frac{5}{6}$ ft. If the longer shelf is $5\frac{3}{4}$ ft long, how long is the shorter shelf?

F $4\frac{1}{2}$ ft   H $5\frac{1}{2}$ ft
(G) $4\frac{11}{12}$ ft   J $5\frac{3}{4}$ ft

7. There were 17 people in a restaurant. Three groups of 4 came in before anyone left. After that, two groups of 3 finished dinner and left. Which expression tells how many people remained in the restaurant?

(A) $17 + 3 \times 4 - 2 \times 3$
B $(17 + 3) \times 4 - 2 \times 3$
C $17 + 3 \times (4 - 2) \times 3$
D $17 - 3 \times 4 + 2 \times 3$

8. Peter, Charles, Joann, and Linda all began a race at the same time. The table shows the distances they had run after 9 minutes. Who was leading the race?

RUNNER	DISTANCE
Peter	$\frac{3}{4}$ mi
Charles	$\frac{1}{2}$ mi
Joann	$\frac{5}{6}$ mi
Linda	$\frac{7}{8}$ mi

F Peter   H Joann
G Charles   (J) Linda

9. Which expression represents the square root of 64, times the difference between the squares of 5 and 3?

A $64^2 \times 5^2 - 3^2$
B $\sqrt{64} \times 5^2 - 3^2$
(C) $\sqrt{64} \times (5^2 - 3^2)$
D $(\sqrt{64} \times 5^2) - 3^2$

10. What is the probability that a card selected at random will be a multiple of 4?

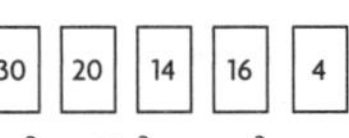

F $\frac{2}{5}$ (G) $\frac{3}{5}$ H $\frac{2}{3}$ J $\frac{3}{2}$

Go On

Name ______________________________

11. What is the probability that if you choose a marble, do not replace it, and then choose a second marble, they will both be red?

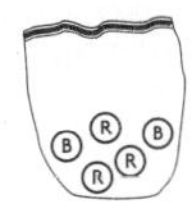

Key
R = Red Marble
B = Blue Marble

(A) $\frac{3}{10}$ B $\frac{6}{25}$ C $\frac{1}{4}$ D $\frac{1}{10}$

12. Which equation represents the function shown in the table?

x	$^-1$	0	1	2	3
y	6	7	8	9	10

(F) $y = x + 7$ H $y = x + 6$
G $y = x - 7$ J $y = x - 6$

13. How many degrees of rotational symmetry does the figure have?

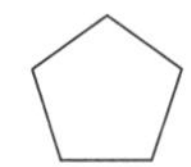

A 70°   (B) 72°   C 90°   D 140°

14. Which inequality describes the graph?

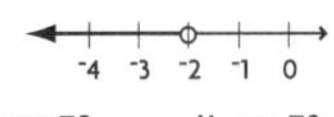

F $x \geq {}^-2$ H $x > {}^-2$
G $x \leq {}^-2$ (J) $x < {}^-2$

15. Which expression is equivalent to $27.18 \div 0.14$

A $2,718 \div 0.14$ C $271.8 \div 14$
(B) $2,718 \div 14$ D $2.718 \div 14$

16. For the set of data, which are the same?

SCORES ON A TEST									
82	86	80	90	75	87	74	86	98	86

(F) mode and median
G mean and mode
H median and mean
J mean, median, and mode

17. What type of graph would best show how a teenager divided her money among her expenses?

A bar graph   (C) circle graph
B line graph   D histogram

18. The graph shows the change in the price of a gallon of gasoline over 4 months. If the trend continues, estimate the price of gasoline in the next month.

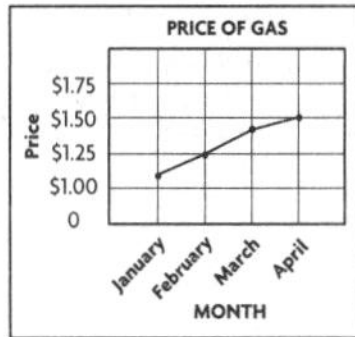

F $1.45   (H) $1.60
G $1.50   J $1.85

19. Aaron is building a frame for a rectangular picture that measures 18 in. by 26 in. He has cut the wood for two adjacent sides. What is the least length of wood he still needs in order to complete the frame?

A 18 in.   C 35 in.
B 26 in.   (D) 44 in.

Go On

Name ______________________________

For 20–21, use the following information.

A large tree has a circumference of 25 ft.

20. To the nearest foot, what is the length of the tree's diameter? Use 3.14 for the value of π.

(F) 8 ft   G 12 ft   H 16 ft   J 20 ft

21. To the nearest whole number, what would be the area of the cut surface of the tree if the tree was cut parallel to the ground? Use 3.14 for the value of π.

A 25 ft^2 (C) 50 ft^2
B 48 ft^2 D 96 ft^2

22. Three friends won some money in a contest. They were able to share the money equally. How much could they have won?

F $949   H $1,333
G $1,025   (J) $1,407

23. A line segment is 40 cm long. If it is bisected, how long will each of the smaller segments be?

A 40cm   (B) 20cm   C 10cm   D 5cm

24. Callers from a research company asked every 8th person they phoned about their favorite TV show. They asked every 12th person about their favorite newspaper. Which was the first person they asked about both?

F 16th person   (H) 24th person
G 20th person   J 96th person

25. After one week of work, Antonio recorded his earnings as $^+$\$45. The next week he did not work, but spent \$60. What integer describes the change in Antonio's wealth over the two weeks?

(A) $^-$\$15   C $^+$\$15
B $^-$\$5   D $^+$\$105

26. Use the figure to find the unknown angle measure.

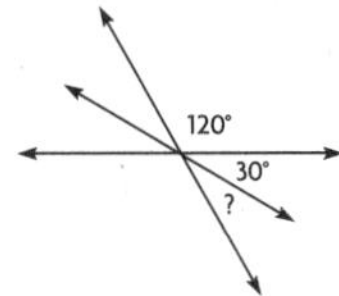

(F) 30°   H 50°
G 40°   J 60°

27. A quadrilateral that has 4 congruent sides must be a ____.

A trapezoid   C rectangle
(B) rhombus   D parallelogram

28. The side view of a solid figure is a rectangle. Which of the following could the figure be?

F cone
(G) cylinder
H rectangular pyramid
J triangular pyramid

29. The formula $h = \frac{m}{60}$ relates the number of hours, h, to the number of minutes, m. How many hours are there in 150 minutes?

A 2 hr   C 3 hr
(B) 2.5 hr   D 3.5 hr

Go On

Name ______________________________

30. $-\frac{3}{4} \times 1\frac{1}{5}$

F $-\frac{10}{9}$ H $\frac{9}{10}$
(G) $-\frac{9}{10}$ J $\frac{10}{9}$

31. The scale of a map is 1 cm equals 40 km. On the map, two cities are 3.5 cm apart. What is the actual distance between the cities?

A 40 km   (C) 140 km
B 120 km   D 1,400 km

32. A factory found that 4% of its TVs had defects. Out of 2,000, how many TVs would be expected to have defects?

F 8 TVs   (H) 80 TVs
G 40 TVs   J 800 TVs

33. A spinner has 8 equal sections. If 2 of them are red, what percent of the spinner is **not** red?

A 2%   B 25%   (C) 75%   D 80%

34. Which measurement is the most precise?

(F) 270 mm   H 6 m
G 14 cm   J 2 km

35. Find the volume.

5 in.
3 in.
4 in.

A 15 $in.^3$
B 20 $in.^3$
(C) 30 $in.^3$
D 60 $in.^3$

36. Annie waits by the entrance to her school and asks the first 50 students that come in a question. What type of sample is she using?

F random   H structured
G systematic   (J) convenience

37. Which measure is equivalent to 56 oz?

(A) $3\frac{1}{2}$ lb   C $4\frac{1}{2}$ lb
B 4 lb   D 7 lb

38. The line plot shows the number of people living in each house on one street. What is the median number of people living in the houses on this street?

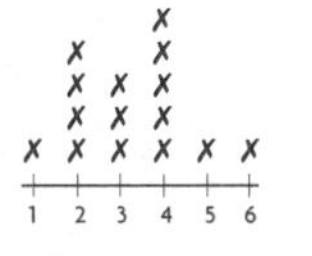

F 2   (G) 3   H 4   J 5

39. Which set shows three numbers in order from *least* to *greatest*?

A $1\frac{5}{8}$, $1\frac{2}{3}$, 1.42
(B) 1.24, $1\frac{2}{5}$, 1.55
C $3\frac{1}{4}$, 3.14, 3.24
D 2.65, $2\frac{5}{6}$, $2\frac{3}{5}$

40. The square field has an area of 1,600 ft^2. The owner of the field wants to put a fence around it. How many feet of fencing will be needed to completely enclose the field?

F 40 ft   H 120 ft
G 80 ft   (J) 160 ft

Stop

…ect answer.

…41

548 r1 or 548.2

2. Order 3.895, 3.905, 3.985, and 3.899 from *least* to *greatest*.

3.895, 3.899, 3.905, 3.985

3. Ken has completed 65 of the 100 questions on his science test. What percent of the questions does he still have to finish?

35%

4. Stephen and Leticia shared $1\frac{1}{2}$ pizzas. If Stephen ate $\frac{7}{8}$ of a pizza, could Leticia have eaten $\frac{3}{4}$ of a pizza? Explain.

No. $\frac{7}{8} + \frac{3}{4} > 1\frac{1}{2}$

5. Solve.

$d - 9 = 12$

$d = 21$

6. The difference in length between two ropes is $\frac{3}{8}$ ft. If the shorter rope is $4\frac{3}{4}$ ft long, how long is the longer rope?

$5\frac{1}{8}$ ft

7. There were 23 people on the bus. Three couples got on before anyone got off. After that, groups of 4 people got off at each of the next two stops. Write an expression you could evaluate to find out how many people remained on the bus.

$23 + (3 \times 2) - (2 \times 4)$

8. Ed, Shelley, Hank, and David all walk to school. The table shows the distance each lives from the school. Who lives nearest the school?

Ed	$\frac{2}{3}$ mi
Shelley	$\frac{3}{4}$ mi
Hank	$\frac{5}{6}$ mi
David	$\frac{3}{8}$ mi

David

9. Write the expression that represents the square root of 49 times the sum of the squares of 9 and 4.

$\sqrt{49} \times (9^2 + 4^2)$

10. What is the probability, expressed as a percent, that if one card is drawn from a stack of cards numbered 1 to 100, it will be a multiple of 5?

20%

Go On

Name

11. What is the probability that if you choose a marble from a bag containing 5 red and 5 black marbles, do not replace it, and then choose a second marble, they will both be red?

$\frac{2}{9}$

12. Write an equation that represents the function shown in the table.

x	⁻2	0	2	4	6
y	3	5	7	9	11

$y = x + 5$

13. How many degrees of rotational symmetry does the figure have?

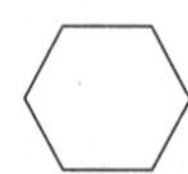

60°, 120°, 180°, 240°, 300°

14. Write an inequality that describes the graph.

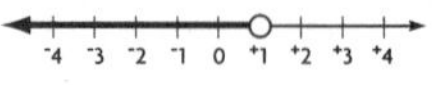

$x < 1$

15. Write an equivalent expression.
$47.61 \div 0.23$

Possible answer: $4761 \div 23$

16. For the set of data, give the mean, median, and mode.

77, 81, 75, 85, 70, 82, 69, 81, 93, 81

79.4, 81, 81

17. What type of graph would best show how the student council divided the money it spent on the school dance among the expenses?

circle graph

18. The graph shows the change in the price of a movie ticket over 4 years. If the trend continues, estimate the price of a movie ticket in the fifth year.

$6.50

19. Felicia is building the sides of a rectangular sandbox that will measure 6 ft by $4\frac{1}{2}$ ft. She has cut the wood for two adjacent sides. How much wood does she still need to complete the sides?

$10\frac{1}{2}$ ft of wood

Go On

Name

For 20–21, use the information below.

A giant sequoia tree has a circumference at its base of 90 ft.

20. To the nearest foot, what is the tree's diameter? Use 3.14 for π.

29 ft

21. To the nearest foot, what is the area of the base of the tree? Use 3.14 for π..

about 645 ft^2

22. Andrea wants to donate a total of $50.00 to three of her favorite charities. Will she be able to give each of the charities an equal amount? Explain.

No; 50 is not evenly divisible by 3

23. A line segment is 6 in. long. If it is bisected, how long wil each of the smaller segments be?

3 in.

24. Researchers asked every 6th person entering the mall about their favorite radio stations. They asked every 8th person about their favorite television stations. Which was the first person they asked about both?

the 24th person

25. Last week, Erik deposited $55 in his bank account. This week, he withdrew $65. What integer describes the change in Erik's bank account balance over these two weeks?

⁻10

26. What is the measure of the unknown angle?

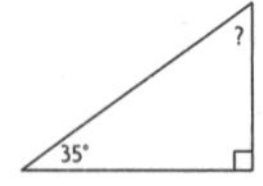

55°

27. A quadrilateral that has 4 congruent sides and congruent opposite angles is a __?__ .

rhombus

28. Identify the solid that has these views.

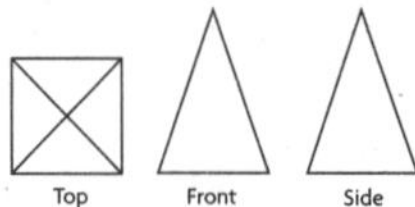

square pyramid

29. The formula $h = 24d$ relates the number of days, d, to the number of hours, h. How many days are there in 80 hours?

$3\frac{1}{3}$ days

Go On

Name

30. $^{-}\frac{2}{3} \times 2\frac{1}{4}$

$^{-}1\frac{1}{2}$

31. The scale of a map is 1 in. equals 30 mi. On the map, two mountains are 4.5 in. apart. What is the actual distance between the mountains?

135 mi

32. A prize is included in 3% of the boxes of a certain cereal. Out of 3,000 boxes, how many are expected to contain a prize?

90 boxes

33. A spinner has 8 equal sections. If 6 of them are blue, what percent of the spinner is **not** blue?

25%

34. Which metric measurement is generally used to measure the distance between two cities?

km

35. Find the volume.

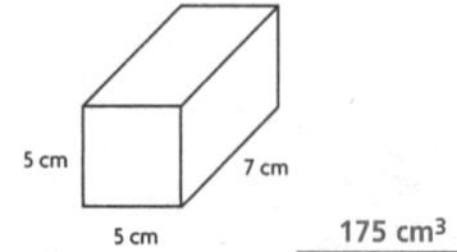

175 cm^3

36. Chris conducts a survey at his school by questioning every third person who walks into the cafeteria at lunch time. What type of sample is he using?

systematic

37. How many pounds are in 72 oz?

4.5 lb

38. The line plot shows the age of ten kids at the roller skating rink. What is the median age of those ten kids?

11 years old

39. Order $5\frac{2}{3}$, 5.23, and 5.32 from *least* to *greatest*.

5.23, 5.32, $5\frac{2}{3}$

40. A square field has an area of 2,500 ft^2. The owner of the field wants to put a fence around it. How many feet of fencing will be needed to enclose the field completely?

200 ft of fencing

Stop